LIONS, LOCUSTS, AND THE LAMB

LIONS, LOCUSTS, AND THE LAMB

INTERPRETING KEY IMAGES IN THE BOOK OF REVELATION

MICHAEL KUYKENDALL

WIPF & STOCK · Eugene, Oregon

LIONS, LOCUSTS, AND THE LAMB
Interpreting Key Images in the Book of Revelation

Wipf & Stock
An Imprint of Wipf and Stock Publishers
199 W. 8th Ave., Suite 3
Eugene, OR 97401

www.wipfandstock.com

PAPERBACK ISBN: 978-1-5326-4086-5
HARDCOVER ISBN: 978-1-5326-4087-2
EBOOK ISBN: 978-1-5326-4088-9

Manufactured in the U.S.A.   01/16/19

For my Mom,
who led me to the Lord,
Hazel Carol Blose Kuykendall Woodard

Contents

Permissions

Scripture quotations marked CEB are taken from the Common English Bible®, copyright © 2010, 2011 by Common English Bible™. Used by permission. All rights reserved worldwide.

Scripture quotations marked CEV are taken from the Contemporary English Version, copyright © 1995 by the American Bible Society. Used by permission.

Scripture quotations marked CSB are taken from the Christian Standard Bible®, copyright © 2017 by Holman Bible Publishers. Used by permission.

Scriptures quotations marked ESV are taken from The Holy Bible, English Standard Version (ESV)®, copyright © 2001 by Crossway, a publishing ministry of Good News Publishers. Used by permission.

Scripture quotations marked GNT are taken from the Good News Translation, 2nd edition, copyright © 1992 by American Bible Society. Used by permission. All rights reserved.

Scripture quotations marked GW are taken from GOD'S WORD®, copyright © 1995 by God's Word to the Nations. All rights reserved.

Scripture quotations marked HCSB are taken from the Holman Christian Standard Bible (HCSB), copyright © 1999, 2000, 2002, 2003 by Holman Bible Publishers. All rights reserved.

Scripture quotations marked NABR are taken from the New American Bible, revised edition, copyright © 2010, 1991, 1986, 1970 by the Confraternity of Christian Doctrine, Washington, DC. Used by permission. All Rights Reserved.

Scripture quotations marked NASB are taken from the New American Standard Bible, copyright © 1960, 1962, 1963, 1968, 1971, 1972, 1973, 1975, 1977, 1995 by the Lockman Foundation. Used by permission.

Preface

MANY PEOPLE HAVE CONTRIBUTED to my understanding of the book of Revelation. I knew the book was special as a young person, especially when I heard adults at my church setting dates for the Lord's return in the 1970s. My pastor tabbed Henry Kissinger as the antichrist, and could prove it mathematically. College and seminary training helped assuage me from being a date-setter. But I maintained my fascination with this mysterious book of the Bible. A major "aha" moment for me occurred when I realized that my dispensationalist upbringing was only one of several possible interpretive methods. My life of study on Revelation started in that moment. Eventually, my dissertation was on a comparison of apocalyptic literature with John's Apocalypse.

In 1989 I began teaching for Gateway Seminary (formerly Golden Gate Seminary). I have taught Revelation as part of the New Testament introductory courses for almost thirty years. For the past twenty years, I have taught Revelation as a masters-level elective, online, and on three regional campuses. For the past ten years, I have taught Revelation to doctoral-level students in Gateway Seminary's PhD program. Each opportunity helped sharpen my skills and motivate my interest in more detailed research. The numerous questions from students have shaped my thinking and teaching on the topic.

I have also benefitted from local churches that allowed me to lecture on Revelation. I always prepared the pastor in advance that I was not going to give a popular dispensationalist study. I am positive I have disillusioned my fair share of conservative church members. In fact, I recall the young woman who cornered me in 2008 as I sat on the first row, prayerfully preparing to speak to her church. She wanted confirmation (before I began my lecture) that Obama was the antichrist. Normally, I work slowly through such issues, but she forced my answer, which was, "No, ma'am, Obama is not the antichrist." She was kind enough to stay for every lecture. I hope my teaching helped her in the long run. Her concerns, however, constantly remind me of the need for local church leaders to teach the book of Revelation, and to find and use the best resources when they do. This book is my own small effort to aid the church and academy.

A consistent thematic question in seminary classes and church settings has been, "What do the symbols mean?" This study is the culmination of thirty years of research and teaching on Revelation with that question in mind. I want to thank Gateway Seminary for their generous sabbatical policy, which gave me the time needed to complete this project. I am thankful for Gateway Seminary's rich library system and helpful staff. I also want to thank my brother, Terry, for his encouragement and generosity throughout the research and writing of this project. I dedicate this book to my mother, Carol, who led me to the Lord. Finally, I am grateful to my patient wife, Terri, who for the past year did not see her husband until late at night.

Abbreviations

Dictionaries, Encyclopedias, and Lexicons

ABD   *The Anchor Bible Dictionary. Edited by David Noel Freedman. 6 vols. New York: Doubleday, 1992.*

BDAG   *Walter Bauer, Frederick W. Danker, W. F. Arndt, and F. W. Gingrich. Greek-English Lexicon of the New Testament and Other Early Christian Literature. 3rd ed. Chicago: University of Chicago Press, 2000.*

DBTEL   *A Dictionary of Biblical Tradition in English Literature. Edited by David Lyle Jeffrey. Grand Rapids: Eerdmans, 1992.*

DDD   *Dictionary of Deities and Demons in the Bible. Edited by Karel van der Toorn, Bob Becking, and Pieter W. van der Horst. 2nd ed. Grand Rapids: Eerdmans, 1999.*

DDL   *Edwin M. Yamauchi and Marvin R. Wilson. Dictionary of Daily Life in Biblical and Post-Biblical Antiquity. Peabody, MA: Hendrickson, 2017.*

DPT   *Dictionary of Premillennial Theology. Edited by Mal Couch. Grand Rapids: Kregel, 1996.*

EDNT   *Exegetical Dictionary of the New Testament. Edited by Horst Balz and Gerhard Schneider. 3 vols. Grand Rapids: Eerdmans, 1990–1993.*

ISBE   *The International Standard Bible Encyclopedia. Edited by Geoffrey W. Bromiley. 4 vols. Grand Rapids: Eerdmans, 1979–1986.*

L&N   *Johannes P. Louw and Eugene A. Nida. A Greek-English Lexicon of the New Testament Based on Semantic Domains. 2 vols. 2nd ed. New York: UBS, 1989.*

LBD   *The Lexham Bible Dictionary. Edited by John D. Barry. Bellingham, WA: Lexham, 2012. https://www.logos.com/product/36564/lexham-bible-dictionary.*

NDT   *New Dictionary of Theology: Historical and Systematic. Edited by Martin Davie, Tim Grass, Stephen R. Holmes, John McDowell, and T. A. Noble. 2nd ed. Downers Grove, IL: InterVarsity, 2016.*

NIDB   *New Interpreter's Dictionary of the Bible. Edited by Katharine D. Sakenfeld. 5 vols. Nashville: Abingdon, 2006–2009.*

NIDNTT   *New International Dictionary of New Testament Theology. Edited by Colin Brown. 4 vols. Grand Rapids: Zondervan, 1975–1978.*

NIDNTTE   *New International Dictionary of New Testament Theology and Exegesis. Edited by Moisés Silva. 5 vols. 2nd ed. Grand Rapids: Zondervan, 2014.*

TDNT   *Theological Dictionary of the New Testament. Edited by Gerhard Kittel and Gerhard Friedrich. Translated by Geoffrey W. Bromiley. 10 vols. Grand Rapids: Eerdmans, 1964–76.*

UBS5   *The Greek New Testament. Edited by Kurt Aland et al. 5th rev. ed. New York: United Bible Society, 2014.*

ZEB   *The Zondervan Encyclopedia of the Bible. Edited by Merrill C. Tenney and Moisés Silva. 5 vols. Rev. ed. Grand Rapids: Zondervan, 2009.*

Bible Translations

CEB   *Common English Bible*

CEV   *Contemporary English Version*

CSB   *Christian Standard Bible*

ESV   *English Standard Version*

GNT   *Good News Translation*

GW   *God's Word for the Nations*

HCSB   *Holman Christian Standard Bible*

KJV   *King James Version*

NABR   *New American Bible, Revised Edition*

NASB	*New American Standard Bible*
NCV	*New Century Version*
NET	*New English Translation*
NIV	*New International Version*
NKJV	*New King James Version*
NJB	*New Jerusalem Bible*
NLT	*New Living Translation*
NRSV	*New Revised Standard Version*
REB	*Revised English Bible*

Journals, Major Reference Works, and Commentaries

AB	*Anchor Bible*
ACCS	*Ancient Christian Commentary on Scripture*
ACNT	*Augsburg Commentary on the New Testament*
AJPS	*Asian Journal of Pentecostal Studies*
ANTC	*Abingdon New Testament Commentaries*
AUSS	*Andrews University Seminary Studies*
AYBC	*Anchor Yale Bible Commentaries*
BBC	*Blackwell Bible Commentaries*
BBR	*Bulletin for Biblical Research*
BECNT	*Baker Exegetical Commentary on the New Testament*
BZNW	*Beihefte zur Zeitschrift fur die Neutestamentliche Wissenschaft*
Bib	*Biblica*
BNTC	*Black's New Testament Commentaries*
BSac	*Bibliotheca Sacra*
BST	*Bible Speaks Today*

BT   *The Bible Translator*

BTB   *Biblical Theology Bulletin*

BTC   *Brazos Theological Commentary*

CBC   *Cambridge Bible Commentary*

CBR   *Currents in Biblical Research*

CBQ   *Catholic Biblical Quarterly*

CC   *Continental Commentaries*

CCT   *Chalice Commentaries for Today*

ConcC   *Concordia Commentary*

CTJ   *Calvin Theological Journal*

CTQ   *Concordia Theological Quarterly*

CurTM   *Currents in Theology and Mission*

Dir   *Direction*

EBC   *Expositor's Bible Commentary*

EvQ   *Evangelical Quarterly*

GTJ   *Grace Theological Journal*

HeyJ   *Heythrop Journal*

HNTC   *Harper's New Testament Commentaries*

HolNTC   *Holman New Testament Commentary*

HTR   *Harvard Theological Review*

HTS   *Harvard Theological Studies*

HvTSt   *Hervormde teologiese studies*

IBC   *Interpretation: A Bible Commentary for Teaching and Preaching*

ICC   *International Critical Commentary*

IJTP   *International Journal of Transpersonal Studies*

Int	*Interpretation*
IVPNTC	*InterVarsity Press New Testament Commentaries*
JATS	*Journal of the Adventist Theological Society*
JBL	*Journal of Biblical Literature*
JCTR	*Journal for Christian Theological Research*
JETS	*Journal of the Evangelical Theological Society*
JPT	*Journal of Pentecostal Theology*
JSNT	*Journal for the Study of the New Testament*
List	*Listening: Journal of Religion and Culture*
L&S	*Letter & Spirit*
LNTS	*Library of New Testament Studies*
MNTC	*Moffatt New Testament Commentary*
NAC	*New American Commentary*
NBBC	*New Beacon Bible Commentary*
NCB	*New Century Bible*
NCCS	*New Covenant Commentary Series*
Neot	*Neotestamentica*
NIB	*New Interpreter's Bible*
NIBCNT	*New International Biblical Commentary*
NICNT	*New International Commentary on the New Testament*
NIGTC	*New International Greek New Testament Commentary*
NIVAC	*New International Version Application Commentary*
NovT	*Novum Testamentum*
NTC	*New Testament Commentary*
NTL	*New Testament Library*

NTS	*New Testament Studies*
OHE	*Oxford Handbook on Eschatology*
PC	*Proclamation Commentaries*
PCNT	*Paideia Commentary on the New Testament*
PCS	*Pentecostal Commentary Series*
QR	*Quarterly Review*
ResQ	*Restoration Quarterly*
RTR	*Reformed Theological Review*
SBJT	*Southern Baptist Journal of Theology*
ScrB	*Scripture Bulletin*
SHBC	*Smyth & Helwys Bible Commentary*
SJT	*Scottish Journal of Theology*
SNTSU	*Studien zum Neuen Testament und Seiner Umwelt*
SP	*Sacra pagina*
StBibLit	*Studies in Biblical Literature (Lang)*
STDJ	*Studies on the Texts of the Desert of Judah*
TFCBC	*Twenty-First Century Biblical Commentary*
THNTC	*Two Horizons New Testament Commentaries*
TJ	*Trinity Journal*
TMSJ	*The Master's Seminary Journal*
TNTC	*Tyndale New Testament Commentaries*
TR	*Textus Receptus*
TPINTC	*TPI New Testament Commentaries*
TTCS	*Teach the Text Commentary Series*
TynBul	*Tyndale Bulletin*

VE	*Vox Evangelica*
VeE	*Verbum et Ecclesia*
WBC	*Word Biblical Commentary*
WEC	*Wycliffe Exegetical Commentary*
WTJ	*Westminster Theological Journal*
WW	*Word and World*
ZIBBC	*Zondervan Illustrated Bible Backgrounds Commentary*

Introduction

REVELATION IS A BOOK saturated with symbols. Its story is told through images. If readers are to grasp the meaning of the book, then they must be prepared to interpret its images. The present study offers readers a handy, interpretive guide into John's symbolic world. The following introduction lays the groundwork for studying the images. It is divided into three sections. First, background matters are addressed. John's chosen genres, methodological options, millennial choices, and safe steps for interpreting Revelation's numerous images are presented. Second, the structure of Revelation is discussed. The external and internal choices and evidences are considered. The results found, along with adopting a progressive recapitulation approach, produce an outline of Revelation that is composed of twelve visions. Finally, a master list of the categories of symbols and their individual entries is offered for easy reference.

Background Matters

This book approaches Revelation from an evangelical viewpoint. It assumes the apostle John is responsible for its content. The best date of composition is around AD 95. John wrote a circular letter to seven churches in Asia Minor (1:4, 11). Each church experienced pressure and persecution from Rome and its imperial cult, from hostile Jews (2:9; 3:9), and from false teachers who enticed the churches to compromise their faith (2:6, 14–15; 20–24).

Therefore, the primary purpose of Revelation was to encourage Christians who faced pressure and persecution from the outside and to exhort Christians who faced heresy and accommodation from the inside. Revelation challenges readers to remain faithful, even to the point of martyrdom. This purpose applies to readers of every generation—not just the first or the last.[1] This section is divided into short discussions on Revelation's genre, methodological and millennial options, and steps for interpreting John's symbols.[2]

---

1. For in-depth background see Aune, *Revelation*, 1:xlvii–ccxi; Beale, *Revelation*, 3–177; Koester, *Revelation*, 3–150; Osborne, *Revelation*, 1–49.

2. This section is drawn from my chapter on Revelation found in Jim Wilson et al., *Impact Preaching*, 214–33.

Three Genres of Revelation

Revelation reflects a mixed literary genre. John's images are drawn from three distinct literary types, and they are intertwined. Scholars have called Revelation "prophetic-apocalyptic."[3] Perhaps a better designation is an "epistolary-prophetic apocalypse." Such a label reveals the literary mixture as well as what appears to be the weightier of the three genres—apocalypse.

Epistle

Revelation reveals itself as a typical epistle written to seven churches in the province of Asia Minor (1:4). Each church receives its own message from the glorified Christ, and each church hears the messages of the other churches (2:1–3:22). The book concludes with an epistolary postscript (22:21). The implication is that Revelation is one letter intended for all seven churches.[4] The genre of epistle reminds readers to accent the original audience and to follow the basic rule that "a text cannot mean what it never could have meant to its author or readers."[5] John's images were certainly understood by his own audience. Thus, interpreters must try to reconstruct as accurately as possible the original historical circumstances. Moreover, epistles are occasional in nature—intended for a specific occasion occurring among the original author and audience.[6]

Prophecy

Prophecy is the second genre of Revelation (1:3). OT prophecy included prediction, but it mainly concerned itself with calling the prophet's own generation to repentance and obedience. Gordon Fee and Douglas Stuart clarified that less than 2 percent of OT prophecy is messianic, less than 5 percent specifically describes the new covenant, and less than 1 percent concerns events yet to come.[7] Thus, in such this-generational preaching, the prophet hints with less detail of a time in the future of one who was to come and make a new covenant (Jesus' first coming), and in even less detail of an ultimate and eschatological end (Jesus' second coming).

Interpreters must keep a "near view-far view" approach in mind. The prophet prophesied what would happen *soon* if repentance was missing. He was specific in the predictions of the *near* future. Yet he also prophesied more generally about a day when a Messiah would come, only with less specificity (after all, the Pharisees—the very people looking for the Messiah—rejected Jesus because he did not come in the way they expected). Likewise, when the prophet envisioned even *farther* into the future to the last days, his words were even more unspecific. Therefore, the NT prophet John should be

---

3. So Beale, *Revelation*, 37; Osborne, *Hermeneutical Spiral*, 276.

4. Bauckham, *Theology of Revelation*, 12–17.

5. Fee and Stuart, *How to Read the Bible*, 77.

6. Ibid., 60–61, 90–91, 262.

7. Ibid., 188.

read the same way. He is specific when speaking to the churches. But interpreters must think in broader strokes when John speaks of the end of days, or else risk falling into the same trap the Pharisees did—expecting the second coming of the Messiah in a certain, specific, detailed way.[8] In addition, the symbols and images which the prophets used for their prophecies must be interpreted primarily with the original audience in mind. The NT prophet John draws from his OT counterparts for many of his symbols. He redelivers and reinterprets their prophecies for his own audience.

Apocalypse

The third genre of Revelation is apocalypse. The very first word of the book is *apokalypsis*—"revelation" (1:1). Apocalyptic literature was popular in John's day. Its rules and guidelines for interpretation must be followed by modern readers. Apocalyptic literature such as Revelation is similar to parables in that the details are often simply a part of the overall scenery. We must not expect every brushstroke on the painting to carry meaning and demand exegesis. The big picture is the best picture. Notice the following traits in apocalyptic literature.

> *Visions.* Apocalypses display a structure that revolves around multiple visions. For example, both *4 Ezra* and *2 Baruch* follow seven visions. Scholars note multiple visions within Revelation as well. This study asserts that John produced twelve visions.

> *Time and space dimensions.* The *spatial* aspect discloses the supernatural world of beings such as angels and demons. The *temporal* aspect involves imminent eschatological judgment. This judgment often involves cosmic catastrophe and the final judgment of humanity.

> *Dualism.* Two types of dualism are evident in apocalyptic literature. The first is *cosmic* dualism. Two worlds are emphasized—heaven and earth; God versus Satan; present suffering versus future salvation; and present age versus the age to come. Second, there is *social* dualism. Humanity is divided into good and evil, those being saved and those perishing. There are no fence-riders in apocalyptic literature. People are either believers or unbelievers.

> *Determinism and God's justice.* For the apocalypticist, the course of history is predetermined. Earth and humanity have run their course. The end of the age will be in the writer's own lifetime or soon afterward. This determinism often led to ethical passivity. Yet apocalyptic literature also revealed a deep concern for defending the justice of God. God will vindicate his people.

> *Recapitulation.* Apocalyptic literature often recycles or recaps its visions. When a new vision begins, the seer temporally goes back in time and

---

8. Duvall and Hays, *Grasping God's Word*, 411–15. For an excellent discussion on the subgenres in prophecy, see Köstenberger and Patterson, *For the Love of God's Word*, 164–81.

marches forward toward the end again. There may be numerous "ends" in the book. Scholars note this literary technique in Isaiah, Ezekiel, Zechariah, and especially Daniel (chapters 2, 7, 8, 9, 10–12 offer five parallel visions on the same general period of the future). Many scholars note recapping in Revelation as well. The seals, trumpets, and bowls, for example, are not three separate plagues. They offer an intensifying repetition. This study argues that John recaps his visions.

Tribulation. A consistent theme found in apocalypses is the intense period of suffering that precedes the end of time and/or advent of a new era. For some apocalypses the tribulation was already in the past. For others it was present. For some it was in the near future. Those who suffer might be God's people or gentiles/unbelievers or both. The function of the tribulation also varied. Tribulation for believers was a test to produce steadfastness and faithfulness. For unbelievers tribulation was judgment and a final opportunity to repent. Revelation correlates closely to these ideas.

Symbolism. In order to express the inexpressible scenes revealed, John abandoned common narrative and opted for apocalyptic imagery. Such language is filled with fantastic, bizarre symbolism and often includes weird creatures, earthquakes, and supernatural upheavals. The symbolism also extends to numbers, colors, places, and institutions as well.[9] This study examines close to three hundred of John's symbols.

Differences in Revelation. Although Revelation exhibits the characteristics listed above, there are differences between apocalyptic literature and John's Apocalypse. John does not use pseudonymity whereas other apocalypses do. John's symbolism is rooted in Christianity. Unlike other apocalypses, John drew from five primary sources—his own genuine experience (1:9–10), the OT, Jewish pseudepigrapha, the NT, and ancient mythology (the contemporary combat myth found in chapter 12). Thus, Revelation is a unique contribution within its own genre.[10]

Five Approaches to Interpreting John's Images

There are five options available for interpreting Revelation's images. Each option has numerous supporters.

Preterist

First, the *preterist* approach stresses the historical context of John's original audience. Its emphasis rests in the first century. All or almost all of its prophecies have already

9. For a fuller discussion on features of apocalyptic literature, see Osborne, *Hermeneutical Spiral*, 276–82; Carey, *Ultimate Things*, 5–10; and John Collins, *Apocalyptic Imagination*.

10. See Bauckham, *Theology of Revelation*, 9–12; Koester, *Revelation*, 104–12; Lioy, *Revelation in Christological Focus*, 25–44.

occurred. Thus, the symbols refer to people and events of John's immediate audience and situation. The catastrophic images most often refer to the fall of Jerusalem in AD 70.

Historicist

Second, the *historicist* approach attempts to trace history from John's original audience to the second coming. Revelation serves as a chronological roadmap as each chapter advances temporally forward. Its symbols predict major events and persons who spanned church history from the first century to the end of time. Thus, parts of Revelation refer to past events and parts to future events. This view was popular among the Reformers. Today, Seventh Day Adventists are most often associated with it.

Futurist

Third, the *futurist* approach understands the majority of Revelation as events that will transpire in the last days. Revelation, therefore, mainly deals with prophecies yet to be fulfilled. The symbols refer to people and events which appear near the end of earth's history. There are two futurist views—historic premillennialism and dispensational premillennialism. This view generally understands Revelation's structure in sequential terms. In addition, John's images refer to literal people and events in the near future.

Idealist

Fourth, the *idealist* approach emphasizes searching for the meaning of Revelation's images over any specific references to time or events. The symbols picture timeless truths, such as the struggle between good and evil that exists in each generation from the first to the last. Idealists, therefore, do not search for literal correspondence to Revelation's images. Every generation should apply John's symbols for their own contexts.

Eclectic

Finally, the *eclectic* approach attempts to combine the strengths and limit the weaknesses of the aforementioned approaches. Few eclectics follow the historicist model. But most attempt to interact with the other approaches. Thus, like every other NT book, Revelation's original audience must be heard first (preterist). The symbols must have meant something to John's first readers. Yet Revelation's symbolic world presents timeless truths which every generation is challenged to reapply (idealist). Ultimately, interpreters must recognize that future events such as the second coming, final judgment, and eternity await fulfillment (futurist).[11] Although eclectics attempt to interact more with all the

---

11. See the discussions by Beale (*Revelation*, 44–49), deSilva (*Seeing Things John's Way*, 2–8), and Köstenberger and Patterson (*For the Love of God's Word*, 274–77). A resource that summarizes preterist, idealist, progressive dispensationalist, and classical dispensationalist is Pate, *Four Views on Revelation*.

views, they nevertheless end up emphasizing one view while incorporating the others less. This study draws from all of the approaches. It eventually lands, however, on the eclectic approach with an idealist emphasis. Readers who support the other options should still receive benefit, especially since they will often find their viewpoints listed in numerous entries.

Four Millennial Options

The five methods mentioned above help in understanding John's reference to a thousand years in Rev 20. Modern evangelicals normally accept one of the following four viewpoints.

Amillennialism

First, amillennialism means "no millennium" since the Greek letter alpha (*a*) negates it. Actually, inaugurated or realized millennialism is a more accurate designation. Features include the understanding that the millennium covers the era between the first and second comings of Christ. The kingdom of God and Christ is happening now in an already-but-not-yet fashion. The kingdom consummates at the return of Christ. The church will go through the great tribulation. Thus, it rejects a rapture of the church and a future earthly millennial period. It also stresses that Revelation's visions are primarily symbolic. Amillennialists are found among preterists, idealists, and eclectics the most.

Postmillennialism

Second, postmillennialism teaches that Christ will return *after* (post-) a one-thousand-year millennial kingdom concludes. Thus, the gradual success of the gospel message will eventually experience much of humanity converted and society transformed. Christ will then return. Chapter 20, therefore, refers to the golden age that is established over a long period of time. Postmillennialists are found among preterists and historicists the most.

Historic Premillennialism

Historic premillennialism is the third option. It asserts the second coming occurs *before* (pre-) the start of an earthly millennium. Historic premillennialists affirm that OT prophecies are fulfilled in spiritual Israel, that is, church. Nevertheless, the prophetic symbols in the Bible do refer to future, literal events. A great tribulation is coming but it may not be seven years. God will use Jews near the end in a mighty way, but Scripture is ambivalent on whether it will be as Jewish people or the Jewish nation. Historic premillennialists are usually post-tribulational. The church will pass through the great tribulation. This view draws primarily from futurists, but idealists and eclectics are often included.

Dispensational Premillennialism

The fourth option is dispensational premillennialism. Dispensationalists stress reading Revelation in a sequential fashion. Thus, chapter 20 clearly indicates a thousand-year earthly reign of Christ after Armageddon and the second coming which occurred in chapter 19. The end of the millennium leads to another end-time battle before the arrival of the new Jerusalem. Other features include interpreting the prophetic and apocalyptic genres of the Bible as literally as possible. The many symbols of Revelation must refer to actual things. Names, people, places, and numbers are understood literally. The church is not the "new Israel" or "spiritual Israel." The church does not replace or fulfill God's intentions concerning the Jews. God has separate end-time programs—one for the church and one for the nation of Israel. This distinction calls for a rapture of believers to occur before Christ's second coming. Most dispensationalists are pre-tribulational, but some are mid-tribulational or prewrath. This viewpoint is primarily futurist, but many dispensationalists accept a historicist understanding of the churches in chapters 2–3.[12]

This study appreciates the optimism expressed by postmillennialists, and the meticulous dedication of the premillennialists. The amillennial view, however, is the best approach for understanding the symbols of John, and the way he structures his work into twelve visions.[13]

Seven Interpretive Steps

Readers must interpret the symbols according to John's intent. It is a better approach to assume symbolic meaning first and foremost in John's images. Readers must ask what is the *meaning* associated with this image? Here are seven helpful steps that provide a pathway for interpreting the symbols of Revelation.[14]

Look for Symbolic Imagery

First, interpreters must recognize that symbolic imagery permeates all of Revelation. Symbols are attached to names, people, beings, clothing, colors, numbers, time designations,

---

12. Classic dispensationalism was slightly modified in the 1980s and called progressive dispensationalism. Proponents agree on the basic tenets but understand the distinction between national Israel and the church not as separate arrangements between God and humanity but as successive arrangements. Thus, the OT promises are fulfilled in Christ. The church is not a parenthesis in history but rather a progression. However, no full-fledged commentary on Revelation has been produced by a progressive dispensationalist, and their input in this study will be minimal. Introductory resources include Blaising and Bock, *Progressive Dispensationalism*; and Pate, *Four Views on Revelation*, 133–75; idem, *Interpreting Revelation and Other Apocalyptic Literature*.

13. For further details on millennial views, including their historical development, see Gregg, *Revelation: Four Views*, 48–72; Grenz, *Millennial Maze*; Koester, *Revelation*, 29–65; Weber, "Millennialism," 365–83.

14. The seven steps are modified from Bandy, "Hermeneutics of Symbolism," 46–58. See also Bandy's contributions found in Köstenberger and Patterson, *For the Love of God's Word*, 293–97; and Bandy and Merkle, *Understanding Prophecy*, 213–20.

heavenly bodies, nature, animals, places, institutions, and events.[15] Readers must come to the text with symbolic readiness. A lion is not a lion; a head is not a head; a sickle is not a sickle; a mountain is not a mountain. These are symbols drawn from the animal kingdom, body parts, and cosmic imagery. This study places these images into identifiable categories.

Look for Intratextual Interpretations and Connections

Second, readers must look for the interpretations of symbols within the context of all of Revelation. There are several examples where John or an angel interprets a symbol (1:20; 4:5; 5:6, 8; 7:14; 11:4; 14:4; 17:9; 19:8).[16] When John interprets a symbol it should become the fixed meaning of that symbol throughout the rest of Revelation. Moreover, intratextual allusions help in confirming the structure of John's work. For example, if allusions to a final battle are found in several places in Revelation, an intratextual awareness suggests a conclusion to an individual vision. This study emphasizes these intratextual markers. Many interpreters and modern Bible translations do poorly on this step.

Look for Intertextual Allusions

Third, Bible students must determine if a symbol is drawn from an allusion to the OT. Although scholars disagree on an exact definition of an allusion (echo, allusion, or near quote) and on their total number (250–500 allusions), they do agree that John's book is saturated with the OT. The entries in this book will include relevant and representative examples from the OT.[17]

Look for Extratextual Allusions

The term extratextual technically relates to something outside a literary text. It is applied in this study to refer to extra-canonical writings (outside the biblical text). Therefore, this fourth step compares Revelation's images with other similar writings to discover whether the image is a common symbol with a relatively standard meaning. The writings considered include apocalyptic, pseudepigraphal, Qumran, and early Christian writings. Like OT allusions, representative but not exhaustive extratextual works will be noted in the entries.[18]

---

15. John uses metaphor, simile, metonymy, synechoche, and other figures of speech for his images. For a recent study on how John's original readers would have heard these images, see Shargel, "Hearer-Centric Approach to Revelation."

16. Rainbow (*Pith of the Apocalypse*, 50–53) discusses several of these glosses.

17. For an introduction on OT allusions in the NT, see Beale, *Handbook on the New Testament Use*.

18. For example, see Charlesworth, *Old Testament Pseudepigrapha*; and Bauckham, Davila, and Panayotov, *Old Testament Pseudepigrapha*.

Look for Cultural-Historical Allusions

The fifth step is to look for possible connections between the symbol and the cultural-historical context of first-century Asia Minor. John wrote to people who shared common cultural assumptions. His images would be understood to the original audience. Modern interpreters must use the culture and history of John's era to interpret his symbols accurately. For example, the image of a woman flying on the wings of an eagle toward the desert (12:14) was understandable to John's audience. Today's readers must use John's cultural cues to interpret the image correctly.[19]

Look to Scholarly Experts

The sixth step is to consult scholarly treatments in commentaries and other specialized works. How have Revelation's images been interpreted by the experts? This present study attempts to add another scholarly resource to the mix. Readers will discover what the basic views are on John's images in several ways. This includes fifty full-fledged commentaries on Revelation, hundreds of articles and detailed studies on specific entries, and twenty English Bible versions.[20]

Remain Humble in Conclusions

Finally, this step reminds all readers and interpreters of Revelation to remain open and honest and humble on their findings. This study lists the major views but makes its own appeal to accept the best or better views on individual images. Nevertheless, a goal of this book is to reflect the best scholarship available on the symbols of Revelation and to show respect toward opposing views.

With these background matters out of the way, the remainder of the introduction discusses how Revelation is structured. Understanding its structure significantly aids in how to interpret John's images.

The Structure of Revelation

That Revelation comprises a single document is widely accepted.[21] Those who find multiple sources and later redactors are in the minority.[22] John's visionary document is intri-

---

19. John's original audience would certainly have understood protection and deliverance for God's people (Exod 19:4), and not as Lindsey (*New World Coming*, 179) suggests, "aircraft from the U.S. Sixth Fleet in the Mediterranean" providing a massive airlift out of Petra, Jordan.

20. This also means there are more detailed footnotes than other studies. Trail (*Exegetical Summary of Revelation*) provides a similar but less in-depth attempt at categorizing scholars. The footnotes also reveal an indebtedness to major dictionaries and encyclopedias—Hays, Duvall, and Pate, *Dictionary of Biblical Prophecy*; and Ryken *Dictionary of Biblical Imagery*.

21. This section is summarized from Kuykendall, "Twelve Visions of John," 533–55.

22. For a recent discussion on the unity of Revelation's composition, see Paul, "Source, Structure, and Composition," 41–54.

cately woven and divided into numerous individual visions. This study asserts that John incorporated twelve visions within his work.

Structural Options

Options for structuring Revelation can be divided into external approaches and internal approaches.[23] The external approaches provide important insights. It is, however, the internal approaches that deliver key clues into John's structure.

External Approaches

Numerous interpreters utilize external approaches to structure Revelation. For example, chiasm, dramatic play (Greek drama), liturgy (hymns, doxologies, feasts), and *ekphrasis* (work of art) have been proposed.[24] The best external prospect, however, is centered on intertextuality. In other words, John utilized previous biblical books in structuring his own composition. John immerses his work with OT language and imagery without direct citation. Some OT books are used extensively by John, especially Exodus, Isaiah, Ezekiel, Daniel, and Zechariah. Not only does John allude to these books, he actually makes use of their structure. Another intertextual possibility is the prophetic lawsuit oracles. Alan Bandy finds a threefold pattern of judgment, oracles against nations, and promises of salvation/vindication in the prophets and in Revelation.[25]

Internal Approaches

Many interpreters stress internal approaches for structuring Revelation. John provides key literary features that aid in recognizing the book's structure. Because "sevens" dominate Revelation, many commentators select a septenary pattern. This is easily done for seven letters, seals, trumpets, and bowls, but what about the large portions without numbering indicators? Scholars typically find seven unnumbered sections in chapters 12–14 and 17–22.[26] G. B. Caird, however, speaks for many when he says, "If we attempt to do what John himself has so explicitly refrained from doing and force these chapters into a sevenfold scheme, we soon find that this can be done only at the cost of extreme artificiality."[27] Some exegetes select the tripartite structure of 1:19 as their external guide. All three clauses, however, relate to the past, present, and future of the entire book. The verse reflects a common apocalyptic formula, similar to the one "who is, and who was,

---

23. Several resources discuss in detail what this section will abbreviate. See Aune, *Revelation*, 1:xci–cv; Bauckham, *Climax of Prophecy*, 1–37; Beale, *Revelation*, 108–51; Michaels, *Interpreting Revelation*, 51–71; Prigent, *Apocalypse*, 84–103; Yarbro Collins, *Combat Myth*, 5–55.

24. For resources see Kuykendall, "Twelve Visions of John," 534–38.

25. Bandy, "Layers of the Apocalypse," 485–87; and idem, *Prophetic Lawsuit in Revelation*.

26. The most meticulous effort at finding sevens throughout Revelation is Wendland, "Hermeneutical Significance," 447–76.

27. Caird, *Revelation*, 105.

and who is to come" (1:4). Therefore, no temporal or structural distinctions should be forced upon 1:19, especially with so many other acceptable literary indicators available. Five internal features, however, merit closer attention.

First, many interpreters agree that the phrase "in the Spirit" (*en pneumati*) comprises a major structural marker for Revelation (1:10; 4:2; 17:3; 21:10). Several commentators divide John's visions into four major segments based on this marker.[28] While a significant marker, there are certainly more than four visions in Revelation. Two of the four "in the Spirit" sections are especially long (4:1–16:21; 17:1–21:8). To place the visions of the seals, trumpets, bowls, and the three interludes under the umbrella of one visionary section lessens the impact for those visions to stand on their own. The outline followed in this study lists seven visions within the 4:1–16:21 section, and three visions within the 17:1–21:8 section.

Second, the discourse markers "and I saw" (*kai eidon*) and a closely linked phrase "and behold" or "look" (*kai idou*) are important. *Kai eidon* is found thirty-five times and most often functions to introduce a new vision or new scene or action within a vision (5:1; 6:1; 7:2; 8:2; 9:1; 10:1; 13:1, 11; 14:1, 6, 14; 15:1, 2, 5; 19:11; 20:1; 21:1). *Kai idou* occurs twenty-six times but is generally not translated in modern versions for stylistic reasons.[29] Yet when *idou* is combined with *kai eidon*, it deserves attention as a potential structural marker (4:1; 6:2, 5, 8; 7:9; 14:1, 14; 19:11).

Third, another vital marker is "after these things" (*meta tauta*). Long ago R. H. Charles recognized that these words were utilized by other apocalypses as a literary marker that separates or divides up vision episodes, including Daniel, *1 Enoch*, *4 Ezra*, *2 Baruch*, *Testament of Joseph*, and *Testament of Levi*.[30] *Meta tauta* is a discourse marker, not a temporal marker.[31] This is enhanced through its association with prominent narrative participants. Heavenly voices are mentioned in 4:1 and 19:1 and angels are mentioned in 7:2 and 18:1. The phrase occurs ten times in Revelation. Six times, however, the verbs "I saw" (*eidon*) or "I heard" (*ēkousa*) are attached (4:1; 7:1, 9; 15:5; 18:1; 19:1). These reflect strategic markers as well. Three commence a new vision (4:1; 7:1; 15:5) and three serve as major transitions within the vision (7:9; 18:1; 19:1).[32]

A fourth internal indicator is John's usage of "interlocking" or "chain link" construction.[33] This ancient model is unfamiliar to modern readers. Essentially, it is a preliminary

---

28. Filho, "Apocalypse of John," 215; Heil, *Book of Revelation*; Herms, *Apocalypse*, 147–54; Ladd, *Revelation*, 14–17; Mazzaferri, *Genre of Revelation*, 338–43; Michaels, *Revelation*, 26–32; Skaggs and Benham, *Revelation*, 14; Christopher Smith, "Structure of Revelation," 373–93; Thomas and Macchia, *Revelation*, 2–5; Tõniste, *Ending of the Canon*, 44; Waddell, *Spirit of Revelation*, 138–50.

29. An exception is the NASB, which helpfully translates *idou* as "behold" each time. Inserting "behold" in modern versions might diminish readability but *idou* stresses the validity of what happens next in the text.

30. Charles, *Revelation*, 1:106–7.

31. So Aune, *Revelation*, 1:xciii; Beale, *Revelation*, 316–17; Beasley-Murray, *Revelation*, 142; Charles, *Revelation*, 1:106; Murphy, *Fallen Is Babylon*, 198.

32. Korner ("And I Saw," 160–83) makes a case for *meta tauta eidon* as a major marker and *kai eidon* as minor visions within the textual boundaries of a major vision.

33. Yarbro Collins (*Combat Myth*, 15–16) was apparently the first to use this term (her original work was in 1976). Longenecker ("Linked Like a Chain," 105–17) notes chain-linking in Quintillian (late first

hint of what is to come. The conclusion of one vision includes words or phrases that prepare for the introduction to the following vision, affording a stronger tie between the two sections. Bruce Longenecker states that these chain links help with marking "text-unit closures" and "springboards into the text-unit that follows."[34] The recognition of the interlocking technique allows interpreters to structure Revelation with more exactness. The two major examples are 8:1–5 and 15:1–4. Although 8:2 introduces the trumpets and 15:1 introduces the bowls, the subsequent verses actually conclude the previous seals series (8:3–5) and trumpet series (15:2–4).[35]

The final literary indicator is the intratextual repetitions. Intratextuality refers to the recurring words, phrases, and images found within Revelation that work together "to create a complex network of textual cross-reference, which helps to create and expand the meaning of any one passage by giving it specific relationships to many other passages."[36] These lexical signifiers become the structural aids that bind the whole book. They also offer interpretive guidance. For example, in 1974 Charles H. Giblin listed numerous connections of terms and subject matter between the introductions and conclusions of 17:1–19:10 and 21:9–22:9, confirming the parallel structure for those two visions.[37] Many scholars have since agreed with his findings. When the content of these two intratextual connections is studied, we find a contrast between two cities—Babylon, the great prostitute and the new Jerusalem, the bride of Christ. The numerous repeated patterns give cross-referenced structural and temporal clues. Key words and phrases are consistently found near the end of an individual vision. Before analyzing these intratextual repetitions, the question of sequence versus recapitulation must be addressed.

Sequence or Recapitulation?

How interpreters structure the Apocalypse underscores the methodology they bring to the table. Futurists and historicists tend to emphasize chronological progression throughout Revelation. Preterists, idealists, and eclectic interpreters tend toward recapitulation. There are exceptions and nuances, but most scholars may be placed in one of the following two categories.

Sequence

Many interpreters understand Revelation's structure in sequential, linear terms. The seals chronologically lead to the trumpets which lead to the bowls which lead to the eschaton

---

century) and Lucian of Samosata (late second century).

34. Longenecker, "Linked Like a Chain," 117.

35. For other interlocking candidates, see Bauckham, *Climax of Prophecy*, 5–6; Beale, *Revelation*, 113–15; and Yarbro Collins, *Combat Myth*, 15–16. Mark Hall ("Hook Interlocking Structure," 278–96) considers 10:1—11:18 to be the interlocking center of Revelation and 10:11—11:1 to be the center of the center.

36. Bauckham, *Climax of Prophecy*, 22.

37. Giblin, "Structural and Thematic Correlations," 487–504.

at the conclusion of Revelation. A modified sequential approach labeled "telescoping" is another possibility. In this case, the seventh seal breaks to reveal the seven trumpets. Then the seventh trumpet sounds to reveal the seven bowls.[38] Supporters of this approach recognize that it is impossible to be strictly sequential. Thus, phrases such as "John anticipates" and "John previews" assist in handling chronology that seems out of order. For example, John Walvoord accepts 14:17–20 to describe the divine harvest at the final judgment, stating "This passage speaks prophetically of that which will chronologically follow the return of Christ to the earth" (i.e. 19:11–21).[39] The modified sequential approach recognizes that Revelation cannot be presented in strictly linear terms. Thus, it attempts to answer the problem by suggesting the visions preview or anticipate the end.

Recapitulation

Other interpreters follow some form of recapitulation. In the third century, Victorinus noted that the trumpets and bowls were parallel accounts of the same events. Later, the seven seals were added, extending the principle of recapitulation. Modern scholars went beyond the septenaries, finding repeated features in the presentation of the beast and the eschatological earthquake.[40] Adela Yarbro Collins, for example, affirms repetition that starts with persecutions, moves to the punishment of the nations, and ultimately to the triumph of God or the Lamb or the faithful.[41]

John therefore repeats his visions. Nevertheless, there is sequence within the individual visions. William Hendriksen proposed that Revelation's sections "are parallel: each spans the entire new dispensation, from the first to the second coming of Christ."[42] However, interpreters must be cautious not to fall into the trap of parallelism (e.g. first seal equals first trumpet equals first bowl). Instead, spiraling, ascending, expanding, and developing progress is made so that later visions describe more fully earlier echoes.[43] Subsequent visions expand and develop the same subject matter but from different, fuller, and deeper perspectives. Therefore, sequence plus recapitulation takes place. A better term is "progressive recapitulation." Several commentators on Revelation utilize various aspects of recapitulation.[44] This study follows the progressive recapitulation approach.

38. Robert Thomas, *Revelation*, 2:525–43; idem, "Structure of the Apocalypse," 45–66; Jauhiainen, "Recapitulation and Chronological Progression," 543–49; Alan Johnson, "Revelation," 13:669–70; Ladd, *Revelation*, 122; Walvoord, *Revelation*, 150.

39. Walvoord, *Revelation*, 223.

40. Giblin, "Recapitulation and the Literary Coherence," 81–95. Beale (*Revelation*, 135–37) discusses several OT and intertestamental books that display a recapping structure.

41. Yarbro Collins, *Combat Myth*, 32–34. In her view, this recapping dealt with the confrontation (combat motif) between Jesus' followers and the Roman Empire.

42. Hendriksen, *More than Conquerors*, 28.

43. Ibid., 47. See Dennis Johnson, *Triumph of the Lamb*, 45–46.

44. Beale, *Revelation*, 121–51; Beasley-Murray, *Revelation*, 30–31; Boxall, *Revelation*, 17–18; Brighton, *Revelation*, 18; Duvall, *Revelation*, 7–8; Dennis Johnson, *Triumph of the Lamb*, 44–47; Keener, *Revelation*, 33–34; Kistemaker, *Revelation*, 65–66; Koester, *Revelation*, 115; Mangina, *Revelation*, 30–31; Mounce, *Revelation*, 33, 369–70; Murphy, *Fallen Is Babylon*, 51–53; Osborne, *Revelation*, 303, 339–40; Reddish, *Revelation*, 21. Beasley-Murray, Duvall, Mounce, and Osborne are premillennial interpreters,

Images Clustered at the Conclusion of Visions

When the key literary indicators are noted and progressive recapitulation is followed, readers begin to find certain words, phrases, and concepts at the conclusion of individual visions. These intratextual clues serve not only as structural indicators but as chronological markers. Each one of the following five motifs occurs not only at the end of a vision but at the conclusion of history. A sixth motif is also found at the conclusion of visions. It does not hold temporal significance, but does assist in delineating the structure of Revelation.

The Last Battle

Revelation presents several images to what is called only once "Armageddon" (16:16). In fact, there are seven allusive portrayals of this end-time battle. Armageddon is echoed in the sixth seal (6:15), given more development in the sixth trumpet (9:13–21), the third interlude (14:19–20); the sixth bowl (16:12–16); the fall of Babylon (17:12–14); the rider on the white horse (19:17–21); and the millennial reign (20:7–10). Each depiction is located near the end of its respective vision. Key words found at end of several visions confirm that Armageddon is in mind. These words include "battle," "kings of the earth (east, world)," "generals," "horses," "nations," "small and great," "the rest," and "inhabitants of the earth." In addition, "demons" is found three times at the end of three visions and demonic "spirits" is found twice at the end of two visions. This suggests an increase in demonic activity leading up to the end.

The Great Earthquake and Cosmic Storm

Cosmic imagery occurs throughout Revelation—earthquakes, falling heavenly bodies, and the dissolution of the world. Specifically, John utilizes two apocalyptic formulas—the earthquake and the cosmic storm—to signify the appearance of God and end-time judgment. First, the end-time cosmic storm ("lightning," "thunder," "rumblings," "hail") is related four times in Revelation (4:5; 8:5; 11:19; 16:18–21). Second, the "earthquake" (*seismos*) is found exactly seven times (6:12; 8:5; 11:13 [twice]; 11:19; 16:18 [twice]). All repeat the one final great earthquake at the end of earth history (Heb 12:26–27). Four times the adjective "great" is added to emphasize full earth coverage. Significantly, the great earthquake and accompanying end-time cosmic storm are located at the conclusion of several individual visions. This establishes that John reserves this usage of cosmic imagery not only as a structural clue, but as a picture of the end of history.

The Second Coming

When Jesus comes, he comes to judge the wicked and to vindicate the righteous. For believers, the second coming is a time of celebration and vindication. Allusions and

---

thus underscoring the breadth of recapitulation scholars.

descriptions of his return are found in all twelve visions as well as the prologue and epilogue. It is a major theme of Revelation. John mentions *erchomai* ("coming") thirty-six times, and twenty-one of those refer to the coming of Christ at the conclusion of history. "Coming" stresses the imminence of his appearance (2:16; 3:11; 16:15; 22:7, 12, 20), but the second coming is most often in mind (6:16; 11:15–19; 14:1–5, 14–16; 16:15; 17:14; 19:6–8, 11–16; 20:9, 11). Each instance appears near the end of an individual vision. Another second coming image is the "harvest," "firstfruits," and the instrument of the harvest—the "sickle." Although placed under nature and clothing accoutrements in this study, these words are used for the end-time harvest of believers (and unbelievers). The harvest is found four times, sickle is found seven times (with "sharp" attached four times), and firstfruits occurs once, and all their references are in 14:14–20. Another image that appears often is the posture of "standing." The victorious "stand" on judgment day (7:9; 11:11; 14:1; 15:2).

The Final Judgment

By contrast, when Jesus comes, he comes not only to vindicate the righteous but to judge the wicked. This image then emphasizes the second coming from the perspective of unbelievers. All of the intratextual allusions to the great day of wrath, fall of Babylon, and eternal punishment anticipate the consummative judgment of the great white throne which is more fully developed in chapter 20. Several key images are linked to the final judgment. They are found most often at the conclusion of an individual vision. Among these are "great day," "wrath" (*orgē* and *thymos*), "cup," "wine," "grapes," "great winepress," "fire," "smoke," "sulfur," and "lake of fire."

Furthermore, the careers of the "beast" and "false prophet" fill up chapter 13, and imply their oppression covers the interadventual age. However, all other references are found at the end of visions in the context of final judgment. Alongside the beast and false prophet is the "image of the beast" and the "mark of the beast." These also appear at end of individual visions. "Babylon the Great" is found six times at the end of three visions. The "great city" is found nine times at or near the end of three visions. God's posture of "sitting" depicts his authority to judge, and is found most often in connection with final judgment. Finally, just as believers stand in victory at the return of Christ, the wicked "stand" to face their judgment (6:17; 18:10, 15, 17; 20:12).

New Heaven and New Earth

Allusions associated with eternal bliss, heavenly rewards, new heaven and new earth, and the intimate, eternal presence, worship, and fellowship with God and the Lamb are not confined to chapters 21–22. They are scattered throughout Revelation. Rewards for overcomers permeate the seven letters. These images show up again in chapters 21–22. End-time rewards, fulfilled promises, heavenly worship, and eternal bliss are major components of several throne room scenes. The initial and longest throne room scene is chapters 4–5. The remaining seven heavenly throne room scenes are located at or near the conclusion of six visions (7:9–17; 8:1–5; 11:15–19; 14:1–5; 15:2–4 [two throne room scenes supports marking the final section of the third interlude as 14:1–15:4]; 19:1–10; 21:1–8). A consistent feature of heavenly throne room scenes is the hymns. The exact number of hymns and doxologies is debated but the hymns typically appear toward the end of individual visions. The "four living creatures" and "twenty-four elders" show up most often at the end of visions. "Harps," "incense," and "altar" are parts of heavenly worship. Other entries that are found at the end of individual visions include "great multitude," "bride," "fine linen," and "river of the water of life."

Therefore, the above five motifs not only assist in structuring Revelation, but in interpreting it—there is one earthquake, one end-time storm, one end-time battle, one return of Christ, and one end-time judgment.

Other Words and Images Found Near the End

Other words and images consolidate toward the end of a vision and become suggestive of literary indicators. First of all, several titles of deity show up near the end of individual visions. Since the throne room scenes appear near the end of visions, the titles of deity follow suit. These could be placed above under second coming or final judgment. The titles include "God of heaven," "Lord God Almighty," "one who is and was and is to/has come," "one who sits on the throne," the vocative form of "God" (*ho theos*), "Lamb," and "King of kings and Lord of lords." Other words assigned for the end of visions for emphasis include the "loud voice," "throne," "face," "prophets," and "servants." Finally, John places the seven beatitudes ("blessed") near the end of visions.

These examples do not display the same temporal importance as the previous examples. Nevertheless, their presence becomes another intratextual clue that John is nearing the end of a vision. John therefore reserves key words, phrases, and images for the end of his individual visions. These clusters assist not only in structuring the vision, but interpreting it. John recaps his visions so that the end of a vision pictures the end of history.

An Outline of Revelation

Aided by the above external and internal clues, and a progressive recapitulation methodology, an outline for Revelation is now attempted. It is based on John producing twelve visions. Most of the visions begin with John's audience and progress to eternity. Chapters 1–3 stress John's immediate audience. By extension, every generation and each believer should heed the challenges of what the Spirit says to the churches. The mighty throne room vision of chapters 4–5 pictures the result of what God did in creation and what the Son accomplished via the cross. His death opens the scroll and reveals its contents. The seals, trumpets, and bowls reveal the ups and downs of history from three different angles. Specifically, the first five of each series reflect this—earthly, natural, resultative judgments on humanity and nature—from John's day through the Middle Ages and Reformation up to the present day and especially toward the end. The final two seals, trumpets, and bowls, however, usher us to the brink of the eschaton.[45] They include allusions, images, and phrases that reveal the final battle, parousia, cosmic imagery (earthquake), end-time judgment, and eternal bliss.

Similarly, the three interludes reveal the same progressive recapping—7:1–8; 10:1–11:6; and 12:1–13:18 present the ongoing battle between the devil and believers throughout the centuries. It is a spiritual war and believers are called to witness until they die. But at the conclusion of each interlude, the end-time images reappear, signaling the eschaton. Thus, 7:9–17; 11:7–13; and 14:1–15:4 are end-time pictures.[46] The fall of Babylon is prefaced by a survey of history in 17:1–11 but 17:12–14 depicts end-time images. Babylon's fall is described (18:1–24), leading to a portrayal of end-time bliss (19:1–10).[47] The rider on the white horse begins abruptly with the parousia and leads to final judgment. The millennial vision, however, depicts history in 20:1–6, leading to the eschatological battle (20:7–10), final judgment (20:11–15), and new heaven and new earth (21:1–8).[48] The new Jerusalem vision completes John's visions, stressing eternal bliss (21:9–22:9).

Here then is an outline on Revelation based on John's twelve visions. As readers study the symbolic entries in this book, they will need to refer to this often.

Prologue (1:1–8)

Vision One: Inaugural Vision and Seven Letters (1:9–3:22)

45. Numerous scholars agree that the seventh seal extends to 8:5, including Bauckham (*Climax of Prophecy*, 70–83), Beasley-Murray (*Revelation*, 149–52), Brighton (*Revelation*, 210), Caird (*Revelation*, 106), Fee (*Revelation*, 118), Giblin (*Revelation*, 13), Harrington (*Revelation*, 103), Dennis Johnson (*Triumph of the Lamb*, 136–38), Kiddle (*Revelation*, 143–48), Koester (*Revelation*, 114), Morris (*Revelation*, 44), Prigent (*Apocalypse*, 297), Reddish (*Revelation*, 161), Thomas and Macchia (*Revelation*, 175–79), Waddell (*Spirit of Revelation*, 148), Mark Wilson ("Revelation," 300). Beale (*Revelation*, 459) adds, "That 8:5 is about the Last Assize is confirmed from 14:18–19, where the Judgment Day is commenced apparently by the same angel described in the same language as here in 8:3–5 . . ."

46. Several scholars extend the third interlude to 15:4, including Bauckham (*Climax of Prophecy*, 16–18), Beale (*Revelation*, 113–14), Boxall (*Revelation*, 20), Koester (*Revelation*, 114), Murphy (*Fallen Is Babylon*, 329), Waddell (*Spirit of Revelation*, 148), Wilcock (*I Saw Heaven Opened*, 137), and Yarbro Collins (*Combat Myth*, 15–19). Mulholland (*Revelation*, 214) extends it to 15:5; Giblin (*Revelation*, 95) and Dennis Johnson (*Triumph of the Lamb*, 199) extend it to 15:8.

47. A growing consensus of scholarship extends the fall of Babylon vision to 19:10, including Aune, *Revelation,* 3:905; Bauckham, *Climax of Prophecy*, 2–6; Beasley-Murray, *Revelation*, 32; Blount, *Revelation*, 347; Boxall, *Revelation*, 18; Fee, *Revelation*, 228; Giblin, *Revelation*, 16; Harrington, *Revelation*, 185; Alan Johnson, "Revelation," 13:593; Dennis Johnson, *Triumph of the Lamb*, 241; Kistemaker, *Revelation*, 69; Koester, *Revelation*, 637; Lambrecht, "Structuration of Revelation," 86; Mulholland, *Revelation*, 276; Murphy, *Fallen Is Babylon*, 348; Paul, *Revelation*, 42; Poythress, *Returning King*, 159; Leonard Thompson, *Revelation*, 166; Tõniste, *Ending of the Canon*, 55; Waddell, *Spirit of Revelation*, 149; Witherington, *Revelation*, 233–34. Those who end the vision with 19:5 include Duvall (*Revelation*, 244), Mounce (*Revelation*, 35), and Osborne (*Revelation*, 31).

48. The pre-, post-, and amillennial question revolves around whether *kai eidon* in 20:1 is used as a literary indicator for the next vision or a historical sequence marker of subsequent events. Following the majority of other uses of *kai eidon* and a progressive recapitulation approach, this study understands it as a literary indicator. Interpreters who extend the vision to 21:1–8 include the resources who follow "in the Spirit" (see footnote 28) as well as Aune (*Revelation*, 3:1040;), Campbell ("Antithetical Feminine-Urban Imagery," 95), Giblin (*Revelation*, 17), Ladd (*Revelation*, 16), and Witherington (*Revelation*, 256).

Vision Two: Throne Room (4:1–5:14)

Vision Three: Seven Seals (6:1–17; 8:1–5)

Vision Four: First Interlude (7:1–17)

Vision Five: Seven Trumpets (8:6–9:21; 11:15–19)

Vision Six: Second Interlude (10:1–11:14)

Vision Seven: Third Interlude (12:1–15:4)

Vision Eight: Seven Bowls (15:5–16:21)

Vision Nine: Fall of Babylon (17:1–19:10)

Vision Ten: Rider on the White Horse (19:11–21)

Vision Eleven: Thousand Years (20:1–21:8)

Vision Twelve: New Jerusalem (21:9–22:9)

Epilogue (22:10–21)

Master List of Entries

The rest of this study places John's images into identifiable categories. Under each category, numerous entries are listed alphabetically. Several entries overlap categories. A thousand two hundred and sixty days is an element of time but also a symbolic number. The Lamb is an animal yet refers to a heavenly being as well as a title of deity. The sixth seal begins with the sun turning "black as sackcloth" (6:12), an image that includes colors, clothing, and cosmic imagery. Where does the "the rider on the white horse" settle? It symbolizes a demonic being (6:2) and a heavenly being (19:11), but also refers to animals and colors. A final example is "A woman clothed with the sun, with the moon under her feet and a crown of twelve stars on her head" (12:1). This image can be placed under people, numbers, cosmic imagery, or body parts. Therefore, decisions must be made on where to place certain entries.

The titles of the entries follow the NIV 2011. The reason is that since it is the best-selling modern version, most readers will have access to it.[49] Each entry begins with an italicized topic sentence(s) which gives the essential essence of the symbol. The rest of the entry broadly follows the seven steps for interpretation. Here then is the master list of entries for handy reference.

---

49. The most recent editions are used, e.g. NRSV, NJB, REB. There are a few exceptions. Since the HCSB came out in 2003 and its revision, CSB, came out in 2017, the HCSB is noted if it has a different reading than the CSB. Likewise, if the NIV 1984 edition is different than NIV 2011, it is mentioned. The KJV is also referred to at times.

Conclusion

Readers now have the necessary background for launching a study of the symbols of Revelation. This introduction will need to be accessed regularly, primarily for the master list. The twelve-vision outline, however, must always be kept in mind when studying an image. Where the image is found within a vision is often just as important as its meaning. This study does not exhaust John's images found in Revelation. The amount, however, should guide readers, teachers, and preachers of Revelation. For interested readers, the book can be browsed via the categories and used as a handy reference when studying Revelation. The entries offer explanations and options on John's symbols. For teachers and preachers, the entries supply background and helps necessary for balanced instruction on Revelation. For scholarly exegetes, it supplies the necessary range of options which Revelation's interpreters offer, and perhaps serves as a springboard for deeper study.

1

Heavenly Beings and Demonic Beings

THE BOOK OF REVELATION is chock-full of heavenly and demonic beings. Heavenly beings include persons of the Trinity, angels, and titles of deity. Because there are so many titles of deity a separate category is set aside for them. But the titles are not exhaustive, and a few titles (Lamb and the Lion of Judah) are found in the chapter on animals. The devil, demons, and Abaddon and Apollyon are examples of demonic beings. As with titles of deity, some designations are placed in the animal kingdom (dragon, serpent, locusts, scorpions). Finally, the four angels is an example of both heavenly and demonic beings.

Heavenly Beings

This section discusses John's treatment of angels and the Trinity. Some of these can be placed just as easily in other categories. The seven spirits and the rider on the white horse (chapter 19) work just as well as titles of deity. Again, the point is not to be exhaustive. For example, God is mentioned ninety-six times in Revelation but is designated for only a couple of entries under titles of deity.

Angel

Angels are spiritual beings, typically heavenly messengers of God who carry out his will, but on occasion they refer to evil beings who carry out the wicked intentions of the devil. Angels are found throughout Scripture and intertestamental literature.[1] They appear prominently in Revelation (38% of all NT references).[2] Broadly speaking, there are good angels and bad angels. Elsewhere in the NT, good angels are called "the holy angels," "the

---

1. See Noll, *Angels of Light*, 63–66, 148–49, 166–67, 183–84.

2. There are too many references to give individual treatment of passages. Helpful starting points for further research include Carrell, *Jesus and the Angels*, 20–23; Davidson, "Angel," 148–55; Funderburk, "Angel," 183–91; Newsom and Watson, "Angels," 248–55 ; Ryken, *Dictionary of Biblical Imagery*, 23–25; J. Macartney Wilson, "Angels," 124–27.

angels of God," "angels in heaven," and "his powerful angels" (Matt 24:31; Luke 9:26; Heb 1:6). In Revelation, John reflects a ranking of angels. Archangel Michael is mentioned (12:7). Some scholars recognize allusions to the traditional seven archangels of apocalyptic literature found in the seven trumpets.[3] Other suggestions of ranking include the mighty angels, the four living creatures, the twenty-four elders, and the angels of the seven churches. The angel coming from the east is obviously high-ranking since he commands the four angels holding back the four winds (7:2).[4]

John also mentions bad angels (12:9; see Matt 25:41). Although some disagree, demonic angels are mentioned at 9:14.[5] Satan is the highest ranking fallen angel, and there are also higher level evil angels (Abaddon/Apollyon, Wormwood), and the angel over the Abyss (who could be Satan). There are also demons and evil spirits.[6]

The roles and duties of angels are observable in Revelation. They have a role over nature (7:1–3; 8:7–12; 19:17). They serve as interpreters for John (1:1; 10:1–10; 14:6–11; 17:1, 7–18; 21:9). They serve humanity by carrying the prayers of the saints to God (8:3–5). Primarily, however, angels worship and serve the Lord. They make proclamations (5:2; 14:6–9), bind the devil (20:1–3), and measure the new Jerusalem (21:9–27). A major role is executing God's wrath at the end (8:6; 14:14–20; 15:1; 19:11–21). Thus, the work of angels is to implement God's will in heaven and on earth.

Angel in Charge of the Waters

Following the Jewish tradition of angels in charge of the elements, this angel renders end-time judgments upon the wicked on behalf of God. This angel is mentioned only once (16:5). It is possible the angel is the same one mentioned in 16:4, and that this phrase simply reflects his actions, not a title. After all, nowhere else in Scripture does an angel have authority over the waters.[7] Most commentators, however, recognize John is carrying forward a common motif from apocalyptic literature that reveals angels to be assigned to certain parts of creation (*1 En.* 60:11–22; 66:1–2; *2 En.* 19:4–5; *Jub.* 2:2), a motif that is found elsewhere in Revelation (7:1; 14:18). Ben Witherington avers, "There is little doubt that the author is following apocalyptic ideas here, as he does at 7.1ff where he speaks of angels that control the wind and, at 14.18, control the fire . . ."[8] James Resseguie calls the

---

3. Smalley, *Revelation*, 29.

4. This angel literally ascends from "the rising of the sun." Since he is called "another angel" he may be the same one that is mentioned later (8:3; 10:1; 14:6–9, 15–18; 18:1–2). Although debated, the angel from the east brings divine blessings. For other viewpoints see Osborne, *Revelation*, 307–8; and Smalley, *Revelation*, 181. Kovacs and Rowland (*Revelation*, 100–101) list historical attempts to identify this angel, including Elijah, Constantine, a saintly pope, Francis of Assisi, and Queen Elizabeth.

5. See the entry "Four Angels."

6. See the entry "Demons."

7. So Kistemaker, *Revelation*, 442; Stefanovic, *Revelation*, 483.

8. Witherington, *Revelation*, 208. So also Aune, *Revelation*, 2:884–85; Beale, *Revelation*, 817–18; Caird, *Revelation*, 202; Harrington, *Revelation*, 163; Hughes, *Revelation*, 171; Keener, *Revelation*, 393; Lupieri, *Apocalypse*, 238; Mounce, *Revelation*, 294; Osborne, *Revelation*, 581–82; Patterson, *Revelation*, 307; Smalley, *Revelation*, 402; Sweet, *Revelation*, 244; Robert Thomas, *Revelation*, 2:252.

angel of the waters "a spokesperson for the entire environment."[9] The third bowl (16:4–7) parallels the third trumpet (8:10–11), and both evoke the first Egyptian plague (Exod 7:14–24). God punishes the wicked for their persecution, especially economic persecution of believers.[10] Many interpret this plague literally, and reserve it for the very end of history.[11] Others understand this bowl more symbolically as any suffering that can lead to death.[12] Eclectically speaking, since it is the third bowl, the end is not yet in sight.

Angel Who Had Charge of the Fire

This angel, mentioned twice, serves God in delivering fiery, end-time judgment upon the earth. Near the conclusion of the third interlude (12:1–15:4) stands a depiction of the grape harvest, a picture of divine judgment on the wicked at the end of history. An angel "who had charge of the fire" calls out "Take your sharp sickle and gather the clusters of grapes from the earth's vine, because its grapes are ripe" (14:18). Jewish tradition often spoke of angels having authority over the elements such as wind, water, earth, stars, thunder, rain, sea, frost, and fire (*1 En.* 60:11–22; *Jub.* 2:2). In fact, an archangel named Purouel is credited with this assignment over fire (*T. Ab.* 12:14; 13:11–14).[13] Following a progressive recapitulation approach, this action of judgment takes place at the second coming.

Many interpreters connect this angel to the one at 8:3–5 who hurls a censer filled with fire upon the earth. If so, then this relates the same recapped episode. Thus, 8:3–5 and 14:18 both picture final judgment at the end of history. The first passage concludes the seals judgments and the latter passage concludes the third interlude. The fire is representative of fiery, final, end-time judgment. The earthquake symbolizes the end at other visions, as does the reaping of the wicked who are cast into the winepress of God's final judgment.[14]

Angels of the Seven Churches

These are angelic beings who represent the prevailing character of each one of the seven churches. The expression is found only at 1:20 when the risen Christ interprets the inaugural vision: "The seven stars are the angels of the seven churches, and the seven lampstands are the seven churches." Each church's angel is then addressed (2:1, 8, 12, 18; 3:1, 7, 14). There are two main proposals for identifying these angels. First, several Bible students understand these angels to refer to human beings. This view places stress on the

---

9. Resseguie, *Revelation*, 211.

10. Osborne, *Revelation*, 580–85.

11. Hindson, *Revelation*, 169; LaHaye, *Revelation Unveiled*, 252; Patterson, *Revelation*, 306–8; Robert Thomas, *Revelation*, 2:251–55; Walvoord, *Revelation*, 233–34.

12. Aune, *Revelation*, 2:884–88; Beale, *Revelation*, 816–21; Smalley, *Revelation*, 402–4.

13. Osborne, *Revelation*, 553; Smalley, *Revelation*, 375.

14. Numerous scholars agree that the seventh seal extends to 8:5. See the listing in the Introduction, n. 46.

basic understanding of the word as "messenger" (Luke 7:24; Jas 2:25). They could be messengers to the churches or they could be the church leaders or delegates of the church.[15] Second, they refer to heavenly beings who are either guardian angels of the churches or the personified spirits of the churches. In other words, they represent the prevailing "spirit" of a particular church, the spiritual and heavenly counterpart to the earthly reality.[16] Evidence to support this view includes the fact that the rest of the nearly seventy references to angels in Revelation denote spiritual beings. Moreover, angels are never used for human messengers in other apocalyptic literature. This latter view is the better proposal. Thus, the angels identify with and serve the seven churches, and represent them before God (8:3–5; 19:10; 22:9).[17] Most would agree with Paige Patterson's assessment. "Dogmatism is not appropriate on the point and, fortunately, is not necessary to grasp the full intent of the text."[18]

Four Angels

A group of four angels is mentioned twice in Revelation, once referring to good angels and once to evil angels, but in both instances drawing attention to the worldwide effects of the events that involve them. The first interlude mentions four angels standing at the four corners of the earth, holding back the four winds (7:1). The sixth trumpet also mentions "four angels who are bound at the great river Euphrates" (9:14). Many interpreters understand both references to be good angels, God's agents of judgment, tasked with restraining evil.[19] But more scholars interpret the first group as good angels and the sec-

15. Buchanan, *Revelation*, 78; Hughes, *Revelation*, 31; Kistemaker, *Revelation*, 103; Mulholland, *Revelation*, 91–92; Patterson, *Revelation*, 72; Tenney, *Interpreting Revelation*, 55; Robert Thomas, *Revelation*, 1:117–18; Walvoord, *Revelation*, 49. Interestingly, GW translates "angels" as "messengers," suggesting its interpretive preference. Several versions maintain "angels" as the translation but also provide an option in the footnote of "or messengers" (CEV, CSB, NET, NIV, NLT). Ferguson ("Angels of the Churches," 371–86) uniquely suggests they are members of the congregation who leads in prayer and Scripture reading.

16. Aune, *Revelation*, 1:110; Beale, *Revelation*, 217–19; Beasley-Murray, *Revelation*, 69–70; Blount, *Revelation*, 47; Boring, *Revelation*, 86–87; Brighton, *Revelation*, 61; Duvall, *Revelation*, 33; Fee, *Revelation*, 21; Hailey, *Revelation*, 115–16; Alan Johnson, "Revelation," 13:608; Dennis Johnson, *Triumph of the Lamb*, 62–63; Keener, *Revelation*, 100; Ladd, *Revelation*, 35; Lupieri, *Apocalypse*, 114; Michaels, *Revelation*, 63; Minear, *I Saw a New Earth*, 41–42; Morris, *Revelation*, 57; Mounce, *Revelation*, 63; Osborne, *Revelation*, 99; Paul, *Revelation*, 74: Reddish, *Revelation*, 43; Resseguie, *Revelation*, 81; Roloff, *Revelation of John*, 38–39; Rowland, "Revelation," 12:567; Schüssler Fiorenza, *Vision of a Just World*, 52; Smalley, *Revelation*, 58; Stefanovic, *Revelation*, 97; Sweet, *Revelation*, 73; Worth, *Seven Cities of the Apocalypse*, 109–11. Both Murphy (*Apocalypticism*, 102) and Mark Wilson (*Victor Sayings*, 67) remark that patron angels are customary of apocalyptic literature. Ryrie (*Revelation*, 21) opts for guardian angels or human leaders.

17. Duvall, *Revelation*, 33. Noll (*Angels of Light*, 146) states, "Christ and the seven church angels replace the imagery of the seven archangels in other Jewish apocalypses."

18. Patterson, *Revelation*, 72.

19. Aune, *Revelation*, 2:536–37; Brighton, *Revelation*, 243–44; Kiddle, *Revelation*, 161–63; Lupieri, *Apocalypse*, 148; Michaels, *Revelation*, 130; Mulholland, *Revelation*, 197; Murphy, *Fallen Is Babylon*, 146; Paul, *Revelation*, 156, 180; Patterson, *Revelation*, 223; Stefanovic, *Revelation*, 315; J. C. Thomas, *Apocalypse*, 301.

ond group as demonic angels, bound and restrained from performing evil until loosed near the eschaton to raise end-time havoc.[20] Thus, the four angels of 9:14 have more in common with the four winds of 7:1 than they do with the four angels who release the winds.[21] The former stand at the extreme limits of the earth whereas the latter stand at the Euphrates River. Altogether, the four angels, four corners, and four winds (7:1) along with the four angels, four occurrences of time (hour, day, month, year), and four horns of the altar (9:13–15) highlight numerical symbolism and accentuate full coverage and the worldwide effects of both passages.

Four Living Creatures

The four living creatures are a high order of angelic beings that represent the animate world, lead in the worship of God the creator, and execute end-time judgment on behalf of God. This entry could also be placed under the heading of animals. John uses *zōon* ("living thing/being") exclusively for the four living "creatures" whereas *therion* is his word choice for "beast." Most English translations follow this distinction.[22] The identity of these beings has stimulated countless interpretations. R. C. H. Lenski listed one writer who tallied twenty-one efforts at a solution, then proffered his own which was equally unsatisfactory.[23] The four living creatures are closely allied to the twenty-four elders. Whereas the elders are angelic representatives of special creation, God's people, the living creatures are angelic representatives of general creation, the animate life of the world. John combines, adapts, and expands upon the descriptions of previous angels, namely the cherubim (Ezek 1:5–21; 10:12–22) and the seraphim (Isa 6:1–4). The creatures are covered with eyes and have six wings. The eyes underscore all-seeing vigilance, intelligence, and watchfulness.[24] Their six wings is not a sinister number here but rather three sets of two wings, each with their own distinct function.[25] The four creatures are like a lion, an ox, the face of a man, and a flying eagle (4:6–8).[26]

---

20. Beale, *Revelation*, 505–8; Beasley-Murray, *Revelation*, 163; Blount, *Revelation*, 182; Boxall, *Revelation*, 147; Keener, *Revelation*, 271; Kistemaker, *Revelation*, 295; Ladd, *Revelation*, 136; Morris, *Revelation*, 133; Mounce, *Revelation*, 194; Osborne, *Revelation*, 379; Resseguie, *Revelation Unsealed*, 159; Roloff, *Revelation*, 118; Smalley, *Revelation*, 326; Sweet, *Revelation*, 172; Robert Thomas, *Revelation*, 2:43; Walvoord, *Revelation*, 165; Witherington, *Revelation*, 154.

21. So too Osborne, *Revelation*, 378 n. 5.

22. The NLT selects "four living beings." The KJV's unfortunate English translation of "four living beasts" masks John's Greek words and several commentators mention it. Fee (*Revelation*, 72 n. 6) laments how this has led to "centuries of unfortunate understanding, not to mention pictures (!)" Patterson (*Revelation*, 154), however, defends the KJV, opting that "creatures" conjures up some ominous biological life form. Fortunately, NKJV follows modern versions by revising them to "living creatures."

23. Taken from Mounce, *Revelation*, 124.

24. Ladd, *Revelation*, 77.

25. Kistemaker, *Revelation*, 191.

26. The creatures are "in the midst of the throne." Robert Hall ("Living Creatures in the Midst of the Throne," 609–13) suggests this means they are integral components of the throne. Hays (*Temple and Tabernacle*, 115–21) identifies the four living creatures as cherubim.

Why these four descriptions? First of all, the number four prompts readers to the numerical symbol of completeness with regards to creation. Generally, they stand as heads of their respective orders. The eagle, the most majestic of birds, is over the air. The lion, the fiercest of wild animals, is over the wilderness. The ox, the strongest of the domesticated animals, is over cultivated land. The man, ruler over the animals, is over creation. Together, they represent the totality of creation.[27]

These four angelic creatures perform two activities which often overlap. First, they serve as worship leaders for the heavenly host. This is exemplified through their eleven references in the throne room vision of chapters 4–5. Resseguie remarks that the "creatures illustrate that worship is not merely something the creation does; rather *worship of God signifies the perfect harmony that exists between God and the creation as heaven and earth are brought together in unity*."[28] A second activity is their role in divine judgment. Five times they shout "Come!" as the end-time judgments of the seals commence (6:1–8). In 15:7, one of the four living creatures gives the bowls to the seven angels to initiate end-time judgment. Finally, they also show up in scenes found at the end of three visions (7:11; 14:3; 19:4) where worship and judgment merge. Therefore, the four living creatures consist of a special order of angels who represent God's total creation. They are worship leaders who also participate in God's end-time judgment.

(Holy) Spirit

Although the familiar title of "Holy" Spirit (as well as "Spirit of God" and "Spirit of Christ") is absent from Revelation, the third person of the Trinity plays a major role as the one sent by the Father and Son to be their eyes in the world, to represent the present and effective work of God, to inspire John's visions, and to join the Father and Son in delivering end-time judgment. Some commentators do not find a developed role of the Holy Spirit or the Trinity in the NT. This holds true for them with regard to John's Apocalypse.[29] On the contrary, the Spirit enjoys an expansive role in Revelation, and coupled with the Gospel of John, the apostle has much to say about the Trinity.[30] The Spirit is referenced less than God and Christ yet still plays a major role.[31]

27. So Barr, *Tales*, 106; Beale, *Revelation*, 329–30; Brighton, *Revelation*, 126–27; Hays, Duvall, and Pate, *Dictionary of Biblical Prophecy*,166–67; Dennis Johnson, *Triumph of the Lamb*, 101; Kistemaker, *Revelation*, 191; Morris, *Revelation*, 88–89; Mounce, *Revelation*, 124; Osborne, *Revelation*, 234–35; Robert Thomas, *Revelation*, 1:358.

28. Resseguie, *Revelation Unsealed*, 130 (original italics).

29. So Aune, *Revelation*, 1:34; Charles, *Revelation*, 1:11.

30. Rainbow (*Pith of the Apocalypse*, 73–74) notes the similar usage of "the Spirit" in the Gospel of John and Johannine epistles.

31. Reynolds ("Trinity in Revelation," 55–72) finds 124 names, titles, designations of God, eighty for Jesus, and seventeen for the Holy Spirit. The Spirit in Revelation is receiving more attention. Bruce ("Spirit in the Apocalypse," 333–44) was the first in-depth contributor to the topic, and revealed John's careful structuring. Bauckham ("Role of the Spirit in the Apocalypse," 66–83; *Climax of Prophecy*, 150–73; and *Theology of Revelation*, 109–25) has produced several cogent studies. More recent studies, usually accenting one area, include Archer, *I Was in the Spirit*; J. C. de Smidt, "Holy Spirit," 229–44; Kobus de Smidt, "Spirit in the Book of Revelation," 27–47; Jeske, "Spirit and Community," 452–66; H. Y.

John's numerical symbolism aids in identifying the Spirit's significance. There are four references to the "seven spirits" (1:4; 3:1; 4:5; 5:6).[32] There are fourteen (7 x 2) references to "the Spirit." Seven of these are commands to the seven churches to hear what the Spirit says (2:7, 11, 17, 29; 3:6, 13, 22). Four of the remaining seven references make up the phrase "in the Spirit" (1:10; 4:2; 17:3; 21:10), which also serves as a key structural marker for John since each one of the four is located at the beginning of a new vision. Two references quote the Spirit (14:13; 22:17) and the final one is the phrase "the Spirit of prophecy" (19:10).[33] This meticulous use of numerical symbolism reveals John's intention to accentuate the Holy Spirit.

John's mention of the Spirit revolves around several major themes. First, the Spirit is intimately connected to God and Jesus. He is the Spirit "of God" (3:1; 4:5; 5:6) who gives the "breath of life" (11:11). Moreover, the Spirit speaks the words of Jesus, and these words are discerned "in the Spirit" to the churches.[34] Second, the theme of discipleship is woven throughout Revelation. The seven exhortations to "hear (*akouō* implies "obey") what the Spirit says to the churches" fit here. These appeals also include the call to endure suffering, be faithful to the point of death, and undergo self-evaluation in order to repent.[35] Third, the theme of witness is observable. The "seven spirits" (found four times) is taken from Zech 4 and closely identifies the Spirit with Christ as the seven eyes sent from God throughout the earth. The numerical symbolism of seven (completeness, totality) and four (full coverage with the earth in mind) highlight the theme of the full presence and effective work of the Holy Spirit. Richard Bauckham adds that the close association of the seven spirits with the Lamb in these four references "indicates that the Lamb's victory is implemented throughout the world by the fulness of divine power."[36] Fourth, the theme of prophecy is evident. The stress here is on the activity of the Spirit through Christian prophets within the church such as John. The Spirit enables John to see the visions and inspires him to write Revelation.[37] Fifth, the presence of the Spirit in Revelation has implications for worship. John was "in the Spirit" on the Lord's day (1:10), suggesting that the Spirit was the path to worship. John is told to worship God, for the Spirit of prophecy is the testimony of Jesus (19:10).[38] Sixth, the Spirit's role in end-time judgment is noticeable. When Christ comes in judgment, God and the Spirit come with him. Bauckham calls this the theme of eschatology. It is the Spirit who fills the saints with

---

Lee, *Dynamic Reading*; Thomas and Macchia, *Revelation*, 475–85; and Waddell, *Spirit of of Revelation*. The role of the Spirit in Revelation is discussed in the final six chapters of Keener, Crenshaw, and May, *But These Are Written*.

32. See the entry "Seven Spirits."

33. Bauckham, *Theology of Revelation*, 110. See the entry "Prophecy."

34. Thomas and Macchia, *Revelation*, 476.

35. Kobus de Smidt, "Spirit in the Book of Revelation," 37; Wall, *Revelation*, 47.

36. Bauckham, *Theology of Revelation*, 109.

37. Bauckham (*Climax of Prophecy*, 160–62) understands the prophets as a special group within the church. See the entry "Prophets."

38. Thomas and Macchia, *Revelation*, 478. Filho ("Apocalypse of John," 213–34) stresses "in the Spirit" not only as a structural guide, but as a grounding in the worshipping community. Archer (*I Was in the Spirit*) devotes her entire study to the Spirit and worship in Revelation.

the expectation of Jesus' return, and to prepare for the second coming by bearing witness to his return.[39] Furthermore, the Spirit has a role in ultimate judgment. The Spirit actualizes God's presence in the present and in eternity, even the lake of fire.[40] Therefore, even though the Holy Spirit appears to be less prominent in Revelation when compared to the Father and the Son, his role is nevertheless thoroughly active.

Jesus

Jesus is the faithful witness and suffering savior who leads the church to victory. This entry is limited to how John uses "Jesus" in Revelation.[41] "Jesus" (*Iēsous*) occurs fourteen times (7 x 2) in Revelation, highlighting John's penchant for numerical symbolism. This also aids readers on how John structures his visions. Seven of the fourteen occurrences are closely connected with "witness" or "testimony" (*martys* and *martyria*) (1:2, 9; 12:17; 17:6; 19:10 [twice]; 20:4).[42]

The Hebrew word *moshiach* means "anointed one." Its transliteration into Aramaic (*messias*), however, is found only twice in the NT, both times with the explanatory, "that is, the Christ" (John 1:41; 4:25). Although the Greek *Christos* is the preferred term for NT writers (over 500 times) to describe God's anointed one, both words were used identically in the first century. Nevertheless, "Jesus" often stresses his humanity. Thus, his suffering is for salvation and the church must be ready to suffer as well. Jesus is the lamb who was slain (5:6, 12; 13:8) and his blood cleanses believers (7:14). His blood is also the pathway to their own victory (12:11).[43] His witness effected salvation and the church must be ready to witness as well. As Bauckham notes, "what matters most about the humanity of Jesus in Revelation is the witness which he bore and which his followers continue."[44] He is the faithful witness who leads an army of martyrs (7:4–14; 11:3–13). They give their lives in witness and ironically overcome and are vindicated by their own deaths.[45]

Michael

Michael is an archangel who—at the time of the resurrection and ascension of Christ—leads the angelic host in a spiritual cosmic war against the dragon and his rebellious angels, casting them out of heaven and effectively binding Satan from deceiving the nations until near the end of history. John draws from several extratextual resources to relate his vision of this archangel.[46] In Daniel, Michael is presented as a guardian protector of Israel in the

---

39. Bauckham, *Climax of Prophecy*, 166–73.

40. Umstattd, *Spirit and Lake of Fire*, 143–49.

41. For background on Jesus see Donald Guthrie, "Jesus Christ," 567–661; Martin, "Jesus Christ," 1034–49; Meyer, "Jesus Christ," 773–96; Ryken, *Dictionary of Biblical Imagery*, 437–51.

42. Bauckham, *Climax of Prophecy*, 34.

43. Ryken, *Dictionary of Biblical Imagery*, 443.

44. Bauckham, *Theology of Revelation*, 66.

45. Ibid., 76–94.

46. Stefanovic (*Revelation*, 395), following Seventh Day Adventist convictions, understands Michael

end times (Dan 10:13, 21; 12:1). In apocalyptic traditions, seven archangels are named. Four stood in God's presence—Michael, Gabriel, Raphael, and Uriel. Michael is called "mediator and intercessor" (*1 En.* 20:5; *T. Levi* 5); a warrior who is "the Lord's greatest archangel" (*2 En.* 22:6); he is active in final judgment (*Ascen. Isa.* 9:22); and he will deliver Israel in the last days (*1 En.* 90:14; and according to the *Apocalypse of Elijah*, Michael is the angel who has information about the future that is revealed to Elijah).

Michael is mentioned by name twice in the NT (Jude 9; Rev 12:7). Jude's reference probably alludes to the pseudepigraphal *Testament of Moses*. Michael tells Satan, "The Lord rebuke you," and Jude utilizes this as an example of how to deal with the false prophets of his own era.[47] John carries forward these themes of Michael as a vindicator of God and his people, and as an angelic commander. Rev 12:7–9 relates that a war broke out in heaven. Michael and his angels defeated the dragon who was then hurled to earth. Exactly when this war breaks out has divided scholars into three camps. First, it may refer to a primordial expulsion of Satan that occurs before earth's history. Grant Osborne, for example, understands the allusion to this primordial expulsion occurs in 12:4 and is expanded upon in 12:7–9.[48] Second, at the other end of the chronological spectrum, some scholars who pursue a sequential structure to Revelation place this event in the final three and a half years of earth's history.[49] The third camp houses the majority of scholars. The war in heaven is a cosmic spiritual battle waged at *the* key moment in history—the cross, resurrection, and ascension of Jesus Christ. Fee exemplifies this approach. John's point is to picture the defeat of Satan "not at some prehistoric point, but at the point of his ultimate defeat through the cross and resurrection, as made clear in verses 10–11."[50]

---

to be none other than Christ himself. This understanding does go back in history. An excellent study is Hannah (*Michael and Christ*, 127–30), who contends that angelological conceptions influenced earliest understandings of Christology. Martin Luther accepted this identification, followed by many early Lutheran scholars. Hannah argues against Michael being the Son of God. See also Gieschen, "Identity of Michael," 139–43.

47. Aune, *Revelation*, 2:693–95; Brighton, *Revelation*, 321–22; Cousland, "Michael," 77–78; Hays, Duvall, and Pate, *Dictionary of Prophecy*, 284; van Henten, "Archangel," 80–82; Watson, "Michael," 811.

48. Osborne, *Revelation*, 470–73. So too Patterson, *Revelation*, 267; and Ryrie; *Revelation*, 90.

49. Several dispensationalists such as Robert Thomas (*Revelation*, 2:124–29) agree that the "tail sweeping the stars" (12:4) refers to a primordial expulsion, but that that Michael's battle is at the end of history. So too LaHaye (*Revelation Unveiled*, 202–3), who places this battle "immediately after the Rapture of the Church." In fact, Michael will continue to fight the devil and his angels in the heavenlies throughout the seven-year great tribulation. See also Easley, *Revelation*, 211; Hindson, *Revelation*, 139; and Walvoord, *Revelation*, 194. Less dispensational readings that favor an end-of-history view include Krodel, *Revelation*, 242; and Mounce, *Revelation*, 235–36.

50. Fee, *Revelation*, 169. So Aune, *Revelation*, 2:691–93; Bauckham, *Climax of Prophecy*, 186; Beale, *Revelation*, 636–37; Beasley-Murray, *Revelation*, 202; Blount, *Revelation*, 234; Brighton, *Revelation*, 333–36; Caird, *Revelation*, 153–54; Duvall, *Revelation*, 166; Hailey, *Revelation*, 274; Alan Johnson, "Revelation," 13:698; Dennis Johnson, *Triumph of the Lamb*, 184; Keener, *Revelation*, 320–21; Kistemaker, *Revelation,* 360–61; Ladd, *Revelation*, 171; Mangina, Revelation, 153; Michaels, *Revelation,* 150; Mulholland, *Revelation*, 221; Paul, *Revelation*, 219; Reddish, *Revelation*, 235–36; Resseguie, *Revelation*, 174; Skaggs and Benham, *Revelation*, 129; Smalley, *Revelation*, 322; Stefanovic, *Revelation*, 388; Sweet, *Revelation*, 199; J. C. Thomas, *Apocalypse*, 367; Wilcock, *I Saw Heaven Opened*, 121; Witherington, *Revelation*, 170. Others emphasize the combat myth at work, including Yarbro Collins, *Combat Myth*, 84–85; and Murphy, *Fallen Is Babylon*, 279–82.

Perhaps Osborne is correct after all when he suggests that John had all three "bindings" in mind as he envisioned the events of chapter 12—primordial past, ministry and death of Jesus, and eschaton.[51] Such a picture confirms the role of Michael as the vindication representative and angelic commander, and who ultimately anticipates the triumphant return of Christ and final judgment.

Mighty Angel

The mighty angels mentioned by John are high-ranking heavenly beings (perhaps archangels) who represent Christ, and deliver significant information at crucial points. A "mighty angel" is mentioned three times (5:2; 10:1; 18:21).[52] Throughout history, some Christians who follow a historicist approach attempted to identify the mighty angel (especially the one in 10:1) with a human figure—emperor Justin, emperor Justinian, monk Benedict, Francis of Assisi, or a pious pope. Not to be outdone, Joachim of Fiore apparently outed himself as this angel, and Peter Olivi's followers claimed their mentor was the angel in question.[53] Most expositors, however, recognize the mighty angel as a heavenly being. But is he "just" an angel or perhaps Christ himself? Generally, Greek fathers understood the mighty angel as an angel whereas the Latin fathers preferred to view him as Christ. The notes of the Geneva Bible (1560) opted for Christ, a choice that is still popular today. Gregory Beale, for example, offers solid arguments for 10:1 being a Christophany.[54] Nonetheless, the overwhelming majority of modern scholars interpret the mighty angel as a high-ranking angel who is a representative of Christ. He may be an archangel like Michael[55] or Gabriel.[56] Louis Brighton effectively points out that "Whether this was from Christ *in the guise of an angel* or from the Lord Christ *through an angel* chosen for the role, *it was still the Lord Christ who commissioned John*."[57]

Modern commentators likewise agree that three distinct angels are mentioned at 5:2, 10:1, and 18:21. A few, however, posit that the revelatory angel of 1:1 and 22:16 may be linked to the mighty angel of 10:1.[58] The mighty angel appears as John's guide. Each

---

51. Osborne, *Revelation*, 469. Ladd (*Revelation*, 170) adds, "We misunderstand the character of John's thought if we try to place this heavenly battle somewhere in the stream of time."

52. Most English versions prefer "mighty" angel. NASB opts for "strong." CEB, GW, NCV, and NET have "powerful" angel.

53. See Brighton, *Revelation*, 274–78; Kovacs and Rowland, 118–19; Wainwright, *Mysterious Apocalypse*, 54–58; Weinrich, *Revelation*, 146.

54. Beale, *Revelation*, 522–26. So also Margaret Barker, *Revelation*, 181; and Mulholland, *Revelation*, 62–64. Stefanovic (*Revelation*, 318) notes that many Seventh Day Adventists interpret the mighty angel as Christ. Jehovah's Witnesses use the confusion to suggest that Christ is Michael, an archangel, and less than deific. Waddell (*Spirit of Revelation*, 59–163) makes a case for the Holy Spirit.

55. So Alan Johnson, "Revelation," 13:677; Smalley, *Revelation*, 258.

56. So Beasley-Murray, *Revelation*, 170; Charles, *Revelation*, 1:258–59; Easley, *Revelation*, 173; Mounce, *Revelation*, 130; Sweet, *Revelation*, 177. Patterson (*Revelation*, 229) suggests an archangel without naming him.

57. Brighton, *Revelation*, 277 (original italics).

58. Aune, *Revelation*, 1:347; Bauckham, *Climax of Prophecy*, 253–57. In fact, John may have had in mind one mighty angel for three (5:2; 10:1; 18:21) or even all five references (1:1; 22:16).

arrival on the scene occurs at a key moment because a "regular" angel does not satisfy the import of their announcements or actions. Thus, in 5:2, the mighty angel functions as a herald in the heavenly court, announcing, "Who is worthy to break the seals and open the scroll?" In 10:1, he majestically brings revelation of the nearness of the end, announcing "no more delay!" Finally, in 18:21, his symbolic action of casting a millstone into the deep represents the fall of Babylon the Great at the conclusion of history. Thus, a mighty angel appears at three crucial points and delivers significant information for John's narrative visions.

Rider on the White Horse
(Chapter 19)

There are two riders on white horses in Revelation, reflecting the dualism of the image. In chapter 19 the rider is the conquering Christ who arrives in righteous judgment at his second coming. The second rider on a white horse is mentioned in 19:11–16. John begins the section, "I saw heaven standing open and there before me was a white horse, whose rider is called Faithful and True. With justice he judges and wages war" (19:11). There is near unanimity that this rider represents Christ at his second coming. Those who disagree are preterist interpreters who understand this passage to refer to the power and triumph of the gospel message, and the continuing warfare of the church through the proclamation of the gospel. For these scholars, the verses reflect Christ's ascension, not his physical return at the consummation of history.[59] Overwhelmingly, however, the numerous descriptions and actions of the rider confirm him to be Jesus Christ, the Warrior Messiah, who consummates history at his return and delivers universal and complete end-time judgment.[60]

Seven Angels

The seven angels may be the seven archangels. They are tasked with delivering the trumpets and the bowls, and guiding John in his vision of the final judgment on the great prostitute and the introduction of the bride of the Lamb. Although "angels" are mentioned regularly, "the seven angels" are connected only with the trumpets and the bowls. The use of the definite article "the" may indicate a specific group of angels, perhaps the seven archangels of Jewish apocalyptic tradition—Uriel, Raphael, Raguel, Michael, Sariel, Gabriel, and Remiel (*1 En.* 20:2–8). The Angels of the Presence are mentioned often in *Jubilees* (1:27–29; 2:1–2; 15:27; 31:14).[61]

---

59. Adams, *Time Is at Hand*, 12; Chilton, *Days of Vengeance*, 481–82; Clark, *Message from Patmos*, 119–24; Mathison, *Postmillennialism*, 154; Russell, *Parousia*, 364.

60. See Osborne, *Revelation*, 679–86, which efficiently lists seven descriptions of the rider in vv. 11–13 and four actions in vv. 14–16.

61. Morris, *Revelation*, 172–73. So too Beckwith, *Apocalypse*, 551; Mounce, *Revelation*, 172; and Swete, *Apocalypse*, 105. Robert Thomas (*Revelation*, 2:7), however, disagrees.

The anaphoric definite article normally requires an antecedent. This leads some interpreters to suggest a reordering of the text.[62] More plausible is that the article use accentuates their connection as the same angels who will pour out the seven bowls. This might suggest a link to the seven seals as well even though they are not mentioned by name. Stephen Waechter, for example, notes that the definite article in 8:2 strengthens a recapitulation view concerning the interplay between the seals, trumpets, and bowls.[63] If so, the seven angels are presented at 8:2 in an interlocking introduction (8:1–5) that completes the seals and introduces the trumpets (8:6). They are reintroduced in a subsequent vision, pouring out the seven bowls of wrath (16:1). Thus, they form part of a parallel vision that suggests the bowls and the trumpets (and seals) are synchronous ways of expressing the same judgments. Next, one of the seven angels shows John a vision of the punishment of the great prostitute (17:1). Lastly, at the beginning of the final vision, one of the seven angels invites John to "Come, I will show you the bride, the wife of the Lamb" (21:9).[64]

Seven Spirits

The seven spirits refers to the full presence and effective work of the Holy Spirit over the whole earth. John mentions "the seven spirits" four times (1:4; 3:1; 4:5; 5:6), a hint that numerical symbolism is at work.[65] Many interpreters understand the seven spirits to refer to the group of seven angels connected to the trumpets or bowls or to the seven watchful archangels or even more broadly to some part of a heavenly entourage.[66] Most, however, identify the phrase as a figure of speech specifying the divine fullness of the Holy Spirit.[67] A few English versions (NASB, NKJV) capitalize "seven Spirits" to confirm the Holy

62. For example, Charles (*Revelation*, 1:224) suggests placing 8:2 after 8:5.

63. Waechter, "Analysis of the Literary Structure," 129.

64. Because of the similarity of words, and the "in the Spirit" structural marker, this is probably the same angel that is mentioned in 17:1.

65. Bauckham (*Theology of Revelation*, 109) cites the Spirit as one of John's major avenues for numerical symbolism. He classifies the fourteen references (7 x 2) into four groups. These identifiable patterns reflect a deliberately crafted theological message embedded in the text. See Sorke, "Identity and Function of the Seven Spirits."

66. So Aune, *Revelation*, 1:34–35, Boring, *Revelation*, 75; Boxall, *Revelation*, 86; Charles, *Revelation*, 1:11; Ford, *Revelation*, 377; Giblin, *Revelation*, 71–72; Krodel, *Revelation*, 83; Mounce, *Revelation*, 46–48; Murphy, *Fallen Is Babylon*, 69; Roloff, *Revelation*, 24; Leonard Thompson, *Revelation*, 49; Witherington, *Revelation*, 75; Yarbro Collins, *Apocalypse*, 7. Some, like Aune and Charles, consider the reference to be a later interpolation. Buchanan (*Revelation*, 49, 154–55) states the phrase comes from Isa 11:2 without reference to the Spirit.

67. So Bauckham, *Climax of Prophecy*, 164, 336; Beale, *Revelation*, 189; Beasley-Murray, *Revelation*, 55–56; Blount, *Revelation*, 34; Brighton, *Revelation*, 41–42; Bruce, "Spirit in the Apocalypse," 333–37; Caird, *Revelation*, 15; J. C. de Smidt, "Holy Spirit," 229–44; Easley, *Revelation*, 26; Fee, *Revelation*, 6; Hemer, *Letters to the Seven Churches*, 142; Hughes, *Revelation*, 18; Alan Johnson, "Revelation," 13:599; Dennis Johnson, *Triumph of the Lamb*, 99; Keener, *Revelation*, 70; Kistemaker, *Revelation*, 82; Ladd, *Revelation*, 24; H. Y. Lee, *Dynamic Reading*, 83; Lupieri, *Apocalypse*, 102; Mangina, *Revelation*, 43; Michaels, *Revelation*, 54; Morris, *Revelation*, 49; Mulholland, *Revelation*, 71; Osborne, *Revelation*, 61, 74; Patterson, *Revelation*, 59–60; Paul, *Revelation*, 62; Prigent, *Apocalypse*, 117; Reddish, *Revelation*, 35; Resseguie, *Revelation*, 66; Rotz, *Revelation*, 48; Skaggs and Benham, *Revelation*, 18; Smalley, *Revelation*, 33–34;

Spirit is indeed intended, even though the plural is retained. The NIV and CSB include a footnote that states that the phrase can be rendered "sevenfold Spirit." The NLT uniquely inserts "sevenfold Spirit" into its text. A primary reason for equating "seven spirits" with the Holy Spirit is that all four references place the phrase on the same level of authority as God and Christ. This suggests that John intended to underscore the Trinity. The plural form is probably an allusion to the seven lamps of Zech 4:1–10 and sevenfold description of Isa 11:2. Throughout Revelation the number seven signifies completeness, fullness, and perfection.

Significantly, the phrase occurs four times, signifying full coverage of the earth. First, the Spirit empowers the church to be effective witnesses in the world (1:4). Second, Christ holds the seven spirits in his hand; he is the Spirit of the risen Christ, distinct therefore from the seven angels (3:1). Third, John sees seven lamps blazing, alluding to the lampstand with seven lamps (4:5; Exod 25:31–40) which stood before God's presence. Finally, the seven spirits appear as a characteristic of the Lamb himself who has seven horns and seven eyes, "which are the seven spirits of God sent out into all the earth" (5:6). Once again, the allusion to Zechariah underscores Jesus' omnipotence and sovereignty and the Spirit's omniscience.[68] The sevenfold (Holy) Spirit is God's active presence and energizing witness sent out to all the earth.[69]

Twenty-Four Elders

These are a high order of angelic beings who represent OT and NT saints, and who lead in worship before the heavenly throne, especially at the parousia. "Elders" (*presbyteroi*) is found twelve times in Revelation, always with reference to the twenty-four elders, often in combination with the four living creatures, and usually placed in visions nearest the second coming. Their twelve references accents the numerical symbol of totality and completeness with God's people in mind. Alan Johnson relates that there are at least thirteen different views on their identity.[70] The two major views understand the elders either as human or angelic, and scholars are evenly divided. First, many surmise that the elders are representative human beings. After all, the word "elders" is more easily applied to humans than angels. This argument is lessened when all Scripture passages come into play. The LXX reading of Isa 24:23 refers to the heavenly assembly as elders. Others point to the white clothing the elders wear since elsewhere it is the clothing of the saints. But angels also wear white elsewhere (Matt 28:3; John 20:12; Acts 1:10; *1 En.* 71:1; 87:2). A final argument is their crowns of gold, which seem more associated with humans than

---

Stefanovic, *Revelation*, 60–61; Sweet, *Revelation*, 65; J. C. Thomas, *Apocalypse*, 92; Robert Thomas, *Revelation*, 1:67.

68. Beale, *Revelation*, 355; Hays, Duvall, and Pate, *Dictionary of Prophecy*, 424–25; H. Y. Lee, *Dynamic Reading*, 102–4.

69. Bauckham, "Spirit of Prophecy," 113. See Waddell, *Spirit of Revelation*, 11–21; and for pastoral applications, see Duvall, *Heart of Revelation*, 67–81.

70. Alan Johnson, "Revelation," 13:641. The most in-depth discussions are Aune, *Revelation*, 1:287–92; Beale, *Revelation*, 322–26; Smalley, *Revelation*, 116–18; and Robert Thomas, *Revelation*, 1:344–48.

angels. But again, such crowns can easily denote royal dignity. Nevertheless, many cogent voices view humanity being represented in the twenty-four elders.[71]

Second, numerous Bible students interpret the twenty-four elders as a high order of angelic beings. They represent the saints. They are not the saints themselves.[72] Most proponents from both groups understand the elders to represent the twelve apostles and the twelve tribes of Israel (21:12–14). Thus, they symbolize the entire community of the redeemed from both testaments.[73] The number twenty-four is significant and stands part and parcel with John's frequent pattern of numerical symbolism. The number twelve is doubled to emphasize fullness and completion.

In the throne room vision (4:1–5:14) they fall down and worship near the throne and instruct John not to weep. Strikingly, the remainder of their references occurs near the conclusion of individual visions. An elder asks John a question typical of apocalypses (7:9–14); they sing a song at the second coming (11:16); they are pictured before the throne again at the second coming (14:3); and they shout and worship at the second coming (19:4). Thus, it appears better to regard them as angels. Like the seven angels of the churches, they are angels who represent humanity. Like the four living creatures who represent animate creation, so the elders represent human creation. They are angelic representatives of the whole body of faithful believers. Since adoration and praise are continually found on their lips, they offer a present challenge to God's people of living in an attitude of daily worship.

Heavenly Titles

In addition to actual titles there are scores of metaphors, similes, and participial constructions that denote deity. Edwin Reynolds uncovered 231 titles.[74] Thus, several titles are left out of this discussion. But these are sufficient enough to give readers a panoramic

71. Brighton, *Revelation*, 117; Buchanan, *Revelation*, 153; Chilton, *Days of Vengeance*, 151; Ford, *Revelation*, 72; Harrington, *Revelation*, 79; Hughes, *Revelation*, 72; Keener, *Revelation*, 171–72; Kistemaker, *Revelation*, 186–87; Mangina, *Revelation*, 77; Mulholland, *Revelation*, 143; Murphy, *Fallen Is Babylon*, 180–82; Paul, *Revelation*, 122; Prigent, *Apocalypse*, 227; Resseguie, *Revelation Unsealed*, 69; Sweet, *Revelation*, 118; Swete, *Apocalypse*, 69. Dispensationalists understand these elders as redeemed and glorified saints after the rapture (Hindson, *Revelation*, 58–59; LaHaye, *Revelation Unveiled*, 118–20; Patterson, *Revelation*, 152; Walvoord, *Revelation*, 106–7). Gromacki ("Revelation, Twenty-Four Elders of," 377–78) and Ryrie (*Revelation*, 43) state that they are redeemed human beings who represent all human beings.

72. Beale, *Revelation*, 322; Beasley-Murray, *Revelation*, 113–14; Caird, *Revelation*, 63; Charles, *Revelation*, 1:129–33; Duvall, *Revelation*, 83; Easley, *Revelation*, 76; Alan Johnson, "Revelation," 13:641; Dennis Johnson, *Triumph of the Lamb*, 100; Krodel, *Revelation*, 155; Ladd, *Revelation*, 75; Mounce, *Revelation*, 121–22; Morris, *Revelation*, 87; Noll, *Angels of Light*, 144–46; Osborne, *Revelation*, 229; Reddish, *Revelation*, 96; Smalley, *Revelation*, 116; Stefanovic, *Revelation*, 185; Robert Thomas, *Revelation*, 1:348.

73. Some scholars, however, understand their function in worship connects them to the twenty-four courses of priests in the OT (1 Chr 24:4). So Buchanan, *Revelation*, 153; Keener, *Revelation*, 172; Skaggs and Benham, *Revelation*, 60.

74. Reynolds, "Trinity in Revelation," 55–72. Johns (*Lamb Christology*, 218–22) lists four pages of titles of Christ in Revelation. Tõniste (*Ending of the Canon*, 87) lists ten christological titles from Isaiah alone and states that this is perhaps Isaiah's most significant contribution to Revelation.

view of the weightiness of the titles of deity in Revelation. Some titles are listed elsewhere in this study. For example, Lamb and Lion of the Tribe of Judah are entries placed under Animals.

Alpha and Omega

This is a title of God and Christ which emphasizes their divinity, complete oneness and sovereignty over history and eternity, and their salvation and judgment at the second coming. The divine title composed of the first and last letters of the Greek alphabet forms a merism that is closely connected with two other merisms in Revelation, namely, "the First and the Last" and "the Beginning and the End."[75] A merism is a figure of speech (synecdoche) in which totality is expressed by contrasting parts. Such polar opposites stress that since God is, for example, the first and the last, then he is everything in between as well. The phrase "Alpha and Omega" (*to Alpha to Ō*) occurs three times in the NT, all in Revelation (1:8; 21:6; 22:13).[76] Similarly, "the First and the Last" (1:17; 22:13) and "the Beginning and the End" (21:6; 22:13) are found two times each. It is commonly accepted that John's application of all three merisms to Christ emphasizes his deity and unity with the Father.[77] The listings for all three merisms are:

- God: I am the Alpha and Omega (1:8)
- Christ: I am the First and the Last (1:17)
- God: I am the Alpha and the Omega, the Beginning and the End (21:6)
- Christ: I am the Alpha and the Omega, the First and the Last, the Beginning and the End (22:13)

Bauckham notes that when all three merisms are added it equals seven, underscoring numerical symbolism. Furthermore, the titles appear four times, suggesting full coverage as well.[78] The self-declaration of "I am" offers further emphasis on deity. These merisms are used interchangeably for God and Christ and accent the deity of Christ, his oneness and equality with the Father, and his complete sovereign control of all history. Finally, the placement of the last and fullest title occurs between the emphasis on Christ coming as judge (22:12) and the warnings to believers and the wicked (22:14–15). As Osborne relates, "Christ is sovereign over all and therefore the one who has authority over the destiny of everyone."[79]

75. Modern English versions capitalize Alpha and Omega (GW offers "A and Z"), but many do not capitalize the other two titles. Translations that capitalize all three titles and thereby aid in connecting the merisms include NCV, NJB, NKJV, NIV, and NLT. Unfortunately, GNT translates Alpha and Omega at 22:13 as "first and last," which causes it to lose one-third of its titles.

76. The Greek text looks odd with *alpha* spelled out but *ōmega* not spelled out. However, Mathewson (*Revelation*, 8) explains that *ōmega* was not written out in manuscripts until the seventh century AD.

77. Prigent (*Apocalypse*, 123–24) relates that the earliest commentators on Revelation understood only Christ uttering this self-designation, a position he confirms as untenable.

78. Bauckham, *Climax of Prophecy*, 33–34.

79. Osborne, *Revelation*, 789. See Aune, *Apocalypticism*, 266–70; Beale and McDonough,

Amen

As a title of Christ, the Amen stresses his deity and the certainty that God's promises will be fulfilled. "Amen" has passed from Hebrew to Greek to English as well as other languages through transliteration, and is often left untranslated. It is mentioned nine times in Revelation. Eight of these correspond to usage found elsewhere in the NT, revealing the finality, certainty, and trustworthiness of something (Matt 5:26; Luke 23:43; John 1:52; 2 Cor 1:20), often in the context of prayer (Rom 1:25; Gal 1:5; 1 Pet 4:11; 1 Thess 5:28). It is an emphatic "Yes!" attached to a prayer or doxology. This authentication of solemn truth may be seen in Rev 7:12, where "amen" serves as bookends for the seven attributes.

But in one instance John forms the word into a title for the risen Christ (3:14). Most interpreters understand "The Amen" to be drawn from Isa 65:16, making these the only two passages in the Bible where Amen is used as a name or title. In addition, the Isaiah allusion affirms that another title originally reserved for God is now being applied to Christ in the Apocalypse.[80] Thus, the lukewarm Christians at Laodicea are challenged to snap out of their spiritual doldrums. The title "The Amen" accents the truthfulness and divine origin of the message received from the risen Christ as well as the confirmation that God's promises will certainly be accomplished.

Christ

This title is applied to Jesus and emphasizes his authority as the Messiah, God's anointed one, who is victorious over Satan through the means of his shed blood, and who will reign forever. This entry is limited to how John utilizes the title of "Christ" in Revelation.[81] That Christ (*Christos*) is found exactly seven times (1:1, 2, 5; 11:15; 12:10; 20:4, 6) highlights its perfection and completeness through the apocalyptic feature of numerical symbolism. That John uses numerical symbolism is corroborated by his fourteen (7 x 2) uses of "Jesus," the seven uses of *erchomai* ("coming") in combination with *Christos* to stress the threat or promise of his parousia, and the twenty-eight (7 x 4) uses of the Christological title "Lamb."[82] These are strong arguments in favor of numerical symbolism.

Some modern versions regrettably select "Messiah" (GW, GNT, HCSB, NIV), "Anointed" (NABR), or "Chosen One" (CEV) in place of "Christ" at 11:15 and 12:10. Although they are used identically, this masks the intratextual connections and numerical symbolism.[83] John enhances the symbolism by limiting its use to only seven times. This

"Revelation," 1091; Hays, Duvall, and Pate, *Dictionary of Prophecy*, 20–22; Reddish, "Alpha and Omega," 161–62; Vos, "Alpha and Omega," 128–29.

80. Beale (*New Testament Biblical Theology*, 338–44) argues that all the titles in 3:14 derive from the Isaiah text and serve as allusions to Isaiah's prophecies of the new creation, thereby emphasizing Jesus as the inaugurator of the new creation. See also Beale, *Revelation*, 298–301; and Funderburk, "Amen," 147–48.

81. For background on Christ see de Jonge, "Christ," 914–21; Donald Guthrie, "Jesus Christ," 567–661; and Martin, "Jesus Christ," 1034–49.

82. See the entry "Jesus."

83. HCSB also singularly chose "Messiah" for 20:4, 6. Fortunately, CSB revised all seven instances to "Christ."

is aided by giving the full title of "Jesus Christ" three times at the beginning (1:1, 2, 5). The final four references include the article, "the Christ." It occurs at the commencement of the second coming related in the seventh trumpet (11:15). It is mentioned in the third interlude at the heavenly hymn celebrating the victory of the saints over Satan (12:10). Lastly, it is located twice in the millennial vision where the saints will reign with Christ for a thousand years (20:4, 6). These final four are used together with the noun *basileia* ("kingdom"; "rule") or the verb *basileuō* ("to reign"; "to rule").[84] Thus, the placement of this title stresses to John's original audience that this revelation comes from the authority of the risen Christ himself (1:1–5). He is the one who is victorious over Satan, and his followers overcome and enjoy spiritual victory through his shed blood (12:7–10). Jesus is the Lord over the millennial reign (the period spanning the interadvental age) and his followers already reign spiritually with him (20:4–6). Ultimately, when Christ returns, he will reign over the universe for ever and ever (11:15–19).[85]

Faithful Witness

This title describes the faithfulness of Christ's earthly witness while encouraging persecuted believers to remain faithful witnesses as well. The messianic title "faithful witness" (*ho martys ho pistos*) forms one part of the threefold description of the risen Christ in 1:5 (and repeated in 3:14): "and from Jesus Christ, who is the faithful witness, the firstborn from the dead, and the ruler of the kings of the earth." Some scholars take the two words as standalone substantives—"the witness, the trustworthy one" (GW). Most, however, understand "faithful" to be modifying "witness."[86] Thus, the title applies to Christ's role in mediating this revelation he received from God (1:1; 22:16). Several scholars note an allusion to Ps 89:37 which would emphasize Jesus as Davidic Messiah.[87]

Nevertheless, the title also applies to the larger purpose of Jesus' life as the one who obediently bore witness to the truth (John 3:32; 5:31; 18:18) with particular emphasis placed on his death.[88] This receives support when it is remembered that the word "witness" derives from *martys*, from which comes the English word "martyr." Christ's faithful, sacrificial witness is the believer's example even as it leads to earthly death. Such a witness assumes suffering and persecution and even death for Christians. This is confirmed in 2:13 when the martyr, Antipas, is given the title of "my faithful witness." It is implied elsewhere. For instance, John is a brother and companion in the suffering and patient

---

84. De Jonge, "Use of the Expression *ho Christos*," 267.

85. Resseguie (*Revelation Unsealed*, 206–7) stresses the same idea through the three tenses—past, present, future. The slaughtered Lamb reflects Christ's past work on the cross. The Son of Man is the image of Christ's present work in his church. The faithful and true warrior is the image of Christ's future work at his second coming.

86. An enlargement of the title is found at 3:14. Rissi (*Future of the World*, 21) states that the formula "faithful and true witness" is nothing but a translation and explanation of the title "Amen."

87. So Aune, *Revelation*, 1:39; Beale, *Revelation*, 190; Kistemaker, *Revelation*, 83; Osborne, *Revelation*, 62 n. 19; Reddish, *Revelation*, 34; Smalley, *Revelation*, 34; Robert Thomas, *Revelation*, 1:73; Mark Wilson, "Revelation," 4:253.

88. Mounce, *Revelation*, 48; Tenney, *Interpreting Revelation*, 118.

endurance (1:9); the two witnesses (*dysin martysin*) are faithful unto death (11:3, 7); and "the woman was drunk with the blood of God's holy people, the blood of those who bore testimony (*martyrōn*) to Jesus (17:6)."

Firstborn from the Dead

This title emphasizes the privileged position of authority and sovereignty that Christ possesses as a result of his resurrection from the dead. Furthermore, it serves as a promise of inheritance for the faithful who follow after him. Although "firstborn" is found only once at Rev 1:5, it nonetheless evokes a rich image for John's readers. Revelation comes from "Jesus Christ, who is the faithful witness, the firstborn from the dead, and the ruler of the kings of the earth." The figurative use of "firstborn" to denote priority or supremacy can be traced to Exod 4:21–23, where the Lord tells Moses to deliver Israel, "my firstborn son." This figure of a nation as firstborn continues into the monarchial period as Israel becomes its representative son under the Father, the Davidic king, who is promised perpetual favor and dominion (2 Sam 7:14–17). The Davidic son previews the ideal king in messianic prophecy, establishing the Father's dominion over all the earth (Exod 19:5; Pss 2, 89, 110).

The shift from primogeniture to adoption is complete by the NT, and all who believe in Jesus are now God's sons. Thus, Paul develops the imagery by calling Jesus the firstborn of the dead and firstborn over all creation (Col 1:15, 18), a clear message of Christ's rule, sovereignty, salvific deliverance, as well as the believer's eschatological inheritance (Rom 8:29–30; Heb 12:23).[89] Beale states, "Christ has gained such a sovereign position over the cosmos, not in the sense that he is recognized as the first-created being of all creation or as the origin of creation, but in the sense that he is the inaugurator of the *new* creation by means of his resurrection . . ."[90]

Thus, the description forms part of the threefold title given to Christ, along with "faithful witness" and "ruler of the kings of the earth." Combined, they hearken back to Ps 89:27, 37, and describe Christ's full and completed work as faithful witness while in the flesh, firstborn of many who would be resurrected, and ultimately, universal king of the world. In addition, his faithful followers receive the prestige, status, and inheritance privileges as well.

God of Heaven

This title of deity is reserved for the Father and emphasizes his sovereignty over heaven and earth, and thus his righteous judgment of sinners at the end of history. "God of Heaven" is a frequent OT title, peculiarly found in the later books (2 Chr 36:23; Ezra 1:2; 5:11; 6:9; Neh 1:4–5; Dan 2:18–19).[91] In all instances, it accents God as sovereign over all earthly

89. Rosscup, "Firstborn," 577–78; Ryken, *Dictionary of Biblical Imagery*, 97; Archie T. Wright, "Firstborn," 457–58.

90. Beale, *Revelation*, 191.

91. CEV masks the title with "God who rules in heaven." No English version capitalizes "heaven," but

affairs.[92] The title is found twice in Revelation, but similar to other titles of deity, John uses it as a signal that he is nearing the end of an individual vision (11:13; 16:11), and the conclusion of earth history. Therefore, the title is highly appropriate since the wicked ultimately acknowledge the one true God.[93]

King of Kings and Lord of Lords

This is a title depicting the sovereignty, authority, and ultimate rulership of Christ over all, displayed at his second coming. This was a familiar title for Near Eastern kings and found in the OT period (Ezra 7:12; Ezek 26:7; Dan 2:37). Yet it was applied foremost to the true supreme ruler, God (Deut 10:17; Ps 136:3; Dan 2:47; Zech 14:9). The intertestamental and NT periods continued to apply the title almost exclusively to God (1 Tim 6:15; *1 En.* 9:4; 84:2; *3 Macc.* 5:35; *3 En.* 22:15).[94] In Revelation, the title is applied solely to Christ (17:14; 19:16). The connection to *1 En.* 9:4 is usually mentioned as the primary resource for John, but Beale argues the probable source of the title comes from the LXX of Dan 4:37.[95]

Since the title is found only twice (the phraseology is reversed for emphasis), it raises issues on how they are connected. Several English versions capitalize all the letters at 19:16 (CEV, CSB, NASB, NCV, NIV, NKJV), but not at 17:14, which diminishes their intratextual connection. A few scholars understand 17:14's title to be out of place; the rearranging work of a later editor.[96] Other interpreters suggest 17:14 serves as a glimpsing preview of the second coming which John does not describe until chapter 19.[97] However, because 19:16 is an obvious second coming context, then 17:14 should also be identified as another picture of the same end-time battle.[98] Both passages depict language and images of the Divine Warrior decisively routing the kings of the earth gathered for battle.[99] Like numerous other titles of deity, John reserves this for the end of an individual vision.[100]

---

doing so would call attention to its use as a title of God.

92. Only a few commentators discuss this title. See Beale, *Revelation*, 604; Osborne, *Revelation*, 589; Smalley, *Revelation*, 287; Tenney, *Interpreting Revelation*, 106.

93. So Bauckham (*Climax of Prophecy*, 279) and Robert Thomas (*Revelation*, 2:99), although the latter would not agree with the assessment that the passage reflects the end of history. Mounce (*Revelation*, 224) disagrees, understanding the title to reflect the majesty and wisdom of God without any specific contrast with the gods of the Chaldeans.

94. Keener, *Revelation*, 454.

95. Beale, "King of Kings and Lord of Lords," 618–20; and followed by Slater, "King of Kings and Lord of Lords' Revisited," 159–60. Aune (*Revelation*, 3:954), however, states this cannot be determined for certain.

96. Aune, *Revelation*, 3:953; Charles, *Revelation*, 2:429–30; Ford, *Revelation*, 282.

97. Walvoord (*Revelation*, 255) calls it "a brief anticipation" of the final triumph of chapter 19. So Hindson, *Revelation*, 179; Koester, *Revelation*, 692; Robert Thomas, *Revelation*, 2:302.

98. Beasley-Murray, *Revelation*, 258; Bauckham, *Climax of Prophecy*, 20; Brighton, *Revelation*, 453; Kistemaker, *Revelation*, 476; Murphy, *Fallen Is Babylon*, 362.

99. Herms, *Apocalypse*, 235.

100. See the entry "Kings of the Earth." John reserves this designation for the climactic end as well.

It stresses the rulership of Christ over all at the time of his victorious coming. John uses superlative nouns so that it reads as "the greatest King" and "the greatest Lord."[101]

Living One

This emphasizes Jesus' resurrection and eternal deity, and therefore his power over death and Hades. This title is found at 1:18 and is a continuation from the previous verse where Christ proclaims that he is "the First and the Last" and "the Living One" (*ho zōn*). This expression stresses his resurrection from the dead. The additional phrase "I was dead, and now look, I am alive for ever and ever" is an ascription to his deity and eternality. The phrase was attributed to God in the OT (Deut 32:40; 1 Sam 17:36; Isa 57:15; Jer 23:36; Dan 4:34; 12:7; see Sir 18:1) and the NT (Acts 10:42; Heb 7:24; 1 John 2:17).[102] It may appear redundant, but actually serves to underscore the uniqueness of Jesus.[103] In order to emphasize the phrase as a reference to deity, and due perhaps to the artificial insertion of a new verse number, many Bibles include an extra "I am" or capital letters to draw attention to the Christological title (GNT, NCV, NIV, NJB, NKJV, NLT). On the other hand, a few versions tend to mask the title with "and the one who lives" (NABR, NET). Jesus declares himself as the Living One, and establishes his deity by contrasting his death with the triumph of his resurrection.[104] Thus, he has authority over death and Hades.

Lord God Almighty

This divine title highlights the majesty of God on account of his true and righteous deeds, and especially for his powerful sovereignty and authority over all history and the universe. In the OT "Almighty" (*shaddai*) was frequently mentioned as a title for God.[105] Its Greek equivalent (*pantokratōr*) literally means "all-power." Thus, "All-Powerful" is chosen by some versions (CEV, NET). Nine of ten NT uses of "Almighty" are in John's Apocalypse (1:8; 4:8; 11:17; 15:3; 16:7, 14; 19:6, 15; 21:22). However, seven of those nine instances are found in the fuller phrase "Lord God Almighty," the clue that numerical symbolism is at work. Even the other two occurrences in which the shortened form "God Almighty" occurs (16:14; 19:15) "perform a literary function, helping to link 16:12–16 to 19:11–21, in which the battle the former passage presages takes place . . ."[106] The fuller expression, therefore, is kept in order to keep the number of occurrences at seven. The title has an additional layer of meaning as a numerical symbol, emphasizing the completion and perfection of the title "Almighty."

---

101. Kistemaker, *Revelation*, 524. A few translations aid this: "Lord over all lords, King over all kings" (CEV, NLT).

102. Beale and McDonough, "Revelation," 1093.

103. Resseguie, *Revelation*, 80.

104. Rotz, *Revelation*, 56.

105. Thirty-one of its forty-eight occurrences are in Job. See Barabas, "Almighty," 125; Feldmeier, "Almighty," 20–23.

106. Bauckham, *Climax of Prophecy*, 33.

Moreover, John reserves the title for special literary placement in his visions. Most often the title is placed at the end of an individual vision and is coupled with statements of God's deeds ("great and marvelous are your deeds"), his justice ("true and just are your judgments), and especially his sovereignty over history ("who is, was, and is to come" and "has come"). Therefore, it appears sparingly enough to notice a preference for the conclusion of an individual vision that accents the eschaton.

Whereas other titles denoting God in the OT are now being applied to Christ (Alpha and Omega, first and the last, beginning and the end, Amen, King of kings and Lord of lords), the title of "Almighty" (as well as "the one who is and was and is to come") is reserved for the Father alone.[107] In the LXX, this title is primarily translated from the Hebrew word that means "Sabaoth, hosts, armies." This conveys the idea that God is over everything—"the heavens and the earth were finished, and all the host of them" (Gen 2:1 ESV)—and all powers, human and angelic. Thus, it expresses God's sovereign power and majesty over the entire history of the human race, especially at the end of human history.[108]

Morning Star

This title of Christ symbolizes his glorious nature, eternal presence, and victorious rule as well as the believer's share in them. The "morning star" (*astēr prōinos*) is found twice in Revelation (2:28; 22:16). Osborne lists six possibilities among scholars on the background to the "morning star." He settles on two, explaining that it "is probably best to see the two as intertwined here."[109] To his conclusion a third one should be added.[110]

First, it is an allusion to Balaam's prophecy. On the heels of the previous promise of shared victorious rule (2:26–27), John connects an allusion to the royal, authoritative scepter of Christ to Ps 2:8–9 and Num 24:17. Balaam prophesies "a star will come out of Jacob; a scepter will rise out of Israel." Jesus' messianic reign was set in motion by his resurrection. Thus, a symbol of a scepter leads to a symbol of a star. Both are symbols of royalty and both are shared by believers. In this context, then, believers reign with Christ and shine as morning stars.[111] Second, the title also refers to the planet Venus. Roman emperors claimed to descend from the goddess Venus. Generals built temples dedicated to the star. It was a sign carried on the standards by the Roman legions.[112] Moreover,

---

107. So Brighton, *Revelation*, 44; Prigent, *Apocalypse*, 124; Witherington, *Revelation*, 77–78. Contra Hindson, *Revelation*, 25; Kistemaker, *Revelation*, 87–88; Lupieri, *Apocalypse*, 106; and Walvoord, *Revelation*, 40; which attribute the self-title to Christ. In addition, many red-letter editions of modern Bible versions place 1:8 in red, signifying Christ as the speaker, and further advancing the confusion.

108. Brighton, *Revelation*, 493–94.

109. Osborne, *Revelation*, 168. Beale (*Revelation*, 269) also treats them as intertwined.

110. Which Osborne (*Revelation*, 793) later assumes.

111. Blount, *Revelation*, 64; Brighton, *Revelation*, 654; Hemer, *Letters to the Seven Churches*, 125–26: Kistemaker, *Revelation*, 142; Keener, *Revelation*, 136; Koester, *Revelation*, 302; Mounce, *Revelation*, 90–91; Sweet, *Revelation*, 97.

112. Beale, *Revelation*, 269. Those who accept Venus include Aune (*Revelation*, 1:212), Barr (*Tales*, 58), Beasley-Murray (*Revelation*, 93), Fee (*Revelation*, 44), Murphy (*Fallen Is Babylon*, 141), Reddish

since Venus is the brightest star in the heavens, it suggests the approach of dawn and a new day in Christ.[113] Third, a fuller interpretation is possible when both passages are taken together. At the conclusion of Revelation, Christ calls himself "the bright Morning Star" (22:16). Thus, the messianic allusion from Numbers and the new age allusion to Venus are reapplied to Christ. "Jesus promises his people not merely dominion but a better treasure, a deeper joy: himself."[114] Many exegetes, therefore, emphasize this third understanding of the title.[115]

The morning star is Jesus. The prophesied messianic deliverer who inaugurated righteous judgment with his death, burial, and resurrection will complete it at the second coming. Yet the glorified Christ promises to give the morning star to the overcomers. This emphasizes not only eternal life and divine presence in glory with Christ, but a share in his victorious rule.

One Like a Son of Man

"One Like a Son of Man" is a messianic title, symbolizing the risen Christ who oversees his church and who comes in judgment and victory at the second coming. John adds "one like" (*homoion*) to this title.[116] This signals John's propensity to use similes and metaphors in describing his visions as well as the mystical language of apocalypses.[117] There is a surplus of scholarly discussion on the "son of man."[118] Traditionally, the title has been understood to emphasize Jesus' humanity in distinction from his divinity. In actuality, the title was highly volatile at the time of Jesus. Thomas Slater notes different ways in which apocalyptic literature understood the son of man figure. Any study of the son of man

---

(*Revelation*, 65), Smalley (*Revelation*, 79), Thomas and Macchia (*Revelation*, 111), and Witherington (*Revelation*, 105).

113. Hailey, *Revelation*, 142.

114. Dennis Johnson, *Triumph of the Lamb*, 82.

115. Caird, *Revelation*, 46; Chilton, *Days of Vengeance*, 579; Duvall, *Revelation*, 61; Easley, *Revelation*, 42; Hughes, *Revelation*, 52; Alan Johnson, "Revelation," 13:625; Mulholland, *Revelation*, 117; Morris, *Revelation*; Patterson, *Revelation*, 117; Roloff, *Revelation*, 56. Sandy (*Plowshares and Pruning Hooks*, 30) lists the morning star as one of ten examples of rewards that primarily describe the one reward—deity and humanity in perfect unity in eternity (21:3).

116. The most literal renderings ("someone/one like a son of man"), some which include quote marks to show dependence on Dan 7:13, include ESV, NABR, NASB, NET, and NIV. NCV and NJB cap it with "One who looked like a Son of Man." Several versions insert the article: "someone/one like the Son of Man" (CEV, CSB, GW, NKJV, NRSV). CEB produces its unique contribution with "someone who looked like the Human One." The weakest offerings are "figure like a man" (REB) and "what looked like a human being" (GNT). Blount (*Revelation*, 44) uses "child of humanity" throughout his commentary. Leonard Thompson (*Revelation*, 58) renders it "Likeness of a Human." Some of these examples might be efforts to soften the title's relationship to Jesus. Most, however, are simply efforts toward gender inclusive concerns. Although language revisions that incorporate gender accuracy are crucial updates for modern translations, the technical title "son of man" has been around since the time of Daniel.

117. Murphy, *Apocalypticism*, 45–46.

118. See Bowker, "Son of Man," 19–48; Hurtado and Owens, *"Who Is This Son of Man?"*; Yarbro Collins, "Son of Man," 536–68. For overviews see Aune, "Son of Man," 574–81; Charles Carter, "Son of Man," 579–81; Nickelsburg, "Son of Man," 137–50.

in the NT should take into account these distinctions within first-century Judaism.[119] Primarily, however, biblical literature understood the title in four ways, and Revelation hits all four even if the expression "son of man" is absent: (1) heavenly being (Dan 7:13; Matt 25:31; Mark 14:62; Rev 1:13; 14:14); (2) eternal ruler (Dan 7:14; Matt 16:27; Rev 1:5; 3:21; 17:14); (3) end-time judge (Matt 13:41–43; 19:28; 25:31–46; Rev 1:18; 14:14; 19:11); and (4) victorious warrior (John 14:30; 16:8–11; Rev 2:16; 3:21; 17:17; 19:11).[120]

John specifically cites the title of "like a son of man" twice. First, in the inaugural vision (1:9–20), John sees the exalted Christ as one "like a son of man" standing "among the lampstands" (1:13). Later, he is "holding" the seven stars in his hand (1:16), and "walking among the seven golden lampstands" (2:1). Such images "depict Christ involved in the lives of his people and sovereignly protecting them."[121] Furthermore, the image is drawn from Dan 7 and 10. Since these texts refer to the kingly and priestly nature so too is Christ's kingly and priestly nature emphasized. He is dressed in priestly attire to confirm this role. As priest, he tends to the seven lampstands which represent his church. This role includes commending, correcting, and warning the churches.[122]

Second, "one like a son of man" reappears at the harvest of believers at the second coming (14:14). Some scholars understand the son of man to be an angel, not Jesus. The key reason is that this figure receives a command from an angel, something Christ would not do.[123] The context, however, confirms it is Christ. He sits in judgment on a cloud and wears a royal crown. Moreover, 14:14 recalls the Gospels' usage of Jesus as the son of man on clouds at harvest time (Matt 25:31; Mark 13:27; 14:62). That Christ "receives" instructions from a lower "another angel" is not an issue. It is a clear allusion to Joel 3:13. It is a petition from an angel, not a command. John reserves the use of this messianic title for emphasis. It occurs once to stress his kingly and priestly role over the universal church, and once for the harvesting of his church.

One Who Is and Who Was and Who Is to Come

This is a threefold divine title of God that emphasizes his authority, infinity, and sovereign reign over all history. The phrase also temporally signals the end of an individual vision. This title of God, with variations, is found five times (1:4, 8; 4:8; 11:17; 16:5).[124] No such

---

119. Slater, "One Like a Son of Man," 183–98. Tõniste (*Ending of the Canon*, 127) applies Richard Hays's famous seven criteria for judging allusions. She is convinced that John's use of the son of man title is drawn from the Gospel of Matthew.

120. Hays, Duvall, and Pate, *Dictionary of Prophecy*, 432–33.

121. Osborne, *Revelation*, 87.

122. Beale, *Revelation*, 208–9.

123. So Aune, *Revelation*, 1:90; 2:800–801; Kiddle, *Revelation*, 277; Michaels, *Revelation*, 61, 177–78; Morris, *Revelation*, 54, 179; Rowland, "Revelation," 12:668; Leonard Thompson, *Revelation*, 58, 147. Roloff (*Revelation*, 177) accepts the reference to Jesus but suggests early Jewish tradition for the reason Jesus receives instruction from an angel.

124. The parody of this phrase should be noted (17:8, 11). The threefold formula is mocked three times by the beast who was, is, and is yet to come.

expression is found in the OT, but the phrase certainly alludes to Exod 3:14.[125] The LXX reads this as "I Am the One Who Is," and refers to timeless eternity or the totality of history.[126] Sayings and formulas in three tenses were used of Greek gods or the supreme God (*Sib. Or.* 3:16).[127] Significantly, the exchange of the final future tense "is to come" with a past tense "has come" in the last two references assists in understanding temporal aspects of Revelation. In other words, the past tense phrase reveals that John is at the end of an individual vision, and is picturing the end of history at 11:17 and 16:5. Bauckham agrees. "At these points in the vision the eschatological coming of God is taking place."[128]

The first instance of the title occurs at the very beginning (1:4) and emphasizes God's sovereign guidance over everything and all time.[129] Robert Mounce remarks it "calls attention to the fact that all time is embraced within God's eternal presence."[130] A few verses later this is accentuated with the addition of the title "the Almighty" (1:8), an expression of God's complete control of this world and the world to come.[131] The third reference is in the throne room vision. The four living creatures continually praise God with, "Holy, holy, holy, is the Lord God Almighty, who was, and is, and is come" (4:8). A clear allusion to Isa 6:3 and holiness is evident. But eternality is what is stressed the most since the following two verses append "who lives for ever and ever" twice (4:9–10).

The last two occurrences of the title serve as temporal markers. At the conclusion of the seventh trumpet (11:15–19), the great multitude is picture in heaven at the end of history. Significantly, the last third of the threefold phrase is absent at 11:17.[132] In its place a verbal shift from the expected future "is to come" is replaced with a past tense "you have taken your great power, and have begun to reign." This confirms that the trumpets judgments have reached their end. It is a vision of the second coming and the triumph of the Lamb at the consummation but also the judgment of the wicked. "The time has come for judging the dead" (11:18).[133]

125. Other allusions include Isa 41:4; 43:10; 44:6; 48:12.

126. McDonough (*YHWH at Patmos*, 57, 195) notes the wide use of the "three-times-formula" (*Dreizeitenformel*) in antiquity.

127. Bauckham, *Theology of Revelation*, 29. Bauckham footnotes Aune, *Prophecy in Early Christianity*, 280–81.

128. Ibid.

129. Literally the phrase is "from he who is and the he was and he who is coming." Wallace (*Greek Grammar*, 63) remarks that this "is the first and worst grammatical solecism in Revelation, but many more are to follow."

130. Mounce, *Revelation*, 45–46.

131. Resseguie, *Revelation*, 69.

132. Regrettably, a later scribe added the third part ("is to come") at both 11:17 and 16:5. This made its way into the TR/KJV/NKJV tradition, thereby weakening the teaching point John makes in deleting the phrase. UBS5 gives the additional phrase a {B} rating for omission. The absence of the third phrase has superior external evidence and best explains the origin of other readings. See Metzger, *Textual Commentary*, 672.

133. Preterist Chilton (*Days of Vengeance*, 290) posits that this is when God took control of the situation in AD 70 and severed Christianity from Judaism. Dispensationalist Robert Thomas (*Revelation*, 2:108–10) considers the passage as "proleptic," and anticipates the real end that occurs in chapters 16–20. Among those who find John envisioning the end, see Bauckham, *Theology of Revelation*, 29; Beale, *Revelation*, 613–14; Duvall, *Revelation*, 155; Dennis Johnson, *Triumph of the Lamb*, 54 n. 12;

The final reference comes at the third bowl when the angel of the waters cries out for God's justice. "You are just, the Holy One, who is and who was, because you have passed judgment on these things" (16:5 CSB).[134] In this case, "is to come" has been excised in favor of another past tense phrase, this time emphasizing end-time judgment. This is deliberate on John's part. It is yet another way to emphasize the end is arriving "because the final act of God has been inaugurated, and the future is here . . . In other words, we are at the eschaton."[135] This implies that the fourth through sixth bowls are at the end and the seventh bowl is the end.

Like the title "Lord God Almighty," this threefold titular phrase applies only to the Father. However, the Father "comes" at the second coming of Christ. This is done in order to "preserve the prime position of God the Father while at the same time displaying the equality of the Father and the Son."[136]

One Who Lives for Ever and Ever

The emphasis on this title is God's sovereignty over all creation, his control of eternity, and his righteous end-time wrath. This title is found four times in Revelation and probably derives from Dan 4:34 and 12:7. Bauckham serves as a starting point. He notes, "Since . . . the number of occurrences of divine titles in Revelation is usually significant, it is probably not insignificant that one of them occurs four times: 'the one who lives for ever and ever' (4:9, 10; 10:6; 15:7). Four is appropriate because it designates God the eternal Creator who is sovereign over his creation (cf. 4:11; 10:6)."[137]

Looking at the context of each of the four occurrences, the throne room vision clearly stresses God's power over his creation with the first two uses of "for ever and ever" (see 4:9–11). At the start of the second interlude in chapter 10, the mighty angel, "swore by him who lives for ever and ever, who created the heavens and all that is in them, the earth and all that is in it, and the sea and all that is in it, and said, 'There will be no more delay!'" (10:6). This emphasizes the "eternality of God as a major basis for the finality of the proclamations."[138] Finally, the fourth reference is found at the commencement of the seven bowl plagues. "Then one of the four living creatures gave to the seven angels seven golden bowls filled with the wrath of God, who lives for ever and ever" (15:7). Its context

---

Koester, *Revelation*, 515; Murphy, *Fallen Is Babylon*, 271; Osborne, *Revelation*, 443; and J. C. Thomas, *Apocalypse*, 347.

134. The phrase in question has been understood differently by modern versions. A few take it as a dependent clause "in these judgments" (NABR, NIV, NLT, REB). However, because of its parallel to 11:17, it should be taken as a causal clause "because you have judged" (CEB, CSB, ESV, GW, NASB, NET, NKJV, NLT, NRSV).

135. Osborne, *Revelation*, 582–83. So too Bauckham, *Climax of Prophecy*, 32; and McDonough, *YHWH at Patmos*, 226. Many, however, would agree with Beale (*Revelation*, 817), who states "this does not mean that the third bowl occurs only immediately prior to or at Christ's final coming . . ."

136. Brighton, *Revelation*, 44.

137. Bauckham, *Climax of Prophecy*, 31–32. The phrase "for ever and ever" is found thirteen times in Revelation but only four times as the "one who lives for ever and ever."

138. Osborne, *Revelation*, 399.

places the emphasis of the phrase on the righteous end-time judgment of the eternal creator.

One Who Sits on the Throne

This title of God stresses the fullness and perfection of his authority, sovereignty, and especially his consummative judgment. Descriptions of God seated on a throne are found often in the OT (1 Kgs 22:19; 2 Chr 18:18; Ps 47:8; Isa 6:1; Dan 7:9). John alludes to these passages, particularly the last two. He expands upon the description of majesty and praise given by others by adding the element of end-time judgment. Bauckham notes the numerical symbolism of this important title since the phrase is found exactly seven times (4:9; 5:1, 7, 13; 6:16; 7:15; 21:5). For stylistic reasons most English Bible translations mask the "the one who" or shift the verb to past tense on some of the examples. But *ho kathemēnos epi tou thronou* is the complete phrase. Bauckham adds that there are five variations of the words (4:2, 3; 7:10; 19:4; 20:11), "but it looks as though John used these variations quite deliberately in order to keep the number of occurrences of the precise phrase to seven."[139]

That the consummation of the world is in view is confirmed by the fact that all twelve references (exact phrase and variations) are placed near the end of their respective visions or with emphasis on final, end-time judgment. The six references in chapters 4–5's throne room vision stress that coming judgment is about to commence because the Lamb is the only person worthy enough to take the scroll from the one seated on the throne and to break its seals. The lone usage in chapter 6 is located at the end of the seals vision in which God's judgment at the second coming is related, and unrepentant humanity cries out to hide from end-time judgment from him "who sits on the throne and from the wrath of the Lamb!" (6:16). This image, coupled with the imagery of creation fleeing from his presence, occurs only here and at the great white throne judgment (20:11).[140] The next two references appear in the final part of the first interlude that pictures the redeemed in heaven at the second coming (7:10, 15). The next mention is at the end of the fall of Babylon vision in which the twenty-four elders praise the one seated on the throne for the arrival of consummative judgment (19:4). As mentioned above, in 20:11 John "saw a great white throne and him who was seated on it." This serves as an expansion of 6:16–17 and 7:9–14. Finally, John sees the new heaven and new earth and "He who was seated on the throne said, 'I am making everything new!'" (21:5). Therefore, John reserves this title of God for the conclusion of his visions. It confirms the power, authority, and sovereignty of God to effect end-time judgment.

Root and Offspring of David

This title for Christ stresses the power of his messianic kingship to triumph over his enemies and deliver end-time judgment. The phrase "Root of David" is found twice in Revelation

139. Bauckham, *Climax of Prophecy*, 33.
140. Beale, *Revelation*, 400.

(5:5; 22:16). First, in 5:5, it is tied closely to another title (Lion of the Tribe of Judah), and together the images converge key OT messianic ideas that carry forward (Gen 49:8–12: Isa 11:1–10; *4 Ezra* 12:31; Sir 47:2). The NT clearly reveals this messianic deliverer to be Jesus of Nazareth. One of Matthew's favorite titles for Jesus is "son of David," used nine times. The OT passages contained military overtones. Ironically, as 5:6 reveals, this military triumph is achieved not through might but through sacrificial death.[141]

The second use of the title is found at the conclusion of Revelation. Christ proclaims "I am the Root and the Offspring of David, and the bright Morning Star" (22:16). Once again it is coupled with another title. Morning Star stresses the victorious rule of the coming Christ. Some scholars treat the additional word "offspring" as a metaphor for origin. This would provide a hint of Jesus' preexistent nature.[142] It is better, however, to understand its stress on Jesus as the descendent of David, who is the hoped for Messiah, the ultimate fulfillment of the promise from Isaiah.[143] The point of the title at the end of Revelation confirms Jesus as the one "who fulfills the prophecy that one of David's descendants will be the Messiah. Therefore, the genitive 'David' should be rendered 'the root and offspring *from* David.'"[144] This prophesied messianic deliverer who inaugurated righteous judgment with his life, death, and resurrection will complete his righteous deliverance at the second coming.

Demonic Beings

The final section of this chapter addresses demonic beings. The following eight titles, names, or designations give readers insights into John's understanding of demonology.

Abaddon and Apollyon

The name (or title) of an evil angel (perhaps Satan himself) who rises from the Abyss to unleash a demonic horde of locusts that inflict end-time suffering on unbelievers prior to the second coming. The names Abaddon and Apollyon are found once in the NT at Rev 9:11. John describes the fearsome locusts of the fifth trumpet that were released from the Abyss (9:7–10), adding that they had as king over them one whose name in Hebrew is Abaddon and in Greek is Apollyon. A few English Bible translations insert the parenthetical statement that translates the two names as "Destroyer" (GNT, NIV, NLT, REB).

In the OT, Abaddon was used as a proper noun to connote the subterranean realm of the wicked dead (Job 26:6; 31:12), and the Psalmist used the word as "destruction"

---

141. Bauckham, *Climax of Prophecy*, 182; Koester, *Revelation*, 375–76; Osborne, *Revelation*, 253–54; Smalley, *Revelation*, 130; Thomas and Macchia, *Revelation*, 146–47.

142. So Beasley-Murray, *Revelation*, 342; Wilcock, *I Saw Heaven Opened*, 217; Robert Thomas, *Revelation*, 1:388. The NLT's "Source of David and heir to his throne" implies this.

143. So Koester, *Revelation*, 856; Osborne, *Revelation*, 792; Smalley, *Revelation*, 577.

144. Beale, *Revelation*, 1147. This comes through forcefully in "David's Great Descendant" (CEV) and "I am descended from the family of David" (GNT, NCV).

(Ps 88:11).[145] Twice Abaddon was personified (Job 28:22; Prov. 27:20). John personifies the word as well. A few scholars suggest John is delivering a dig at the emperors Nero or Domitian, both who claimed to be the incarnation of the god Apollo.[146] John's focus, however, seems more fixed on the spiritual destroyer rather than on a veiled reference to an earthly despot.[147]

Abaddon is closely related to the angel ("star") mentioned at the fifth trumpet (9:1). Some scholars believe this star symbolizes a good angel, similar to the destroying angel of Exodus, who was tasked with carrying out God's righteous judgment.[148] It seems more likely that this is an evil angel who is permitted by God to inflict end-time harm. A key is the perfect tense found in 9:1. John sees that this angel "had fallen" (*peptōkota*), a common characteristic of fallen angels.[149] Is the "star" angel of 9:1 the same evil angel of 9:11? It appears that they are one and the same. Who, then, is Abaddon and Apollyon? Some believe it is none other than Satan himself.[150] Others disagree, settling for a highly ranked evil angel.[151] Perhaps it is best to allow for both of these latter possibilities.[152]

That the appearance of Abaddon/Apollyon occurs nearer to the conclusion of history appears likely since it is mentioned at the end of the fifth trumpet. The sixth trumpet paints images of Armageddon and the seventh trumpet is the second coming. Evil and demonic influence has worked in the world through the centuries. Near the end, however, unprecedented evil and demonic influence arises prior to the coming of Christ.

Demons

Demons are evil spiritual beings which perform physical, psychological, and spiritual harm to humans on behalf of Satan, particularly through deceptive idolatry, and especially near the end. In Revelation, "spirit" (*pneuma*) receives twenty-four references, but only two refer to evil spirits (16:14; 18:2). There are a considerable number of allusions to demons as fallen angels (*angeloi*) and stars (*asteras*) (8:10; 9:1, 14–15; 12:4, 9) as well as the devil himself (12:9; 20:2).[153] But "demon" (*daimonion*) is specifically mentioned only three times

---

145. Kenneth Barker, "Abaddon," 7; Hutter, "Abaddon," 1.

146. So Caird, *Revelation*, 120; Ford, *Revelation*, 152.

147. Kistemaker, *Revelation*, 292.

148. So Ladd, *Revelation*, 129; Osborne, *Revelation*, 362. Paul (*Revelation*, 176) states "the star appears to be a neutral character rather than a malevolent one . . ."

149. Beale, *Revelation*, 491, 503.

150. Aune, *Revelation*, 2:534; Blount, *Revelation*, 179 (who sees him as a literary personification of death which is allied with Satan); Brighton, *Revelation*, 240; Fee, *Revelation*, 132; Hughes, *Revelation*, 111; Lupieri, *Apocalypse*, 163; Mulholland, *Revelation*, 193; Patterson, *Revelation*, 215; Stefanovic, *Revelation*, 305.

151. Keener, *Revelation*, 269; Mounce, *Revelation*, 191; Reddish, *Revelation*, 176; Rowland, "Revelation," 12:632; Robert Thomas, *Revelation*, 2:38.

152. So Beale, *Revelation*, 503; Kistemaker, *Revelation*, 292; Osborne, *Revelation*, 373; Smalley, *Revelation*, 233.

153. See Aune, "Demonology," 919–23; Reese, "Demons," 140–42; Twelftree, "Demon," 91–100; Yamauchi, "Demons," 410–27.

(9:20; 16:14; 18:2). Thus, each time an evil spirit or a demon is mentioned it is located near the end of a vision. If the conclusion of John's individual visions signal the end of history, then these references to demons portends a rise in demonic activity at that time.

First, at the end of the sixth trumpet and in spite of the worsening end-time conditions that include an Armageddon-like gathering, wicked unbelievers do not stop worshipping demons or idols (9:20). Next, at the sixth bowl, which clearly relates the end-time gathering, John sees three "demonic spirits that perform signs, and they go out to the kings of the whole world, to gather them for the battle on the great day of God Almighty" (16:14). Finally, an image of Babylon's fall at the end of history reveals that it was a dwelling place for demons and a haunt for every impure spirit (18:2). This is a picture of a world without God that is in the power of evil spirits which freely vex people.[154] But now that dwelling place is routed. It has fallen at the return of Christ. Demonic influence pervades every generation. But the fact that demons are mentioned only near the end of John's visions lends support for heightened demonic activity, influence, and deception near the conclusion of history.

Devil

Devil is one of four names attributed to the spiritual being who is the mortal enemy of God and his people. This name emphasizes his role as adversary, accuser, deceiver, and persecutor. The word "devil" (*diabolos*) normally means "slanderer" or "false accuser" and is the Greek equivalent to the Hebrew "Satan" (which is translated as *diabolos* in the LXX). The idea of accuser and slanderer comes through in both names.[155] The devil is found five times in Revelation. The first reference occurs in the letter to Smyrna. The devil will test and persecute the faithful, but Christ will give them the victor's crown" (2:10). Thus, poverty, slander, imprisonment, and even death should be anticipated. The second reference presents all four names in one verse: "The great dragon was hurled down—that ancient serpent called the devil, or Satan, who leads the whole world astray. He was hurled to the earth, and his angels with him" (12:9). Emphasis is laid on the accompanying statement that mentions deception. The third reference occurs a few verses later. A spontaneous song of praise erupts in heaven at the defeat and expulsion of the devil who "is filled with fury because he knows his time is short" (12:12). Most interpreters place this event at the cross and resurrection of Christ, although others understand the timeframe as primordial or occurring at the very end of history.[156] The context emphasizes the devil's fury and his intention to persecute God's people. The fourth occurrence is at the beginning of the millennial vision (20:2). Since the phrase is almost verbatim to the four titles found in 12:9 it appears likely that they refer to the same event—the cross and resurrection of Christ. Finally, the end of the devil is promised with his fifth mention. He is thrown into the lake of fire (20:10). Once more the added insight into his deception is noted. The devil was defeated by the death and resurrection of Christ (Matt 25:41), and his eternal

---

154. Kistemaker, *Revelation*, 486.

155. Twelftree, "Devil, Devils," 117–18; Watson, "Devil," 183–84.

156. See the entry "Michael" for supporters of these views.

defeat, along with the beast and false prophet, is assured. Therefore, all four names (devil, Satan, serpent, and dragon) are interchangeable terms, but John uses each one in different contexts for emphasis. In this case, it closely matches the usage of Satan in that accusations, deception, and persecution are stressed.

Rider on a Black Horse

The rider on a black horse represents the arrival of suffering and terror through poverty and famine, the resultant effects of war. This rider is the third of four horsemen that make up the first four seal judgments (6:5–6). The results of the white horse (war, invading armies) and the red horse (bloodshed, civil strife) now lead to sorrow, suffering and mourning, hunger and the scarcity of goods, and famine. This is confirmed by the pair of scales in the rider's hand and the exorbitant prices for wheat and barley. In the OT, scales were a metaphor indicating famine (Lev 26:26; 2 Kgs 7:1; Ezek 4:10). Beale estimates the prices to be between eight and sixteen times the average price in the Roman Empire.[157] Nevertheless, the final statement "but do not damage the oil and wine" indicates that conditions, though unbearable, are limited and do not constitute the very end. The olive tree and grape vine are not as susceptible to drought due to their deep root systems. This connotes a limitation to the famine.[158] Interpreting this eclectically, John's audience was enduring this, as have many throughout the centuries. Famine, scarcity, and price-gouging will be a part of the very end as well.

Rider on a Pale Horse

The rider on a pale horse represents the coming of violence and terror, death and judgment, and brings John's readers to the brink of the second coming. This is the fourth of the four horsemen, and the fourth of the seven seals (6:7–8). The Greek word *chlōros* has produced translations such as "pale" (ESV, GW, NCV, NIV, NKJV), "pale green" (CEB, CEV, CSB, NABR, NET, NLT, NRSV), "deathly pale" (NJB), "sickly pale" (REB), "pale-colored" (GNT), and "ashen" (NASB). Pale is the color of a corpse or someone who is deathly sick.[159] The war, famine, pestilence, and wild beasts narrated in the first three seals results in death. The rider is named Death, and alongside is his companion, Hades. Thus, death and hell are personified to indicate the ultimate conclusion to the four horsemen. This grim reaper's arrival signals death. The eclectic interpreter views the fourth seal as nearing the threshold of history. John's readers would certainly find social and religious parallels in their own generation. Every era can likewise point to the tensions and upheavals of their generations. All of these elements repeat themselves in history, and will be found

---

157. Beale, *Revelation*, 381.

158. J. C. Thomas, *Apocalypse*, 244–45. See the entry "Pair of Scales."

159. Henri Volohonsky ("The Color of that Horse," 167–68) singularly suggests that *chlōros* should match the color of the fourth horse of Zech 6:3: "a dappled, vigorous horse." Volohonsky asserts "One should not make a drawing of the Fourth Rider in a medieval or renaissance style as a skeleton. He looks rather like a Bedouin dressed in black, on a dappled horse, and a lance is probably his weapon."

in the final generation as well.[160] The added fraction, a fourth, however, indicates that the end has not arrived yet.[161]

Rider on a Red Horse

The rider on a red horse represents the coming of war and horrific bloodshed, perhaps more specifically civil strife and/or the persecution of believers. The imagery of the four horsemen of Rev 6:1–8 is drawn from Zech 1:7–11 and 6:1–8. The second horsemen (6:3–4) rides a "fiery red" horse. He "was given power to take peace from the earth and to make people kill each other. To him was given a large sword" (6:4). Many accept that the second rider heightens what the first rider brought—general warfare, the wars and rumors of wars on the earth (Matt 24:6–7). Indeed, the logical progression of conquest (6:2) to bloodshed (6:4) to famine (6:5–6) to widespread death (6:7–8) is easily observable.[162] The second rider, however, seems to emphasize internal strife over external strife. Whereas the first horseman on the white horse signifies the external lust for war or war in general, the second horseman appears to be a metaphor for civil war. To "make people kill each other" is not necessarily a military phrase.[163] The "large" (*megas* is usually translated "great") sword is a Roman knife or dagger known for in close fighting, another allusion to internecine warfare.[164] On the other hand, the second rider may infer the persecution of believers (6:9–11). Beale, for example, does not limit any of the four horsemen to literal, physical wars only. They also symbolize the spiritual war of oppression and persecution against believers.[165] It appears best to see that John is alluding to both ideas.

Rider on a White Horse (Chapter 6)

There are two riders on white horses in Revelation, reflecting the dualism of the image. In 6:2, the rider is evil and comes as a conqueror bent on bringing war, bloodshed, persecution, and perhaps false prophecy upon the earth. This horseman is presented in the first seal. John relates, "I looked, and there before me was a white horse! Its rider held a bow, and he was given a crown, and he rode out as a conqueror bent on conquest" (6:2). The rider's identity is disputed. Several scholars understand the horseman as Christ. Hendriksen, for example, marshals no less than seven arguments to support this view.[166] This preference

160. See Morris, *Revelation*, 105; Smalley, *Revelation*, 156.

161. Resseguie (*Revelation*, 129) views the "heaping-up of fours" to accentuate the nature and extent of the plagues over the earth.

162. So Keener, *Revelation*, 203; Kistemaker, *Revelation*, 226; Patterson, *Revelation*, 180; Witherington, *Revelation*, 133.

163. The NIV's "kill" (*sphazousin*) is more precisely translated as "slaughter" (CEV, CSB, GW, NABR, NLT, NRSV, REB) or "butcher" (NET).

164. So Beasley-Murray, *Revelation*, 132; Mounce, *Revelation*, 143; Osborne, *Revelation*, 278–79; Reddish, *Revelation*, 126; Roloff, *Revelation*, 86.

165. Beale, *Revelation*, 379. So also Hendriksen, *More than Conquerors*, 120–22; Alan Johnson, "Revelation," 13:653; Stefanovic, *Revelation*, 237.

166. Hendriksen, *More than Conquerors*, 113–17. Beale (*Revelation*, 175), though not favoring the

goes as far back as Ireneaus, and several moderns continue to favor it.[167] The color white, the crown, the rider's conquering nature, and the obvious connection to Christ found later in 19:11 apparently tip the scale in its favor. This understanding, however, has more against it than for it. The other three horsemen are certainly evil, and it appears better to see this rider on the white horse as part of the same wicked group. Thus, many scholars take the opposite approach, and interpret the first rider as none other than the end-time antichrist, underscoring the futurist view that the seals predict events that occur near the very end of human history.[168]

The majority of commentators, however, recognize the evilness of the first rider, but without the specific, end-time antichrist tag. The rider, like the other three horsemen, is a demonic being, not a human being. He is "a demonic parody of Christ, evil masquerading as good."[169] This rider, therefore, represents a malevolent or satanic figure or force found throughout history, and especially nearer the end, and who in context with the other three horsemen combine to produce an evil fearsome foursome. The "bow" is a negative image of the lust for power and conquest through war.[170] The use of "white" reflects parody, and emphasizes false "purity," "evil" victory, and conquest. The "crown" is parody as well, reflecting the desire for authority and power.[171] Moreover, it is possible that the rider symbolizes false prophecy and spiritual persecution through deception and oppression.[172] This is an appealing idea, but the images of military conquest, tyranny, and violence appear to take priority over it.

---

view, lists several elements to support it.

167. So Caird, *Revelation*, 80; Chilton, *Days of Vengeance*, 186–88; Ford, *Revelation*, 106; Hailey, *Revelation*, 188–89; Ladd, *Revelation*, 97–98; Lupieri, *Apocalypse*, 143; Mulholland, *Revelation*, 168–69 (who interestingly adds that the rider of the second horse is Satan [171]); Stefanovic, *Revelation*, 227; Sweet, *Revelation*, 137; J. C. Thomas, *Apocalypse*, 240–41. Kistemaker (*Revelation,* 224) falls short of identifying Christ, but still understands the first rider positively as representing the proclamation of God's Word. Boxall ("'Who Rides the White Horse," 76–88) lists ancient commentators.

168. Hindson, *Revelation*, 81; Alan Johnson, "Revelation," 13:652–53; LaHaye, *Revelation Unveiled*, 142–44; Patterson, *Revelation*, 179; Ryrie, *Revelation*, 55; Robert Thomas, *Revelation*, 1:420–24 (who does not clearly mention antichrist but does connect the rider to the beast of 13:1–10); Walvoord, *Revelation*, 126; Wong, "First Horseman of Revelation 6," 212–26.

169. Resseguie, *Revelation*, 127.

170. So Beale, *Revelation*, 375–78; Beasley-Murray, *Revelation*, 131–32; Boring, *Revelation*, 122; Caird, *Revelation*, 80–81; Fee, *Revelation*, 93; Harrington, *Revelation*, 91; Alan Johnson, "Revelation," 13:652–53; Keener, *Revelation*, 201; Morris, *Revelation*, 101–2; Osborne, *Revelation*, 277; Patterson, *Revelation*, 178–79; Smalley, *Revelation*, 147–50; Witherington, *Revelation*, 133.

171. So Aune, *Revelation*, 2:393–94; Beale, *Revelation*, 375–77; Beasley-Murray, *Revelation*, 132; Blount, *Revelation*, 123–24; Brighton, *Revelation*, 162–65; Charles, *Revelation*, 1:164; Duvall, *Revelation*, 101; Easley, *Revelation*, 106; Dennis Johnson, *Triumph of the Lamb*, 119; Keener, *Revelation*, 202; Mangina, *Revelation*, 98; Morris, *Revelation*, 101–2; Mounce, *Revelation*, 141–42; Murphy, *Fallen Is Babylon*, 205; Osborne, *Revelation,* 276–77; Prigent, *Apocalypse*, 266–67; Reddish, *Revelation*, 125; Resseguie, *Revelation*, 127; Rowland, "Revelation," 12:611–12; Smalley, *Revelation*, 150–51; Witherington, *Revelation*, 133. Many believe John was making a reference to the contemporary Parthian warriors, including Boring, *Revelation*, 122; Farmer, *Revelation*, 74; Harrington, *Revelation*, 89; Kiddle, *Revelation*, 113–14; Osborne, *Revelation,* 276–77; and Roloff, *Revelation*, 86.

172. So Beale, *Revelation*, 377; Boxall, "Who Rides the White Horse," 76–88; de Villiers, "Role of White Horse," 125–53; Kerkeslager, "Apollo and the Rider," 116–21; Michaels, *Revelation*, 101; Paul, *Revelation*, 144; Mark Wilson, "Revelation," 4:289.

Satan

Satan is one of four names attributed to the spiritual being who is the mortal enemy of God and his people. This name emphasizes his role as adversary, accuser, deceiver, and persecutor. "Satan" is a Hebrew noun that means opponent, adversary, or accuser. It is transliterated into Greek as *satanas*. In the OT it referred to a human enemy (1 Sam 29:4; 1 Kgs 11:14) or an angelic adversary sent by God (Num 22:22). Job 1–2 includes references to the judicial prosecutor of the heavenly court, a slanderer and enemy of God who incites God's people to sin and who persecutes them.[173] The NT relates two identifiable aspects of Satan's activities—his hostility toward humanity and his animosity toward God.[174]

"Satan" is found eight times in Revelation (2:9, 13 [twice], 24; 3:9; 12:9; 20:2, 7). The first five occurrences are in the letters to the churches. Those who falsely claim to be God's people at Smyrna and Philadelphia, yet who slander and persecute his followers, are called "the synagogue of Satan" (2:9; 3:9). Christians at Pergamum, the official Asian center for emperor worship, dwell "where Satan lives" and where "Satan has his throne" (2:13). Lastly, the remnant at Thyatira includes those who do not follow Jezebel and do not know about "Satan's so-called secrets." These five references underscore Satan's deceptive practices and especially his opposition to the communities of Christ.

The sixth reference is near the beginning of the third interlude (12:9). Four names or titles are listed—the great dragon, the ancient serpent, the devil, and Satan—along with the added description as one "who leads the whole world astray." The series of names is given for at least three reasons: "to identify the one whom Christ has conquered; to alert the dwellers on earth of the devil's grim power; and to illustrate this monster's capability to both destroy and deceive."[175] Interpreters differ over exactly when this war in heaven breaks out which results in Satan being hurled to earth. A few say it refers to a primordial expulsion of Satan and a third of the angelic host before earth's history began. Others place the event in the future, during the last three and a half years of earth's history. The majority of scholars, however, view this spiritual battle waged at the key moment in all of history—the cross, resurrection, and ascension of Jesus Christ.[176]

The final two references of "Satan" (20:2, 7) probably parallel this same cross event.[177] The series of names are reduplicated from 12:9 at the beginning of the millennial vision (20:2). Premillennialists, however, place this "binding" after the second coming, serving as part of the ushering in of a millennial reign of Christ on earth that is free from Satan's activities. Then, at the conclusion of the millennium, Satan will be released from his prison. He will deceive and gather the nations for another final battle (20:7–8). On the other hand, amillennialists—or better termed, inaugurated millennialists—place the

---

173. See Conrad, "Satan," 112–16; Daniel Fuller, "Satan," 340–44; Victor Hamilton, "Satan," 985–89. A full study is presented in Wray and Mobley, *Birth of Satan*.

174. Hays, Duvall, and Pate, *Dictionary of Prophecy*, 399–400; Ryken, *Dictionary of Biblical Imagery*, 760–61. Most interpreters view Satan and the devil as interchangeable terms. Beale (*Revelation*, 655–56), however, emphasizes "devil" and "Satan" to mean respectively "slanderer" and "adversary."

175. Kistemaker, *Revelation*, 361.

176. See the entry "Michael" for supporters of these views.

177. So also Beale, *Revelation*, 988, 991; Brighton, *Revelation*, 553.

binding of Satan at the cross of Christ, like in 12:9. Thus, the millennial vision envisions the time period between the first and second comings of Christ. Satan remains active, prowling like a roaring lion, and seeking to devour sinners (1 Pet 5:8). But he can go only as far as the Lord allows. Satan continues to be kept in line. Nonetheless, near the end of the millennium, he is released from restrictions, and leads the world to Armageddon. The end-time battle of 20:8, then, becomes another picture of Armageddon.

2

Nature and Cosmic Imagery

JOHN USES NATURE IMAGES and cosmic images often, and the length of this chapter confirms it. Significant overlap is noticeable. It is difficult to decide on whether to place some entries under nature images or under cosmic images. Broadly, the chapter is divided into "everyday" natural earth images and images that signify the dissolution of the world at the end of history.

Nature

The following entries describe symbols which John takes from nature. Each entry is symbolic, not literal. Among other things, they reveal contrasts, reflect idioms, and symbolize eternal life and the majesty of God.

Bronze

Bronze symbolizes the stability, strength, and purity of the risen Christ. The literal understanding of bronze is detected at 9:20 and 18:12. The symbolic nature of bronze, however, is discernible at 1:15 ("His feet were like bronze glowing in a furnace") and 2:18 ("These are the words of the Son of God, whose eyes are like blazing fire and whose feet are like burnished bronze"). The uniqueness of the word leads some scholars to assume it refers to some unknown metal. It is probably connected with an alloy of copper and zinc or tin.[1] But some take it as an alloy of copper and gold.[2] Most modern English versions choose "burnished" or "polished bronze," although "fine brass" (CEB, NKJV) and "polished brass" (GNT, NABR) are also offered. The bronze is glowing and polished. Thus, the point appears to center on its shiny brightness and uniqueness, but most of all as an image of strength and stability, based on an allusion to Dan 10:6.[3] Furthermore, the risen

---

1. Bowes, "Bronze," 679–80. See Hemer, *Letters to the Seven Churches*, 111–17; Kistemaker, *Revelation*, 96; Osborne, *Revelation*, 90.

2. Lupieri, *Apocalypse*, 110; Prigent, *Apocalypse*, 138; Roloff, *Revelation*, 36.

3. Morris, *Revelation*, 54; Smalley, *Revelation*, 54.

Christ embodies a moral purity that by implication is demanded from the churches.[4] A final allusion is in order. Christ's feet are refined in a furnace, which underscores the consistent theme of judgment found in Revelation.[5]

Firstfruits

At the second coming, all believers are pictured as a dedicated offering to God, evidence of their faithful discipleship, guaranteeing a harvest of eternal, divine fellowship. The offering of "firstfruits" is located in seven places in the NT, and each instance is used figuratively. One of the seven usages is Rev 14:4. In a vision of the second coming, the Lamb stands on Mount Zion surrounded by the hundred and forty-four thousand. Who are these people? John gives a fourfold identification of these faithful followers of Christ. They are: (1) virgins (i.e. pure); (2) followers of the Lamb; (3) firstfruits; and (4) blameless. For the third characteristic most English versions choose a literal translation of "firstfruits." Several, however, attempt to define what "firstfruits" means for modern audiences. Thus, we have "special offering" (NLT); "as people to be offered" (NCV); "first ones offered" (GW, GNT); "the most precious people" (CEV); and a less helpful "purchased from among humankind as early produce" (CEB).

Firstfruits is a common sacrificial metaphor, a technical term, denoting the first portion of the harvest or animals that had been set aside and offered to God (Exod 23:19; Lev 23:9–14; Deut 18:4). It was offered back to God in thankfulness and total indebtedness for a good harvest and the hope that God would bless the remainder of the crops. The firstfruits become a token for the coming abundant harvest.[6] The whole nation of Israel, delivered from Egypt, is considered firstfruits as well (Jer 2:2–3). Thus, the firstfruits serves as another already-not-yet metaphor which is found throughout the NT for something that is first in a sequence of more to come. For example, Paul informs the Romans (Rom 8:23), the Corinthians (1 Cor 15:20–23; 16:15), and the Thessalonians (2 Thess 2:13) that they are at the present time "firstfruits." Jas 1:18 does the same, calling gentile readers the firstfruits of a new creation in Christ. In its lone instance in Revelation, John confirms what these previous Bible writers stated. The hundred and forty-four thousand (representing all believers, the church) are called the firstfruits. They are the first and best parts of a harvest dedicated to God, the guarantee of the final harvest of all believers at the second coming (14:14–16).[7]

---

4. Beale, *Revelation*, 209–10; Robert Thomas, *Revelation*, 1:102.

5. Blount, *Revelation*, 44.

6. Reddish, *Revelation*, 275. See Minear, *Images of the Church*, 112–13; Jack Lewis, "Firstfruits," 578; Rigsby, "First Fruits," 796–97.

7. Beale, *New Testament Biblical Theology*, 581; Mounce, *Revelation*, 266–69; Osborne, *Revelation*, 528–31; Smalley, *Revelation*, 359.

Harvest

Harvesting or reaping is a common symbol for end-time judgment on the wicked and end-time gathering and deliverance for the faithful. The OT presented the harvest frequently in the literal sense, particularly since Israel was an agrarian society. Harvest as a symbol, however, was also common. It pictured a blessing for the returning captives of Judah (Hos 6:11). The law of reaping what one sows was either for righteousness (Hos 10:12) or unrighteousness (Prov 22:8), and carried over to the NT (Gal 6:7–9). Harvesting also served as a metaphor for divine judgment (Isa 17:5; Jer 12:13; Joel 3:13).

Harvesting and reaping, therefore, evolve into natural symbols in NT. It could be understood positively (Matt 9:37–38; Mark 4:26–29; John 4:35–38; Jas 3:18), negatively (Matt 25:24–26; Luke 19:21; Jas 5:4; see also *4 Ezra* 4:28–32), or even placed side-by-side for comparison (Matt 13:24–30; Gal 6:7–9). Jesus, the master of metaphors, uses the picture of the harvest in two distinct ways—first, as an immediate opportunity to respond and second, as a reference to end-time judgment.[8]

John uses the harvest metaphor in 14:14–20. The noun "harvest" (*thērismos*) is found once (14:15). The verb "to reap" or "to harvest" (*thērizō*) is found three times (14:15–16). Both shades of meaning—judgment for the wicked and deliverance for the saints—are pictured, and laid side-by-side. Verses 14–16 depict a grain harvest as an image of the gathering of the saints at the end whereas verses 17–20 describe a grape harvest as an image of the judgment on the wicked. Several interpreters understand both harvests to portray scenes of judgment on the wicked, particularly since a sickle and reaping often appear in judgment.[9] The majority of scholars, however, support a distinction between the two harvests.

The positive image of the grain harvest is supported by the biblical passages cited above. Contextually, it also appears connected with the hundred and forty-four thousand "firstfruits" (14:4).[10] The image of the "one like a son of man," identified by most interpreters as Christ, plus the absence of judgment that is plainly present in the grape harvest, contributes to the positive picture. By contrast, the image of a grape harvest as judgment upon the wicked has much support from the OT (Isa 63:2–6; Joel 3:13–14).

Positively, therefore, the grain harvest is redemptive and depicts the ingathering of the faithful at the second coming of Christ.[11] Negatively, the grape harvest portrays

---

8. Ryken, *Dictionary of Biblical Imagery*, 366; Wolf, "Harvest," 45–46.

9. Aune, *Revelation*, 2:803; Beale, *Revelation*, 770–78; Duvall, *Revelation*, 203; Hendriksen, *More than Conquerors*, 187–88; Alan Johnson, "Revelation," 13:725; Lupieri, *Apocalypse*, 232; Mounce, *Revelation*, 277–81; Patterson, *Revelation*, 296; Resseguie, *Revelation*, 200; Skaggs and Benham, *Revelation*, 152; Robert Thomas, *Revelation*, 2:219–20; Walvoord, *Revelation*, 220–22; Witherington, *Revelation*, 196. LaHaye (*Revelation Unveiled*, 242) states the passage refers to the last three and a half years of earth history. Brighton (*Revelation*, 389–94) interprets the grain harvest to reap both believers and unbelievers while the grape harvest reaps only unbelievers.

10. Bauckham (*Climax of Prophecy*, 291–96) presents an extended discussion on this.

11. Easley (*Revelation*, 254–55, 262–64, 407) points to 14:14–16 for evidence of the rapture. Hence, Easley adopts an offshoot of the dispensationalist view called the prewrath rapture, popularized by Rosenthal (*Pre-Wrath Rapture of the Church*), and Van Kampen (*Sign*). Recent proponents include Alan Hultberg ("Case for the Prewrath Rapture," 109–54), and Kurschner (*Antichrist before the Day of the Lord*).

the condemnation of unbelievers and final judgment.[12] Philip Hughes offers an effective summary. "There is the reaping of the wheat and the reaping of the tares, the reaping of the redeemed and the reaping of the unregenerate, the reaping to glory and the reaping to condemnation."[13]

Palm Branches

Waving palm branches evokes images from the Feast of Tabernacles and is a gesture of thanksgiving and praise to signify the triumphant arrival of Christ at his second coming, delivering his people from tribulation, and rewarding the faithful in eternity. "Palm branches" (*phoinikes*) is found twice in the NT.[14] First, the Gospel of John mentions them in the triumphal entry of Jesus at the last Passover (John 12:13). By Jesus' day, palm branches were a customary national symbol of victory (2 Macc 10:7), and often associated with military victory (1 Macc 13:51; *T. Naph.* 5:4). The act of waving palm branches provocatively signaled nationalistic hopes that Jesus had arrived as messianic liberator. Palms were also a feature of apocalyptic end-time hopes. At both Jewish insurrections (AD 66–70 and 132–135), palms appear on newly minted coins.[15]

John picks up this theme of end-time victory for the saints in the second half of the first interlude (7:9–17). John sees "a great multitude" that is "standing before the throne and before the Lamb" and "were holding palm branches in their hands" (7:9). Thus, God and the Lamb are being praised with the faithful in heaven for effecting salvation for humanity and for protecting the church through tribulation.

Several scholars note an allusion to the Feast of Tabernacles in the phrase "holding palm branches in their hands" (Lev 23:40; Neh 8:13–17).[16] If so, then the imagery of celebrating both the harvest and delivery from slavery in Egypt—twin themes of Tabernacles—fits nicely. The end-time harvest and new exodus deliverance are found often in Revelation. J. A. Draper argues that this particular feast is the origin of the concept of the eschatological day of the Lord.[17] This idea has merit since the harvest is used of-

---

12. Farmer (*Revelation*, 104, 126–30) presents a more universalistic interpretation. The two harvests are two different aspects of a single in-gathering of all people—all are judged and all are saved.

13. Hughes, *Revelation*, 165–66.

14. The place name Phoenix is a third reference at Acts 27:12.

15. Köstenberger, *John*, 369.

16. So Aune, *Revelation*, 2:468–70; Beale, *Revelation*, 428; Blount, *Revelation*, 151; Boxall, *Revelation*, 125; Brighton, *Revelation*, 194–95; Buchanan, *Revelation*, 214; Harrington, *Revelation*, 100; Patterson, *Revelation*, 200; Paul, *Revelation*, 161; Prévost, *How to Read the Apocalypse*, 96; Prigent, *Apocalypse*, 290; Rotz, *Revelation*, 125–26; Rowland, "Revelation," 12:621; Smalley, *Revelation*, 192; Stefanovic, *Revelation*, 265–66; Sweet, *Revelation*, 152; Leonard Thompson, *Revelation*, 108. A few interpreters understand the entire feast cycle to be represented in the structure of Revelation, including Farrer (*Rebirth of Images*, 157–84), Goulder ("Apocalypse as an Annual Cycle of Prophecies," 342–67), and Stefanovic (*Revelation*, 33–35).

17. See Draper, "Heavenly Feast of Tabernacles," 133–47. Allusions to the Tabernacles are not confined to 7:9–17. Reynolds ("Feast of Tabernacles and Revelation," 245–68) notes twelve allusions throughout Revelation. Another attempt at connecting Jewish feasts is Stramara (*God's Timetable*), who attempts to anchor Pentecost as the hermeneutical key for understanding the structure of Revelation.

ten as a symbol for the end-time ingathering. Hakan Ulfgard has produced the most thorough analysis on this connection. He states it is not the Feast of Tabernacles itself which is John's focus in 7:9–17, but rather what the feast represents, namely, "it is a joyful celebration of God's past salvation . . . [and] the redeemed Christian people of God in accordance with the biblical 'type' of Israel, liberated from Egypt and on its way to the Promised Land . . ."[18]

Primarily, though, the palm branches signify end-time victory and rejoicing. John applies this image to the people of all nations, who now rejoice in their exodus deliverance and redemption at the second coming.[19] The allusion to palm branches is a fitting climax to the end of the first interlude, which pictures the redeemed in heaven praising God.

Rainbow

The rainbow is a reminder to God's people that although righteous end-time judgment must happen, it will nonetheless be tempered by gracious divine mercy. "Rainbow" (*iris*) is found twice in the NT, both in Revelation (4:3; 10:1). The OT uses the Hebrew word for "bow," a weapon, to refer to the bow-shaped object in the sky. The "bow in the sky" serves as a potent symbol of God's mercy and peace after the storm of judgment. The judgment of the flood led to a covenant with Noah, and the bow in the sky served as a promise never again to destroy humanity with a flood for sinfulness (Gen 9:13–17).[20] Ezekiel alludes to this Genesis event by beginning his prophecy with an awe-inspiring image of God surrounded by the appearance of a rainbow (Ezek 1:28). Thus, Ezekiel hearkens back to the flood story in order to tell his own generation that God will exercise mercy even in the context of imminent judgment. John does the same in the Apocalypse. In the throne room vision a rainbow encircled the throne (4:3). Thus, the connection drawn from Ezekiel and Genesis is repeated in Revelation, along with its symbolic teaching.[21]

The other reference is found in the introduction of the second interlude. There the mighty angel's description included "a rainbow above his head" (10:1). John sees the rainbow, an allusion to the covenant with Noah and the promise of majestic grace and mercy in the middle of end-time judgment. The rainbow also intimates that just as creation was renewed after the flood, so too a new creation is on its way.[22]

---

18. Ulfgard, *Feast and Future*, 150–51.

19. Osborne, *Revelation*, 320. See Keener, *Revelation*, 243–44. Apparently, no one has connected the eleven references to decorated palm trees in the vision of the Ezek 40–41, that is, the vision of the eschatological temple. Perhaps John has in mind the connection between the final dwelling place of his people. Yet this, too, must not be pressed.

20. Kissling, "Rainbow," 729.

21. Shargel ("Hearer-Centric Approach to Revelation," 312) calls this a window allusion.

22. See Aune, *Revelation*, 1:285–86; 2:557; Beale, *Revelation*, 320–21; 522–26; Brighton, *Revelation*, 114–16; 258–59; Osborne, *Revelation*, 227, 394; Ryken, *Dictionary of Biblical Imagery*, 695; Robert Thomas, *Revelation*, 1:343–44; 2:61.

River

River is used contrastingly by John. It is pictured as both a threat to people but is also associated with the life-sustaining water of the new Jerusalem. Rivers and springs figure prominently throughout the Bible. More than a hundred and fifty references are found and they fall into six categories—source of life, source of cleansing, geographical boundary, place of human-divine encounter, agent of God's acts of provision and rescue, and as a symbol. Many of its references draw from the original river in paradise (Gen 2:10–14), including those in the book of Revelation. [23]

Since river is used contrastingly, this entry discusses its bad side. "River" (*potamos*) is found eight times (8:10; 9:14; 12:15, 16; 16:4, 12; 22:1, 2). Resseguie explains that three topographical references in Revelation are ambiguous—river, mountain, and wilderness. The river is a dangerous place and poses a threat to humanity. The third trumpet reveals a third of the rivers and springs turning poisonous (8:10). It is the boundary crossed by the four angels that dispense the sixth trumpet plagues (9:14). The third bowl reveals all the rivers and springs turning to blood (16:4). The great river Euphrates is the place where the kings from the east cross over to fight at Armageddon (16:12). Indeed, "The Euphrates, which flows through Babylon, is a parody of the river of water of life, which flows through Jerusalem."[24]

The river threatens God's people as well—a river of water gushes from the mouth of the serpent in an attempt to destroy the woman (12:15–16). The symbolic nature of the flood of water is one of the few instances where most interpreters from all persuasions agree. This passage poses a difficulty for literalist interpreters. When trumpet and bowl judgments come, they envision poisonous waters and seas turned to blood. But for these verses, most resort to symbolism. Only a few interpreters venture a literal gushing of water let loose to sweep away the woman.[25] The majority of interpreters understand the river as a "river of lies" that the serpent spews in an attempt to drown the church. It "represents Satan's, lies, deceit, false teaching, slander, accusations, counterfeit miracles, and persecution aimed at destroying God's people (cf. Matt. 24:24; 2 Cor. 2:11; 11:3, 13–15; 2 Thess. 2:9–10; 1 Tim. 4:1; 5:15; 2 Tim. 2:23–36; Rev. 13:13–15; 16:14)."[26] Yet the river also symbolizes eternal life for God's people. The next entry unfolds this.

---

23. Ryken, *Dictionary of Biblical Imagery,* 729–30. Gilchrest ("Topography of Utopia," 289–99) produces an excellent study that compares Greco-Roman and Jewish end-time utopias with Rev 21–22's use of water imagery.

24. Resseguie, *Revelation Unsealed,* 84. See the entry "Great River Euphrates."

25. Only Ryrie, *Revelation,* 93; and tentatively, Robert Thomas; *Revelation,* 2:140. Walvoord (*Revelation,* 195) considers the literal view implausible. LaHaye (*Revelation Unveiled,* 205) and Lindsey (*New World Coming,* 179) envision the flood of water as a flood of soldiers of the antichrist who are pursuing great tribulation Jews. This obviously limits the reference to the very end of earth history. See the entry "Serpent."

26. Duvall, *Revelation,* 173. See Beale, *Revelation,* 671–73, for OT and intertestamental support. Keener (*Revelation,* 323) stresses slander the most. Mouths are typically used as symbols for speech, especially God's Word, but what supports the slander interpretation most clearly is the serpents' mouths that appear as slander in Ps 140:1–5. Resseguie (*Revelation Unsealed,* 85) suggests that John intended to make a sharp contrast between what comes out of the serpent's mouth with what comes out of the Lamb's mouth—a sharp, two-edged sword (1:16; 19:15). One is evil but the other is "the Word of God."

River of the Water of Life

The river of the water of life (and associated expressions) symbolizes eternal salvation and the never-ending fellowship that believers enjoy with God, the Lamb, and the Spirit in the new Jerusalem. "River" is one of the many images John uses contrastingly. This entry deals with the good side of river. The Bible frequently uses the figure of thirst to depict the desire to know God (Pss 36:9; 42:1; 63:1; Isa 55:1). John links four references to this image—"springs of living water," "spring of the water of life," "river of the water of life" and "water of life."[27] Each reference is reserved for the conclusion of an individual vision.

The first image connects to glorified saints in heaven at the end of history (7:9–17). Believers are promised, "'Never again will they hunger; never again will they thirst. The sun will not beat down on them,' nor any scorching heat. For the Lamb at the center of the throne will be their shepherd; 'he will lead them to springs of living water.' 'And God will wipe away every tear from their eyes'" (7:16–17). The phraseology derives from Isa 49:10. Just as God shepherded the exiles, freed from Babylon, to fountains of water, so too will the Lamb guide his redeemed to eternal "springs of the water of life." For those who believe, their spiritual thirst is forever quenched.[28]

The last three references are found in chapters 21–22. At the conclusion of the thousand years vision John is told to write down, "It is done. I am the Alpha and the Omega, the Beginning and the End. To the thirsty I will give water without cost from the spring of the water of life" (21:6). Stephen Smalley states this "stands for the salvific presence of God through faith in the redeeming Lamb, and the life which results for the saints from eternal fellowship with them."[29]

Next, an angel shows John "the river of the water of life, as clear as crystal, flowing from the throne of God and of the Lamb" (22:1). This end-time river is "clear as crystal," symbolizing purity and holiness. Brighton asserts that this "refers to the spiritual power of God and of the Lamb that will sustain forever the communal life of God's people with him in the new heaven and earth."[30] Several exegetes detect an allusion to the Holy Spirit here as well, and it does make sense (Ezek 36:25–27; John 3:5; 4:10–14; 7:38–39; 1 John 5:7–8; 1QS 4:21).[31] The river is the main thoroughfare in the new Jerusalem. It hearkens

---

One holds the threat of evil while the other holds the promises of God. This is possible, but a better contrast is the water of evil that flows from the serpent compared to the river of the water of life that flows in the new Jerusalem which the subsequent entry discusses.

27. See the entry "Water." Whitaker ("River of Life," 667) states the river of life signifies fertility, rejuvenation, joy, and eternal life, and that the Middle Ages used the image often for its iconography.

28. Smalley, *Revelation*, 200–201.

29. Ibid., 541. See Beale, *Revelation*, 1056.

30. Brighton, *Revelation*, 625.

31. This is noted in Duvall, *Revelation*, 299; Dennis Johnson, *Triumph of the Lamb*, 320; Lindsey, *New World Coming*, 295; Mulholland, *Revelation*, 331; Swete, *Apocalypse*, 298; and Walvoord, *Revelation*, 329. However, Beale and McDonough ("Revelation," 1154) appropriately add, "Although the Holy Spirit may be in mind, the water metaphor primarily represents the life of eternal fellowship with God and Christ, which is borne out by the way 22:3–5 develops 22:1–2 . . ." Barr (*Tales*, 145) understands the water of life to allude to the cross of Christ. Robert Thomas (*Revelation*, 2:481–82), ever the literalist, envisions a pollution-free river that imparts spiritual life.

back to Ezekiel who himself referred back to the garden of Eden (Gen 2:10; Ezek 47:1–12).[32] "In the Apocalypse, John connects this spring of life-giving water to the Eden-like river whose water of life runs through the heart of the new Jerusalem (22:1)."[33]

Lastly, "The Spirit and the bride say, 'Come!' And let the one who hears say, 'Come!' Let the one who is thirsty come; and let the one who wishes take the free gift of the water of life" (22:17). The imagery is drawn from Isa 55:1. Jesus uses the phraseology as well (John 7:37–38). There is debate on whether it is John or Jesus who is speaking. But the point is that God's people will eternally live at the source of the life-giving river that figuratively flows from the very presence of God.

Sand on the Seashore

This is a common expression that signifies an innumerable multitude, specifically of armies. It is found in the OT to note an incalculably large number (Gen 22:17; 2 Sam 17:11), often in the context of a large army (Josh 11:4; 1 Sam 13:5).[34] In the NT, four of the five references to "sand" (*ammos*) include "sea" (Rom 9:27; Heb 11:12; Rev 13:1; 20:8). "Sand on the seashore" (*ammos tēs thalassēs*), then, is found twice in the Apocalypse. A few English versions helpfully translate the phrase the same way at both locations: "sand of the sea" (CSB, ESV, NABR, NKJV) or "sand of the seashore" (NASB).

First, the dragon is pictured standing expectantly on the shore of the sea (13:1).[35] He faces the sea, not the land, ready to call on beastly reinforcement in his fight against the woman's offspring. Few commentators mention this part of the verse, emphasizing instead the evil symbolism of the sea from which the beast rises. Smalley alone mentions the sand, now invaded by the powers of evil, forms a marked contrast to the rock of Zion in 14:1.[36]

The hyperbolic expression comes through clearly in the final reference to sand and sea. The dragon will deceive the nations and gather them for battle. "In number they are like the sand on the seashore" (20:8). The idiom comes through forcefully in idiomatic translations: "as many followers as there are grains of sand along the beach" (CEV), "as many as the grains of sand on the seashore" (GNT), and "as numberless as sand along the seashore" (NLT). The point is that this end-time battle is worldwide and that the evil forces are overwhelming and incalculable in number. Only God can help his people.

---

32. Shargel ("Hearer-Centric Approach to Revelation," 122–23, 203) calls these references window allusions.

33. Blount, *Revelation*, 382.

34. Osborne, *Revelation*, 711.

35. Alongside the NIV, the NASB, NKJV, and REB place this phrase at the beginning of 13:1. ESV places it at the end of 12:17. Most versions add a verse 18 (CEB, CEV, CSB, GW, GNT, NET, NJB, NLT, NRSV). The TR/KJV/NKJV tradition follows the textual variant "I [John] stood" instead of "he [dragon] stood." The difference is only one letter (*estathē* or *estathēn*). See Metzger, *Textual Commentary*, 748.

36. Smalley, *Revelation*, 335.

Sea

The sea functions as a versatile image for John. It is a literal geographical feature but also a sinister symbol of evil and chaos, death and Hades. It is the place of origin for the beast, a symbol of wicked humanity, and therefore symbolically has no place in the new heaven and new earth. The sea is used regularly as a symbol in Scripture. The idiom "sand of the sea" was a blessing of many descendants (Gen 22:17) and huge armies (Josh 11:4). The stirring of the sea described human restlessness (Isa 57:20), a doubter's instability (Jas 1:6), and shameful carousing (Jude 13). God's forgiveness was as great as the sea's depth (Mic 7:19). Yet there was a sinister side to the sea. The ancient world commonly associated the sea with chaos and evil. It was the home of the great mythical sea monster Leviathan (or Rahab or the dragon), which God defeated (Job 26:12; Pss 74:13; 89:9; Isa 27:1; 51:9). It also held associations with death (Jonah 2:1–6) and the rise of satanic power (Dan 7:2–3).[37]

John uses the sea as a literal, natural body of water, often in close connection with the earth. This signifies synecdoche in which the sea is a part of the old creation and represents its totality.[38] As a part of creation, the sea suffers along with the earth from the devil's onslaughts (12:12) and from judgments carried out by God (8:8–9; 16:3). This literal understanding of the sea accounts for the majority of occurrences in Revelation.

Nevertheless, John often draws figuratively from the sea and in line with previous OT use. There are three ways that the sea is evil in John's universe.[39] First, it is revealed as the origin of cosmic evil. John visualizes a sea of glass, clear as crystal (4:6) and later mixed with fire (15:2). This image symbolizes that the chaos of evil is destroyed by God's sovereignty from the viewpoint of believers. The tranquility of overcoming is suggested by "clear as crystal." But the addition of "mixed with fire" hints at judgment from the viewpoint of unbelievers.[40] Second, the sea symbolizes the realm of evil and wicked humanity (13:1). In a dramatic scene, the dragon stands on the seashore and the beast rises from the sea. This alludes to Dan 7 and hints first of all to the origin of cosmic evil. The sea may infer evil humanity as well. If so, the accompanying persecution of the wicked against the faithful is a consequence.[41] This is reasonable when coupled with other watery images (17:15).[42] Third, the sea symbolizes the place of the dead and the demonic realm (20:13). Most interpreters correctly understand the phrase "the sea gave up the dead that were in it" to refer to all those who perished at sea. Alongside those buried on land it

---

37. Coogan, "Sea," 139–40; Follis, "Sea," 1058–59; Hays, Duvall, and Pate, *Dictionary of Prophecy,* 84, 402–3; Paterson, "Sea," 370–72; Ryken, *Dictionary of Biblical Imagery,* 765–66; Stolz, "Sea," 737–42.

38. Beale, *Revelation,* 1042.

39. The lone exception is "sand on the seashore" (20:8), a figure of speech that denotes incalculability of armies.

40. See the entry "Sea of Glass."

41. Hughes, *Revelation,* 143; Kiddle, *Revelation,* 243; Prigent, *Apocalypse,* 396; Skaggs and Benham, *Revelation,* 134; Smalley, *Revelation,* 335. Walvoord (*Revelation,* 198) distinguishes even more. The beast from the sea arises from "Gentile humanity" in comparison to the second beast "from the land" who represents Israel.

42. Beale (*Revelation,* 1042) adds that the sea is the location of the world's idolatrous trade activity (18:10–19). Murphy (*Apocalypticism,* 173–74) comments that chapter 10 of the *Testament of Moses,* written near the time of Christ, depicts the "sea shall retire into the abyss" in the eschaton.

accents that all the dead will stand before the great white throne. Thus, no one can escape the final judgment, not even the unburied dead, which was a concern of the ancients.[43] Moreover, sea and death and Hades are virtual synonyms and thereby represent the demonic realm of death.[44]

Because John symbolizes the sea in these three ways, it becomes easier to understand why there is no more sea in the new heaven and the new earth (21:1).[45] This forms part of John's *via negativa* found in chapters 21–22.[46] Symbolically, no more devil, no more evil, and no more persecution is perfectly pictured in the phrase "no more sea."[47] The disappearance of the sea in the eschaton confirms God's victory over evil, chaos, death, and hell.

Sea of Glass

This image before the heavenly throne symbolizes God's sovereignty and judgment. From the perspective of believers, the sea of glass accentuates the majesty of God and the absence of chaos and evil. The sea of glass mixed with fire symbolizes the testing which they have safely passed through. For unbelievers, however, the sea of glass mixed with fire represents end-time judgments poured out. Water imagery is significant in prophetic literature, especially in Revelation where over fifty references occur. Some of these are literal but the majority serve as contrasting symbols of good (4:6; 7:17; 16:5; 21:6) or evil (12:15; 17:1, 15; 20:13; 22:17). Specifically, the "sea" (*thallasa*) is mentioned twenty-six times in Revelation, primarily as a literal body of water. Four times, however, the sea is clearly intended to be symbolic (4:6; 13:1; 15:2; 21:1). On two of those four occasions the "sea of glass" is mentioned.

First, John's throne room vision reveals "what looked like a sea of glass, clear as crystal" (4:6). Some understand this sea of glass positively. It emphasizes God's awesomeness, transcendence, holiness, and therefore, serves as a metaphor for the majesty of God.[48] But others understand the sea of glass negatively. The sea represents the chaos and evil that

43. Aune, *Revelation*, 3:1102; Robert Thomas, *Revelation*, 2:432–33. This similarly fits the concerns of other apocalyptic works (*4 Ezra* 7:32–35; *1 En.* 61:5). Bauckham (*Climax of Prophecy*, 56–60) lists other extratextual examples.

44. Osborne, *Revelation*, 722–23. Several commentators note the demonic aspect of the sea, including Bauckham, *Climax of Prophecy*, 67–70; Beale, *Revelation*, 1034; Kiddle, *Revelation*, 406–7; Kistemaker, *Revelation*, 547; Resseguie, *Revelation*, 250; Roloff, *Revelation*, 232; and Smalley, *Revelation*, 518.

45. LaHaye (*Revelation Unveiled*, 357) demonstrates the literalistic approach when he opines that there will be rivers and water in the new heaven and new earth, but "it will have no land surface wasted by seas." So too Hindson, *Revelation*, 215; and Walvoord, *Revelation*, 311.

46. See the entry "No More." Mathewson ("New Exodus as a Background," 243–58) understands the phrase to form part of the eschatological new exodus motif common throughout Revelation. Moo ("Sea That Is No More," 148–67), however, sees the new exodus motif within the larger framework of new creation typology which differs from Gen 1. See also Thomas Schmidt, "And the Sea Was No More," 233–49.

47. Beale (*Revelation*, 1042) states 21:1 encompasses all nuances of "sea" in Revelation, including the literal body of water.

48. Fee, *Revelation*, 71; Michaels, *Revelation*, 92–93; Mounce, *Revelation*, 122–23; Osborne, *Revelation*, 231–32.

is now calmed in heaven. This tumultuous evil includes unredeemed humanity, Satan, and demonic forces. This chaos no longer exists since John sees a calm sea.[49] These views are not incompatible. Like many of the symbols in Rev 4, John's image of a sea of glass alludes to Ezekiel's vision of heaven (Ezek 1:22). The understanding of the sea and waters in heaven is common in the OT (Pss 104:3; 148:4), and relates back to Gen 1:7 where God separated the sky as an expanse between the upper and lower waters. This certainly underscores God's majesty. Yet the sea is often symbolized as chaos. Thus, putting the two ideas together, the calmness of the sea serves as an example of God's sovereign authority over such powers (Job 9:8; Ps 74:13).[50]

Second, at the conclusion of the third interlude John perceives "what looked like a sea of glass glowing with fire and, standing beside the sea, those who had been victorious over the beast and its image and over the number of its name" (15:2). It is possible to interpret the sea that glows (most English versions have "mixed") with fire as a picture of purity stemming from God's holiness.[51] "Mixed with fire" may reflect back to the flashes of lightning that emerge from the throne (4:5). It may also evoke the common apocalyptic image of a "river of fire flowing" from God's presence (Dan 7:10; *1 En.* 54:7; *3 En.* 18:19). Yet fire often symbolizes divine judgment (Isa 66:15; Mal 3:2), especially in Revelation (8:4–5; 9:17–18; 14:10; 16:8; 17:6; 18:8; 19:20; 20:9). The addition of a saturating fire then stresses a scene of judgment. This is a picture of judgment day, the great white throne where God judges saints and sinners (20:11–15). Moreover, John probably alludes to the fiery Red Sea deliverance of the exodus, thereby symbolizing end-time deliverance and salvation for believers on the one hand, and judgment for the beast and his followers on the other hand.[52] Therefore, John's contrasts are at work again. He emphasizes the sovereignty of God through the lack of chaos and evil. The sea of glass stresses tranquility in 4:6 and end-time judgment in 15:2.

Stones

On one hand, precious stones symbolize the alluring beauty and abusive wealth and power of the great prostitute. On the other hand, they represent the majesty, beauty, holiness, and eternality of a sovereign God. Jewels and precious stones fall into four categories when used symbolically: adornment and beauty (Gen 24:22; Song 1:10; Prov 1:9), wealth and power (Exod 11:2; 2 Chr 21:3; Matt 13:44), holiness and worship (Exod 28:17–20; Ezek 28:12–14), and transcendent permanence (Isa 54:11–12).[53] John taps into these four images when he mentions precious stones in Revelation (4:3; 17:4; 18:12, 16; 21:9–21).

---

49. Beale, *Revelation*, 327; Caird, *Revelation*, 68; Resseguie, *Revelation Unsealed*, 80; Thomas Schmidt, "And the Sea Was No More," 233–49.

50. See Hylen, "Sea of Glass, Glassy Sea," 140; Kuykendall, "Sea of Glass,"; Moo, "And the Sea Is No More," 151–54.

51. Robert Thomas, *Revelation*, 1:353.

52. Beale, *Revelation*, 789; Caird, *Revelation*, 197; Osborne, *Revelation*, 562.

53. Ryken, *Dictionary of Biblical Imagery*, 451–52. Platt ("Jewelry, Ancient Israelite," 823–34) discusses historical, archaeological, and manufacturing processes of precious stones. Bullard ("Stones, Precious," 623–30) describes the background on several precious stones found in the Bible. Draper ("Twelve

First, adornment and beauty is part of the great prostitute's allure (17:4). The precious stones and other extravagant accessories are used to entice earth's inhabitants. The same description is given to Babylon the Great (18:16). Second, the great prostitute's allure reflects her wealth and power which she abuses and forces on people. The precious stones mentioned in the list of cargoes characterize her wealth and power that now faces divine judgment (18:12). By contrast, the jewels mentioned in the construction of the new Jerusalem portray God as a king of unimaginable power and wealth (21:14, 19–21). The stones along with the gates of pearls and streets of gold also represent the saints' pure, untainted, eternal wealth.[54] Third, the holiness and worship imaged in the high priest's dazzling breastplate is pictured again in the twelve foundation stones that serve the heavenly city. The high priest's ephod had the names of the twelve tribes displayed. New Jerusalem has the tribes and the apostles. The high priest ministered in the holy of holies. The new Jerusalem is a holy of holies. Fourth, transcendent permanence is pictured in the precious stones that surround the throne of God (4:3). Moreover, the Isaiah passage envisioned the restored Jerusalem, a city fashioned from precious stones (Isa 54:11–12). John fulfills this prophecy as he paints a similar picture of a jeweled heavenly city (21:9–21).[55]

Sulfur

Sulfur presents a fearful image of burning, odorous judgment, particularly when viewed through the final judgment of the fiery lake of burning sulfur at the end of history. Sulfur is a frequent image of divine judgment in the OT. For example, the fall of Sodom and Gomorrah commences with burning sulfur (Gen 19:24) and Sodom is mentioned in 11:8. Edom's downfall is compared to that of Sodom and Gomorrah (Isa 34:9) and John draws from this Isaiah passage for his vision of the end of history in the sixth seal (6:12–14). The fall of Gog mentions burning sulfur (Ezek 38:22), a passage from which John richly draws (16:14–16; 19:17–21; 20:9–10).

"Sulfur" (*theion*) is found six (of seven NT) times in Revelation (9:17, 18; 14:10; 19:20; 20:10; 21:8).[56] Strikingly, each mention is located near the conclusion of an individual vision. Sulfur was a type of asphalt found in volcanic deposits. It produced both an intense heat and foul smell. Its yellow color "burns with a blue flame with the formation of noxious, suffocating sulfur dioxide gas."[57] It is easy to imagine how this image developed into a common symbol of terrible suffering and divine judgment.[58] The traditional yet archaic reading of "brimstone" is still translated in NKJV and NASB.

Apostles as Foundation," 41–63) and Mathewson ("Note on the Foundation Stones," 487–98) take note of the interpretive tradition from the Qumran community (1QS 8:1–16; 9:3–7; 11:7–9; 4Qp Isaiah).

54. Reader, "Twelve Jewels of Revelation," 456.

55. Most commentators mention John's allusion to Isa 54:11–12. See Fekkes, "His Bride Has Prepared Herself," 277–78.

56. If the cognate "yellow like sulfur" (*theiōdēs*) in 9:17 is included then the number comes to seven, a sure sign that John's numerical symbolism is intended.

57. Bowes, "Brimstone," 678.

58. Osborne, *Revelation*, 541.

"Sulfur" is found twice in 9:17–18 plus "yellow like sulfur" (*theiōdēs*) once (NET reads "sulfurous yellow"). Some versions diminish the symbolism attached with sulfur by listing only its yellow color (although sulfur may be mentioned elsewhere in the verse), including CEV, GW, and NLT. The three references to sulfur in the sixth trumpet (9:17–18) coupled with the cavalry heighten an allusion to Armageddon, the final battle. The mention of sulfur as one facet of the end-time cavalry serves as a proleptic reference to its use at final judgment.

The last four usages of sulfur specifically refer to final judgment for unbelievers, the beast and the false prophet, and the devil. In 14:10, unbelievers "will be tormented with burning sulfur in the presence of the holy angels and of the Lamb." In 19:20, the beast and the false prophet "were thrown alive into the fiery lake of burning sulfur." Then in 20:10, the devil "was thrown into the lake of burning sulfur, where the beast and the false prophet had been thrown." These three visions parallel one another temporally. The final reference is the vice list that concludes the millennial vision (21:8). Unbelievers "will be consigned to the fiery lake of burning sulfur. This is the second death." Thus, the image of sulfur is reserved as an end-time symbol by John, limited to Armageddon and final universal judgment in the lake of fire.

Tree of Life

To "eat from the tree of life" symbolizes immortality in the presence and intimate fellowship of God. This immortality was originally lost in the garden of Eden but is regained in the new heaven and new earth. God planted two trees in the middle of the garden of Eden—"the tree of life and the tree of the knowledge of good and evil" (Gen 2:9). Adam was commanded not to eat of the tree of the knowledge of good and evil (Gen 2:16–17), implying that eating from the tree of life was not only acceptable but a necessary provision for immortality. Adam and Eve, however, ate from the forbidden tree, and were expelled from God's paradise and intimate presence. God barred them from access to the tree of life not as punishment, but as protection, as an act of mercy, for fear that the first couple doom themselves to endless physical life in a fallen state. God stationed cherubim with flaming swords to guard the garden and keep access from the tree of life (Gen 3:24).[59]

The OT recalls this story often, using the tree of life as a metaphor for life, longevity, fertility, and even wisdom (Prov 3:18; 11:30; Ezek 47:12). Apocalyptic works are more explicit. Fallen humanity will be restored to the tree of life at "the great judgment," given to "the righteous and the holy" as a food of immortality. This tree will be transplanted into the temple of the Lord, the heavenly city (*1 En.* 24:4–5; *4 Ezra* 2:1–13; 8:50–52; *T. Levi* 18:10–14; *2 Bar.* 4:1; *T. Dan.* 5:12).[60]

After Genesis, the clearest biblical teaching on the tree of life (*zylon tēs zōēs*) is found in four passages in Revelation (2:7; 22:1–2, 14, 18–19). First, to the overcomer at Ephesus, Christ promises, "I will give the right to eat from the tree of life, which is in the paradise

---

59. Hays, Duvall, and Pate, *Dictionary of Prophecy*, 450; Ryken, *Dictionary of Biblical Imagery*, 889.

60. Declaisse-Walford, "Tree of Knowledge, Tree of Life," 659–61; Hemer, *Letters to the Seven Churches*, 41; Smick, "Tree of Knowledge," 901–3.

of God" (2:7). Since one does not eat the actual tree of life, some translations choose to add words such as "fruit of" the tree of life (CEV, GNT, NCV, NLT). The important issue, however, is to note the clear reference to the tree of life ("life-giving tree" CEV) from the garden of Eden, given further support by the additional phrase "which is in the paradise of God." Thus, in the final Eden, the curse of the first Eden will be reversed, and God's people are granted eternal life.[61] This promise is expanded upon in chapter 22.

Second, John is shown "the river of the water of life" and on "each side of the river stood the tree of life, bearing twelve crops of fruit, yielding its fruit every month. And the leaves of the tree are for the healing of the nations" (22:1–2). Some scholars attempt to assist John by suggesting the tree rests in the middle of the river with watery streams diverging around it.[62] It is best to understand it as a collective singular to denote a forest of trees. Thus, the English versions (CEV, NABR, NJB, NLT) translating the singular "tree" as "trees of life" are actually more on target. The point is that the one tree of life in the first garden has become many trees of life in the escalated garden, the new heaven and new earth.[63] In addition, "the healing of the nations" does not mean that medicine and therapy are still needed in the eschaton or that nations will continue to exist outside of the new heaven and new earth. Instead, much like 21:24, John uses imagery borrowed from the present state carried over to the eternal state. The healing leaves indicate a complete absence of physical and spiritual want. Eternal life is one of abundance and perfection.[64]

The last two references are contained in a blessing (22:14) and a warning (22:18–19). The blessing gives believers the "right" (*exousia*) to the tree of life. Adam and Eve had access to the tree of life, but not authority over it. But in the new Jerusalem, God's people have authority over the tree of life. This is yet another image of the assurance of the possession of eternal life.[65] But John adds a warning as well. Those who add or take away the words of this prophecy will not share in the tree of life in the Holy City. This warning is intriguing for two reasons. First, the TR reads "book of life" in place of "tree of life," a rendering that came from the Byzantine Greek text of Erasmus in 1516. He had no access to Greek manuscripts for this part of Revelation, and translated from the Latin Vulgate back into Greek. But an earlier Vulgate scribe had miscopied *libro* ("book") for *ligno* ("tree"). This variant reading made its way into early English Bibles, including the KJV, and is

---

61. Osborne, *Revelation*, 124. Several scholars suggest that "tree of life" connotes a play on words for the "wooden" cross of Christ (Barr, *Tales*, 56, 145; Hemer, *Letters to the Seven Churches*, 41–44; Lupieri, *Apocalypse*, 117–18; Minear, *Images of the Church*, 132; Osborne, *Revelation*, 124; Patterson, *Revelation*, 91; Leonard Thompson, *Revelation*, 48). Others, however, consider such a connection baseless (Kistemaker, *Revelation*, 120; Robert Thomas, *Revelation*, 2:484). Beale (*Revelation*, 235) relates that it does not refer to the cross, but to the redemptive effects of the cross that brings about the restoration of God's presence.

62. Beasley-Murray, *Revelation*, 331.

63. Beale, *Revelation*, 1106; Keener, *Revelation*, 500–501; Osborne, *Revelation*, 770; Smalley, *Revelation*, 562; Robert Thomas, *Revelation*, 2:484.

64. Mounce, *Revelation*, 400; Smalley, *Revelation*, 563. Contra Resseguie (*Revelation Unsealed*, 90) who argues the collective translation destroys John's imagery of an amazing singular tree with twelve kinds of fruit, thereby symbolizing completeness and perpetual, ample provisions.

65. Osborne, *Revelation*, 790; Brighton, *Revelation*, 623–29. Thus, translating "right" as "access" (NET), "right of access" (CEB), and "permitted" (NLT) are not forceful enough renderings.

perpetuated in the NKJV today.[66] The second intriguing point is the warning that God will take away "any share in the tree of life" for the one who takes away from the words of John's prophecy. This has prompted debate between Calvinist scholars who suggest it does not imply apostasy of the believer and Arminian scholars who imply that it does. Readers should be aware of this discussion when studying this passage in commentaries.

The tree of life, therefore, is much more than a vision of tasty, fruit-laden branches on a tree.[67] It symbolizes immortal life in the full presence and intimate fellowship of God, reclaimed from the fall of Adam, and realized at the end of history. It is one more example of how John portrays eternal life in chapters 21–22—as a new heaven and new earth (21:1), a new creation (21:1, 4–5), a Holy City (21:2), a holy of holies (21:16–18), a new temple (21:3, 22), and a restored garden of Eden (22:1–5).

Trees

Trees are positive images that symbolize all living things on the earth, possibly including humans. Ultimately, the new Jerusalem with its tree of life symbolizes eternal life in the presence of God. Salvation history begins and ends with trees, underlining their symbolic significance. There is the tree of life and the tree of the knowledge of good and evil in Eden in Gen 2, and the tree of life in the new Jerusalem in Rev 22. Sandwiched between those two passages is *the* tree, that is, the cross of salvation (Gal 3:13; 1 Pet 2:24). Trees picture blessings and goodness (Gen 2:9; Song 2:3; Prov 13:12) as well as judgment and curse (Ezek 6:13; 1 Kgs 14:23; Isa 2:13). Interestingly, trees are even personified (Judg 9:15; 2 Kgs 14:9).[68] The glory of humanity, the blessing of God, and the curses of the covenant are all pictured in the tree metaphor.[69] The NT utilizes trees as symbols often (Matt 3:10; 7:17–19; 12:33; Mark 8:24; John 1:48; Rom 11:24; Jude 12).

Trees (*dendron*) are mentioned ten times in Revelation, five of which refer to the tree of life. Concerning the rest, at the sixth seal, the earth dissolves like a fig tree shaken by a strong wind (6:13). The two witnesses are described as "olive trees" (11:4), an allusion to Zechariah's vision of the anointed leaders who serve the earth (Zech 4:14). These examples are surely figurative uses of trees, and the last one personifies humans. The literal use of trees is also found in the plagues that come upon the earth (7:1, 3; 8:7; 9:4). Most scholars understand trees to symbolize the whole plant kingdom. In such earthly judgments trees are particularly vulnerable. Yet the expression "on the land or on the sea

---

66. Metzger, *Textual Commentary*, 690.

67. Some maintain that the tree of life is a literal tree, including LaHaye, *Revelation Unveiled*, 368; Walvoord, *Revelation*, 330; and Wong, "Tree of Life in Revelation 2:7," 213. However, Sandy (*Plowshares and Pruning Hooks*, 28–31) cogently describes it as one of numerous images (crown of life, white stone, pillar, morning star, etc.) that all visualize the singular reward of deity and humanity in perfect unity (21:3).

68. Smalley (*Revelation*, 180) notes that trees are interpreted as people in Tg. Isa. 2:13; 14:8; 61:3.

69. Ryken, *Dictionary of Biblical Imagery*, 890–92; Tucker, "Trees," 1632–58.

or on any tree" (7:1) is a grouping by metonymy that probably stands for the world and its inhabitants.[70] Thus, it is possible that trees are personified here as well.[71]

Water

Water is a multifaceted image in Revelation. It symbolizes persecution, judgment, and wicked people yet also represents the sovereignty of Christ and eternal life. Since water is essential to life it is no surprise that there are over six hundred references in Scripture. It became a vivid symbol used in a variety of ways. Water was a commonly used in the OT to picture salvation and eternal life (Pss 23:2; 36:8; Isa 43:19; 55:1; 58:11). Its earliest connection is with the tree of life from the original garden of Eden (Gen 2:10) and to which the prophets alluded (Ezek 47:1–12; Joel 3:18; Zech 14:8). These themes continue into the NT. Jesus is Lord over water (Matt 14:22–33; 17:24–27; Luke 8:22–25).[72] An added feature is the divine revelation that comes through the Holy Spirit by way of Jesus (John 3:5; 4:10–14; 7:38–39; 19:34).[73]

Water then is a consistent symbol in Johannine literature. The Gospel of John (21 times), 1 John (4 times), and Revelation (18 times) represent 57 percent of all NT uses of *hydor*. An associated word, "springs" (*pēgē*), is found three times in John's Gospel and five times in Revelation, constituting eight of the eleven NT usages. When "river," "springs," "sea," and "lake" are included, Revelation contains a greater concentration of water imagery than found anywhere else in biblical literature.[74] As with many of John's symbols, water is used in contrasting ways—it can be good or bad. The following five images surface in Revelation. The first three are negative and the last two are positive images.

First, water depicts persecution. In 12:15, water like a river spews from the serpent's mouth after the woman. This alludes to Ps 18:4 and Isa 43:2. It depicts a flood of lies, deceit, and delusions.[75] Second, water pictures judgment. Water is mentioned three times in the third trumpet as the waters turn bitter and people die (8:10–11). In another allusion to the exodus plagues, the two witnesses have the power to turn the waters to blood (11:6). The third bowl's judgment is upon the rivers and springs of water (16:4), and the angel in charge of the waters confirms the justice of God's judgments (16:5). In the sixth bowl, the waters of the Euphrates dry up in preparation for Armageddon (16:12). Third, water can represent people. The great prostitute sits on many waters (17:1, 15). This is a direct reference to the destruction of Babylon in Jer 51:13 where "waters" once helped Babylon to flourish economically and provided security. John interprets the "waters" for

---

70. Beale, *Revelation*, 407. The Greek has a more literal rendering of "against any tree" (ESV, NABR, NRSV). See Mulholland, *Revelation*, 180–81, for discussion.

71. So Ford, *Revelation*, 115.

72. Harrison, "Water," 1024–26; Hays, Duvall, and Pate, *Dictionary of Prophecy*, 392; Klingbeil, "Water," 818–21; Ryken, *Dictionary of Biblical Imagery*, 810–11, 929–32.

73. See Song, "Water as an Image of the Spirit."

74. Thomas Schmidt, "And the Sea Was No More," 245.

75. See the entry "River."

his readers as multitudes of humanity which served as the basis for Babylon the Great's economic trade and security.[76]

Fourth, by contrast water symbolizes the sovereign power and greatness of Christ at his second coming. The risen Christ has a powerful voice "like the sound of rushing waters" (1:15). At the second coming, John hears a voice (*phonē*; ESV, NASB) from heaven like the roar of rushing waters (14:2). Then an angel declares the hour of judgment has come. The world must worship him who made the heavens, the earth, the sea and the springs of water" (14:7). Next, John hears what sounds like "a great multitude, like the roar of rushing waters" (19:6). All heaven rejoices at the marriage of the bride and the Lamb at the second coming. Fifth, water is a symbol of eternal life. Christ will lead his people to "springs of living water" (7:17), and they will drink without cost from "the spring of the water of life" (21:6). An angel shows John "the river of the water of life" in the heavenly city (22:1), and the believer is invited to drink "the water of life" freely for eternity (22:17).[77] Interpreters will continue to debate on whether or not water should be understood literally or figuratively in Revelation. It is, however, the figurative explanation that holds the teachable significance.

White Stone

The white stone might be John's most elusive symbol. Out of numerous possibilities, it probably symbolizes for the overcomer admission and membership into eternal fellowship with God and Christ. "Stone" (*psēphos*) is mentioned three times in the NT. Paul testified how he cast his "vote" (*psēphos*) against the fledgling Christian group (Acts 26:10). A "white stone" (*psēphon leukēn*) is mentioned by John in Rev 2:17. The final *psēphos* is also in 2:17, but often replaced by modern versions with "it" for stylistic reasons.[78]

The reception of a "white stone" is one of the two promises offered to the victorious saints at Pergamum: "I will give some of the hidden manna. I will also give that person a white stone with a new name written on it, known only to the one who receives it." This intriguing white stone has received no less than dozen plausible explanations, but none have won over Bible students. Among these are a jewel of the OT; a casting vote of acquittal; a token of gladiatorial discharge; a process of Asclepian initiation; writing material whose form or color is significant; an amulet with a divine name; or a token of admission, recognition, and membership.[79] The last two have more supporters.

---

76. Beale and McDonough, "Revelation," 1139.

77. See the entry "River of the Water of Life."

78. Those versions that mention "stone" twice include CEV, CSB, ESV, NASB, NET, NKJV, NLT, NRSV. John uses the more common word for "stone" (*lithos*) when speaking of precious stones. See the entry "Stones."

79. For example, Hemer (*Letters to the Seven Churches*, 96–102, 242) spends one page interpreting the hidden manna compared to nearly seven pages discussing ten options on the white stone. Others who list options include Aune (*Revelation*, 1:189–90), Kistemaker (*Revelation*, 134), Morris (*Revelation*, 68), Osborne (*Revelation*, 148–49), Smalley (*Revelation*, 70–71), Robert Thomas (*Revelation*, 1:199–201), Mark Wilson (*Victor Sayings*, 125–26), and Wong ("Hidden Manna and White Stone," 349–53). The NET's study notes also list several choices.

Most English translations are satisfied with the rendering "white stone." The NABR makes an interpretive choice with "white amulet," adding a footnote: "literally, 'white stone, on which was written a magical name, whose power could be tapped by one who knew the secret name. It is used here as a symbol of victory and joy."[80] The CEV footnote mentions a "ticket" or a symbol of victory. The best option appears to be that of a "ticket" of admittance, recognition, and membership given to the overcomer who now comes into eternal fellowship and eats the hidden manna at the wedding supper of the Lamb (19:6–9).[81] Pierre Prigent reminds that "whatever interpretation we may give to the stone, it must be recognized in the end that it is the conqueror who is seen as the stone."[82] Yet Brent Sandy pointedly states that the white stone visualizes one of several images that refer to the singular promise of deity and humanity in perfect eternal unity (21:3).[83]

Wilderness

The wilderness symbolizes a place of both testing and protection for believers but temptation and evil for unbelievers. The wilderness period extends from the first coming to the second coming. This entry could be placed under good places or bad places since it illustrates John's penchant for contrasts. On the one hand, it hearkens back to the forty-year Israelite sojourn, and therefore signifies a place of refuge and safety yet also a place of testing for God's people, which is now the church. On the other hand, it symbolizes a place of evil, temptation, and the demonic realm.

The wilderness represents an important motif in Scripture, and is utilized in a variety of ways.[84] The OT prophets pictured a new beginning of a restored Israel and a second exodus through the wilderness that was to be a flourishing garden with safety from wild beasts (Isa 35:1–10; 40–55; Jer 23:7–8; 31:7–12). A new covenant will be made (Jer 31:31–34), and Israel will be transformed from a wilderness to the garden of Eden (Ezek 36:8–36). Later, the Qumran community chose to live ascetically in the wilderness "preparing the way" through repentance (4Q171 2:11; 3:1) and Torah study (1QS 8:13–15; 4:19–20), and also preparing for battles that were to precede the arrival of the

---

80. This choice is also followed by Aune (*Revelation*, 1:190), Charles (*Revelation*, 1:66–67), Murphy (*Fallen Is Babylon*, 132), Roloff (*Revelation*, 52), and Sandy (*Plowshares and Pruning Hooks*, 31).

81. So Beale, *Revelation*, 253; Beasley-Murray, *Revelation*, 88; Beckwith, *Apocalypse*, 461; Blount, *Revelation*, 60; Buchanan, *Revelation*, 109; Caird, *Revelation*, 42; Easley, *Revelation*, 40; Hailey, *Revelation*, 134; Harrington, *Revelation*, 62; Alan Johnson, "Revelation," 13:621; Keener, *Revelation*, 126; Ladd, *Revelation*, 49; Mounce, *Revelation*, 83; Mulholland, *Revelation*, 110; Reddish, *Revelation*, 62; Resseguie, *Revelation*, 92; Rotz, *Revelation*, 73; Smalley, *Revelation*, 71; Robert Thomas, *Revelation*, 1:201. Brighton (*Revelation*, 76) chooses acquittal. Patterson (*Revelation*, 110) settles on the association of white with holiness and righteousness. Paul (*Revelation*, 90) suggests a composite meaning of Jesus' intimate knowledge and approval of those who reject the surrounding culture.

82. Prigent, *Apocalypse*, 178.

83. Sandy, *Plowshares and Pruning Hooks*, 31.

84. Brian Jones, "Wilderness," 848–52. For examples, see Davies, "Wilderness Wanderings," 912–14; Ryken, *Dictionary of Biblical Imagery*, 949–50; Watts, "Wilderness," 841–43. For an excellent in-depth study, see Robertson, *God's People in the Wilderness*, 9–30.

messianic age (1QM 1:2–3). Popular messianic expectations held that the Messiah would first appear in the wilderness (Matt 24:46; Acts 21:38).

These expectations stood in the background at the arrival of the forerunner of the Messiah, John the Baptist. He came from the Judean wilderness (Matt 3:1), prepared the way for the Lord (Mark 1:3), and called for repentance (Mark 1:2–8; Luke 1:13–17).[85] Other NT references maintain these connotations with a stronger emphasis on recalling the wilderness wanderings of the Israelites (Matt 4:1–2; Mark 1:12–13; Luke 4:1–2; John 3:14–15; 6:31–32; Acts 7:30–44; 1 Cor 10:5; Heb 2:1–4; 3:8–11). Just as Jesus recapitulates Israel's wilderness wanderings, so too must Jesus' followers go through the wilderness of the new exodus. John consummates these images into his end-time visions, connecting wilderness and eschatology through two characters—the woman clothed with the sun (12:6, 14) and the woman sitting on the scarlet beast (17:3).[86]

The wilderness then represents both good and evil.[87] Two women reside in the wilderness. First, the woman clothed with the sun personifies the church, the true Israel of God from which the Messiah comes. She takes flight into the refuge of the wilderness (12:6). The stress here is on God's provision for his people ("prepared") in times of distress, while at the same time a period of testing and trial.[88] This continues in the subsequent reference to wilderness, which is a "recapitulation of 12:6."[89] "The woman is given the two wings of a great eagle, so that she might fly to the place prepared for her in the wilderness" and be protected for time, times, and half a time (12:13–14). Once again, the themes of protection, security, and provision, alongside testing and trial, are observable. What does the escape into the wilderness by the woman symbolize? It coincides with the other references of God's eternal protection and security. It is not necessarily physical, but spiritual. The added component of "testing" is also important. Believers must not shrink back from being witnesses for Christ, even to the point of martyrdom. There is no "get out of jail free" card in John's theology. Christians persevere to the end. Thus, the wilderness references in chapter 12 are patterned after the wilderness wanderings of the exodus and symbolize the current wilderness-like experiences of believers, pictured through the woman. Life in this world is a pilgrimage through a desert in which only God can care and sustain his people.[90]

The final mention of wilderness, however, unveils a sharp contrast. At the beginning of the fall of Babylon vision, an angel carries John away in the Spirit to the wilderness

---

85. Ibid., 851.

86. English Bible versions are evenly divided over translating *erēmos* as "wilderness" (CSB, ESV, GW, NET, NIV, NKJV, NLT, NRSV, REB) or "desert" (CEB, CEV, GNT, NABR, NASB, NCV, NJB).

87. Resseguie (*Revelation Unsealed*, 71, 84–85) mentions three places that are ambiguous in Revelation—river, mountain, and wilderness. In other words, John used these places contrastingly and context must decide whether it is understood as a threat or as a place of refuge.

88. Osborne, *Revelation*, 463–64. See Beale, *Revelation*, 645–46; Buchanan, *Revelation*, 321; Smalley, *Revelation*, 320–21.

89. Ibid., 482.

90. Brighton, *Revelation*, 439. Dispensationalists literalize the woman into national Israel (Patterson, *Revelation*, 270; Robert Thomas, *Revelation*, 2:139); her flight takes her to the actual desert locale of Sinai or perhaps Petra (Walvoord, *Revelation*, 195); and the time period is the final three and a half years prior to the second coming (Hindson, *Revelation*, 139; LaHaye, *Revelation Unveiled*, 205).

and shows him the punishment of the great prostitute (17:3). Thus, the dualism noted elsewhere in Revelation is expressed here as well. The wilderness is understood positively (chapter 12) or negatively (chapter 17). Here it is connected with Babylon the Great which will soon become a "home for demons" (18:2).[91] The wilderness found in the fall of Babylon, therefore, emphasizes evil and temptation. Several scholars take note of the revelatory aspect of "the angel carried me away in the Spirit into a wilderness." With its probable allusion to Isa 21:1–10, it apparently provides a more positive light of the wilderness.[92] But any positive spin must be subordinate to its negative emphasis. Chapter 17 stands in stark contrast to chapter 12. The wilderness of 17:3 reflects the haunt of demons. It is evil. It represents death and destruction. It is a region devoid of good. The great prostitute and the beast dwell there.[93]

Therefore, believers are at this time in the wilderness, awaiting the coming of the garden at the arrival of the new Jerusalem. The wilderness period extends from the first advent to the second advent. Until that great day of the Lord, God delivers, protects, nourishes, fellowships, and tests his people.

Wormwood

This is the name (or title) of an evil angel which unleashes bitter, end-time judgment on the unbelieving world. Wormwood was a bitter-tasting shrub found in the Near East. The plant produced greenish oil that was used medicinally to kill intestinal worms, hence the English translation of "wormwood." By John's day it had become a symbol of bitter sorrow (Prov 5:4), the bitter poison of idolatry (Deut 29:18), and particularly the bitterness of judgment and death (Jer 9:15). Wormwood is found twice in the NT, both times at Rev 8:11. The third trumpet relates a great star named Wormwood falling to earth and poisoning a third of the waters. This recalls the bitter, polluted waters of Marah (Exod 15:23). Thus, wormwood best symbolizes divine judgment.[94]

For many interpreters, the "great star" is a literal star falling from the skies or a meteor.[95] Some futurists posit a modern nuclear explosion that generates radioactive fallout.[96] It is better to understand the star as an evil angel who is permitted to unleash

---

91. Osborne, *Revelation*, 610.

92. So Aune, *Revelation*, 3:933; Beale, *Revelation*, 850–52; Boxall, *Revelation*, 241; Caird, *Revelation*, 213; Dennis Johnson, *Triumph of the Lamb*, 244; Kistemaker, *Revelation*, 464; Ladd, *Revelation*, 222–23; Morris, *Revelation*, 199; Mounce, *Revelation*, 309; Smalley, *Revelation*, 428; Sweet, *Revelation*, 254; Thomas and Macchia, *Revelation*, 293.

93. So Beasley-Murray, *Revelation*, 251–52; Brighton, *Revelation*, 439; Paul, *Revelation*, 280; Resseguie, *Revelation Unsealed*, 71, 80–81; Roloff, *Revelation*, 196; Robert Thomas, *Revelation*, 2:285.

94. Reddish, *Revelation*, 167. See Aune, *Revelation*, 2:520–22; Osborne, *Revelation*, 355; Smalley, *Revelation*, 222. English translations are consistent in rendering both words with the same translation, except for NIV, which chooses "Wormwood" and "bitter."

95. So Beasley-Murray, *Revelation*, 158; Brighton, *Revelation*, 227; Easley, *Revelation*, 145; Fee, *Revelation*, 125; Dennis Johnson, *Triumph of the Lamb*, 145; Kistemaker, *Revelation*, 276; Ladd, *Revelation*, 127; Mounce, *Revelation*, 180; Osborne, *Revelation*, 354; Robert Thomas, *Revelation*, 2:21; Walvoord, *Revelation*, 155; Witherington, *Revelation*, 149.

96. Hindson, *Revelation*, 102; Patterson, *Revelation*, 211–12. Although LaHaye (*Revelation Unveiled*,

havoc. This is supported by passages such as Isa 14:12–15; 24:21 where the falling star is connected to evil angels. Apocalyptic literature also equated falling stars with fallen angels (*1 En.* 6–8). In addition, a similar falling star mentioned a few verses later (9:1) is generally identified as an evil angel or even Satan. If so, this angel is permitted by God to deliver divine judgment on the wicked.[97]

Names in Revelation are often characteristic of their nature and this angel is aptly named, delivering bitter divine judgment for the sin, rebellion, and idolatrous apostasy of the wicked. Brian Blount concludes, "The angelic 'poisoning' of the waters is a deliciously ironic way of punishing a people who have so poisoned their faith."[98]

Cosmic Imagery

Cosmic imagery pictures nature and cosmology. Again, there is overlap here with the nature images, and some of the cosmic images have more than one use, but end-time judgment and world-shaking events is more in view with the following entries.

Black as Sackcloth

The "sun turned black as sackcloth made of goat hair" combines the cosmic image for the darkening of the heavens and the dissolution of the world at the end of history along with a period of mourning. This entry can be easily placed under nature, colors, clothing, or animals. It is placed here because it forms one of four similes that depict the end of the cosmos (6:12–14). English translations offer several variations. Literally, it is "black as sackcloth made of hair" (CSB, NASB, NET, NKJV). Some drop the "hair" (ESV, NRSV); others specify it as "goat hair" (NIV); others drop "sackcloth" in favor of "dark," "coarse," or "rough" cloth (GNT, NABR, NCV, NLT, NJB), and a few choose modern similes of "black as a funeral pall" (REB) and "black as funeral clothing" (CEB). This odd expression originates from the stockpile of the language of cosmic imagery for the dissolution of the world. Isaiah resides in the background: "I clothe the heavens with darkness and make sackcloth its covering" (Isa 50:3). So does Joel: "The sun will be turned to darkness and the moon to blood before the coming of the great and dreadful day of the LORD" (Joel 2:31). The image refers to the coarse coat of black hair that comes from a goat and was worn during times of mourning.[99] Such mourning is apropos since the sixth seal pictures the end of history and the time for judgment.

---

167) opts for a meteorite, he speculates its exact destination: "Evidently there is a place in the earth where the headwaters of three great rivers come together. When this 'Wormwood' meteorite strikes that place, it will embitter great rivers, and those who are dependent on them will die."

97. Beale, *Revelation*, 478–80; Blount, *Revelation*, 169; Boxall, *Revelation*, 139; Caird, *Revelation*, 114–15; Kiddle, *Revelation*, 155; Resseguie, *Revelation*, 145; Rotz, *Revelation*, 136; Smalley, *Revelation*, 222; Stefanovic, *Revelation*, 292–93; Sweet, *Revelation*, 163–64. Beale (*Revelation*, 478–79) argues that the star is to be identified with the evil angelic representative of Babylon (Isa 14:12–15).

98. Blount, *Revelation*, 170.

99. Resseguie (*Revelation*, 132) calls the black goat hair "a mourning sign of the spiritual and moral decay of the world."

Thus, the darkening of the heavens is one of the many elements found throughout Revelation that depict the end has arrived. They form part of a well-established tradition that is traced back to apocalyptic literature that itself is traceable to OT portrayals of the day of the Lord.[100] Taken all together, the four cosmic events unfurled on the sun, moon, stars, and heavens, each followed with the same literary pattern of four similes, pictures the final day of God's judgment on the world. This darkening and destruction of the cosmos appears frequently in the OT (Isa 13:9–10; Ezek 32:6–8; Joel 2:10; 3:15; Amos 8:9; Zeph 1:15), apocalyptic literature (*T. Levi* 4:1; *4 Ezra* 7:39; *Sib. Or.* 5:346–385), and the NT (Matt 24:29; Mark 13:24–25; Acts 2:20; 2 Pet 3:10).[101]

Clouds

Clouds symbolize the arrival of divine judgment for unbelievers and glorious salvation for believers at the second coming. Clouds are essentially symbols throughout the Bible and consistently picture divine visitation (Exod 19:9; Num 11:25; Isa 19:1; Jer 4:13; Dan 7:13; Joel 2:2; Zeph 1:15); God's protection (Exod 13:21; Josh 24:7; Ps 104:39; Ezek 38:9); covering his glory (Exod 40:34; Lev 16:2; Ps 17:2; Isa 4:5; Ezek 1:28); and representing his dwelling place (Zech 2:17; Isa 14:14; Ezek 31:10).[102] All twenty-five NT references to "clouds" (*nephelē*) refer to divine visitation. The transfiguration (Matt 17:5; Mark 9:7; Luke 9:34); ascension (Acts 1:9); and second coming (Matt 24:30; 26:64; Mark 13:26; 14:62; Luke 21:27; 1 Thess 4:13–18) serve as examples. Seven references appear in Revelation, signifying numerical symbolism on John's part (1:7; 10:1; 11:12; 14:14–16 [4 times]).

Clouds display John's affection for contrasts. Their appearance for unbelievers reflects divine, end-time judgment. For believers, however, clouds are connected to their salvation and vindication, and to the glory of God occasioned at the second coming. Concerning unbelievers, John pronounces the coming of the Lord, "'Look, he is coming with the clouds,' and 'every eye will see him, even those who pierced him'; and all peoples on earth 'will mourn because of him.' So shall it be! Amen" (1:7). There are two near verbatim quotations of Dan 7:13 and Zech 12:10.[103] John universalizes the language of both passages, expanding them from Israel to "every eye." This divine visitation of judgment matches the selections from the Gospels above.

The remainder of John's cloud images is positive. The mighty angel, "robed in a cloud" (10:1), echoes Exod 13:21, where God guided the Israelites in a pillar of cloud. The two witnesses come back to life and ascend to heaven in a cloud (11:12). This pictures the vindication of the church, represented by the two witnesses. This rapturous event is either proleptic or an actual vision of the end since it is found at the conclusion of the second interlude. The image parallels Paul's words (1 Thess 4:17). Simon Kistemaker adds, "This

---

100. Mounce, *Revelation*, 150.

101. Smalley, *Revelation*, 166–67.

102. Alden, "Cloud," 936; Joy, "Cloud," 725–26; Ryken, *Dictionary of Biblical Imagery*, 157.

103. Only a few English versions attempt to set off John's strongest candidates for OT quotes. CSB uses bold print; NIV uses quote marks; and NET italicizes the phrases. NASB caps Dan 7:13 but not the allusion to Zech 12:10.

undoubtedly is a specific reference to the glory cloud which appeared when Jesus was transfigured (Matt. 17:5) and which enveloped him when he ascended from the Mount of Olives (Acts 1:9)."[104]

The key passage is 14:14–16 where clouds are mentioned four times. These verses depict the second coming as a grain harvest. "One like a son of man" harvests the earth. He is seated on a "white" cloud signifying purity and victory. The cloud is not a mode of transportation but a throne upon which he sits (perhaps alluding to Joel 3:12). This could be a throne of judgment, but since it is believers who are harvested, it appears better to see an image of salvation and victory (like 10:1 and 11:12). Nevertheless, believers will also experience a judgment of works (20:12; 2 Cor 5:10).[105] Therefore, it is not necessary to understand clouds to be part of literal atmospheric entourage that accompanies Jesus' return. They are best understood as figurative. They represent a metaphor for the glorious divine visitation of Christ, signaling end-time judgment for the wicked and eternal salvation for the faithful.

Darkness

Darkness characterizes the spiritual blindness of an evil world, and is a common feature of cosmic imagery that heightens coming end-time judgment. Darkness is rich in figurative usage. Throughout the Bible it is the implied opposite to light, both physically and symbolically. In fact, sixty OT verses present light and darkness as a contrasting pair, and being brought out of darkness into the light is a major image for redemption. If light represents insight and understanding, then darkness symbolizes ignorance (Ps 82:5), folly (Eccl 2:13), and moral depravity (Job 12:22). The NT continues the symbolism of darkness with spiritual blindness (John 1:5; 3:18–21; 1 John 2:11). The major usage of darkness, however, is found in cosmic imagery. The day of the Lord will be darkness and disaster (Isa 3:10; Ezek 32:7; Joel 2:2; 3:1–5; Amos 5:18; Zeph 1:15). Extratextual literature follows suit, including apocalyptic writings (*T. Levi* 4:1; *4 Ezra* 7:39; *Sib. Or.* 5:346–385; *Jub.* 5:14; *1 En.* 17:6; 63:6; *2 En.* 7:1; *Pss. Sol.* 14:9) and the Dead Sea Scrolls (1QS 4:11–13). This darkening and destruction of the cosmos continues into the NT (Matt 8:12; 24:29; Mark 13:24–25; Acts 2:20; 2 Pet 2:17; 3:10; Jude 13).[106]

John utilizes all these rich images for his three uses of darkness. First, the verb *skotizō* is used at the fourth trumpet as a third of the stars "turned dark" (8:12).[107] This plague is based partly on Exod 10:21 when God caused darkness to envelop Egypt. Beale relates that the fourth trumpet punishes the wicked because of their idolatry and oppression of the saints. It is partial, not consummative judgment. Yet it is emblematic of humanity's

---

104. Kistemaker, *Revelation*, 337–38.

105. Osborne, *Revelation*, 551. See Beale, *Revelation*, 777–78, for more of an emphasis on judgment.

106. Joy, "Dark; Darkness," 868–69; Osborne, *Revelation*, 356; Ryken, *Dictionary of Biblical Imagery*, 191; Smalley, *Revelation*, 166–67. See Scott M. Lewis ("Light and Darkness," 662–63) for numerous Dead Sea Scroll examples.

107. *Skotizō* is found only four other times, including the consummative passages of Matt 24:49 and Mark 13:24.

separation from God and inevitable final condemnation to come.[108] Second, the cognate verb *skotoō* is used as the sun and sky "were darkened" by the smoke rising from the Abyss in the fifth trumpet (9:2). Third, *skotoō* is used again as the beast's kingdom plunges into darkness at the fifth bowl (16:10).[109]

Some Bible students press for literalism in John's usages of darkness. For example, Hal Lindsey prophesies that the fourth trumpet's darkness is the result of tremendous pollution from nuclear explosions.[110] Tim LaHaye states that after the sun-induced heat wave of the fourth bowl (16:8–9), the fifth bowl's darkness gives relief to humanity. The "darkness may be the singular expression of God's mercy to the rebellious citizens of the earth during the Tribulation period."[111] Literal fulfillment, however, is not confined to popular dispensational authors. Several scholars assume literal darkness. Mounce rightly cautions against over-interpretation. The darkness is one part of the cumulative effect of the vision.[112] Nevertheless, although such literalism can happen, it limits the meaning of the symbol to a specific future event. This darkness represents judgment and death and should be enlarged. "This spiritual darkness began in the past, continues to the present, and is widespread."[113] Therefore, it is more significant to understand darkness as an incredible symbol of the world's evil spiritual darkness and ultimately the end-time judgment that surrounds all who do not know Jesus.[114]

Fall on Us and Hide Us

This is the response of the unrepentant wicked to the reality of universal judgment at the second coming. This phrase is found at the end of the sixth seal. It reveals the reaction of unbelievers to the arrival of end-time judgment. The expression is traceable to the OT. The idea is evident in Adam's attempt to hide from God in the garden of Eden (Gen 3:8). Hosea uses the phrase for the response of wicked Israelites to God's judgment (Hos 10:8). On the way to the cross Jesus predicts the destruction of Jerusalem by quoting Hosea (Luke 23:29–31). Especially significant is Isaiah's prophecy of the great day of the Lord when the unrighteous go into rocks and hide in the ground (Isa 2:10–11). John has universalized this anguished cry of the wicked for the last, true great day. After the end-time cosmic imagery in 6:12–14, he writes, "Fall on us and hide us from the face of him who sits on the throne and from the wrath of the Lamb! For the great day of their wrath has come, and who can withstand it?" (6:16–17). The sevenfold listing of different categories of humans (6:15) reveals the universality of the event (see also 13:16; 19:18).

---

108. Beale, *Revelation*, 482.

109. The ninth plague is again alluded to (Exod 10:21–29), but here the darkness is total and worldwide, and thus intensifies the fourth trumpet (8:12).

110. Lindsey, *New World Coming*, 133.

111. LaHaye, *Revelation Unveiled*, 253.

112. Mounce, *Revelation*, 186.

113. Kistemaker, *Revelation*, 446.

114. So Beale, *Revelation*, 824; Blount, *Revelation*, 301; Hughes, *Revelation*, 109; Osborne, *Revelation*, 588; Reddish, *Revelation*, 307; Smalley, *Revelation*, 406. Caird (*Revelation*, 204) finds darkness to be a metaphor of Satan's influence on society and politics.

The point is that no one escapes judgment day. Thus, the unrepentant reveal their terror and hopelessness at the second coming. They attempt to run away and hide from this day, but they cannot escape ultimate justice. It is too late. The sixth seal, then, is John's first of several snapshots of the end of history, each vision culminating in the second coming, shaking of the cosmos, divine judgment for the wicked, and heavenly bliss for the faithful.

Fire

With few exceptions, the appearance of fire signals divine, end-time judgment on the wicked, culminating in the lake of fire. In the OT, fire was used in religious ceremonies for sacrifices and burnt offerings. The smoke rising up served as a symbol of appropriate sacrifice from earth to heaven. Fire was a symbol of divine presence (Gen 15:17; Exod 3:2). Fire also symbolized God's desire to destroy sin and purify his people (Isa 6:6–7). Jesus baptized with fire and the Holy Spirit (Matt 3:10; Luke 3:16). Fire as a metaphor for the divine judgment of God is found abundantly throughout the Bible (2 Kgs 1:9–12; Ezek 22:21; 38:22; Nah 1:6; Zeph 1:18; Luke 9:51–54; 1 Cor 3:13; 2 Pet 3:7). Extratextual references also abound (4 Ezra 13:8–11; *Sib. Or.* 2:196–205; 1QM 11:16–18). This fiery judgment would accompany the day of the Lord (Joel 2:30; Dan 7:9–11; Luke 17:29; 2 Thess 1:7).[115]

These metaphors reoccur in Revelation. "Fire" (*pyr*) is mentioned twenty-six times, accounting for 37 percent of all NT uses. In partnership with smoke, sulfur, and the lake of fire, it is clearly an end-time symbol of judgment. Some of these overlap, but the following five emphases are connected with fire in the Apocalypse. First of all, there is an emphasis on purity and testing and purifying the righteous. Christ's eyes are like blazing fire (1:14; 2:18). Laodicea needs gold from Christ refined in fire (3:18). The seven lamps blaze before the throne (4:5). The angel's legs are fiery pillars (10:1). The sea of glass mixed with fire contains the idea of the faithful who have persevered by living pure lives (15:2).[116] The returning Christ's eyes are like blazing fire (19:12). These images represent purity and especially the penetrating spiritual discernment that leads to righteous end-time judgment.

Second, judgmental fire is depicted as coming from the mouths of humans and beasts. In a picture of the near end, the demonic cavalry of the sixth trumpet shoot fire from their mouths (9:17–18). Likewise, in a clear allusion to Elijah (2 Kgs 1), fire comes from the mouths of the two witnesses (11:5). David Aune states this refers to the proclamation of the Word in rebuke and condemnation.[117]

Third, fire falls or is hurled from heaven in judgment. The seventh seal pictures the end. The angel commences end-time judgment on the earth by hurling fire (8:4–5). Accompanied by thunders, rumblings, lightnings, and the earthquake, it parallels the final

---

115. Van Broekhoven, "Fire," 305–6; Ryken, *Dictionary of Biblical Imagery*, 286–89; Schöpflin, "Fire," 454–55.

116. See the entry "Sea of Glass." This image is used as one of John's contrasts. Thus, it is also below under the fourth emphasis.

117. Aune, *Revelation*, 2:684. This matches metaphorical fire from the mouths of individuals (Prov 16:27; Song 8:6; Ps 39:3) and God in the OT (Isa 30:27; Jer 23:39).

judgments pictured in 11:19 and 16:18.[118] Elsewhere, hail and fire mixed with blood falls in partial judgment of the first trumpet (8:7), and a fiery mountain falls in the second trumpet (8:8). The fraction "a third" suggests the partial, ongoing judgment of these two trumpets. In a parody of Elijah's sign (and the two witnesses; 11:5), the false prophet causes fire to fall from heaven (13:13). Finally, the fourth bowl scorches people with fire (16:8). Scholars fall into their respective camps on the literality or symbolism of the fourth bowl. What is especially prescient is the people's response: "They were seared by the intense heat and they cursed the name of God, who had control over these plagues, but they refused to repent and glorify him" (16:9).

Fourth, fire punishes the wicked as a part of end-time judgment. Allusions to Armageddon, second coming, and final judgment are coupled with fire. The angel of the seventh seal hurls the fire in judgment (8:4–5). The threat of fiery, final punishment is heralded at the conclusion of the third interlude (14:10), accompanied by the angel in charge of the fire (14:18). The sea mixed with fire recalls the fiery test of believers but also symbolizes the soon-to-come judgment that the angels bring (15:2). The judgment of the great prostitute is expressed in "they will eat her flesh and burn her with fire" (17:16) and "she will be consumed by fire (18:8). When Jesus returns, he is described with "eyes like blazing fire" (19:12). This image can be viewed not only as purity but as the penetrating end-time judgment of God.[119] Concomitantly, in an image of Armageddon, fire comes down and devours God's enemies (20:9).

Fifth, John mentions the lake of fire with its emphasis on final judgment and eternal torment. Anyone who worships the beast will be judged with "burning" (*pyri*) sulfur (14:10). The beast and false prophet are thrown into the lake of fire (19:20) as is the devil (20:10). Death and Hades are cast into the lake of fire (20:14) along with anyone whose name is not written in the book of life (20:15). Finally, the vice list cataloguing all the wicked is cast into the fiery lake (21:8).

On a few occasions the appearance of fire symbolizes God's desire to purify his people. Primarily, however, fire is a component of cosmic imagery. It comes down in divine judgment and punishment on the wicked.

Flashes of Lightning, Rumblings, Peals of Thunder . . .

This cosmic storm symbolizes God's majesty, power, and sovereignty at the arrival of the eschaton. Numerous Jewish writings describe storm theophanies, an important aspect of the awe of God (Judg 5:4; 1 Sam 12:17–18; 2 Sam 22:8–10; Ps 18:7–9; *Jub.* 2:2; Heb 12:18). The primary background, however, is the Sinai theophany of Exod 19:16 and the chariot vision of Ezek 1:13.[120] The phrase "flashes of lightning, rumblings, peals of thunder" and added accoutrements "earthquake" and "hail" is found four times in Revelation (4:5; 8:5; 11:19; 16:18). All four occurrences depict images of the end of history and the day of judgment. John builds upon the cosmic storm, expanding it each time it is mentioned.

---

118. Beale, *Revelation*, 458.

119. See the entry "Eyes."

120. Osborne, *Revelation*, 230.

Astrapai is translated as "lightning" but more often as "flashes of lightning" in English versions. It heads three of the four listings. *Phonai* is a favorite word for John (29% of all NT uses). Elsewhere in Revelation it is translated as "voice," "sound," and "shout." At these four locations, however, the most common rendering is "rumblings" (CSB, ESV, GNT, NABR, NIV, NRSV). But there is also "noise(s)" (GW, NCV, NKJV ["voices" at 4:5]), "sounds" (NASB), "voices" (CEB), and "roaring" (NET). *Brontai* is most often translated as "thunder(s)" or "peals of thunder" (ESV, GNT, NASB, NIV, NRSV). Some versions hamper intratextual connections in their search for synonyms. NLT, for example, offers "rumble of thunder" (4:5), "thunder crashed" (8:5), "thunder crashed and roared" (11:19), "thunder crashed and rolled" (16:18). Moreover, *phonai* is left untranslated in NLT and REB.

The first reference is near the beginning of the throne room vision (4:5). The subsequent three references, however, appear at the conclusion of their respective visions, implying the final judgment. This suggests that the throne room vision should also be viewed as an end-time vision, depicting heavenly images that temporally parallel the earthly visions of the seals, trumpets, and bowls. The scroll the Lamb opens is composed of these later visions. Bauckham explains that at 4:5 "the expectation of God's coming to judge and rule the world in this initial vision of his rule in heaven."[121] Thus, the first use of the formula is introductory, anticipatory, and expectant. Final judgment is being introduced at 4:5. Final judgment concludes with the last three references.

Each one of the final three occurrences enlarges and elaborates, offering more information on the eschaton.[122] The end-time earthquake is added at 8:5. Following the interlocking approach, the phrase constitutes the end of the seventh seal (8:3–5).[123] At 11:19, the formula expands again with the addition of a "severe hailstorm."[124] The final iteration of the cosmic storm is the seventh bowl (16:18–21). The hailstorm and earthquake are enlarged again, giving the fullest description of the end.

Beale observes the numerical symbolism of this phrase. It appears four times at major literary joints to introduce (4:5) or conclude (8:5; 11:19; 16:18) final judgment. "This fourfold repetition underscores the finality and universality of the last judgment. The climactic nature of the judgment is heightened by progressive expansion of the wording of the allusion."[125] Therfore, these are not four separate celestial phenomena events that give preliminary judgments. All four depict the end. All are linked tightly together.

---

121. Bauckham, *Climax of Prophecy*, 203.

122. Contra Blount (*Revelation*, 164–65), who sees the four references stressing God's majesty, not his judgment.

123. Moreover, Beale (*Revelation*, 459) affirms the end is apparent at 8:5 because the same angel is mentioned at 14:18–19, which is a clearer depiction of judgment day.

124. See the entry "Hail."

125. Beale, *Revelation*, 61.

Four Winds

The four winds serve as destructive agents of God who deliver divine judgment on wicked humanity. Wind is used symbolically throughout Scripture, both in negative and positive imagery. Significantly, the OT prophets utilized the image of wind for God's wrath, punishment, and imminent judgment (Jer 4:11–13; Ezek 5:12; Zech 2:6).[126] NT apocalyptic literature carries forward these pictures. The Gospels mention that God will send his angels to gather the elect "from the four winds, from the ends of the earth to the ends of the heavens" (Mark 13:27; see Matt 24:31), thereby emphasizing end-time totality and comprehensiveness.

John mentions "wind" (*amenos*) three times in two passages in Revelation. The motif of end-time judgment comes through clearly. First, it forms part of the end-time shaking of the cosmos (6:13). Second, "four winds" is found twice at the beginning of the first interlude (7:1) in which the four angels hold the winds back. The four winds are clearly agents of destruction sent by God. Several scholars connect the four winds with the four riders of the first four seals (6:1–8). After all, the first four seals allude to the four horsemen of Zech 6 where they are identified as "four winds" (Zech 6:5).[127] Others scholars, however, reject any connection to the four horsemen. Kistemaker, for example, explains "to turn these four winds into four horses (6:2–7) on the basis of Zech. 6 is questionable."[128] Mounce adds that since winds as destructive agents of God were a regular feature of Jewish apocalyptic literature, and that angels elsewhere in Revelation are in charge of the elements (14:18; 16:5), the four winds should be distinct from the four horsemen.[129] This latter view appears stronger, especially when all passages of nature are included. Wind is a common image found often in the OT as a metaphor for divine punishment (Jer 51:36; Hos 13:15) as well as of the fragility of life (Ps 103:16; Isa 40:6).[130] Therefore, in the end, nothing hinges on either position. Like other passages where John's allusions are debated, he may have intended this elusiveness.

---

126. Ryken, *Dictionary of Biblical Imagery*, 951–52.

127. So Beale, *Revelation*, 406–8; Beasley-Murray, *Revelation*, 142; Boxall, *Revelation*, 121; Brighton, *Revelation*, 182; Caird, *Revelation*, 94; Harrington, *Revelation*, 99; Kiddle, *Revelation*, 131–32; Michaels, *Revelation*, 111; Morris, *Revelation*, 110; Roloff, *Revelation*, 96; Stefanovic, *Revelation*, 254; J. C. Thomas, *Apocalypse*, 258–59; Leonard Thompson, *Revelation*, 106; Wilcock, *I Saw Heaven Opened*, 79.

128. Kistemaker, *Revelation*, 246 n. 11.

129. Mounce, *Revelation*, 155. So Osborne, *Revelation*, 305–6; Smalley, *Revelation*, 179–80; Witherington, *Revelation*, 136. Likewise Robert Thomas (*Revelation*, 1:463), who rejects it because to connect the four winds to the four horsemen means to stop the chronological sequence and go backward in time to before the seals visions begin, a view he deems untenable. Lupieri (*Apocalypse*, 148) and Murphy (*Fallen Is Babylon*, 217) actually push the reference temporally forward, positing the four winds are the angels of the sixth trumpet (9:14). Alan Johnson ("Revelation," 13:658) does not identify the four winds as angels but does say they represent the earthly catastrophes of the trumpets and bowls.

130. Osborne, *Revelation*, 306.

Great Earthquake

The great earthquake is a feature of cosmic imagery that refers to the dissolution of the world, ushering in the conclusion of history, end-time judgment, and the new heaven and new earth. Some earthquakes in Scripture are simple historic events with no symbolic value (Amos 1:1; Zech 14:5; Acts 16:26). The majority of earthquakes, however, appear as symbols, theophanies that manifest God's direct presence, action, and power in the world (Ps 97:4–5; Isa 64:2–3).[131] The earthquake that is referenced and alluded to the most occurred when the law was given at Mount Sinai (Exod 19:18). In the poetic reviews of the exodus, the Psalmist stressed this feature (Pss 68:8; 77:18; 114:4–7), but broadened it to include the whole exodus event. When Matthew linked the earthquake to the ripping of the temple veil at the crucifixion (Matt 27:51–54), it was much more than a mere geological event—it was profoundly symbolic. The covenant inaugurated at Sinai had ended. A new covenant was in effect.[132]

Another symbolic teaching concerning earthquakes was divine judgment, particularly end-time judgment. God shook the earth when he judged nations or wicked people, ushering in the day of the Lord (Isa 13:10–13; 24:18–23; Jer 10:10; Ezek 38:18–23; Joel 2:1–11; 3:16; Mic 1:3–4; Nah 1:3–6; Hag 2:5–7; Zech 4:3–5). This final shaking carries over to apocalyptic literature (1 *En.* 1:3–9; 102:1–2; *T. Mos.* 10:1–7; 2 *Bar.* 32:1; *Sib. Or.* 8:232–238) and the NT (Heb 12:26–27). Thus, the earthquake becomes a cosmic, universal quake that shakes the heavens and the earth at the day of the Lord.[133] The Gospels mention earthquakes as a part of general prophecies being fulfilled in the present age (Matt 24:7; Mark 13:8; Luke 21:11), but the OT day of the Lord passages concerning the shaking of the earth are tied to the return of Christ (Matt 24:29–30; Mark 13:24–27; Luke 17:24).[134] In addition, apocalyptic texts declare the destruction of the cosmos makes way for God's new world (1 *En.* 83:3–5; 4 *Ezra* 6:11–16).

The apostle John adapts, synthesizes, and universalizes these aspects of earthquakes. He adapts Exod 19 and universalizes the prophets' judgment passages that once referred to Israel or a wicked nation to the whole world at the end of history. Allusions by John to Sinai or to the day of the Lord are keys for his universalizing the eschaton. Thus, the imagery of the earthquake emphasizes the last, great, one-time shaking and dissolution of the world at the return of Christ.

It is markedly significant that "earthquake" (*seismos*) is found exactly seven times in Revelation (6:12; 8:5; 11:13 [twice]; 11:19; 16:18 [twice]). The adjective "great" (*megas*) is attached to four of those seven references. Seven is the number for completeness and four is the number for full coverage (often in regards to the surface of the earth). Furthermore,

---

131. Even early interpreters did not always picture earthquakes literally. For example, Wainwright (*Mysterious Apocalypse*, 42–43) mentions Primasius (sixth century AD), who interpreted the earthquakes of Revelation as descriptions of persecution.

132. Ryken, *Dictionary of Biblical Imagery*, 224–25; Schnabel, *40 Questions*, 240–41.

133. Osborne, *Revelation*, 291. Silva ("σείω," 279) adds, "all mentions of earthquakes in the New Testament refer to divine intervention."

134. Hays, Duvall, and Pate, *Dictionary of Prophecy*, 126–27. See Beale, *Revelation*, 413; Blomberg, *Matthew*, 353–54; Bock, *Luke*, 2:1667–68.

John places every earthquake at the conclusion of a vision. The numerical symbolism prepares readers not to think of seven individual, sequentially-spaced earthquakes, but one great earthquake repeated in four different visions. All recapitulate the one, final, last, great earthquake.

The first mention is in the sixth seal (6:12–17).[135] There are numerous OT allusions behind these verses (Isa 13:10–13; 24:1–6, 9–23; 34:4; Ezek 32:6–8; Joel 2:10, 30–31; 3:15–16). The earthquake joins many other cosmic end-time elements. Elisabeth Schüssler Fiorenza summarizes that "The portents in the heavens are so terrible that they can only be understood in apocalyptic terms to mean the final dissolution of the whole world."[136]

The second occurrence is in the seventh seal (8:1–5). This study understands John utilizing an interlocking technique in the structure of his visions. This means the seventh seal encompasses 8:1, 3–5. It thus serves as a recapitulation of earthquake of the sixth seal as well as an introduction to the seven trumpets (8:2). Beale comments "In 8:5 the climactic end of the cosmos is in mind, since there is allusion to Sinai together with mention of the earthquake."[137]

Seismos is mentioned twice at the conclusion of the second interlude (11:13). A great earthquake destroys a tenth of the city and seven thousand people are killed. The earthquake heralds the end of history. The two numbers (tenth, seven thousand) serve as numerical symbols representing the totality of unbelievers at the end.[138] Allusions include Ezek 38:19 where the great earthquake represents final judgment on Gog at the end of history. This also associates 11:13 with final denouement, since that is how John utilizes Ezek 38–39 elsewhere (19:17; 20:8–9).[139]

The fifth occurrence is located at the seventh trumpet (11:19). Numerous commentators understand John to give a fore-glimpse of the end, usually to emphasize their sequential structure.[140] Other scholars believe John uses realized eschatology in 11:15–19. That is, John's final judgment language in the seventh trumpet introduces the end played out in chapters 12–22.[141] Still others understand the seventh trumpet to picture the very end. The heavenly celebration, the aorist tense verbs, the final wrath, and judging the dead all combine with the cosmic storm that includes the earthquake.[142] This last view fits the structure of Revelation the best.

---

135. The accompanying elements of the earthquake and its allusion to Sinai are found first at 4:5. But John limits his uses of *seismos* to exactly seven for symbolic reasons.

136. Schüssler Fiorenza, *Revelation*, 64. See Beale, *Revelation*, 123, 396–97, for more examples.

137. Beale, *Revelation*, 458.

138. See the entries "Tenth of the City" and "Seven Thousand."

139. Beale, *Revelation*, 602.

140. Ladd, *Revelation*, 163; Reddish, *Revelation*, 225; Ryrie, *Revelation*, 87; Robert Thomas, *Revelation*, 2:104; Walvoord, *Revelation*, 184. By contrast, preterist Chilton (*Days of Vengeance*, 290–92) remarks that the seventh trumpet has God taking control of the situation in AD 70.

141. Boring, *Revelation*, 149; Hailey, *Revelation*, 264; Michaels, *Revelation*, 147; Mounce, *Revelation*, 230; Stefanovic, *Revelation*, 369; J. C. Thomas, *Apocalypse*, 351; Wall, *Revelation*, 151.

142. Bauckham, *Climax of Prophecy*, 209; Beale, *Revelation*, 615; Beasley-Murray, *Revelation*, 188; Blount, *Revelation*, 219; Brighton, *Revelation*, 309; Duvall, *Revelation*, 154; Dennis Johnson, *Triumph of the Lamb*, 176; Kistemaker, *Revelation*, 341; Prigent, *Apocalypse*, 363.

Finally, *seismos* is mentioned twice in the seventh bowl (16:18). Numerous OT allusions converge at the seventh bowl (16:17–21). Bauckham notes the parallelism between the earthquake of 11:13 and 16:18, and offers evidence that both passages herald the end.[143] Fowler White considers 6:12–17; 16:17–21; and 20:9–11 to refer to "the cosmic shaking that accompanies the advent of the Divine-Warrior Judge."[144] Therefore, earthquakes in Revelation play no role in preliminary judgments. All seven uses portray images of the very end. The shattering of the world ushers in end-time judgment and the formation of a new world.

Hail

Hail is an element of the storm theophany and symbolizes God's righteous wrath which culminates in final, end-time judgment. In the OT, hail and hailstorms comprise common features of God's judgmental wrath against the wicked (Josh 10:11; Job 38:22; Isa 28:2; Ezek 13:11–13; 38:22; Hag 2:17).[145] "Hail," "hailstones," and "hailstorm" all derive from *chalaza* and originate from the stockpile of cosmic imagery that was available to John and his audience. For John, this storm imagery includes lightning, thunder, rumblings, and a final earthquake. Although common in the OT, hail is found only four times in NT, all in Revelation (8:7; 11:19; 16:21 [twice]).[146] The twin themes of divine wrath and punishment appear prominently.

The first trumpet includes "hail and fire mixed with blood" that is hurled to earth (8:7). This judgment replicates the seventh Egyptian plague (Exod 9:13–35). Blood and fire are often combined as symbols of judgment (Isa 9:5; Ezek 38:22). John adds hail to the mix.[147] Futurists generally understand the first trumpet to take place toward the very end of earth history, within a seven-year tribulation period. Such symbolic judgments, however, may be found within history and throughout history and first four trumpets are "in history" judgments. Nevertheless, the final three references to hail are clearly images of the very end of history and form part of the end-time storm theophany.

The seventh trumpet concludes with "Then God's temple in heaven was opened, and within his temple was seen the ark of his covenant. And there came flashes of lightning,

---

143. Bauckham, *Climax of Prophecy*, 207–8.

144. Fowler White, "Reexamining the Evidence," 331. Although 20:11 does not mention *seismos*, the cosmic destruction affords yet another end-time glimpse. Robert Thomas ("Analysis of the Seventh Bowl," 73—95) postulates that the seventh bowl judgment extends from 16:17—22:5.

145. See Beck, *Dictionary of Imagery*, 118–20; Hawkins, "Hail, Hailstones," 718–19; Ryken, *Dictionary of Biblical Imagery*, 359.

146. John limits the number of references to four to emphasize worldwide fulfillment. Lightning is also limited to four occurrences.

147. Osborne, *Revelation*, 350.

rumblings, peals of thunder, an earthquake and a severe hailstorm" (11:19).[148] Concisely stated, the seventh trumpet is a picture of the final judgment of God.[149]

The final two occurrences of hail are located at the seventh bowl (16:17–21), another day of judgment image. The elements of 11:19 are listed again, followed by expanded descriptions of the earthquake and hail. "From the sky huge hailstones, each weighing about a hundred pounds, fell on people. And they cursed God on account of the plague of hail, because the plague was so terrible" (16:21). Scholars choose between 60–120 pounds to translate *talantiaios* ("talent"). Most English versions choose "about one hundred pounds" for the weight of the hailstones. The NLT reads "as much as seventy-five pounds." NJB and NKJV transliterate with each hailstone the "weight of a talent." Closer to the idea, however, are GW's "large, heavy hailstones" and NABR's "like huge weights." These renderings recognize "talent" is not a measure of exactness but rather a symbol of vastness. David Barr concurs. "But the expression is best understood to mean they were impossibly big. In our idiom, we might say they weighed a ton."[150] Hail, therefore, is a symbol of the righteous wrath of God. Expecting a barrage of literal hundred-pound hailstones is not necessary to make the point. This is an image of the end. The unrighteous cannot escape final judgment.

Heavens Receded Like a Scroll Being Rolled Up

This phrase is a part of the cosmic imagery that depicts the collapse of the world, ushering in the end of history. The phrase is found in the sixth seal: "The sky was split apart like a scroll when it is rolled up, and every mountain and island were moved out of their places" (6:14). Taken all together, the four cosmic events in the sixth seal upon the sun, moon, stars, and heavens, each followed with the same literary pattern of four similes, pictures the final day of God's judgment on the world. This darkening and destruction of the cosmos appears frequently in the OT (Isa 13:9–10; Ezek 32:6–8; Joel 2:30–31; Amos 8:9; Zeph 1:15), apocalyptic literature (*T. Levi* 4:1; *1 En.* 102:2–3; *4 Ezra* 7:39; *Sib. Or.* 5:346–385; *Barn.* 15:5), and the NT (Matt 24:29; Mark 13:24–25; Acts 2:20; 2 Pet 3:10).

Not everyone views this as the description of the collapse of the universe at the conclusion of history. Smalley, for example, reminds us that the splitting of the heavens is a regular biblical image used to introduce the disclosure of God, and not necessarily in final, end-time judgment.[151] Likewise, those who adopt a sequential approach to the

---

148. Smalley (*Revelation*, 296) represents those who recognize that 11:19 serves as a transitional verse. It ties together structurally what comes before and after. Some commentators begin the third interlude with 11:19: see Aune, *Revelation*, 2:647; Boxall, *Revelation*, 173; Koester, *Revelation*, 523; Mulholland, *Revelation*, 214; Wilcock, *I Saw Heaven Opened*, 16.

149. Bauckham, *Climax of Prophecy*, 202–4; Beale, *Revelation*, 618; Brighton, *Revelation*, 308–9; Duvall, *Revelation*, 156; Hendriksen, *More than Conquerors*, 132; Kistemaker, *Revelation*, 346; Dennis Johnson, *Triumph of the Lamb*, 175; Osborne, *Revelation*, 449. Moreover, many futurists accept the seventh trumpet as a proleptic picture of judgment day: Hindson, *Revelation*, 127; Ladd, *Revelation*, 163; Robert Thomas, *Revelation*, 2:113–15; Walvoord, *Revelation*, 189.

150. Barr, *Tales*, 133.

151. Smalley, *Revelation*, 166–67.

seals, trumpets, and bowls would certainly agree with that assessment. Robert Thomas states, "This is the human perception of the magnitude of the disturbance, but is not the ultimate passage of the heavens, which does not occur until Rev. 20:11 . . ."[152] Many soften the end-time dissolution of the cosmos with depictions of literal of physical phenomena. Patterson, for example, asserts "Almost certainly what is being described here are meteo-rological storms of such increased magnitude that tornado and hurricane-like effects are created everywhere in the sky, giving the look of the rolling up of a scroll."[153]

Nevertheless, many others recognize that John is relating the final, great day of the Lord, whether hyperbolic or literal.[154] He alludes to Isa 34:4, a favorite passage that portrays final judgment. Modern versions help in understanding what John meant by the separation of the sky. Selections include "split apart" (CSB, NASB, NET), "divided" (NABR), "receded" (NIV, NKJV), and "separated" (HCSB). Other translations choose "vanished" (ESV, GW, NRSV, REB) or "disappeared" (CEB, GNT, NCV, NJB).[155] Most ver-sions choose to translate the simile literally with "like a scroll rolled up." NABR does well with "the sky was divided like a torn scroll rolling up." The verb *apochōrizō* literally means "to separate." Thus, to separate "like a scroll" the heavens (most versions choose "sky") means separated into two halves, each one rolled up.[156] No stronger language or similes can be imagined for the collapse of the world.

For numerous scholars, therefore, this phrase depicts the dissolution of the cosmos at the conclusion of history. Ian Boxall relates, "We are now presented with the shaking of the cosmos, which will herald the final coming of the Son of Man in judgement (Mk 13:24–25). In other words, it is particularly this section of the seals sequence which will be recapitulated, and viewed from different angles, in the visions yet to come."[157] In sum, this pictures the universe falling apart, not storms, tornados, and hurricanes hitting here and there over the earth's surface. The cosmic signs depicted in 6:12–14 are stock ele-ments of the final great day of the Lord. Creation trembles, crumbles, and flees at the arrival of the eschaton (6:17; 20:11).

Island

Every island removed from its place or fleeing pictures the collapse of the world at the end of history, and the totality of judgment. Most of the OT's references to islands occur in Isaiah where they form "an image of the far-flung and little-known nations across the

---

152. Robert Thomas, *Revelation*, 1:454.

153. Patterson, *Revelation*, 188.

154. So Bauckham, *Climax of Prophecy*, 208; Beasley-Murray, *Revelation*, 138; Blount, *Revelation*, 139–40; Boxall, *Revelation*, 117; Schüssler Fiorenza, *Revelation*, 86; Ford, *Revelation*, 112; Harrington, *Revelation*, 96; Alan Johnson, "Revelation," 13:655; Kistemaker, *Revelation*, 236; Morris, *Revelation*, 109; Mounce, *Revelation*, 150–51; Mulholland, *Revelation*, 117; Osborne, *Revelation*, 291; Sweet, *Revelation*, 143; Wilcock, *I Saw Heaven Opened*, 73.

155. NLT omits this important verb.

156. Beale, *Revelation*, 396.

157. Boxall, *Revelation*, 117. Osborne (*Revelation*, 293) agrees: "There can be no better image for the end of the world as we know it."

Mediterranean world."[158] Thus, God will gather the remnant from far off islands (Isa 11:11). They tremble in fear before the Lord (Isa 41:5). They wait in hope for God to exercise his saving power (Isa 51:5). Notably, islands will not escape the judgment of God (Isa 59:18). For Isaiah, "the islands are images of the ends of the earth, borders of the known world that nevertheless fall under the sovereignty of Yahweh."[159] "Island" (*nēsos*) is found three times in Revelation. In 1:9 it refers to the specific island of Patmos on which John is exiled and receives his visions. The other two instances, however, reflect cosmic imagery of the dissolution of the world at the conclusion of history. In the sixth seal, "The heavens receded like a scroll being rolled up, and every mountain and island was removed from its place" (6:14). This pictures the collapse of the world. Nothing escapes the day of wrath of the God and the Lamb. A parallel account is found at the seventh bowl. "Every island fled away and the mountains could not be found" (16:20). "Fled away" (*ephygen*) is also rendered "vanished" (GW, NJB, REB) and "disappeared" (GNT, NLT). Again, the consummation of history is pictured.[160] The mention of islands, therefore, is a reminder that the farthest reaches of the world cannot offer asylum or sanctuary when end-time judgment arrives. Nothing can hide from or escape the great day of the Lord.

Moon

The moon is used by John either as part of the end-time cosmic imagery or as signifying the eternal honor and glory of God's presence for eternity. The moon is referenced often in the OT to demarcate time through its lunar cycle. Its regularity became an image of both longevity and even eternity (Pss 72:5–7; 89:37). Prophetic literature utilized the moon as a player in earth's final collapse. Usually the moon's light ceased (Isa 13:10–13; 24:1–23; 34:4; Ezek 32:6–8; Joel 2:10; 3:15–16; Hab 3:6–11) or it turned blood red (Joel 2:31). Isaiah envisioned a time when there would be no moon or sun, because "The LORD will be your everlasting light" (Isa 60:19–20).[161]

Revelation maintains these images. The moon (*selēnē*) is found four times, always in connection with the sun. Two of the four instances refer to the cosmic imagery associated with end-time judgment. First, the sixth seal, depicting the end of history, is opened to reveal "the whole moon turned blood red" (6:12). Preterists and historicists generally understand this verse to describe social and governmental upheavals against Rome or Jerusalem in the first century.[162] Many futurists believe the cosmic events depicted in the sixth seal will happen literally.[163] Lindsey attributes the blood red moon to nuclear explosions. LaHaye envisions volcanic ash. Robert Thomas proposes a total lunar eclipse that

---

158. Ryken, *Dictionary of Biblical Imagery*, 429.

159. Ibid.

160. Caird (*Revelation*, 209) attempts to draw all three references to "islands" together, suggesting an allusion to Patmos here.

161. Mare, "Moon," 308–10; Ryken, *Dictionary of Biblical Imagery*, 565–66; Brian Schmidt, "Moon," 585–93.

162. Chilton, *Days of Vengeance*, 196–97; Clark, *Message from Patmos*, 55.

163. Patterson, *Revelation*, 188; Walvoord, *Revelation*, 136.

panics the world's population. Edward Hindson foresees nuclear or cosmic disaster.[164] However, the moon turning to blood and the darkening of the moon are two common images found often in OT (see above) and apocalyptic literature (*T. Mos.* 10:3–6; *4 Ezra* 5:4–8; 7:39; Matt 24:29; Mark 13:24; Acts 2:20). [165] Taken altogether, the four cosmic events of 6:12–14 upon the sun, moon, stars, and heavens, each followed with the same literary pattern of four similes, pictures the final day of God's judgment upon the world.

Second, backing up temporally, the fourth trumpet figuratively and physically depicts cosmic disturbances throughout history. The trumpet sounds and "a third of the sun was struck, a third of the moon, and a third of the stars, so that a third of them turned dark" (8:12). The choices for interpretation are the same—some understand this darkening of the moon to occur literally in the past or the future. Instead, it is best to understand it as cosmic imagery that occurs tumultuously throughout history and especially near the end.

The other two references to the moon reflect glory and honor given to God and coming from God. A great sign appears at the beginning of the third interlude. A woman is "clothed with the sun, with the moon under her feet and a crown of twelve stars on her head" (12:1). The picture of being clothed with the sun signifies her glory. She also has the moon under her feet, perhaps suggesting dominion.[166] This certainly fits the passage to which it alludes (Gen 37:9) where honor and glory are bestowed. In the Genesis account, the sun is symbolized by Jacob, the moon by his wife, and the stars are the eleven tribes of Israel who bow down to Joseph. In Rev 12, then, the radiance surrounding the woman connotes heavenly identity, protection, purity, and glory.[167]

The final reference to the moon is found in the vision of the new heaven and new earth. The heavenly city "does not need the sun or the moon to shine on it, for the glory of God gives it light, and the Lamb is its lamp" (21:23). Thus, the lack of the sun and the moon in the heavenly Jerusalem implies that God himself, by means of his glory and honor, will eternally illuminate the city. John is not referring to a literal physical sun or moon. Rather, he describes what it will be like for God's people, who are the new Jerusalem, who are the holy of holies, to live forever in his presence (22:5).

Mountain

John uses the image of a mountain contrastingly. It is the place of divine presence at the second coming and a vantage point of the new Jerusalem. But mountains represent powerful kingdoms, and in cosmic imagery the fall of Babylon the Great and the collapse of the world on judgment day is symbolized. The biblical landscape flourishes with mountains. With five hundred references, it is easy to see why symbolism became attached to them.

164. Lindsey, *New World Coming*, 110; LaHaye, *Revelation Unveiled*, 146; Robert Thomas, *Revelation*, 1:453; Hindson, *Revelation*, 84.

165. Smalley, *Revelation*, 166–67.

166. So Brighton, *Revelation*, 326.

167. Beale, *Revelation*, 627. Blount (*Revelation*, 227) adds that the moon under her feet signals elevated status.

God's divine presence is frequently associated with mountains (Gen 22:2; Deut 11:29). The Psalms and prophets used mountains to express God's power (Ps 65:6; Isa 40:4; Jer 4:24; Hab 3:6). They symbolize his eternal nature (Gen 49:6), righteousness (Ps 36:6), love (Isa 54:10), majesty (Ps 76:4), and anger (Deut 32:22). In response, the mountains leap (Ps 114:4), sing (Isa 49:13), rejoice (Ps 98:8), and praise God (Ps 89:12). Mountains also figure prominently in eschatological passages (Jer 51:25; Ezek 38:20; Joel 3:18; Amos 9:12; Zech 14:4). Jewish tradition placed the final eschatological city on a mountain (Isa 2:2; 4:1–5; Mic 4:1–2; *1 En.* 24:1–3; *Jub.* 4:26). *Oros* occurs over sixty times in the NT, most often in the Gospels. Theological significance becomes attached when Jesus teaches authoritatively (Matt 5:2), seeks isolation (Matt 14:23), and is transfigured (Matt 17:1) on mountains. His apocalyptic discourse is on the Mount of Olives (Matt 24:1), and his final words usher forth from a mountain (Matt 28:16).[168]

Although mentioned only eight times in Revelation, *oros* forms an important piece of John's geographical symbolism. Resseguie relates that three topographical references are ambiguous—river, mountain, and wilderness. "The mountain is a symbol of divine presence in the created order. The mountain, however, may also represent humankind's striving towards the heavens to achieve dominance over the created order—a type of tower of Babel lurching towards the heavens."[169] John uses mountains symbolically in the following ways.

First, mountains are depicted as part of cosmic imagery for the world's collapse at the second coming. Every mountain is "removed" (*ekinēthēsan*) in the sixth seal (6:14).[170] Every mountain "disappears" (*ouch heurethēsan*) in the seventh bowl (16:20 CEB, CSB, NABR). Surrounded with other end-time cosmic images (6:12–17; 16:17–21) it becomes evident the end of history is being depicted here. These passages parallel one another and proclaim that the end has come.[171] Furthermore, the sixth seal reveals the response of the wicked to the certainty of end-time judgment. They cry out to the mountains to hide them (6:15–16).[172]

Second, a mountain is used to envision the collapse of Babylon the Great or perhaps a fallen angel. The second trumpet includes an allusion to the first exodus plague (Exod 7:20) when "something like a great mountain, all ablaze, was thrown into sea, and a third of the sea turned to blood" (8:8). Modern scholars disagree on what John intended to say about this flaming mountain. He may have envisioned a meteorite.[173] Numerous exegetes

168. Green, "Mount, Mountain," 159–60; G. A. Lee, "Hill, etc.," 713–16; Ryken, *Dictionary of Biblical Imagery*, 572–74; Silva, "ὀρός," 548–53.

169. Resseguie, *Revelation Unsealed*, 71; see 81–85. Four mountains in particular have spiritual significance—Zion, Armageddon, new Jerusalem, and the seven mountains of chapter 17.

170. English translations have "moved" or "removed" except for "shaken" (NJB) and "dislodged" (REB).

171. Those who follow a sequential structure do not see the end of history pictured. In addition, some scholars lessen the impact by interpreting 6:14 as political and social decay or upheaval (Beckwith, *Apocalypse*, 528; Charles, *Revelation*, 1:181; Hailey, *Revelation*, 197; Swete, *Apocalypse*, 93). Chilton (*Days of Vengeance*, 198) intones that this de-creation language "is not speaking of the End of the World, but of the *End of Israel* in A.D. 70."

172. See the entry "Fall on Us and Hide Us."

173. Dispensationalists favor this, including LaHaye (*Revelation Unveiled*, 167), Patterson (*Revelation*,

suggest volcanic eruptions similar to Mount Vesuvius in AD 79.[174] Other scholars posit a link to Jeremiah's burned out mountain depicting the fall of Babylon (Jer 51:25). If so, John has in mind the end-time Babylon the Great.[175] Lastly, John may be alluding to fallen angels. Apocalyptic literature portrays fallen angels as stars who are like "burning mountains" (1 En. 21:3–4) and come down to the sea and Babylon (Sib. Or. 5:158–159). This receives more support when a few sentences later (9:1) a star falls from the sky and is usually interpreted as a fallen angel.[176] A picture of fallen Babylon and fallen angel are better interpretive choices. Since the second trumpet does not envision the very end, partial judgment is in mind. Perhaps Osborne is correct when he writes that all the scenarios are possible, and perhaps purposefully intended by John, and there is no need to choose only one.[177]

Third, a picture of the new Jerusalem that arrives at the eschaton is pictured with Mount Zion (14:1) and the great and high mountain (21:10). The hundred and forty-four thousand servants rest on the mount with Christ. The earthly Mount Zion is equated with the new Jerusalem which "comes down from heaven" (21:2) which John observes from the vantage point of a great and high mountain (21:10). Many exegetes understand this scene in simple terms. John is whisked in the Spirit to a mountain perch which allows him a panoramic view of the descending heavenly city.[178] Others, however, suggest that John envisions the heavenly city sitting on the mountaintop. Understood in this light, the mountain sharply contrasts with the evil city, Babylon the Great, which sits on seven mountains (17:1–3). It also fulfills Ezekiel's vision (Ezek 40:1–2). John intertextually parallels this mountain with Mount Zion (14:1).[179] Victory, vindication, and security in the eternal presence of God and the Lamb are stressed.

Fourth, mountains are mentioned to represent the oppressive nature of evil. The scarlet beast is identified with seven heads, seven kings, and seven mountains (17:9). Most scholars agree that John makes a reference to oppressive Rome, the city on seven hills. But John does not limit himself to first-century or last days Rome. Instead, Resseguie

---

211), Robert Thomas (Revelation, 2:19), and Walvoord (Revelation, 154). Lindsey (New World Coming, 131) speculates "more likely, a colossal H-bomb."

174. Blount, Revelation, 169; Brighton, Revelation, 226; Chilton, Days of Vengeance, 238; Easley, Revelation, 144; Fee, Revelation, 124; Swete, Apocalypse, 111; Witherington, Revelation, 149. Aune (Revelation, 519–20), Mounce (Revelation, 179), Murphy (Fallen Is Babylon, 240), and Skaggs and Benham (Revelation, 96) agree but add fallen angels, whereas Duvall (Revelation, 126) and Kistemaker (Revelation, 274) add fall of Babylon.

175. Beale, Revelation, 476; Caird, Revelation, 114; Hailey, Revelation, 220; Resseguie, Revelation, 144; Stefanovic, Revelation, 296. Ford (Revelation, 133), Harrington (Revelation, 106), Smalley (Revelation, 220–21), and Sweet (Revelation, 163) agree but add fallen angels.

176. Charles, Revelation, 1:234; Koester, Revelation, 449; Prigent, Apocalypse, 307. So too Keener (Revelation, 257), who adds a volcano, and Roloff (Revelation, 110), who adds a meteorite.

177. Osborne, Revelation, 353.

178. Aune, Revelation, 3:1151; Fee, Revelation, 297; Kistemaker, Revelation, 564; Morris, Revelation, 242; Mounce, Revelation, 389; Patterson, Revelation, 369; Robert Thomas, Revelation, 2:459.

179. Bauckham, Theology of Revelation, 132–33; Beale, Revelation, 1065; Beasley-Murray, Revelation, 319; Boxall, Revelation, 301; Brighton, Revelation, 609; Caird, Revelation, 269; Ford, Revelation, 339; Keener, Revelation, 491–92; Michaels, Revelation, 241; Mulholland, Revelation, 320–21; Resseguie, Revelation Unsealed, 83; Smalley, Revelation, 546; Witherington, Revelation, 268.

explains, "the seven mountains symbolize the archetypal human city, the tower of Babel, lurching towards the heavens—to be godlike. Since seven is emblematic of completeness, seven mountains represent the whole civilized world, the city of this world, reaching heavenward—a striking parody to the New Jerusalem that comes down out of heaven to sit on a mountain."[180] Mountains, therefore, are a versatile symbol in John's arsenal. Their contrasting use accents the fulfillment of the eschaton and eschatological judgment.

Smoke

Smoke is a common portent of cosmic end-time judgment, but John also uses it as a symbol of sacrifice and worship rising up to God. In the OT, smoke often accompanied a theophany (Exod 19:18; 2 Sam 22:9; Isa 6:4), communicated the wrath of God (Deut 29:20; Ps 18:8), was a sign of destruction (Gen 19:28; Isa 34:10), and signaled a portent of God's judgment (Joel 2:30). But smoke could also symbolize sacrificial offerings and worship, and the aromatic smoke of the incense ascended to heaven to please God (Exod 29:18; Lev 1:9).[181] Thus, smoke may be understood positively or negatively, and even both at the same time. The very offerings of incense intended to please God might provoke his wrath instead (Isa 65:5).[182]

Both OT motifs are found in Revelation. Twelve of the thirteen occurrences of "smoke" (*kapnos*) in the NT are in the Apocalypse.[183] Two of those twelve are used as positive symbols of sacrifice and worship. First, the angel with the golden censer stood at the heavenly altar with the smoke from incense (8:3–5). Here smoke either symbolizes the fragrant prayers of the saints (Ps 141:2) or accompanies their prayers to the heavenly altar. Either way, they represent imprecatory prayers of justice and vindication on behalf of all the saints (6:9–11). Structurally-speaking, then, this continues God's answer to the martyrs' request in the fifth seal (6:9–11) with judgment day (6:12–17; 8:1, 3–5). Application-wise, such imagery is powerful—the believer's prayers are central to the final judgment of God's enemies. Second, a positive reference is played out at the commencement of the bowl judgments (15:8). Most recognize allusions to Isa 6:4, and perhaps Exod 19:18; 40:34; and Ezek 10:2–4. The three images of smoke, glory, and power combine to make the outpouring of wrath subsequently found in chapter 16, "an act of worship. The name of God is vindicated, and his glory is demonstrated in these bowls of wrath." [184]

The other ten references to smoke confirm it as a common feature of end-time judgment. Smoke is mentioned four times in the fifth trumpet (9:2–3) and twice in the sixth trumpet (9:17–18). The smoke of the Abyss darkens the skies and locusts come forth. The demonic horses spew fire, sulfur, and smoke from their mouths. The final references to smoke narrate the final judgment of Babylon the Great along with her wicked followers. The angel states, "the smoke of their torment will rise for ever and ever" (14:11). Those

---

180. Resseguie, *Revelation*, 83. See the entry "Seven Heads/ Seven Hills/ Seven Kings."

181. Lemon, "Smoke," 308–9.

182. Chamberlain, "Smoke; Smoking," 554.

183. The other reference is Acts 2:19, which is Peter's quotation from Joel 2:30.

184. Osborne, *Revelation*, 571–72.

who share in her persecuting luxuries "see the smoke of her burning, they will weep and mourn over her" (18:9, 18). Finally, the great multitude in heaven will shout, "Hallelujah! The smoke from her goes up for ever and ever" (19:3). This last phrase coincides temporally with 14:11, and both use the same wording.

Osborne notes an interesting contrast between the smoke of the martyrs' prayers for vengeance (6:9–11) and the smoke that depicts the torment of evildoers that rises forever. "In the theology of this book, the smoke of the latter is God's response to the smoke of the former."[185] Therefore, John uses "smoke" as yet another end-time contrast. It is a symbol of worship for believers but a sign of judgment for unbelievers. In both cases the end is in view.

Split into Three Parts

The expression "split into three parts" signifies universal, total, and complete destruction of the worldwide city, Babylon the Great, at the conclusion of history. A great earthquake occurs at the seventh bowl and "the great city split into three parts, and the cities of the nations collapsed. God remembered Babylon the Great and gave her the cup filled with the wine of the fury of his wrath" (16:19).[186] The phrase is unique to Revelation but probably alludes to Ezek 5:2, 12 where unfaithful Israelites were divided into three parts, each dying because of God's judgment.[187] If so, then John is customarily expanding and universalizing the allusion. Witherington suggests that the city is split into three parts "perhaps because it is ruled by the unholy trinity, so that the punishment fits the crime."[188] Older scholars proposed the division via three ways dealt with people groups, not geography.[189]

The majority, however, recognize that Babylon the Great is in mind for the great city (NLT actually reads "great city of Babylon"). But does John intend for the great city to refer to the historic earthly city of Jerusalem,[190] Rome,[191] or the ungodly worldwide city?[192] The last option is the best option. Babylon the Great is theological and symbolic, not geographical and literal. The phrase is an idiomatic expression symbolizing the total

185. Ibid., 345.

186. English versions are consistent in translating this phrase. Exceptions include choosing the verb "divided" (NKJV) for "split," and exchanging "parts" in favor of "sections" (NLT).

187. Brighton, *Revelation*, 429.

188. Witherington, *Revelation*, 211. So also Stefanovic, *Revelation*, 505.

189. For names, see Beale, *Revelation*, 844; Gregg, *Revelation*, 390; and Robert Thomas, *Revelation*, 2:275.

190. Followed by futurists such as Patterson (*Revelation*, 314), Robert Thomas (*Revelation*, 2:275), and Walvoord (*Revelation*, 240). LaHaye (*Revelation Unveiled*, 258) envisions a future rebirth of the ancient city of Babylon. Preterists select first-century Jerusalem, including Chilton (*Days of Vengeance*, 168), Ford (*Revelation*, 264, 274), and Lupieri (*Apocalypse*, 246).

191. Either Rome or an end-time Rome is followed by Aune (*Revelation*, 2:900–901), Charles (*Revelation*, 2:52), Keener (*Revelation*, 397), Krodel (*Revelation*, 288), Mounce (*Revelation*, 303), Osborne (*Revelation*, 598), and Reddish (*Revelation*, 314).

192. So Beale, *Revelation*, 843; Boxall, *Revelation*, 236; Hughes, *Revelation*, 179; Dennis Johnson, *Triumph of the Lamb*, 238; Kiddle, *Revelation*, 332–33; Kistemaker, *Revelation*, 454–55; Morris, *Revelation*, 195; Resseguie, *Revelation*, 216; Smalley, *Revelation*, 414–15.

destruction of the rebellious, wicked worldwide city at the end of time. There is no hint that survival is possible, and that the cities of the world "collapsed" (NET, NIV, NJB, REB) or are "destroyed" (GNT, NCV) finish the picture of universal devastation at the conclusion of history. The word "fell" (*epesan*) implies that the great earthquake was worldwide, total, and catastrophic. It is the same word used for the "fall" of Babylon (14:8; 18:2–3) and implies the same event is being described.[193]

Star(s)

Depending on the context, stars symbolize people, angels, or serve as part of the cosmic imagery that ushers in judgment at the second coming. Stars are mentioned nearly seventy times in Scripture. They came to symbolize transcendence (Job 22:12), God's artistry (Ps 8:3), and God's glory (Ps 148:3; 1 Cor 15:41). Stars personified angels (Judg 5:20; Job 38:7). In apocalyptic texts, stars become participants in God's end-time story, ceasing to give light (Isa 13:10; Joel 2:10) or falling from heaven (Matt 24:29; Mark 13:25). Stars also symbolize people. The wise will be rewarded with glory and "will shine like the stars for ever and ever" (Dan 12:3). In 2 Pet 1:19, Peter refers to Christ as the morning star. In Isa 14:12, the king of Babylon, perhaps a reference to Satan, imagines himself as the "morning star, son of the dawn." Similarly, Jude 13 mentions false teachers who are figuratively called "wandering stars."[194]

These images converge in Revelation. "Star" (*astēr*) is found fourteen times. Five times it is singular (2:28; 8:10, 11; 9:1; 22:16) and nine times it is plural (1:16, 20 [twice]; 2:1; 3:1; 6:13; 8:12; 12:1, 4). The following three images surface. First, stars symbolize people. These people can be good or evil. The crown of twelve stars on the woman's head clearly symbolizes believing Israel, God's people, who are expanded to include all Christians (12:1, 17). This metaphor is taken from Gen 37 and Joseph's dream of stars (representing his brothers) bowing down to him. Likewise, the title "Morning Star" also references people. It denotes Christ and those believers who overcome (2:28; 22:16).[195]

Second, stars symbolize angels. These angels can be good or evil. The good angel motif is most noticeable in Christ's holding of the "seven stars," found in five of the nine plural references (1:16, 20 [twice]; 2:1; 3:1). These angels represent the prevailing character of the seven churches.[196] The falling star of 9:1 is usually understood as an angel although scholars differ over whether it is a good angel or an evil angel.[197] If it is a good

---

193. Kistemaker, *Revelation*, 455; Mulholland, *Revelation*, 273; Osborne, *Revelation*, 598–99.

194. Hartley, "Star," 611–12; Ryken, *Dictionary of Biblical Imagery*, 813–14.

195. See the entry "Morning Star."

196. Many interpreters understand the seven stars to refer to human leaders of the churches, and would therefore place these references to stars as people. See the entry "Angels of the Seven Churches."

197. It is a good angel according to Aune, *Revelation*, 2:525; Boxall, *Revelation*, 142; Duvall, *Revelation*, 131; Easley, *Revelation*, 156; Hughes, *Revelation*, 108; Keener, *Revelation*, 266; Koester, *Revelation*, 455; Ladd, *Revelation*, 129; Morris, *Revelation*, 124; Mounce, *Revelation*, 185; Osborne, *Revelation*, 362; Paul, *Revelation*, 176; Smalley, *Revelation*, 225. It is a bad angel according to Beale, *Revelation*, 492; Blount, *Revelation*, 173; Boring, *Revelation*, 136; Hailey, *Revelation*, 225; Hendriksen, *More than Conquerors*, 120; Kistemaker, *Revelation*, 285; Mulholland, *Revelation*, 192; Patterson, *Revelation*, 215;

angel then it may be the same angel that is mentioned in 20:1. In other words, he is an angelic messenger and the word "fallen" simply means "descended" from heaven. That the star angel of 9:1 is evil also garners support. Jewish apocalyptic literature often refers to "falling angels" as evil angelic beings (1 En. 18:15; 88:1–3; T. Sol. 20:14–17). In fact, it might represent the devil himself (1 En. 86:1; Apoc. El. (H) 4:11–12) which also draws biblical support (Isa 14:12; Luke 10:18; Rev 12:9). The disagreement on the identity of the star in 9:1 does not carry over to 12:4. Everyone agrees that when the dragon sweeps one-third of the stars from heaven it refers to bad angels (12:4).

Third, stars form a stock feature of end-time cosmic imagery. The plural usage and context with other heavenly bodies connote cosmic imagery is at work. John must surely be aware of the apocalyptic sections of the Gospels that relate stars as end-time accoutrements (Matt 24:29; Mark 13:25). He utilizes this metaphor twice—"stars of the sky fell (6:13) and "a third of the stars" turned dark (8:12).

A final reference to stars, however, engenders debate. Interpreters argue on the identification of the "great star blazing like a torch" whose name is Wormwood (8:10–11). Most interpreters select bad angel whereas literalist interpreters opt for an actual falling star, comet, meteorite, or nuclear bomb.[198] The close context with 9:1, however, favors a bad angel as the best choice. Therefore, stars serve John's symbolic world in a multitude of ways, signifying people, angels, and end-time cosmic imagery. Context, intertextual, and extratextual allusions aid the reader in understanding John's intent.

Sun

The sun is utilized by John either as part of cosmic imagery or as signifying the eternal honor and glory of God's presence for eternity. The overwhelming majority of references to the sun in Scripture are literal. Nevertheless, two symbolic images are noticeable. First, the failure of the sun to shine and produce light and heat evoked images of God's judgment that became part of the day of the Lord (Isa 13:10; Ezek 32:7; Joel 2:10; Mark 13:24; Acts 2:20). Second, the glory of God's presence is linked to the sun. Following the day of the Lord the righteous will not need the sun anymore. God will be the everlasting source of light (Isa 24:23; 60:19–20).[199]

"Sun" (*hēlios*) is found thirteen times in Revelation, and may be divided in the same two ways. First, the sun is another stock image of cosmic imagery. In the sixth seal, at the end of history, the "sun turned black like sackcloth" (6:12). John sees an angel "ascending from the rising of the sun" (7:2, ESV).[200] A vision of heaven, taken from Isa 49:10,

---

Reddish, *Revelation*, 176; Sweet, *Revelation*, 167; Walvoord, *Revelation*, 158 .

198. See the entry "Wormwood."

199. Ryken, *Dictionary of Biblical Imagery*, 827; Schley, "Sun," 662–64; William White, "Sun," 632–34.

200. Most English translations have the angel "rising from the east." Its eastern origins could simply be the direction of the sunrise, the source of light (Easley, *Revelation*, 124; Keener, *Revelation*, 234; Kistemaker, *Revelation*, 246), or perhaps the direction of Palestine (Alan Johnson, "Revelation," 13:658; Ladd, *Revelation*, 111; Mounce, *Revelation*, 157; Robert Thomas, *Revelation*, 1:467). A few suggest it alludes to the Messiah entering the temple from the east (Prigent, *Apocalypse*, 281; Roloff, *Revelation*, 96; Sweet, *Revelation*, 148). Many suggest the angel brings divine blessings (Beale, *Revelation*, 408; Beasley-Murray,

includes the sun not beating down on the faithful (7:16). The fourth trumpet shows a third of the sun struck (8:12). The fifth trumpet produces smoke from a gigantic furnace that darkens the sun and sky" (9:2). The fourth angel poured out his bowl on the sun, and the sun was allowed to scorch people with fire (16:8). Finally, John sees "an angel standing in the sun" who calls for the birds to devour the dead at Armageddon (19:17). This image could also fit under the second section since the angel reflects the glory of God. Many commentators, especially dispensationalists, disagree with several of the references above. Instead, they interpret references to the sun more literally.

Second, the sun is used to represent God's glory and majesty. Christ's face was like the sun shining in all its brilliance (1:16). The mighty angel's face was like the sun (10:1). The woman clothed with the sun reflects glory and honor (12:1). In the new Jerusalem, there will be no need for the sun "for the Lord God will give them light" (21:23; 22:5). Thus, John's contrasts shine through once again. The darkening of the sun represents judgment on the wicked. For believers, the lack of a sun reflects the glory and splendor of the eternal source of light.

Revelation, 142; Hailey, *Revelation*, 202; Osborne, *Revelation*, 307; Smalley, *Revelation*, 181; J. C. Thomas, *Apocalypse*, 259). Conversely, some find God's permissive will to judge the peoples of the earth (Blount, *Revelation*, 142; Brighton, *Revelation*, 183). Alongside this latter view, some (Beale *Revelation*, 408; Duvall, *Revelation*, 113) find parody since evil comes from the kings of the east (16:12).

3

Good Places and Bad Places

JOHN USES PLACES AND place names symbolically. They form part of his spiritual geography. Readers must look at John's spiritual map, not a physical map. Most often, places refer to good people or bad people, not geographical locales. Places also reveal John's proclivity for dualism. For every good city there is an evil city. For every heavenly dwelling there is a hellish domain. Once again, decisions must be made for categorizing purposes. Some entries in this chapter could be listed under nature images.

Good Places

The good places mentioned in Revelation are symbols for heaven, God's presence, and God's people. In several ways, this section confirms the title of Robert Gundry's 1987 study: "The New Jerusalem: People as Place, Not Place for People."[1]

Camp of God's People

This phrase symbolizes the Holy City, which in Revelation depicts God's people, the faithful followers of Christ. It is found only in the millennial vision (20:1–21:8). Satan is released and gathers the nations for the end-time battle. "They marched across the breadth of the earth and surrounded the camp of God's people, the city he loves" (20:9). The Greek text literally reads "the camp of the holy ones," and alludes to the twelve tribes encamped around the tabernacle during the wilderness years (Exod 14:19-20; Num 2:1-34). In these camps the *shekinah* glory, the utter presence of the Lord, shone forth. "Camps" may also suggest a military background, but it appears more likely an ecclesiological picture of God's wandering people is intended, protected by his presence, even from an overwhelming invading army (Ezek 38:18–23). The camp is a description of God's people, the church, and serves as a reminder of its spiritual, pilgrim-like nature.[2]

1. Gundry, "New Jerusalem," 254–64.

2. So Beale, *Revelation*, 1026-27; Blount, *Revelation*, 370-71; Caird, *Revelation*, 257; Hughes, *Revelation*, 217; Alan Johnson, "Revelation," 13:773; Koester, *Revelation*, 790; Lupieri, *Apocalypse*, 323;

The "camp" is equated with "the city he loves." Most English translations insert "and" which tends to separate the phrase into two locations—a camp and a city. Only a few versions (CSB, NIV, NJB) recognize the epexegetical nature of the phrase. Most scholars take it this way as well. Smalley writes, it "is probably epexegetic, and explanatory: 'the camp, *that is* the city.'"[3] "The city he loves" summons the phraseology of the OT for Jerusalem, the Holy City of Zion (Ps 78:68; Isa 7:1; Jer 11:15; Zeph 3:17).

Many interpreters literalize the symbol. Patterson, for example, explains, "This city has to be Jerusalem; and although the reference to camp may seem strange, probably the armies of the Lord would be camped around Jerusalem."[4] In Revelation, however, the ideal, true "Jerusalem" is the new Jerusalem, the Holy City that is populated with faithful followers of Christ. This pictures, therefore, the people of God, the true followers of the Lamb who are elsewhere envisioned as the new Jerusalem.[5] Thus, John draws upon rich OT imagery, describing the church, the true people of Israel, as an "encampment" and "the beloved city." When the two images are combined, they symbolize God's people both on the move and also arriving at their destination.[6] John does not intend his metaphor to be literalized into a specific geographical location. The community of the redeemed is the symbol, and is in harmony with previous references to the city (3:12; 11:2, 8).[7] Whenever and wherever God's people are gathered together, "there is the city of God."[8] Temporally, this is an allusion to Armageddon, the final end-time battle depicted elsewhere (16:12–16; 17:12–14; 19:17–21).

Dwelling Place

The dwelling place refers not only to the heavenly temple or Jesus as the temple, but symbolizes believers as well who will enjoy the eternal presence of God in the new heaven and earth. The Bible frequently refers to God residing in heaven, using the imagery of a great patriarch stretching his tent in which to dwell (Ps 104:2–3; Isa 40:22). Moreover, God sits on his heavenly throne and the temple is described as the place of his reign. Thus, the dual concept of temple residence and royal palace are noticeable (Ps 11:4; Heb 8–9).[9] Most occurrences of "dwelling place" in the OT are used figuratively to mean God's temple in Jerusalem (2 Chr 6:54; Ps 74:7). In one passage God becomes the people's dwelling place

---

Mounce, *Revelation*, 373; Reddish, *Revelation*, 387; Resseguie, *Revelation*, 248; Smalley, *Revelation*, 514. For Paul (*Revelation*, 330) it "symbolizes the vulnerability of God's people and their dependence on God for guidance, sustenance, and security."

3. Smalley, *Revelation*, 514; emphasis his. Similarly, Robert Thomas (*Revelation*, 2:425) states it "is a further definition of the camp of the saints."

4. Patterson, *Revelation*, 357. So too Hindson, *Revelation*, 204; Robert Thomas, *Revelation*, 2:425; Walvoord, *Revelation*, 304.

5. Beasley-Murray, *Revelation*, 278. Kistemaker (*Revelation*, 543) agrees: "But here the 'camp of the saints' includes true Christians from all peoples, nations, languages, and races."

6. Walker, *Jesus and the Holy City*, 260–61; Smalley, *Revelation*, 514.

7. Alan Johnson, "Revelation," 13:773.

8. Caird, *Revelation*, 257. See Gundry, "New Jerusalem," 254–64.

9. Hays, *Temple and Tabernacle*, 19.

(Ps 90:1), underscoring the idea of rest and communion.[10] Significantly, this tabernacling presence arrived on the scene with Jesus. "The Word became flesh and made his dwelling (*skenoō*) among us" (John 1:14). Jesus proclaimed himself to be the temple, God with us (Isa 7:14; Matt 1:23; John 2:13–22).

The noun *skēnē* is found twenty times in the NT. Ten times it occurs in Hebrews, and is usually translated as "tabernacle" or "tent." Revelation mentions the word three times (13:6; 15:5; 21:3). In 13:6 and 21:3 it is most often rendered "dwelling" or "dwelling place."[11] In 15:5, the context requires a translation of "tabernacle" or "tent."[12] The verb *skēnoō* is found five times in the NT (John 1:14; Rev 7:15; 12:12; 13:6; 21:3). At 7:15, the context fits best with a translation of "shelter."[13] The final three passages are usually translated as "dwell" or "lives," and accent how John understands the term.

First, a reference to God's dwelling in heaven is found near the beginning of the third interlude. The heavens and those who "dwell" therein rejoice because the devil's time is short (12:12). It is possible that this refers to or at least includes angels.[14] But many scholars understand the phrase to refer to believers.[15] This serves to contrast believers with unbelievers who are consistently referred to as "inhabitants of the earth." The point of the verse is that blaspheming God's people is to blaspheme God's place. The two are identical and synonymous. The equation of the heavenly tabernacle with the saints is essentially the same identification made in 11:1–2 where believers on earth are equated with the temple and the altar.

The second reference is also found in the third interlude. The beast utters blasphemous words against God and his people and slanders "his name and his dwelling place and those who live in heaven" (13:6). Several modern versions correctly place "dwelling place" and "those who dwell in heaven" in direct apposition, thereby equating the two. For example, "It opened its mouth to utter blasphemies against God, blaspheming his name and his dwelling, that is, those who dwell in heaven" (ESV; see also CEB, CSB, GW, NASB, NET, NLT, NRSV, REB).[16]

Third, the conclusion of the thousand years vision confirms this understanding of dwelling place. "And I heard a loud voice from the throne saying, "Look! God's dwelling place is now among the people, and he will dwell with them. They will be his people, and

---

10. Knutson, "Dwell; Dweller; Dwelling," 999–1000; Koosed, "Dwelling Place," 168.

11. For 13:6 there is also "tent" (GW), "heavenly Tent" (NJB), "tabernacle" (NASB), and "where he lives" (GNT, NCV). For 21:3 there is "God's home" (CEV, GNT, NLT, NRSV), "lives" (GW), "residence" (NET), and "tabernacle" (NASB).

12. See the entry "Tabernacle of the Covenant Law."

13. For 7:15, there is also "dwell" (NKJV), "tabernacle" (NASB), "tent" (CEV, GW, NJB), 'protect' (GNT, REB), and "be present" (NCV).

14. So Brighton, *Revelation*, 345; Easley, *Revelation*, 228; Fee, *Revelation*, 182; Koester, *Revelation*, 565; Michaels, *Revelation*, 159; Mounce, *Revelation*, 250; Roloff, *Revelation*, 158; J. C. Thomas, *Apocalypse*, 374.

15. So Beale, *Revelation*, 697; Blount, *Revelation*, 239; Caird, *Revelation*, 166–67; Farmer, *Revelation*, 95; Ladd, *Revelation*, 180; Morris, *Revelation*, 158; Osborne, *Revelation*, 500; Reddish, *Revelation*, 254; Smalley, *Revelation*, 341; Robert Thomas, *Revelation*, 2:162–63.

16. Beale (*Temple and the Church's Mission*, 277) states that John picks up on the synonymous use of "sanctuary" and "hosts" in Dan 8:10–13.

God himself will be with them and be their God" (21:3). In this statement, the marvelous promises of the OT are now fulfilled. God declared in Leviticus, "I will put my dwelling place among you, and I will not abhor you. I will walk among you and be your God, and you will be my people" (Lev 26:11–12; see also Exod 29:45; Jer 31:33; Ezek 37:26–27; Zech 2:10–11; 2 Cor 6:16). God's dwelling place is not in some far off distant heaven, high and lifted up above his people. He tabernacles among them.[17] The dwelling place, then, is no longer a building or a location—it is an eternal sphere, relationship, and presence. God is tabernacle. He spreads his tent of presence and protection over his people. They will live in harmony and unity forever.

Holy City

The Holy City represents the Christian community on earth and in the new Jerusalem, the place where God's people are and God's presence dwells. It contrasts with Babylon the Great, the evil city. In Revelation, there are good cities and bad cities. The tale of two cities comprises a significant portion of Revelation (17:1–22:9). John sets up a comparison to contrast the two cities.[18] Kistemaker summarizes the career of the Holy City. In the OT, Jerusalem is called the Holy City, the place where God chose to dwell with his people (Ps 48; Isa 48:2; Dan 9:24; Neh 11:1). Jerusalem is also called the Holy City during Jesus' ministry (Matt 4:5; 27:53). At Pentecost, however, God began to dwell not in Jerusalem but in his church (Acts 2:1–4, 38–39). The term "Holy City" is not used again until Revelation when John describes the new Jerusalem as the Holy City (21:2, 10; 22:19). Kistemaker concludes, "the NT shows that earthly Jerusalem lost its claim to be called holy city when the Holy Spirit changed his dwelling place from Jerusalem to the hearts and bodies of God's people, the saints (1 Cor 6:19)."[19]

The Holy City is used dualistically not only between itself and Babylon the Great. It also contrasts the earthly Holy City (11:2; 20:9) and the heavenly Holy City (3:12; 14:20; 21:2–22:19). However, this is not a geographical location. The Holy City refers to God's people and God's presence on earth and in heaven.

The earthly Holy City, therefore, is mentioned twice. First, gentiles will trample the Holy City for forty-two months (11:2). This pictures the people of God who represent the presence of God on earth. They are the believers throughout the generations who face persecution, and particularly near the end of history. The church will be protected and enabled to carry out her mission and complete it.[20] The Holy City serves as one of five complementary descriptions of the earthly Christian community, the new people of

---

17. Osborne, *Revelation*, 734. This understanding is confirmed in Gundry, "New Jerusalem," 254–64.

18. The literature on "city" in Revelation continues to grow, underscoring its significance. See Bauckham, *Theology of Revelation*, 129–32; Campbell, "Antithetical Feminine-Urban Imagery," 81–108; Gill, "City, Biblical Theology of," 713–15; Räpple, *Metaphor of the City in the Apocalypse*; Rasmussen, "City, theology of," 917; Rossing, *Choice between the Two Cities*; Ryken, *Dictionary of Biblical Imagery*, 150–54; Zerbe, "Revelation's Expose of Two Cities," 46–60.

19. Kistemaker, "Temple in the Apocalypse," 437.

20. Brighton, *Revelation*, 289.

God in 11:1–2, including the temple, altar, worshippers, and the outer court.[21] Second, a reference to the earthly Jerusalem is found in the phrase "the camp of God's people, the city he loves" (20:9). As with 11:2, this pictures the faithful Christian community under suffering. The image stresses their pilgrim-like nature again as God's people, and alludes to their persecution, especially near the end of history.[22]

The heavenly Holy City is mentioned several times. John pictures the city as "the city of my God, the new Jerusalem" (3:12). The wicked are "outside the city" (14:20). This is a bad place. The phrase means outside the Holy City, the new Jerusalem, and refers to the final judgment of unbelievers.[23] Lastly, in the final two chapters of Revelation there are twelve references to "the city," "Holy City," and "new Jerusalem." "Holy City" is referred to three times (21:2, 10; 22:19). Each one of these references provides details on the heavenly Holy City. Strikingly, the promise of people and presence, not place, is emphasized.[24]

Therefore, there are only two cities in Revelation. One is evil and the other one is good. One is the city of Satan where the beast and the great prostitute reign while the other one is the city of God inhabited by God, the Lamb, and his people. The evil city is called by many names, including Sodom, Egypt, Babylon the Great, the great city, and the city where our Lord was crucified. The good city is known by many names, too, such as new Jerusalem, the Holy City, the city of my God, Mount Zion, the camp of God's people, and the city he loves. But neither the good nor the evil city is a geographical locale. The evil city is composed of the idolatrous, unrepentant, evil people inspired by the devil who populate the entire earth. Conversely, the good city is not a place, but a people—faithful believers who follow the Lamb wherever he goes, and serve as his witnesses throughout the earth.

Kingdom of God

The kingdom of God reflects inaugurated eschatology. The kingdom was launched with Christ's first coming and consummates at his second coming. The kingdom is delivered to the saints who, as a kingdom of priests, are witnesses of the gospel. The kingdom of God is a central theme of Scripture. God is the king of Israel (Exod 15:18; Isa 43:15) and the earth (2 Kgs 19:15; Jer 46:18). Yet this present reign gives way to a glorious future reign (Isa 24:23; Zech 14:9). The kingdom of God appears over a hundred times in the NT. By Jesus' day, the hope for such a kingdom was relegated to the end of the age. But Jesus asserted the kingdom of God arrived with him (Mark 1:15; Luke 17:21), and was inaugurated

21. Beale, *Revelation*, 570–71. Preterists and futurists customarily understand the Holy City to be limited to earthly Jerusalem of the first century (Chilton, *Days of Vengeance*, 274) or the last days of earth history (Robert Thomas, *Revelation*, 2:84). A better understanding is to see the Holy City as one of John's various symbols for God's people.

22. See the entry "Camp of God's People."

23. See the entry "Outside the City." As Osborne (*Revelation*, 555) states, "Thus, the judgment of unbelievers 'outside the city' emphasizes their absolute rejection by God and is in contrast with the blessed state of the faithful."

24. See Beale, *Revelation*, 568–71; Minear, *Images of the Church*, 91–96; Walker, *Jesus and the Holy City*, 246–50.

through his miracles, teachings, death, and resurrection. Yet it will not be fully consummated until his return. This already-not-yet understanding that the Gospels portray is confirmed in Paul's letters. The kingdom is a present (Rom 14:17) and future reality (1 Cor 6:9–10), and both at the same time (1 Cor 15:24).[25]

John sustains the already-not-yet aspect in Revelation. "Kingdom" (*basileia*) is found nine times. Its dualistic nature is apparent in that the first five references are good (1:6, 9; 5:10; 11:15; 12:10) while the last four are evil (16:10; 17:12, 17, 18). This confirms that the devil remains a threat until the eschaton. Nevertheless, the earthly kingdom of the great prostitute and the beast will fall.

By contrast, Christ has delivered his kingdom over to his followers to be a kingship of priests (1 Pet 2:9–10).[26] Through inaugurated eschatology believers serve and reign with Christ now and forever.[27] The saints' reign may appear embattled and persecuted, but the ultimate victory is assured. The beast and his minions might kill the body but cannot kill the soul. Because this is true, believers should live victoriously now (1 John 4:4).

Mount Zion

Mount Zion is a symbol of the new Jerusalem, which arrives at the eschaton, emphasizing the victory, vindication, and security found in the eternal presence of God and the Lamb with their people. "Mount Zion" is found thirty-one times in Scripture, but only twice in the NT (Heb 12:22; Rev 14:1). In the OT, Zion was a metaphor for the earthly, historical city of Jerusalem. "But behind this metaphor lies a complex cluster of interlocking themes of immense theological significance."[28] Some of the connected concepts include the temple, covenant people of God, Davidic kingship that leads to the Messiah, and the renewed heaven and earth. The prophets alternated between references to historical Zion under judgment and the glorified Zion of the last days (Isa 2:2–4; 65:17–25; 66:1–24; Ezek 47:1–12; Mic 4:1–2).[29]

Geographically, Mount Zion referred to the fortress-like outcropping of rock that David captured and which eventually became Jerusalem (2 Sam 5:7; 1 Kgs 8:1). Later, the temple was built on it. Over time, Mount Zion moved from a reference to the hilly area of southeast Jerusalem to the temple mount, then to the whole city of Jerusalem, to the whole land of Judah, and then the whole Israelite nation.[30] God declared that he would install his "anointed one" (Ps 2:2: LXX has "his Christ"), his king, on "Zion," God's holy mount (Pss 2:6; 87:1–3). Zion came to signify, therefore, not only the temple mount but

---

25. Duling, "Kingdom of God," 49–69; Hays, Duvall, and Pate, *Dictionary of Prophecy*, 243–45; I. H. Marshall, "Kingdom of God," 911–22; Ryken, *Dictionary of Biblical Imagery*, 478–81.

26. See the entry "Priests."

27. Dispensationalists disagree. The references to the kingdom are promises that specifically refer to a future millennial kingdom on earth. See Patterson, *Revelation*, 252–53; Robert Thomas, *Revelation*, 2:105–6, 133; and Walvoord, *Revelation*, 184, 193.

28. Ryken, *Dictionary of Biblical Imagery*, 980.

29. Ibid., 980–81.

30. Alan Johnson, "Revelation," 13:719.

the location where the Messiah would stand to deliver his people and gather them to himself (Joel 2:32; Ps 48:1–11; Isa 2:2; Mic 4:1–8; *4 Ezra* 13:35–40; *2 Bar.* 40:1–2).[31]

John fulfills these themes when he states, "Then I looked, and there before me was the Lamb, standing on Mount Zion, and with him 144,000 who had his name and his Father's name written on their foreheads" (14:1). Many interpreters maintain that John's mention of Mount Zion is an earthly reference to the geographical location across the Kidron Valley in Jerusalem. After all, its high elevation assures that everyone will see Jesus at his second coming. The phrase "sound from heaven" favors an earthly view as well.[32] On the other hand, numerous Bible students picture Mount Zion as a reference to the heavenly throne room. After all, the context mentions the four living creatures and the twenty-four elders who are always before the throne.[33]

It appears better to allow both emphases to work. A third interpretation, then, equates earthly Mount Zion with the new Jerusalem which "comes down from heaven" (21:2) at the return of Christ. It becomes a part of the new creation after the old has passed away. It is part of the already-not-yet attitude the rest of the NT supports. The writer of Hebrews adopts this view of the inauguration of the end times, applying it to first-century believers: "But you have come to Mount Zion, to the city of the living God, the heavenly Jerusalem. You have come to thousands upon thousands of angels in joyful assembly, to the church of the firstborn, whose names are written in heaven" (Heb 12:22–23).[34]

Like other topographical features throughout Revelation, Mount Zion is a spiritual locale. The mountain is neither in heaven nor on earth, but is "nowhere and everywhere at the same time."[35] Thus, the coming ultimate city of God has already invisibly, proleptically arrived in this present age, and because of Christ, believers presently participate in it. John's vision of the triumphal Lamb standing on Mount Zion, along with the hundred and forty-four thousand, pictures the consummative arrival of Christ at the second coming. Mount Zion becomes yet one more majestic symbol of the new heaven and new earth, the Holy City, the new Jerusalem, the new garden of Eden, all emphasizing the complete victory and vindication of God, and the promise of his forever presence.

31. Brighton, *Revelation*, 364–65; Osborne, *Revelation*, 525.

32. Aune, *Revelation*, 2:803; Blount, *Revelation*, 266; Charles, *Revelation*, 2:4–5; Hughes, *Revelation*, 157; Kistemaker, *Revelation*, 369; Krodel, *Revelation*, 261; Michaels, *Revelation*, 168; Mulholland, *Revelation*, 240; Patterson, *Revelation*, 285; Roloff, *Revelation*, 170; Swete, *Apocalypse*, 177; Wall, *Revelation*, 179; Walvoord, *Revelation*, 214; Wilcock, *I Saw Heaven Opened*, 132.

33. Easley, *Revelation*, 246; Fee, *Revelation*, 190; Hendriksen, *More than Conquerors*, 151; Kiddle, *Revelation*, 262–63; Dennis Johnson, *Triumph of the Lamb*, 201; Morris, *Revelation*, 170; Mounce, *Revelation*, 264–65; Paul, *Revelation*, 244; Sweet, *Revelation*, 221.

34. So Beale, *Revelation*, 732; Beasley-Murray, *Revelation*, 222; Boxall, *Revelation*, 200; Alan Johnson, "Revelation," 13:720; Keener, *Revelation*, 369; Ladd, *Revelation*, 189–90; Osborne, *Revelation*, 525; Resseguie, *Revelation*, 194; Smalley, *Revelation*, 354. Likewise, Robert Thomas (*Revelation*, 2:189–91) understands it more in terms of a future millennial reign.

35. Boxall, *Revelation*, 200.

New Heaven and New Earth

The new heaven and new earth refers to the renovation, renewal, transfiguration, and trans-
formation of the existing universe at the end of history. Ultimately, it symbolizes the eternal
presence of God and the Lamb with the saints. The new heaven and new earth is synonymous with Mount Zion, camp of God's people, the new Jerusalem, and the Holy City.
That is, they all represent the faithful in eternal presence and fellowship with God and the
Lamb. John sees "a new heaven and a new earth, for the first heaven and the first earth
had passed away" (21:1). Although the expression is mentioned only here, it anticipates
his vision of the new Jerusalem (21:9–22:9).

The imagery forms part of the common motif in apocalyptic literature of cosmic
upheaval that commences at the end of history. However, OT prophetic and apocalyptic
literature reveals two different ideas. Several writings suggest destruction of the whole (or
at least part) cosmos and its replacement (Isa 65:17; 66:22; *1 En.* 45:4–5; 72:1; 83:3; 91:16;
4 Ezra 7:31; *2 Bar.* 44:12; *Jub.* 1:29; *Sib. Or.* 3:83). By contrast, other writings—sometimes
the same writing—suggest a renewal of the cosmos (*1 En.* 45:4; 91:16; *4 Ezra* 7:29–32; *2*
Bar. 32:6; 44:9–12).[36] These two views carry into the NT as commentators debate what
"passes away," "disappears," "liberates," and "destroys" mean (Matt 5:18; Mark 13:31; Luke
16:17; Rom 8:19–22; 2 Pet 3:10–13; 1 John 2:17).

The same choices are presented in Revelation. Many scholars opt for destruction
and replacement.[37] The present physical earth and sky are destroyed and replaced. Destruction is pictured (6:12–14; 20:11) and a brand new heaven and earth takes its place
(21:1). Destruction is further supported by 2 Pet 3:10: "The heavens will disappear with
a roar; the elements will be destroyed by fire, and the earth and everything done in it will
be laid bare."

Nonetheless, numerous scholars make a case for renovation over replacement.[38]
For these supporters emphasis is made on spiritual renewal and a purified world. The
second coming does not annihilate creation; it fulfills creation. Just as a believer's body
is changed from perishable to imperishable in the eschaton (1 Cor 15:35–58), so too the

---

36. Hays, Duvall, and Pate, *Dictionary of Prophecy*, 306–7; Hylen, "New Heaven, New Earth," 263–64;
Watson, "New Earth, New Heaven," 1094–95.

37. Aune, *Revelation*, 3:1117; Beasley-Murray, *Revelation*, 307; Charles, *Revelation*, 2:204; Fekkes,
Isaiah and Prophetic Traditions, 228–29; Hindson, *Revelation*, 215; Keener, *Revelation*, 485; Ladd, *Rev-*
elation, 276; LaHaye, *Revelation Unveiled*, 356; Michaels, *Revelation*, 233; Osborne, *Revelation*, 730;
Patterson, *Revelation*, 361; Rissi, *Future of the World*, 54; Roloff, *Revelation*, 235; Stefanovic, *Revelation*,
586; J. C. Thomas, *Apocalypse*, 619; Robert Thomas, *Revelation*, 2:439; Walvoord, *Revelation*, 311. Dispensationalist Lindsey (*New World Coming*, 287) theorizes a quadrillion megaton explosion will destroy
the earth and pave the way for a new one.

38. Bauckham, *Theology of Revelation*, 49; Beale, *Revelation*, 1041; Blount, *Revelation*, 376; Boring,
Revelation, 220; Boxall, *Revelation*, 293; Brighton, *Revelation*, 631; Caird, *Revelation*, 265; Dumbrell, *End*
of the Beginning, 166–74; Duvall, *Revelation*, 281; Farmer, *Revelation*, 134; Harrington, *Revelation*, 207;
Alan Johnson, "Revelation," 13:778; Kistemaker, *Revelation*, 554; Morris, *Revelation*, 236; Mounce, *Rev-*
elation, 380; Mulholland, *Revelation*, 315; Murphy, *Fallen Is Babylon*, 407; Paul, *Revelation*, 338; Prigent,
Apocalypse, 591; Smalley, *Revelation*, 524; Stefanovic, *Revelation*, 587; Sweet, *Revelation*, 297; Wilcock,
I Saw Heaven Opened, 198. Stephens (*Annihilation or Renewal*, 171–257) produces a full-fledged study
that supports a renewed creation, not a destroyed and replaced creation. See also Mathewson, *New*
Heaven and a New Earth, 37–39, 186–215.

world is changed. The common apocalyptic principle of a new Eden reveals the end is like the beginning (Ezek 36:33–35; *1 En.* 23, 32). Concerning the 2 Pet 3 passage, the strong verbs "destroy," "burn," and "melt" reflect apocalyptic language of cleansing judgment. Like the flood "destroyed" the earth, so will the second coming "destroy" the earth. Gold is burned and melted (purified) to rid its impurities.[39]

In addition, if renovation is correct, then the appeal toward contemporary environmental concerns is more compelling. Numerous studies have been produced on Revelation's challenge to care for the environment.[40] Richard Middleton explains that "holistic eschatology" means consummate redemption includes the renewal of human cultural life on earth. It is the reversal of damage done by sin. Thus, Middleton accents ethics as well as ecology and eschatology: "To focus our expectation on an otherworldly salvation has the potential to dissipate our resistance to societal evil and the dedication needed to work for the redemptive transformation of this world."[41]

Thus, a radically transformed world at the eschaton is the best option. The words and phrases that infer total destruction of the cosmos should take into account the idea of a transformation that accompanies purging destruction. It is renewal of God's original intent. This view also challenges the saints on the ethical and moral responsibility to care for the present earth and its social ills.

New Jerusalem

The new Jerusalem is the heavenly city of the new heaven and new earth which stresses people over place, and thus represents the intimate presence and fellowship that believers will eternally enjoy with God. The tale of two cities comprises a significant portion of Revelation (17:1–22:9). John sets up a comparison to contrast Babylon the Great to the new Jerusalem.[42] The "new Jerusalem" is found only twice in the Bible (3:12; 21:2) yet is described in detail in chapters 21–22. Its concept developed out of postexilic prophetic expectations of the restoration of Jerusalem and the return of God to his temple. The restoration of Jerusalem was a focus of numerous promises (Isa 2, 49, 52, 54, 60–62; 65; Jer 31; Mic 4; Zech 14). However, the excitement of the actual restoration during the Persian Period degenerated into disillusionment. As a result, later Jewish literature replaced

---

39. See Bauckham, *Theology of Revelation*, 49–50; Hays, Duvall, and Pate, *Dictionary of Prophecy*, 448–50; Heide, "What Is New," 46–55. Some exegetes refuse to be placed in the renewal or the replacement category, including Easley (*Revelation*, 394), Koester (*Revelation*, 803), Resseguie (*Revelation*, 252), Skaggs and Benham (*Revelation*, 213), and Witherington (*Revelation*, 253), who asserts "the symbolic nature of this material prevents one from pressing the issue."

40. Bredin, "God the Carer," 76–86; Cate, "How Green Was John's World," 145–55; Heide, "What Is New," 37–56; Rossing, "River of Life," 487–99; Woods, "Seven Bowls of Wrath," 64–75; Zerbe, "Ecology according to the New Testament," 15–26.

41. Middleton, *New Heaven and New Earth*, 237. Middleton's preliminary work on this topic is "New Heaven and New Earth: The Case for a Holistic Reading," 73–97.

42. Reddish (*Revelation*, 405) provides a handy graph of Babylon contrasted with new Jerusalem with fourteen characteristics each. Hock ("From Babel to the New Jerusalem," 109–18) stresses the contrast between Babel (manmade, human initiative, human accomplishment, leads to dispersion) and the new Jerusalem (God-made, initiative, accomplished, leads to unity).

physical expectations of restoration with supernatural transformation (Tob 13:8–18; *T. Dan* 5:12–13; *Sib. Or.* 5:420–427; *1 En.* 90:28–29). Other writers envisioned a Jerusalem from heaven which would replace the earthly Jerusalem (*4 Ezra* 7:26; 10:25–28; *2 Bar.* 4; 32:1–4).[43]

The idea of Jerusalem in heaven is adopted by NT writers (Gal 4:26; Heb 11:10–16; 12:22) and finds its ultimate fulfillment in Revelation. The first mention of new Jerusalem is the promise extended to the Philadelphians. "The one who is victorious I will make a pillar in the temple of my God. Never again will they leave it. I will write on them the name of my God and the name of the city of my God, the new Jerusalem, which is coming down out of heaven from my God; and I will also write on them my new name" (3:12). All four symbols in this verse (pillar, name of God, name of city of God, Christ's new name) are different aspects of the same promise. The person who conquers receives as a reward eternal fellowship and identification with Christ. Second, John states "I saw the Holy City, the new Jerusalem, coming down out of heaven from God, prepared as a bride beautifully dressed for her husband" (21:2). John draws from Isa 62:1–5, where a new and intimate marriage relationship that Israel will enjoy with God is enlarged to Christ the bridegroom and his bride at the consummation of time. The new Jerusalem completes the transformation from the old order to the new, symbolized through marital imagery. The new creation as a new, invisible and heavenly Jerusalem was inaugurated at the cross and now receives fulfillment here in chapter 21.[44]

Interpreters are divided on whether the new Jerusalem symbolizes a place or symbolizes the saints. Those who express or assume a geographical location tend to find literalness in all of Revelation's symbols.[45] Many interpreters, however, stress the idea of saints over place. The new Jerusalem is the church, composed of a body of believers in eternity.[46] Gundry provides the fullest development on this theme. He states that "John is not describing the eternal dwelling place of the saints; he is describing them and them alone."[47]

A few scholars suggest that both concepts of people and place should be kept in mind.[48] Beale adds an emphasis on God's presence. The image of the city is figurative, "representing the fellowship of God with his people . . . [49] Similarly, Smalley does not see the perfected church but rather stresses the new Jerusalem as the new covenant—the

---

43. Hays, Duvall, and Pate, *Dictionary of Prophecy*, 309–11; Rosscup, "New Jerusalem," 461–62; Ryken, *Dictionary of Biblical Imagery*, 436–37; Watson, "New Jerusalem," 1095–96.

44. Beale, *Revelation*, 1044.

45. Lindsey, *New World Coming*, 289; Patterson, *Revelation*, 363; Ryrie, *Revelation*, 138; Robert Thomas, *Revelation*, 2:441–42; Walvoord, *Revelation*, 313.

46. Bauckham, *Theology of Revelation*, 126–28; Brighton, *Revelation*, 595–96; Hays, Duvall, and Pate, *Dictionary of Prophecy*, 311; Hughes, *Revelation*, 222; Kistemaker, *Revelation*, 556; Mounce, *Revelation*, 382; Michaels, *Revelation*, 235; Mulholland, *Revelation*, 316; Prigent, *Apocalypse*, 595; Skaggs and Benham, *Revelation*, 215.

47. Gundry, "New Jerusalem," 256.

48. So Ladd, *Revelation*, 276; Osborne, *Revelation*, 733.

49. Beale, *Revelation*, 1045.

relationship between God and people.[50] Thus, the idea of people, place, and the presence of God is at work. William Dumbrell summarizes that the new Jerusalem "asserts the fact of final Kingdom of God rule, combining people, place, and divine presence."[51]

"People" and "presence" should be kept at the forefront of defining the new Jerusalem because the mention of "place" invariably leads to limitations. John has enlarged, universalized, and spiritualized the new Jerusalem far beyond the limitations of any spatial concepts. It can no longer be held to measurable statistics. It is universal—the people of God are with their God forever.

Paradise of God

This is a symbol for the regained garden of Eden—the new heaven and the new earth— the eternal dwelling place and perpetual fellowship of God with his people. "Paradise" is a loan word from Persia. It expanded its meaning from "enclosure" to "park" to "beautiful garden." The LXX adopted it to translate the Hebrew word for "garden" in Gen 2–3. Thus, paradise embraces strong allusions to the garden of Eden. In apocalyptic literature, paradise is sometimes perceived as the intermediate abode of the righteous (*1 En.* 37–70) or an eschatological hiding place for the righteous (*2 En.* 8). Other Jewish apocalypses mention a final age will be characterized by the blessed state that characterized Eden (*Apoc. Ab.* 21). This influence carries over to the NT's three occurrences of the word.[52] Jesus tells the repentant sinner on the cross that he will experience paradise (Luke 23:43). Paul refers to a vision of paradise (2 Cor 12:4). The last reference is found in Revelation and alludes not only to Genesis but to Ezekiel (28:13; 31:8–9; 36:35). The glorified Christ extends a promise to the victorious in Ephesus: "To the one who is victorious, I will give the right to eat from the tree of life, which is in the paradise of God" (2:7). The equation of paradise with the tree of life confirms both a connection to the garden of Eden as well as the same understanding. Some Bible versions make a clearer connection with "God's wonderful garden" (CEV) or "garden of God" (GNT, NABR, NCV, REB). Thus, the victorious in Christ will be rewarded with a blessing of eternal life originally intended at creation yet never realized due to the fall of humanity. Paradise then is a symbol of heaven, the dwelling place of God and his people. The paradise once lost will be regained in the new heaven and new earth.[53]

Bad Places

Bad places are scattered throughout Revelation. Readers must not limit them to actual locales. Instead, they symbolize hell, the evil world, and wicked unbelievers.

---

50. Smalley, *Revelation*, 535–36.

51. Dumbrell, *End of the Beginning*, 31. So too Koester, *Revelation*, 828–29.

52. Charlesworth, "Paradise," 154–55; Gordon, "Paradise," 660–61; Gordon Lewis, "Paradise," 665–67.

53. Hemer, *Letters to the Seven Churches*, 50; Smalley, *Revelation*, 64.

Abyss

The Abyss is the interim prison house for evil spirits and the devil. This derives from imagery originally connected with the bottomless, immeasurable depths of the ocean (Gen 1:2). Later, it became an idiom for the realm of the dead (Pss 33:7; 63:9; 71:20). Apocalyptic literature connected it with a "pit" or "prison house" where fallen angels were held (*1 En.* 10:4–6; 18:9–16; *Jub.* 5:3–11). In its two usages outside of Revelation, the NT presents the Abyss as the place of the dead (Rom 10:7) and as the place of evil spirits (Luke 8:31). Other biblical connections are 2 Pet 2:4 and Jude 6 where "these he has kept in darkness, bound with everlasting chains for judgment on the great Day."[54]

Several modern versions translate "Abyss" as "bottomless pit" (ESV, GW, NLT, NRSV) or "deep pit" (CEV). Connected closely to the Abyss is the "shaft" (*phrear*) found four times at 9:1–2. Other English offerings for shaft include "tunnel" (CEV) and "deep hole" (NCV). The coupling of the word "shaft" with "Abyss" lends support to the idea of its fathomless depth. John uses the word Abyss exactly seven times (9:1, 2, 11; 11:7; 17:8; 20:1, 3) which numerically symbolizes total completion and fullness on the topic.[55]

John's imagery builds on what has been written before, and so the Abyss is presented as a prison house for evil angels. The word also serves as a strong emotive metaphor of the devil's spiritual realm.[56] It forms part of John's spiritual geography and is intended to be contrasted with its opposite—heaven.[57]

Smoke rises when the angel opens the Abyss (9:2). It has an evil angel over it called Abaddon and Apollyon (9:11). From the Abyss the beast surfaces and attacks the two witnesses (11:7). If the Abyss emphasizes the abode of evil angels, then proof is found in that the beast is supernaturally empowered by Satan. Nevertheless, the beast from the Abyss will go to its destruction (17:8). The final reference to the Abyss (20:1–3) begins with the descent of an angel holding the key to the Abyss along with a great chain. He seizes the dragon and binds him for one thousand years, casting him into the Abyss, to be set free for a short time afterward. The Abyss, then, is not the final "resting" place for the devil and his angels. For premillennialists, the Abyss holds the dragon for one thousand years of a millennial reign on earth before being set loose again to raise a second round of end-time havoc. For amillennialists, the binding of Satan reflects the interadvental age. For them, Satan was "bound" at the resurrection of Christ but will be loosed near the end of history. Either way, the final stop for the devil, his angels, his wicked followers, as well as death and Hades is the lake of fire (19:20; 20:11–15; 21:8).

---

54. Grether, "Abyss," 49; Osborne, *Revelation*, 362–63.

55. Bauckham (*Climax of Prophecy*, 35–36) suggests the number seven in this case is coincidental. However, its seven occurrences combined with four related words ("shaft") is a common pattern of John's (e.g. "great" earthquake and "sharp" sickle).

56. So Beale, *Revelation*, 987–88; Rotz, *Revelation*, 139.

57. Resseguie, *Revelation Unsealed*, 88–89.

Armageddon

Armageddon refers to the one, final, consummative battle at the end of history that immediately precedes the second coming. The great day of God often includes allusions to a battle where God decisively judges the unrighteous, and often includes a location (Isa 13:1–13; 34:1–17; 63:1–19; Ezek 38:2–8; 39:2; Joel 2:11, 31; 3:2; Mic 4:6–12; Zeph 1:14–16; Zech 12:3–11; 14:13–14; *4 Ezra* 13:8–11; *1 En.* 56:7; *Sib. Or.* 3:663–68). John likewise utilizes the final battle motif.[58] Armageddon is mentioned by name in the Bible only once (Rev 16:16). Demonic spirits assemble the kings of the world for the battle on the great day of God Almighty. The location of the battle in Hebrew is called "Armageddon."[59] Many attempts have been made to decode this unique word. Most agree with a definition of "mountain of Megiddo." Megiddo was associated with important OT battles (Judg 5:19; 2 Kgs 9:27; Zech 12:11).[60] But since there is no mountain at Megiddo, various interpretations have arisen. Osborne provides a helpful list of eight proposed solutions, divided equally into geographically-based interpretations and etymologically-based interpretations.[61] In the end, all attempts of the actual meaning of the word whether literal or symbolic fails to satisfy. Therefore, Osborne, followed by many others, opts for a more general reference, building upon the OT connection of Megiddo with warfare.[62]

Revelation presents numerous images of Armageddon. In fact, there are seven allusive portrayals of this end-time battle. Each depiction is located near the end of an

58. Schnabel (*40 Questions*, 234–35) supplies a chart on OT prophecies of a final battle and their match in Revelation under the rubrics of date, location, phenomena, enemy, weapons, God's army, God's action, and the enemy's defeat.

59. "Armageddon" is spelled and pronounced differently in Greek manuscripts. The best reading, reflected in UBS5, is *Harmagedōn*. Metzger (*Textual Commentary*, 681) mentions several other variant spellings. This variety makes its way into English Bibles. Most versions settle on "Armageddon." There is also "Armagedon" (CEV, HCSB), but closer to the Greek pronunciation is "Harmagedon" (CEB, NRSV) and Har-Magedon (NASB).

60. John Day ("Origin of Armageddon," 315–26) is the first to connect Armageddon to a conflation of "Megiddo" in Zech 12:11 and "mountains of Israel" in Ezek 38–39. Many scholars agree with Day, including Beale (*Revelation*, 840–41), Boxall (*Revelation*, 233–34), Koester (*Revelation*, 660), Osborne (*Revelation*, 596), Resseguie (*Revelation*, 214), and Schnabel (*40 Questions*, 233). However, Jauhiainen ("OT Background to *Armageddon* Revisited," 381–93) disagrees, finding Isa 13 and Jer 50–51 to be its etymological background. J. C. Thomas (*Apocalypse*, 486) notes both emphases and rightly suggests that the original hearers would recall a variety of images converging at this point.

61. Osborne, *Revelation*, 594–96. Other lists are found in Aune, *Revelation*, 2:898–99; Koester, *Revelation*, 660–61; Robert Thomas, *Revelation*, 2:268–70. Paulien ("Armageddon," 394–95) offers a short history of interpretation. A few exegetes take Armageddon to refer to past events, not the second coming. Chilton (*Days of Vengeance*, 412) and Russell (*Parousia*, 479) envision the Waterloo of apostate Israel in AD 70, delivered at Mount Carmel. Clark (*Message from Patmos*, 103) chooses Rome in the fifth century.

62. So Aune, *Revelation*, 2:898; Beasley-Murray, *Revelation*, 245; Brighton, *Revelation*, 423; Hughes, *Revelation*, 178; Alan Johnson, "Revelation," 13:734–35; Kistemaker, *Revelation*, 453; Ladd, *Revelation*, 216; Morris, *Revelation*, 194; Mounce, *Revelation*, 302; Mulholland, *Revelation*, 271; Reddish, *Revelation*, 314; Smalley, *Revelation*, 412–13; Witherington, *Revelation*, 211. Resseguie (*Revelation Unsealed*, 82) explains, "None of these suggestions is satisfactory, for they attempt to locate Harmageddon on a physical map, whereas John has in mind a spiritual map. The battle takes place on a mountain because the mountain is a natural location for the divine/human encounter, and therefore is the appropriate arena for the final battle between good and evil, God and Satan, Christ and Antichrist."

individual vision. Armageddon is echoed in the sixth seal (6:15), and developed more in the sixth trumpet (9:14–19), the third interlude (14:19–20), the sixth bowl (16:12–16), the fall of Babylon vision (17:12–14), the rider on the white horse vision (19:17–21), and the thousand years vision (20:7–10).[63] The references are not simple repetition but information elaborated on from different angles and audiences.[64]

Armageddon is first and foremost a symbol. It is an event, not a place. It is a horrific metaphor, not an actual geographical location.[65] The different locations for the final, end-time battle from the OT have been universalized by John. It now covers all locations and blankets the whole earth. For example, just as the temple of Jerusalem has been expanded and universalized to be the church over the earth, so too has the end-time battle been expanded and universalized into one final, end-time event that encompasses the world. This study, therefore, supports the view of one end-time battle depicted by John in several of his visions, offering numerous points of views and angles, including participants, location, and accompanying descriptions.[66] Thus, like other place names found in Revelation (Babylon, Egypt, Sodom, Euphrates), Armageddon does not indicate a geographic locale. John is utilizing imagery that is spiritual not physical. It is a symbol for the final battle.

Babylon the Great

This title evokes the OT's metaphor of an ungodly city, refers to Rome for John's original audience, and ultimately symbolizes unredeemed humanity and the evil worldwide system that is opposed to God and his people, and will be eternally judged at the end of history. Babylon the Great is the great city, the great prostitute, and the woman sitting on a scarlet

---

63. "Battle" (*polemos*) occurs nine times in Revelation (9:7, 9; 11:7; 12:7, 17; 13:7; 16:14; 19:19; 20:8). Five times it refers to the final battle (11:7; 13:7; 16:14; 19:19; 20:8).

64. Mathewson ("Re-Examination of the Millennium," 240–42) connects 19:17–21 with 20:7–10. Fowler White ("Reexamining the Evidence," 325–30) connects 16:12–16 and 19:17–21 with 20:7–10. Bauckham (*Climax of Prophecy*, 19), Beale (*Revelation*, 400), Boone ("Five Armageddons of Revelation," 109–10), and Osborne (*Revelation*, 294) connect 6:15 to 19:18. Beale (*Revelation*, 513), Brighton (*Revelation*, 248), Caird (*Revelation*, 122), and Osborne (*Revelation*, 384) connect 9:14–19 to 16:12–21 and19:17–21. Bauckham (*Climax of Prophecy*, 19), Patterson (*Revelation*, 295), and Robert Thomas (*Revelation*, 2:220) connect 14:19–20 with 19:17–21. Bauckham (*Climax of Prophecy*, 20), Beasley-Murray (*Revelation*, 258), Brighton (*Revelation*, 453), and Kistemaker (*Revelation*, 476) connect 17:14 with 19:14.

65. Some dispensationalist interpreters (Hindson, "Armageddon, Battle of," 57; Lindsey, *New World Coming*, 223) do not see a climactic, isolated battle but rather an extended military campaign that extends through the final three and a half years of history. LaHaye (*Revelation Unveiled*, 299–316) exemplifies the hazards of hyper-literalism. He finds four earthly battles at the second coming. First, Jesus goes to Edom to fight (Isa 63:1–6). Second, Jesus travels to the valley of Megiddo for the battle of Armageddon (16:12–16; 19:17–21). Third, the battle of the Valley of Jehoshaphat commences (Joel 3:1–17; Rev 14:14–20). Fourth, what is left of antichrist and his armies descends on the Holy City for "The Battle of Jerusalem." But Christ delivers her at the last moment (Zech 12:1–9; Rev 16:17–21). After these four earthly battles, Jesus will then finally set his foot on the Mount of Olives (Zech 14:1–4; Rev 14:1–5).

66. Kline ("Har Magedon," 219–22) favors the etymological solution of Mount Zion. Although few agree with Kline, many more agree with his assessment that the connection of Armageddon to Ezek 38–39 and Rev 20:7–10 warrants only one eschatological battle at the coming of Christ.

beast.[67] "Babylon" appears nearly three hundred times in the OT. By the time of the prophets it took on the symbolism of an ungodly city (Isa 23:15–18; Nah 3:4–5). Babylon is mentioned twelve times in the NT. Four times it is found in Matthew's genealogy (Matt 1:11–17) and once in Stephen's sermon (Acts 7:43). Peter's reference is surely symbolic of Rome (1 Pet 5:13). Rome is also designated as Babylon in extratextual literature (*4 Ezra* 3:1–31; *2 Bar.* 10:1–3; 11:1–2; *Sib. Or.* 5:155–161). John refers to Babylon six times in the Apocalypse. He, too, uses the term as a metaphor for Rome and the evil Roman Empire.[68]

Thus, the consensus since earliest times is that the Babylon of Revelation symbolizes Rome.[69] Yet not all agree with the consensus. Preterist interpreters believe Babylon symbolizes Jerusalem.[70] Moreover, some moderns contend for a literal understanding of Babylon. For them, the ancient city will once again rise to world power in the near future.[71] Another futurist offshoot is to advance a revival of Rome into end-time prominence, a melding of the ecclesiastical and political power of ancient Rome.[72] If, however, Babylon is reserved more strictly as a symbol then John's words challenge every Christian and each generation, not merely the first generation or the last generation. John has universalized any remnant of geography associated with the term. Babylon is to be understood today as the evil, anti-God world empire which is already in existence.[73]

In Revelation, the very first reference reveals its final destruction. The angel proclaims, "Fallen! Fallen is Babylon the Great" (14:8). "Fallen, fallen" is a customary phrase indicating ruin, and derives from Isa 21:9. The title "Babylon the Great" alludes to Dan 4:30. Just as Nebuchadnezzar glories in the Babylon he built only to experience God's judgment, so too Rome—the Babylon of John's day—is ripe for downfall for its own hubris. Rome's fate, therefore, will be the same as ancient Babylon (Isa 13:19–22; Jer

67. See the entries "Great City," "Great Prostitute," and "Woman Sitting on a Scarlet Beast."

68. Beck, *Dictionary of Imagery*, 14–16; Fortune, "Babylon," 391; Hays, Duvall, and Pate, *Dictionary of Prophecy*, 49–57; Ryken, *Dictionary of Biblical Imagery*, 68–69; Seebass, "Babylon," 140–42. All six references occur at the end of three visions: the third interlude (14:8); the seventh bowl (16:19), and the fall of Babylon vision (17:5; 18:2, 10, 21).

69. Wiseman ("Babylon," 479) lists Tertullian, Jerome, and Augustine as early proponents. A few modern examples include Bauckham, *Climax of Prophecy*, 172; Beale, *Revelation*, 755; Beasley-Murray, *Revelation*, 185–86; Blount, *Revelation*, 314; Brighton, *Revelation*, 298; Keener, *Revelation*, 295; Kistemaker, *Revelation*, 333–34; Morris, *Revelation*, 146; Mounce, *Revelation*, 221; Osborne, *Revelation*, 426–27; Smalley, *Revelation*, 281.

70. So Beagley, *Sitz im Leben*, 92–112; Chilton, *Days of Vengeance*, 362; Ford, *Revelation*, 286–89; Mathison, *Postmillennialism*, 152–53; and Russell, *Parousia*, 482–504; 563–69, the latter including thirty pages of arguments in favor of Jerusalem. However, Biguzzi ("Is Babylon Rome or Jerusalem," 371–86) interacted with twenty preterists, and concludes that the traditional understanding of Babylon as Rome still stands.

71. Popular dispensationalists promote this. For example, Dyer (*Rise of Babylon*) and Hitchcock (*Second Coming of Babylon*) contend for a literal revival of the city of Babylon located by the Euphrates. Scholarly dispensationalists also support it, such as Walvoord (*Revelation*, 218) and Robert Thomas (*Revelation*, 2:207), who states, "The best solution is to assign Babylon its literal significance of the city on the Euphrates by that name."

72. So Hindson, *Revelation*, 156; Patterson, *Revelation*, 292; Walvoord, *Revelation*, 246–48. LaHaye (*Revelation Unveiled*, 266–77) is more specific: Babylon represents the Roman Catholic Church. See also Couch and Chambers, "Babylon," 61–62.

73. See Heater, "Do the Prophets Teach that Babylonia Will Be Rebuilt," 23–43.

50:35–40; 51:24–26). The second reference to Babylon is the seventh bowl and recaps its destruction, offering more information on how it falls. "The great city split into three parts, and the cities of the nations collapsed. God remembered Babylon the Great and gave her the cup filled with the wine of the fury of his wrath" (16:19). The complete devastation of the city is depicted by the expression "split into three parts."

The fall of Babylon vision provides the fullest details on its own destruction at the end of history. The connection between Babylon and Rome is made explicit by the reference to the woman, the great prostitute (17:5; 18:2, 10, 21). Babylon's demise is assured because of economic persecution and exploitation (18:3, 19), arrogance (18:7), corrupt lifestyle of luxury (18:9–14), deception of the world (18:23), and violence against all people (18:24).[74]

The numerous refrains of "fallen, fallen is Babylon" are not descriptions of separate sequential events but rather of the same cataclysmic judgment at the coming of Christ. Eclectically-speaking, the anti-God, persecuting, corrupting "Babylon" has always been here. For John it was Rome; for subsequent generations of believers it reflected their own circumstances. For the last generation, it will be even worse. Babylon signifies the world power in opposition to God and his people. Therefore, Babylon does not indicate a geographic locale. As a symbol, Babylon embraces much more than a reference to Rome's power and cultural influence. It symbolizes evil, idolatry, worldliness, pride, celebrity, immorality, satanic control, and the painful persecution of God's people. Babylon is the antithesis of the church as the bride of Christ, the new Jerusalem.

Death and Hades

The phrase "death and Hades" refers not only to the realm of the dead but also to personified evil powers. "Death" is mentioned nineteen times in Revelation. "Hades" is found four times, but each time in tandem with death.[75] Some scholars understand John to be emphasizing a spatial aspect—stressing death and the realm of the dead in the underworld. Hades translates the Hebrew word *sheol* which means death or grave in almost every instance in the LXX. In the NT, its usage is twofold. First, it may denote the place of all the departed dead (Acts 2:27). Second, it is the place only of the departed wicked (Luke 16:23; Rev 20:13–14). Others, however, believe that John has personified death and Hades into an evil power. In Greek mythology, Hades was the god of the underworld. Death and Hades together, therefore, represent death's power. It is best to see both emphases at work. It is not necessary to personify two separate entities.

In 1:18, the risen Christ holds the keys to death and Hades. They have lost their grip of terror for Christ holds the keys to eternal life. Nevertheless, the fourth seal's horseman who was "named Death, and Hades follows closely behind" (6:8), serve as a reminder that malignant cosmic forces are at work in the world. Ultimately, at the great white throne

74. Friesen, "Babylon," 379. See Beale, *Revelation*, 755.

75. Exactly four occurrences of the phrase suggest its worldwide nature, numerically speaking. Numerous translation attempts have been proffered for this latter word, including "hell" (GW), "world (or "place") of the dead" (NCV, GNT), "death's kingdom" (CEV), "the grave" (CEB, NLT), and "netherworld" (NABR). Most often it is simply transliterated as "Hades."

judgment, death and Hades give up their dead and are "thrown into the lake of fire" (20:14). The evil partnership of death with Hades adds another layer of meaning to the idea of hell. These companions personify evil and represent destructive cosmic forces. Through Christ's victory, however, they lose their death grip and are eternally judged.

Earth

Earth refers to the whole world and all the people in it. Therefore, it is essentially a bad place that will ultimately be renovated into a new heaven and new earth. In the OT, the land is understood as a part of God's creation and also as a covenant promise—the promised land—a land flowing with milk and honey, a land lost because of sinfulness and regained because of faithfulness. The prophets envisioned an ultimate restoration of the land (Isa 14:1; Jer 16:15; Ezek 28:25; Amos 9:15). The NT universalizes the land.[76] Jesus taught "land" as ultimately fulfilled in himself. He changes the rootedness for the people of God from geography to relationship (John 2:13–22; 4:19–24; 15:1–17). Paul continues the theme, claiming that the descendants of Abraham (the church) would "inherit the world" (Rom 4:13; Gal 3:26–29).[77] This is necessary background when reading Revelation. Every reference to *gē* in Revelation is a universal reference to the whole earth.[78] *Gē* is found over eighty times in Revelation, accounting for one-third of its NT usages. In the NIV, it is translated as "earth" sixty-three times, "land" seven times (7:1, 2, 3; 10:2, 5, 8; 16:2), and as "world" twice (13:3; 18:23).

Following John's proclivity for dualism, there are positive and negative images of the earth. Positively, the earth aids the woman by opening its mouth (12:16), and there are references to the new heaven and new earth.[79] But the kings of the earth, merchants of the earth, inhabitants of the earth, and the earth as recipient of the judgments reflect the negative side of *gē*. Thus, the earth reveals spiritual geography. It has been universalized to mean the whole earth and all its people. Ultimately, in the new heaven and new earth, it becomes the whole universe and all God's people.

76. N. T. Wright (*New Testament and People of God*, 226–27) observes that along with temple and Torah, the land was a symbol of what it meant to be Jewish. Yet the virtual absence of land as a theme in the NT implies it has been superseded.

77. Beale, *New Testament Biblical Theology*, 750–72; Burge, "Land," 570–75; Hays, Duvall, and Pate, *Dictionary of Prophecy*, 250–53; Millar, "Land," 623–27. On the topic of land, see the significant studies of Brueggemann, *Land*; Burge, *Jesus and the Land*; Habel, *Land Is Mine*; and Johnston and Walker, *Land of Promise*.

78. Nevertheless, some commentators attempt to limit *gē* to specific geographical locales. For example, preterist Gentry (*Before Jerusalem Fell*, 128–32) understands Revelation to be God's judgment on the land of first-century Palestine. Popular dispensationalists suggest a reference to end-time Petra or Israel for 12:16. Furthermore, the "beast from the land" (13:11) is a Jew arising from Israel or at least the Middle East (LaHaye, *Revelation Unveiled*, 205, 223; Lindsey, *New World Coming*, 179, 192).

79. Resseguie (*Revelation*, 34, 176) comments that the personified earth, Ge, is overlooked as a feminine actor in 12:16.

Egypt

"Egypt" represents hostility toward God, wickedness, and particularly an enslaving persecution of God's people. Ultimately, it pictures the evil world apart from Christ that is positioned for end-time judgment. After the exodus, "Egypt" transported into a negative symbol. The name came to signify slavery and oppression. Israel was reminded throughout the OT never to forget the awful experience of slavery in Egypt. Neither were they to treat the alien in their land as Egypt had treated them. Thus, when the prophets rhetorically call on Egypt to bear witness to the oppression and injustice within Israel, it served as a great lesson on the victim becoming the victimizer (Amos 3:1–10; 8:1–10).[80]

The singular reference to Egypt in Revelation reads: "Their bodies will lie in the public square of the great city—which is figuratively called Sodom and Egypt—where also their Lord was crucified" (11:8). John assists readers by prefacing "figuratively called" (CSB, NIV).[81] This signals that Egypt—indeed, all four "cities" listed in the verse—should be understood symbolically. Egypt, of course, is a country, not a city. Alan Johnson points out, however, that by John's day Egypt had become a symbol for "antitheocratic world kingdoms that enslaved Israel . . ."[82] In fact, if John has Rome in mind, then there are five places—Babylon, Sodom, Egypt, Jerusalem, and Rome—that embody one evil place opposed to God and his people for those readers who are spiritually discerning.[83]

In sum, the four "cities" picture the world at odds with God and his people. An eclectic chronology may be viewed this way: at the conclusion of the three and a half-year period (the time between the first and second comings of Christ) the two witnesses (the church) "finished their testimony, the beast that comes up from the Abyss will attack them, and overpower and kill them" (11:7). This coincides with the fifth seal (6:9) and places us near the end of history as persecution against believers intensifies.[84] Thus, like many other place names found in Revelation (Armageddon, Babylon, Sodom, Euphrates), Egypt no longer indicates a geographic location. John is utilizing imagery that is spiritual, not physical. Egypt represents ungodly people who oppress God's people. Finally, the placement of these four cities at 11:8, near the end of the second interlude and just before the commencement of the seventh trumpet which heralds the second coming, confirms that such cities—exemplified by first-century Rome and reproduced in part throughout the centuries—will conglomerate themselves near the end of history into an anti-Christian world system bent on destroying the church.

---

80. Ryken, *Dictionary of Biblical Imagery*, 228–29; Smalley, *Revelation*, 282.

81. Other possibilities include "mystically called" (NASB), "spiritually called" or "spiritual meaning" (CEB, CEV, NCV), "symbolically called" (ESV, NET) or "symbolic name" (GNT, NABR, NJB), and "prophetically called" (HCSB, NRSV, REB). RSV regrettably rendered it "allegorically."

82. Alan Johnson, "Revelation," 13:687.

83. Ibid.

84. So Beale, *Revelation*, 590–93; Kistemaker, *Revelation*, 333–34; Osborne, *Revelation*, 426–27.

Great City

The great city is Babylon the Great. This invokes the OT's metaphor of an ungodly city, refers to Rome for John's original audience, and ultimately symbolizes the evil world system that is opposed to God and will in the end be judged. "The great city" (*hē polis hē megalē*) is mentioned in Revelation nine times at or near the end of three visions (11:8, 13; 16:19; 17:18; 18:10, 16, 18, 19, 21).[85] Interpreters agree that the great city is Babylon the Great, the great prostitute, the woman sitting on the beast, especially since John makes the connections himself (17:3, 18; 18:10, 21). However, a few references are disputed. Many preterists and futurists label the reference at 11:8 as Jerusalem. A few also accept 16:19 to be Jerusalem.[86] It is consistent, however, to maintain Babylon the Great as the great city throughout Revelation. This means that in 11:8 Jerusalem has become like the great city. It is no better than an apostate city, another representative of an oppressive city that persecutes believers. Osborne states it well. The great city "is every city that embodies self-sufficiency in place of dependence on the creator, achievement in place of repentance, oppression in place of faith, the beast in place of the Lamb, and murder in place of witness to God."[87]

Great City Where Their Lord Was Crucified

The great city (Babylon the Great) has been universalized by John to symbolize all evil, oppressive people such as Sodom, Egypt, and even earthly Jerusalem—"the great city where their Lord was crucified." There are no specific references in Revelation by name to the earthly Jerusalem. The three times the word shows up refer to the heavenly Holy City, the new Jerusalem. Similarly, the phrases "outside the city" (14:20) and "the camp of God's people, the city he loves" (20:9), which some scholars will note as references to earthly Jerusalem, are better understood as references to the new Jerusalem, that is, God's people.

There is, however, one reference to the earthly Jerusalem found at 11:8, even though the name does not appear. John prophesies that the bodies of the two witnesses will lie in the public square of the great city—which is figuratively called Sodom and Egypt— "where also their Lord was crucified." John's symbols tumble out in this verse. Not one, not two, not even three, but four "cities" are listed and universally equated. First, John lists "the great city," Babylon the Great. Many interpreters, however, assume that "great city" here must refer to Jerusalem in light of the fourth city listed. NLT reads "And their bodies will lie in the main street of Jerusalem, the city that is figuratively called "Sodom" and "Egypt," the city where their Lord was crucified."[88] Yet every other reference in Revela-

---

85. GW consistently opts for "important city." Yet this version inconsistently switches to "great" elsewhere to translate *megas* (Babylon the Great, great river Euphrates, great supper).

86. Buchanan, *Revelation*, 466; Chilton, *Days of Vengeance*, 414; Ford, *Revelation*, 264; Patterson, *Revelation*, 314; Ryrie, *Revelation*, 114; Robert Thomas, *Revelation*, 2:275.

87. Osborne, *Revelation*, 427.

88. Preterist interpreters understand first-century Jerusalem ripe for its AD 70 collapse: Aune, *Revelation*, 2:618–19; Buchanan, *Revelation*, 286–87; Chilton, *Days of Vengeance*, 281; Clark, *Message from Patmos*, 77; Ford, *Revelation*, 180; Gentry, *Before Jerusalem Fell*, 170; Rissi, *Future of the World*, 55–56; Russell, *Parousia*, 432; Swete, *Apocalypse*, 237–38. Futurist interpreters envision an end-time Jerusalem:

tion to "the great city" consistently refers to evil Babylon, a euphemism for Rome, and it fits here as well.[89] The second city-symbol is Sodom, whose immorality is historically enacted. The third city mentioned is Egypt, the place of persecution where God's people endured slavery for four hundred years. The fourth "city" on John's list is "where also their Lord was crucified." This is assuredly an allusion to earthly Jerusalem. In striking fashion John equates Babylon the Great (the great city), Sodom, and Egypt with earthly Jerusalem as wicked partners of the system that persecutes God's people. That Jerusalem joins this wretched list is confirmed by the fact that they rejected and crucified the Lord, thus forfeiting their place as the Holy City. Jerusalem is a great city, not the Holy City. The new Jerusalem is now the Holy City, and Jesus' followers are its citizens, unfettered by geography or ethnicity.

Therefore, John has combined all four cities, rolling them into one antichrist-like world system.[90] All of these cities represent opposition to God and hostility to Christians. This is not new information for John's original readers. Jerusalem and its leadership had already been linked with Sodom (Isa 1:9–10; Jer 23:14; Ezek 16:46–49) and Egypt (Hos 8:13; Joel 3:19). Similarly, the earthly city of Jerusalem failed to respond to Jesus. Thus, Paul dismisses "the present city of Jerusalem because she is in slavery with her children" (Gal 4:25). Now the faithful must focus their thoughts on "the Jerusalem that is above . . ." (Gal 4:26).[91] When all the geographical locations of 11:8 are taken together they reveal every city that opposes God and his people. This is spiritual geography on display, not physical geography.

Great River Euphrates

Euphrates represents an evil threat to humanity. It is a symbol for universal foreign invasion that inaugurates the final battle called Armageddon, ushering in the second coming. In the OT, the Euphrates River separated Israel from her enemies. It also served as Rome's eastern boundary. Many of the horrific invasions of Palestine—Assyrians, Babylonians,

---

Hindson, *Revelation*, 125; Ladd, *Revelation*, 156–57; Patterson, *Revelation*, 248–49; Ryrie, *Revelation*, 85; Stefanovic, *Revelation*, 350; Robert Thomas, *Revelation*, 2:94; Walvoord, *Revelation*, 181.

89. So Beale, *Revelation*, 590–93; Bauckham, *Climax of Prophecy*, 172; Beasley-Murray, *Revelation*, 185–86; Blount, *Revelation*, 214; Brighton, *Revelation*, 298–99; Caird, *Revelation*, 137–38; Duvall, *Revelation*, 151; Easley, *Revelation*, 194; Hailey, *Revelation*, 338; Hughes, *Revelation*, 127; Alan Johnson, "Revelation," 13:686–87; Dennis Johnson, *Triumph of the Lamb*, 173; Keener, *Revelation*, 295; Kistemaker, *Revelation*, 333–34; Krodel, *Revelation*, 226; Morris, *Revelation*, 150; Mounce, *Revelation*, 220–21; Mulholland, *Revelation*, 206–7; Murphy, *Fallen Is Babylon*, 266–67; Osborne, *Revelation*, 426–27; Paul, *Revelation*, 201; Poythress, *Returning King*, 130; Prigent, *Apocalypse*, 355; Reddish, *Revelation*, 212; Resseguie, *Revelation*, 164; Roloff, *Revelation*, 133; Rowland, "Revelation," 12:642; Smalley, *Revelation*, 281–82; Sweet, *Revelation*, 187; J. C. Thomas, *Apocalypse*, 336. Years ago, de Villiers ("Lord Was Crucified in Sodom and Egypt," 125–38) cautioned interpreters on the quest of finding historical referents to these cities. The key is to understand the cities symbolically.

90. Actually, there are five cities since Rome lurks in the background. See Tõniste, *Ending of the Canon*, 72 n. 85; and Waddell, *Spirit of Revelation*, 182. See the entries "Egypt," "Sodom," and "Jerusalem."

91. See Walker, *Jesus and the Holy City*, 127–32, 248–59. Beale (*Revelation*, 592) keenly notices that "where" (*hopou*) often introduces symbolic, spiritual geography, not literal locales, such as "wilderness," (12:6, 14), "heads" and "mountains" (17:9), and "lake of fire" (20:10).

Persians—crossed the Euphrates on their way to conquering Palestine (Jer 2:18; 51:63). Therefore, it is understandable why the ancients utilized this river as a metaphor for foreign invasion.[92] In addition, some prophecies mention the image of God drying up the Euphrates in order for enemies to cross reminiscent of the crossing of the Red Sea, demonstrating that God will act powerfully in the future as he has in the past (Josh 4:23–25; Isa 11:15; 50:2).[93] Euphrates is found only twice in the NT (Rev 9:14; 16:12). Following a progressively parallel structure, both references depict the same event and inform and expand on one another. In fact, Euphrates echoes in the background of the sixth seal (6:15). It is then given more detail through later visions of the sixth trumpet (9:14–19), the third interlude (14:19–20), the sixth bowl (16:14–16), the rider on the white horse vision (19:18–19), and the thousand years vision (20:8–9).[94]

Nevertheless, some interpreters sustain any references to Euphrates as literally as possible.[95] Robert Thomas, for example, states "the unmistakable geographic usage of the river's name in Scripture is a staunch refutation against any symbolic meaning."[96] Most interpreters, however, agree with Kistemaker who asserts, "when the name Euphrates occurs in a chapter filled with symbolism, it is wise to affirm that next to a literal reading there is room for a figurative version. The name marks the boundary between good and evil, between the kingdom of God and that of Satan."[97] George Eldon Ladd adds, "the drying of the river is represented symbolically as the removal of the barrier which holds back the pagan hordes."[98] John is recounting a vision, not detailing a military exercise.[99]

Euphrates represents a potent symbol for the end. Like many other place names found in Revelation Euphrates does not indicate a geographic site. John is utilizing imagery that is spiritual not physical. Euphrates stands as a symbol for foreign invasion at the final judgment. The drying up of the Euphrates symbolizes no more hindrances toward end-time events. God allows demonically-driven beings to influence ungodly earthly forces to gather together in order to judge them all at Armageddon, the end-time battle.

---

92. Duvall, *Revelation*, 137; Alan Johnson, "Revelation," 13:674; Osborne, *Revelation*, 379.

93. Hays, Duvall, and Pate, *Dictionary of Prophecy*, 142. See Scurlock, "Euphrates River," 356.

94. So Beale, *Revelation*, 507; Brighton, *Revelation*, 248; Osborne, *Revelation*, 589; Smalley, *Revelation*, 237; Yarbro Collins, *Apocalypse*, 114. Resseguie (*Revelation Unsealed*, 84) confirms it as an evil symbol of threat against humanity, and states, "The Euphrates, which flows through Babylon, is a parody of the river of water of life, which flows through Jerusalem."

95. As with John's other symbols, Euphrates has been interpreted contemporarily. Kovacs and Rowland (*Revelation*, 175) mention sixteenth-century Samuel Sewall's understanding of the destruction of the Spanish Empire in the Americas. Foxe pointed to the Saracens.

96. Robert Thomas, *Revelation*, 2:262. Similarly, Easley, *Revelation*, 248; LaHaye, *Revelation Unveiled*, 174; Patterson, *Revelation*, 310; Walvoord, *Revelation*, 236.

97. Kistemaker, *Revelation*, 295.

98. Ladd, *Revelation*, 212.

99. Smalley, *Revelation*, 237. Osborne (*Revelation*, 590) enlarges on this.

Jerusalem

Although the earthly Jerusalem is not mentioned by name in Revelation, it plays a significant albeit negative role for John as the location of Christ's crucifixion and partner with an antichrist-like world system. "Jerusalem" is mentioned by name only three times in Revelation (3:12; 21:2, 10), each time with reference to the new Jerusalem. But earthly Jerusalem is certainly in the background of John's symbolic universe. Because of Jerusalem's pivotal role in the history of Israel, the name inevitably attained broad metaphorical usage. The city often stood for the nation as a whole (Jer 2:2; Mic 3:10; Zeph 1:12). Significantly, God's approval of allowing David to bring the ark to Jerusalem signified the city as his place of presence (Ps 132:13), fulfilling expectations of a dwelling place for God (Deut 12:5), the nation of the great king, the city of God (Ps 48:1–3; Matt 5:35). Remarkably, Jerusalem is also universalized—"born of Zion" represents the salvation of those who know God, yet it is used by the Psalmist for Rahab (or "Egypt"; see CEV, GW, GNT, NCV, NLT), Babylon, Philistia, Tyre, and Ethiopia as "among those who acknowledge me" (Ps 87:4–6). In like fashion, Isaiah lists Egypt and Assyria as nations added to the roll call of Israel as people of God (Isa 19:18–25). The NT extends these figurative attachments to Jerusalem. Now, however, believers must set aside earthly Jerusalem, and give their allegiance to new Jerusalem (Gal 4:25–26; Heb 12:22–23).[100]

When these preexisting pictures are kept in mind it becomes easier to see how John uses references to Jerusalem. Again, there are no specific references by name to the earthly Jerusalem. Similarly, the phrases "outside the city" (14:20) and "the camp of God's people, the city he loves" (20:9), which some scholars point to as references to earthly Jerusalem, are better understood as references to the new Jerusalem, that is, not a place, but God's people.[101] The one allusion to the earthly Jerusalem is found at 11:8. In one sentence, John relegates earthly Jerusalem to the great city (Babylon, Rome), Sodom, and Egypt. Thus, John expands the hopes of a restored, future, earthly Jerusalem in favor of the new Jerusalem, the Holy City of God's eternal presence at the end of time.

Lake of Fire

The lake of fire refers to the eternal destination and damnation of the dragon, the beast and the false prophet, death and Hades, and all unbelievers; this is the second death. The lake of fire is a graphic depiction of hell. In Matt 25:41 it is called "the eternal fire prepared for the devil and his angels." Some Bible students attach the lake of fire with Gehenna where fire and hell are connected (found twelve times in Matthew and in Jas 3:6). Gehenna is a place of fire where the evil dead resided. Daniel mentions "a river of fire" (Dan 7:9–11).

---

100. Hays, Duvall, and Pate, *Dictionary of Prophecy*, 225–28; Murphy-O'Connor, "Jerusalem," 246–59; Payne, "Jerusalem," 528–64; Ryken, *Dictionary of Biblical Imagery*, 437.

101. Dispensationalists accent the literal city of Jerusalem in Revelation. For them, earthly Jerusalem remains distinct from the heavenly city of Rev 21–22, and will continue into the millennial period. The promises of OT will be literally fulfilled during this millennium. See Foos, "Jerusalem in Biblical Prophecy," 207–10.

In other apocalyptic literature, it is the place of final punishment, located in the depths of the earth (*1 En.* 54:1; *2 En.* 10:2; *Sib. Or.* 4:184–86).[102]

John uses "the lake of fire" and "the fiery lake of burning sulfur."[103] These phrases are found five times at the conclusion of two visions. Four groups are cast into the lake of fire. First, immediately after the battle of Armageddon and return of Christ, the beast and the false prophet are captured and "thrown alive into the fiery lake of burning sulfur" (19:20). Next, in the same way the devil is "thrown into the lake of burning sulfur, where the beast and the false prophet had been thrown. They will be tormented day and night for ever and ever" (20:10). Third, "death and Hades were thrown into the lake of fire. The lake of fire is the second death. Anyone whose name was not found written in the book of life was thrown into the lake of fire" (20:14–15). Finally, "the cowardly, the unbelieving, the vile, the murderers, the sexually immoral, those who practice magic arts, the idolaters and all liars—they will be consigned to the fiery lake of burning sulfur. This is the second death" (21:8). Thus, all God's enemies—the evil trinity, death and Hades, and all unbelievers will be consigned to the lake of fire at the end of history.

This study understands the thousand years vision (20:1–21:8) as another separate vision, not a chronological advancement from chapter 19. It covers the same chronological territory as the recapped visions found throughout the rest of Revelation. This means that one point of view of judgment at the second coming is shown in 19:17–21 and another point of view appears in 20:7–10. Thus, the four groups cast into the lake of fire are thrown in at essentially the same time, at the great white throne judgment (20:11–15). John is simply giving his readers another camera angle.

The lake of fire is best understood not as a literal huge lake with flames licking up the sides. It is much more than that. The lake of fire, Beale comments, "is not literal since Satan (along with his angels) is a spiritual being. The 'fire' is a punishment that is not physical but spiritual in nature."[104] Ladd concurs, "The devil and his angels are spirits, not physical beings; fire belongs to the material physical order. How a lake of literal fire can bring everlasting torture to nonphysical beings is impossible to imagine."[105] Thus, the point is conscious, final, and ceaseless punishment that is spiritual and psychological in nature.

Some interpreters, however, do not accept a doctrine of eternal punishment and instead follow either annihilationism or universalism. An example of the former is Ranko Stefanovic, who states that this is not everlasting burning hell, but a metaphorical expression describing complete destruction, and "continues until it completes God's purpose."[106] An example of the latter is Ronald Farmer, who states that the goal of final judgment "is not eternal punishment but redemptive transformation."[107] Nevertheless, if the same language of eternity and presence is used for believers, it seems suitable to interpret the

---

102. Hays, Duvall, and Pate, *Dictionary of Prophecy*, 246–47; Osborne, *Revelation*, 690.

103. All English versions render this consistently except for the NABR's "burning pool of fire and sulfur."

104. Beale, *Revelation*, 1020.

105. Ladd, *Revelation*, 270. See Kistemaker, *Revelation*, 544; Smalley, *Revelation*, 515.

106. Stefanovic, *Revelation*, 580.

107. Farmer, *Revelation*, 132.

same for those who have, like the devil himself, rejected God. Eternality of the judgment is confirmed by the phrase "for ever and ever."

Outside the City

This phrase means outside the Holy City, the new Jerusalem, and refers to the final judgment of unbelievers. Near the conclusion of the third interlude, John pictures the second coming from the perspective of the saints (14:14–16) and from the perspective of unbelievers (14:17–20). The latter's judgment is visualized as trampled in the winepress "outside the city" (*exōthen tēs poleōs*), and appears just once (14:20). However, the identity of the city and the time of its trampling are disputed. The following four options have supporters. First, some scholars take it as a general reference to no specific city. It is simply a vivid image of judgment.[108] Second, a few scholars find an allusion to Babylon/Rome. After all, Babylon the Great is mentioned a few verses earlier (14:8). If so, then the trampling could refer to the persecution of believers (11:2).[109] Third, many interpreters choose the city to be Jerusalem. Among these interpreters are those who find a reference to literal, earthly Jerusalem either of the first century or the last days.[110] But most who select this option do so in light of the contextual allusions to the earthly city. These scholars usually interpret John to be universalizing the final battle to cover the earth.[111]

Fourth, several scholars interpret the reference to the new Jerusalem, the heavenly Holy City.[112] This view fits best. Earthly Jerusalem is certainly the backdrop and serves as a contrast to the heavenly Jerusalem. "Outside the city" is surely an allusion to the crucifixion of Christ, which was accomplished outside the city of Jerusalem (John 19:20; Heb 13:11–13). But earthly Jerusalem falls into the same category as Sodom, Egypt, and Babylon the Great (11:8). It has become reflective of the evil city.[113] It is better to see the city of 14:20 as the heavenly Holy City, composed of God's people who are separate from unbelievers.[114] This relates closely to other passages that mention the heavenly Holy City

---

108. Beasley-Murray, *Revelation*, 230; Easley, *Revelation*, 257; Alan Johnson, "Revelation," 13:726; Ladd, *Revelation*, 201; Morris, *Revelation*, 180; Reddish, *Revelation*, 282; Witherington, *Revelation*, 196–97.

109. Caird, *Revelation*, 193–94; Fee, *Revelation*, 206; Keener, *Revelation*, 377; Kiddle, *Revelation*, 294.

110. Preterists such as Buchanan (*Revelation*, 424), Chilton (*Days of Vengeance*, 376–77), and Russell (*Parousia*, 474) understand apostate Israel judged outside Jerusalem by Vespasian and Titus in AD 70. Futurists such as Hindson (*Revelation*, 159), Lindsey (*New World Coming*, 205), Patterson (*Revelation*, 297), Ryrie (*Revelation*, 106), and Robert Thomas (*Revelation*, 2:223) find a glimpse of the final battle here that covers a large portion of Palestine.

111. Aune, *Revelation*, 2:847; Blount, *Revelation*, 282; Brighton, *Revelation*, 393; Mounce, *Revelation*, 281; Prigent, *Apocalypse*, 452; Smalley, *Revelation*, 377; Stefanovic, *Revelation*, 468; J. C. Thomas, *Apocalypse*, 446.

112. Beale, *Revelation*, 780–81; Hailey, *Revelation*, 315; Hendriksen, *More than Conquerors*, 156; Hughes, *Revelation*, 167; Dennis Johnson, *Triumph of the Lamb*, 214; Kistemaker, *Revelation*, 420; Koester, *Revelation*, 630; Krodel, *Revelation*, 276; Mulholland, *Revelation*, 255; Osborne, *Revelation*, 555; Roloff, *Revelation*, 179; Rowland, "Revelation," 12:668; Leonard Thompson, *Revelation*, 149.

113. See the entry "Great City Where Their Lord Was Crucified."

114. See the entry "Holy City."

(20:9; 21:27; 22:14–15). The last reference mentions that the faithful will go through the gates into the eternal city while sinners are judged "outside" the Holy City. Outside the city means outside the new Jerusalem. "To be outside the city, then, is not to be outside the earth. It means to be on earth not at all; rather, in the lake of fire."[115]

Sodom

Sodom symbolizes depravity, immorality, corruption, and hostility to God and his people, and ultimately is an image of the rebellious world apart from Christ, and ripe for end-time judgment. The sin and subsequent destruction of Sodom (and Gomorrah) described in Gen 19 reverberates through the rest of Scripture as a perpetual reminder of and model for divine judgment. These evil cities became figures for sexual immorality, unnatural sin, and ungodliness. The character and fate of Sodom reappear often as examples of warning. Sodom and Gomorrah are cited as bywords for what is unnatural (Deut 32:32) and oppressive (Isa 1:10; Jer 23:14). The divine punishment of Sodom developed into a symbol for irrevocable judgment (Isa 13:19; Jer 49:18; Ezek 16:46–58; Amos 4:6; Zeph 2:9; *Ascen. Isa.* 3:10). In the NT, Sodom and Gomorrah continue as metaphors for the final day of judgment (Matt 10:1–15; 11:20–24; Luke 17:28–36; 2 Pet 2:6–11; Jude 7).[116]

Although found only once in Revelation, Sodom nonetheless is significant. John expands on the imagery of end-time judgment. In 11:8, John combines Sodom with three other "cities"— the great city (Babylon, i.e. Rome), Egypt, and the "city where their Lord was crucified" (earthly Jerusalem). Altogether these cities synthesize into one horrific, evil world city. Sodom—indeed, all four "cities" listed—should be understood figuratively. John's use of this biblical symbol emphasizes the rebellious moral degradation of those who are aligned against God.[117] Thus, Sodom represents ungodly, persecuting people who oppress God's people. Final judgment awaits them just like it did the original Sodom.

115. Gundry, "New Jerusalem," 263.

116. Alden, "Sodom," 550–52; Hays, Duvall, and Pate, *Dictionary of Prophecy*, 432; Howard, "Sodom," 560–61; Mulder, "Sodom and Gomorrah," 99–103; Ryken, *Dictionary of Biblical Imagery*, 802–4. See Howard, "Sodom and Gomorrah Revisited," 385–400.

117. Beale, *Revelation*, 592; Smalley, *Revelation*, 282; Resseguie, *Revelation*, 164. For an in-depth study see Reynolds, "Sodom/Egypt/Babylon Motif."

4

Good Things and Bad Things

JOHN OFTEN ATTACHES SYMBOLISM to objects. These objects are normally presented dualistically. There are good things and there are bad things. Each one of the entries listed in this chapter should be considered symbolically, not literally.

Good Things

The following entries are essentially good things. Their contrasting audiences, however, would receive them as bad things. For example, the great white throne is good for believers but bad for unbelievers. The seals are judgment for the wicked but the seal of God is protection for the faithful. The scroll reveals judgment for unbelievers yet the promise of eternal security for believers. Doors, keys, and gates can be open or closed, locked or unlocked.

Book of Life

The book of life—the divine ledger of names (and deeds) of all believers—signifies the promise of eternal, intimate fellowship with God. The equivalent words *biblios* and *biblion* are found twenty-five times in Revelation.[1] The expression "book of life" is mentioned five times (3:5; 13:8; 17:8; 20:15; 21:27). Modern versions translate the words either as "book" or "scroll." The book of life as a register of the names of the faithful is a symbol found throughout Scripture (Exod 32:32; Ps 9:5; Isa 4:3; Mal 3:16; Luke 10:20; Phil 4:3; Heb 12:23). Especially significant is Dan 7:9–10 and 12:1 where the context is final judgment and from which John draws heavily.[2]

Aune lists three types of ancient books: (1) the book of life records the names of the righteous; (2) the book of deeds keeps track of all the good and bad deeds a person has performed (1 Cor 3:12–15; 2 Cor 5:10); and (3) the book of destiny records the history

---

1. See the entry "Scroll."

2. Ryken, *Dictionary of Biblical Imagery*, 114. Osborne (*Revelation*, 180) and Beale (*Revelation*, 281) list intertestamental references. See Silva, "βιβλίος," 510–15.

of the world and/or the destinies of people before birth (Ps 139:16 possibly refers to this). Although the NT does not mention Aune's third type, the first two books are mentioned, and seem to be combined in one place in Revelation. The third book may also be inferred.[3]

The phrase is identified twice as belonging to the Lamb (13:8; 21:27) and twice it includes the statement "from the foundation of the world" (13:8; 17:8). The five references are, first of all, a promise to faithful members of Sardis (3:5). Sardis housed the royal archives. Thus, John draws from this contemporary picture to emphasize that Christ will never blot out the names of the faithful from the heavenly ledger.[4] The second appearance is in the third interlude where it offers security to persecuted believers (13:8). They are the citizens of heaven no matter what the beast or wicked inhabitants of the earth might do to them. Third, the fall of Babylon vision includes a reference (17:18). This passage, like the one previous (13:8), link Revelation with themes of sovereignty of God, omniscience, and predestination. Moreover, both passages appear to echo Aune's third description above. The beast and his followers will not inhabit the new heaven and the new earth. Only those whose names are written in the book of life enter. Fourth, the book of life receives additional description at the great white throne (20:12, 15). Here the first two of Aune's designations combine. The phrases "and books were opened" and "another book was opened, which is the book of life" merge allusions to Dan 7:10 (which focuses on deeds of end-time persecutors of God's people) and Dan 12:1–2 (which focuses on redemption at the end of time). Thus, the great white throne confirms that those whose names are found in the book of life will receive eternal life.[5] The last mention of the book of life relays the roll call for entrance into the new Jerusalem (21:27). This confirms one final time that those who will reside eternally with God and the Lamb in the new heaven and new earth have their names written in the book of life.

The popular image of Saint Peter sitting by the gate of heaven with the books opened will endure until the second coming. But the book of life is ultimately a metaphor for "God's unfailing memory" and "a metaphor for elect saints" whose salvation has been sovereignly determined.[6] Thus, themes of eternal security accompany these references as well as the call to stand up and deliver a faithful witness for Christ. For those who know their names are written in this heavenly book, earthly persecution holds no threat.

Door

The door is a symbol for spiritual entrance or exclusion, for access or denial of access, and offers a glimpse of eternal bliss and union with Christ now and forever. Doors are valuable symbols for Bible writers. The opening or closing of a door affords images of hiding (Gen 4:7; 1 Kgs 14:6; Matt 6:6), opportunity (Acts 14:27; 1 Cor 16:9; Col 4:3), and spiritual entry (Matt 7:7; John 10:7–9) or spiritual exclusion (Matt 25:10; Luke 13:22–28). The door is also a figure for the eschaton (Mark 13:29; Jas 5:9). Apocalyptic literature mentions

---

3. Aune, *Revelation*, 1:224. See Hays, Duvall, and Pate, *Dictionary of Prophecy*, 71.

4. Beale, *Revelation*, 279–82.

5. Beale, *New Testament Biblical Theology*, 512.

6. Beale, *Revelation*, 1037, 1102.

a door into heaven to symbolize access to God and eternal bliss (3 *Macc.* 6:18; *1 En.* 14:10; 104:2; *T. Levi* 5:1).[7] John carries forward these figurative usages in his Apocalypse. "Door" is found four times in three verses (3:8, 20 [twice]; 4:1). Primarily, he views the door in its apocalyptic sense as a signal for spiritual and revelatory entry, but secondarily the element of exclusion is noticeable.

The first mention occurs with the church at Philadelphia. The risen Jesus states, "I have placed before you an open door that no one can shut" (3:8). Several proposals on the meaning of this open door have arisen. Two are the most viable. First of all, it serves as an open door for the spread of the gospel, similar to the passages found in Paul's letters.[8] This view cannot be discounted, but another interpretation conforms better to the context. The second understanding is to view the open door to the heavenly kingdom. Philadelphian believers were being excluded from the synagogue, but Christ reminds them that it is he who holds the keys to the final, eschatological kingdom. Christ has opened the door and no one can shut it.[9]

The next two occurrences are found in the letter to the Laodiceans. Christ proclaims, "Here I am! I stand at the door and knock. If anyone hears my voice and opens the door, I will come in and eat with that person, and they with me" (3:20). Here the door illustrates a call to enter the fellowship and community of Christ himself. This is not a call to be evangelized since it is written to the church. Evangelism is popularly applied to the verse, but it is at best a secondary application. Patterson relates, "Verse 20 might qualify as the most misused verse in the entire New Testament. The verse has been preached enumerable times as an evangelistic text."[10] It is first and foremost a call for repentance to backslidden Christians, a challenge to reverse half-hearted discipleship. Jesus is on the outside, requesting entrance into his own church.[11] The invitation issued by Christ suggests the future wedding supper of the Lamb (2:17; 19:9).[12] But more so it reflects a present foretaste of the intimacy available to each person who responds to Christ. "Jesus

---

7. See McKim, "Door," 983–84; Ryken, *Dictionary of Biblical Imagery*, 215–16; Marvin Wilson, "Doors and Keys," 536–46.

8. So Beale, *Revelation*, 285–86; Brighton, *Revelation*, 92; Caird, *Revelation*, 51; Hailey, *Revelation*, 151; Harrington, *Revelation*, 72; Hemer, *Letters to the Seven Churches*, 171, 175; Hendriksen, *More than Conquerors*, 75; Hindson, *Revelation*, 46; Kistemaker, *Revelation*, 158–59; LaHaye, *Revelation Unveiled*, 79–80; Patterson, *Revelation*, 125; Stefanovic, *Revelation*, 139–40; Walvoord, *Revelation*, 85–86.

9. So Aune, *Revelation*, 1:236; Beasley-Murray, *Revelation*, 100; Blount, *Revelation*, 74–75; Boxall, *Revelation*, 72; Easley, *Revelation*, 57; Fee, *Revelation*, 53; Alan Johnson, "Revelation," 13:632; Dennis Johnson, *Triumph of the Lamb*, 87; Keener, *Revelation*, 150; Ladd, *Revelation*, 59; Lupieri, *Apocalypse*, 126; Michaels, *Revelation*, 84; Morris, *Revelation*, 78; Mounce, *Revelation*, 101; Mulholland, *Revelation*, 126; Murphy, *Fallen Is Babylon*, 153; Osborne, *Revelation*, 188–89; Paul, *Revelation*, 106; Prigent, *Apocalypse*, 203–4; Reddish, *Revelation*, 75; Resseguie, *Revelation*, 98; Roloff, *Revelation*, 61; Rotz, *Revelation*, 83; Rowland, "Revelation," 12:584; Smalley, *Revelation*, 89; Sweet, *Revelation*, 103; Robert Thomas, *Revelation*, 1:277–78; Wall, *Revelation*, 83; Wilcock, *I Saw Heaven Opened*, 55; Witherington, *Revelation*, 106.

10. Patterson, *Revelation*, 143. Alan Johnson ("Revelation," 13:638), for example, believes the words are directed toward professing Christians who lack authentic conversion.

11. Resseguie, *Revelation*, 102. Nevertheless, some advocate for an evangelistic appeal, including Hailey, *Revelation*, 162; Robert Thomas, *Revelation*, 1:308; Walvoord, *Revelation*, 96. Wiarda ("Revelation 3:20," 212) suggests the image is general enough to assume an evangelistic appeal.

12. So Kiddle, *Revelation*, 60; Sweet, *Revelation*, 109; Robert Thomas, *Revelation*, 1:321–22.

is inviting the Laodicean Christians to realize how they have shut him out of their lives with their own self-sufficiency."[13]

The final reference initiates the throne room vision (4:1). This image appears closely connected to the idea of an open heaven (Gen 28:17; Ps 78:23; Matt 3:16; John 1:51; Acts 7:56; 2 Cor 12:1–4). The emphasis here is on the realm and presence of God, a glimpse of bliss, glory, and eternity through visionary revelation.[14] The door, therefore, serves as a symbol of spiritual entry in Revelation. Although unbelievers (3:9) or even believers (3:19) may attempt to exclude or deny access, it is God who ultimately holds the key and permits entrance.

Great White Throne

The great white throne refers to the final judgment at the conclusion of history where all the dead—believers and unbelievers—are judged. This entry is listed under good things but reflects John's dualism. For believers, the great white throne is a good thing. For unbelievers, it is a bad thing.[15] Many scholars understand the great white throne to be final judgment aimed only at the unsaved. The audience is the same "dead" who have come back to life to face judgment in 20:5. They encompass the unsaved "small and great" (13:16; 19:18) who must now stand before God (6:17; 18:10, 15, 17).[16] Dispensationalists especially follow this, finding various judgments in various phases. These events include judgment at rapture, judgment at the second coming (divided into judgments of Israel, gentiles, OT, and tribulation saints), and multiple judgments following a millennial kingdom which is the great white throne (judgment of Satan, fallen angels, unsaved dead, present heavens and earth).[17] But most scholars simply note a general judgment for everyone. Believers are judged in 20:12 and unbelievers in 20:13–15. This means the martyrs of 20:4 are in view. Thus, believers encompass the believing "small and great" (11:18; 19:5) who stand before the throne victorious (7:9; 11:11; 14:1; 15:2).[18]

---

13. Keener, *Revelation*, 161. So also Beale, *Revelation*, 308–9; Beasley-Murray, *Revelation*, 107; Easley, *Revelation*, 61; Fee, *Revelation*, 60; Hemer, *Letters to the Seven Churches*, 206; Hindson, *Revelation*, 50; Kistemaker, *Revelation*, 174; Ladd, *Revelation*, 67; Mounce, *Revelation*, 113; Osborne, *Revelation*, 217; Patterson, *Revelation*, 143; Smalley, *Revelation*, 102; Stefanovic, *Revelation*, 150.

14. Osborne, *Revelation*, 223–24.

15. See the entry "Throne."

16. Beckwith, *Apocalypse*, 748; Chilton, *Days of Vengeance*, 532; Duvall, *Revelation*, 275–76; Fee, *Revelation*, 287; Hughes, *Revelation*, 218; Alan Johnson, "Revelation," 13:774; Keener, *Revelation*, 469; Koester, *Revelation*, 779; Ladd, *Revelation*, 272; LaHaye, *Revelation Unveiled*, 349; Michaels, *Revelation*, 230; Reddish, *Revelation*, 387; Resseguie, *Revelation*, 249; Schnabel, *40 Questions*, 289; Swete, *Apocalypse*, 272.

17. Hindson, *Revelation*, 206; Patterson, *Revelation*, 359; Ryrie, *Revelation*, 134; Robert Thomas, *Revelation*, 2:430–31; Walvoord, *Revelation*, 306. See the various phases in Nicholas, "Judgments, Various," 225–27; and MacLeod, "Sixth Last Thing," 315–30.

18. Beale, *Revelation*, 1032; Beasley-Murray, *Revelation*, 301; Blount, *Revelation*, 373; Boring, *Revelation*, 210; Brighton, *Revelation*, 584; Easley, *Revelation*, 380; Farmer, *Revelation*, 126; Hailey, *Revelation*, 401; Hays, Duvall, and Pate, *Dictionary of Prophecy*, 195; Hendriksen, *More than Conquerors*, 196; Dennis Johnson, *Triumph of the Lamb*, 298; Kistemaker, *Revelation*, 546; Mangina, *Revelation*, 233; Morris, *Revelation*, 235; Mounce, *Revelation*, 376; Mulholland, *Revelation*, 312; Osborne, *Revelation*, 721–22;

The background for God sitting on his throne in final judgment can be traced to the OT (Dan 7:9–10) and apocalyptic literature (*4 Ezra* 7:33; *1 En.* 90:20). Judgment is based on "the books," which refers to the words and actions of a person's lifetime.[19] Another book, the book of life, refers to the ledger of those who are saved or unsaved (Dan 12:1–2).

Therefore, universal judgment is intended at the great white throne. There is one final judgment at the climax of history. All people great and small, righteous and unrighteous, appear before the judge (Matt 25:31–46; John 5:24–29; Acts 24:15; Rom 14:10). The righteous who are judged in 20:12 recaps the grain harvest of 14:14–16. The unrighteous who are judged in 20:13–15 recaps the grape harvest of 14:17–19. In addition, the sea (the personification of evil in 12:12; 13:1) and death and Hades are judged as well. These all join the devil, the beast, and the false prophet in the lake of fire. Craig Keener delivers a fitting application. "This passage, like most others in Revelation, provides preachers and teachers an adequate transition for what many nineteenth- and twentieth-century evangelicals called an 'altar call.' The knowledge of final judgment calls all to repentance in the present, for someday—when it is no longer possible to ignore God and his perfect way—it will be too late to repent."[20]

Key of David

This image depicts the trustworthiness, sovereign ownership, and absolute authority of Christ over Satan, the realm of the dead, and the new Jerusalem. "Key" is simple to unravel, especially since its symbolism continues today. It is a tool for locking or unlocking something. Thus, power and authority rests in the hand of the one who holds the key. In the ancient world, people understood that spiritual realms had doors, and that gods and demons had access via keys.[21] A key passage in the OT is Isa 22:20–25 where access to the king was symbolized with the key. Shebna was to be removed from his office and replaced with Eliakim. God placed on Eliakim's shoulder "the key to the house of David; what he opens no one can shut, and what he shuts no one can open" (Isa 22:22).[22] Later Jewish writings used similar language (*3 Bar.* 11:2). The idea of authority possessed (Matt 23:13; Luke 4:25) or granted (Matt 16:19) continued into Jesus' day.[23]

John's Apocalypse mentions a key (*kleis*) four times. The verb form (*kleiō*), usually translated "lock" or "shut," is found six times. In the inaugural vision, the risen "Son of Man" holds the key over death and Hades (1:18). Therefore, Jesus' sovereignty over death and final judgment is asserted. In 9:1, the keys of the Abyss are given to the fallen star. The

---

Prigent, *Apocalypse*, 579; Roloff, *Revelation*, 231; Smalley, *Revelation*, 516; Stefanovic, *Revelation*, 582; Sweet, *Revelation*, 294; J. C. Thomas, *Apocalypse*, 615–16.

19. Hays, Duvall, and Pate, *Dictionary of Prophecy*, 256–57.

20. Keener, *Revelation*, 482.

21. The symbolism of keys is so pervasive that only one reference in the Bible is non-figurative (Judg 3:25).

22. Beale (*Revelation*, 284–85), Fekkes (*Isaiah and Prophetic Traditions*, 131) and Osborne (*Revelation*, 187) mention this passage was interpreted as a messianic text in early Judaism.

23. Keylock, "Key," 898–900; Ryken, *Dictionary of Biblical Imagery*, 476.

star does not own the keys, but is given them by the one who has ultimate authority. The two witnesses—like Elijah before them—possess the power to lock up the sky (11:6). In 20:1–3, an angel has a key to the Abyss and a chain in his hand with which he shackles the dragon. Here then the authority is power over the Abyss and over the dragon. His chain is symbolic of helplessness. Lastly, in the heavenly Jerusalem, at no time will its gates be locked (21:25).

The major passage on the "key of David," however, is in Christ's message to Philadelphia (3:7–8). It is a near quote of Isa 22:22 and a development from 1:18. The emphasis is on Christ's sovereign authority over who enters the kingdom of heaven and who does not. The next few verses confirm that although the earthly synagogue doors are closed to the faithful, the heavenly door is open. Thus, Jesus, not the synagogue rulers, has sovereign control over who enters into the eternal city of David—the new Jerusalem.[24]

Measuring Rod

To measure the earthly temple or the heavenly city signifies God's ownership, protection, and eternal presence. In the OT, measuring the temple became a common metaphor either to rebuild it (Ezek 40:1–6), destroy it (2 Sam 8:2; 2 Kgs 21:13; Isa 34:11; Amos 7:7–9), or protect and preserve it along with the saints (2 Sam 8:2; Ezek 40:1–6; Zech 2:1–5; see also *1 En.* 61:1–4). Every NT reference to "measuring" something contains a figurative understanding (Matt 7:2; Mark 4:24; Luke 6:38; 2 Cor 10:12).[25] John continues this tradition. The verb *metreō* means "to measure" and is found five times in two passages (11:1–2; 21:15–17). The measuring is accomplished by a measuring rod.[26] This instrument is a small, lightweight, hollow reed often used for measuring the length of something.[27]

In the first passage, John is instructed to measure the temple, the altar, and the worshippers, but exclude the outer court (11:1–2). When John measures the temple, he is measuring the church. The majority of commentators understand the temple as a symbol for the people of God.[28] The measuring means to secure and establish, and connotes

---

24. Beale, *Revelation*, 283; Mounce, *Revelation*, 100; Osborne, *Revelation*, 187.

25. Aune, *Revelation*, 2:604; Osborne, *Revelation*, 409–10.

26. Two words need clarity due to multiple English translations. First, the noun *rhabdos* is found four times, three of which "scepter" (2:27; 12:5; 19:15) is usually translated. See the entry "Iron Scepter." Once it is translated as a measuring "rod" (11:1) by most versions, but there is also "stick" (CEV, GW, GNT, NCV, NLT) and "reed" (CSB). Second, the noun *kalamos* is found three times. In 11:1, *kalamos* is rendered "reed" (CSB, NIV, NKJV), "staff" (ESV, NABR, NASB, NET, NRSV), "cane" (NJB, REB), and "pole" (CEB). In 21:15–16, *kalamos* is rendered most often as "rod" but there is also "stick" (CEV, GW, GNT, NLT) and "reed" (NKJV).

27. Osborne, *Revelation*, 409. He adds that it was ten feet, four inches in length.

28. See the entry "Temple." Because some interpreters envision a literal future temple, then the measuring with a measuring rod is literal as well (LaHaye, *Revelation Unveiled*, 182; Lindsey, *New World Coming*, 160; Ryrie, *Revelation*, 83). Other dispensationalists, however, follow symbolic measuring (Patterson, *Revelation*, 238; Robert Thomas, *Revelation*, 2:80; Walvoord, *Revelation*, 176). Preterists also refer to a literal first-century temple, but understand the measuring as a symbolic act (Chilton, *Days of Vengeance*, 273).

divine protection for believers.[29] John also measures the altar. The believer's response to God's protection combines the two major emphases of worship (altar of incense) and sacrifice (altar of burnt offering).[30] The worshippers are also measured. Several translations unfortunately add the word "count" to render the phrase "count the worshippers" (CSB, GNT, GW, NABR, NCV, NLT, REB).[31] However, adding this word tends to limit the measuring to the temple and the altar. Yet all three (temple, altar, and worshippers) are measured. This aids in recognizing that all three reflect multi-dimensional aspects of the same thing.[32] This also matches imagery found elsewhere in the NT (1 Cor 3:16–17; 2 Cor 6:16; Eph 2:19–22; 1 Pet 2:4–10) and early Christian literature (Ign. *Eph.* 9:1; Barn. 4:11; 2 Clem. 9:3).

The purpose of the measuring is to protect and secure God's temple, altar, and people. This signifies the utter presence of God, where he dwells with his people (Matt 27:51; Heb 9:12). Whoever is "measured" is just like the person who is "sealed" (7:1–8). Yet the outer court is not measured. Many scholars understand this to mean the outer court belongs to unbelieving Jews or gentiles.[33] But it appears best to interpret the outer court as yet another metaphor for the church viewed from a different perspective. In this case, it reminds believers that although they are spiritually and eternally protected, they must nevertheless be subject to the enemies of God. Rejection, persecution, and even martyrdom await the believer.

In the second passage, the angel measures the new Jerusalem with a measuring rod of gold.[34] The measuring includes the city which is twelve thousand stadia, and the walls which are a hundred and forty-four cubits (21:15–17). The measuring of the heavenly Holy City is similar to chapter 11 in that the emphasis is on people and presence, not inches and miles. The measurements form a perfect square, a cube that pictures the holy of holies (1 Kgs 6:20). It confirms the city is actually unmeasurable and immeasurable, composed of God's presence with his people. It is a symbolic figure of incalculable dimensions.

Neither measuring applies to an actual structure but to people, presence, and protection. Thus, John fulfills and expands the promise of God concerning the measuring of the temple. For Ezekiel, the measuring of the temple was a promise that it would be rebuilt and that God would live among his people forever. It signified ownership and protection. For Zechariah, the measuring symbolized that God would protect the city and be its glory. This is exactly the point of John's vision of the earthly temple and heavenly city being measured. God's temple—his people, the church—represent the earthly temple (chapter 11). The church is a symbol itself of the heavenly temple, the heavenly Jerusalem,

29. See Bauckham, *Climax of Prophecy*, 272; Beasley-Murray, *Revelation*, 182; Hailey, *Revelation*, 250.

30. See the entry "Altar."

31. Because it sounds odd to measure people, some scholars agree with the added word "count," including Aune (*Revelation*, 2:578), Michaels (*Revelation*, 137), and Robert Thomas (*Revelation*, 82).

32. Tavo, *Woman, Mother, Bride*, 218–19.

33. See the entry "Outer Court."

34. The verb *metreō* is found three times and the noun *metron* ("measuring," "measurement") is found twice.

the Holy City where God will dwell with his people forever in the new heaven and new earth (chapter 21).

Scroll

The scroll (chapters 5 and 10) represents God's message and divine plan for human history. Its contents mean judgment for the wicked and suffering (yet eternally protective) witness for the faithful. Chapter 5 relates a double-sided "scroll" (*biblion*) lying open in the hands of God. Only the Lamb is worthy to break its seals and open the scroll. This image is traced to Ezekiel's call where a two-sided scroll includes the message of "lament and mourning and woe" (Ezek 2:10; also Isa 29:11; Jer 36:1–25; Dan 12:4). Osborne conveniently lists six possibilities on interpreting the scroll.[35] The best view identifies the scroll as a contract deed containing God's redemptive, future plan for humanity. The contract is composed of future prophecies and is written on the inner side, rolled up, and sealed with seven seals. The outer side contains a short description. Osborne states that it summarizes "the whole of biblical truth, beginning with the foreshadowing of the plan in the OT and the progressive unveiling of it in Christ."[36] In chapter 10, a "little scroll" (*biblaridion*) is mentioned three times in a renewed commission for John (10:2, 9–10). Once again Ezekiel is referenced. John's vision has the same meaning as Ezekiel's but the audience is now enlarged. John is instructed by the mighty angel to eat the scroll. The eating confirms that John's message though sweet to him is bitter for the rest of the world. This bitterness implies persecution for believers.[37]

There is disagreement over whether these are two separate scrolls or the same scroll. Scholars are evenly divided and base their decision on the similarity or dissimilarity between the scrolls. Many scholars distinguish two scrolls. One scene is in heaven, the other on earth. One scroll is great, the other is small. One is closed, the other open. One is taken by Christ, the other given by an angel. The content of one is judgment, the topic of the other is recommissioning.[38] Other scholars, however, conclude the scrolls of 5:1 and 10:2 are one and the same. Both passages allude to Ezek 2:8–3:3. *Biblion* and *biblaridion* are used interchangeably. Both scrolls are eventually opened. Both are held by divine or angelic figures. Both have a mighty angel who shouts. Bauckham notes this pathway: God>Jesus>angel>John.[39] The content of both scrolls apparently deals with the destiny of all human beings.[40]

---

35. Osborne, *Revelation*, 248–49. Other possibilities are found in Aune, *Revelation*, 1:341–46; Beale, *Revelation*, 339–42; Caird, *Revelation*, 70–73; and Koester, *Revelation*, 373.

36. Ibid., 249.

37. See the entries "Bitter" and "Sweet as Honey."

38. So Aune, *Revelation*, 1:xcviii–xcix; Blount, *Revelation*, 190; Easley, *Revelation*, 173; Hailey, *Revelation*, 242; Hughes, *Revelation*, 116; Alan Johnson, "Revelation," 13:677; Kistemaker, *Revelation*, 306–7; Ladd, *Revelation*, 142; Mounce, *Revelation*, 202; Paul, *Revelation*, 188; Prigent, *Apocalypse*, 328; Roloff, *Revelation*, 123; Swete, *Apocalypse*, 126; Robert Thomas, *Revelation*, 2:62; Leonard Thompson, *Revelation*, 122; Witherington, *Revelation*, 156.

39. Bauckham, *Theology of Revelation*, 81–82.

40. So Bauckham, *Climax of Prophecy*, 243–46; Beale, *Revelation*, 527–32; Beasley-Murray,

Thus, it appears that there is one scroll which is further unrolled. The little scroll elaborates upon the double-sided scroll. Its full contents are chapters 6–22, and reveal the customary contrasts of John.[41] On the one hand, God's purposes are carried out by the Lamb in judgment. On the other hand, this purpose reveals the role of John and the church. The scroll unveils judgments against the wicked and an expectant suffering witness for the saints.

Seal of God

The seal of the living God identifies believers. It metaphorically stamps them with God's eternal ownership, security, and protection, and stands in stark contrast to the mark of the beast which identifies unbelievers. Seals served various purposes in ancient daily life, including personal identification and the labeling and securing of property. Primarily, however, seals secured and verified official documents. Metaphorically, sealing can mean securing (Job 14:17; Matt 27:66) or showing God's ownership (2 Cor 1:22; Eph 1:14). In addition, prophetic messages and visions are sealed until the proper time (Isa 8:16; Dan 8:26; 12:4). Ezek 9 is particularly helpful in understanding how John uses the seal. An angel of God puts a mark on true believers to protect them from the wrath of God coming upon the Babylonians. Unfaithful Israelites without the mark are killed.[42]

John utilizes the seal of God in the same way. Those who have the seal of God are protected from the coming wrath of God and the Lamb (6:17; 16:14). The noun "seal" (*sphragis*) occurs thirteen times in Revelation, eleven of which refer to the seven seals.[43] The remaining two refer to the "seal of the living God" (7:2; 9:4).[44] The verb "to seal" (*sphragizō*) is found eight times in Revelation. Five of those occur in chapter 7 with the sealing of the hundred and forty-four thousand (7:3, 4 (twice), 5, 8).[45] Thus, John makes

---

Revelation, 171; Boring, *Revelation*, 140; Boxall, *Revelation*, 153; Brighton, *Revelation*, 263; Caird, *Revelation*, 126; Duvall, *Revelation*, 143; Hays, Duvall, and Pate, *Dictionary of Prophecy*, 401; Keener, *Revelation*, 280; Koester, *Revelation*, 476–77; Mazzaferri, *Genre of Revelation*, 271–74; Michaels, *Revelation*, 133–34; Murphy, *Fallen Is Babylon*, 250; Osborne, *Revelation*, 395; Resseguie, *Revelation*, 153; Schüssler Fiorenza, *Revelation*, 73–74; Smalley, *Revelation*, 258–59; Stevanovic, *Revelation*, 331; Sweet, *Revelation*, 177; J. C. Thomas, *Apocalypse*, 312; Tõniste, *Ending of the Canon*, 99; Wall, *Revelation*, 135–36.

41. Interpreters, of course, disagree on the contents of the scroll. Keener (*Revelation*, 280–81) agrees the singular scroll constitutes the entire message of Revelation, which may also include the book of life as well. Osborne (*Revelation*, 250) believes chapter 6 is outside the first scroll. Charles (*Revelation*, 1:260), Kistemaker (*Revelation*, 307), Morris (*Revelation*, 138), and Mounce (*Revelation*, 210) understand the little scroll to cover only chapter 11. Blount (*Revelation*, 100–101) finds a case for three or four scrolls. Resseguie (*Revelation Unsealed*, 95–99) detects four scrolls—the book John is writing, the book of life, the Lamb's scroll, and the little scroll.

42. Bean and Harrison, "Seals," 1505–14; Drinkard, "Seal," 141; Hays, Duvall, and Pate, *Dictionary of Prophecy*, 403–4; Schnabel, *40 Questions*, 89–91.

43. See the entry "Seven Seals."

44. In the first interlude (7:1–17), the four angels are not permitted to harm the hundred and forty-four thousand servants until they received the seal of the living God. Then in the fifth trumpet (9:13–21) the demonic locusts were not allowed to harm those who have the seal of God on their foreheads.

45. The other uses of the verb confirm the metaphorical understanding of the seal. This includes the scroll in God's hand which is "sealed thoroughly" (*katasphragizō*; 5:1), the seven thunders sealed up

an intentional connection between the seals of chapter 6 and the sealing of God in chapter 7.[46]

All believers are sealed just as all unbelievers are marked. Beale describes the hundred and forty-four thousand sealed in 7:3–8 with the entire community of the redeemed. First, all the redeemed believers are included when "servants" is used elsewhere in Revelation.[47] Second, Ezek 9, the backdrop to the passage, distinguishes only true believers from unbelievers, not various groups of believers. Third, if Satan puts a seal on all his followers, then presumably God does likewise for all his followers. Consequently, those sealed are not a special group of martyrs or a last generation of believers or a remnant of Jewish believers protected through tribulation. Rather, all who know Christ are sealed by the Holy Spirit (2 Cor 1:22; Eph 1:13; 4:30).[48]

Resseguie observes how "sealing" is a verbal thread running through Revelation. Key words or phrases tie together sections or even an entire book, and often elaborate a main theme or subtheme of a passage. Another verbal thread is the mark of the beast. Thus, these two threads of "seal" and "mark" bring out the two choices of Revelation. One either receives the seal or the mark, there is no in between. Both are placed on the forehead and are intimately linked to their owner, either God and the Lamb or the beast. Ownership is confirmed by how John compares the seal to the "name" of God and the Lamb (2:3, 13; 3:8, 12; 11:18; 14:1; 21:12; 22:4) in contrast to the "name" of the beast (13:17; 14:11; 15:2). The former is sealed for salvation (2 Tim 2:19). The latter is sealed for condemnation. Some are sealed, some are marked. No one receives both a seal and a mark.[49] Therefore, the seal of the living God symbolizes ownership (chapter 7) and protection (chapter 9) for believers. The faithful may suffer and die (6:9–11; 12:11–17), but the seal confirms their eternal status. It authenticates the personal relationship with God and the promise of eternal life.

Throne

The throne is a symbol for God's presence, authority, majesty, sovereignty, and righteous judgment filled with grace. There are physical, human, and symbolic thrones in Scripture, but the most common usage is God's throne. In Revelation, "throne" (*thronos*) is found forty-seven times, accounting for 76 percent of all NT usages. It is found in all but

---

(10:4), the devil sealed in the Abyss (20:3), and the angel's instructions not to seal the words of this book (22:10).

46. Lemcio (*Navigating Revelation*, 19–20) notes seven terms found in both chapters (four, seal, number, servants, stand, throne, and Lamb). Moreover, three questions are asked (one is implied) in chapter six and answered in chapter seven. First, "how long?" (6:9); when the number of fellow servants killed is completed (7:3). Second, the implied "how many?" receives the implied answer of a hundred and forty-four thousand (7:4). Third, "who can stand?" (6:17); the great multitude can stand (7:9).

47. See the entry "Servants."

48. Beale, *Revelation*, 412–15. Many dispensationalists believe the seal of God is a literal mark on the forehead, including Hindson (*Revelation*, 88), LaHaye (*Revelation Unveiled*, 150), Lindsey (*New World Coming*, 119), Patterson (*Revelation*, 192), and Walter Wilson (*Dictionary of Bible Types*, 176).

49. Resseguie, *Revelation*, 25–26. See also Duvall, *Revelation*, 114; Hays, Duvall, and Pate, *Dictionary of Prophecy*, 403; Lemcio, *Navigating Revelation*, 19–20.

four chapters. Revelation opens with God on his throne (1:4) and closes with God and the Lamb sitting on the throne of the heavenly city (22:3). When John ascends in the Spirit, the first image he sees is the throne (4:2). John's vision of chapters 4–5 is especially "throne-heavy." Nineteen references are found in these two short chapters, underscoring the centrality of the throne image.[50] Indeed, some recognize the throne motif to be John's central symbol. Resseguie, for example, affirms, "The primary setting of the Book of Revelation is the throne of God."[51] Chapters 4–5 also lay out a foundation for major motifs in the rest of the book, including the call to be faithful witnesses in the midst of suffering and persecution, the promise of spiritual protection, and the confirmation that God is supreme over all, and worthy of worship.

Although heavenly thrones are mentioned multiple times, a competing throne is present as well. The parodic throne of Satan (2:13; 13:2) and the beast (16:10) serve as contrasts to God's throne. Scholars affirm that the background of cult emperor worship is found in these references.[52] Since Revelation describes the ultimate victory of the Lamb that ushers in the consummative kingdom of God, it is appropriate to find the throne mentioned so often, culminating in the great white throne judgment.[53] For believers, therefore, the throne bursts forth images of sovereign majesty and just judgment.

Twelve Gates

The twelve gates of the heavenly city are a symbol of free access to the presence of God and eternal protection for the saints. Gates serve an important function throughout the Bible. They played a practical role of protection since they were the weakest part of a city's defense, and most sieges started at the gates. Because they were public thoroughfares, gates also took on social and legal aspects. It was where people met and where the community made decisions. Gates naturally took on symbolic meaning. They might serve as synecdoche for an entire city (Isa 3:26; Ps 87:2). Since gates provide entry they became figurative aspects for entrance into other realms. Thus, we read of the gate of heaven (Gen 28:17) and the gates of righteousness (Ps 118:19), but also the gate of death (Job 38:17; Ps 9:13), gates of Sheol (Isa 38:10), and gates of Hades (Matt 16:18). The coming of the Messiah meant the arrival of a new age, an era of universal peace. "Lift up your heads, you gates; be lifted up, you ancient doors, that the King of glory may come in" (Ps 24:7). When the Messiah arrives, "Your gates will always stand open, they will never be shut, day or

---

50. Beale (*Revelation*, 320) and Smalley (*Revelation*, 114) among others mention seventeen, but there are actually nineteen. Major studies on the throne imagery in chapters 4–5 include Gallusz, *Throne Motif in Revelation*; Morton, *One upon the Throne and the Lamb*; and Williamson, "Thrones in the Book of Revelation."

51. Resseguie, *Revelation Unsealed*, 72. So too Bauckham, *Climax of Prophecy*, 31, 141–42; Hays, Duvall, and Pate, *Dictionary of Prophecy*, 444; Schüssler Fiorenza, *Revelation*, 58, 120. Gallusz (*Throne Motif in Revelation*, 300–329) claims it is the major interpretive key for the theology of the book.

52. Beale, *Revelation*, 246; Reddish, *Revelation*, 94. See an extended discussion in Williamson, *Thrones in Revelation*, 151–71.

53. For introductory studies, see Beck, *Dictionary of Imagery*, 257–59; Hays, Duvall, and Pate, *Dictionary of Prophecy*, 444–45; Drinkard, "Throne," 589–90; Ryken, *Dictionary of Biblical Imagery*, 868–69. See the entry "Great White Throne."

night" (Isa 60:11). Jesus uses the figure of a gate for entrance into life or destruction (Matt 7:13–14) and figuratively pictured himself as the gatekeeper, the provider and protector of his people, the sheep (John 10:1–17).[54]

It is this image of gates as entry and protection that John adopts, but expanding it for his vision of the heavenly city. "Gate" (*pylon*) is found eleven of eighteen NT times in Revelation.[55] All eleven references are found in 21:12–22:14 in connection with the great, high wall of the heavenly city. The wall has twelve gates with twelve angels at the gates, and three gates each face east, north, south, and west (21:12–13). An angel had a measuring rod to measure the city, its gates, and its walls (21:15). The twelve gates are twelve pearls, each gate made of a single pearl (21:21). Significantly, on no day will its gates ever be shut (21:25; see Isa 60:11), and believers enjoy free access to the tree of life and go through the gates into the heavenly city (22:14).[56]

Added to this description is the numerical symbolism of twelve, underlining complete and abundant entrance for God's people. Yet this is not new information for John's audience. Twelve gates were a part of the temple vision of Ezek 48:30–35. Whereas those twelve gates meant that each Jewish tribe had entry to their own tribal territory, John universalizes the heavenly temple to provide access for all believers, that is, the overcomers who have inherited the city of God (21:3, 7). Thus, John's vision of the heavenly city with its open twelve gates is one of safety and security, access and freedom. Will there be a cubed city with two hundred-foot walls and twelve open gates in eternity? To literalize the heavenly city in this fashion serves only to limit it. What believers are assured of is eternal access to and protection of God. This cannot be limited.

Bad Things

The following bad things involve divine judgment from God, most often in the context of end-time judgment. Except for the bed of suffering, these bad things are targeted at unbelievers.

Bed of Suffering

A bed of suffering symbolizes someone who is seriously ill as a result of divine judgment. The risen Christ addresses the church at Thyatira concerning its toleration of the false prophetess, Jezebel. He warns Jezebel and her followers that he will "cast her on a bed of suffering, and I will make those who commit adultery with her suffer intensely, unless they repent of her ways" (2:22). To "cast her on a bed" is a common Hebrew idiom that indicates causing someone to be sick or seriously ill (Exod 21:18; 2 Kgs 1:4–6; Ps

---

54. Beck, *Dictionary of Imagery*, 104–6; Hays, Duvall, and Pate, *Dictionary of Prophecy*, 177–79; Ryken, *Dictionary of Biblical Imagery*, 321–22.

55. Specifically, *pylōn* denotes a gateway or gate tower and should probably be distinguished from an actual gate (*pyle*). So Mounce, *Revelation*, 390 n. 12; Smalley, *Revelation*, 548; Robert Thomas, *Revelation*, 2:462.

56. See Rissi, *Future of the World*, 73–74.

6:6).[57] "Bed" (*klinēn*) is metonymy for a debilitating illness in which a person is confined to bed. It is used ironically for those who commit spiritual adultery with Jezebel. Most English translations, therefore, add something to communicate the full meaning of the idiom. Thus, "bed of suffering" (NCV, NIV, NLT), "sickbed" (CEB, CSB, ESV, GW, NABR, NKJV), "bed of pain" (NJB, REB), and "bed of violent illness" (NET).[58] The context confirms what the Bible states elsewhere: the Lord chastens and disciplines those he loves (1 Cor 11:30; 2 Cor 12:6–10; Heb 12:1–13). This warning fits every generation, beginning with John's. This is especially appropriate as a call to repentance and perseverance in light of the second coming.

Dust on Their Heads

This is a common idiom for grief, sorrow, and mourning, and perhaps anger at the prospect of divine, end-time judgment. Although found only once in Scripture (Rev 18:19), throwing dust on one's head is a common Jewish symbol designating sorrow and mourning. The word translated "dust" (*chous*) is found at only one other location. Jesus instructs his followers to leave an unreceptive locale by shaking "the dust off your feet as a testimony against them" (Mark 6:11). Another word for dust (*koniortos*) is used in similar expressions (Matt 10:14; Luke 9:5; Acts 13:51). The Jews of Jerusalem flung dust in the air when they heard Paul's "blasphemy" that Christ had sent him to witness to the gentiles (Acts 22:23). Therefore, sorrow and grief coupled with anger appears to be expressed. The OT shows the phrase as a familiar sign of mourning (Josh 7:6; 1 Sam 4:12; 2 Sam 13:19; Job 2:12). All these references echo John's main source of allusion from Ezek 27:30 where the seafarers "sprinkled dust on their heads" at the destruction of Tyre. In like manner, this will happen at the fall of Babylon at the end of history (18:17–19). Thus, John universalizes the Ezekiel passage to include mourning from the whole evil world system of Babylon at its end-time judgment.[59]

Furnace

A furnace envisions heat, smoke, and hell, and ultimately pictures end-time judgment. Most references to a furnace are used metaphorically to indicate God's judgment or testing. For example, the destruction of Sodom and Gomorrah was likened to "the smoke of a furnace" (Gen 19:28) whereas the fiery furnace of Dan 3 was a place of testing and deliverance. "Furnace" is found only four times in the NT, two of which are in Revelation (1:15; 9:2). The other two references are in parables (Matt 13:42, 50) and afford background. Twice

57. So Aune, *Revelation*, 1:205; Beale, *Revelation*, 263; Brighton, *Revelation*, 83; Hemer, *Letters to the Seven Churches*, 120–21; Osborne, *Revelation*, 159. Robert Thomas (*Revelation*, 1:219–20) agrees as well but assigns the suffering specifically to the great tribulation at the end of history.

58. Patterson (*Revelation*, 116) criticizes NIV translators for moving "from translation to interpretation" by adding the words "of suffering," when in actuality there is no one-to-one correspondence in words. In agreement with the majority of other Bible translations the extra words are appropriately added to clarify the original meaning. See L&N, 1:23, 152.

59. Mounce, *Revelation*, 336; Osborne, *Revelation*, 653.

Jesus concludes the parable with "and will cast them into the furnace of fire. There will be wailing and gnashing of teeth." Both pictures allude to fiery end-time judgment. This theme of end-time judgment continues in John's Apocalypse. In 1:15, the risen Christ's feet are "like bronze glowing in a furnace." This emphasizes the purity and strength of Christ, but stressed within the context of his coming. Judgment, however, is a noticeable secondary motif. Not so for 9:2. Thus, John pictures the Abyss, the bottomless pit of end-time punishment. "When he opened the Abyss, smoke rose from it like the smoke from a gigantic furnace. The sun and sky were darkened by the smoke from the Abyss." Thus, the image of a furnace with its heat, smoke, and choking fumes forms an apt description of judgment that ultimately ends in the lake of fire.

Great Winepress

This is a graphic symbol of end-time judgment upon the wicked. Just as grapes are crushed in a winepress, so too shall the wicked be eternally crushed in the great winepress of God's divine wrath at the second coming. The physical image of trampling the grapes of the harvest was an opportunity for joy and singing (Isa 16:10; Jer 48:33; Joel 2:23). As a metaphor, however, the winepress is consistently presented as a negative image, depicting destruction and judgment.[60] John uses "winepress" (*lēnos*) four times which suggests worldwide coverage. The first three uses are found in 14:19–20 in the grape harvest vision of judgment upon the wicked at the second coming. John adds a favorite apocalyptic adjective—"great winepress."[61] The grape harvest is clearly judgmental, and unbelievers are the intended audience. John evokes Joel 3:13 and Isa 63:1–6. The angel picks the grapes and throws them into the great winepress, a striking figure of divine judgment. Yet many interpreters do not find a picture of the final judgment at this point. Instead, this is one of several judgments that form a proleptic lead up to the final judgment at the second coming.[62] It is better, however, to view this passage as another one of John's visions of the end, and that the treading of the winepress pictures final, end-time judgment that arrives at the second coming.[63] Osborne adds, "It is hard to imagine a stronger picture of final judgment than the graphic image of blood rising like juice from grapes trodden in a winepress."[64]

---

60. Beck, *Dictionary of Imagery*, 274–76; Ryken, *Dictionary of Biblical Imagery*, 954. Beale (*Revelation*, 775) states that treading the winepress, "is without exception a metaphor of judgment in the OT."

61. "Great" is left untranslated by some versions (CEV, GNT, GW), and there is debate on what the adjective modifies since "great" is masculine and "winepress" is feminine. See Beale, *Revelation*, 779–80; and Osborne, *Revelation*, 554, for discussion.

62. So Easley, *Revelation*, 254–55; Alan Johnson, "Revelation," 13:725; LaHaye, *Revelation Unveiled*, 242; Mounce, *Revelation*, 277–81; Patterson, *Revelation*, 296; Robert Thomas, *Revelation*, 2:219–20; Walvoord, *Revelation*, 220–22.

63. So Bauckham, *Climax of Prophecy*, 291–96; Beale, *Revelation*, 770–76; Beasley-Murray, *Revelation*, 230; Brighton, *Revelation*, 388; Hughes, *Revelation*, 165–66; Dennis Johnson, *Triumph of the Lamb*, 214; Mounce, *Revelation*, 279; Mulholland, *Revelation*, 251–53; Smalley, *Revelation*, 379; J. C. Thomas, *Apocalypse*, 446–47.

64. Osborne, *Revelation*, 555.

The last mention of a winepress presents a clearer vision of the second coming. The rider on the white horse is described with allusions to Isaiah and Psalms: "Coming out of his mouth is a sharp sword with which to strike down the nations. 'He will rule them with an iron scepter.' He treads the winepress of the fury of the wrath of God Almighty" (19:15). The last phrase matches closely with 14:19–20, including echoes from Joel 3:13 and Isa 63:1–6. Most English translations prefer the verb "tread" or "trample," but there is also "stomp" (NET), "crush" (NCV), and "release" (NLT). The rest of the sentence is especially powerful, doubling up on wine, wrath, and God's name. Literally, it reads "the winepress of the wine of the wrath of the fury of God, the Almighty." The "treading of the winepress" then is a prophetic symbol of the destruction of God's enemies. John reshapes and universalizes this into an end-time image of final judgment.

Image of the Beast

This symbolizes the deceived and enforced allegiance of unbelievers by the false prophet to the beast. The image (*eikōn*) of the beast is mentioned ten times in Revelation.[65] Four times it is found in 13:14–15. The second beast sets up an image in honor of the first beast. It gives breath to the image so that it can speak and cause all who refuse to worship the image to be killed. The final six occurrences feed off this introduction and are almost always mentioned near the conclusion of an individual vision. Each instance mentions the downfall of those who worship the image (14:9, 11; 16:2; 19:20) or the victory of those who refuse (15:2; 20:4).

Preterists interpret the image from a first-century perspective. It is a statue of the emperor or the institution of the synagogue.[66] Many futurists understand the image of the beast to be a literal statue erected in the last days.[67] Most scholars, however, identify the image of the beast as a cult image in honor of the emperor. The image then is closely connected to idolatry.[68] Resseguie suggests that the second beast's ability to enliven a mute statue is an ironic commentary on idolatry. It is not so much a testimony to magical

---

65. Most English versions have "image" but a few offer "idol" (CEV, NABR, NCV) and "statue" (GW, NJB, NLT). Liu ("Backgrounds and Meaning," 64–78) traces *eikōn* to three meanings: from prototype (idol image of a pagan god) to outward forms and appearances to figurative (living image or a representation of something else).

66. Hailey (*Revelation*, 295) suggests an image of Domitian. Russell (*Parousia*, 468) opts for Nero. Chilton (*Days of Vengeance*, 344) claims it is the synagogue. Buchanan (*Revelation*, 368) interprets it as enforced cooperation with Roman procurators.

67. LaHaye, *Revelation Unveiled*, 225; Ryrie, *Revelation*, 98; Robert Thomas, *Revelation*, 2:177; Walvoord, *Revelation*, 207. Easley (*Revelation*, 232) and Patterson (*Revelation*, 281) suggest ventriloquism is employed to make the statue speak. Hindson (*Revelation*, 148) speculates a projected three-dimensional holographic image to be worshipped around the world. Lindsey (*New World Coming*, 194) states the image will be erected in the middle of the reconstructed temple. For a history of interpreting the image of the beast see Liu, "Backgrounds and Meaning," 13–62.

68. Numerous scholars accept John being more concerned with believers compromising themselves by participating in Roman culture rather than from actual persecution. Thus, a perceived crisis of oppression was on the horizon. Fuller studies include deSilva, "Image of the Beast," 185–208; Friesen, "Beast from the Land," 49–64; idem, *Imperial Cults and the Apocalypse of John*; Kraybill, *Imperial Cult and Commerce*; and Leonard Thompson, *Book of Revelation*.

powers as it is the compelling rhetoric that persuades people to worship creation rather than creator.[69]

Rebekah Yi Liu produces a detailed study of the image of the beast. She depicts the attempt of an unholy trinity to counteract God's goal for the plan of salvation—the restoration of *Imago Dei* in human beings. For her, the image is an end-time entity, comprised of people who reflect the character of the dragon, and impose false worship. The image is best identified with the end-time Babylon the Great of chapters 17–18.[70] Liu's research has merit, especially if it is enlarged to include every generation, not solely the last.

Nebuchadnezzar's golden image (Dan 2), Antiochus Epiphanes's altar to Zeus in the temple (2 Macc 6), Caligula's attempt to do the same, and Domitian's twenty-foot statue in the temple at Ephesus form the historical context for John's image of the beast. The image, however, transcends any narrow reference. Throughout history images have been raised and people have bowed to them whether by deceptive idolatry or forced allegiance. The substitute for the truth of God is available for every generation. Hitler's swastika and the hammer and sickle of the former Soviet Union are recent examples. Believers, therefore, must resist the forced participation into the culture of the age. Overcomers will not succumb to such pressure even when faced with death.[71]

Mark of the Beast

This is a symbol of the worship, allegiance, and ownership of the unholy trinity upon unbelievers, and the pressure for them to submit. It stands in contrast to the seal of God for believers. The mark of the beast is introduced in the third interlude. The second beast (later referred to as the "false prophet") enforces worship of the first beast's image and requires all people to receive a "mark" (*charagma*) on their foreheads and right hands, a mark which is the name of the beast and the number of its name (13:16–17).[72] The mark is mentioned again most often in passages depicting end-time judgment (14:9, 11; 16:2; 19:20; 20:4). It is closely aligned with the image of the beast and the number of its name. The ten references to the image and seven references to the mark accent John's numerical symbolism. These numbers of completion and totality are used as parody.

Smalley succinctly lists major alternatives for the background of the mark: (1) Jewish custom of wearing phylacteries; (2) branding slaves or defeated soldiers or devotees to gods; (3) reference to imperial red seals bearing the emperor's effigy or name; and (4) reference to Roman coinage.[73] The first two are stronger possibilities than the last two. The meaning of the mark stems from Exod 13:9 and Deut 6:8, where God's people are instructed to place the Shema on their hands and foreheads. In other words, Jews were to

---

69. Resseguie, *Revelation*, 187. Mounce (*Revelation*, 258) and Smalley (*Revelation*, 348) remark that breathing life into the image is a satanic parody of the gift of God's Spirit to believers.

70. Liu, "Backgrounds and Meaning."

71. Beale, *Revelation*, 711; Kistemaker, *Revelation*, 391; Smalley, *Revelation*, 348.

72. TR/KJV/NKJV reads "the mark of the beast or his name." Comfort (*New Testament Text*, 845) confirms the best reading is "the mark, the name of the beast, and so most English versions." This means that the mark and the name are appositional—they mean the same thing.

73. Smalley, *Revelation*, 349. See Aune, *Revelation*, 2:767–78; and Koester, *Revelation*, 595–96.

live their lives for God, thinking (forehead) and doing (hands) what the Shema and the law instructed.[74] Another passage from Ezekiel unlocks the meaning. God instructed an angel to put a mark on the foreheads of those who grieve over the detestable things done in Jerusalem (Ezek 9:4–6; also *Pss. Sol.* 15:9).[75]

The seal of God and the mark of the beast, therefore, are contrasting stamps of ownership and loyalty. For the sake of consistency, they both should be understood either figuratively or literally. The seal of God is readily understood as symbolic. The mark of the beast should as well.[76] The mark as a literal, futuristic stamp on the hand and forehead popularly persists for dispensationalists.[77] Yet several scholars—recognizing the symbolism attached to the mark—also agree to a literal manifestation of the mark. For them, such marks had literal historical reality and therefore may imply a futuristic possibility.[78] However, it does not need to be a literal future mark in order to accomplish the purpose of the symbol. In fact, the mark is much more powerful when it is understood figuratively. It reflects all unbelievers, not a partial number of duped followers at history's end. This mark is observable in everything that is thought about and the actions and behaviors performed. Thus, most scholars fully stress the symbolic nature and do not limit the mark to a literal appearance in human history. The mark of the beast reflects the sold out ideological commitment to self, sin, and the devil.[79] Therefore, some follow the Lord, some follow the beast. No one, however, receives both a seal and a mark. Those who refuse the mark (proving that they are believers) will be persecuted and killed (13:15; 14:12–13).

74. Ironically, this figurative teaching point became literalized. By Jesus' day phylacteries were worn by observant Jews. Even today, orthodox Jews wear tefillin on their foreheads and arms.

75. Mulholland (*Revelation*, 237) lists several other metaphorical uses of hand and forehead (Num 24:17; Isa 48:14; Jer 3:3; Ezek 3:7; 2 Chr 26:16–21) and concludes, "All these references have one thing in common, the forehead represents a perceptual framework, particularly an inner orientation of being that is in rebellion against God," and the right hand "is a symbol of action. It represents the practical outworking of the inner orientation of being characterized by the forehead."

76. Nevertheless, the mark has received a bevy of interpretations throughout history. Chilton (*Days of Vengeance*, 342) agrees the mark describes enforced submission to the emperor. But for him, this means only that first-century Israel was "marked" with the seal of Rome's total lordship. Emmerson ("Mark of the Beast," 481–82) mentions that Augustine interpreted it as those who pretend to be Christians but remain members of the godless city. Other church fathers noted Teitan (pagan gods), Lateinos (Roman Empire or church), Genseric (Goths), Mohammed (Islam), the Turks, or simply antichrist as the mark of the beast. During the Reformation the mark was identified with both the Reformers and the papacy. Recently, David R. Johnson ("Mark of the Beast and Early Pentecostal Literature," 184–202) examines the fluidity of interpretation among Pentecostals in the early twentieth century.

77. LaHaye, *Revelation Unveiled*, 227; Patterson, *Revelation*, 281–82; Ryrie, *Revelation*, 99; Robert Thomas, *Revelation*, 2:181; Walvoord, *Revelation*, 209. Seventh Day Adventists purport the mark is a counterfeit Sabbath-like or anti-Sabbath mark that will be enforced on people. See MacPherson, "Mark of the Beast," 267–83; and Stefanovic, *Revelation*, 423–24.

78. Beasley-Murray, *Revelation*, 218–19; Ladd, *Revelation*, 185; Morris, *Revelation*, 168; Mounce, *Revelation*, 260; Osborne, *Revelation*, 517–18; Rowland, "Revelation," 12:658–59; Smalley, *Revelation*, 349–50; Witherington, *Revelation*, 185.

79. Beale, *Revelation*, 715–17; Blount, *Revelation*, 259; Boxall, *Revelation*, 196; Brighton, *Revelation*, 361–62; Caird, *Revelation*, 172–73; Duvall, *Revelation*, 187; Easley, *Revelation*, 233; Hendriksen, *More than Conquerors*, 150; Hughes, *Revelation*, 153; Dennis Johnson, *Triumph of the Lamb*, 196; Keener, *Revelation*, 353; Kistemaker, *Revelation*, 393; Mulholland, *Revelation*, 237; Murphy, *Fallen Is Babylon*, 312; Resseguie, *Revelation*, 188; Schnabel, *40 Questions*, 203; Wilcock, *I Saw Heaven Opened*, 128.

Those who accept the mark (proving they are unbelievers) will be eternally condemned (14:9–11; 16:2; 19:20; 20:4).

Millstone

The symbolic action of the mighty angel hurling the large millstone into the sea represents complete destruction of wicked Babylon at the end of history. Near the end of the fall of Babylon vision "a mighty angel picked up a boulder the size of a large millstone and threw it into the sea, and said: 'With such violence the great city of Babylon will be thrown down, never to be found again'" (18:21). "Millstone" refers to the huge, grain-grinding stone that might weigh tons and must be driven by animals. The image derives from Jeremiah's prophecy of the fall of Babylon. Jeremiah instructs a staff officer to tie a stone around a scroll that lists the disasters placed by God upon Babylon. After reading it to the king he threw it into the Euphrates River (Jer 51:53–64). God proclaims, "So will Babylon sink to rise no more because of the disaster I will bring on her. And her people will fall" (Jer 51:64).

In the Gospels, Jesus warns that "If anyone causes one of these little ones—those who believe in me—to stumble, it would be better for them if a large millstone were hung around their neck and they were thrown into the sea" (Mark 9:42; Matt 18:6; Luke 17:2). Ramsey Michaels makes the application that "Babylon the Great was thrown into the sea for one main reason: because she harmed the 'little ones' who belonged to Jesus! The saying of Jesus is here transformed into a vision and acted out in a violent and unforgettable drama."[80] John universalizes Jeremiah's symbolic action for the end-time judgment of Babylon the Great. In addition, the verb translated "with such violence" (*ormēmati*) is unique in the NT, and denotes a sudden, violent rushing action, further underscoring the consummate judgment of Babylon at the end of history.[81]

Pair of Scales

The pair of scales which the rider on the black horse carries symbolizes famine and scarcity. "Scales" (*zygos*) normally have two dishes balanced by a stand. On one side a precious metal or money is placed while the other dish holds a weight. The OT often pictures God as the righteous judge holding heavenly scales and weighing earthly motives and actions (1 Sam 2:3; Job 6:2; Ps 62:9; Prov 16:2; Isa 40:12; Dan 5:27).[82]

In the NT, implicit "weighing" is found when Jesus enjoins listeners to judge justly (Matt 7:2–5; Mark 4:24–25; Luke 7:34–38). The idea of justice is prominent. The sole explicit reference to scales, however, is found in the Apocalypse. At the third seal, John sees a black horse, its rider holding a "pair of scales." One of the four living creatures states, "Two pounds of wheat for a day's wages, and six pounds of barley for a day's wages, and do not damage the oil and the wine!" (6:5–6). Although details on wheat, barley, oil, and

---

80. Michaels, *Interpreting Revelation*, 127.

81. Osborne, *Revelation*, 656 n. 20.

82. Bond, "Scales," 683–84.

wine differ among Bible scholars, all agree that the context clearly symbolizes famine and scarcity. The foods mentioned are daily staples of life, scarcely enough to survive on for one slave family. The price is exorbitant, manifold times more than the normal rate. The mention of "oil and wine" cause debate among interpreters, but if John's original audience is allowed the first shot for interpretation, then it may be an allusion to the recent grain shortage (AD 92). Emperor Domitian demanded half of the vineyards to be cut down in order to increase grain production. This certainly would reflect the severity of the situation. Since the roots of olive trees and grapevines go deep into the soil, it might also imply that one day the oil and wine may return. God, then, is allowing the famine, but limiting its extent. Conditions are bad, but not unbearable. This situation can be found throughout the centuries, including the present generation. Famine and scarcity will be a part of the universal landscape at the end of history as well.[83]

Seven Bowls

The seven bowls are the last in a series of three righteous judgments (along with seals and trumpets) delivered upon unrepentant humanity. Each series culminates with the eschaton. Bowls are mentioned often in the OT. About thirty times they are found in connection with the priestly service at the altar in the tabernacle or the temple. "Bowl" (*phialē*) is found twelve times in the NT, all in Revelation, and all in conjunction with the seven bowl judgments (15:5–16:21). John alludes to the golden bowls filled with incense found in the holy of holies. These saucer-like pans were placed on the table of the bread of Presence and served as instruments of worship and praise (Exod 25:29).[84] The golden bowls may also derive from the early Jewish belief that angels functioned as heavenly priests of God. John, however, combines these images to produce a negative effect—God's end-time wrath poured out. The bowls form part of the answer to the prayers of the righteous (5:8).[85] One of the four living creatures gives the golden bowls to the seven angels (15:7) who then deliver the seven bowls of wrath (16:1–21).[86] The order is significant. The bowls come first from the heavenly temple, are delivered from the throne by the four living creatures, who in turn give them to the seven angels to dispense upon the earth.

Exegetes agree that the sixth and seventh bowls reflect the gathering for an end-time battle and the eschaton. But John repeats, expands, and offers different viewing angles from previous and subsequent references to Armageddon and the end (6:12–17; 9:13–21; 11:15–19; 19:17–21; 20:7–10). Therefore, following a progressive recapitulation approach, the seals, trumpets, and bowls are temporally parallel. Many interpreters, of

---

83. Aune, *Revelation*, 1:399–400; Mounce, *Revelation*, 144–45; Osborne, *Revelation*, 280–81.

84. Beale, *Revelation*, 806; Hays, Duvall, and Pate, *Dictionary of Prophecy*, 73–75; Ryken, *Dictionary of Biblical Imagery*, 115–16; Smalley, *Revelation*, 134.

85. Hays, Duvall, and Pate, *Dictionary of Prophecy*, 189. Woods ("Seven Bowls of Wrath," 64–75) examines the bowls from an ecological standpoint, and attempts to connect them to climate change, pollution, and other global calamities. Thus, the bowls become a warning and summons to repent of these ecocatastrophes. See the entry "New Heaven and New Earth."

86. Two final references occur. The fall of Babylon vision is introduced by one of the seven angels who deliver the bowls (17:1), and perhaps the same angel shows John the new Jerusalem (21:9).

course, disagree. In particular, the use by John of fractions such as a fourth (seals) and a third (trumpets) compared to the full coverage of the bowls is a potent argument for sequence or at least partial judgments being depicted in the seals and trumpets. Words such as "every," "all," and "last" intersperse the bowls. Nevertheless, the weight of the rest of the context favors temporally parallel events. Beale explains that "the difference in extent of effect may merely suggest that the trumpets are part of a larger process of judgment, which at the same time strikes the entire world."[87] The similarities between the trumpets and the bowls overshadow any differences. Both judgments draw heavily from the Exodus plagues.[88] Both present their judgments in the same order—earth, sea, rivers, sun, darkness, Euphrates/Armageddon, and final judgment.[89] The bowls are last in their order of literary presentation, not in chronology. Eckhard Schnabel clarifies, "The events described in the three series of judgments are indicators of the last period of human history on this earth in the sense that the last period of history is the period between Jesus' first and second coming."[90]

Seven Seals

The seven seals form one of the three series of righteous judgments (along with trumpets and bowls) delivered upon unrepentant humanity. Each series covers the interadvental age. Seals were sometimes used by OT prophets to emphasize that their messages and visions were sealed until the proper time (Isa 8:16; 29:11; Dan 8:26; 9:24; 12:4).[91] John uses the same formula. The seven seals are the first in a series of three judgments that comprise the heart of the Rev 6–16.[92] In all three series the first four judgments are briefer and focus on earth whereas the last three are longer and more cosmic in nature. They picture the very end of history.[93]

In the throne room vision the mighty angel asks who can break the seals and open the scroll. Only the Lamb is worthy to do so (5:1–14). The seals vision immediately follows. There is disagreement on where to end the seals judgments. Most scholars select 8:1 because the trumpets are introduced in 8:2.[94] Numerous scholars, however, recognize that John is utilizing an interlocking or chain-linking approach. In other words, John

---

87. Beale, *Revelation*, 808.

88. Gallusz, "Exodus Motif in Revelation 15–16," 21–43.

89. Beale (*Revelation*, 128, 809–10) includes excellent charts on the seals and comparing the trumpets and bowls.

90. Schnabel, *40 Questions*, 74.

91. See the entry "Seal of God."

92. For a history of how the seal judgments are interpreted, see Kovacs and Rowland, *Revelation*, 80–93; and Reeves, "Seven Seals," 703–6.

93. Hays, Duvall, and Pate (*Dictionary of Prophecy*, 405) and Koester (*Revelation*, 405) suggest that since the seals and trumpets are interrupted by interludes, it may be more accurate to see a 4+2+1 pattern for them.

94. Osborne (*Revelation*, 341) speaks for many when he says 8:2–6 serves as the introduction to the trumpet judgments.

is introducing the forthcoming trumpets before concluding his seals series.[95] Thus, the seventh seal extends to 8:5.[96]

Bible students argue over the chronology of the seven seals (and trumpets and bowls). Some attempt a straight sequence with occasional forward and backward looks.[97] Others find a modified sequential progression in which the seventh seal opens to reveal the trumpets. The seventh trumpet opens to reveal the seven bowls.[98]

But many scholars recognize repetition between the seals, trumpets, and bowls.[99] This study favors the three judgments progressively recapitulating the same time frame between the resurrection of Christ and his second coming. The first four judgments of each series reflect the progression of history while the last three judgments appear to be reserved closer to the conclusion of history. Thus, the judgments of first four seals (the famous four horsemen of the Apocalypse) can be found throughout the centuries. Wars, civil wars, famine, and death have not escaped any generation. They reflect the partial judgment that will one day become judgment day. The final three seals, however, reflect events closer to the second coming. The cry of the martyrs is a cry for vindication. Their question of "how long?" is answered in the sixth and seventh seals which depict the second coming and the day of judgment.

Seven Thunders

This is another sevenfold cycle of judgments that temporally parallel the seals, trumpets, and bowls, but are never described. They accent the fact that God is sovereign and in complete control of end-time judgment. People of the ancient Near East believed thunder was a manifestation of God's voice. It metaphorically portrayed God's awesome majesty or divine displeasure (Exod 19:16; 2 Sam 22:14; Ps 18:13). Thunder becomes a common image that accents the presence, power, and judgment of God, particularly at the end of history. In response, it elicits the awe and dread of humanity.[100] *Brontē* is found ten times in Revelation. In four locations, thunder forms part of the end-time cosmic storm of "flashes of lightning, rumblings, peals of thunder (and earthquake and hailstorm; 4:5; 8:5; 11:19; 16:18).[101] Thunder is featured three times to reflect power and authority and judgment which originates from heaven (6:1; 14:2; 19:6).

This leaves three references to the "seven thunders," one of John's most mysterious revelations (10:3–4). At the beginning of the second interlude where John is

95. Beale (*Revelation*, 454), for example, explains "The primary thematic function of the parenthesis in vv. 3–5 is to pick up and conclude the description of final judgment begun in 6:12–17 and 8:1."

96. See the Introduction n. 46, for scholars who extend the seals to 8:5.

97. Patterson (*Revelation*, 34), for example, allows for "flashbacks to historical events (12:7–9) and contemporary events (John's frequent participations in his own visions)."

98. Alan Johnson, "*Revelation*," 13:669–70; Ladd, *Revelation*, 122; Robert Thomas, *Revelation*, 2:525–43; Walvoord, *Revelation*, 150.

99. See the Introduction n. 44, for scholars who follow recapitulation.

100. Lawlor, "Thunder and Lightning," 590–91; Ryken, *Dictionary of Biblical Imagery*, 869; William White, "Thunder," 852.

101. See the entry "Flashes of Lightning, Rumblings, Peals of Thunder . . ."

recommissioned to be a witness, the mighty angel gives a loud shout. "And when the seven thunders spoke, I was about to write; but I heard a voice from heaven say, 'Seal up what the seven thunders have said and do not write it down'" (10:4). John includes the article, "the" seven thunders, an assumption that the readers knew what he was referencing. Most scholars detect Ps 29:1–9 in the background. For certain, the number seven emphasizes fullness or totality of what is numbered. This would therefore represent the complete word on the matter. Yet it is not known exactly what John was referencing. Some conclude, therefore, that to speculate anything adds little value to understanding the passage.

There are enough allusions and structural clues, however, to permit a few conjectures. First, some posit that the seven thunders may picture another series of further judgments, but that God has canceled them. For the sake of the elect or because of the lack of repentance on the part of humanity, God canceled the judgments of the seven thunders.[102] Second, several scholars state the seven thunders are too sacred to be revealed, and it is unwise to speculate further. Kendell Easley, for instance, relates, "we have sufficient but not exhaustive information on the end."[103] Other speculations have been offered as well.[104] A third view, however, holds the most promise. The seven thunders are another temporally parallel series of seven plagues patterned after the seals, trumpets, and bowls, but which are never launched. This is similar to the first view above but advances beyond it. The seven thunders are not canceled; they are simply not described. Thus, they follow in the same temporally parallel vein as the seals, trumpets, and bowls. Beale reasons that a fourth sevenfold plague is modeled to match the fourfold plagues found in Lev 26. The thunders remain hidden "perhaps because they are so repetitive of the previous synchronous sevenfold cycles that they reveal nothing radically new."[105] John Christopher Thomas adds, "it is exceedingly difficult to imagine that mention of the seven thunders would not be taken by the hearers as the introduction of yet another series of sevens, along the lines of the seven seals and seven trumpets."[106] Several scholars appear to support this viewpoint.[107] Following a progressively parallel structure for Revelation, this means the seven thunders would have been yet another synchronous series of judgments, with the sixth

---

102. Caird, *Revelation*, 126–27; Kiddle, *Revelation*, 169–70; Mounce, *Revelation*, 203–4; Sweet, *Revelation*, 176–77.

103. Easley, *Revelation*, 173–74. So also Beasley-Murray, *Revelation*, 173; Brighton, *Revelation*, 267–68; Fee, *Revelation*, 142; Keener, *Revelation*, 281; Kistemaker, *Revelation*, 311; LaHaye, *Revelation Unveiled*, 179; Morris, *Revelation*, 139; Mulholland, *Revelation*, 200; Osborne, *Revelation*, 396–97; Patterson, *Revelation*, 231.

104. Hughes (*Revelation*, 116), for example, argues that the words of the thunders are subsequently recorded in the rest Revelation. Schüssler Fiorenza (*Revelation*, 75) suggests the thunders may have revealed the date for the end. Lupieri (*Apocalypse*, 168–69) personifies the seven thunders into seven angels.

105. Beale, *Revelation*, 536 n. 177. See his full discussion at 533–37.

106. J. C. Thomas, *Apocalypse*, 313.

107. Alan Johnson, "Revelation," 13:677; Ladd, *Revelation*, 143; Murphy, *Fallen Is Babylon*, 253; Resseguie, *Revelation*, 154; Schnabel, *40 Questions*, 62. Possibly followed by Bauckham (*Climax of Prophecy*, 259–61), Boxall (*Revelation*, 154), and Smalley (*Revelation*, 262–63). So too Paul (*Revelation*, 189), who notes the complete series adds up to twenty-eight, but understands the seals, trumpets, and bowls are for the present while the thunders are for the future.

and seventh thunders picturing the end of history. Therefore, the major message is one of sovereignty. God is in control. The numerical symbolism described in a fourfold series of seven judgments heightens the complete, total world coverage of these judgments.

Seven Trumpets

The seven trumpets form the second of three series of righteous judgments (along with seals and bowls) delivered upon unrepentant humanity, culminating in the second coming. Trumpets in ancient Greek, Roman, and Jewish worlds were primarily used as heralds of significant events, not as musical instruments. The blow of a trumpet signaled warfare (Judg 3:27; Ezek 7:14). It heralded the coming of a dignitary or king (2 Sam 15:10; 1 Kgs 1:34). It formed part of worship activities such as festive processions (2 Sam 6:15; Neh 12:35) and sacrificial offerings (2 Chr 29:27). Trumpets became associated with eschatological events (Joel 2:1; Zeph 1:14–16; 4 Ezra 6:23; Matt 24:31; 1 Cor 15:52; 1 Thess 4:16).[108] These images continue in Revelation, especially as symbolic harbingers that usher in the eschaton.

The majority of John's uses are connected to the seven trumpets. All ten verbs "to sound a trumpet" (*salpizo*) and four of the six nouns (*salpinx*) deal with the seven trumpets.[109] The seven trumpets cover parts of three chapters (8:2, 6–13; 9:1–21; 11:15–19). Like the bowls, they recap the Egyptian plagues of Exod 7–10.

The seven trumpets recapitulate the seals and bowls and span the time from the first coming of Christ to his second coming. Thus, the first four trumpets deliver judgments on earth. The final three trumpets are called "woes." The fifth and sixth trumpets deliver judgments to unbelievers, and envision events nearer the end time, including allusions to Armageddon (9:13–21). The seventh trumpet is the eschaton (11:15–19). The heavenly choir announces that God's wrath has arrived. It is now time to judge the unrighteous and reward the righteous.

Resseguie capably relates the symbolic connections between the seals, trumpets, and bowls. Since the Lamb breaks the seals, the emphasis for the first plague series is not upon the destruction released as much as it is on the one worthy to accomplish God's plan. The trumpets announce the day of the Lord but also summon people to repentance before it is too late (9:20–21). The bowls are used in the context of worship and prayers to the saints, so they emphasize God's vindication of his people's prayers.[110]

---

108. Beale, *Revelation*, 465–72; Caird, *Revelation*, 108–11; Hays, Duvall, and Pate, *Dictionary of Prophecy*, 454–57; Peach, *Paul and the Apocalyptic Triumph*, 64–67; Resseguie, *Revelation Unsealed*, 99–100; Ryken, *Dictionary of Biblical Imagery*, 900.

109. There are two references to a voice "like a trumpet" (1:10; 4:1) and the cognate "trumpeter" (*salpistēs*; 18:22). The other two NT instances are also used symbolically (Matt 6:2; 1 Cor 14:8).

110. Resseguie, *Revelation Unsealed*, 101–2.

5

Good People and Bad People

THIS CHAPTER RELATES THE key images and figures of speech found in people and names. The length of the chapter attests that John's Apocalypse is more about people than it is about events. The division into good and bad people assists in understanding John's theology. There is no fence-sitting in Revelation. You are either a believer or you are not. Nevertheless, there are a few phrases which John uses to encompass all people. Thus, the chapter is divided into all people, good people, and bad people.

All People

The following three phrases appear to include everyone on earth, good and bad, believer and unbeliever.

Every Tribe and Language and People and Nation

This fourfold phrase, found in varying word order, indicates everyone on earth without exception. Numerical symbolism is prominently on display in this expression. It is mentioned exactly seven times in Revelation (5:9; 7:9; 10:11; 11:9; 13:7; 14:6; 17:15). Bauckham states, "The sevenfold use of this fourfold phrase indicates that reference is being made to all the nations of the world. In the symbolic world of Revelation, there could hardly be a more emphatic indication of universalism."[1] Thus, universality and completeness is noted in John's usage of both numbers. This idiom for universality probably derives from Gen 10:5, 20; Dan 3:4; 5:19; 6:25; 7:14. The phrase is found seven times in Daniel as well.[2]

---

1. Bauckham, *Climax of Prophecy*, 326; see 326–37. Although most commentators identify the universal coverage of the phrase, it is Bauckham who adds keen insights into the genius of John's compositional technique.

2. The Danielic passages reveal three ethnic units (peoples, nations, and languages) and a universal audience is in view. Similarly, Smalley (*Revelation*, 137) notes a fourfold phrase is used in *4 Ezra* 3:7.

The various orderings include "kings" for "tribes" (10:11) and "multitudes" for "tribes" (17:15). Intriguingly, in none of the seven listings is the same order given. Nor do any of the seven listings begin with "languages." This suggests the listings are not random. Rather, the order is specific and tied to the immediate context.[3] Broadly, "tribe" (*phylē*) conveys the meaning of physical descent. "Language" (*glōssa*) emphasizes linguistic communication. "People" (*laos*) refers to ethnicity. "Nation" (*ethnos*) can and does include the previous three, but probably emphasizes political and geographical distinctions and boundaries. Thus, the overlapping nature of the four terms plus the fact they are all classed together confirms the phrase as an all-encompassing idiom. No national, political, cultural, or racial boundaries are exempt in the definition. Most modern English versions do well in listing all four words each time to aid the intratextual connections. A few select "race" over "people" for *laos* (CEV, GNT, NJB, REB) and "tongue" over "language" for *glōssa* (NABR, NASB, NKJV).[4]

In Heaven, on Earth, and under the Earth

This common idiom denotes all created beings in the universe and is not limited to humans. This phrase is used by John in contexts of worship. In the throne room vision, John weeps because there is no one in the whole universe who is worthy enough to open the scroll (5:3). The threefold division of the universe into heaven, on earth, and under the earth follows the Jewish understanding of a three-tiered universe (Exod 20:4: Job 11:8–9; Ps 146:6). By the time of the NT the third division became synonymous with Hades and departed spirits, including demons (Phil 2:10; Rom 10:6–7).[5] That the residents of Hades are included matches the possible forced homage found elsewhere (11:13; 14:6–7).[6] John flexes the idiom into a fourfold division later in the vision, adding "on the sea, and all that is in them" (5:13). The add-on phrase enhances the numerical symbol of four and stresses the totality of God's creatures. The threefold division (heaven, earth, sea) is mentioned in the second interlude (10:6). John also relates a dualistic twofold division of heaven and earth/sea (10:5; 12:12; 14:6; 21:1). Thus, John uses stock phrases to emphasize the totality of creation. Everything witnesses God's actions and gives glory, either voluntarily or by compulsion.

Small and Great

This figure of speech indicates all people and stresses that everyone is on equal footing in the eyes of God either for reward or for judgment. This merism is common (Gen 19:11;

---

3. Bauckham, *Climax of Prophecy*, 326–27; J. C. Thomas, *Apocalypse*, 232. See the helpful chart in Duvall, *Revelation*, 96.

4. See Aune, *Revelation*, 1:351; Beale, *Revelation*, 359; Kistemaker, *Revelation*, 211; Morris, *Revelation*, 97; Osborne, *Revelation*, 260; Robert Thomas, *Revelation*, 1:401.

5. Osborne, *Revelation*, 251; Smalley, *Revelation*, 130; Robert Thomas, *Revelation*, 1:384–85.

6. Most commentators understand one last chance to repent. Beale (*Revelation*, 749–53), however, understands forced submission since the context (fall of Babylon) reflects judgment day.

1 Sam 5:9; 2 Kgs 23:2; Ps 104:25; Jer 16:6). "The small and great" is found five times in Revelation, most often at the conclusion of an individual vision. The first four instances mention "small and great" and the last one mentions "great and small," but the change is insignificant.[7] Several modern versions follow this Greek word order closely (CEB, CSB, ESV, NASB, NET). The NIV, however, translates all five references as "great and small." For readability reasons, some English translations end up masking the repetition of this figure of speech with alternate phrases and switching the word order. For example, CEV favors "no matter who they are" and for the last reference "no matter who they had been." GW follows "the important and unimportant" but adds other phraseology as well.

Whereas other figures of speech are consistently used by John to refer to all people ("every tribe and language and people and nation"), unbelievers ("inhabitants of the earth"), or believers ("great multitude"), the phrase "the small and the great" refers twice to all believers (11:18; 19:5), twice to all unbelievers (13:16; 19:18), and once to both believers and unbelievers (20:12). Not everyone understands 13:16 to refer to unbelievers. Osborne, for example, states that "small and great" in this instance refers to the socially important and unimportant. In other words, it stresses all humanity.[8] Other commentators likewise interpret this passage's "small and great" universally—Christians and non-Christians. But it seems more consistent to maintain the contrast between those who follow the Lamb and receive the seal of God and those who follow the beast and receive his mark. The point for believers (small and great) is not to bow to the beast. Similarly, 20:12 is debated. Primarily, believers are in mind here, but since the very next sentence begins the judgment of unbelievers, and the proximity could easily imply full coverage, an all-inclusive reference is in order.[9] Thus, this merism stresses universality. One either follows God and the Lamb, resulting in eternal life and rewards or one does not, which means following the beast and resulting in eternal judgment.

Good People

Except for the singular Antipas, the entries listed in this section all reflect the church or the totality of believers in both the OT and NT. John's assorted images force readers to observe the church from many different perspectives.

Antipas

Antipas is a martyr for Christ mentioned by John in order to encourage persecuted Christians to remain steadfast in their witness until the end. One of the few non-symbolic designations found in Revelation is John's reference to a person named Antipas from the

---

7. Most scholars see the inverse as insignificant. J. C. Thomas (*Apocalypse*, 615), however, suggests that the switch to "great and small" means that absolutely no one, "beginning with the great people of the earth and going to the least, is absent or exempted."

8. Osborne, *Revelation*, 517. Patterson (*Revelation*, 255–56) singularly suggests that 11:18 refers to the "small or great (in the church)."

9. So Beale, *New Testament Biblical Theology*, 513. See Aune, *Revelation*, 2:766.

church at Pergamum. Christ states, "You did not renounce your faith in me, not even in the days of Antipas, my faithful witness, who was put to death in your city—where Satan lives" (2:13). Nothing is known of Antipas except his name and description as a faithful witness of Christ, stressed by a double title of "my faithful one, my witness" (*ho martys mou, ho pistos mou*; NASB, NRSV). Evidently, he was well-known to the church at Pergamum and neighboring congregations as well. A later writing called *The Menologia* claimed he was killed under Domitian (AD 81–96). *The Martyrologia* added that he was cast into a heated brazen bull and slowly roasted to death.[10]

Beheaded

"Beheaded" refers not only to those who have died as martyrs for Christ, but to all believers who must be ever ready to suffer persecution because of their Christian testimony. "Beheading" is mentioned five times in the NT, four times in connection with John the Baptist, and once in connection with the martyrs of Rev 20:4. The Gospels record the literal beheading of John the Baptist. The apostle James suffered the same fate (Acts 12:2). Tradition states that Paul was beheaded. But what does the apostle John mean when he mentions "beheading?" Is it literal and limited or figurative and broad? Bible students debate over the exact identity of these martyrs. Some limit them to the first century, some see them as martyrs throughout the centuries, and still others relegate them to the final days of history.

Scholars do agree that beheading is a metaphor for martyrdom, whatever shape it takes. The word is periphrasis for "put to death."[11] Therefore, most understand the beheaded of 20:4 more simply as those who are put to death— martyrdom for one's testimony for Christ. This opens up the fuller context of Revelation that repeatedly mentions perseverance in the face of persecution and possible martyrdom (1:2; 2:13; 6:9–11; 12:17; 13:10; 14:12; 19:10), as well as the assumption of the rest of the NT (Matt 10:38; Rom 6:3–11; Gal 5:24). A few English Bibles lend support at this point. GNT translates the word "beheaded" as "executed." NCV opts for "killed." These dynamic equivalent renderings for modern audiences actually come closer to the meaning.[12] Thus, the dreadful image of "beheading" refers primarily to martyrdom. Just as the sword is used as an example of capital punishment and does not necessarily mean a genuine sword, so too martyrs for Christ die in a variety of ways, and are not limited to beheadings.

Nevertheless, does the image of beheading remain limited only to those who die for Christ? Does John refer only to a select class of saints?[13] Or does "beheading" refer

---

10. Koester, *Revelation*, 287; Mounce, *Revelation*, 80; Smalley, *Revelation*, 69.

11. Blount, *Revelation*, 364–65; Brighton, *Revelation*, 558–59; Robert Thomas, *Revelation*, 2:415; Walvoord, *Revelation*, 296.

12. The HCSB reads "beheaded" but a footnote is supplied that states: "All who had given their lives for their faith in Christ." The updated CSB, however, deletes the note.

13. For example, Michaels (*Revelation*, 223) states they are indeed actual martyrs "because in John's visions all faithful Christians have been killed. They are not an elite group that is more 'spiritual' than other believers." So Beasley-Murray, *Revelation*, 293; Mounce, *Revelation*, 365; Mulholland, *Revelation*, 309; Resseguie, *Revelation*, 246.

to all Christians since everyone who is in Christ will—in one way or another—suffer in their witness? If the latter view is in John's mind, then the martyrs serve as outstanding examples of the suffering that may come to everyone who follows the Lamb (6:9–11). Rebecca Skaggs and Priscilla Benham state it "is probably a general term representing all those who have wholly committed themselves to Christ."[14] Thus, if a more general understanding of persecution is in mind then "beheaded" serves as a brutal reminder for all believers that to live for Christ means the possibility of following the Lamb wherever he goes, even all the way to martyrdom.

Blameless

At the second coming, believers are pictured as a dedicated offering to God. This is evidenced by their moral lifestyles which guarantee a harvest of eternal, divine fellowship with the Father and the Lamb. "Blameless" (*amōmos*) is found only once in Revelation, but it is a word rich in symbolism. John describes the redeemed as firstfruits, with no lie in their mouths, blameless (14:5). "Blameless" basically means without blemish or fault and derives from sacrificial imagery. Alternative translations include "without fault" (NCV, NKJV, REB), "no fault" (NJB), "faultless" (GNT), "unblemished" (NABR), and "innocent" (CEV).

John presents a fourfold identification of believers—(1) virgins (i.e. pure); (2) followers of the Lamb; (3) firstfruits; and (4) blameless. The last two terms refer to sacrificial offerings. "Blameless" applied to humans takes on the idea of one's ethical lifestyle. The picture of an offering given to the Lord with no defect (Exod 29:1; Lev 4:3) is adopted by NT writers to refer to Jesus, the perfect sacrificial lamb (Heb 9:14; 1 Pet 1:19) as well as to believers for living faithfully and morally (Eph 1:4; Phil 2:15; Col 1:22; Jude 24). Therefore, the redeemed are pictured as without blemish. They live pure, ethical lives, sacrificially offering themselves fully to the Lamb. "Of course, this does not entail absolute perfection but rather a total walk with Christ and an absolute commitment to God, in keeping with its use elsewhere in the NT."[15]

Bride of the Lamb

The bride of the Lamb is a metaphor for the church, including OT saints as well as NT saints, who will enjoy intimate, eternal fellowship with their bridegroom in the new Jerusalem. Brides, bridegrooms, and weddings comprise a rich resource for symbolism in the Bible. Many interpret the entire Song of Solomon, with its sensual story of an intimate relationship, as a figure for the ultimate relationship between God and his people. Israel became symbolized as the wife of God in the OT (Isa 49:18; 54:5–6). Conversely, infidelity was

---

14. Skaggs and Benham, *Revelation*, 206. So too Beale, *Revelation*, 998; Boxall, *Revelation*, 284; Brighton, *Revelation*, 558–59; Keener, *Revelation*, 467; Rotz, *Revelation*, 274; Smalley, *Revelation*, 506. Perhaps Osborne (*Revelation*, 705) states it best: "I believe it is indeed the martyrs who are the focus throughout 20:4 but that all the saints are also intended in the larger context."

15. Osborne, *Revelation*, 531; see 528–31; Mounce, *Revelation*, 266–69.

also a prevalent symbol. Hosea's story symbolizes the warped relationship between Israel and God. Israel became a prostitute (Hos 2:1–23; see Ezek 16:15–63).

The NT expands on the marriage imagery. The popular phrase "bride of Christ" does not appear. The concept, however, is expressed in several passages to describe the church. Jesus uses the figure of a bridegroom (Matt 9:14–17; 25:1–13; John 3:22–30). Paul adopts the bride as a metaphor for the church (2 Cor 11:2; Eph 5:25–27). Wedding imagery reaches its climax in the last book of the Bible. John symbolizes the believing community as the new Jerusalem who unites with Christ—the eschatological bridegroom.[16]

This nuptial imagery is found in five places (18:23; 19:7–9; 21:2; 21:9; 22:17).[17] The first is a negative reference. The finality of Babylon's doom includes the phrase the "voice of the bridegroom and the bride will never be heard in you again" (18:23). Thus, just as the new Jerusalem will be pictured as a bride (21:2), Babylon the Great is a city without a bride.[18] Second, the wedding supper of the Lamb pictures the commencement of the believer's intimate relationship and eternal fellowship with Christ (19:7–9). The bride has made herself ready and is given to wear "fine linen, bright and clean," signifying a life of faith and good works and holding fast to the testimony of Jesus (19:10).[19] The third use is found near the conclusion of the thousand years vision. John declares, "I saw the Holy City, the new Jerusalem, coming down out of heaven from God, prepared as a bride beautifully dressed for her husband" (21:2). The merging of these two metaphors is significant and natural. The bride is the city, a common Jewish depiction (Isa 1:18; Jer 4:31; Gal 4:22–31; 4 Ezra 9:38–47).[20] The fourth mention is only a few verses later but in the subsequent vision. John begins the new Jerusalem vision with "One of the seven angels who had the seven bowls full of the seven last plagues came and said to me, "Come, I will show you the bride, the wife of the Lamb" (21:9). The bride that John is permitted to see is the end-time city of God, where his glorious presence establishes an eternal, redeemed community.[21] The final bride reference is found near the conclusion of Revelation. "The

---

16. There are rich resources for the study of this image. See Batey, *New Testament Nuptial Imagery*, 53–58; Fekkes, "His Bride Has Prepared Herself," 269–87; Hays, Duvall, and Pate, *Dictionary of Prophecy*, 76–78; Huber, *Like a Bride Adorned*, 134–89; Minear, *Images of the Church*, 54–56; Ryken, *Dictionary of Biblical Imagery*, 120–22, 537–39. Two studies are particularly in-depth. First, Hartopo ("Marriage of the Lamb") investigates the background to marriage imagery in Jewish literature to shed light on John's purposes. John employs marriage imagery to warn the seven churches against the sin of idolatry. Second, Villeneuve (*Nuptial Symbolism*, 1–55, 247–64) traces four key moments of this motif. Marriage was established yet damaged at Eden; restored on Mount Sinai, perpetuated in temple liturgy on Mount Zion, and consummated at the eschaton.

17. Zimmerman ("Nuptial Imagery in Revelation," 153–83) finds nuptial imagery coursing throughout Revelation, and not limited to the final chapters. It is glimpsed in the bridal wreath (2:10; 3:11) and the virgins (14:4–5). Thus, John structures his wedding metaphors to contrast with metaphors on fornication and adultery, which is idolatry (2:20–22; 14:8; 17:1–5; 18:3; 19:2).

18. Huber (*Like a Bride Adorned*, 185–89) notes that the nuptial reference is placed at the end of the list of the things no longer found in Babylon, accenting its importance.

19. See the entry "Wedding Supper of the Lamb." Since the context is the wedding supper most English translations prefer "bride" (19:7) although the word is actually "woman" or "wife" (*gynē*). A few translations adopt the more literal translation of "wife" (HCSB, NKJV).

20. Smalley, *Revelation*, 536. See Fekkes, "His Bride Has Prepared Herself," 274–78.

21. Beale, *Revelation*, 1063. See Huber, *Like a Bride Adorned*, 163–76.

Spirit and the bride say, 'Come!' (22:17). Although the fulfillment of all the marital imagery awaits future consummation, the marriage of the Lamb is coming soon (22:20).

The metaphor of marriage, therefore, creates a compelling picture of the intimate, loving, personal relationship the Lamb has with his bride. John hearkens back to the OT prophecies about God marrying his people Israel once again for the end times, but moving beyond ethnic designations to include all who believe in Jesus.

Brothers and Sisters

The Greek word for "brothers" refers to "brothers and sisters," that is, Christians. It underscores the intimate familial relationship of believers with the Father. The OT's use of "brother" for fellow Israelites is taken up in the NT (Acts 2:29; Rom 9:3; Gal 6:10; Eph 2:19). Since Christ's followers are the new people of God (2 Cor 6:16–18; Heb 8:8–12; 1 Pet 2:9–10), the word brother (*adelphos*) is applied to fellow believers. In plural form, *adelphoi* normally includes both male and female members of the church.[22] Thus, Christian fellowship is modeled along biological lines of siblingship and family ties.

In Revelation, *adelphos* is used once (1:9) and *adelphoi* is found four times (6:11; 12:10; 19:10; 22:9).[23] The singular form refers to John himself. Each one of the plural usages is gender inclusive and means "brothers and sisters." Accordingly, numerous English versions attempt gender accuracy at some or all four of these locations. "Brothers and sisters" is consistently chosen by CEB and NCV. GW selects "Christians." NRSV opts for "comrades" except for "brothers and sisters" at 6:11.[24] NIV has "brothers and sisters" except for "fellow prophets" at 22:9. CEV has "followers," "our people," and "everyone who tells about Jesus."

Many moderns, however, assume there are only male prophets at 22:9. A few English versions reflect this. CSB and NLT utilize "brothers and sisters" at the other three locations but switch to "brothers" at 22:9. NET opts for "brothers" at 6:11 and 22:9. GNT uses "believers" except for "brothers" at 22:9. ESV, HCSB, and NABR retain "brothers" at all four locations. These choices indicate modern complementarian translation concerns that prophets are only male.[25] Yet there were prophetesses in the OT (Exod 15:20; Judg

---

22. Aasgaard, "Brother, Brotherhood," 505–7; Silva, "ἀδελφός," 150–51.

23. It is possible that John had numerical symbolism in mind for the four plural references of *adelphoi*. If so, totality and the full coverage of the earth by believers is in mind.

24. NRSV'S choice of "comrades" is peculiar considering that the RSV had "brethren" at these passages. A major attack against the RSV when it was published in 1952 was the charge of being a "Red Bible" because "comrade" was translated in three places (Judg 7:13–14; Heb 1:9). The story of this charge of Communist conspiracy against a Bible translation is detailed in Thuesen, *In Disconcordance with the Scriptures*, 94–144. RSV's revision into NRSV dropped one "comrade" (Heb 1:9) but then added seven more, including three in Revelation (12:10; 19:10; 22:9). The selection of "comrade" by NRSV is due to its desire for gender inclusive translation, but few contemporary English speakers utilize the term.

25. ESV and HCSB were spurred to completion partly out of reactions to the inclusive language found in the NRSV and TNIV. NABR incorporated inclusive language in earlier editions, but the 2011 revision lessened inclusive language considerably. HCSB's revision (CSB) relaxed some of their restrictions and used "brothers and sisters" three of the four times in Revelation. Finally, a few versions hold on to the archaic "brethren" (NASB, NKJV).

4:4; 2 Kgs 22:14; Neh 6:14; Isa 8:13), and John mentions a prophetess (2:20). Moreover, John uses "prophets" as a general description for all believers.[26]

John's structure also helps to confirm the gender inclusiveness of all four passages. The fall of Babylon vision and the new Jerusalem vision reveal similar conclusions.[27] Many commentators find it odd that John has to be instructed twice not to worship the angel.[28] The scenes look identical because they are identical, temporally speaking. Thus, 19:10 parallels 22:9, offering the same information from a different angle and contrast.[29] In a tale of two cities, one vision describes the fall of Babylon and the other the rise of new Jerusalem. The "brothers and sisters" of 19:10 parallels the "fellow prophets" of 22:9. Therefore, John's use of *adelphoi* becomes another of his many synonyms to designate all believers.

Called, Chosen, and Faithful

This expression refers to Christians and is found in a vision picturing the victorious return of Christ, and thus underscores perseverance. Within the fall of Babylon vision, John makes a reference to the glorious return of Christ. "They will wage war against the Lamb, but the Lamb will triumph over them because he is Lord of lords and King of kings—and with him will be his called, chosen and faithful followers" (17:14). The majority of scholars agree that this verse refers to the second coming, and parallels 19:11–16.[30]

The "called, chosen, and faithful" accompany Christ at his return. "Faithful" (*pistos*) is found regularly, and is used of Christ (1:5; 3:14; 19:11), of believers (2:10, 13; 17:14), and of the content of John's vision (21:5; 22:6). But this is the lone occurrence of

---

26. See the entry "Prophets." John also uses "priests" and perhaps "apostles" as general descriptions of the faithful, not necessarily specialized ministries.

27. The openings of the two visions are also closely parallel (17:1–3; 21:9–10).

28. Swete (*Apocalypse*, 304), for example, suggests John forgot the warning he so recently received. Osborne (*Revelation*, 783) relates that John "has already been rebuked for the same thing in 19:10, but like so many of us, he has not learned his lesson." Robert Thomas (*Revelation*, 2:500) thinks that John mistook the angel for the Lord himself. Other scholars (Aune, *Revelation*, 3:1038; Charles, *Revelation*, 2:130) attribute the duplication to careless final editors. Many scholars (Bauckham, *Climax of Prophecy*, 133; Beale, *Revelation*, 1128; Boring, *Revelation*, 224; Kistemaker, *Revelation*, 587; Smalley, *Revelation*, 569; Sweet, *Revelation*, 315) address the repetition not as an oversight but a deliberate decision to stress prohibition against angel worship or to address the problem of idolatry in John's churches. The lengthiest treatment is supplied in Bauckham, *Climax of Prophecy*, 120–40. The simplest explanation is that recapitulation is taking place.

29. Mulholland (*Revelation*, 334) recognizes that the passages repeat the same events, adding 1:17 as well. Thus, he sees Christ as the mighty angel of 19:10 and 22:9. But his explanation for why Christ forbids John to worship is unconvincing.

30. For many, particularly sequence-minded futurists who envision only one detailed picture of the second coming (19:11–21), this means that John is relating a parenthetical statement or anticipatory fore-glimpse of the end (Beasley-Murray, *Revelation*, 258; Brighton, *Revelation*, 453; Easley, *Revelation*, 312; Hindson, *Revelation*, 179; LaHaye, *Revelation Unveiled*, 263; Mangina, *Revelation*, 200; Patterson, *Revelation*, 324; Stefanovic, *Revelation*, 526; Robert Thomas, *Revelation*, 2:302; Walvoord, *Revelation*, 255). This study affirms 17:12–14 to be one of John's many iterations of Armageddon and the second coming (6:15; 9:14–19; 14:14–20; 16:12–16; 19:17–21; 20:7–10).

"called" (*klētos*) and "chosen" (*eklektos*) in Revelation.[31] Perhaps little can be drawn from the single appearance of these two words. The rest of the NT, however, uses "called" to show God's action in drawing people out of their separation and alienation from him into fellowship. Likewise, "chosen" carries same idea.[32] It is important to recall that "chosen" is another Jewish term for the people of God which NT writers adapted and expanded to picture the church, the whole company of God's people. At least a dozen NT books utilize this.[33] Thus, the threefold designation is three different ways to refer to the same group, and underscores their character and perseverance. It answers the question posed in 13:4: who is able to make war with the beast? The answer is the called, elect, and faithful who accompany the Lamb and fight alongside him. They represent the vindication of the persecuted saints of Dan 7:21 and Rev 6:9–11; 12:11; 13:10, 15–17.[34] Ultimately, it is another of John's many designations for believers.

God's People

God's people signify the saints, the redeemed in Christ who faithfully follow the Lamb in spite of persecution and therefore will enjoy eternal fellowship with God in the new Jerusalem. God's people in both the OT and NT are those who respond to him in faith. They may be summed up in the phrase, "I will be their God and they will be my people" (Exod 6:6–7; Lev 26:9–14; Jer 32:37–40; Acts 15:14; 2 Cor 6:16).[35] Two words in the NT are regularly used to depict the people of God—*hagioi* and *laos*. John utilizes both words in his Revelation.

Modern Bibles are evenly divided on how to translate *hoi hagioi*. "The saints" (literally "the holy ones") is used in CEB, CSB, ESV, NASB, NET, NJB, NKJV, and NRSV. "God's (holy) people" is found in CEV, GW, GNT, NCV, NIV, NLT, NABR ("holy ones"), and REB. *Hoi hagioi* has become a generic term that means "Christians." Yet it is more than a mere synonym. Rooted in the OT concept of holiness, it came to mean Christlikeness, and emphasizes one's service, faithfulness, and compassion.[36] John uses the term in two ways. First, when *hagios* is singular, its adjectival nature comes through, and is normally translated as "holy" (3:7; 4:8 [3 times]; 6:10; 11:2; 14:10; 20:6; 21:2, 10; 22:11, 19). When it is plural, its noun aspect comes through, and it is rendered as "saints" or

---

31. Although the three words are nouns, many English versions make them into adjectives. GNT, NCV, and NIV add "followers" after the phrase, and NLT adds "ones."

32. Mulholland, *Revelation*, 282.

33. Minear, *Images of the Church*, 81–82.

34. Beale, *Revelation*, 880. See J. C. Thomas, *Apocalypse*, 513–14; Witherington, *Revelation*, 224.

35. Hays, Duvall, and Pate, *Dictionary of Prophecy*, 329–30. See Fitzpatrick, "People of God," 440–41; Millar, "People of God," 684–87; Minear, *Images of the Church*, 66–68, 272–73; Ryken, *Dictionary of Biblical Imagery*, 750–52; Silva, "ἅγιος," 124–33.

36. Sadly, modern saints have lost the significance of this word. F. E. Hamilton and R. Laird Harris ("Saint," 261) remark the designation has "almost totally lost its original denotation, that is, of being set aside for the exclusive ownership and use of the Triune God. Very few people in the Christian church would consider themselves to be 'saints,' for the original meaning of the word, unfortunately, has largely fallen into disuse." So too Fee (*Revelation*, 219) and Gorman ("Saint," 43).

"God's people." The contexts may be divided into prayer (5:8; 8:3–4), praise (11:18; 18:20, 24; 19:8), patience (13:10; 14:12) within persecution (13:7; 16:6; 17:6; 20:9), and a benediction (22:21).[37]

The other word used by John to refer to God's people is *laos* ("people"). This word is found nine times. The first seven form part of the fourfold formulaic phrase "every tribe and people and language and nation," and means everyone on earth. The final two instances, however, depict God's people. First, the voice from heaven says "Come out of her, my people (*ho laos mou*), so that you will not share in her sins" (18:4). "My people" is a singular noun treated as a collective. It is a semitechnical term in the Bible that indicates a special relationship with God.[38] Second, the voice from the throne proclaims that "they will be his people (*laoi autou*) and God himself will be with them" (21:3). All other references in Scripture use the singular *laos*. John alone switches to the plural *laoi* in this passage. Thus, John purposefully shifts from the singular to plural for emphasis.[39]

At issue for many dispensationalists is whether God's people should be a term reserved for biological Jews in certain instances.[40] Although dispensational interpreters prefer to stress two peoples of God (Jews and Christians), none of John's uses of *hagioi* or *laoi* is a cause for debate.[41] Thus, John continues the application from other NT authors of expanding and universalizing what were previously Jewish designations. In the eschaton, there are no racial or ethnic distinctions.

37. There is a textual issue at 22:21. UBS5 gives a {B} rating for the exclusion of *hagion* and most modern interpreters take this shorter reading. After all, a general principle for textual critics is that it is usually easier to account for additions to the text than for omissions. Thus, Sweet (*Revelation*, 320) asks if "the words were original, why were they ever dropped?" So too Beale, *Revelation*, 1157; Blount, *Revelation*, 416; Metzger, *Textual Commentary*, 690–91; Omanson, *Textual Guide*, 552; Osborne, *Revelation*, 799; Ross, "Ending of the Apocalypse," 338–44; Robert Thomas, *Revelation*, 2:522–23. Nevertheless, there are seven different endings for Revelation found in the Greek witnesses. Although only a few modern English versions retain the word *hagion* (HCSB, NIV, NLT, NRSV), several scholars support its original presence in the text (Aune, *Revelation*, 3:1239, 1241; Charles, *Revelation*, 2:226; Beasley-Murray, *Revelation*, 349; Hailey, *Revelation*, 433; Patterson, *Revelation*, 386; Swete, *Apocalypse*, 313; Wall, *Revelation*, 272). In particular, Wall treats this textual problem as a theological issue because some use the shorter reading to bolster their view of universalism (e.g. Boring, *Revelation*, 226; Farmer, *Revelation*, 141–42). For a different reason altogether, if the variant that includes "saints" at 22:11 is indeed original, then the word is found exactly fourteen times, a sure sign that John is once more utilizing numerical symbolism (7 x 2).

38. Osborne, *Revelation*, 638; Smalley, *Revelation*, 446. Beale (*Revelation*, 897–98) lists Jer 50:8; 51:6, 45; Isa 48:20; 52:11 for background.

39. The plural use produces a textual problem. UBS5 gives a {B} rating for the plural *laoi* over the singular *laos*. Omanson (*Textual Guide*, 549) succinctly states the option. If the original reading was plural, then copyists made it into a singular in order to be consistent with the other uses of the phrase. If it was originally singular, then a later copyist changed it into the plural to conform to the plural pronoun preceding it (*autoi*). Two versions (CEB, NRSV) choose the plural "peoples."

40. See Hays, Duvall, and Pate, *Dictionary of Prophecy*, 329–30.

41. Premillennialists, however, do reserve 20:9 to refer to saints at the close of the millennium. So Decker, "People of God," 297–300; Ladd, *Revelation*, 270; Osborne, *Revelation*, 714; Patterson, *Revelation*, 357; Robert Thomas, *Revelation*, 422–26; Walvoord, *Revelation*, 303. Roman Catholics use 11:18 and 19:8 to support the veneration of saints after death (Gordon, "Saints," 282–83).

Great Multitude

The great multitude is composed of all the redeemed of history. They praise God for salvation, perfect judgment against Babylon the Great, and for eternal fellowship symbolized by the wedding supper of the Lamb. The "great multitude" (*ochlos polys*) is mentioned three times (7:9; 19:1, 6) near the conclusion of two parallel visions (7:9–17; 17:1–19:10).[42] In the first vision, after listing the hundred and forty-four thousand among the twelve tribes (7:1–8), John initiates a new section, and pictures a vast crowd in heaven. He sees "a great multitude that no one could count, from every nation, tribe, people and language, standing before the throne and before the Lamb. They were wearing white robes and were holding palm branches in their hands" (7:9). Many interpreters make a distinction between the two groups of this interlude. Robert Thomas, for instance, understands the hundred and forty-four thousand as a specific number of "Jewish believers" but identifies the vast crowd as an innumerable number of "Gentile and Jewish believers" who died in the great tribulation.[43]

Yet many others understand the hundred and forty-four thousand and the great multitude as one and the same—a symbol of the church. Eugene Boring states, "As 7:1–8 presents the church militant on earth, sealed and drawn up in battle formation before the coming struggle, 7:9–17 presents the church after the battle, triumphant in heaven."[44] Thus, only one group is portrayed, but from two different perspectives. The hundred and forty-four thousand picture the militant witnessing church on earth throughout history. The great multitude represents the redeemed church in heaven at the end of history.[45]

42. Numerous English versions render the three instances consistently, either as "great multitude" (ESV, NABR, NASB, NIV, NKJV, NRSV), "vast multitude" (CSB), "vast throng" (REB), "vast crowd" (NLT), and "large crowd" (GW). Other versions, however, use a variety of terms, thereby weakening the intratextual connections. "Great" derives from *polys*, not *megas*. *Polys* is found fifteen times in Revelation. English versions translate it elsewhere as "many," "rushing," and "more." Most English versions, however, follow NIV and translate *polys* as "great" in these three passages.

43. Robert Thomas, *Revelation*, 1:485. Other dispensationalists agree: Hindson, *Revelation*, 91; Patterson, *Revelation*, 199–200; Ryrie, *Revelation*, 62; Walvoord, *Revelation*, 144. Yet many non-dispensationalists also find a distinction between the two groups, but see images, not real people, including Beasley-Murray (*Revelation*, 139), Blount (*Revelation*, 149–50), Murphy (*Fallen Is Babylon*, 222–24), Rowland ("Revelation," 12:621), Skaggs and Benham (*Revelation*, 85), Skaggs and Doyle ("Revelation 7," 161–81), Leonard Thompson (*Revelation*, 108), and Wall (*Revelation*, 118). Aune (*Revelation*, 1:445–47) lists others. Osborne (*Revelation*, 318) and Mounce (*Revelation*, 154) find a distinction between the saints and the saints who are martyred.

44. Boring, *Revelation*, 131. Quoted by several commentators, including Barr (*Tales*, 87–88), Bauckham (*Climax of Prophecy*, 222–24), Beagley (*Sitz im Leben*, 47), Beale (*Revelation*, 426–27), Boxall (*Revelation*, 125), Brighton (*Revelation*, 193), Charles (*Revelation*, 1:201–4), Dalrymple (*Revelation and the Two Witnesses*, 92–97), Duvall (*Revelation*, 118), Easley (*Revelation*, 131), Harrington (*Revelation*, 100), Hendriksen (*More than Conquerors*, 112), Hughes (*Revelation*, 95), Alan Johnson ("Revelation," 13:664), Keener (*Revelation*, 243), Kistemaker (*Revelation*, 253), Koester (*Revelation*, 419), Ladd (*Revelation*, 117), Mayo (*Those Who Call Themselves Jews*, 102–4), Michaels (*Revelation*, 113), Mulholland (*Revelation*, 182), Prigent (*Apocalypse*, 121), Reddish (*Revelation*, 148), Resseguie (*Revelation*, 138), Roloff (*Revelation*, 98), Rotz (*Revelation*, 125), Schnabel (*40 Questions*, 90), Smalley (*Revelation*, 190), Stefanovic (*Revelation*, 264), Swete (*Apocalypse*, 99), Tavo (*Woman, Mother, Bride*, 161), J. C. Thomas (*Apocalypse*, 268), Witherington (*Revelation*, 137).

45. Bauckham (*Climax of Prophecy*, 224) suggests that "multitude" (*ochlos*) could also be translated

The great multitude is mentioned again in a subsequent vision. Near the conclusion of the fall of Babylon vision the great multitude appears twice. The saints in heaven praise the Lord for Babylon's demise and for the wedding supper of the Lamb. John hears "the roar of a great multitude in heaven shouting: "Hallelujah! Salvation and glory and power belong to our God" (19:1). John says later, "I heard what sounded like a great multitude, like the roar of rushing waters and like loud peals of thunder, shouting: 'Hallelujah! For our Lord God Almighty reigns'" (19:6). Debate persists over whether the great multitude is believers or angelic multitudes or both. A few scholars choose angels.[46] Numerous scholars identify the great multitude in 19:1 as angelic beings and the great multitude of 19:6 as the redeemed (or angels plus believers).[47] Yet it is more consistent (and matches with 7:9) to see God's people praising God at both locations in chapter 19. The saints, apostles, and prophets are called to rejoice over the fall of Babylon the Great (18:20). This great throng declares God's salvation (7:9–10; 12:10). Those who are victorious over the beast sing God's justice by the sea of glass (15:3; 19:2).[48] Therefore, all references to the great multitude picture the church triumphant at the consummation of history. John uses it sparingly, but when all three occurrences are analyzed, this metaphor stresses heavenly praise which believers deliver at the eschaton for their salvation, righteous judgment, and eternal fellowship.

One Who Is Victorious

This phrase signifies the believer who is faithful in spite of enduring persecution and even martyrdom, thus ironically becoming victorious like the Lord. The idea of victory is a major theme in Revelation.[49] The verb *nikaō* is found seventeen times. It is most often used as part of a substantive present participle which can be rendered "the one who is victorious."

---

as "army," thus accentuating his theme of the militant church on earth victorious in heaven. Resseguie (*Revelation Unsealed*, 66) appends that John *hears* the number of those sealed (7:4) but *sees* the great multitude (7:9). Elsewhere in Revelation what John hears interprets what he sees.

46. Ladd, *Revelation*, 244–46; Robert Thomas, *Revelation*, 2:355–63.

47. Aune, *Revelation*, 3:1024–40; Beasley-Murray, *Revelation*, 270–76; Beckwith, *Apocalypse*, 720–26; Easley, *Revelation*, 346–48; Hendriksen, *More than Conquerors*, 178–79; Hughes, *Revelation*, 196, 199; Alan Johnson, "Revelation," 13:755; Michaels, *Revelation*, 211; Murphy, *Babylon Is Fallen*, 378; Reddish, *Revelation*, 360; Schüssler Fiorenza, *Revelation*, 101; Swete, *Apocalypse*, 242–45; Wall, *Revelation*, 220–21; Witherington, *Revelation*, 232.

48. Bauckham, *Climax of Prophecy*, 331; Boxall, *Revelation*, 266; Caird, *Revelation*, 232–33; Duvall, *Revelation*, 246, 250; Dennis Johnson, *Triumph of the Lamb*, 260–62; Koester, *Revelation*, 726–28; Mounce, *Revelation*, 341–47; Mulholland, *Revelation*, 291–93; Osborne, *Revelation*, 663, 671; Resseguie, *Revelation*, 234; Roloff, *Revelation*, 210–11; Sweet, *Revelation*, 278–79; Stefanovic, *Revelation*, 554–56; J. C. Thomas, *Apocalypse*, 553, 560; Walvoord, *Revelation*, 268–70. Some interpreters (Beale, *Revelation*, 926; Brighton, *Revelation*, 487–88; Keener, *Revelation*, 449–50; Kistemaker, *Revelation*, 509–13; Prigent, *Apocalypse*, 519–24; Smalley, *Revelation*, 476–80) suggest angels and the faithful for 19:1 and/or add that the heavenly court (twenty-four elders and four living creatures) may join in with the great multitude at 19:6.

49. Sweet (*Revelation*, 80) calls it a keyword and basically confined to Johannine writings. Moreover, Strand ("Overcomer," 237–54) notes a progressive thematic development of the theme throughout Revelation. See Mark Wilson, *Victor Sayings*, 79, for word study statistics.

The present tense underscores the continual struggle for victory, not the completed action. "Jesus is not giving promises to the ones who have conquered, but to the ones who are in the process of conquering."[50]

The majority of exegetes recognize that the victors represent all believers.[51] The word receives three variations from English translations—"to overcome" (NASB, NIV 1984, NKJV); "to conquer" (CSB, ESV, NET, NRSV); and to be "victors" or "victorious" (CEB, CEV, GNT, GW, HCSB, NABR, NCV, NIV, NJB, NLT, REB).[52] Mark Wilson notes well the differences. "Overcomer" may be the weakest of the three options. In modern parlance it suggests someone who has overcome some addiction, such as drugs or gambling. "Conqueror," on the other hand, produces a militaristic tone. This certainly fits Revelation's war imagery and the spiritual warfare of the believer. But the best nuance is that of "victor." It recalls the ancient games (wreaths, palm branches, white robes), and secondarily is a military term.[53]

Nikaō is used in three different ways.[54] First, it stresses the moral, spiritual victory of Christ and the saints. This matches the promises given the victors of the seven churches (2:7, 11, 17, 26; 3:5, 12, 21).[55] Second, it reflects the permissive (*edothē*; "was given") physical and military victory of Satan over the saints. The first rider is given power to conquer (6:2), and the dragon (11:7) and the beast (13:7) overcome the saints. Third, it reflects the moral and military victory by Christ and the saints. The Lamb has triumphed by his blood (5:5) and believers have overcome the dragon by the blood of the Lamb (12:11).[56] In an end-time picture of heaven, the faithful are victors over the beast and his image (15:2). At his return, the Lamb will conquer them for he is Lord of lords and King of kings (17:14). Finally, those who are victorious will inherit "these things" in the new Jerusalem. This refers to eternal life, fellowship, promises, rewards, and blessings.

Rest of Her Offspring

The offspring of the woman clothed with the sun is composed of believers of every generation—the church—who must be ready to withstand the dragon's attempts to annihilate them

---

50. Mulholland, *Revelation*, 96 n. 9. Also emphasized by Mark Wilson (*Victor Sayings*, 80). Beale (*Revelation*, 269–72) speaks well to the ironic, paradoxical notion of overcoming while undergoing persecution.

51. Rosscup ("Overcomer in the Apocalypse," 261–63) mentions a few scholars who limit the victors to only the martyrs or to conquering (as opposed to defeated) Christians.

52. These options refer to their usage only in the seven letters. Only CEB, ESV, and NRSV remain consistent with all seventeen references.

53. Mark Wilson, *Victor Sayings*, 85. Homcy ("To Him Who Overcomes," 193–201) emphasizes that such victor language must provoke believers to forsake the world and embrace the Lord.

54. Ibid., 81.

55. Waechter ("Analysis of Literary Structure," 140) adds that if the occasion for several of the churches was the threat of heretical teaching, then overcoming might be designed to admonish as much as comfort and encourage.

56. Shin ("Conqueror Motif," 207–23) takes note of the switch from the usual present tense to past tense (*enikēsan*). This refrain pictures the eschaton and proclaims the victory of God from the heavenly perspective. This switch also applies to 5:5. The future tense (*nikēsei*) is found in 11:7 and 17:14.

and their witness for Christ. The dragon, frustrated at being defeated in heaven and in snatching the child (12:1–6), becomes enraged at the woman and wages war against the rest of her offspring (12:17). *Sperma* is rendered as "offspring" (CSB, ESV, NABR, NIV, NKJV, REB), "children" (CEB, CEV, GW, NASB, NCV, NET, NJB, NLT, NRSV), and "descendants" (GNT). The identity of these offspring has produced differences of opinion. Preterists, for example, interpret both the woman and her offspring as the predominately gentile Christian church in the first-century Roman Empire.[57] Many dispensationalists, however, believe the woman represents ethnic Israel. This means that her offspring must also be Jewish, a remnant of believing Jews converted after a rapture, and bearing witness during the final few years of earth history.[58] Another idea is that the woman represents Jewish Christians but her offspring represent gentile Christians.[59]

The majority of scholars, however, understand the symbolism of both the woman and her offspring as the believing community, demolishing all ethnic restrictions. In the OT, Israel could be designated as Zion, daughter of Zion, or children of Zion (Pss 9:11–14; 149:2; Song 3:11). So too the NT church could be described as both a woman and her children. In concert with other NT teachings, there is no longer Jew or gentile, but "if you belong to Christ, then you are Abraham's seed (*sperma*)" (Gal 3:29; see Rom 4:13–18; 9:27–28). This likewise fits with the rest of Revelation's use of images that were formerly limited by ethnicity, but are now enlarged beyond racial distinctions. The woman represents the messianic community—the ideal church—composed of faithful believers of both testaments. Her offspring alludes to Gen 3:15: "And I will put enmity between you and the woman, and between your offspring and hers; he will crush your head, and you will strike his heel." Paul understood this prophecy to be fulfilled in the church: "The God of peace will soon crush Satan under your feet" (Rom 16:20).[60]

The phrase represents the church of every generation. Human history is rife with examples of persecution and martyrdom of the faithful. Ultimately, it also represents the church of the final generation which must be prepared to suffer for their witness.[61] Even though the dragon wages war and attempts to quash the church, he will not succeed. Nevertheless, individual Christians are targets of his desperation. The challenge from Revelation for believers of every generation is to remain vigilant and faithful to the Lord.

---

57. So Chilton, *Days of Vengeance*, 323. Buchanan (*Revelation*, 336), however, opts for pious diaspora Jews.

58. So Hindson, *Revelation*, 139–40; LaHaye, *Revelation Unveiled*, 205; Ryrie, *Revelation*, 93; Walvoord, *Revelation*, 196. Robert Thomas (*Revelation*, 2:142), however, believes the woman represents Christian Jews, and Patterson (*Revelation*, 271) enlarges the offspring to the whole church.

59. Hughes, *Revelation*, 142–43. Stefanovic (*Revelation*, 396) states, "The remaining ones of the woman's offspring are, then, the followers of Christ living in the last period of this earth's history." Many Seventh Day Adventists view "the rest" as a remnant of their own group.

60. Morris (*Romans*, 541) relates, "Nothing in the context indicates that Paul is looking to the parousia, and it is better to see the promise of a victory over Satan in the here and now." Schreiner (*Romans*, 804–5) similarly agrees.

61. So Aune, *Revelation*, 2:708; Beale, *Revelation*, 676–77; Blount, *Revelation*, 241–42; Brighton, *Revelation*, 341; Keener, *Revelation*, 324; Kistemaker, *Revelation*, 370; Michaels, *Revelation*, 153; Mounce, *Revelation*, 242; Mulholland, *Revelation*, 225; Osborne, *Revelation*, 485; Smalley, *Revelation*, 334; Sweet, *Revelation*, 203–5.

Servants

A servant signifies a devoted follower of Christ who obediently does his will. The word *doulos* is usually translated as "servant" or "slave" in the Apocalypse. It is found fourteen times.[62] In three cases it refers to all unbelievers, and forms part of the phrase "free and slave" (6:15; 13:16; 19:18). All English translations consulted translate *doulos* as "slave" at these three locations, and the surrounding context confirms the word is used for unbelievers as a whole.

The other eleven uses (1:1; 2:20; 7:3; 10:7; 11:18; 15:3; 19:2, 5; 22:3, 6) refer to believers and is regularly translated as "servant/s" by most modern versions. There are a few exceptions to this. "People" is substituted in a few of the references (CEV, NCV) and "bond-servant" is chosen all but once by NASB.[63] In addition, the cognate word *syndoulos* is found three times (6:11; 19:10; 22:9). Most versions translate this word as "fellow servants," but there is also "fellow slaves" (HCSB) and "coworkers" (GW). "People" and "coworkers," however, comprise weaker English offerings. Scriptural usage points toward the legal subordination of a slave as property of the owner. Still, the emphasis is on superior-inferior relationship, not on chattel slavery. In a religious context, prominent individuals, even kings, were servants of God. The slave language designating a special and honored relationship to God in the OT is carried over to the NT (Rom 1:1; Phil 1:1; Jas 1:1; 2 Pet 1:1).[64]

Scripture often employs the term servant as a general reference for God's people. A few of John's uses nevertheless produce debate. At 7:3, the seal of God is placed on the foreheads of the servants, the hundred and forty-four thousand. Some futurist interpreters reserve this use of "servants" for Jewish believers.[65] Yet Revelation consistently emphasizes the Jewishness of all believers, and numerous formerly Jewish-only terms are expanded and universalized by NT writers, including John. Since "servants" refer to those who obediently follow Christ elsewhere in Revelation with no limitations of ethnicity or gender or marital status, so too should the servants be interpreted here.[66] At 10:7, John incorporates a frequent OT phrase—"his servants the prophets" (2 Kgs 17:13; Ezra 9:11; Jer 7:25; Dan 9:6; Amos 3:7). This refers to the prophets of both the OT and NT eras.[67]

---

62. At first glance, this may reflect numerical symbolism (7 x 2). But *doulos* is used three times for unbelievers. However, if John considers *syndoulos* to be included then there are in fact fourteen references to "servants." Interestingly, seven of the occurrences of *doulos* appear at the end of four visions.

63. HCSB translated "servants" eight times and "slaves" three times. The CSB revised all uses to "servants."

64. See Bartchy, "Servant," 420–21; DeFelice, "Slavery," 1515–39; Michaels, "Servant," 429–31; Minear, *Images of the Church*, 156–58; Margaret Barker, "Servant in Revelation," 493–511; Silva, "δοῦλος," 767–73. The premier study on this topic is Murray Harris, *Slave of Christ*. Aune (*Revelation*, 1:13), however, argues that "servants" in 1:1 and 22:6 specify a circle of Christian prophets.

65. Hindson, *Revelation*, 89–90; LaHaye, *Revelation Unveiled*, 149–50; Patterson, *Revelation*, 194; Robert Thomas, *Revelation*, 1:473; Walvoord, *Revelation*, 141. See Bauckham, *Climax of Prophecy*, 217–19.

66. Keener, *Revelation*, 231–32. See the chart in Tavo, *Woman, Mother, Bride*, 149–50.

67. Mounce, *Revelation*, 208. Koester (*Revelation*, 211) shares that *douloi* should be rendered as "servants" for believers "to avoid the impression that they are the mere property of God, the slaveholder."

The phrase resurfaces in 11:18 with the addition of "saints." In both cases the reference to *doulos* means believers, the faithful Christian community. John may appear to draw out a special class of servants—the prophets. But he is more likely speaking of the prophethood of all believers.[68]

Souls under the Altar

The slain under the altar refers not only to martyrs but to all believers who must be ever ready to suffer persecution and death because of their testimony for Christ. This is another of the numerous terms that John uses to identify the people of God. In this instance, it stresses persecution and death because of their witness for Christ. The fifth seal is unique. John sees "under the altar the souls of those who had been slain because of the word of God and the testimony they had maintained" (6:9).[69] Scholars debate on what the altar symbolizes. Most accept the altar of burnt offering as the backdrop, especially since "blood under the altar" stresses sacrifice.[70] But several recognize the altar of incense, especially since prayers are mentioned and elsewhere in Revelation this altar seems the best choice.[71] Mounce offers a common ground by suggesting that John intended readers to understand both ideas. The theme of sacrifice suggests the former, but the prayers that rise indicate the latter.[72]

"Souls" (*psychē*) has various meanings, but "lives" or "persons" are best understood.[73] But who are these souls? Many interpreters limit them to a select group of saints. Preterists view them as martyrs from the persecution by Jews before AD 70 or from Romans.[74] Dispensationalists interpret them as saints who will be martyred during the great tribulation at the end of earth history.[75]

Most scholars, however, understand this group as the martyred believers throughout the ages.[76] Yet is this limited only to martyrs? Even better is to understand these

68. See the entry "Prophets."

69. English versions include "slain" (ESV, NASB, NIV, NKJV); "killed" (CEV, GNT, NCV, NJB); "violently killed" (NET); "martyred" (NLT); and "slaughtered" (CEB, CSB, GW, NABR, NRSV, REB).

70. Aune, *Revelation*, 2:405; Blount, *Revelation*, 133; Boring, *Revelation*, 125; Chilton, *Days of Vengeance*, 194; Easley, *Revelation*, 109; Keener, *Revelation*, 219; Murphy, *Babylon Is Fallen*, 208; Osborne, *Revelation*, 285; Reddish, *Revelation*, 130; Smalley, *Revelation*, 158; Thomas and Macchia, *Revelation*, 159; Roloff, *Revelation*, 89; Sweet, *Revelation*, 142.

71. Beale, *Revelation*, 392; Brighton, *Revelation*, 171; Kistemaker, *Revelation*, 232; Ladd, *Revelation*, 102; Morris, *Revelation*, 105; Alan Johnson, "Revelation," 13:655; Robert Thomas, *Revelation*, 1:442.

72. Mounce, *Revelation*, 146. So also Duvall, *Revelation*, 106.

73. Alan Johnson, "Revelation," 13:654; Osborne, *Revelation*, 284.

74. Charles, *Revelation*, 1:172; Chilton, *Days of Vengeance*, 194; Gentry, *Before Jerusalem Fell*, 233 n. 1.

75. LaHaye (*Revelation Unveiled*, 145–47) states they are martyred in the first half of the great tribulation. Robert Thomas (*Revelation*, 1:441) and Walvoord (*Revelation*, 133–34) view them as martyred in the second half. Hindson (*Revelation*, 83–84) and Patterson (*Revelation*, 184) opt for the whole great tribulation period.

76. Easley, *Revelation*, 109; Keener, *Revelation*, 218–19; Ladd, *Revelation*, 104; Kistemaker, *Revelation*, 232; Mounce, *Revelation*, 146–47; Osborne, *Revelation*, 284; Smalley, *Revelation*, 157; Stefanovic,

souls more generally as believers as a whole. Beale explains that "more likely 'slain' is metaphorical and those spoken of represent the broader category of all saints who suffer for the sake of their faith (so 13:15–18 and perhaps 18:24; 20:4)."[77] This is also consistent with figurative use of sacrificial martyr language found elsewhere (Matt 16:24–26; Rom 8:35–39; 12:1–2; Phil 2:17). Brighton affirms, "The *martyred* saints of God, then, portray a picture of the suffering church all during the time period that the four horsemen are ravaging the earth, from the time of the ascension of Christ to the End. For *all* Christians are martyrs in the sense that they *all* give witness by their faith, their mouths, and their lives to the victorious Lamb, who died and rose again."[78] The fifth seal then symbolizes the persecution (and martyrdom) of all believers. Like "beheaded" (20:4), the image is one of the many terms and phrases that John uses to describe faithful followers of the Lamb.

Tribes of Israel

"Tribes of Israel" is one of the many Jewish designations expanded in Revelation to symbolize the church, that is, all those who believe in Christ regardless of ethnic identification. The phrase is found at two locations in Revelation.[79] First, John hears the number of those sealed: "144,000 from all the tribes of Israel" (7:4).[80] The second occurrence of the phrase is near the beginning of the vision of the new Jerusalem. The heavenly Holy City includes gates that have "the names of the twelve tribes of Israel" (21:12). These accompany the foundation with its names of the twelve apostles (21:14). It is customary to view the twelve tribes and twelve apostles together as accenting the unity of the two covenant peoples.

The tribes of Israel, therefore, becomes one of the many terms John uses to denote the people of God, the church. As Paul Minear explains, the use of twelve tribes "asserts the oneness, the fullness, and the wholeness of the people of God."[81] Several NT passages

---

Revelation, 246; J. C. Thomas, *Apocalypse*, 248–49.

77. Beale, *Revelation*, 390. See Pattemore, *People of God*, 79–82, 114.

78. Brighton, *Revelation*, 172 (italics original).

79. There is one other occurrence of "Israel" at 2:14, an actual historical event that refers to Israelites during the wilderness period.

80. The order of the listing of the twelve tribes in 7:5–8 has generated several studies. Farrer (*Revelation*, 106–7) theorizes it derives from Ezek 48:30–35. Winkle ("Another Look," 53–67) expands on Farrer, and affirms that John incorporates a list that runs counterclockwise from Ezekiel, partly for the tribe of Judah to fit first, but also to show that Dan was dropped because of connections to Judas Iscariot. Independently, Christopher Smith ("Portrayal of the Church," 111–18) agrees, adding that the sons of the handmaidens are moved up the list to represent the inclusion of gentiles into the church. Bauckham ("List of Tribes," 99–115), however, finds such arguments unconvincing. Smith writes later ("Tribes of Revelation 7," 213–18) in hopes of keeping the discussion moving forward. Mayo (*Those Who Call Themselves Jews*, 79–87) interacts with these scholars and concludes John's listing is unique. Tavo (*Woman, Mother, Bride*, 151–58) compares the list with twenty-four other OT lists. He tempers scholars who stress the uniqueness of John's listing as evidence for spiritual Israel. Nevertheless, Koester (*Revelation*, 418) characterizes modern scholarship on the variety in the sequence of names with "The list simply gives a sense of the whole."

81. Minear, *Images of the Church*, 73. Numerous dispensationalists understand John's listing as literal Jews from literal tribes, including Hindson (*Revelation*, 89), LaHaye (*Revelation Unveiled*, 149),

infer that the church is assuming Jewish terms once reserved only for Israel. In Matt 19:28, Jesus appears to compare the twelve disciples with the twelve tribes to highlight "the theme of the church replacing Israel as the locus of God's saving activity in the new age."[82] Gentile believers are considered Jews "inwardly" and possess a true "circumcision of the heart" (Rom 2:26–29; Phil 3:2–3; Col 2:11). Paul announces that Christians are "sons of God" (Gal 3:26), "Abraham's seed" (Gal 3:16, 29), and the "Israel of God" (Gal 6:16).[83] Strikingly, Paul does not fall back upon a concept of two Israels, the old and the new, or the false and the true. Instead, he defines God's Israel as one people, measured qualitatively by God's mercy through the cross.[84]

Therefore, "tribes of Israel" is one of the numerous originally ethnic terms that is expanded, universalized, and redefined by Jesus and the NT writers to refer to everyone who believes in Christ.[85]

Two Witnesses

The two witnesses represent the church, particularly its distinguishing characteristic as militant witnesses for Christ despite persecution and death. The story of the two witnesses is found at the conclusion of the second interlude (11:3–13). They wear sackcloth, a symbol of the call to repentance. They are given authority to prophesy for a thousand two hundred and sixty days. They perform miracles similar to what Moses and Elijah did. The beast kills them but they are raised from the dead and transported to heaven. The two witnesses have borne a variety of interpretations over the centuries.[86] Preterists and historicists interpret them not as people to come, but rather past heroes to emulate. Proposals include Jesus and John the Baptist, James and John, Stephen and James, and Peter and Paul.[87] Other historicists find fulfillment within church history. Hence, first-century high priests Ananus and Joshua, anti-papal witnesses, the Reformation, or the French Revolution are suggested.[88]

Modern interpreters advance their own speculations. The majority fall into the familiar categories of literal or symbolic. A few, however, attempt to combine the literal with the symbolic viewpoint. They stress the message of the two witnesses represents the

---

Patterson (*Revelation*, 196), Ryrie (*Revelation*, 61), Robert Thomas (*Revelation*, 1:476), and Walvoord (*Revelation*, 141). See the entry "Hundred and Forty-Four Thousand."

82. Blomberg, *Matthew*, 301.

83. Beale, *New Testament Biblical Theology*, 672.

84. Minear, *Images of the Church*, 71–72.

85. For names and images of Israel applied to the church, see Beale, *New Testament Biblical Theology*, 669–79; Minear, *Images of the Church*, 71–84; and Provan, *Church Is Israel Now*, 3–46.

86. For example, Rodney Petersen (*Preaching in the Last Days*, 257–65) traces interpretations found in the sixteenth and seventeenth centuries. See Aune, *Revelation*, 2:599–603; Koester, *Revelation*, 439–40; Kovacs and Rowland, *Revelation*, 126–30.

87. Ian Brown, "Two Witnesses," 385–90. For a list of preterist views and critique see Tan, "Preterist Views on the Two Witnesses," 72–95; idem, "Critique of Preterist Views," 210–25.

88. For a critique of historicist as well as idealist views see Tan, "Critique of Idealist and Historicist Views," 328–51.

need for the church to witness in every generation. Yet they also hold out for a possible literal unfolding of two unknown end-time prophets in the future.[89] Futurists, preterists, and historicists offer literal possibilities. Many dispensationalists select Elijah and Moses coming back to life.[90] Most futurists, however, propose two unknown saints who come in the spirit of Elijah and Moses at the end of history.[91] The literal approach falls prey to losing the message which John seeks to convey to readers. Relegating the two witnesses to a specific time in the past or the future undercuts application for readers in the present.

A symbolic understanding of the two witnesses is better. Many scholars accept their identity as the church with its stress on witness bearing.[92] Beale provides six effective reasons why the two witnesses symbolize the whole church. First, John explicitly refers to lampstands (11:4) as churches (1:20). The seven symbolizes all the churches whereas the two symbolizes their role as witnesses (Deut 17:16; 19:15; Num 35:30). Second, the beast of 11:7 fights the people of God in 13:7. This alludes to Dan 7:21 where the whole nation of Israel is meant. Thus, the formula is Israel equals the two witnesses and Israel equals the church. Therefore, the two witnesses equal the church. Third, the worldwide witness of 11:9 is the responsibility given to the church. Their witness is everywhere—not centered in Jerusalem or Israel alone. This presupposes witness done by Christians over the earth. Fourth, their prophetic timeline (thousand two hundred and sixty days) matches the same timeline as other metaphors for the whole church, including the "Holy

89. So Ladd, *Revelation*, 154; Osborne, *Revelation*, 418; and Siew, *War between the Two Beasts*, 84–122. Yet this approach faces the same trap of limitation that strict literalists fall into, namely that the ministry of the two witnesses takes place in the future. Thus, if there are two witnesses in the future, then will there be exactly a hundred and forty-four thousand servants in the future as well? It is best to understand both numbers as representing the whole church.

90. LaHaye, *Revelation Unveiled*, 186; Lindsey, *New World Coming*, 162; Robert Thomas, *Revelation*, 2:88–89.

91. Mayhew, "Revelation 11," 364–66; Ryrie, *Revelation*, 84; Tan, "Futurist View," 471; Walvoord, *Revelation*, 179; Wong, "Two Witnesses," 348. Patterson (*Revelation*, 245) states they are "two remarkable Jewish witnesses . . ." Hindson (*Revelation*, 125) adds they preach the gospel "to the Jews in Jerusalem." Ian Brown ("Two Witnesses," 368–84) lists numerous other writers.

92. Bauckham, *Climax of Prophecy*, 273–83; Beale, *Revelation*, 573; Beasley-Murray, *Revelation*, 184; Boring, *Revelation*, 145; Boxall, *Revelation*, 155; Brighton, *Revelation*, 293–94; Duvall, *Revelation*, 149–150; Easley, *Revelation*, 192; Fee, *Revelation*, 150; Hailey, *Revelation*, 254; Harrington, *Revelation*, 123; Hendriksen, *More than Conquerors*, 155; Hughes, *Revelation*, 123; Dennis Johnson, *Triumph of the Lamb*, 170–71; Keener, *Revelation*, 291; Kistemaker, *Revelation*, 328–29; Koester, *Revelation*, 505; Mangina, *Revelation*, 134; Mounce, *Revelation*, 217; Mulholland, *Revelation*, 206; Pattemore, *People of God*, 160–64; Paul, *Revelation*, 198; Resseguie, *Revelation*, 162; Roloff, *Revelation*, 114; Schnabel, *40 Questions*, 218; Smalley, *Revelation*, 275; Sweet, *Revelation*, 184; Swete, *Apocalypse*, 134; Tavo, *Woman, Mother, Bride*, 218–23; Tõniste, *Ending of the Canon*, 117; Wilcock, *I Saw Heaven Opened*, 71. A few interpreters (Boxall, *Revelation*, 164; Wall, *Revelation*, 145; Witherington, *Revelation*, 158) accept the church as well but add it may refer to two specific churches (Smyrna and Philadelphia). Similarly, Mazzaferri (*Genre of Revelation*, 325) and Michaels (*Revelation*, 138–39) add the two witnesses symbolize John himself. A few scholars select a smaller group within the church, such as martyrs (Caird, *Revelation*, 134; Kiddle, *Revelation*, 183; Morris, *Revelation*, 143) or Christian prophets (Alan Johnson, "Revelation," 13:685; Murphy, *Babylon Is Fallen*, 263; Schüssler Fiorenza, *Revelation*, 77). Finally, Müller ("Two Witnesses of Revelation 11," 30–45) and Strand ("Two Witnesses of Rev 11:3–12," 127–35; idem, "Two Olive Trees of Zechariah 4," 257–61) interpret the two witnesses as the OT and the NT. Stefanovic (*Revelation*, 353) appreciates this view but ultimately adopts the symbol of the church. Ian Brown ("Two Witnesses," 399–416) lists others.

City" (11:2), the woman (12:6, 14), and "those tabernacling in heaven" (13:6). Therefore, if these other metaphors symbolize all Christians, it seems most plausible that the two witnesses represent all Christians. Fifth, their witnessing parallels the witnessing of the church elsewhere in Revelation (6:9; 12:11, 17; 19:10; 20:4). Sixth, both witnesses function as Moses and Elijah. They are a singularity. Since they share each other's characteristics it is easier to understand them as a metaphor for all Christians.[93]

Rob Dalrymple lays out four main themes for the two witnesses. First, although the outer court is trampled, the temple is secure (11:1–2). This symbolizes the divine protection of God's people—the church. Moreover, this protection lasts until the witness of the church is complete (11:7). Second, they are two "witnesses." Their portrayal reveals God's purpose for the church—to be a witness of Christ's work. Third, God's people must expect to face suffering, persecution, and even death. Fourth, the church will ultimately be vindicated. This is demonstrated by the resurrection of the two witnesses (11:11–12).[94] These themes fit not only the two witnesses, but also the other references to God's people scattered throughout Revelation.

Dalrymple's four themes clearly reveal John's purposes for his original audience. He challenges the faithful to live for Christ and to witness for Christ. He exhorts the churches to be prepared to endure persecution and perhaps martyrdom. Therefore, it is best to understand the two witnesses as yet one more example of the marvelous symbolism of John that refers to the church. In particular, chapter 11, from differing angles and allusions, reveals the church as the temple, altar, outer court, Holy City, and the two witnesses. Emphases include eternal ownership and protection (temple), persecution and sacrifice (outer court), fellowship with God (Holy City), and their witness (two witnesses).

Virgins

Believers are depicted as "virgins" to symbolize their pure and moral lifestyles as the bride of Christ as well as their single-minded loyalty and devotion for being soldiers in his spiritual army. One way that virginity was utilized in the OT was as a sign of purity and newness (Gen 24:16; Song 6:8). This concept was applied to Israel, anticipating future blessings (Jer 31:4) or facing failures (Jer 18:13).[95] "Virgins" (*parthenoi*) occurs fifteen times in the NT, normally in the context of unmarried people. But Paul uses the term once symbolically to refer to the church (2 Cor 11:2).

The word is found once in Revelation within the third interlude (12:1–15:4) in a description of the triumphant redeemed who "are those who did not defile themselves with women, for they remained virgins" (14:4). "Virgins," coupled with a literal understanding of the numeric symbol a "hundred and forty-four thousand," has caused interpretive problems throughout church history. Tertullian, Methodius, Primasius, and Venerable

---

93. Beale, *Revelation*, 574–75. See also the discussions by Aune (*Revelation*, 2:599–603), Schnabel (*40 Questions*, 213–18), and Tavo (*Woman, Mother, Bride*, 158–71). Blount ("Reading Revelation Today," 398–412) presents a strong word for bold witness against modern institutional evils.

94. Dalrymple, *Revelation and the Two Witnesses*, 47–58.

95. Ryken, *Dictionary of Biblical Imagery*, 917–18. For ancient Near East background see Branch, "Virgins and Virginity," 1659–80.

Bede are examples of influential people who chose simple literalism. Tertullian, for instance, understood these as male virgins who castrated themselves for the sake of the kingdom of heaven. In nineteenth-century Russia, Kondrati Selivanov and his followers likewise understood this passage as a call for the "fiery baptism" of castration.[96] Perhaps recognizing this, some modern versions introduce a softer translation such as "kept themselves pure" (NCV, NIV 1984) and "kept themselves chaste" (REB). But this does not project a strong enough rendering as the word *parthenoi* requires. Although the majority of modern versions sustain "virgins," the word continues to tempt some interpreters to understand literal celibacy.[97] Yet such a stress on the literalness of virginity implies a denigration of marriage and the evilness of sexuality. Perhaps closer to John's intention for the meaning of the word is the simile "pure as virgins" (NLT). John has already introduced sexual imagery to symbolize spiritual unfaithfulness (2:14, 20). With "virgins," he is emphasizing spiritual faithfulness.

How then is John using the symbol of "virgins"? Two metaphors are promoted. First, the "bride of Christ" metaphor is a possibility. On many occasions Israel was depicted as a virgin (2 Kgs 19:21; Isa 61:10), and when she lapsed into sin she was called a prostitute (Jer 3:6; Hos 2:5). This figure carries over to the NT in Paul (2 Cor 11:2) and perhaps Jesus as well (Matt 25:1–13).[98] Thus, the redeemed are pictured as the promised bride of Christ, devoid of defiling relationships with the pagan world system known as Babylon the Great. Spiritual monogamy means that everyone—man, woman, single, and married—the whole church, is the virgin bride of her husband (John 3:29; Eph 5:21–33; Rev 19:7; 21:2, 9; 22:17).[99]

A second possibility is the "holy war" metaphor. Several scholars note that the male celibacy pictured here hearkens to the Mosaic law's instructions for Israelite warriors to maintain sexual purity while engaged in the Lord's holy war against pagan enemies (Deut 23:9–11; 1 Sam 21:5; 2 Sam 11:8–11). This fits statements found elsewhere in Revelation where the saints accompany their divine commander in battle at the end (17:14; 19:14). Thus, this ceremonial purity is now spiritually symbolized for the whole church.[100]

It is hard to decide between these two metaphors. The context slightly favors "holy war," but the "bride of Christ" metaphor is evident elsewhere in Revelation. Perhaps John

96. Kovacs and Rowland, *Revelation*, 162; Wainwright, *Mysterious Apocalypse*, 28, 41.

97. So Gromacki, "Witnesses, 144,000," 425; Hindson, *Revelation*, 123, 154; Patterson, *Revelation*, 288. Likewise, Robert Thomas (*Revelation*, 2:195–97), who limits this sexless lifestyle to a hundred and forty-four thousand male virgins in a future great tribulation. Charles (*Revelation*, 2:8–9) believes the verse is an interpolation by a monk who stressed celibacy. See Kiddle, *Revelation*, 268; Buchanan, *Revelation*, 389–94; Yarbro Collins, *Crisis and Catharsis*, 129.

98. Minear, *Images of the Church*, 52–53.

99. So Beale, *Revelation*, 738–40; Duvall, *Revelation*, 191–92; Easley, *Revelation*, 247–48; Hailey, *Revelation*, 304; Alan Johnson, "Revelation," 13:721; Kistemaker, *Revelation*, 405; Ladd, *Revelation*, 191; LaHaye, *Revelation Unveiled*, 232; Morris, *Revelation*, 171–72; Mounce, *Revelation*, 266–67; Smalley, *Revelation*, 357–58; Walvoord, *Revelation*, 216.

100. Bauckham, *Climax of Prophecy*, 230–32; Beasley-Murray, *Revelation*, 223; Blount, *Revelation*, 269; Fee, *Revelation*, 192; Dennis Johnson, *Triumph of the Lamb*, 202–3; Keener, *Revelation*, 370–71; Michaels, *Revelation*, 170–71; Osborne, *Revelation*, 529; Reddish, *Revelation*, 274; Rowland, "Revelation," 12:664; Skaggs and Benham, *Revelation*, 145; Sweet, *Revelation*, 222; Tavo, *Woman, Bride, Mother*, 156–58; Witherington, *Revelation*, 185–86.

has it secondarily in mind. Both metaphors stress the characteristics of discipleship that followers of the Lamb maintain—pure, moral lives and single-minded devotion.[101]

Woman Clothed with the Sun

The woman clothed with the sun pictures the totality of God's people, both faithful OT Israel and true, NT spiritual Israel. "Woman" is a major image in John's arsenal of contrasts. *Gynē* is found nineteen times in Revelation. There is Jezebel (2:20); locusts with "women's hair" (9:8); virgins who do not defile themselves with women (14:14); and the bride of the Lamb (19:7; 21:9). John's dualism especially comes through in the woman clothed with the sun (eight references in chapter 12) compared to the woman sitting on the scarlet beast (six references in chapter 17). The third interlude begins with an image of a woman clothed with the sun, with the moon under her feet, and a crown of twelve stars on her head (12:1). This woman has received her fair share of eccentric identifications over the centuries.[102] Moderns argue over her identity as well. Many interpreters believe she is patterned after a widespread multicultural combat myth.[103] Even so, John has fully adapted the story and "Christianized it." Identifying the woman as Mary also remains popular in some circles.[104]

The two major choices, however, are that the woman represents the Jewish community or the Christian community.[105] First, the Jewish community is championed by dispensationalists. The woman symbolizes ethnic, national Israel. Her crown of twelve stars represents the twelve tribes. She gives birth to the Lord. This also infers that the rest of her offspring (12:17) are Jewish, a remnant of believing Jews converted after a rapture near the end of history.[106]

Second, and better, the woman symbolizes the Christian community. Specifically, she represents the church (the people of God) of both the OT and NT. The majority of interpreters accept this view.[107] The picture of her being clothed with the sun signifies her victory and glory. She also has the moon under her feet, which suggests dominion.

---

101. Resseguie, *Revelation*, 22. See Boxall (*Revelation*, 249–51) and Olson ("Those Who Have Not," 492–510) for a discussion on feminist responses to sexual imagery in Revelation.

102. See historical examples in Downing, "Women Clothed with the Sun," 265–80; Emmerson, "Woman Clothed with the Sun," 846–47; Koester, *Revelation*, 525–27, 560–63; Kovacs and Rowland, *Revelation*, 136–38; and Wainwright, *Mysterious Apocalypse*, 93–97.

103. For background on the combat myth, see Aune, *Revelation*, 2:667–74; Caird, *Revelation*, 147–48; Murphy, *Fallen Is Babylon*, 279–86; Prigent, *Apocalypse*, 366–74; Witherington, *Revelation*, 164–66; and especially Yarbro Collins, *Combat Myth in Revelation*, 57–100.

104. For references, see Aune, *Revelation*, 2:680–81; Koester, *Revelation*, 526–27; and Tavo, *Woman, Mother, Bride*, 232 n. 25. Mulholland (*Revelation*, 224) accepts the woman as a symbol of God.

105. See the entry "Rest of Her Offspring."

106. Hindson, *Revelation*, 137; LaHaye, *Revelation Unveiled*, 197–98; Patterson, *Revelation*, 261; Ryrie, *Revelation*, 90; Robert Thomas, *Revelation*, 2:142; Walvoord, *Revelation*, 196. Some preterists also select Jews or Jewish Christians only, including Buchanan (*Revelation*, 313), Charles (*Revelation*, 1:315), and Ford (*Revelation*, 198).

107. Fuller discussions supporting this view include Beale, *Revelation*, 624–32; Koester, *Revelation*, 542–44; Osborne, *Revelation*, 455–58; and Tavo, *Woman, Mother, Bride*, 228–30, 289–94.

The woman is fitted with a crown of twelve stars. This image derives from Gen 37:9. The sun, moon, and eleven stars in Joseph's dream represented Jacob, his wife, and the eleven brothers who would one day submit to Joseph. Thus, Israel is the initial understanding of the twelve stars. But the woman's starry crown is more clearly determined by looking elsewhere in Revelation, where "crowns" speak of God's people sharing in Christ's kingship and being rewarded for their faithfulness (2:10; 3:11; 4:4; 14:14). These passages do not refer to ethnic Jews but rather speak of the church.[108] The number twelve represents the fullness and completeness of God's people. Here the twelve stars epitomize the totality of God's people—OT saints and NT saints.[109]

The woman suffers in labor. This portrayed Israel in the OT (Isa 26:17; Jer 4:31; Mic 4:10). Her birth pangs represent the persecution of the faith community leading up to Christ's birth (Isa 66:7–11; Ezek 16:8). The woman therefore is faithful Israel, the messianic community, the true believing remnant, who longed for the coming of the Messiah, and who by their faith are metaphorically the mother of Christ. After the birth and ascension of Christ the woman becomes and represents the church of the apostles. Her offspring hold fast to the testimony of Jesus. Thus, she represents the church as well (2 Cor 11:2; Eph 5:23–27; Rev 21:2). The woman clothed with the sun symbolizes the ideal people of God throughout Scripture.[110]

Bad People

In Revelation, bad people are comprised of wicked unbelievers, false believers, and evil leaders. In John's dualistic world, there is no neutral position. If you are not a believer, you belong with Satan, the beast, and the other bad people.

Balaam

Like his OT counterpart, Balaam represents false, idolatrous, greedy teachers who tempt and try to entrap believers into sexual immorality and idol worship. Balaam's story is found in Num 22–25, 31. He was a pagan prophet hired by Balak, king of Moab, to curse the invading Israelites prior to their invasion of Canaan. Later, he successfully entices the Israelites to succumb to fornication and idolatry. Balaam thus becomes a symbol for false teachers who accept money in order to influence naïve listeners to compromise in physical and spiritual morality, and thereby fall into apostasy. In addition, the context of Num 24 confirms that it was understood as an eschatological passage, especially Num

---

108. Smalley, *Revelation*, 315.

109. So Aune, *Revelation*, 2:681; Beale, *Revelation*, 626–27; Beasley-Murray, *Revelation*, 197–98; Blount, *Revelation*, 227; Brighton, *Revelation*, 326–27; Ladd, *Revelation*, 167; Murphy, *Fallen Is Babylon*, 278; Osborne, *Revelation*, 457; Swete, *Apocalypse*, 148–49.

110. Beale (*Revelation*, 676–80), followed by others, recognizes a contrast between the heavenly ideal church (woman) and the earthly church (offspring). Such a contrast fits well with the rest of Revelation's emphasis on the earthly church's charge to be a witness in spite of deadly persecution.

24:14–19 where "in the last days" a Messiah-like king will come to defeat Israel's enemies. Such symbolism is noted in the first two NT citations of Balaam (2 Pet 2:15; Jude 11).[111]

The last mention of Balaam is Rev 2:14. Christ rebukes the church at Pergamum for having "some among you who hold to the teaching of Balaam, who taught Balak to entice the Israelites to sin so that they ate food sacrificed to idols and committed sexual immorality" (2:14). The trouble is not so much doctrine as it is practice—tempting the faithful to indulge in sexual immorality and food sacrificed to idols. In fact, the immorality mentioned may not be actual, but serving as a metaphor for idolatry (similar to the reference to Babylon in 14:8; 17:2–4; 18:3, 9). Either understanding is possible; perhaps both are intended. Most interpreters understand Balaam, Jezebel, and the Nicolaitans to be closely related, if not identical. This fits with the rest of Revelation toward warning the faithful not to compromise despite the enormous pressures which wicked unbelievers place on them. Just as the original Israelites were punished, so too will Pergamum-like churches and people be punished, starting with the original audience, throughout the church age, and especially nearer the end.[112]

Cowardly

The cowardly are false believers who turn their backs on Christ when faced with persecution, thereby revealing their lack of faith and their deserved destiny in the lake of fire. The adjective "cowardly" (*deilos*) is mentioned three times in the NT. Jesus calls his disciples "cowards" for their lack of faith at his calming of the storm (Matt 8:26; Mark 4:40). Most translations soften this to "terrified," "fearful," "frightened," or "afraid." Only a few modern Bibles render it as "cowards" or "cowardly" (GW, NET, REB). The final occurrence heads the list of those who will not enter the new Jerusalem (21:8). The majority of modern versions have "cowards" or "cowardly" here, except for "fearful" (KJV). The fact that this list of sinners begins with the cowardly and concludes with "all liars" underscores the view that these two vices describe the complete failure of so-called believers. When faced with the threat or reality of persecution they turn away from Christ, thereby revealing their true lack of faith. The cowardly reflect the contrasting opposite of those who live victorious lives for Christ in spite of persecution and even martyrdom.[113] Some modern readers might question the severity of relegating "cowards" and "liars" to the lake of fire. But John's dualism means there are no fence-sitting believers. Either one lives (and possibly dies) for Christ or one follows the devil—there is no in between. Therefore, believers must consider the call to persevere despite the tremendous pressure to conform to the world, the flesh, and the devil.

---

111. Hackett, "Balaam," 569–72; Waite, "Balaam," 404–5. Some interpreters suggest that Pergamum's "Balaam" was an actual rival prophet, including Barr (*Tales*, 50), Yarbro Collins (*Crisis and Catharsis*, 44–45), and Murphy (*Fallen Is Babylon*, 114). It seems more likely to view the symbol as stressing false teaching by many.

112. See Beale, *Revelation*, 248–50; Hays, Duvall, and Pate, *Dictionary of Prophecy*, 57; Kistemaker, *Revelation*, 130–32; Osborne, *Revelation*, 143–45.

113. Beale, *Revelation*, 1059. See Michaels, *Interpreting Revelation*, 42–43; Osborne, *Revelation*, 740–41.

False Prophet

The false prophet is the third part of the unholy trinity alongside the dragon and the beast. In parody of the Holy Spirit, he performs signs and wonders to deceive unbelievers into following Satan, and to pressure believers to accommodate to the prevailing culture. "False prophet" occurs eleven times in the NT. Jesus teaches his followers to "Watch out for false prophets. They come to you in sheep's clothing, but inwardly they are ferocious wolves" (Matt 7:15). This coincides with the apparently harmless nature of "he had two horns like a lamb" (13:2). On the Mount of Olives, Jesus teaches that "many false prophets will appear and deceive many people" (Matt 24:11), and "false messiahs and false prophets will appear and perform great signs and wonders to deceive, if possible, even the elect" (Matt 24:24). This matches the deceptive signs and wonders of the second beast. Rev 13:11–18 describes the nefarious career of the false prophet. He is introduced as "another beast" (13:11), comes "out of the earth," is empowered by Satan (13:11, 14), deceives the world with signs and wonders (13:13–15), promotes and demands that the world worship the first beast (13:12–15), puts to death those who refuse to worship the first beast (13:15), and economically persecutes the world (13:16–17). Such characteristics imply a heavy religious role.[114]

This religious role is confirmed in the final three references in Revelation. It is here where he is called the "false prophet" and the false trinity is clearly mentioned. First, demonic, frog-like spirits come out of the mouths of the false trinity at the sixth bowl, inspiring and deceiving the world to gather for the final battle of Armageddon (16:13). Next, the end for the false prophet is noted at the second coming. The beast and the false prophet are captured and "The two of them were thrown alive into the fiery lake of burning sulfur" (19:20). Lastly, in the subsequent thousand year vision, the devil "was thrown into the lake of burning sulfur, where the beast and the false prophet had been thrown" (20:10).

But who or what is the false prophet? Several possibilities have arisen over the centuries, generally tied to current events of the interpreter's era.[115] Today, many understand a future, end-time religious leader of the apostate church. This is the futurist reading. It usually promotes an individual, not an institution, a religious leader who becomes an ecumenical spokesperson and enforces the worship of the antichrist. He is

---

114. For extended exegesis of 13:11–18, see Beale, *Revelation*, 707–18; Osborne, *Revelation*, 513–22; Siew, *War between the Two Beasts*, 175–81; Smalley *Revelation*, 344–53; J. C. Thomas, *Apocalypse*, 397–414; Robert Thomas, *Revelation*, 2:171–88.

115. Alan Johnson ("Revelation," 13:711–12), Weinrich (*Revelation*, 204–10), and Wainwright (*Mysterious Apocalypse*, 49–66) trace contemporary interpretations on both beasts from the early church to the Reformers. Papal abuse in the Middle Ages led many to pinpoint the church as the false prophet. Ubertino of Casale, as an example, outed Pope Benedict XI. The historicist readings of the Reformers targeted papal Rome. Puritan theology, including Jonathan Edwards, promoted Muhammad because of the rise of Muslim population (Kovacs and Rowland, *Revelation*, 156–57). Adventist theologians understand the false prophet as an alliance of the United States with the papacy for an enforcement of Sunday worship. Thus, Stefanovic (*Revelation*, 432–33) relates, "It appears that no single religious or political entity in modern history matches the description of the earth beast as does the United States of America . . . Revelation 13 seems to foretell a key religious-political role for the United States in the final crisis."

the "Satan-inspired leader of apostate Christendom."[116] This view tends to minimize the original audience and must be continually updated.[117]

The majority of interpreters recognize the necessity to begin with John's original audience. The prevailing view of scholarship understands the false prophet to represent supporters of the imperial cult that aided emperor worship. Many scholars attempt to narrow this view further. The false prophet may symbolize aristocratic supporters of Asia Minor. These wealthy families formed the social elite, and funded the building of temples, statues, and worked in civic administration.[118] Others point to the Asia Minor provincial council. The council appointed priests/priestesses and oversaw sacrifices and festivals. They were in the position to enforce worship.[119] Still others opt for imperial priesthood found throughout the empire. John's readers would have linked the first beast with Roman imperial system (and leader/s within that system).[120] The second beast would be the imperial priests active in ensuring the expansion of emperor worship everywhere.[121]

Such specificity may be correct. John, however, does not limit the symbol. He broadens it. A better view, therefore, is to see the false prophet represents all evil religious authority. This includes pagan worship and culture in general, supporters of Greco–Roman religion, the imperial cult, society at large, and the idolatrous teaching found within the church (2:14). This can also include Christians who accommodate to pagan practices.[122]

Nailing down John's original image must give way to how the symbol should be utilized today. This study follows an eclectic approach that stresses the need for each generation to come to grips with John's words. Thus, the original audience could swiftly see the false prophet all around them. The close tie between economics, religion, and politics suggests the use of trade guilds in promoting false worship. Trade guilds were organizations that expected participation in worship rituals, a practice that placed pressure on believers to compromise their faith.[123] Moreover, it symbolizes false religion and

---

116. Hindson, *Revelation*, 148. So also Easley, *Revelation*, 23; Ladd, *Revelation*, 177; LaHaye, *Revelation Unveiled*, 222–26; Patterson, *Revelation*, 280–81; Ryrie, *Revelation*, 98; Walvoord, *Revelation*, 204–5. Lindsey (*New World Coming*, 192) and Robert Thomas (*Revelation*, 2:173) suggest he comes from Jewish lineage.

117. On the other hand, preterist interpreters are content to leave the identification to the first century. Chilton (*Days of Vengeance*, 337) tabs Jewish religious leaders. Others are more specific. Buchanan (*Revelation*, 359) posits Herod Agrippa I, and Russell (*Parousia*, 467) selects procurators Albinus or Gessius Florus.

118. Adams, *Time Is at Hand*, 72; Clark, *Message from Patmos*, 86; Friesen, "Beast from the Land," 62–63; Koester, *Revelation*, 600–601; Murphy, *Fallen Is Babylon*, 309; Prigent, *Apocalypse*, 416; Yarbro Collins, "What the Spirit Says," 82.

119. Aune, *Revelation*, 2:756–57; Blount, *Revelation*, 257; Caird, *Revelation*, 171; deSilva, "Image of the Beast," 204–5; Mounce, *Revelation*, 256.

120. See the entry "Beast."

121. Bauckham, *Climax of Prophecy*, 446; Charles, *Revelation*, 1:357; Fee, *Revelation*, 185; Keener, *Revelation*, 340; Schnabel, *40 Questions*, 195; Schüssler Fiorenza, *Revelation*, 86.

122. Beale, *Revelation*, 707–8; Beasley-Murray, *Revelation*, 216–17; Brighton, *Revelation*, 352; Boring, *Revelation*, 157; Duff, *Who Rides the Beast?*, 114; Duvall, *Revelation*, 185; Osborne, *Revelation*, 513; Reddish, *Revelation*, 258; Resseguie, *Revelation*, 188; Roloff, *Revelation*, 161; Smalley, *Revelation*, 345; Sweet, *Revelation*, 214–15; Swete, *Apocalypse*, 167.

123. Hays, Duvall, and Pate, *Dictionary of Prophecy*, 152–53.

philosophy in all their forms throughout the centuries. Counterfeit miracles and signs and wonders typify false teachers throughout the history (Deut 13:1–4; 2 Pet 2:3). Religious pressure and persecution is found in every era. The church must resist this pressure to accommodate to the false prophet in every generation. Finally, the fact that the false prophet is always mentioned near the end of a vision lends support to increased religious persecution at the conclusion of history.

Free and Slave

The phrase "free and slave" is a metaphor that means all unbelievers without exception. "Free" (*eleutheros*) occurs three times in Revelation, each time companioned with "slave" (*doulos*).[124] In two instances the phrase appears in a vision of judgment upon unbelievers at the second coming. First, it is found in the sevenfold list of wicked humanity at the sixth seal (6:15). This end-time scene is repeated in the listing found in the rider on the white horse vision (19:18). The third occurrence is found in chapter 13. The false prophet requires everyone, "great and small, rich and poor, free and slave, to receive a mark on their right hands or on their foreheads" (13:16). It is possible that this last reference to "free and slave" includes believers as well. If so, then stress must be placed on the word "all" (*pantas*) and a comprehensive universality that cuts across all social lines.[125] Yet this suggests the possibility that believers receive the mark, and capitulate to the beast for economic reasons. This study contends that believers receive the seal of God and unbelievers receive the mark of the beast—there is no overlapping. It appears more likely therefore that "free and slave" is a metaphor reserved solely for unbelievers. "The expression *all* does not signify that every single human being is included but rather that people from all walks of life are intended.[126] True servants of God do not accept the mark. One is either marked and sealed by God or marked and sealed by the devil. When all three uses of the phrase are considered, it confirms that all unbelieving humanity is meant.

Generals

The mention of generals alludes to the gathering of armies at Armageddon, the final battle. The word *chiliarchoi* is found twenty-one times in the NT, seventeen of which are in Acts. It is mentioned twice in Revelation in sevenfold lists that include all wicked humanity (6:15; 19:18). Elsewhere, the NIV translates the word as "commanders," but for some reason "generals" is chosen for Revelation. "Generals" is also preferred by other English versions (CEB, GW, NCV, NET, NLT). Different selections include "military

---

124. *Doulos* is found a total of fourteen times in Revelation, and is usually translated "servant" in English versions. *Eleutheros* is usually rendered "free," or "free man/person/people" in English versions. NJB uniquely renders it "citizens."

125. So Aune, *Revelation*, 2:765–66; Brighton, *Revelation*, 361–62; Mounce, *Revelation*, 259; Osborne, *Revelation*, 517; Smalley, *Revelation*, 348–49; Stefanovic, *Revelation*, 425; Robert Thomas, *Revelation*, 2:179–80.

126. Kistemaker, *Revelation*, 393.

officers" (NABR) and "commanders" (NASB, REB). Slight variations between the two passages include "military leaders" and "leaders" (CEV), and "military commanders" and "commanders" (HCSB). Some versions, however, translate *chiliarchoi* differently at these two locations, masking a significant intratextual link. This includes "military commanders" and "generals" (CSB); "military chiefs" and "generals" (GNT); "commanders" and "captains" (NKJV); "governors" and "generals" (NJB), and particularly "generals" and "captains" (ESV, NRSV) which modern readers would certainly distinguish as separate ranks.[127] The point is that these are parallel passages and the same word refers to the same group of people at the same place and time (Armageddon).[128] Since Armageddon is specifically mentioned only at 16:16, then that passage comes into play as well. Thus, all three passages (6:15; 16:16; 19:18) parallel one another and offer more details on the final battle.[129] The sevenfold lists are similar and both draw from Ezek 38–39. They compose a rhetorical listing of everyone from the lofty to the lowly.[130] John's mention of generals, therefore, evokes an image of the universal gathering of armies for the end-time battle of Armageddon.

Gog and Magog

Gog and Magog represent the whole world, the enemies of God's people, who Satan deceives into gathering for the climactic, end-time battle of Armageddon. Gog and Magog derives from Ezek 38–39. Gog (the king of northern lands) and Magog (which means "land of Gog") gather to wage war against God and his people. Ezekiel envisions a vast enemy army from the north invading Israel. The words lost their geographical distinction and extratextual sources confirm they became a symbol of the archetype evil force that rises up at the end of history (*Sib. Or.* 3:319–322, 512) in which a last great battle is often mentioned (*1 En.* 56:5–8; *Jub.* 8:25; *Sib. Or.* 3.657–732; *4 Ezra* 13:5–11, 25–29). Qumran writers also universalized Ezekiel's prophecy, equating "nations" with Gog and Magog (1QM 11:15–16 and 4QIsa).[131]

John mentions Gog and Magog once (20:8). Its location in the text and how it relates to Ezek 38–39 has generated a multitude of interpretations. Attempts at a literal approach are noticeable throughout the centuries as interpreters identify Gog and Magog with contemporary peoples and places. The phrase has been attached to the Goths, Huns, Arabs,

127. Curiously, Smalley (*Revelation*, 179, 497) makes the same mistake. In 6:15 he states they are "high-ranking generals . . . the commander of a cohort of about six hundred soldiers." Yet in 19:18 he relates, "The word strictly means military commander of one thousand soldiers."

128. Beale (*Revelation*, 400) points out that the sevenfold list of people in 6:15 "shows that all unbelievers living on earth at the time of final judgment are in mind, as the parallel in 19:18–19 bears out . . ." Osborne (*Revelation*, 294) concurs: "Therefore, there is probably a connection between these two events."

129. Although the word "generals" is not found at the sixth bowl (16:12–16), it does mention the gathering of kings for the end-time battle called Armageddon.

130. Resseguie, *Revelation*, 132–33.

131. Barabas, "Gog," 806; Emmerson, "Gog and Magog," 311–12; Reddish, "Gog and Magog," 1056. For further research, Bøe (*Gog and Magog*) and Tooman (*Gog of Magog*) provide definitive background on the topic.

Saracens, Hungarians, Mongols, Roman emperors, the Reformers, and Catholic popes. Then in the twentieth century Russia became a popular pick for dispensationalists.[132] Since the fall of the Soviet Union, more distinctions became required. Renald Showers proposes modern Iran, Sudan, Libya, central Turkey, eastern Turkey, and Russia. Their Islamic fundamentalism is a key. Mark Hitchcock agrees on the Russian-Islamic axis of nations invading Israel.[133] The intricate details of these invaders and their fulfillment from Ezek 38–39 are usually attached to Armageddon (Rev 16, 19). Yet Gog and Magog are mentioned only in 20:7–10, at the conclusion of the millennium. The solution is to posit a second, similar end-time battle and that John uses the same language from Ezek 38–39.[134]

Schnabel critiques the literalist methodology: "These various and very different interpretations have one element in common: they all depend on contemporary political and military threats. These identifications can be justified only temporarily and then must be modified to match the ever-changing regional or global political climate changes."[135]

However, numerous non-dispensationalist scholars also follow a sequential outline with two battles separated by a thousand years. For example, Osborne explains that the battle of 19:17–21 is the defeat of armies whereas 20:7–10 is the defeat of the rest of world.[136] Still other scholars understand only one end-time battle.[137] This means that the singular NT reference to Gog and Magog is part of one more retelling of Armageddon with expanded details.[138] This latter understanding fits well with John's intratextual cross-referencing style. The fact that John references Ezek 38–39 in 16:12–21 and 19:17–21 favors the idea that 20:7–10 is yet one more iteration of the same events.

Thus, at the conclusion of the thousand years (church age), Satan is released and allowed to deceive the nations—Gog and Magog—to gather for "the battle" (*ton polemon*).

---

132. See specific details in Lindsey, *Late Great Planet Earth*, 59–71. Wainwright (*Mysterious Apocalypse*, 47, 74) relates an eccentric historical example. Thomas Burnet, based on burgeoning seventeenth-century discoveries, explained that Gog and Magog would be a horde of fearsome creatures "generated from the slime of the ground." Railton ("Gog and Magog," 23–43) provides numerous historical examples.

133. Showers, "Gog and Magog," 124–26; Hitchcock, *Russia Rising*, 117–18.

134. Ryrie, *Revelation*, 133–34; Robert Thomas, *Revelation*, 2:422–25; Walvoord, *Revelation*, 303–4. Patterson (*Revelation*, 357) offers that there is one final conflict occurring at two different times separated by the millennium. By contrast, Tanner ("Rethinking Ezekiel's Invasion," 29–46) differs from other premillennialists by limiting the reference of Gog and Magog and Ezek 38–39 to Rev 20:7–10 only.

135. Schnabel, *40 Questions*, 220. Chilton (*Days of Vengeance*, 521–22) notes the inconsistencies of literalists who do not literally follow the text. Railton ("Gog and Magog," 23) is more trenchant toward popular dispensationalists. Their rhetoric to interpret the signs of the times "has entrenched religious believers in an inflexible, nationalistic and self-righteous mindset . . . ever tighter with the chains of bigotry tinged with racism."

136. Osborne, *Revelation*, 713, in agreement with Beasley-Murray, *Revelation*, 297. Others who recognize two battles include Blount, *Revelation*, 369; Duvall, *Revelation*, 270; Easley, *Revelation*, 377; Alan Johnson, "Revelation," 13:772; Keener, *Revelation*, 467; Ladd, *Revelation*, 270; Michaels, *Revelation*, 226; Mounce, *Revelation*, 372; Paul, *Revelation*, 330; J. C. Thomas, *Apocalypse*, 611.

137. Bauckham, *Climax of Prophecy*, 208–9; Beale, *Revelation*, 1022–23; Boxall, *Revelation*, 286; Brighton, *Revelation*, 574–76; Boring, *Revelation*, 210; Hendriksen, *More than Conquerors*, 193–95; Hughes, *Revelation*, 217; Dennis Johnson, *Triumph of the Lamb*, 294–95; Kistemaker, *Revelation*, 544; Mulholland, *Revelation*, 307; Smalley, *Revelation*, 513; Fowler White, "Reexamining the Evidence," 319–44.

138. See the entry "Armageddon."

The definite article denotes previous reference to this battle elsewhere.[139] The same "the battle" is mentioned in 16:14; 19:19; and 20:8.[140] The deceived "nations" of 20:8 are the same opponents of God who are judged in chapters 16 and 19.[141] They come from everywhere ("four corners of the earth"; "like sands on the seashore") and surround God's people.[142] But like its parallel vision in chapter 19, the battle is over before it starts. The devil is thrown into the lake of fire with the beast and the false prophet.[143]

Similar to previous apocalyptic writers, John expands and universalizes this end-time element, symbolizing Gog and Magog into all the nations of the earth and worldwide opposition to Christ and his followers to describe the final attack of evil forces against the people of God. The final battle of Armageddon is pictured yet one more time (6:15–17; 9:13–21; 14:19–20; 16:17–21; 19:17–21) from one more angle.

Great Prostitute

The great prostitute is Babylon the Great, the great city, the woman who sits on the scarlet beast. Rome is John's original referent, but ultimately she symbolizes the evil, immoral world system that opposes God and persecutes his people, and will be eternally judged at the end. The images associated with the great prostitute originate from the prophets. Regularly, Jerusalem and Israel are depicted as an adulteress to her husband, the Lord (Hos 1–3; Isa 23, 57; Jer 3–4; Ezek 16, 23). Spiritual unfaithfulness runs throughout these passages. In Revelation, the connection to these previous metaphors is on clear display in the fall of Babylon vision where the great prostitute is mentioned five times (17:1, 5, 15, 16; 19:2).[144]

139. Wallace (*Greek Grammar*, 218) states, "But subsequent mentions of it (the substantive) use the article, for the article is now pointing back to *the* substantive previously mentioned . . . It is the most common use of the article and the easiest usage to identify." See Fowler White, "Reexamining the Evidence," 328–30.

140. Only NASB and NET include the article at 20:8. Regrettably, no English version offers consistent renderings at 16:14; 19:19; and 20:8, thereby undercutting a significant intratextual connection.

141. Premillennialists answer the question of how evil nations can rise again after end-time judgment has been rendered in different ways. Hindson (*Revelation*, 204) adheres to a survivor theory, i.e. not all died on the battlefield of 19:17–21. Duvall (*Revelation*, 270–71), Mealy (*After the Thousand Years*, 140–42), Schnabel (*40 Questions*, 276), and Stefanovic (*Revelation*, 579) propose the wicked dead who were killed in 20:5 are raised to life to fight again. Some scholars (Rissi, *Future of the World*, 35–36; Roloff, *Revelation*, 228; Schüssler Fiorenza, *Revelation*, 107; Sweet; *Revelation*, 290–91) suggest a demonic or ghostly army.

142. See the entry "Camp of God's People."

143. Some English versions unfortunately assume a sequential, not synonymous, understanding of 20:10. There is no second verb ("throw") to connect with the first verb "to throw." It is supplied by translators. Thus, "And the devil, who deceived them, was thrown into the lake of burning sulfur, where the beast and the false prophet *had been thrown*" (NIV; see also GNT, REB). But the italicized words are not in the Greek text. Such renderings suggest a sequential translator is at work. The Greek text implies that the two "throwings" are simultaneous. Most English versions supply "are" or "were" and allow readers to decide. One version does well here: "And Satan, who tricked them, was thrown into the lake of burning sulfur with the beast and the false prophet" (NCV).

144. For *pornē*, most English versions choose "prostitute" (CEB, CEV, CSB, ESV, GNT, GW, NCV, NET, NIV, NJB, NLT), but there is also "harlot" (NABR, NASB, NKJV) and "whore" (NRSV, REB). For the adjective *megalē* (17:1; 19:2), the rendering is usually "great" but there is also "notorious" (CSB, GW),

John relates a scandalous image of a prostitute clothed in purple and scarlet, adorned with gold, jewels, and pearls. She is the mother of all prostitutes. These images portray idolatry and economic luxuries. She glories in culture, consumerism, and affluence. The world becomes drunk with the wine of her immoralities. She persecutes the saints, becoming drunk with their blood. But her end is assured. At the eschaton, the great multitude shouts "for true and just are his judgments. He has condemned the great prostitute who corrupted the earth by her adulteries. He has avenged on her the blood of his servants" (19:2).[145]

As with many of John's images, the great prostitute has been identified in various ways throughout history.[146] Schnabel, however, offers an apt description. "The great prostitute symbolizes the prevailing economic and religious institutions that are in alliance with the political and social systems throughout history."[147] Thus, John's contrasts flow forth. Just as there are two cities, so there are two women. One is the faithful bride of the Lamb but the other is a rebellious prostitute. Immorality, idolatry, and abusive power are evident throughout the centuries. That the great prostitute's name appears only in the fall of Babylon vision underlines her prevalence near the end of the age.

Idolators

Idolatry, the worship of objects and images made with hands, is repulsive and abhorrent to God and will be eternally judged at the end of history. Idols and their worshippers were indigenous to the ancient Near East. Although Israel limited idolatry after the Babylonian exile, it never disappeared. In fact, recent archaeological studies suggest an undercurrent of idol acceptance into the NT period.[148] Idolaters are mentioned only a few times in Revelation but their influence pervades the text. Christ rebukes the churches of Pergamum and Thyatira for allowing idolatrous infiltration the same way the Israelites had done with Balaam and Jezebel (2:14, 20).[149] Revelation includes three vice lists (9:20–21; 21:8; 22:15). The word "idol" is found on the first list and "idolaters" appear on the other two lists. The lists essentially draw together all the sins found in the book. Their purpose is to sum up the wickedness of all unbelievers. For moderns, idols are symbolized in materialism, consumerism, celebrity, sex, success, status, and power. Worshipping such things made by

---

"famous" (GNT), and "shameless" (CEV). GNT and NCV leave *megalē* untranslated at 19:2.

145. Blount and Blickenstaff, "Whore of Babylon," 845–46; Hays, Duvall, and Pate, *Dictionary of Prophecy*, 189–91; Ryken, *Dictionary of Biblical Imagery*, 676–78; Schnabel, *40 Questions*, 205–12.

146. See the entry "Babylon the Great." See also Schnabel, *40 Questions*, 205–6, for other speculations. Valentine ("Cleopatra," 310–30) suggests a connection to Cleopatra as a model. Bond ("Whore of Babylon," 826–28) traces how the great prostitute was interpreted and appropriated from anti-Nicene fathers to James Joyce's *Ulysses*.

147. Schnabel, *40 Questions*, 211–12.

148. See Curtis, "Idol, Idolatry," 380–81; Huey, "Idolatry," 3:270–75; Laughlin, "Idol," "Idolatry," 8–14; Ryken, *Dictionary of Biblical Imagery*, 416–18. A strong case for idolatry as the foundational sin that leads to all other sins is made by Beale (*New Testament Biblical Theology*, 357–80; and *We Become What We Worship*).

149. Murphy (*Apocalypticism*, 103) observes a close biblical connection of idolatry with fornication. This tightens the parallel to the Balaam story.

hands is detestable to a holy God who should be worthy of all our focus. Those who run after such things reveal a mind toward self and Satan. In the end, idolaters will be judged.

Inhabitants of the Earth

This expression refers to all unbelievers. They persecute the faithful, worship the beast, and follow the great prostitute to their eternal destruction. This phrase is one of several used by John to refer to the totality of wicked unbelievers.[150] It is found eleven times (3:10; 6:10; 8:13; 11:10 [twice]; 13:8, 12, 14 [twice]; 17:2, 8).[151] The NIV consistently renders the phrase as "inhabitants of the earth" (so also NABR, NRSV, REB). Alternate English translations include "those who live/dwell on the earth" (CEB, CSB, ESV, NASB), and "people who belong to this world" (NLT). Some translations, however, use a variety of English renderings for the same Greek phrase (CEV, GNT, NCV, NET, NJB). This practice masks the repetition of the phrase and undercuts its symbolism as a technical term for all unbelievers throughout Revelation. Bauckham notes the phrase is common in apocalyptic literature (*1 Enoch, 2 Baruch, 4 Ezra*) and is also found in the OT (Isa 24:1–6; 26:9; Dan 4:1, 35; 6:25). But whereas other apocalypses do not necessarily include negative overtones for the phrase, Revelation consistently does. Mounce, for example, calls it "a semitechnical designation for the human race in its hostility to God."[152] Osborne adds that the term "is important in the book and always refers to the unbelievers, the enemies of God who not only worship and follow the beast but also persecute the believers."[153]

Thus, the phrase is used by John to refer to the idolatrous earth-dwellers who persecute believers, follow the beast, and receive righteous condemnation at the end of history. Although unbelievers who persecute are documented throughout history, the placement of this phrase near the conclusion of individual visions in Revelation is intriguing. It is found in the fifth seal that is immediately prior to the second coming depicted in the sixth seal. It is found as the fifth, six, and seventh trumpets are blasted. It is found near the end of the second interlude where Christian witness appears to have been stamped out. There are four references found in the third interlude. Finally, there are two references in the vision of the fall of Babylon. Thus, a case can be made that persecuting nature of "the inhabitants of the earth" will get worse and worse toward the end of history.

---

150. See Herms, *Apocalypse*, 185–88.

151. Although the phrase is not found in 12:12, it is possible to add this passage as well. Bauckham (*Climax of Prophecy*, 240) and Osborne (*Revelation*, 478) rightly note the verse's strong contrast. Preterist interpreters such as Beagley (*Sitz im Leben*, 34–36), Buchanan (*Revelation*, 132), and Chilton (*Days of Vengeance*, 129) limit the phrase to the "inhabitants of the land," i.e. first-century Palestine. Charles (*Revelation*, 1:289) limits Palestine only to 11:10. Ice ("Meaning of Earth-Dwellers," 350–65) limits them to persistent unbelievers during the great tribulation period at history's end.

152. Mounce, *Revelation*, 148. So too Resseguie, *Revelation Unsealed*, 152.

153. Osborne, *Revelation*, 193. So too Aune, *Revelation*, 1:240; Bauckham, *Climax of Prophecy*, 239; Beale, *New Testament Biblical Theology*, 209; Beasley-Murray, *Revelation*, 101; Blount, *Revelation*, 77; Caird, *Revelation*, 88; Duvall, *Revelation*, 73; Herms, *Apocalypse*, 185; Resseguie, *Revelation*, 98–99; Rotz, *Revelation*, 85; Smalley, *Revelation*, 92; Robert Thomas, *Revelation*, 1:289. Keener (*Revelation*, 151) prefers to add the word "normally" because he sees 2:13 as another location for the word. Beale (*Revelation*, 595–96) notes that each usage in chapters 13–17 is attached to idolatry.

Jezebel

Like her OT counterpart, Jezebel represents false teachers who tempt believers into idolatrous worship and sexual immorality. Jezebel is mentioned only once in the NT. Christ challenges the church at Thyatira to stop tolerating Jezebel, "who calls herself a prophet. By her teaching she misleads my servants into sexual immorality and the eating of food sacrificed to idols" (2:20). It was Queen Jezebel (1 Kgs 16–21) who incited her husband, Ahab, and the rest of Israel to compromise their faith by worshipping Baal. Jezebel's name became symbolic of apostasy and is used in Revelation with reference to a false prophetess that is probably representing a larger group at Thyatira.[154] Jezebel's namesake is simply unknown but she is presumed to be an influential member of the church.[155] Jezebel and the great prostitute are closely linked, and serve as antithetical imagery to the woman clothed with the sun and the bride of Christ.[156] Thus, Thyatira is chastised for allowing the idolatrous activities of pagan culture to infiltrate their congregation. John draws upon a familiar story from Jewish history to warn first-century Christians not to follow a similar-styled prophetess in their church. She stands as a symbol of uncontrolled power, unrestrained sexuality, and spiritual adultery. John's mention of her is a poignant reminder to any church that rebuke is on the horizon if it allows such sinfulness to breed unchecked.

Kings of the Earth

The kings of the earth represent the evil power and authority of human rulers who support the beast and persecute the faithful. However, those kings who convert to Christ will participate in the new Jerusalem. "Kings" (*basileis*) is mentioned twenty-one times in Revelation, and "kings of the earth" is mentioned nine times (1:5; 6:15; 17:2, 18; 18:3, 9; 19:19; 21:24). John normally reserves the phrase for the end of individual visions. This confirms that the kings of the earth play a specific role at the end of history as antagonists of God and his people. Ronald Herms declares, "In the majority of cases 'kings of the earth' functions as a stock apocalyptic phrase with pejorative connotations."[157]

John also mentions "kings from the east" (16:12) and "kings of the world" (16:14). This leads many interpreters to distinguish them from kings of the earth. The kings from the east either war against or more likely coalesce with kings of the world in a lead up to Armageddon.[158] "From the east" literally means "from the rising sun" (*apo anatolēs*

---

154. Culver, "Jezebel," 670–71; Hays, Duvall, and Pate, *Dictionary of Prophecy*, 229–30; Eleanor Johnston, "Jezebel," 1057–59. Interpretations of Jezebel through church history are found in Parsons, "Jezebel," 401–2. On the other hand, Duff ("I Will Give to Each," 116–33) stresses witchcraft is in the background of Jezebel and the church at Thyatira. Many dispensationalists follow historicist methodology for Rev 2–3. Thus, Ryrie (*Revelation*, 30) understands Jezebel and Thyatira to depict "the Middle Ages and the ascendancy of the Roman Catholic Church."

155. Hemer, *Letters to the Seven Churches*, 117–23, 128. See Appler, "Jezebel," 313–14; Dutcher-Walls, *Jezebel*.

156. Campbell ("Antithetical Feminine-Urban Imagery," 81–108) and Duff (*Who Rides the Beast?*, 83–96) discuss the integration of the good and evil cities.

157. Herms, *Apocalypse*, 199.

158. Beasley-Murray, *Revelation*, 243; Blount, *Revelation*, 302; Easley, *Revelation*, 289; Koester,

hēliou). This is the clue for dispensationalists to find Asian nations involved with the final conflict, usually China.[159]

The "kings from the east," however, is a spiritual symbol, not a geographical location. John alludes to the prophecies of judgment upon sinful Israel from an enemy who crosses the Euphrates (Isa 11:15; Mic 7:12). John universalizes this to symbolize the whole world arriving for the end-time battle. Like the Euphrates River they cross, the kings from the east represent an overwhelming force that cannot be stopped. It is better therefore to view the kings from the east and the kings of the world as synonymous with the kings of the earth. It is a generic term for human leaders who support the beast and persecute the faithful. Numerous commentators agree with this assessment.[160]

Thus, kings from the earth form part of John's imagery for Armageddon and final judgment in several visions. They are in the comprehensive list of people who cower on the day of judgment depicted in the sixth seal (6:15–17). They are present at the sixth bowl, a recap of the preparation for Armageddon (16:12–16). Several references are noted in the fall of Babylon vision (17:1–19:10). They are in league with the beast and the great prostitute (17:2, 18) yet turn against her in end-time self-destruction (17:16). Although the kings of the earth participate in her downfall they mourn their own loss of wealth (18:3, 9). They appear again in yet another vision of Armageddon when they are among "the rest" who are "killed with the sword coming out of the mouth of the rider on the horse" (19:21).

Consummative judgment is the destiny of the kings of the earth. This is why their final mention is startling. In stark contrast to previous passages, the kings of the earth are present in the new Jerusalem. The city needs no sun or moon because the glory of God gives it light, and "the nations will walk by its light, and the kings of the earth will bring their splendor into it" (21:24). Scholars are perplexed by this sudden turnabout, and many minimize any significance or do not discuss the tension at all. Robert Thomas discusses and dismisses nine proposals, then posits his own unsatisfactory suggestion.[161] Most scholars are satisfied with understanding this as human leaders who convert to Christ some time before the second coming. Their military victory and plunder is exchanged for conversion and worship of God. Those who refuse to repent are still destined

---

Revelation, 659; Ladd, *Revelation*, 213; Morris, *Revelation*, 191; Mounce, *Revelation*, 298; Osborne, *Revelation*, 590–91; Reddish, *Revelation*, 310; Skaggs and Benham, *Revelation*, 164.

159. Hitchcock, *Russia Rising*, 26–27; LaHaye, *Revelation Unveiled*, 256; Lindsey, *New World Coming*, 221; Robert Thomas, *Revelation*, 2:263; Walvoord, *Revelation*, 236. However, Hindson (*Revelation*, 170) cautions against China, Japan, or Korea. Instead, he speculates it is Muslim nations under the yoke of Islam.

160. Beale, *Revelation*, 827, 834; Boring, *Revelation*, 176; Boxall, *Revelation*, 232; Brighton, *Revelation*, 418; Hughes, *Revelation*, 176; Dennis Johnson, *Triumph of the Lamb*, 232; Kistemaker, *Revelation*, 449; Michaels, *Revelation*, 187; Prigent, *Apocalypse*, 469; Resseguie, *Revelation*, 212; Smalley, *Revelation*, 408, 410; J. C. Thomas, *Apocalypse*, 480, 482. There are alternate views. Aune (*Revelation*, 2:895) explains the tension between 16:12 and 16:14 as an interpolation of a later editor. Chilton (*Days of Vengeance*, 408) links 16:12 to a return of Titus to Jerusalem in AD 70 with further reinforcements. Stefanovic (*Revelation*, 495) believes the "kings from the east" are actually Christ with his armies of saints.

161. Robert Thomas, *Revelation*, 2:475–78. Thomas speculates they are "saved people who survive the millennial kingdom without dying and without joining Satan's rebellion and who undergo some sort of transformation" and "will be like Adam and Eve."

for the lake of fire.[162] Some scholars, however, note a rhetorical function at work. John is utilizing the common "pilgrimage of the nations" motif found in the prophets. In Isa 2, the nations come to Jerusalem. In Isa 60, Jerusalem is restored with wealth and glory. In Zech 14, the Lord is king over the whole earth. He strikes the nations and a remnant emerges who worship on the day of the Lord. Thus, John offers a hortatory challenge to his audience. Both judgment and salvation are purposefully laid side by side. The tension between the two is for rhetorical effect.[163]

Nevertheless, there is only one true king. At the outset of Revelation, John declares Christ as the ruler over the "kings of the earth" (1:5). At the conclusion of the third interlude depicting the eschaton, the victorious sing "Just and true are your ways, King of the nations" (15:3).[164] The returning Christ is "King of kings" (17:14; 19:16). Ultimately, this kingship is shared with believers who are a royal priesthood or kingly priests (1:6, 5:10) who reign with Christ (20:6).[165]

Liars

For John, liars are false believers who live contrary to the lifestyle and values of the Christian community, especially when faced with persecution and who even persecute believers themselves. Revelation mentions "liars" twice (2:2; 21:8), "lying" once (3:9), and "lies" three times (14:5; 21:27; 22:15). The locations include the seven churches which were hampered by false believers and the two vice lists of those who will not enter the heavenly kingdom. The vice lists obviously catalog unbelievers. But false Christians are implied as well. In the first vice list, John relates who is not going to be in the new Jerusalem: "Nothing impure will ever enter it, nor will anyone who does what is shameful or deceitful, but only those whose names are written in the Lamb's book of life" (21:27). This seems to imply that false believers as well as unbelievers are included. For certain, the final vice list includes false believers. John states "the cowardly, the unbelieving, the vile, the murderers, the sexually immoral, those who practice magic arts, the idolaters and all liars—they will be consigned to the fiery lake of burning sulfur. This is the second death" (21:8). This final group of eight sinners, commencing with cowards and ending with all liars, is John's understanding of apostate believers. They are the ones who compromise

---

162. Aune, *Revelation*, 2:1175; Beale, *Revelation*, 1095; Osborne, *Revelation*, 762–63; Smalley, *Revelation*, 558–59.

163. See the entry "Nations." Those who discuss the rhetorical function include Baines ("Identity and Fate," 73–88), Bauckham (*Climax of Prophecy*, 238–337; *Theology of Revelation*, 84–107), Herms (*Apocalypse*, 172–256), Mathewson ("Destiny of the Nations," 121–42), and McNichol (*Conversion of the Nations*, 58–140).

164. There are three variant readings of 15:3 in Greek manuscripts: "nations," "ages," or "saints." UBS5 gives a {B} rating for "nations" (*ethnōn*) and almost all modern versions follow this reading. "Ages" (*aiōnōn*), followed by NIV (1984) and REB, has equal external evidence but the internal evidence weighs more heavily in favor of "nations." The TR/KJV/NKJV tradition has "saints" (*hagiōn*). Omanson (*Textual Guide*, 542) relates that the TR reading arose from confusion of the Latin abbreviations for sanctorum (*sctorum*) and saeculorum (*sclorum* = *hagiōn*).

165. See the entries "King of Kings and Lord of Lords" and "Priests."

under pressure.[166] Therefore, John does not simply condemn those who tell lies. Rather, it is anyone who is living a lie and living as a Christian yet not upholding the truth. "Liars" lie by their actions and practice, and occasionally this includes their speech.

Nations

This term designates unbelievers whom Christ eternally judges at the parousia. However, those people among the nations who repent and believe are promised eternal bliss in the new Jerusalem. "Nations" (*ethnē*) occurs twenty-three times in Revelation.[167] It is another one of John's words that is normally reserved for the end of individual visions. Seven references underscore the universality of the fourfold phrase "every tribe and language and people and nation" (5:9; 7:9; 10:11; 11:9; 13:7; 14:6; 17:15). Most of the remaining references to "nations" depict their end-time judgment. The victorious are promised a share in Jesus' everlasting rule over the nations (2:26). The male child is destined to rule the nations with an iron scepter (12:5; 19:15). The temple's outer court (God's people) is handed over to the nations who persecute the faithful (11:2). The nations raged but destined end-time wrath has come at the seventh trumpet (11:18). The end-time fall of Babylon for enticing and duping the nations is described in the third interlude (14:8) and fall of Babylon vision (18:3, 23). The cities of the nations collapse at the seventh bowl (16:19). At the conclusion of history, Jesus is exalted as King of the nations and all nations bow to worship him (15:3–4). At the cross, the nations as a whole were no longer deceived by the dragon (20:3). At the end of history, however, Satan is loosed and the nations are deceived again and prepare for the final battle of Armageddon (20:8).[168]

The final references to the nations generate the most debate from interpreters. The nations (and the kings of the earth who lead them) are consistent antagonists of God and his people and are judged at the conclusion of history. Surprisingly, they reappear in the new Jerusalem. The nations will walk by God's eternal light, and the glory and honor of the nations will be brought into the new Jerusalem (21:24–26). Moreover, the leaves of the tree of life "are for the healing of the nations" (22:2). How do interpreters address this tension of universal judgment over against universal salvation?

Four proposals are proffered. First, some commentators understand the tension through the lens of universalism. In the end, all people, all kings, and all nations are redeemed.[169] Second, a few scholars find a priority for salvation over judgment. Bauckham,

---

166. Smalley, *Revelation*, 543–44. See Michaels, *Interpreting Revelation*, 42–43.

167. Seven English versions are consistent in translation with all twenty-three instances (CEB, CSB, ESV, GW, NASB, NLT, NRSV). Five other versions are consistent except for exchanging "nations" for "gentiles" at 11:2 (NET, NIV, NJB, NKJV, REB). All other versions use a variety of words. GNT and NCV obscure the intratextual connections with five different renderings for *ethnē*.

168. Since the nations are destroyed in final battle at 19:17–21, premillennialists advance a second end-time battle involving more nations after a thousand years has passed (20:8). See the entry "Gog and Magog."

169. Boring, *Revelation*, 226–31; Caird, *Revelation*, 279–80; Farmer, *Revelation*, 138; Harrington, *Revelation*, 229–235; Pilgrim, "Universalism in the Apocalypse," 235–43; Rissi, *Future of the World*, 71–74. The potential universalism of 21:24 may have caused copyists to add "of those who are saved," a reading perpetuated in NKJV.

for example, maintains that the OT's use and John's use of universal language in relation to the nations envisions the conversion of the nations as a result of the prophetic witness of the church. This falls short of a thoroughgoing universalism. Those who do not repent still face judgment, but the majority of nations come into a renewed creation.[170]

Third, the majority of interpreters suggest that the nations present in the new Jerusalem are those redeemed out of the nations throughout history (5:9; 7:9), and especially nearer the end (9:21; 11:13; 16:9, 11). These believers essentially replace the rebellious kings and nations who served the beast and great prostitute. Therefore, there is no unresolvable conflict between the destruction of the nations in chapter 19 and the conversion of nations in chapter 21. Those among the nations who reject God are destroyed. Those who repent and bow to Christ (15:4) will bring their glory into the celestial city.[171]

Fourth, some scholars stress rhetorical function wherein John purposefully intends to keep the tension in place. Thus, John juxtaposes absolute judgment and absolute salvation for hortatory reasons. John paraphrases Isa 60. Israel was to be a light to the nations and the procession of nations, led by their kings, are drawn to the light. John finalizes this imagery of the nations responding to God. He transforms Isa 60 from military victory to conversion and worship. Herms states the universal language does not presuppose universal salvation but rather vindicates and validates the faithful community. The subservience of the nations portrays the eschatological reversal of Israel's misery in three ways: (1) language of repatriation to the land for the exiles; (2) language of restoration of wealth and prosperity (Isa 60:5–11); and (3) language of acknowledgment of God and status of God's people (Isa 60:3, 14–15). Those nations who remain uncooperative are destroyed (Isa 60:12; 63:1–6; 66:17–18).[172] David Mathewson, however, prefers to see that the tension be kept in balance. John's audience must decide to follow the nations and their kings to destruction or follow them to eternal bliss.[173] Allan McNichol agrees. John's overall message stems from his pastoral interest in the churches.[174]

The last reference to the "healing of the nations" (22:2) figuratively expresses the eternal salvation accomplished by Christ. John draws from Ezek 47:12 where national Israel receives the healing leaves of the tree. John universalizes this to "the nations." This means there is no longer any need for physical healing (no hunger, disease, or suffering) or spiritual healing (eternal presence of God).[175] A synthesis of options three and four has

---

170. Bauckham, *Climax of Prophecy*, 310, 315–16; idem, *Theology of Revelation*, 98–108. See also Beasley-Murray, *Revelation*, 328–29; Blount, *Revelation*, 393–94; and Sweet, *Revelation*, 308–9.

171. The best discussions are found in Aune, *Revelation*, 3:1170–73; Beale, *Revelation*, 1097–1101; Osborne, *Revelation*, 762–67; Schnabel, "John and the Future of the Nations," 243–71; and Smalley, *Revelation*, 557–59.

172. Herms, *Apocalypse*, 245–46, 260. See the entry "Kings of the Earth."

173. Mathewson, *New Heaven and New Earth*, 174–75. So too Baines, "Identity and Fate," 87–88.

174. McNichol, *Conversion of the Nations*, 14–16. McNichol adds (137–38) that the nations will subjugate themselves to Christ at his second coming which places him more in agreement with Bauckham. Koester (*Revelation*, 833) and J. C. Thomas (*Apocalypse*, 654–66) also view the tension rhetorically. Thomas suggests a full-scale end-time conversion takes place.

175. Kistemaker, *Revelation*, 582; Osborne, *Revelation, 772*; Mounce, *Revelation*, 400; Smalley, *Revelation*, 563. Stefanovic (*Revelation*, 605) relates the leaves "heal all wounds—racial, ethnic, tribal, or linguistic—that have torn and divided humanity for ages." Bauckham (*Climax of Prophecy*, 316–18)

merit. The nations represent unsaved and antagonistic people. Only those who repent and accept Christ will enter the new Jerusalem. But John's universalistic language offers a challenge to the church to maintain a witness to the very end. God works for salvation up to the eschaton. The church's job is to witness.

Nicolaitans

The Nicolaitans are unknown, but their activities in the seven churches draw allusions to false teachers from the OT. They tempt the churches into a theological and moral compromise with paganism. Although mentioned only twice (2:6, 15), the Nicolaitans were apparently influencing three of the seven churches John wrote to in Asia Minor. At Ephesus they claimed to be apostles yet at the same time practice wickedness (2:2, 6). At Pergamum they are connected with the teaching of Balaam, the false prophet who enticed Israel to sin (2:14–15).[176] Finally, they are probably identified with Thyatira as well where the false prophetess Jezebel misleads God's servants (2:20). They are best understood as a heretical sect within the church which by the end of the first century had thoroughly compromised with its surrounding pagan culture.[177] Thus, most commentators accept them as synonymous with references to Balaam at Pergamum and Jezebel at Thyatira.[178] Nicolaitan-like people form a segment of every generation. Their names change but their treacherous doctrines stay the same. The churches in John's day were challenged to be on their guard. Each succeeding generation must likewise be vigilant against such heretics. Such people will infiltrate the church even more as the return of Christ looms closer.

Rest, The

John uses this term to picture the unsaved on judgment day. "The rest" (*hoi lopoi*) as a title is found four times (9:20; 11:13; 19:21; 20:5).[179] Many English translations are inconsistent with multiple renderings, thereby masking the intratextual connection. Only seven modern versions consistently render the term "the rest" at all four locations (CEB, ESV,

---

sees this as the climax of the conversion of the nations. The nations are healed of their idolatry and sins so they will not come under God's curse anymore. See Schnabel, "John and the Future of the Nations," 268–70, for critique of Bauckham.

176. Hemer (*Letters to the Seven Churches*, 87–94) has a detailed discussion equating the Nicolaitans with Balaam.

177. Bauckham (*Theology of Revelation*, 124) and Mark Wilson (*Victor Sayings*, 84) note a wordplay for Nicolaitans (literally, "victors over my people") and the strong victor language of the seven letters.

178. Beale, *Revelation*, 251, 260; Hays, Duvall, and Pate, *Dictionary of Prophecy*, 314; Osborne, *Revelation*, 120–21; 155–56. See also Cargal, "Nicolaitans," 270–71. Some interpreters stress Gnostic tendencies, including Patterson (*Revelation*, 108), Rotz (*Revelation*, 65), Schüssler Fiorenza (*Justice and Judgment*, 119–20), and Watson ("Nicolaitans," 1106–7).

179. Actually, there are four other uses of "the rest" in Revelation (2:24; 3:2; 8:13; 12:17). But each instance reveals a different grammatical form. It is the subject nominative or perhaps nominative of appellation usage that takes on a technical understanding. However, Pollard ("Function of *Loipos* in Revelation") appends two more usages and divides them into contexts of salvation (2:24; 11:13; 12:17) and judgment (9:20; 19:21; 20:5).

NABR, NASB, NKJV, NRSV, REB). John employs several terms to designate unbelievers (free and slave, inhabitants of the earth, nations, whole world). "The rest" is another such image. It takes on the role of a technical term, an idiom that describes the unsaved.[180]

The structural placement of each occurrence is significant. John reserves all four instances for late appearances in his visions, each one in conjunction with end-time judgment. First, the conclusion of the sixth trumpet summarizes the depravity of humanity (9:20). The rest of humanity is ripe for judgment day which arrives with the seventh trumpet. Second, the conclusion of the second interlude envisions the end. There is the great earthquake and seven thousand people are killed. The rest are terrified and give glory to God (11:13).[181] The rest is found near another universal idiom of sinful humanity—inhabitants of the earth, found twice in 11:10. Third, at the second coming, "The rest were killed with the sword coming out of the mouth of the rider on the horse, and all the birds gorged themselves on their flesh" (19:21). The slain remnant has birds gorge on their flesh. Thus, their bodies are not given a decent burial, similar to what they did to the two witnesses (11:9). Once again "the rest" have company. The unholy trinity, kings of the earth, free and slave, and small and great are antagonists in Revelation. They oppose God and are now judged.[182] Fourth, in the thousand years vision (20:1–21:8), John inserts the parenthetical statement: "(The rest of the dead did not come to life until the thousand years were ended) (20:5).[183] Unbelievers are raised to face the great white throne judgment (Dan 12:2; John 5:28–29).[184] Therefore, the phrase becomes yet another signal for John's structure. Each use informs and explains the others. "The rest"—unrepentant wicked humanity—remain obstinate to the end. They will face judgment day.

Those Who Say They Are Jews and Are Not

This phrase refers to the persecution of Jews against believers at Smyrna and Philadelphia. John stresses the term "Jew" as a symbol for God's true people, that is, those who believe in Christ, whether they are Jew or gentile. Jakob Jocz summarizes the history of the term "Jew." Technically, a Jew is a descendent of the tribe of Judah, or from the land of Judah (2 Kgs 25:25). After the separation of northern and southern tribes and the fall of the former (722 BC), the Israelites in Judah held on to their land for another century and a half (586 BC). It became natural to identify all Israelites as Judahites, or Jews. By the time of Greek and Roman rule, Jew (*Ioudaios*) became the accepted name. The diaspora

---

180. Herms, *Apocalypse*, 194–95.

181. See the entries "Great Earthquake" and "Seven Thousand."

182. Many scholars understand "the rest" giving glory to God as a signal of repentance and conversion. See Pollard, "Function of *Loipos*," 330–43, for a defense of this position.

183. Herms (*Apocalypse*, 194 n. 59) states that this fourth reference does not belong to the first three. It has no bearing "because it neither reflects an eschatological judgment scene, nor takes as its referent a group actively opposed to God (here 'the dead')." Nevertheless, a case can be made for its inclusion. First, the nominative form is used (*hoi loipoi*). Second, these antagonists may have died, but they rise to face final judgment at the great white throne judgment. Thus, they are the same group as the previous three. Paul (*Revelation*, 329), on the other hand, interprets "the rest" (20:5) as believers.

184. See Kistemaker, *Revelation*, 539–41. See the entry "First Resurrection."

led to understanding the name in a more religious and ethnic sense, not a geographical sense. Paul, for example, was a Jew born in Tarsus (Acts 21:39). But Paul also pressed for a redefinition of the term Jew. It did not mean mere physical descent any longer in light of Christ. Circumcision therefore must be from the heart (Phil 3:3; Col 3:11–12; see Deut 10:16; Jer 4:4). It is the heart that makes a person a "true Jew." This means that all who claimed to be a Jews because they descended from Israel did not necessarily belong to Israel (Rom 9:6). It is on this basis that those who believe in Christ, though originally non-Jews—become Abraham's offspring and heirs according to the promise (Gal 3:29).[185]

John's theology picks up right where Paul's left off. *Ioudaios* is found only twice in Revelation (2:9; 3:9), but both instances confirm the term is being enlarged by John to refer symbolically to God's true people, the church, those who believe in Christ. From the NT's point of view, it is possible to be a "Jew" by faith without being born a Jew by race or religion.

The traditional understanding is that both references relate to the persecution that (gentile and Jewish) Christians endured at the hands of ethnic Jews in the cities of Smyrna and Philadelphia.[186] The cities were hotbeds of imperial worship. Greco-Roman culture did not separate the secular from the sacred. Spirituality, then, had dramatic political implications. It was required by law to sacrifice to the emperor. Those who refused were disloyal and unpatriotic. Apparently, the Jewish communities were helping Rome do their investigative work by informing on believers.[187] True Jews, however, follow God and the Lamb, and resist Satan. Thus, the claim of being the people of God (Jews) is separated by the fact that they persecute God's true people—the church. They are ethnic Jews but not spiritual Jews.[188]

Significantly, the once geographical turned religious turned ethnic term "Jew" that designated God's people has widened its meaning to the NT people of God—those who know Christ, both Jew and gentile (Matt 3:9; Rom 2:28–29; 2 Cor 11:22; Gal 6:15). A true Jew, Abraham's seed, is the follower of Christ. Therefore, "Jew" joins numerous other formerly ethnic images in Revelation, now used to describe the church as the spiritual Israel of God, the universal people of God.

185. Jocz, "Jew," 666–67. See also Gasque, "Jew," 1056.

186. Worth (*Seven Cities of the Apocalypse*, 72) calculates a widespread Jewish population in Asia Minor—one million, or 20 percent of the population.

187. Not everyone recognizes ethnic Jews as the backdrop. Several commentators understand Jewish Christians who accommodated to the values and beliefs of the dominant satanic culture. The opposition, then, is not between Jews and Christians but between true Jews (i.e. Christians) and false Jews (i.e. Christians such as Jezebel). This is followed by Boxall (*Revelation*, 54), Bredin ("Synagogue of Satan Accusation," 160–64), Alan Johnson ("Revelation," 13:617), John Marshall (*Parables of War*, 132–34), Resseguie (*Revelation*, 88–89), and Rowland ("Revelation," 12:577). Others find the term refers to gentile Christians; specifically, gentile Judaizers who convert to Judaism and hide in the churches to avoid persecution. So Frankfurter ("Jews or Not?," 419) and Michaels (*Revelation*, 74). Leonard Thompson (*Revelation*, 68–69) also sees a reference to a gentile Christian group without noting Judaizers.

188. Beale, *Revelation*, 241; Blount, *Revelation*, 53–54. The majority of interpreters favor this view. The most in-depth treatment is Mayo, *Those Who Call Themselves Jews*, 51–76. Duff (*Who Rides the Beast?*, 49–51) agrees with the majority view but minimizes any serious hostilities between Jews and Christians.

Whole World

When John mentions "the whole world" he indicates the totality of unbelievers. The phrase "the whole world" (*tēs oikomenēs olēs*) is found three times in Revelation (3:10; 12:9; 16:14), each time with unbelievers in mind.[189] First, Christ promises the overcomers at Philadelphia, "Since you have kept my command to endure patiently, I will also keep you from the hour of trial that is going to come on the whole world to test the inhabitants of the earth" (3:10). Since they kept his word he will keep them through the hour of testing that is coming on the whole world.[190] John uses two phrases to designate the entirety of wicked humanity—"the whole world" and "inhabitants of the earth." This double idiom accentuates collective humanity and "makes it apparent that whom the author has in mind includes everyone not found among the faithful community."[191] Both phrases reinforce the universal scope of the testing on unbelievers.

The other two instances of the phrase confirm its universalness. In the third interlude John sees "The great dragon was hurled down—that ancient serpent called the devil, or Satan, who leads the whole world astray. He was hurled to the earth, and his angels with him" (12:9). In the sixth bowl, a picture of Armageddon: "They are demonic spirits that perform signs, and they go out to the kings of the whole world, to gather them for the battle on the great day of God Almighty" (16:14). Thus, "whole world" becomes one of several expressions that John uses to indicate wicked unbelievers in entirety.

Woman Sitting on a Scarlet Beast

This symbol refers to the great prostitute—the ungodly world system—who has authority over the beast yet is turned on at the end of history as a part of God's judgment. The woman sitting on a scarlet beast is the great city, the great prostitute, and Babylon the Great. She stands in stark contrast to the woman clothed with the sun. She is mentioned specifically at 17:3, but discussed throughout chapter 17. This epitaph gives more information on the relationship between the woman and the beast. The beast signifies the political strength of Rome.[192] The color "scarlet" typifies the exorbitant luxury that is attached to

189. English Bible versions are consistent in translating these three Greek words as "the whole world." CEV is the exception, rendering the phrase as "all the world" (3:10), "everyone on earth" (12:9), and "every king on earth" (16:14; also NET). The TR/KJV/NKJV text reads "kings of the earth and of the whole world" at 16:14. Balz ("οἰκουμένη," 504) states that *oikoumenē* "focusses on the negative side" and is "exclusively unbelievers and enemies of God . . ."

190. This means protection through, not exemption from. The church is not exempt from going through the hour of trial, but the judgment of God is against unbelievers. See the entry "Hour of Trial." Hemer (*Letters to the Seven Churches*, 164–65) understands the testing to be limited to Philadelphia. But "inhabitants of the earth" and "whole world" are consistently used universally in Revelation.

191. Herms, *Apocalypse*, 188. Beckwith (*Apocalypse*, 483) and Kistemaker (*Revelation*, 163) hold that the phrase in 3:10 refers to both Christians and non-Christians. Many futurists posit a rapture for 3:10, since it is evil humanity that is left behind. Alternatively, those who espouse a partial rapture understand nominal believers who do not believe in a rapture to be left behind. Preterists, on the other hand, limit "the whole world" to first-century apostate Israel (Chilton, *Days of Vengeance*, 129) or the Greco–Roman world (Buchanan, *Revelation*, 126).

192. See the entry "Beast."

the woman as well as the red associated with the dragon (12:3). It also implies suffering and persecution. It might indicate that she has conferred the symbolic color to the beast because she dominates the beast who acts on her behalf. The fact that she rides the beast means she is not only in alliance with the beast but in control as well. As the ungodly world system, she works in tandem with the state for each other's benefit and to persecute believers socially, culturally, economically, and religiously. The beast, however, turns on the woman near the end of history (17:16). Their eschatological civil war fulfills Ezek 38:21 where Gog's judgment includes "Every man's sword will be against his brother." Thus, their mutual hatreds result in mutual destruction. This pictures the self-destroying power of evil and composes part of the end-time judgment of God.[193]

This text applies to nations (and individuals) that pursue economic and political dominance over others. John saw it in his day. It is observable in every generation. But near the end of history (pictured in 17:12–18), the woman's collapse will occur for the final time as a part of God's righteous end–time judgment.

---

193. Caird, *Revelation*, 221; Morris, *Revelation*, 206; Mounce, *Revelation*, 320; Osborne, *Revelation*, 625; Smalley, *Revelation*, 440. Beale (*Revelation*, 883) relates that the woman's demise follows the outline from Ezek 16:37–41; 23:25–34.

6

Body Parts and Animals

THE FIRST HALF OF this chapter discusses John's use of human body parts as symbols. The second half deals with the animal kingdom. Although some of the body parts may infer literal aspects, they are essentially symbols. Likewise, without exception, all of the animal kingdom is used symbolically by John.

Body Parts

The twenty entries below examine John's usage of human body parts, including emotions and bodily postures. On occasion a literal backdrop may be intended, but overall each example is symbolic.

Blind

Blindness symbolizes spiritual sightlessness that is ripe for divine judgment. A common biblical symbol is spiritual blindness (Exod 23:8; Deut 16:19; Isa 42:16–19; Matt 23:16–26; John 9). Blindness also reflects the work of Satan (2 Cor 4:4), and believers who revert to sinful ways (2 Pet 1:9; 1 John 2:11).[1] Although found only once (3:17), "blind" serves as a vivid example of John's use of figurative language. Each item on the list which the lazy Laodicean believers are charged with—"wretched, pitiful, poor, blind, naked"—does not refer to literal, physical problems but rather to symbolic issues. The Laodiceans were the opposite of what they thought they were. They were selling out their faith by idolatrous compromise with the world. In spite of the medical center found in Laodicea and its development of medicinal eye salve, the Christians living there remained in need of spiritual healing. Their earthly accomplishments were meaningless in light of their spiritual blindness.[2] Self-sufficient, Laodicean-type Christians of every era do not perceive the gravity of their condition. They too become candidates for God's divine judgment.

---

1. Ryken, *Dictionary of Biblical Imagery*, 99. This dictionary has been a rich resource for this study, and especially for this chapter.

2. Beale, *Revelation*, 305; Mounce, *Revelation*, 110–11; Osborne, *Revelation*, 210.

Blood

Blood is a potent symbol in Revelation, ranging from its sacrificial aspect to a metaphor for death to its use in cosmic imagery as a portent of the end. Blood forms a major component of biblical revelation, evidenced by its four hundred references. Several metaphors and symbols arise. Blood is a symbol of life, and "flesh and blood" are often paired as a metonymy for humanity (John 1:13; Gal 1:16; 1 Cor 15:50). Blood may connote death (2 Sam 23:17; Acts 1:18–19). Blood could allude to guilt due to violence (Hos 1:4; Ps 139:19; Matt 27:24). The shedding of blood is a part of sacrifice and atonement (Gen 9:6; Lev 16:15; Mark 14:24; Rom 3:25; Heb 9:18). Finally, blood is used by Bible writers as an omen (Exod 4:9; 2 Kgs 3:22; Joel 2:30; Acts 2:19).[3]

Twenty percent (19 of 97) of NT uses of blood (*haima*) are found in Revelation. John draws from these prior biblical symbols for his usage, but particularly from sacrifice and omen. John's references to blood fall into three categories. First, blood is used in a sacrificial and atoning aspect in connection with Christ (1:5–6; 5:9; 7:14; 12:11). The second category finds blood as a metaphor for the persecution and death of faithful followers of the Lamb (6:10; 16:5–6; 17:6; 18:24; 19:2). Third, blood may be categorized as an end-time omen. It is a common element of the cosmic imagery of a hemorrhaging universe found in apocalyptic literature and final battle imagery (*1 En.* 100:3–4; *4 Ezra* 15:35; *Sib. Or.* 3:667–684; Isa 63:2–6; Joel 2:31; Acts 2:20).[4] Nine such uses of blood are mentioned by John in the following passages—the picture of the end found in the sixth seal includes "the whole moon turned blood red" (6:12); the first two trumpets mention cosmic blood and a third of the sea turned to blood (8:7–8); the two witnesses have power to turn the waters into blood" (11:6); in a vision of Armageddon, the wicked "were trampled in the winepress outside the city, and blood flowed out of the press, rising as high as the horses' bridles for a distance of 1,600 stadia" (14:20);[5] the second and third bowls closely match the second trumpet above (16:3–6); and finally, Christ at his second coming, is "dressed in a robe dipped in blood" (19:13). This last reference to blood possibly combines all three metaphoric aspects.

Most scholars recognize the blood symbolism for cosmic imagery (8:7) and for Christ's bloody robe (19:13). Many, however, hold out for a literal understanding of the waters of the earth turning into actual blood, as found in the second trumpet and second and third bowls. Robert Thomas, for example, states that "the sea becomes blood, not *like* blood. On the basis of his vision, John believed that a large part of the sea would, quite literally, turn into blood as it had under the first deliverance in Egypt . . ."[6] Patterson suggests that if it is not real blood, then perhaps it refers to a "red tide" that is notorious

---

3. Ryken, *Dictionary of Biblical Imagery*, 99–101. See Stibbs, *His Blood Works*, 1–24; and K. C. Hanson, "Blood and Purity," 215–30.

4. See Osborne, *Revelation*, 555–56.

5. Bauckham (*Climax of Prophecy*, 40–48) cites numerous Jewish apocalyptic passages that show the widespread use of the horse's height to measure the blood is a signal for slaughter by an army in battle. Thus, the image is hyperbolic.

6. Robert Thomas, *Revelation*, 2:19. Interestingly, the normally literal Walvoord (*Revelation*, 154–55; 233–34) allows for a possible symbolic meaning.

for killing marine life, but now on a grand scale.[7] LaHaye envisions sea creatures "will float to the top, their decaying bodies discharging an unbearable stench and inaugurating potential disease."[8]

Many others agree with similar prolonged judgments upon planet earth. Easley, however, reminds us that "John is viewing a supernatural phenomenon rather than a scientific, explainable event."[9] The point is famine and death for all who depend on earthly resources such as the sea. Thus, a figurative understanding should come first. The imagery of blood represents judgment upon wicked inhabitants of the earth and on the kingdom of the beast. Statistical analysis is not the point—judgment is the point. The sea as symbolic of ungodly humanity (i.e. "flesh and blood"), might suggest the collapse of the world's economic system and everything that humanity places its trust in. Altogether, blood serves as a malleable symbol for John. It recalls Christ's sacrifice and the readiness for sacrifice on the part of the faithful. Finally, while many will hold out for a literal and "liberal spattering of blood"[10] from heaven upon the earth, and on Christ's robe, it is best understood as cosmic imagery and an omen of the end.

Eyes

Eyes are symbolic of all-seeing and spiritual perception, and thus all-knowing and wise. This is especially stressed through the penetrating end-time judgment of God. Eyes and eyesight are used frequently by Bible writers as symbols. Eyes are cited in connection with God to picture his omnipresence (Gen 1:4; Ps 33:18) and omniscience (Gen 3:5; Job 28:10; Ps 139:16). His "sight" leads to protection for those he loves (Ezra 5:5; Neh 1:6). For humans, eyesight symbolizes spiritual perception and knowledge (Prov 20:12; Isa 6:10). Prophets are "seers" gifted with insight from God. Apocalyptic writers such as Daniel and Ezekiel have visions and see the heavens opened (Dan 10:5–6; Ezek 38:23).[11] Bauckham relates, "It is important to realise that the eyes of Yahweh in the Old Testament indicate not only his ability to see what happens throughout the world, but also his ability to act powerfully wherever he chooses."[12] "Eye(s)" are found one hundred times in the NT, and the common metaphor for spiritual sight that leads to powerful actions carries over from the OT (Matt 6:22–23; Mark 8:18; Luke 11:34; John 1:50; Acts 28:27; Rom 3:18; 1 Cor 12:16–21; Eph 1:18).[13]

There are ten references to eyes in Revelation, one singular and nine plural. As with so many of John's symbols, he contrasts between good eyes and bad eyes. The singular "eye" occurs at 1:7 where John says every eye will see the second coming. The lukewarm

---

7. Patterson, *Revelation*, 306–7.

8. LaHaye, *Revelation Unveiled*, 251.

9. Easley, *Revelation*, 285. See Kistemaker, *Revelation*, 441.

10. Walvoord, *Revelation*, 223. Beale (*Revelation*, 781) states that Walvoord "misses the hyperbolic point of the picture in an attempt to rescue a literal interpretation of the [final] battle scene."

11. Ryken, *Dictionary of Biblical Imagery*, 255.

12. Bauckham, *Climax of Prophecy*, 164.

13. Vanzant, "Eye," 386.

Christians at Laodicea do not recognize their spiritual blindness and need for Christ to put "salve" on their eyes to give them spiritual insight (3:18). Three times the glorified Christ's eyes are described as like "blazing fire" (1:14; 2:18; 19:12; see Dan 10:6). This expresses "the penetrating insight of the one who is sovereign, not only over the seven churches but over the entire course of history as well."[14] In the throne room vision, the four living creatures are covered with eyes, front and back. Resseguie states, "Their twenty-twenty vision allows them to see God for who he is and thus to *see* God's attributes: his holiness, omnipotence, and eternality (4:6, 8)."[15] John sees the Lamb, and describes him with seven eyes (5:6). The number emphasizes perfect and complete insight, perception, and wisdom. Commentators agree that the seven eyes allude to Zech 3–4 and God's omnipotent Spirit. The final two references are parallel, and describe the redeemed at history's conclusion (7:17; 21:4). They mention that God will "wipe away every tear," a near quote of Isa 25:8. This phrase could be understood literally. Yet readers must not limit themselves to a literalistic box that means glorified bodies will include retinas, eyelashes, and tear ducts. The visionary point is not to think of actual eyes, but rather that no more suffering is a promise of eternity.[16]

Face

The face refers to one's true character or self or to one's presence in either divine judgment or eternal fellowship. The face is often used as a metaphor for one's true self. Just as the face of Moses showed that he had been with God (Exod 34:29) so too does being in the company of the divine transfigure the face of Jesus (Matt 17:2; see Acts 6:15). Another metaphor for face is presence. The "bread of presence" in the ark of the covenant is literally the "bread of [God's] face" (Exod 25:30). To "see the face" is to gain acceptance in one's presence (Exod 32:20; Acts 20:25). Believers should live in God's presence and daily hearken the call to "Seek my face" (Pss 27:8; 105:4).[17] These two metaphors for face are found several times in Revelation along with the added element of end-time judgment. John's preferred word for face is *prosōpon*, found ten times.[18] First, there are four occasions where face and one's true self are intended (4:7; 9:7 [twice]; 10:1). Second, the idea of face as presence is understood either negatively (6:16; 12:14; 20:11) or positively (7:11; 11:16; 22:4). It appears significant that this understanding of face is found so often at the end of individual visions.

---

14. Mounce, *Revelation*, 59.

15. Resseguie, *Revelation*, 20 (original italics).

16. Some interpret the tears as sorrow for sin or sadness in life. Osborne (*Revelation*, 332) affirms the tears more likely refer to the suffering received as a witness for Christ. See the entry "Blind."

17. Litwak, "Face," 407; Mixter, "Face," 513–14; Ryken, *Dictionary of Biblical Imagery*, 259, 522.

18. John's inaugural vision describes "one like a son of man" who has a face shining like the sun (1:16). Most versions render this singular use of *opsis* as "face" while CEB has "appearance" and NKJV has "countenance."

Fall Down

The posture of falling down is a sign of obeisance and reverence in the worship of God. John mentions falling down or bowing down (*piptō*) twenty-three times.[19] Seven times it is used in the refrain "Fallen! Fallen is Babylon the Great" (14:8; 18:2). Primarily, however, it is connected to the context of worship. Bowing is perhaps the most basic posture of deference mentioned in the Bible. It shows honor, respect, and reverence.[20] Worship is a major—if not the central—theme of John's Apocalypse.[21] Thus, we find John falling down before the risen Christ (1:17). He attempts to do the same before an angel (19:10; 22:8).[22] The angels, the four living creatures, and especially the twenty-four elders fall down before the heavenly throne and worship God and the Lamb (4:10; 5:8, 14; 7:11; 11:16; 19:4). Resseguie affirms that such a reaction is "a stereotypical response to the presence of the numinous (cf. Ezek. 1:28; Dan. 8:17; Matt. 17:6)."[23] It may be an involuntary response by John in 1:17, but the other references imply a voluntary reaction, a sign of reverential worship.

Feet

Feet are used literally and metaphorically by Bible writers, but John reserves them as symbols of power and authority or submission and worship. A number of images involve feet but two stand out. "To be under one's feet" implies being under the power of that person (Ps 8:6; Eph 1:22). "To sit at the feet" means to learn from someone (Luke 10:39; Acts 22:3).[24] These two basic symbols are used by John as well but accompanied with end-time judgment. First, Christ's authority to judge is pictured in his bronze feet (1:15; 2:18). The mighty angel plants his foot, representing the power of God to initiate "no more delay" (10:2). The slain two witnesses stand to their feet in preparation for their heavenly ascent (11:11). The woman clothed with the sun has the moon under her feet, like a footstool, which speaks of her dominion (12:1).[25] The beast had feet like a bear underscoring his swiftness and power (13:2). Second, to fall at someone's feet voluntarily is a mark of reverence. John falls before Christ (1:17), but also inappropriately attempts to do the same with an angel (19:10; 22:8).[26] Finally, one passage contains both ideas. The persecuting "synagogue of Satan" has power over the Philadelphians. But Christ promises that they will "fall down at your feet and acknowledge that I have loved you" (3:9).

19. English versions choose "fall," "bow," "kneel," and "prostrate."

20. Ryken, *Dictionary of Biblical Imagery*, 115.

21. See Brighton, *Revelation*, 7–9; Osborne, *Revelation*, 46–49.

22. Many commentators find it odd that John is instructed twice not to worship the angel. See the entry "Brothers and Sisters" for comments.

23. Resseguie, *Revelation*, 79. See Aune, *Revelation*, 1:99–100.

24. Lay and Vunderink, "Foot," 332–33; Ryken, *Dictionary of Biblical Imagery*, 280; Kevin Wilson, "Foot," 476.

25. Mounce, *Revelation*, 232.

26. See the entry "Brothers and Sisters."

Forehead

The forehead is the symbolic location of either the seal or name of God or the mark of the beast. This underscores its meaning as one of allegiance either to God or the devil. References to the forehead in the Bible fall generally into three categories. First, the condition of the forehead helped a priest determine if someone had leprosy (Lev 13:41; 2 Chr 26:19). Second, a hard forehead was a symbol for stubbornness and rebelliousness (Isa 48:4; Ezek 3:7; "hard-headed" is a modern equivalent) or courage and perseverance (Ezek 3:8). Third, and most common, the forehead was where a person wore an identifying mark, either literal or symbolic. The Passover was to be like an emblematic reminder placed on the forehead (Exod 13:9). Moses commanded that his words be an emblem on the forehead (Exod 6:8). As God's representative, Aaron wore a gold plate on his forehead (Exod 28:36). Ezekiel put a mark identifying God's people (Ezek 9:4).[27]

John uses the third category in his visions, and all are figurative. "Forehead" (*metōpon*) is found eight times in the NT, all in Revelation. They are evenly divided between God's followers and the devil's followers. The seal of God on the forehead is mentioned twice (7:3; 9:4) as is the name of God on the forehead (14:1; 22:4). Conversely, the mark (of the beast) is mentioned three times (13:16; 14:9; 20:4). Finally, a title was written on the forehead of the great prostitute (17:5).

The fact that there are four good references and four bad references to foreheads may suggest numerical symbolism. If so, then full coverage is intended and everyone on earth belongs to one of these two antithetical categories. Revelation demonstrates that there are no theological fence-sitters. One is a follower of and owned by either God or the devil. To declare neutrality merely confirms one's allegiance to Satan. Some Bible readers hold out for an actual physical mark of the beast to be placed on the forehead of his followers.[28] Consistency demands that a similar mark and name be planted on the heads of the Lamb's followers. But such an idea is unnecessary. The forehead is intended as a symbol of one's devotion and submission, the mark of allegiance and true character of a person. One's allegiance—based on what is thought about, worshipped, and adored—confirms who he or she is devoted to, whether to God or to Satan. It is another of the many contrasts found in Revelation; contrasts that demand a choice from its readers.

Hair

Hair is an image of wisdom and power when applied to God, but a picture of dread or deception when applied to the demonic. Surprisingly, hair receives one hundred references in the Bible, several with symbolic overtones. The images of hair could be positive (2 Sam 14:25; Song 4:1) or negative (Ezra 9:3; Jer 7:29). Symbolically, white or gray hair was a sign of old age, and with it came maturity, honor, and wisdom (Prov 20:29). Daniel raised

---

27. Giacumakis, "Forehead," 630–31; Ryken, *Dictionary of Biblical Imagery*, 299–300.

28. See the entry "Seal of God."

this to the transcendent plane with pictures of God having white and fiery hair (Dan 7:9).[29]

"Hair" (*thrix*) is mentioned in two passages in Revelation (1:14; 9:8). One is presented positively and one negatively. In John's inaugural vision, the description of the glorified Christ is drawn from eight OT images. These images connect Father with Son and stress their divine unity. Osborne sums it up this way: "Christ in this simile is pictured in his eternal wisdom and in the respect due his person . . ."[30] The other mention of hair is in the description of the demonic locusts found in the fifth trumpet. Part of their fearsome appearance includes the statement, "Their hair was like women's hair" (9:8). The long hair of these demonic locusts may refer to leg and body hair in order to emphasize speed.[31] Or it may allude to John's original audience's fear of longhaired Parthian warriors. The Parthians were a palpable threat to Rome's borders in the first century.[32] It may also be a simple contrast between the charming hairstyle of a female that is pleasing to the eye that suddenly bares a lion's teeth.[33] Aune adds that a picture of loose, disheveled hair connotes uncleanness (Lev 13:45), mourning (Lev 10:6), proper protocol for a woman accused of adultery (Num 5:18), and perhaps even an appearance of a demon (*T. Sol.* 13:1) or Satan (*Apoc. Zeph.* 6:8).[34] Osborne agrees. "Many of these [Aune's] images would fit the situation here."[35] In sum, John's contrasts are at work again as he utilizes the appearance of hair to symbolize godly wisdom and demonic deception.

Head

This symbolizes the leadership and authority of God or is a parody of power by Satan. The word "head" appears over four hundred times in the Bible. It became a well-known metonym for ruling authority (Judg 11:8; Isa 7:8; 1 Cor 11:3; Eph 1:22). Paul adopts the figure of the head also for nourishment, provision, and growth (Col 1:18; Eph 4:15). Other images include the idea of the head to stand for the whole person (Acts 18:6). To "heap coals of fire on the head" (Matt 5:44; Rom 12:20) meant returning good for evil. Covering or dusting the head symbolized grief or shame (2 Sam 13:19).[36]

In the Apocalypse, "head" (*kephalē*) receives nineteen of its seventy-five NT usages. There is one occasion where the common idiom of "dust on their heads" expresses grief and mourning (18:19). Often, "head" serves as part of a description in a vision (1:14; 4:4; 9:7, 17, 19). Most often, however, it is a symbol that refers to power, authority, and

29. Ryken, *Dictionary of Biblical Imagery*, 359–60. See Cartledge, "Hair, Hairs," 719; Wilson and Rodriquez, "Hair," 765–78.

30. Osborne, *Revelation*, 90. He discusses all eight OT images (88–93).

31. Mounce, *Revelation*, 190.

32. So Blount, *Revelation*, 179; Boxall, *Revelation*, 145; Harrington, *Revelation*, 110; Keener, *Revelation*, 268. Others, however, do not see a Parthian reference at all, including Beale (*Revelation*, 501), Mounce (*Revelation*, 189), and Smalley (*Revelation*, 232).

33. Kistemaker, *Revelation*, 290.

34. Aune, *Revelation*, 2:532.

35. Osborne, *Revelation*, 371.

36. Mixter, "Head," 63–64; Ryken, *Dictionary of Biblical Imagery*, 367–68; Silva, "κεφαλή," 669–74.

leadership. But as is common to John, he contrasts good and evil "heads." Good heads include the authority exuded in the mighty angel's rainbow above his head (10:1); the woman with twelve stars on her head (12:1); and "one like the son of man" (14:4) and the white horse rider (19:12) with crowns on his head. The remainder of the "heads," however, are evil and revolve around the seven heads belonging to the dragon and the beast (12:3; 13:1; 17:3, 7, 9).[37] As Brighton explains, "The dragon's seven heads reflect his deceptive claim that *he*, and *not* the Christ, is the spirit who has all knowledge to supervise all earthly matters."[38] Head, therefore, is a common metaphor for authority, whether it comes from truth or error.

Loud Voice

The "loud voice" is a common apocalyptic symbol that emphasizes authority and sovereignty. A loud voice evinces the need to be heard due to volume or joy (Luke 17:13; 19:37). But it is most commonly connected with authority (Deut 5:22; Matt 27:46; John 11:43) and prophetic announcements (Ezek 11:13; Luke 1:42; John 7:37). In prophetic literature, heavenly messengers use a loud voice (Ezek 9:1; Dan 4:14). The voice of God is also used in the Bible as a metaphor to refer to a person (Num 7:89; 1 Kgs 19:13; 2 Pet 1:17).[39] The phrase is common in extratextual works as well (*2 Bar.* 11:3; *4 Bar.* 2:2; *Sib. Or.* 3:669; *T. Ab.* 5:9).[40]

These same usages are found in Revelation, the "noisiest book" in the NT.[41] "Great" (*megas*) is found eighty times. "Voice" (*phonē*) is found fifty-five times. The combination of the two words into a "loud voice" (*phōnēn megalēn*) is found twenty times, and often near the end of visions. This underscores the auditory nature of John's message, and alludes to the power and the presence of the one who provides the voice, particularly at the eschaton. The loud voice of the risen Christ (1:10), and perhaps Christ or the Father (11:12; 16:1, 17) is found four times. There is also the collective voice of the martyrs who cry out for God's justice (6:10); the great multitude in heaven (7:10; 19:1); and the ominous eagle flying in midair (8:13). The majority of references, however, are associated with angels (5:2, 12; 7:2; 10:3; 11:15; 12:10; 14:7, 9, 15, 18; 19:17; 21:3).[42] In fact, the four references to deity may also be an angelic voice on God's behalf. Even so, all angels speak on behalf of God. Most would agree with Robert Thomas: "As throughout the Apocalypse, the loud sound or voice clearly indicates the importance and solemnity of what is about to be spoken . . ."[43]

37. See the entry "Seven Heads/Seven Hills/Seven Kings."

38. Brighton, *Revelation*, 328.

39. Ryken, *Dictionary of Biblical Imagery*, 918–19.

40. Aune, *Revelation*, 1:85.

41. Maier, *Apocalypse Recalled*, 91. See Resseguie, *Revelation*, 20–21, 73.

42. There is one example of a "loud voice" that uses a different Greek adjective. At 18:2, an angel shouts in a "strong" (*ischyra*) voice, variously translated as "loud" (CEB, GNT), "powerful" (GW, NCV, NET), but most often as "mighty" (CSB, ESV, NABR, NASB, NIV, NLT, NRSV, REB). NJB produces "top of his voice." CEV leaves the adjective untranslated. NKJV offers up "mightily with a loud voice."

43. Robert Thomas, *Revelation*, 1:91.

Additional metaphors capture the loudness of the voices, including the blast of a trumpet, the clap of thunder, the roar of a lion, and the rushing of waters. The content of the loud voice usually revolves around the key themes of redemption (7:2; 11:12; 12:10; 21:3) and judgment (6:10; 8:13; 14:7, 9, 15, 18; 16:1, 17; 19:17).[44] Thus, readers must not think of voices, mouths, and vocal chords. The point of the loud voice throughout Scripture, and especially apocalyptic literature, is to emphasize authority, worthiness, and sovereignty of God in redemption and judgment.

Mouth

The mouth is a symbol of the inner person through which verbal communication uncovers moral character. This is a major biblical image, mentioned over three hundred times. It is often a metonym for a person's speech (Exod 1:14) which unveils the character of the speaker (Ps 5:9; Isa 6:6–7). The mouth is connected to the thoughts and heart of a person (Deut 30:14; Josh 1:8; Ps 19:14). By the NT era, mouth and heart become synonyms (Matt 12:34; Rom 10:10). When the mouth opens, the inner person is disclosed. It may reveal wisdom or folly, good or evil.[45] This dualism of good mouths and evil mouths flows through Revelation, appearing twenty-two times. On the one hand, the Lamb's "good" mouth brings end-time justice and judgment (1:16; 2:16; 19:15, 21). He is ready to spit out the lukewarm Laodiceans (3:16). John obediently puts the scroll into his mouth (10:9–10). Fire comes from the mouths of the two witnesses (11:5). No lies are found in the mouths of the hundred and forty-four thousand (14:5). On the other hand, those with "evil" mouths hubristically self-exalt, persecute, blaspheme, and deceive. Out of the mouths of the demonic cavalry comes fire, smoke, and sulfur (9:18–19). The serpent spews a flood (of lies) from its mouth (12:15).[46] The beast has a mouth like a lion, and the dragon "gives him a mouth" to speak blasphemies (13:2–6). Lastly, deceptive, demonic, impure spirits come out of the mouths of the unholy trinity (16:13).[47] John, therefore, uses the image of a mouth to contrast good and evil. Good mouths praise God and bring righteous judgment. Evil mouths blaspheme and persecute.

Right Hand

The ideas of authority, power, blessing, comfort, action, and swearing are evident in the image of the "right hand." The figurative use of "hand" in the OT includes power, authority, possession, consecration, and sacrifice ("lay hands on"). The hand as an extension of

44. Waechter, "Analysis of the Literary Structure," 130. Seal ("Shouting in the Apocalypse," 339–52) connects the loud voice to the role of acclamations found in the Roman Empire. Thus, John counters the acclamations given to the emperor by offering them to Christ. Similarly, see Humphrey, *And I Turned to See the Voice*, 151–94, for rhetorical analysis of 1:12–13; 4:1–5:14; 11:15–12:17.

45. Ryken, *Dictionary of Biblical Imagery*, 575.

46. Minear ("Far as the Curse Is Found," 74) proposes that John is alluding to Gen 4:1–16.

47. Osborne (*Revelation*, 591) appends that the mouth, which symbolizes royal proclamation in the ancient world, is used by the unholy trinity to send out a deceptive message of propaganda.

a person reflects the wishes and will of the entire person. Actions are produced by the hand.[48] The "right hand" holds even more significance, and is a common biblical metaphor for prominence and favored position. To sit at the right hand reflects prestige (1 Kgs 2:19; Ps 110:1). It also portrays intense power (Exod 15:6; Ps 18:35; Isa 41:10). This OT metaphor carries over to the NT. In particular, writers give special attention to Ps 110:1, a messianic enthronement psalm, quoting from it twenty times.[49] "Hand" (*cheir*) is found fifteen times in Revelation with the same signification as above. The word "right" (*dexios*) is found nine times and seven of those nine times "right hand" is intended (1:16, 17, 20; 2:1; 5:1, 7; 10:2, 5; 13:16). Only 1:16 and 13:16 have both words for emphasis. English translations are consistent in adding "hand" at the other locations.

The right hand is concentrated in four passages. First, the inaugural vision mentions the right hand of Christ that holds the stars (1:16–20; see 2:1). This grasping stresses the idea of the power to preserve, comfort, and possess.[50] Second, in the throne room vision, the Lamb shares the authority of God and he alone is worthy to take the scroll that is in the "right (hand)" of the one who sits on the throne" (5:1, 7). Third, at the beginning of the second interlude, the mighty angel has a little scroll open in his hand (10:2). Then he raises his right hand to swear to heaven (10:5). The immediate background to this is Dan 12:7 where the angel lifts both hands to heaven and swears by God that there will be some delay. In 10:6 the angel announces the fulfillment of Daniel's prophecy with "no more delay."[51] The final "right hand" occurs in the third interlude. The mark of the beast is placed on the right hands and foreheads of the beast's followers (13:16). Osborne declares that this mark of the beast is a parody of Deut 6:8 where Jews were told to place the Shema on their hands and foreheads.[52] Robert Mulholland states that the right hand "is a symbol of action. It represents the practical outworking of the inner orientation of being characterized by the forehead."[53] Resonating behind all these passages is the idea of the authority, promise, and action of end-time judgment.[54]

Sitting

The posture of sitting emphasizes authority, sovereignty, victory, conquering, and privilege. Most of the over three hundred references to this in the Bible denote the posture of sitting

---

48. Appler, "Hand," 731; Mixter, "Hand," 34–35; Ryken, *Dictionary of Biblical Imagery*, 360–62.

49. Aune, *Revelation*, 1:340. Barr (*Tales*, 80) states the right hand is "a cultural code for power and favor. It is always the hand of God's deliverance and blessing . . ." Dispensationalists believe Ps 110:1 will be fulfilled literally only at the second coming, when Jesus is enthroned as king in Jerusalem. Other interpretive approaches apply it to Jesus' resurrection and ascension. Thus, Jesus is enthroned at the right hand of God now. See Hays, Duvall, and Pate, *Dictionary of Prophecy*, 392.

50. Osborne, *Revelation*, 91.

51. Smalley, *Revelation*, 263. Other passages echoing in the background are Gen 14:22; Exod 6:8; Num 14:30; Deut 32:40.

52. Osborne, *Revelation*, 517.

53. Mulholland, *Revelation*, 237.

54. Umstattd (*Spirit and Lake of Fire*, 90–103) reveals the judgment side of "hand." He traces this judgment motif (and its connection to the Holy Spirit) in God's finger, hand, and arm.

as opposed to standing or walking. But metaphorical examples of sitting also abound. For example, "sitting" portrays enthronement, reigning, and honor (1 Sam 4:4; Ps 9:4; Matt 19:28; 25:31). Jerusalem and Babylon "sit on the ground" as a sign of mourning (Isa 3:26; 47:1). Sitting means "living" under various conditions (Isa 9:2; Jer 10:17; Luke 1:79).[55] Sitting is also associated with judgment, "for there I will sit to judge all the nations on every side" (Joel 3:12).

Revelation mentions the verb "sit" (*kathēmai*) thirty-three times, accounting for 37 percent of all NT uses.[56] John stresses the first metaphor above, the posture of authority, sovereignty, conquering, and privilege, particularly with end-time judgment in mind. Once again this pictures John's contrasting nature, prompting the question "who is doing the sitting?" For example, the vision of the throne room reveals God sitting on his throne (4:2–4; 9–10; 5:1, 7, 13). The wicked at the end of time cry out to be hidden from the face of him who sits on the throne (6:16). God is pictured as sitting on his throne in eternity (7:10, 15; 19:4; 20:11; 21:5). The twenty-four elders are seated on their own thrones (11:16). One like the son of man is sitting on a cloud (14:14–16). The rider is sitting on the white horse ("sitting" is masked by English translations for "rider") at the conclusion of history (19:11, 19, 21). The posture of sitting in these examples stresses the final judgment of the world. Joel 3:12–15 stands behind most of these examples. Moreover, the lone promise to the overcomers at Laodicea is "the right to sit with me on my throne, just as I was victorious and sat down with my Father on his throne" (3:21). This visualizes intimate, eternal fellowship with the Lord.[57] Many of these also occur at the conclusion of a vision, lending more support for scenes of final judgment.

Nevertheless, there are other "sitters" in Revelation. These "squatters" attempt to parody or usurp God's sovereign position. God permits the four horsemen ("rider" fills in for "sitter" in English versions) to bring their four seals (6:1–8). In particular, the great prostitute dominates others. She sits on many waters (17:1, 15) and on the scarlet beast (17:3, 9). She boastfully sits as queen (18:7). These passages reflect conquering, authority, and control over the peoples and nations of the earth.

Sores

The festering sores poured out on the unrepentant wicked symbolize righteous judgment from God. The sores are not limited to or primarily understood as outward physical pain, but reflect inward spiritual and psychological harm. The word "sore" (*elkos*) is found twice (out of three NT times) in Revelation, and in the same context of the first and fifth bowl judgments (16:2, 11).[58] Most commentators consider the sores to be literal, physical boils

---

55. Lawlor, "Sit, Dwell," 295–96. See Ryken, *Dictionary of Biblical Imagery*, 796.

56. In addition, the cognate *kathizō* is used three times.

57. Sandy (*Plowshares and Pruning Hooks*, 30) relates that this is one of numerous rewards promised to the faithful but which all visualize the one ultimate reward—deity and humanity in perfect unity in eternity (Rev 21:3).

58. The Greek singular "sore" in 16:2 is followed by CEB, NASB, NKJV, NRSV. The singular noun suggests the possibility that the sore contains a collective idea (the sore of humanity) rather than numerous sores upon a person's body. However, Osborne (*Revelation*, 579 n. 3) understands it oppositely: "The

or ulcers, reserved for the wicked near the end of earth history. All agree that this bowl alludes to the sixth exodus plague where boils broke out on the people and animals (Exod 9:8–12). Thus, the reasoning is that since those plagues on Egyptians were physically literal, then these sores should be taken literally as well. Robert Thomas, for example, speaks for many with, "The sixth Egyptian plague imposed maladies on the Egyptians, so why should these sores be any different?"[59]

However, like numerous other originally literal events in the OT, later writings and the NT symbolize the teachings that accompany such events. In doing this, the Bible writer expands and universalizes what may have been an originally limited situation. The OT often associated sores with leprosy which was representative of idolatry and apostasy.[60] Revelation reveals idolatry and apostasy in the followers of the beast.[61]

If the sores of these two bowls are understood more figuratively (they can also include a literal understanding, but not at the cost of minimizing the symbolic meaning), then they reveal an evil society that is suffering the sores of spiritual and psychological harm.[62] This also permits the bowl judgments to relate not only to a future, end-of-the-world punishment, but to be experienced throughout history. Brighton, for example, states that the plague strikes the human race during the entire prophetic period of Revelation's message, that is, from the ascension of Christ to his return.[63] Following an eclectic approach, then, John's audience would see evidences of this "sore," as would each generation, with the final generation experiencing its increase.

The punishment for the unrepentant wicked becomes ironic justice. Those who have the "mark of the beast" now own a new "mark"—painful sores.[64] But since the mark of the beast is not necessarily visible, the sore may not be necessarily visible. This provides a vivid picture of how the outer person now reflects the inner person. First and foremost, sores are symbolic of spiritual malady that is ripe for end-time judgment.

Spit You Out of My Mouth

This image symbolizes the revulsion and rejection of Christ toward those who compromise their faith during persecution. There is hardly a more sickening image imaginable than

---

singular here is collective, referring not to a single sore on each person but to many such sores breaking out on the earth-dwellers."

59. Robert Thomas, *Revelation*, 2:248. Others who understand physical, futurist earth plagues include Kistemaker, *Revelation*, 446–47; Ladd, *Revelation*, 210, 212; LaHaye, *Revelation Unveiled*, 250–55; Mounce, *Revelation*, 293–97; Osborne, *Revelation*, 579–80; Patterson, *Revelation*, 309–10; Walvoord, *Revelation*, 232, 235. Hindson (*Revelation*, 169) proposes these sores to be the result of nuclear radiation poisoning. Mounce (*Revelation*, 293 n. 10) relates that Deut 28:27 (LXX) speaks of God smiting the disobedient with the boil of Egypt in the seat—"a case of hemorrhoids!"

60. Rotz, *Revelation*, 236; Wall, *Revelation*, 197–99.

61. Smalley, *Revelation*, 400; J. C. Thomas, *Apocalypse*, 467.

62. Beale (*Revelation*, 814) explains, "The sore here represents some form of suffering, presumably like that entailed by the spiritual and psychological 'torment' (βασανισμος) of the fifth trumpet (see on 9:4–6, 10)." See Smalley, *Revelation*, 401, 406.

63. Brighton, *Revelation*, 409, 414.

64. Blount, *Revelation*, 295; Reddish, *Revelation*, 303; Roloff, *Revelation*, 188.

someone vomiting. But that is the exact picture intended with this word. "Spit out" (*emeō*) is found only once in the NT. The risen Christ warns the Laodiceans with "So, because you are lukewarm—neither hot nor cold—I am about to spit you out of my mouth" (3:16). Yet this image of revulsion is mentioned often in the OT. For example, the prophets use the word to describe God's judgment on the nations. Just as God vomited out of the promised land the previous depraved owners (Lev 18:25–28), as well as his own people (Jer 51:34), so too he threatens a similar judgment on Laodiceans who do not take their Christian faith seriously.[65]

This lone NT reference affords modern translators the opportunity to find forceful English words, but most end up taking a weaker course with "spit out." It is hard not to improve upon the KJV's "spue thee out." The CSB, NET, and NKJV adopt "vomit" for their translations. Indeed, no stronger word is available nor is so fitting for such complete disgust and rejection. Therefore, believers are challenged to remain faithful to the end in the face of persecution and suffering. "If the Laodicean Christians will not own up to their identity with Christ, he will not acknowledge them at the judgment but will 'spew them out.'"[66]

Standing

Standing symbolizes one's readiness to act or is understood as a position of authority or is the posture of a victorious saint on judgment day. The posture of standing is a major image in the Bible. Many of its six hundred occurrences are used symbolically. Most refer to location or presence as in "the Lord's tabernacle stands in Israel" (Josh 22:19). But figurative expressions abound as well. Thus, standing may entail a spiritual posture (Ps 122:2) in worship at a sacred place (Jer 28:5). It is an expression of reverence (Neh 8:5) or prayer (1 Sam 1:26; Luke 8:9–14). Standing could represent a godly purpose and resolve (nearly a dozen exhortations in the epistles call to stand firm or stand fast). Standing also gives the image of permanence such as when vows are made (Num 30:4–11).[67] John uses the verb "stand" (*histēmi*) twenty-one times and with the same variety found elsewhere. Three emphases seem prominent and often overlap. First, there is standing in readiness to act (3:20; 5:6; 7:1, 11; 8:2, 3; 11:4; 13:1). Second, standing is mentioned from a position of authority (10:5, 8; 12:4; 19:17). Third, the posture of standing is used for the end-time victor (7:9; 11:11; 14:1; 15:2) or non-victor (6:17; 18:10, 15, 17; 20:12).[68]

---

65. See Aune, *Revelation*, 1:258. See Ryken (*Dictionary of Biblical Imagery*, 810, 919), for several OT examples. Porter ("Why the Laodiceans Received," 143–49) adds support from Greek writers.

66. Beale, *Revelation*, 304.

67. Ryken, *Dictionary of Biblical Imagery*, 812–13.

68. Only a few commentators reflect on how "standing" affects the context. For further research on individual passages, see Aune, *Revelation*; Beale, *Revelation*; Koester, *Revelation*; Osborne, *Revelation*; Smalley, *Revelation*; Robert Thomas, *Revelation*. For 20:12, many would place this "standing" under believers. See the entry "Great White Throne."

Teeth

Teeth symbolize the ferocious, destructive power of the devil upon the unrepentant wicked. Teeth may be considered a positive symbol in some contexts, but they are viewed negatively in most biblical examples. Thus, the Leviathan has "fearsome teeth" (Job 41:14) and Daniel's vision of the second and fourth beasts include crushing, iron-like teeth (Dan 7:5–7). When Israel was invaded Joel likened the destruction to "the teeth of a lion" (Joel 1:6). The idiom "gnashed their teeth" is similarly negative (Ps 35:16; Mark 9:18; Acts 7:54). In fact, most NT references reveal this latter phrase as a descriptor of judgment and hell.[69] The negative image likewise fits the lone reference in Revelation where one of the seven descriptions of the demonic locusts reveals that "their teeth were like lions' teeth" (9:8). Thus, the savage attacks from the demonic locusts of the fifth trumpet (an allusion from Joel) imply cruelty, lack of mercy, and a voracious appetite. The image is a reminder that Satan's goal is to destroy humanity.

Thigh

Christ's title of "King of kings and Lord of lords" is visible on the thigh of his robe, where a soldier's sword rests, thereby stressing his role as warrior-judge at his second coming. The image of the thigh produces several connotations in Scripture, including undertones of sexuality, swearing oaths, and sacrificial offering regulations. Another image is that of a warrior's sword strapped to the thigh for quick defense or attack (Exod 32:27; Judg 3:16; Ps 45:3).[70] This latter usage is what is found in the NT's only mention of "thigh" (*mēros*) at Rev 19:16. The coming Christ has his kingly title on his robe and on his thigh. "Upper leg" (NCV) is the only alternate English translation found for "thigh." Most versions translate the phrase in such a way that it appears as if the written name is placed in two locations—on the robe and on the thigh.[71] Many scholars, however, recognize an epexegetical use of "and" (*kai*). This means there is only one name written "on his robe, namely his thigh [area]."[72] Two modern English translations adopt the epexegetical translation: "on the part of the robe that covered his thigh" (CEV); and "on his robe at his thigh" (NLT). Still others surmise that the rider's robe has blown aside, revealing the name on the thigh.[73] That image, however, is almost too fanciful, despite its apocalyptic elements. It appears better to envision a name on the robe at the thigh area. "In other words, the name is written on that part of his tunic that covered his thigh, the place

---

69. Ryken, *Dictionary of Biblical Imagery*, 847.

70. Beale, *Revelation*, 963; Brighton, *Revelation*, 517–18; Ryken, *Dictionary of Biblical Imagery*, 863–64.

71. Followed by several scholars including Beasley-Murray (*Revelation*, 281–82), Caird (*Revelation*, 246–47), Morris (*Revelation*, 225), Mulholland (*Revelation*, 302), Paul (*Revelation*, 319), Resseguie (*Revelation*, 237), and Wall (*Revelation*, 232).

72. So Aune, *Revelation*, 3:1062; Blount, *Revelation*, 356; Ladd, *Revelation*, 256; Mounce, *Revelation*, 356; Murphy, *Fallen Is Babylon*, 392; Osborne, *Revelation*, 686; Robert Thomas, *Revelation*, 2:390.

73. Beale, *Revelation*, 963; Beckwith, *Apocalypse*, 733–34; Prigent, *Apocalypse*, 547; Smalley, *Revelation*, 495; Swete, *Apocalypse*, 255.

where his sword would rest and where it would be conspicuous on a mounted warrior."[74] Whatever, the point of this symbolism is not to imagine Jesus on a galloping horse with flying robes and a sword protruding from his mouth. Kistemaker reminds us "the fact remains that the picture is purely symbolic. The thigh is a figure of power and the robe a symbol of royal majesty."[75]

Tongues

The phrase "gnawed their tongues" is an expression of agony, suffering, and defiance made by the wicked in response to righteous end-time judgment. This anguished phrase is a straightforward symbol to unravel. The exact expression is found in the NT only at Rev 16:10.[76] However, it is certainly a synonym for the "gnashing of teeth" that is found often in the Gospels (Matt 8:12; 24:51; 25:30; Luke 13:28).[77] Significantly, the gnashing of teeth is done in response to the realization of eternal hellfire. This connection is made by John in his Apocalypse as well. When the fifth bowl was poured out the people gnawed their tongues in agony and cursed God. Several versions select some form of "bit their tongues" (CEB, CEV, GNT, NABR, NET, NJB) or "ground their teeth" (NLT).[78] The point is that the Lord punishes hardened unbelievers especially toward the end by causing them to suffer. This only results in further hardening by the wicked. Like the ninth exodus plague it alludes to (Exod 10:21–29), the response is increased antagonism toward God, further vindicating his righteous judgment. Osborne adds that this expression, coupled with darkness, links it to judgment and suffering of the eternal punishment to come (14:9–11; 20:13–15).[79]

Walking

Walking is a metaphor that describes a person living a godly life. The action of walking functions metaphorically throughout the Bible as a description of conducting one's life in relationship to God. Enoch walked faithfully with God (Gen 5:22–24). Abram was charged by God Almighty to "walk before me faithfully and be blameless" (Gen 17:1). Ten times in Deuteronomy, Israel is charged to "walk in obedience to God." In the NT,

---

74. Osborne, *Revelation*, 686. Beale (*Revelation*, 963) adds that the thigh is the typical location in which the hand was placed for swearing oaths. Several note that it was common in the Greco-Roman world to place inscriptions on the thighs of statues. See Aune, *Revelation*, 3:1062; Ford, *Revelation*, 323; Keener, *Revelation*, 455; Smalley, *Revelation*, 495.

75. Kistemaker, *Revelation*, 524.

76. "Tongue" (*glōssa*) is found seven other times in the fourfold phrase "every tribe and people and language and nation" (5:9; 7:9; 10:11; 11:9; 13:7; 14:6; 17:15).

77. L&N (1:254) confirms the two expressions are virtual synonyms for portraying the agony of intense suffering.

78. Many interpreters, particularly dispensationalists, understand the fifth bowl's contents literally. Thus, the darkness causes unbelievers physically to gnaw their tongues due to extreme cold or perhaps from the sores or burns from previous plagues.

79. Osborne, *Revelation*, 588.

Paul favors this metaphor for the Christian life, using it thirty-two times.[80] "Walking" (*peripateō*) is also a favorite metaphor for John's Gospel (John 6:66; 8:12; 11:9–10; 12:35), letters (1 John 1:6–7; 2:6; 2 John 4; 3 John 3), and Revelation (2:1; 3:4; 9:20; 16:15; 21:24).[81]

Modern versions often translate "walking" as "live," "live your life," "behave," or "conduct." Doing so, however, tends to weaken the force of the metaphor. The first of Revelation's five references is the "one like a son of man" who walks among the golden lampstands (2:1). This symbolizes Christ's presence with his church and his guidance, care, and authority over it. Second, the believers at Sardis have a few people who have not soiled their clothes, but walk with Christ, dressed in white (3:4). This stresses their identification and relationship with the resurrected Lord who grants them eschatological reward. Third, the lone possible "literal" use of walking is found in the sixth trumpet where unrepentant humanity follows "idols that cannot see or hear or walk" (9:20). Fourth, walking is found in a blessing that calls for ethical conduct (16:15).[82] The whole image is figurative, alluding to spiritual clothing and making a good account of oneself, withstanding the temptations and deceit of the devil.[83] Finally, in the vision of the new Jerusalem, the nations will walk by the light of God and the Lamb (21:24). Their light is so intense that the nations walk in it, finalizing the theme of Revelation on the conversion of the nations.[84] Walking, therefore, constitutes a vivid metaphor. Like other postures in Revelation, the action of walking is not to be understood in any literal fashion. It is figurative of one's relationship with God, a statement of how a believer is to live.

Wrath

Although the nations, the dragon, and the great prostitute are angry at their deserved judgment, wrath is primarily connected to the righteous wrath of God and the Lamb on judgment day. Anger is an emotion. When attributed to God it is anthropomorphic. Thus, both humans and God can "burn with anger" (Gen 39:19; Exod 14:14). For humans, anger is usually a loss of self-control that results in sinfulness (Gen 49:6; Ps 37:8; Prov 15:1). The majority of references to anger in the OT, however, relate God's justified response to the sins of Israel or pagan nations (Num 11:10; Deut 6:15; 1 Kgs 14:9). In the NT, Jesus also responded in righteous anger (Matt 21:12; Mark 3:5). In addition, the Lord speaks of the wrath to come (Matt 3:7; Luke 21:23) as does Paul (Rom 1:18; 2:5; 1 Thess 1:10; 2:16). It is Revelation, however, that brings together the fullest teaching on God's wrath.[85]

---

80. See Banks, "Walking as a Metaphor," 303–13.

81. See Knapp, "Walk," 1003–5; Ryken, *Dictionary of Biblical Imagery*, 922–23.

82. Several modern versions select "go" in place of "walk" at 16:15 (CEB, CSB, ESV, NABR, NIV, NJB, NRSV).

83. Kistemaker, *Revelation*, 451.

84. Osborne, *Revelation*, 762. See the entry "Nations."

85. See Grant, "Wrath of God," 932–37; Hays, Duvall, and Pate, *Dictionary of Prophecy*, 474–76; Ryken, *Dictionary of Biblical Imagery*, 25–26; William White, "Wrath," 1153–58.

John uses the two words for "wrath" (*orgē, thymos*) interchangeably.[86] Moreover, he reserves these words for the end of individual visions, emphasizing images of divine wrath on judgment day. The noun *orgē* occurs six times. Each time judgment day is depicted (6:16–17; 11:18; 14:10; 16:19; 19:15). The noun *thymos* occurs ten times. In one instance it refers to the dragon's wrath (12:12). Twice it is the great prostitute's wrath (14:8; 18:3).[87] The other seven occurrences refer to God's divine wrath that comes with the bowls or arrives on judgment day (14:10, 19; 15:1, 7; 16:1, 19; 19:15). At three locations both words are used together for intensity (14:10; 16:19; 19:15). God's wrath is reserved for the dragon and his cohorts and the wicked unbelievers who follow them. Their end is the lake of fire. God's people will not experience this wrath. Strikingly, when God's wrath is mentioned there is often a contrasting statement for believers (7:3; 11:18; 14:12–13). God's wrath "enables the defeat of evil, the vindication of his people, the triumph of his perfect character, and eternal fellowship with his redeemed creation in the new heaven and new earth."[88]

Animal Kingdom

The second half of this chapter addresses the animal kingdom, including animal parts and insects. With few exceptions, the animal kingdom portrays negative images in Revelation.[89] One image (four living creatures) is placed under heavenly beings. Every entry should be understood symbolically.

Bear

The bear symbolizes strength, ferocity, and the ability to crush opposition, which are characteristics of the devil-inspired beast. Bears have essentially disappeared from the ancient Near East. During the biblical period, however, a healthy population of bears kept unprotected travelers on their toes. Their power and fierceness were characteristics which made them easy to symbolize. David was compared to a bear for his military proficiency (1 Sam 17:34–37; 2 Sam 17:8).[90] The word "bear" is found in the NT once at Rev 13:2. There it serves as part of the animal-like description of the beast rising from the sea which is given the dragon's authority and power to persecute believers. The added description of "feet like those of a bear" may also suggest images of swiftness and military proficiency.

---

86. The verb *orgizō* is found twice (11:18; 12:17).

87. Both *orgē* and *thymos* are usually translated as wrath, anger, or fury. For these two references (14:8; 18:3) the NIV produces "maddening." Most other versions have "passion/passionate." CSB is the only version that renders the word clearly: "which brings wrath."

88. Hays, Duvall, and Pate, *Dictionary of Prophecy*, 476.

89. Resseguie (*Revelation Unsealed*, 117–19) lists the demonic animals as locusts, lions, birds, dragon/serpent, and beast. He states demonic animals are characterized by their bizarre hybrid appearance (mutation of human and animal), unnaturalness and ugliness, deceptive nature, destructiveness and strength, and surprising resiliency.

90. Beck, *Dictionary of Imagery*, 20–21.

The bear, along with the beast, leopard, and lion, form a single figure that is drawn from the four beasts of Dan 7.

Beast

The beast implied the Roman Empire and a leader like Nero for John's original audience. Ultimately, it represents the evil world system (and its leader/s) that is empowered by Satan to oppose God and persecute believers. This is apparent in every generation and especially the last. In the OT, beasts might be used literally as vehicles of God's judgment (2 Kgs 2:24; Ezek 14:15). They were also symbols. Daniel used the lion, leopard, and bear to refer to world empires (Dan 7:4–6). Hosea used these same animals to illustrate how God will pounce on Israel in judgment (Hos 13:7–8). "Beast" (*thērion*) is found forty-six times in the NT, thirty-nine (85%) which are in Revelation. The word refers once to dangerous "wild beasts" (6:8) and once to every "detestable animal (18:2).[91] This leaves thirty-seven uses for a possible symbolic understanding. But in actuality there are two "beasts" in Revelation. The second one is introduced in 13:11 as "the beast from the earth," and is later labeled the "false prophet." The remaining thirty-six references, therefore, apply strictly to the first beast, the "beast from the sea." Intriguingly, thirty-six is a triangular number.

Although the word "antichrist" is not found in Revelation, most scholars understand the beast from the sea to be connected. By John's era, two types of anti-Messiah-like figures were prominent in Judaism. One was a political, military tyrant from the outside who opposes and oppresses Israel, and one was a false teacher from within Israel who deceives the people. "Antichrist" is found only five times, once as a plural (1 John 2:18 [twice], 22; 4:3; 2 John 7), and all refer to false teachers infiltrating the first-century church. These antichrists are forerunners of those who harass and persecute Christians throughout the centuries.[92] Another probable reference to the antichrist is 2 Thess 2:3–12. There Paul mentions a "man of lawlessness," probably modeled after Caligula's threat to set up a statue of himself in the temple of Jerusalem.[93] This man of lawlessness is a deceiver, takes a throne in the temple, claims divine authority, depends on Satan's power, and is a sign that the second coming is near. Thus, Paul combines the two anti-Messiah-like figures. John, however, separates them into the first beast (political, military) and the second beast (religious; the "false prophet").[94] For John's audience, Nero was certainly the model for the beast. Such fear of a return of Nero gripped the first century. Since few ever

---

91. Mulholland (*Revelation*, 172–73) theorizes that the wild beasts of 6:8 actually do refer to the beast which comes later in chapter 13. However, John assuredly refers to Ezek 5:16–17; 14:21 which has the same four elements.

92. For a history of interpretation see Koester, "Antichrist," 177–78; and Kovacs and Rowland, *Revelation*, 147–56. McGinn (*Antichrist*) presents an in-depth study, tracing the development from the first to twenty-first centuries. Robert Fuller (*Naming the Antichrist*) accents the American fascination with outing the antichrist.

93. Weima, *1–2 Thessalonians*, 521–22.

94. Murphy, *Apocalypticism*, 376–77; Osborne, *Revelation*, 493–95; Schnabel, *40 Questions*, 163–68. Dan 7 mentions four beasts. John combines them into one fearsome beast. Or perhaps, as Michaels (*Revelation*, 158) reasons, the fourth beast has "swallowed" its three predecessors.

saw Nero's corpse after his suicide in AD 68, a *Nero Redivivus* legend arose. Nero was either still alive or would come back from death to reconquer the empire.[95]

The beast is briefly introduced as originating from the Abyss to make war with the two witnesses, that is, the church (11:7). It is mentioned seventeen times in chapter 13 alone. It comes up from the sea and is empowered by Satan (13:1–4).[96] It parodies the death and resurrection of Christ (13:1–3, 12).[97] It demands worship as God (13:4, 8). It blasphemes and slanders God and his people (13:5–6). It persecutes believers (13:7). It is aided by the second beast which demands worship of the first beast and requires the world to receive the mark of the first beast (13:12–17). The beast's number is revealed to be six hundred sixty-six.[98] Scattered references to the beast continue later in the third interlude on the consequences of following the beast and gaining victory over it (14:9, 11; 15:2). The fifth bowl is poured out on the throne of the beast, and in the sixth bowl the beast inspires the armies of the world to gather for Armageddon (16:2, 10, 13). Chapter 17 has nine references to the beast. It is controlled by the great prostitute (17:3, 7). It is symbolically the eighth Roman emperor who has not yet appeared (17:8, 11). It receives authority from the kings of the earth (17:12–13), and will hate the prostitute and bring her to ruin (17:16–17). The demise of the beast is detailed in chapters 19 and 20. It gathers the forces for Armageddon (19:19), but is captured along with the false prophet and thrown into the fiery lake (19:20). Victory is assured for those who did not worship the beast (20:4), and the dragon is thrown into the lake of fire just as the beast was (20:10).

Most commentators understand the beast to symbolize the Roman Empire, particularly since John draws from Dan 7, which depicted the fourth beastly empire as Rome. The emperors embody the empire, but the empire system is John's intention.[99] Other interpreters, however, stress the beast more as an individual who fulfills the roles of Paul's "man of lawlessness" and Daniel's "little horn." The descriptions of chapter 13 underscore a person. For them, the empire aspect is minimized.[100] These views are not mutually exclusive. It appears best to allow both ideas to work. Therefore, many scholars understand the beast as both an empire and a specific person who represents or heads the empire.[101]

95. See Bauckham, *Climax of Prophecy*, 407–23; Hays, Duvall, and Pate, *Dictionary of Prophecy*, 303; Schnabel, *40 Questions*, 177–78. Preterist Gentry (*Beast of Revelation*) generates two hundred pages of support for Nero as the beast.

96. The beast arises from the Abyss (11:7) and the sea (13:1), but they are used as synonymous terms and are parallel in time. See the entry "Abyss."

97. Resseguie (*Revelation Unsealed*, 124) produces a chart with seven traits of Christ and seven parodies of the beast.

98. See the entry "Six Hundred Sixty-Six."

99. Bauckham, *Climax of Prophecy*, 450–52; Beale, *Revelation*, 680; Blount, *Revelation*, 246; Brighton, *Revelation*, 352; Caird, *Revelation*, 162; Fee, *Revelation*, 178; Harrington, *Revelation*, 140; Hughes, *Revelation*, 145; Mounce, *Revelation*, 244; Murphy, *Revelation*, 297; Paul, *Revelation*, 234; Reddish, *Revelation*, 250; Schüssler Fiorenza, *Revelation*, 84; Sweet, *Revelation*, 207; Swete, *Apocalypse*, 161; Stefanovic, *Revelation*, 412–16.

100. Ladd, *Revelation*, 177; LaHaye, *Revelation Unveiled*, 207–13; Lindsey, *New World Coming*, 183–90; Morris, *Revelation*, 160; Patterson, *Revelation*, 273; Walvoord, *Revelation*, 197–203; Witherington, *Revelation*, 179. Futurists emphasize this person will arise in the last days.

101. Duvall, *Revelation*, 180; Hindson, *Revelation*, 142–44; Alan Johnson, "Revelation," 13:704; Dennis Johnson, *Triumph of the Lamb*, 188–90; Keener, *Revelation*, 335–39; Kistemaker, *Revelation*, 375–76;

Understanding the beast begins with first-century Rome and its evil leaders. But it must be enlarged to include subsequent political, social, and economic systems as well as the individuals who lead them. Thus, the beast *"symbolizes every human authority and everything of the human nature that the dragon can corrupt and control and use in his warfare against the woman (the church) and her seed (individual Christians):* political, governmental, social, economic, philosophical, and educational systems, as well as individuals."[102]

Birds

Birds are unclean animals who are associated with death. "Bird" is found only three times in the NT, all in Revelation. Birds are common in the OT as food, quarry, and symbols of escape and safety, faithfulness and beauty. Yet they are also characterized as detestable scavengers whose nighttime cries symbolized for many ancients collusion with demonic spirits. Their presence around tombs associated them as agents of death and the realm of the dead, and thus animals to be avoided (Isa 13:20–23; Ezek 39:4; Zeph 2:13–15).[103] It is these latter images which John draws from for his three references. First, in the fall of Babylon vision, the idea of uncleanness comes through. Babylon the Great has fallen and become a dwelling for demons and the haunt of every impure spirit and unclean bird (18:2). The vision of the rider on the white horse holds the final two references. The birds are invited by an angel to come and gather for the great supper of God (19:17) and gorge themselves on the flesh of the wicked (19:21).[104] This invitation is drawn from Ezek 39, and highlights the overpowering judgment of God upon his enemies.[105] Most English translations opt for "birds," but the NLT uses "vultures" for all three references, which might aid modern readers in viewing these animals more clearly as symbols of end-time judgment.[106]

Koester, *Revelation*, 580–81; Michaels, *Revelation*, 156–57; Osborne, *Revelation*, 495; Ryrie, *Revelation*, 95; Robert Thomas, *Revelation*, 2:152–54; Wong, "Beast from the Sea," 337.

102. Brighton, *Revelation*, 352 (original italics).

103. Bailleul-Lesuer, "Birds," 176–89; Ryken, *Dictionary of Biblical Imagery*, 92–94; Waltke, "Birds," 511–13.

104. Resseguie (*Revelation Unsealed*, 121) notes the "gruesome dinner is an ironic reversal of the natural order: scavenging birds devour human sacrifices in grim contrast to the normal order of humans feasting on animal sacrifices."

105. Predation by wild beasts is a sign of divine judgment (Num 21:4–9; Ezek 5:17; Jer 12:9; Hos 2:12. For an extended discussion on Jeremiah's reference (12:9), see Foreman, *Animal Metaphors and the People of God*, 222–31. Although birds are singled out in Rev 19:17, 21, it suggests a parallel to the fourth seal (6:8). Farmer (*Revelation*, 122) understands the scene quite differently. This is not a scene of grotesque destruction with bodies on the battlefield for scavenger birds to consume. Instead, following a universalistic approach, he understands the sword from Christ's mouth to reveal the result of the conversion of unbelievers. They are "slain" by the good news, and the birds eat their "flesh," which becomes a reference to the sinful nature of a person.

106. So too Beasley-Murray, *Revelation*, 284; Mounce, *Revelation*, 359; Smalley, *Revelation*, 500.

Dogs

Dogs symbolize unsaved and unrepentant people. In the ancient Near East, dogs herded livestock (Job 30:1) and perhaps served as house pets (Matt 15:26). Overall, however, they were disparaged. The Bible consistently offers a negative portrayal of dogs. Street dogs were unclean and despised (1 Kgs 14:11). A male prostitute was called a dog (Deut 23:18). Dogs served as epithets for fools (Prov 26:11) and greedy rulers (Isa 56:10). A dead dog was a metaphor for "less than nothing" (1 Sam 24:14; 2 Sam 9:8).[107] By NT times, rabbis referred to gentiles as dogs. "Dogs" (*kyon; kynarion*) are mentioned nine times in the NT, two of which are analogous to how John uses the word in Revelation. A proverbial saying found in Matt 7:6 uses dogs to indicate the unsaved. In Phil 3:2, Paul turns the tables on Judaizers who agitate for a requirement of circumcision for gentile Christians, epitomizing them as dogs.

John uses the word once at the head of a vice list (22:15). Most English translations are content to translate the word as "dogs." But a few versions define the symbol for modern audiences. "Dogs" is translated as "perverts" (GNT) and "evil people" (NCV).[108] Thus, dogs are symbolically portrayed as evil, godless, malicious, and depraved, perhaps even suggestive of pederasts or sodomites.[109] J. C. Thomas asserts, "the dogs are those who persecute the people of God, having sold themselves into the sexual immorality of the Great Whore."[110] The fact that dogs are on the same list as liars, sorcerers, murderers, idolaters, and fornicators as those who will not enter heavenly rest confirms the symbolic understanding of the word. These immoral, unrepentant people will be left outside the eternal city.

Dragon

The dragon symbolizes Satan, the ultimate enemy of God and his people. He was defeated at Christ's birth and death, and consummately at the second coming. The dragon is an ancient symbol of evil and chaos, and opposition to God. This legendary animal is found in numerous cultures as a common symbol for cruelty, evil, ferocity, and power. The OT consistently presents the dragon and related images as malevolent and threatening. The oldest depiction of the dragon is the reference to the serpent in Gen 3. Later, he is located in the sea (Amos 9:3), a place of chaos. Only God can vanquish the dragon, sea monster, Rahab, or Leviathan (Job 26:12–13; Ps 74:13–14; Isa 27:1; 51:9–11; Ezek 32:2–8).[111]

---

107. Beck, *Dictionary of Imagery*, 65–67; Alfred Day and Harrison, "Dog," 980–81; Yamauchi, "Dogs," 519–27.

108. REB footnote has "perverts."

109. So Aune, *Revelation*, 3:1223; Patterson, *Revelation*, 382–83; Smalley, *Revelation*, 574. Robert Thomas (*Revelation*, 2:507) suggests "impudently impure, those addicted to unnatural vices."

110. J. C. Thomas, *Apocalypse*, 679. Singularly, Strelan ("Outside Are the Dogs," 148–57) interprets the dogs in a literal fashion. He links the first two items together (dogs and sorcerers) to suggest that pagans used the animals in their purification rituals as a source of power and charms.

111. Carey, "Dragon," 161–62; John Day, "Dragon and the Sea," 228–31; Hays, Duvall, and Pate, *Dictionary of Prophecy*, 124–25; Osborne, *Revelation*, 458–59; Ryken, *Dictionary of Biblical Imagery*, 562–65. For a summary of extratextual myths, see Yarbro Collins, *Combat Myth,* 57–65. Reeves ("Dragon of the

Revelation alludes to all these ideas, depicting the dragon as Satan himself. The dragon becomes one of four names or titles given to the ultimate enemy of God and his people, alongside the devil, serpent, and Satan. Of the four names, however, the dragon is John's favorite. All thirteen NT uses of *drakon* are found in Revelation (12:3, 4, 7 [twice], 9, 13, 16, 17; 13:2, 4, 11; 16:13; 20:2).[112]

Significantly, eleven of the thirteen uses are in chapters 12–13. It is common to label these two chapters as the heart of Revelation. Many understand John drawing from all of the dragon myths of other cultures and historicizing them.[113] Yet John moves beyond these stories and the OT and fulfills them in Revelation.[114] By doing so, the two chapters convey the basic story of Satan—the dragon—who attempts to thwart God and his people at every turn. His power and authority are palpable yet pretentious. He is the "great, red dragon" (12:3, 9), cruel and wicked. He is the enemy of God, the Lamb, and his people. God, however, defeats the dragon, first at the time of Christ's birth (12:4) and then at his resurrection (12:3, 7–10). The dragon's wrath is directed at God's people, but God spiritually nourishes and protects them (12:6, 13–17). The dragon's attempts to destroy the faithful through his agents of deception (13:2, 4, 11; 16:13) will ultimately fail, and all will be thrown into the lake of fire (20:2). The dragon, therefore, culminates all scriptural teachings on the ancient adversary of God and his people, and rolls them into one evil entity, Satan. His cruelty and deception will be forever judged at the second coming.

Eagle

The eagle serves two purposes. On the one hand it is a symbolic harbinger of coming end-time judgment for unbelievers. On the other hand it represents the eternal protection and deliverance which the faithful receive from God. The eagle portrayed speed and power in biblical images from the OT (2 Sam 1:23; Isa 40:31). It also signified God's deliverance for his people as well as his destructive judgment on the unrepentant (Exod 19:4; Deut 32:11). Three of the five uses of "eagle" in the NT are found in Revelation (4:7; 8:13; 12:14). Notably, the other two references are usually translated as "vulture" and both are found in apocalyptic sections (Matt 24:28; Luke 17:37). This aids in understanding the eagle as an end-time omen in John's Apocalypse.

The first mention of an eagle is found in the description of the fourth living creature who was "like a flying eagle" (4:7), accenting the swiftness of God's strength and protection. Second, the eagle appears at the introduction of the final three trumpets (8:13).[115]

Apocalypse," 210–13) relates several historical attempts at identifying the dragon and his heads.

112. GW consistently translates dragon as "serpent" and serpent as "snake."

113. Yarbro Collins (*Combat Myth*, 142–45) presents a strong case for John developing themes from several sources to produce the storyline of chapter 12.

114. Beale, *Revelation*, 624–25; Osborne, *Revelation*, 454; Sweet, *Revelation*, 203.

115. The TR/KJV/NKJV tradition reads "angel" for "eagle." This variant was a scribal mistake, confusing *angelou* for *aetou*. Or perhaps scribes changed "eagle" to "angel" since it seemed more appropriate for an angel to make a proclamation, not a bird. Comfort (*New Testament Text*, 831) adds the change results in eight angels involved in the visionary unveiling. "This is inconsistent with the numerical coding in the book of Revelation, which typically has sevens, twelves, or their multiples."

John hears an eagle cry "Woe!" three times to the earth dwellers.[116] Once again, strength and swiftness are observable. But the probable connection to "vulture" stresses the idea of judgment. The eagle, then, brings a message from God, announcing end-time disaster is on its way.[117] The third mention is at 12:14. Here the eagle symbolizes God's protection and nurture for his people, represented by the woman, who is "given the two wings of a great eagle, so that she might fly to the place prepared for her in the wilderness, where she would be taken care of for a time, times and half a time, out of the serpent's reach." Michaels notes that most English versions conceal the definite article in the phrase "*the great eagle*" in 12:14. This might imply the eagle is the same one who pronounces the three woes in 8:13.[118] Or perhaps the definite article is used to refer to "the great eagle" of Exod 19:4, thereby accenting God's deliverance.[119] Whichever was originally intended, Bible students agree that John adopts the image from the Exodus, Deuteronomy, and Isaiah references listed above. To suggest that a literal eagle suddenly speaks English in a voice loud enough for the whole earth to hear, or that a woman suddenly sprouts eagle's wings, or is transmogrified into modern aircraft undercuts the intention of this symbol. The eagle stands as a metaphor for the swiftness and strength of God's deliverance for believers as well as the swiftness and strength of his destruction for unbelievers.

Frogs

Frogs emphasize uncleanness and impurity of speech, the influence of demonic spirits, and perhaps a caricature of the foolishness of the unholy trinity. The word "frogs" is found once in the NT at Rev 16:13. Three unclean spirits that look like frogs come from the mouths of the satanic trinity—the dragon, the beast, and the false prophet. The majority of English translations choose "unclean" to translate *akarthata*. "Impure" (NIV) and "foul" (NJB, NRSV, REB) are close synonyms. "Evil" is also popular (CEV, GW, NCV, NLT) yet less specific. In other words, the evilness of these frog-like spirits is their unclean, foul speech. "Out of the mouth" occurs three times, suggesting wicked, impure speech, and "persuasive and deceptive propaganda."[120]

Frogs were considered unclean and unfit for eating (Lev 11:9–11). But John is also alluding to the plague of frogs unleashed on unrepentant Egyptians prior to the exodus (Exod 8:1–15; Ps 78:45).[121] Stephan Witetschek offers a further possibility. After analyzing

116. Resseguie (*Revelation Unsealed*, 136), following Roloff (*Revelation*, 111), posits the threefold woe imitates onomatopoetically the cawing of an eagle.

117. So Mounce, *Revelation*, 182–83; Mulholland, *Revelation*, 192–93; Murphy, *Fallen Is Babylon*, 241; Rotz, *Revelation*, 137; Robert Thomas, *Revelation*, 2:24. Stefanovic (*Revelation*, 298) understands the eagle as a vulture. Uniquely, Lupieri (*Apocalypse*, 158) suggests the eagle is an angel, a "spiritual angelomorphic being."

118. Michaels, *Revelation*, 152. Actually, CEB, ESV, GW, NASB, and NRSV retain the article.

119. Yarbro Collins, *Apocalypse*, 87.

120. Mounce, *Revelation*, 299. See Beale, *Revelation*, 832; Kistemaker, *Revelation*, 449; Smalley, *Revelation*, 409. Keener (*Revelation*, 395) adds that ancients saw frogs as "vicious."

121. See the numerous window allusions to the exodus in Shargel, "Hearer-Centric Approach to Revelation," 140–43.

the metaphors of ancient Greek and Jewish writers, he concludes that the primary symbol of the frog is one of foolish talk (like their croaking) and human silliness in general.[122] If so, this adds another layer to John's depiction of the evil trinity. What they have to teach is not only evil but silly, senseless, mere grotesque croaking. What a contrast to the sword that comes from the mouth of Christ. Thus, John identifies frogs with unclean spirits who inspire the unholy trinity to deliver slippery, ridiculous, evil lies as well as great signs to fool the wicked rulers of the earth, compelling them toward the end-time gathering of Armageddon.

Horns

Horns are a common symbol of strength and honor when attributed to God. By contrast, when horns are ascribed to the devil, the beast, and their followers, they accent the aggressive nature of power and authority. Since an animal's horns were an obvious sign of its strength, and functioned as weapons, it is easy to see how they became symbols.[123] A few examples from a variety of biblical genres confirm this (Deut 33:17; 1 Kgs 22:11; Ps 89:17; Zech 1:18; Dan 7–8). The plural noun "horns" (*kerata*)is found ten times in the NT, all in Revelation (the singular "horn" is found at Luke 1:69). Like the contrasting nature of many of John's symbols, horns may imply good power or evil power. In Revelation, good power is understood in the first two references, while evil power is intended by the last eight references.

Positively, the seven horns of the Lamb symbolize the completeness and fullness of his power. Although the Lamb was slain he retains the image of a conqueror (5:6).[124] Second, at the sixth trumpet John hears a voice from "the four horns of the golden altar," (9:13), that is, the four horn-shaped corners of the heavenly altar. Thus, images of the power, strength, and authority of God's voice receive emphasis here, especially in light of the nearness of the eschaton.[125]

The remaining references are negative and underscore the aggressive and abusive power of evil. In 13:11, John sees a second beast with two horns like a lamb. "Two" underscores his testimony on behalf of the first beast as well as his subservient nature to it. Yet it also serves to parody the Lamb of God.[126]

---

122. Witetschek, "Dragon Spitting Frogs," 557–72.

123. Harrison, "Horn," 757; Ryken, *Dictionary of Biblical Imagery*, 400; Suring, "Horn-Motifs," 335–40.

124. Beale (*Revelation*, 351) suggests that horns on the conquering messianic Lamb perhaps allude to *1 En.* 90:6–16 and *T. Jos.* 19:6–8.

125. Whether the addition of the word "four" is original is textually disputed. Metzger (*Textual Commentary*, 670) determines that the evidence for inclusion and exclusion is even, and thus UBS5 gives it a {C} rating for inclusion. English translations that exclude "four" include NCV, NET (with a footnote of explanation), NIV 1984, and REB while the NABR places the word in brackets. The variant reading is not significant since the altar has four corners.

126. Many scholars, however, interpret the two horns as a parody of the two witnesses: Beale, *Revelation*, 707; Ford, *Revelation*, 213; Alan Johnson, "Revelation," 13:712; Morris, *Revelation*, 166; Resseguie, *Revelation*, 187; Sweet, *Revelation*, 215; J. C. Thomas, *Apocalypse*, 398.

The remaining references are to "ten horns." The dragon and the beast have seven heads and ten horns (12:3; 13:1). The seven and ten symbolize the completeness and fullness of their oppressive power. In the fall of Babylon vision John sees the great prostitute riding the scarlet beast with its seven heads and ten horns (17:3, 7). This shows the beast's subservience to the woman. The ten horns receive more description later. They are "ten kings who have not yet received their kingdom" (17:12). This builds on the ten horns of Dan 7:7–8, 20–25 (from which the little horn appears). In Daniel, the kings arise from the final kingdom and prepare for the little horn to take power. Their last mention reflects the self-destroying nature of evil as they turn against the woman (17:16).[127]

The image of the ten horns in chapter 17 has received much speculation over the centuries. Many interpreters suggest John to be originally referencing client kings or kingdoms of the Roman Empire.[128] But these kings are yet to appear, so it is safer not to speculate. Nevertheless, numerous futurists point to the beast being a revived Roman Empire, and since modern Europe embodies that empire, the ten horns are modern European nations. The European Union is often touted by some prophecy writers.[129]

Yet as with all numbers in Revelation, ten is not literal. It commonly represents totality and completeness. Horns reflect power and strength. Therefore, this symbolizes the totality of the all the nations of the world that are submissive to the beast and the prostitute, that is, the antichrist-like world system.[130] The ten horns probably serve as another metaphor for the "kings of the nations" and "kings from the east."[131] The ten horns unite and yield their power to the beast. This occurs in every generation. This turns rampant in the final days when Satan is loosed from restrictions (20:3). They will attempt to make war with the Lamb, but he will conquer them at the battle of Armageddon (17:14). In sum, horns represent the strength and honor of God on the one hand, and the falsely claimed power and honor of the devil and his minions on the other.

---

127. Mounce (*Revelation*, 320) comments, "The wicked are not a happy band of brothers, but precisely because they are wicked they give way to jealousy and hatred and mutual destruction."

128. So Aune, *Revelation*, 2:951; Brighton, *Revelation*, 451; Keener, *Revelation*, 411; Osborne, *Revelation*, 621. Preterists Chilton (*Days of Vengeance*, 437) and Russell (*Parousia*, 502) add that these subject kings represent Rome in their first-century war on Judaism and Christianity.

129. Hindson, *Revelation*, 178–79; Lindsey, *Late Great Planet Earth*, 123; Walvoord, *Revelation*, 254. Ryrie (*Revelation*, 119), however, suggests ten Western nations. Murphy (*Fallen Is Babylon*, 362) criticizes this approach: "Recent commentators have identified the kings with the nations of the European Economic Community, for example, or the oil-producing nations belonging to OPEC. Such identifications are gratuitous and serve merely to lend supposedly divine sanction to individuals' judgments about their own times."

130. Beale, *Revelation*, 878; Caird, *Revelation*, 219; Mounce, *Revelation*, 319–20; Resseguie, *Revelation*, 225; Smalley, *Revelation*, 437.

131. So Beale, *Revelation*, 878; Beasley-Murray, *Revelation*, 258; Duvall, *Revelation*, 228; Easley, *Revelation*, 312; Koester, *Revelation*, 679; Michaels, *Revelation*, 198; Prigent, *Apocalypse*, 494; Schnabel, *40 Questions*, 172; J. C. Thomas, *Apocalypse*, 511. Contra Blount, *Revelation*, 321. See the entry "Kings of the Earth."

Horses

Horses are animals of war and signify end-time conflict and ultimate conquest at the second coming. Since horses are often characterized as aggressive and stubborn, the OT occasionally symbolized people as obstinate horses (Ps 32:9; Prov 26:3; Jer 5:8; Ezek 23:20). Horses appear most often, however, in the context of battle. "Because it was essential for success in battle, the horse became a symbol of military might and national security (Ps 20:7; Is 30:16)."[132] The prophets envisioned future battles in which the Lord would destroy the horses of his enemies (Jer 50:37; Mic 5:10; Hag 2:22; Zech 14:15), and display his power by allowing scavengers to devour the carcasses (Ezek 39:17–21). With the exception of Jas 3:3, all explicit references to horses in the NT are found in symbolic contexts in Revelation.[133]

"Horses" (*hippikoi*) appears sixteen times in Revelation.[134] The first four references are found in the four horsemen of the four seals. They refer to the horses that patrol the earth, signaling the beginning of the messianic age (Zech 1:7–11; 6:1–8).[135] The seals are not reserved for the final few years of earth history, but commence soon after the ascension of Christ, and are fulfilled throughout history.[136] The remaining occurrences cluster toward the end of individual visions. Five references are in the fifth and sixth trumpets. The demonic locusts "looked like horses prepared for battle" (9:7) and "the sound of their wings was like the thundering of many horses" (9:9). Their heads resembled the heads of lions and their power was in their mouths and tails (9:17–19).[137]

A solitary appearance of horses is found near the conclusion of the third interlude. The end-time harvesting of the wicked relates that blood flowed out of the divine winepress, rising as high as the horses' bridles for a distance of 1,600 stadia" (14:20). The mention of horses' bridles alludes to the heavenly army (17:14; 19:14) or the final eschatological battle (16:12–16; 19:17–21).[138] Bauckham cites Jewish apocalypses that reveal

---

132. Ryken, *Dictionary of Biblical Imagery*, 400.

133. Ibid., 400–401. See also Foreman, *Animal Metaphors and the People of God*, 129–39; Donn Morgan, "Horse," 759–60; Yamauchi, "Horses," 817–24.

134. *Hippikos* is found in the NT once (9:16) and is most often translated as "mounted" (CSB, ESV, GNT, NIV, NJB, NLT). But there is also "cavalry" (CEB, NABR, NRSV, REB); "horsemen" (NASB, NKJV); "on horses" (GW, NCV); "horseback" (NET); and "war horses" (CEV). *Strateuma* ("troops," "armies") is found four times (9:16; 19:14, 19 [twice]).

135. Donn Morgan, "Horse," 760.

136. Beale, *Revelation*, 370–71.

137. Patterson (*Revelation*, 222) wisely cautions against modern attempts: "to identify tanks belching forth fire with some sort of automatic weaponry being described by their tails is far-fetched to say the least." Nevertheless, he adds, "The seemingly anachronistic idea of modern employment of horses in battle is not stretching the imagination at all." He then footnotes a book on modern special ops using horses in the Afghanistan conflict.

138. Bauckham, *Climax of Prophecy*, 19; Beale, *Revelation*, 781; Blount, *Revelation*, 282; Keener, *Revelation*, 378; Kistemaker, *Revelation*, 420; Koester, *Revelation*, 630; Smalley, *Revelation*, 378. Some English translations soften the universal battle aspect by using the singular "a horse" instead of the plural (CEV, ESV, GW, NABR, NLT, NRSV). Bauckham, however, relates that this is not simply an abstract measure of height but actual cavalry horses in battle.

the pervasive use of horses to measure the depth of blood. The point of the image is that it represents the complete slaughter of an army in battle.[139]

The final cluster of five occurrences is in the rider on the white horse vision (19:11, 14, 18, 19, 21). In a clear picture of the second coming, the rider is followed by the armies of heaven on their white horses. Then the birds are invited to feast on the carcasses of the horses and their riders after complete end-time slaughter. Thus, the mention of horses in Revelation does not warrant a literalist reading that demands actual horses or a literalizing of the horses into modern day metallic warfare machinery. Horses symbolize war, specifically end-time conflict which results in final victory.

Lamb

The Lamb is a title for Christ which stresses his paradoxical victory—he was sacrificially slain yet by his death we attain eternal life. It also emphasizes his authority as the messianic end-time judge. This entry can be placed easily under heavenly beings or heavenly titles. There are almost two hundred references to "lambs" in Scripture. Two symbolic marks distinguish their appearance. First, lambs symbolize gentleness, innocence, and vulnerability. Thus, God is the shepherd who gathers lambs in his arms (Isa 40:11). The suffering servant is like a lamb led to the slaughter (Isa 53:7; Jer 51:40). Jesus sends out his disciples like lambs (Luke 10:3). Peter is commissioned to feed Christ's lambs (John 21:15). Second are the associations of lambs with sacrifice, something mentioned eighty times in Exodus, Leviticus, and Numbers. Sacrifice reaches its climax in Christ who is the Lamb of God (John 1:29, 36) and the Passover lamb without blemish (John 19:14; 1 Cor 5:7; 1 Pet 1:19). Complete fulfillment of the metaphor is found in Revelation where "Lamb" is used as a title of Christ.[140]

The word *amnos* is found four times in the NT (John 1:29, 36; Acts 8:32; 1 Pet 1:19), and all designate Jesus as the Lamb of God. The synonym *arnion*, however, is John's favorite Christological title. It is found once in John 21:25 and twenty-nine times in Revelation to account for all NT uses. The only time that "lamb" does not refer to Jesus in Revelation appears in the description of the second beast (13:11), who is "like a lamb," stressing the parody of the genuine Lamb. This leaves twenty-eight references (7 x 4) to Jesus as the Lamb, a sure signal that numerical symbolism is intended. Seven of these occurrences couple God with the Lamb (5:13; 6:16; 7:10; 14:4; 21:22; 22:1, 3). Bauckham declares, "Since it is through the Lamb's conquest that God's rule over his creation comes about, the 7 x 4 occurrences of 'Lamb' appropriately indicate the worldwide scope of his complete victory."[141]

Norman Hillyer noted long ago the significance of John's selection of *arnion* over *amnos*. *Amnos* is centered more on the sacrificial aspect whereas *arnion* allows for a

---

139. Bauckham, *Climax of Prophecy*, 40–48. Another solitary reference to horses is in the fall of Babylon vision where merchants of the earth lament the loss of horses (18:13).

140. Hays, Duvall, and Pate, *Dictionary of Prophecy*, 247–48; Hylen, "Lamb," 563; Miles, "Lamb," 132–34; Ryken, *Dictionary of Biblical Imagery*, 484; Skaggs and Doyle, "Lion/Lamb in Revelation," 362–75; Woodbridge, "Lamb," 620–22.

141. Bauckham, *Climax of Prophecy*, 34.

triumphant warrior aspect. Moreover, Hillyer believes *arnion* is deliberately chosen as a special word to describe young Christians (John 21:15). These faithful followers share in Christ's risen life and are entitled to enter into his triumphant works over Satan. Thus, Lamb becomes more than a title. It becomes a description of Christ's relationship to humanity through his redemptive death. This produces six themes for the Lamb: redeemer (7:14; 15:3); object of worship (3:21; 5:8, 12; 7:9–10; 21:22; 22:1–3); ruler (5:6; 12:11; 17:14); judge (6:16; 14:10); pastor (7:17); and married to the church (3:20; 19:9; 21:2, 9; 22:17).[142]

The Lamb, therefore, conquers ironically through his suffering and death, not through military might. His followers must conquer in the same way. Nevertheless, the Lamb will come one day to judge (6:16; 14:10) and rule (12:11; 17:14). The Lamb who appears as slaughtered becomes the conquering lion (5:5–6; 6:17; 19:11–21).[143]

Leopard

The leopard symbolizes cunning, cruelty, agility, and ferocity, all which are characteristics of the devil-inspired beast. The leopard is a close relative of the lion and considered a dangerous animal. This solitary cat was known for surveying the territory from high perches (Song 4:8). Since it did not call out like a lion it was considered more threatening (Jer 5:6; Hos 13:7–8). Daniel's vision reveals the leopard as a malicious predator (Dan 7:6).[144] The leopard is found only once in the NT where it forms part of the grotesque appearance of the beast that also includes a bear and a lion (13:2). This image is taken from Daniel's vision of four animals (Dan 7:1–8; see *4 Ezra* 11–12).[145] John explains, "The beast I saw resembled a leopard, but had feet like those of a bear and a mouth like that of a lion. The dragon gave the beast his power and his throne and great authority." This beast is described with similes (*hōs* means "like"), and "resembles a leopard," not in appearance, but symbolically for its cruel and cunning nature.

Lion

In accordance with John's contrasts, lions signify the power, strength, and wrath of either God or Satan. There are over one hundred references to lions in the OT and many are symbolic. The lion's roar and ruthless nature as a predator evoked images of ferocity,

---

142. Hillyer, "Lamb in the Apocalypse," 228–36. Donald Guthrie ("Lamb in the Structure of Revelation," 64–71) appends Hillyer by noting how the Lamb is used in Revelation's structure. He determines that the Lamb appears most often not in scenes of judgment but in scenes of worship and salvation. Johns (*Lamb Christology*, 22–32) does not see as much a sacrificial metaphor as he does a stress on vulnerability. Johns also shies away from seeing a warrior Lamb.

143. Brighton (*Revelation*, 149) affirms that "*While the Christology of Revelation deals primarily with the exaltation of Jesus Christ and his glorious reign, the foundation for this exalted Christology is the theology of the Lamb of God, who suffered and died and rose again*" (original italics).

144. Ryken, *Dictionary of Biblical Imagery*, 30; Harrison, "Leopard," 102–3.

145. Smalley, *Revelation*, 337. All English versions translate *pardalis* as "leopard."

power, and strength (Judg 14:18; Job 10:16; Dan 7:3–6; Hos 13:7–8; Amos 3:8; Jer 4:7).[146] Six of the nine occurrences of "lion" (*leōn*) in the NT are found in John's Apocalypse. Three are positive references (4:7; 5:5; 10:3) and three are negative references (9:8, 17; 13:2). Positively, the lion is a picture of the power and strength of God in righteous end-time judgment. This is displayed in the throne room vision where the first of four living creatures surrounding the throne "was like a lion" (4:7).[147] The second positive reference comprises one of the most powerful symbols of Revelation—the Lion of the Tribe of Judah. This messianic title is detailed in the next entry. Third, a positive reference is mentioned at the commencement of the second interlude. The mighty angel's shout is likened to a lion in its loudness and intensity, and therefore, its authority and sovereignty (10:3).[148] Negatively, the lion is viewed as a symbol of terrifying strength, wanton destructiveness, and devouring nature.[149] Their power and wrath is a parody of genuine, divine authority. This includes the fearful locusts of the fifth trumpet with "teeth like lion's teeth" (9:8); the horses of the sixth trumpet whose heads "resembled the heads of lions" (9:17); and in the third interlude, a beast that "resembled a leopard, but had feet like those of a bear and a mouth like that of a lion. The dragon gave the beast his power and his throne and great authority" (13:2).

Lion of the Tribe of Judah

This messianic title reveals Christ as Judah's greatest descendant and who has the sovereign power to be the conquering Divine Warrior. When Jacob was on his deathbed, he prophesied to his son, "You are a lion's cub, Judah; you return from the prey, my son. Like a lion he crouches and lies down, like a lioness—who dares to rouse him?" (Gen 49:9). Using the image of a lion, *4 Ezra* 12:31 stated, "This is the Messiah." In John's throne room vision the exalted Christ is presented with two messianic titles—"the root of David" and the "Lion of the tribe of Judah" (5:5).[150] This latter title stresses Christ's prophetic lineage and alludes to Gen 49. It is an intentional contrast to the Lamb. Coupled with the militaristic verb *nikaō* (conquer, vanquish, overcome, triumph), the symbol emphasizes the conquering nature of the allusion. It is Jesus who fulfills both messianic titles. Beale lists several passages from targumic literature and later Jewish literature to bolster the understanding that this text was understood messianically.[151] It is the lion of the tribe of

---

146. Borowski, "Lion," 669–70; Ryken, *Dictionary of Biblical Imagery*, 514–15; Strawn, *What Is Stronger than a Lion?*, 5–16.

147. The imagery of a lion with eagle's wings (Dan 7:3–6) and the first living creature of Revelation stimulated the early church to make symbols for the four Gospels. Mark is the lion's symbol.

148. A significant portion of OT references concerns the lion's voice (Job 4:10; Ps 22:13; Prov 19:12; Jer 2:15; Ezek 22:25; Zech 3:3).

149. Another NT example is 1 Pet 5:8.

150. Bauckham (*Climax of Prophecy*, 214) traces the coupling of the two titles in several apocalyptic texts.

151. Beale, *Revelation*, 349 n. 143. See also Osborne, *Revelation*, 253.

Judah who has the authority and power to overcome his enemies and thus the sovereignty to open the book and loose its seals for end-time judgment.[152]

Locusts

Locusts are demonic beings unleashed from the Abyss who wage war upon the wicked inhabitants of the earth. Locusts are used in the OT as a symbol of divine judgment (Deut 28:42; 1 Kgs 8:37; Ps 78:46). John draws richly from two texts for his vision of the fifth trumpet. First, the locusts are an allusion to the eighth Egyptian plague (Exod 10:1–20; see Ps 105:33–35). Moses predicted that in the latter days the sufferings experienced in Egypt will reoccur, including locusts (Deut 28:38–42). Second, John references Joel where the locust plague is described as an invading army (Joel 1:4; 2:11), and serves as a portent of the "day of the Lord" (Joel 2:31).[153] John consummates this locust imagery in the fifth trumpet. The Abyss is opened, and "out of the smoke locusts came down on the earth and were given power like that of scorpions of the earth . . . The locusts looked like horses prepared for battle. On their heads they wore something like crowns of gold, and their faces resembled human faces" (9:3, 7).

Locusts have received their fair share of interesting interpretations through history, generally in light of contemporary events. Preterists proposed the first-century Roman army or zealots in Palestine.[154] In the sixth century, Primasius likened the locusts to current heretical teachers plaguing the church.[155] The marginal note in the 1560 Geneva Bible reads: "Locusts are false teachers, heretics, and worldly futile prelates, with Monks, Friars, Cardinals, Patriarchs, Archbishops, Bishops, Doctors, Bachelors & Masters which forsake Christ to maintain false doctrine."[156] Nineteenth-century historicists saw locusts in the arrival of Mohammed and rise of Islam in the seventh century.[157] In the twentieth century, popular dispensationalists interpreted locusts as modern weaponry such as tanks and helicopters.[158]

Moderns continue to debate their identity. Some envision demonized human armies, but the majority understands them as supernatural demonic beings. Several interpreters picture actual insects. Ryrie, for example, sees "not ordinary locusts" but "demons who take the form of unique locusts."[159] Yet even a committed literalist such as John Walvoord cautions that "these are not natural locusts, but a visual representation of the hordes of

---

152. Ibid., 350.

153. Keown, "Locust," 149–50; Redditt, "Locust," 684–85; Ryken, *Dictionary of Biblical Imagery*, 516; Yamauchi, "Insects," 886–904.

154. Buchanan, *Revelation*, 247; Chilton, *Days of Vengeance*, 246–47; Ford, *Revelation*, 149.

155. Weinrich, *Revelation*, 134.

156. Taken from Kovacs and Rowland, *Revelation*, 114.

157. Gregg, *Revelation*, 230.

158. Lindsey, *New World Coming*, 138–39; Walter Wilson, *Dictionary of Bible Types*, 264.

159. Ryrie, *Revelation*, 72. So too Patterson, *Revelation*, 218. Hindson (*Revelation*, 108) writes, "These are not hippies on motorcycles! They are either demonic hordes, human armies, or radiation-poisoned and mutated creatures."

demons loosed upon the earth." He adds, "what John is seeing must symbolize demonic possession."[160]

The locusts of the fifth trumpet must be understood symbolically. They represent demonic forces. Actual giant mutated locusts or allegorical attack helicopters limit the intended meaning of this powerful symbol. Literalizing a symbol limits its intended meaning. The demonic locusts terrorize, deceive, and demoralize the wicked inhabitants of the earth—of every generation—and especially the last generation.

Scorpions

The demonic locusts with scorpion-like tails are unleashed from the Abyss to wage war upon the wicked inhabitants of the earth. Much of the discussion on scorpions parallels the entry on locusts. Scorpions are dangerous creatures and effortlessly became symbols for menace and terrible punishment (Deut 8:15; 1 Kgs 12:11; Ezek 2:6). The author of Sir 39:30 included scorpions as one of God's vehicles for punishing the ungodly.[161] Jesus employed scorpions (and snakes) as descriptors of demonic forces (Luke 10:18–20). Scorpions are mentioned three times in Revelation (9:3, 5, 10). They form part of the description of the fifth trumpet where demonic locusts rise from the Abyss. The locusts transform and are given power like that of scorpions, have scorpions' tails that sting, and inflict agony on the unrepentant world.

Popular dispensationalists literalize the fifth trumpet. Walter Wilson, writing after World War II, relates the creature as "a symbol of a modern fighting machine such as a tank or a portable cannon pulled by a tractor. Both have power in the rear end."[162] Lindsey, writing during the Vietnam era, suggests Cobra helicopters with nerve gas sprayed from its tail.[163] The inflicted agony, however, is primarily spiritual, mental, and psychological. For example, Beale notes that spiritual and psychological connotations are found elsewhere in John with reference to trials that both precede and include the final judgment (11:10; 14:10–11; 18:7–15; 20:10). Chapter 18's weeping and mourning are synonymous with the emotional pain as well.[164] Thus, the scorpion-tailed demonic locusts of the fifth trumpet are permitted ("was given"; 9:3) to exact torture on wicked unbelievers. Satan's ultimate purpose is to destroy humanity. This spiritual (and sometimes physical) torment is allowed throughout the centuries, and will be even worse nearer the end.

---

160. Walvoord, *Revelation*, 160, 162. So too LaHaye, *Revelation Unveiled*, 171; Robert Thomas, *Revelation*, 2:35.

161. Aune, *Revelation*, 2:531. See Birch, "Scorpion," 357–58; Cansdale, "Scorpion," 350–51. Beale (*Revelation*, 515–16) lists numerous Jewish texts on the metaphorical associations of serpents and scorpions. Judgment and deception are recurring themes.

162. Walter Wilson, *Dictionary of Bible Types*, 361.

163. Lindsey, *New World Coming*, 139.

164. Beale, *Revelation*, 497.

Serpent

The serpent is another moniker for Satan, the devil, and the dragon. These four names or titles refer to the spiritual being who opposes God and his people. In this instance, deception is stressed through an allusion to the serpent's role in humanity's fall in the garden of Eden. Most of the Bible's nearly fifty references to snakes or serpents are figurative. From the beginning (Gen 3:1) to the end (Rev 20:2), Bible writers are repulsed by these reptiles. This is especially true since they are so closely associated with the devil and his agents.[165] *Ophis* is found five times in Revelation. Once it is in plural form and is usually translated in English Bible versions as "snakes" (9:19). The other four references (12:9, 14–15; 20:2) are singular, include the article, and clearly refer to Satan, alluding to his role in the fall of humanity in Gen 3. "Serpent" is the favored English translation, but some versions select "snake" (CEB, CEV, GW, NCV). Two versions (GNT, NLT) opt for "dragon" at 12:14 but this disguises the distinctive nature of how John uses Satan's four names.

All four names are mentioned near the beginning of the third interlude (12:9). The adjective "ancient" serves to confirm its role in deluding Adam and Eve in paradise. In Gen 3:1 the serpent is introduced as clever, shrewd, and wise. The term may be a play on words with "naked" found in the previous verse (Gen 2:25). If so, then the serpent exhibits its cleverness by seeing through the Lord's command, namely, that humans would not "die" if they ate from the tree of knowledge and good and evil.[166] The serpent points this out to the first couple, and entices them to sin. Thus, John's allusion to this story underscores the role of the serpent as deceiver.

The serpent is mentioned twice more a few verses later (12:14–15). The woman is given two wings of a great eagle so that she may flee the serpent's reach. The enraged serpent pursues and persecutes the woman (the people of God), but she is spiritually and eternally protected by God. Nevertheless, temptation and persecution continues. She is nourished in the wilderness yet also tested. John then supplies a specific example with the serpent's attempt to drown the woman with a torrent of water. Few interpreters hold out for a literalist reading of the watery flood. Two views have emerged. First, some understand this symbol of flood waters from the serpent's mouth to refer to physical force and persecution, usually near the end of earth history.[167] The OT supports this understanding by describing evil nations overflowing Israel (Jer 46:7; 47:1–3). Second, many scholars understand this image as a flood of lies and deceit. This, too, is supported by OT symbolism (Pss 18:4; 32:6; 69:1). In addition, it fits John's use of the serpent and the allusion to Eden-like deception as well as the use of "mouth" as a symbol for deceitful speaking that is found elsewhere in Revelation (13:2–6; 16:13).[168] These two views are not mutually

---

165. See Cansdale, "Serpent," 427–29; Alfred Day and Jordan, "Serpent," 417–18; Handy, "Serpent (Religious Symbol)," 1113–16; McFall, "Serpent," 773–75; Ryken, *Dictionary of Biblical Imagery*, 773; Swanson, "Serpent," 190–91. Farrell and Karkov ("Serpent," 693–95) state that since the time of Augustine, the serpent has taken on an added image of sensuality and sexual license.

166. Swanson, "Serpent," 190.

167. Robert Thomas, *Revelation*, 2:140; Walvoord, *Revelation*, 195. LaHaye (*Revelation Unveiled*, 205) wanders away from a contextual literalist reading to suggest a flood of soldiers invading the desert to kill the children of Israel.

168. So Beale, *Revelation*, 673; Caird, *Revelation*, 159; Kistemaker, *Revelation*, 369; Morris, *Revelation*,

exclusive. Taken together, they refer to the two strategies that Satan uses—force and persecution, deception and false teaching.[169] Nevertheless, because of the context of "serpent" and "mouth," the second view should receive the primary interpretation. This permits the serpent's threat to be real for each generation, not just the last one. The final occurrence of the serpent begins the millennial vision and recapitulates 12:9. All four names are used again, and he is bound for a thousand years (20:2). Although the timing of the "binding" is disputed by scholars, the serpent's eventual end is the lake of fire.

Snakes

In Revelation, snakes (plural) describe the demonic horse's tails, depicting devilish activities and deception. The plural noun "snakes" is found once when the demonic horses of the sixth trumpet had tails like snakes (9:19).[170] Snakes call to mind *the* snake, that is, the serpent, Satan, the devil (Gen 3:1–7). Snakes were universally considered as demonic. Persian and Egyptian religions, for example, considered snakes to be demons. That the tip of the horses' tails were snakes, injuring the inhabitants of the earth, becomes a universal picture of demonic activity.[171] Some interpret the horses more literally, either as a contemporary reference to Parthian soldiers,[172] or a futurist demonically-inspired military army.[173] If John is drawing from the terror of the Parthians then he has expanded it to depict a universal demonically-charged army. Caird suggests that John blends the reference to Parthians with the imagery of a demonic army to produce "a nightmare version of a familiar first-century fear."[174] There appears to be a figurative link with Gog and Magog (Ezek 38–39) as well.[175] This fits if the sixth trumpet is understood as a prelude leading to Armageddon in which Gog and Magog are referenced (16:12–21; 19:11–21; 20:7–10). The infliction of pain which these snakes dole out may certainly be physical. More crucial, however, is to understand that demonic activities and demonic deception are being symbolized here, and not limited to the first or last generation.[176]

159; Mounce, *Revelation*, 246; Osborne, *Revelation*, 483; Smalley, *Revelation*, 331–32. See the entry "River."

169. Stefanovic, *Revelation*, 392.

170. A few versions translate the plural as "serpents" (ESV, NASB, NKJV, NRSV, REB). The singular *ophis* is found four times and refers to the devil. See the entry "Serpent."

171. So Morris, *Revelation*, 132; Osborne, *Revelation*, 384; Mark Wilson, "Revelation," 4:307. Aune (*Revelation*, 2:539) suggests a background to the mythological Chimera, a monster with a lion's head, goat's body, and snake's tail. Resseguie (*Revelation*, 40–41, 149) calls these hybrids.

172. So Beasley-Murray, *Revelation*, 164; Ford, *Revelation*, 146.

173. Hindson, *Revelation*, 110; Patterson, *Revelation*, 224–25; Walvoord, *Revelation*, 167.

174. Caird, *Revelation*, 122. See Keener, *Revelation*, 271; Mounce, *Revelation*, 197.

175. Brighton, *Revelation*, 248; Caird, *Revelation*, 122–23; Mounce, *Revelation*, 197; Osborne, *Revelation*, 384; Smalley, *Revelation*, 241.

176. Beale, *Revelation* 513–15; Smalley, *Revelation* 241.

Tails

Tails are a fiendish, devilish image portraying power over other spiritual beings and the inflictions of pain upon unrepentant people. They are mentioned fifteen times in the OT and occasionally incorporate symbolic ideas (Deut 28:13; Isa 9:14–15). Ancient cultures often connoted evil with dragons and their tails, including the use of their tails to inflict destruction. All five references to "tails" in the NT occur in Revelation—twice at 9:10 and 9:19 and once at 12:4. Each instance is portrayed negatively through demonic locusts, fiendish horses, and the dragon. First, the demonic locusts of the fifth trumpet have "tails with stingers, like scorpions, and in their tails they had power to torment people for five months" (9:10).[177] Second, the demonic cavalry of the sixth trumpet reveal that the "power of the horses was in their mouths and in their tails; for their tails were like snakes, having heads with which they inflict injury" (9:19).

The final mention is in the third interlude. John sees "an enormous red dragon" whose "tail swept a third of the stars out of the sky and flung them to the earth" (12:4). This vivid image has produced varying interpretations. First, Satan's sweeping a third of the stars with his tail might refer to a primordial war in heaven.[178] Second, futurists see the event as part of the last days. Third, because the following verse (12:5) alludes to the birth and ministry of Christ, most scholars understand the temporal aspect of the event to occur within history, specifically at the cross.[179] Thus, the tail is an evil instrument, an image of the power of Satan, the dragon, to inflict persecution and destruction.

Wings

The wings attached to spiritual beings represent either protective security for the faithful or fearsome judgment for the wicked. With few exceptions, the mention of wings in the Bible is understood figuratively. They are present in scenes of protection (Exod 19:4; Deut 32:11; Ps 17:8; Isa 34:15), strength and endurance (Job 39:13; Isa 40:31; Ezek 17:3), and tender care (Ps 91:4; Matt 23:37; Luke 13:34). Most references to wings occur in apocalyptic visions and pertain to spiritual beings. There are seraphs (Isa 6:2), cherubim (Ezek 10:1), apocalyptic beasts (Dan 7:4–6), and even women with wings (Zech 5:9).[180]

John draws from this imagery in his three usages of wings (*ptera*). First, "each of the four living creatures had six wings and was covered with eyes all around, even under its wings" (4:8). This alludes to Ezek 1:5–21; 10:12–22; and Isa 6:1–4. Together the four

---

177. A few futurists (Lindsey, *New World Coming*, 138; Walter Wilson, *Dictionary of Bible Types*, 408) suggest these tails refer modern weaponry.

178. So Beasley-Murray, *Revelation*, 199; Blount, *Revelation*, 230; Brighton, *Revelation*, 329; Hendriksen, *More than Conquerors*, 165; Hindson, *Revelation*, 138; LaHaye, *Revelation Unveiled*, 200; Mulholland, *Revelation*, 218–19; Osborne, *Revelation*, 461; Patterson, *Revelation*, 263–65; Stefanovic, *Revelation*, 382; Robert Thomas, *Revelation*, 2:124.

179. See the entry "Michael."

180. Ryken, *Dictionary of Biblical Imagery*, 954–55.

creatures symbolize the totality of animate creation and what is strong, noble, wise, and swift in nature. The wings suggest swiftness to carry out the will of God.[181]

Second, wings form part of the description of the demonic locusts in the fifth trumpet. The "sound of their wings was like the thundering of many horses and chariots rushing into battle" (9:9). This depicts the sound of an actual locust swarm (Joel 2:4–5; Jer 51:14). Perhaps John is also referencing *T. Sol.* 2:2–4 which speaks of demons who have wings and resemble human-like lions.[182] Such a fearsome portrait stresses powerful judgment. Robert Thomas states, "The loud rushing sound of the swarm creates a formidable psychological problem for mankind and implies the hopelessness of resisting them."[183]

Finally, wings occur at 12:14. "The woman was given the two wings of a great eagle, so that she might fly to the place prepared for her in the wilderness." The woman represents the faithful Christian community. Thus, she is not actually an angelic or demonic being even though she is figuratively transformed with two wings. John's usage of wings, however, surely underscores God's deliverance, security, and nourishment for his people (Exod 19:4; Deut 32:11). Wings, therefore, form a small part of the apocalypticist's symbolic repertoire. Like other images in Revelation, the audience is a mixed contrast. For some, wings represent swift comfort and security. For others, they picture the certain prospect of end-time judgment.

---

181. Mounce, *Revelation*, 125.

182. Beale, *Revelation*, 501–2.

183. Robert Thomas, *Revelation*, 2:37.

7

Food and Clothing

THIS SHORT CHAPTER DESCRIBES images associated with food and clothing. Food (and hunger) is a major symbol in Scripture. It connotes provision, pleasure, and God's divinely intended order. Spiritual food was used by Jesus often in his teachings (Matt 26:26; Luke 12:23; John 4:34; 6:25–59).[1] The characters of Revelation are dressed and decorated. What they wear relates to their identity personally and corporately. The condition and color of clothing is important for John's teachings. Clean, soiled, being clothed and unclothed are his symbolic signals. Once again, some entries that qualify for food and clothing are placed elsewhere in this study. For example, the great prostitute's clothing is significant, but is placed under colors.

Food and Drink

John utilizes food imagery often. The following ten entries on food, drink, taste, and eating instruments are used as symbols for persecution, divine judgment, and eternal bliss.

Bitter

To make something bitter symbolizes persecution toward believers or God's judgment on unbelievers. "Bitter" and "bitterness" are common symbols in the Bible. The Hebrew noun (*mar*) and verb (*marar*) are mentioned as early as the exodus experience. The Israelites ate bitter herbs (*maror*) at Passover to symbolize the bitterness and agony of slavery (Exod 12:8; Num 9:11). When speaking of the immorality of the Canaanites, Moses mentions bitter clusters of grapes (Deut 32:32). The mental attitude of a dethroned David and his followers is expressed as "fierce" which is literally rendered as "bitter of soul" (2 Sam 17:8).[2] The verb "to make bitter" (*pikrainō*) is found three times in Revelation (8:11; 10:9, 10).[3] At the third trumpet a great star fell from the sky and, "the name of the star is

---

1. Ryken, *Dictionary of Biblical Imagery*, 297–99.
2. Feinberg, "Bitter, bitterness," 644. He lists other examples.
3. Col 3:19 is the only other NT use.

Wormwood. A third of the waters turned bitter, and many people died from the waters that had become *bitter*" (8:10–11; "poisoned" [NET]). The other two uses of *pikrainō* are translated "to turn sour" in the NIV.[4]

In John's commission (10:9–10), the bitterness that follows the sweetness speaks of something strong and painful. But is it because the message is directed more toward the wicked as part of their judgment, that is, bitter to his hearers?[5] Or is the emphasis directed more to believers who are commissioned to witness yet recognize that God's sweet message will engender bitter persecution?[6] Scholars are evenly divided over the identification. Certainly both ideas are valid and found elsewhere in John, and both should be intended here. Carol Rotz summarizes, "Whatever the particular nuance for the prophet in this vision, the essence of the sweetness and bitterness metaphor is the great joy of salvation and the anguish of judgment for those who refuse to believe."[7] The waters turning bitter is taken literally by many interpreters, but more likely it is used as a symbol of agony and pain similar to the rest of the Bible's usages.

Cup

The cup symbolizes God's end-time judgment on Babylon the Great and all wicked unbelievers. The cup and its contents might convey love, comfort, prosperity, and fellowship (Ps 16:5; 1 Cor 10:16). The majority of uses, however, convey God's judgment against sin. God is pictured as punishing evil, rebellious people by making them drunk (Isa 51:17; Jer 49:12; Ezek 23:31–34; Ps 75:8; Hab 2:16). This figure carries over to the NT as well, and includes the idea of violence, suffering, and impending death (Matt 20:22; 26:39; John 18:11).[8]

John carries forward this emphasis as well. Ironically, the cup of wrath is voluntarily drunk. "Cup" is found four times in Revelation (14:10; 16:19; 17:2; 18:6). Strikingly, all four examples are found in individual visions that signify the divine judgment of God at the consummation of history. Therefore, Babylon will receive her just retribution from God on the last day. Symbolically, anyone who voluntarily drinks from her cup drinks in the cup of wrath of the eternal judgment of God. Kistemaker applies the cup for modern readers: "But the cup itself is held out to the people at large, who are being seduced to drink its contents. When they do so, they suffer disastrous results, becoming victims

4. Several versions helpfully translate *pikrainō* as "bitter" all three times (CSB, ESV, GW, NASB, NRSV).

5. So Beale, *Revelation*, 552; Beasley-Murray, *Revelation*, 175; Boring, *Revelation*, 142; Brighton, *Revelation*, 271; Dennis Johnson, *Triumph of the Lamb*, 163; Kistemaker, *Revelation*, 316.

6. So Alan Johnson, "Revelation," 13:678; Ladd, *Revelation*, 147; Michaels, *Revelation*, 136; Mounce, *Revelation*, 210; Mulholland, *Revelation*, 202; Osborne, *Revelation*, 403–4; Patterson, *Revelation*, 234–35; Resseguie, *Revelation*, 156; Roloff, *Revelation*, 126; Smalley, *Revelation*, 267–68. Interestingly, Robert Thomas (*Revelation*, 2:74) opts for John literally eating the scroll. But this is surely a symbolic action. Similar to the measuring of the temple in chapter 11, John does not pull out a yardstick. So too here he does not choke down a scroll.

7. Rotz, *Revelation*, 157.

8. See Rea, "Cup," 1111; Ryken, *Dictionary of Biblical Imagery*, 186. Minear (*Images of the Church*, 38–39) discusses the image of the cup in several NT passages.

of pornography, gambling, extravagance, power, and the craving of celebrity status. The great prostitute occupies a central position in an anti-Christian culture."[9]

Drunk

Drunkenness is a powerful symbol of end-time judgment. The wicked who become drunk on Babylon's maddening wine will one day drink God's wrathful wine. Drunkenness is a major biblical symbol. Although the production and consumption of wine formed a central part of ancient Near East culture, the Bible also critiques its misuse (Gen 9:21–27; Prov 23:29–35; Isa 5:22; Rom 13:13; Gal 5:21; Eph 5:18; 1 Cor 6:10; 1 Tim 3:3).[10] The largest number of references to drunkenness occurs in the prophets as a metaphor of God's judgment. In some cases, they reflect God's judgments in history; at other times the nations represent the world as a whole, set to suffer God's end-time destruction (Isa 19:14; Jer 13:13; 51:7; Ezek 23:33).[11] Revelation draws from this metaphor for the eschatological destruction of Babylon the Great.

John utilizes four words to demonstrate intoxication. First, the verb *potizō* simply means to drink. An angel of the third interlude (12:1–15:4) proclaims, "'Fallen! Fallen is Babylon the Great,' which made all the nations drink the maddening wine of her adulteries" (14:8). Thus, the context and the allusion to Jer 51:7 imply that the wicked have (over) drunk the wine of immorality from the great prostitute.[12] Second, "drinking wine" (*pinō*) is mentioned twice. Followers of the beast "will drink the wine of God's fury, which has been poured full strength into the cup of his wrath" (14:10); and the end-time lament over the fall of Babylon includes, "For all the nations have drunk the maddening wine of her adulteries" (18:3).[13] John mixes the concepts of drinking wine and wrath. The two combine to make "the wrathful wine."[14] The third word is *methyskō*, usually translated as "become drunk" but rendered in NIV as "intoxicated": "the inhabitants of the earth were intoxicated with the wine of her adulteries" (17:2). The final word reflecting drunkenness is *methyō*, found a few verses later. John sees "the woman was drunk with the blood of God's holy people" (17:6). Beale proposes that the woman's drunkenness indicates she was dominated by her activity of persecuting Christians.[15] Therefore, John's usage of several words to denote drunkenness, along with connections to the fall of Babylon the Great, depict a forceful image of divine judgment at the end of history.

9. Kistemaker, *Revelation*, 465.

10. See Claassens, "Wine," 860; Edwards and Armerding, "Drunkenness," 994–95; Marvin Wilson, "Alcoholic Beverages," 43–52.

11. Ryken, *Dictionary of Biblical Imagery*, 220–21.

12. Osborne, *Revelation*, 539.

13. One other use of *pinō* is found in 16:6 where the wicked have only blood to drink.

14. Kistemaker, *Revelation*, 410.

15. Beale, *Revelation*, 860.

Eating

Depending on the audience, eating refers either to divine intimate fellowship or divine end-time destruction. The fact that there are over seven hundred references to eating in the Bible underscores its importance as a major image. Although many passages refer to literal physical consumption it is metaphorical eating that occurs the most. Negatively, sexual appetite is pictured in terms of eating (Prov 7:18; Song 2:3). Divine judgment is pictured as devouring (Lev 10:2; Deut 32:42; 2 Sam 18:8; Ps 21:9; Jas 5:3). Positively, to grow spiritually is compared to the process of eating and digesting (Jer 3:15; 1 Cor 3:1; Heb 5:11–14; 1 Pet 2:2). Ultimately, to eat is to participate in salvation. Jesus pictured the messianic banquet in his teachings (Matt 22:1–14; 25:1–13; 26:29; Luke 14:15–24), and all must eat the Bread of Life to inherit eternal life (John 6:25–40).[16]

Eating comprises a major symbol in Revelation as well. Like many of the symbols John employs, the activity of eating has both positive and negative connotations, depending on the audience addressed. John employs three word groups essentially as synonyms. First, *esthiō* (six times) and *katesthiō* (five times) are usually translated "to eat," although the latter word includes a stronger quality "to devour" (2:7, 14, 20). An intimate relationship with God or other gods is intended in these verses. In the second interlude, John eats up, devours, internalizes the scroll, and thus becomes intimate with its contents (10:9–10).[17] Negative connotations are likewise noticeable. Fire comes from the mouths of the two witnesses and "consumes" (CSB, ESV, NET, NJB, NLT, NRSV, REB) or "devours" (NABR, NKJV, NIV) their enemies (11:5). The dragon prepares to devour the child once it is born (12:4). The beast will turn against the great prostitute and eat her flesh (17:16). At Armageddon, the birds eat the flesh of kings, generals, and mighty men (19:18). This utter destruction is recapped in the subsequent vision as the armies of Armageddon "marched across the breadth of the earth and surrounded the camp of God's people, the city he loves. But fire came down from heaven and devoured them" (20:9).

The second word John uses is *chortazō*. It is found only once and implies gorging, satisfaction, and satiation from eating. At the second coming, "all the birds gorged themselves on their flesh" (19:21). Many versions choose "ate their fill," but NIV, ESV, GW, NABR, NET, NLT, NRSV, and REB effectively translate the one Greek word with the one English word "gorged," and NJB has "glutted." The point of this gorging is that the slain are not given decent burial in order to picture the ultimate humiliation of defeat. God is "returning upon the heads of unbelievers what they have done to the saints."[18] They have become "apocalyptic bird food."[19]

The last word group refers to eating supper. John uses the verb *deipneō* once at 3:20. "Here I am! I stand at the door and knock. If anyone hears my voice and opens the door, I will come in and eat with that person, and they with me."[20] This passage emphasizes the

---

16. Jenks, "Eating and Drinking," 250–54; Ryken, *Dictionary of Biblical Imagery*, 226–27; Woudstra, "Eat," 6–8. A deeper study is Klingbeil, "Eating and Drinking in Revelation," 75–92.

17. J. C. Thomas, *Apocalypse*, 319–20.

18. Osborne, *Revelation*, 691.

19. Blount, *Revelation*, 358.

20. Wallace (*Greek Grammar*, 380–82) correctly emphasizes *eiseleusomai pros* to mean "come in to"

invitation to the intimate meal of fellowship and community, a foretaste of the end-time wedding supper of the Lamb. The other three uses of *deipneō* occur in communion passages (Luke 17:8; 22:20; 1 Cor 11:25). Finally, two uses of the noun *deipnon* are connected with the wedding supper of the Lamb and its contrasting meal, the great supper of God. The angel tells John, "Blessed are those who are invited to the wedding supper of the Lamb!" (19:9). Disastrously, those who refuse the invitation will attend their own supper—the great supper of God (19:17–18).

Therefore, when eating is mentioned in Revelation, the reader's first response should be to understand it as a symbol. Consuming actual food spread out on an enormous heavenly table, or eating luscious fruit picked off the tree of life, or observing actual birds picking at the flesh of dead bodies could conceivably occur, but such literalist readings are not the purpose for the image. The meaning of eating is the promise of eternal provision and intimate fellowship for the faithful, and consuming end-time judgment for unbelievers.

Great Supper of God

The great supper of God is a symbol for the comprehensive judgment of the wicked at the second coming. It contrasts with the wedding supper of the Lamb. Although mentioned only once (19:17–18), "the great supper of God" ("God's great feast," CEV, GNT, NABR, NCV, NJB; "great banquet of God," GW, NET, NLT, REB) is a powerful symbol portraying the final judgment of the unrepentant. The invitation for birds to come and gather for this supper serves as a "macabre parody"[21] of the invitation to come to the wedding supper of the Lamb mentioned in 19:9. The list of invitees for this feast comes from all ranks of life, from the mighty to the lowly, from the free to the slave. The overuse of "and" (listed eight times) stresses everyone who has followed the dragon, the beast, and Babylon will be in attendance for this dining experience. J. C. Thomas explains, "The message is clear. Absolutely no one will be exempt from the judgment inherent for those who stand in opposition to the rider on the white horse. No one will escape. No favoritism will be shown."[22] John alludes to Ezek 39:17–21, a sacrificial feast at the end-time, prepared by the Lord on the mountains of Israel. It reverses the natural order since birds eat people, not the other way around. John adapts this image for the great supper of God. Thus, a gruesome contrast is envisioned. While believers celebrate the wedding feast of the Lamb along with its overtones of eternal intimacy, joy, and celebration, unbelievers become the feast themselves in the great supper of God. Osborne states, "A powerful sermon title for chapter 19 could be, 'Will You Be the Eater or the Eaten?'"[23]

(CEB, CSB, ESV, NASB, NKJV, NRSV), not "come into" (GNT, NET). The emphasis is on coming before a person, not penetration into a person.

21. A favorite description apparently coined by Ladd (*Revelation*, 257) and repeated by Beale (*Revelation*, 965), Beasley-Murray (*Revelation*, 282), and Wilcock (*I Saw Heaven Opened*, 185). Resseguie (*Revelation*, 239) appends, "The flesh-eating birds frame this macabre scene and add a Hitchcockian chill to the narrative."

22. J. C. Thomas, *Apocalypse*, 587.

23. Osborne, *Revelation*, 694.

Hidden Manna

The hidden manna represents eternal, intimate fellowship with Christ that a victorious be-
liever experiences now and forevermore. This image fits as a worship accoutrement as well.
"Bread" (*artos*) presents a hearty symbol in the Bible. Common metaphors include the
bread of tears (Ps 80:5), bread of wickedness (Prov 14:17), bread of idleness (Prov 31:27),
bread of adversity (Isa 30:20), and bread of sincerity and truth (1 Cor 5:8). Jesus taught
his followers how to compose a prayer, using bread as a metaphor for the basic daily needs
(Matt 6:11).[24] Bread finds ultimate metaphoric updating in Christ who is the Bread of Life
in John's Gospel. But John does not use the common word for bread. Instead he draws
from the wilderness wanderings and uses the word "manna" three times in John 6:25–59.
Manna served as Israel's food for forty years until the people entered the promised land
(Josh 5:12). Israel "ate the bread of angels" (Ps 78:25). The Lord instructed Moses to place
a jar of manna in the ark of the covenant. Thus, it was "hidden" from sight (Exod 16:32;
Heb 9:4). According to 2 Macc 2:4–7, the prophet Jeremiah hid the ark of the covenant in
a cave on Mount Nebo before Jerusalem fell (586 BC). The tradition developed that when
the messianic age began, Jews would eat this hidden manna.[25] Beale mentions another
tradition that the manna given to Israel in the wilderness was also "hidden in the high
heavens . . . from the beginning" of creation (Tg. Ps.-J Exod. 16:4, 15) and was ultimately
to prosper Israel "at the end of days" (Tg. Neof. 8:16).[26]

This messianic age ushered in with the first advent of Christ. His followers have
eaten the hidden manna and participate in its blessings. Along with the parabolic teaching that came with the forty days of testing (Matt 4:1–11; Luke 4:1–13), Jesus declared
himself a new kind of manna that had come down from heaven. All those who link themselves with this manna will never go hungry and never die (John 6). Thus, the manna
once hidden is now revealed.

From this backdrop, the sole reference to manna in Revelation is more easily interpreted. The risen Christ extends a promise to the overcomers at Pergamum. "To the
one who is victorious, I will give some of the hidden manna" (2:17). Modern versions
retain the transliteration of manna. An exception is "hidden food" (CEV) but with an
explanatory footnote referencing Exod 16. The NLT reproduces the traditional teaching
mentioned by Beale with "manna that has been hidden away in heaven."

Because of Christ's atoning sacrifice, this promise was available not only to the saints
at Pergamum but to all who place their trust in Jesus, the Bread of Life. The hidden manna
"represents God's supernatural and eternal provision that stands in contrast to the idol
food offered at the pagan feasts."[27] This promise finds consummate fulfillment, however,
at the wedding supper of the Lamb (19:6–9). John ties the messianic banquet of the end
times with the hidden manna to picture the eternal bliss of heavenly fellowship.[28]

---

24. Beck, *Dictionary of Imagery*, 33–35, 163–65. See Carr, "Manna," 239–40.

25. So Beale, *Revelation*, 252; Kistemaker, *Revelation*, 133; Koester, *Revelation*, 290; Mounce, *Revelation*, 82; Smalley, *Revelation*, 70. Osborne (*Revelation*, 147–48) agrees but lists other possibilities.

26. Beale, *Revelation*, 252. See Prigent, *Apocalypse*, 177.

27. Duvall, *Revelation*, 54.

28. Ryken, *Dictionary of Biblical Imagery*, 118. See Wong, "Hidden Manna," 346–49.

Sweet as Honey

John uses the common idiom "sweet as honey" to symbolize the pleasurable experience of receiving divine revelation. Honey was recognized for its sweetness (Judg 14:14), as medicine (Prov 16:24), and as a delicacy (Gen 43:11). It became a symbol for prosperity and abundance (Deut 32:13; Ps 81:16; Jer 41:8). The reception of divine revelation was often linked to the sweetness of honey (Ps 119:103; Ezek 3:3).[29] The phrase "sweet as honey" is found twice in Revelation when John relates eating the little scroll (10:9–10). John clearly alludes to the experience of Ezekiel and his reception of God's word (Ezek 3:3; NIV includes quote marks to denote this). John inverts Ezekiel's order, and follows a normal digestive track, thus alerting the reader to the fact they will first encounter sweetness (the promise of divine protection) and then bitterness (the call to martyrdom).[30] Thus, the scroll represents not only the sweetness of God's word but is at the same time a metaphor for brief pleasure, since John's received message is focused more on judgment.[31] This message of judgment against peoples, nations, languages, and kings will result in persecution and perhaps even death for those who witness for Christ.

Twelve Crops of Fruit

The monthly "twelve crops of fruit" imaged in the new Jerusalem figuratively expresses eternal salvation, along with its benefits, which is fully consummated in the new heaven and new earth. "Fruit" is found only twice in Revelation.[32] Both instances are located in one sentence in a passage that summarizes the new Jerusalem with several symbols. The angel shows John "the river of the water of life" along with the "tree of life, bearing twelve crops of fruit, yielding its fruit every month. And the leaves of the tree are for the healing of the nations" (22:1–2). Since there is no sun or moon in the new heaven and new earth (21:23; 22:5), the literal idea of an actual, annual fruit cycle makes no sense. Thus, the tree of life does not produce monthly fruit. Believers will not need to eat to maintain strength. John is simply drawing his symbolism from Ezek 47:12. Both prophets are using imagery "which corresponded to earthly realities that he could understand, to describe eternal realities beyond his comprehension."[33] This continues the picture of 21:4—there will be no more death, pain, or hunger. In sum, the fruit mentioned by John vividly symbolizes eternal life with God, including the benefits of "no more hunger." Thus, the twelve months of fruit-bearing combined with the twelve crops of fruit reinforces the numerical symbol of the completeness and fullness of eternal life for God's people.[34]

---

29. Ryken, *Dictionary of Biblical Imagery*, 396–97, 832–34.

30. J. C. Thomas, *Apocalypse*, 321.

31. Beale, *Revelation*, 551.

32. *Opōra* is found once in the NT at 18:14. It is often translated as "fruit" in English translations but literally means "good things" (see CEV, NCV, NLT).

33. Beale, *Revelation*, 1108. Patterson (*Revelation*, 376) states that since there is no season for productivity, "its production is perpetual."

34. Ibid. See Kiddle, *Revelation*, 442.

Wedding Supper of the Lamb

This image portrays the believer's intimate relationship and eternal fellowship with Christ that commences at the conclusion of history. "The wedding supper of the Lamb" is found once (19:9).[35] It draws on several images from the marriage banquet motif and portrays the blessings of joyful, eternal fellowship. Wedding ceremonies were rich symbols for OT writers. The promise of the messianic age was pictured as a wedding supper (Isa 25:6; 54:1–8; Hos 2:7). Jesus adapted the symbol for his arrival on the scene. His public ministry begins at a wedding feast (John 2:1–11). He is the messianic bridegroom (John 3:27–30) and likens his followers as friends of the bridegroom at a marriage feast (Matt 9:14–17; Mark 2:19–20). The kingdom of heaven is like a wedding banquet (Matt 8:11; 22:1–14; 25:1–13; Luke 14:15–24).[36] The fulfillment of this banquet is pictured at the conclusion of the fall of Babylon vision (19:6–10). The bride has made herself ready for the feast through her faith and good works and testimony of Jesus. At the conclusion of Revelation, the Spirit and the bride entreat the Lamb to "Come!" to the wedding feast (22:17). This feast, therefore, stands in sharp contrast to the "great supper of God" which unbelievers "attend" at history's end (19:17–18). Although the fulfillment of all the marital imagery awaits future consummation, the wedding supper of the Lamb is coming soon (22:20).[37] Thus, John uses imagery of a marriage ceremony to show the believer's eternal relationship and fellowship with God.

Wine

Wine is closely connected with other symbols (cup, drunkenness, great winepress) to emphasize divine, end-time judgment. Contrastingly, there is also the suggestion of wine as an element of joy connected with the wedding supper of the Lamb. The production of wine was intended as a celebratory symbol. People shared in the labor and enjoyed the harvest with shouts of joy, song, and dancing (Judg 21:21; Ps 104:15; Isa 16:10; Jer 48:33). Wine accompanied special occasions such as marriage feasts (Gen 29:22–25; John 2:1–11). The cultivation and care that went into the wine harvest finds its way into images of God's love for his people (Isa 5:1–7), and Jesus who is the true vine and whose followers produce fruit (John 15:1–17). Yet wine was also used as a symbol of divine judgment. Israel's

35. NIV stands alone for its choice of "wedding supper." Other versions choose (with differing word order) "banquet at the wedding celebration" (NET), "marriage feast" (CSB), "wedding meal" (NCV), "wedding banquet" (CEB, GW, REB), "wedding feast" (CEV, GNT, NABR, NJB, NLT), and "marriage supper" (ESV, NASB, NKJV, NRSV).

36. See Fekkes, "His Bride Has Prepared Herself," 269–87; Harrison and Yamauchi, "Banquets," 127–35; Hays, Duvall, and Pate, *Dictionary of Prophecy*, 271–72; Kuykendall, "Marriage of the Lamb," Pitre, "Jesus, the Messianic Banquet," 145–66; Priest, "Note on the Messianic Banquet," 222–38; Ryken, *Dictionary of Biblical Imagery*, 938–39. See the entry "Bride of the Lamb."

37. The majority of interpreters agree this supper image is intended for all saints—OT and NT. Dispensationalist interpreters, however, keep gentile and Jewish believers separate. The audience for the supper is the church, but not the redeemed of national, ethnic Israel. They are either absent or attend as guests of the bridegroom. So Hindson, *Revelation*, 192; LaHaye, *Revelation Unveiled*, 296; Robert Thomas, "Marriage Supper of the Lamb," 248; Walvoord, *Revelation*, 271–72.

disobedience affects the vineyards and wine production. All the hard work of cultivating and treading went for naught since the workers were not able to drink the wine (Deut 28:39). The prophets link disobedience with disaster by depicting wine shortages (Isa 24:7; Hos 2:12; Joel 1:7–12; Amos 5:11; Zeph 1:13). Isaiah describes a grisly picture of judgment as God's Messiah treads the winepress filled with people whose "juice" spatters his divine garments (Isa 63:1–6).[38] The apostle John draws deeply from this last image.

"Wine" (*oinos*) is found eight times in Revelation, seven referring to the fall of Babylon at the end of history, a numerical signal that indicates complete and full judgment. The lone exception is in the third seal where the rider is charged not to damage the oil and the wine, and is generally understood as famine and suffering (6:6). The other seven references to wine, however, are tied closely to Babylon the Great's final judgment. The great prostitute forces the wicked to drink "the maddening wine of her adulteries" (14:8; 17:2; 18:3). This imagery of drinking wine refers to the participation into a lifestyle or destiny.[39]

The Lord, on the other hand, forces the wicked to drink the wine of "the fury of his wrath" (14:10; 16:19). Next, a non-symbolic reference to wine is found in the list of cargoes no longer available to Babylon the Great (18:13). However, it is situated in the fall of Babylon vision and thus accompanies the other more symbolic references to wine. The final mention of wine is left untranslated by most Bible versions, due to stylistic redundancy and perhaps to match more closely its allusions (Isa 63:2–3; Joel 3:13). The NIV renders it, "He treads the winepress of the fury of the wrath of God Almighty" (19:15). This literally reads "the winepress of the wine of the wrath of the fury of God, the Almighty." A few versions do insert "wine" (GNT, NABR, NCV, and CEV renders "grapes" and NLT has "juice"). Thus, images of wine, winepress, drunkenness, and God's wrath are intricately connected, and all are found at the end of John's individual visions, depicting final judgment.

Nevertheless, there is also the hint of restoration and joy and eschatological blessing for God's people. The return of joy accompanied the return of wine production (Jer 31:11–14; Amos 9:13; Joel 2:24).[40] The prophets symbolized the coming messianic age as a marriage feast: "On this mountain the Lord Almighty will prepare a feast of rich food for all peoples, a banquet of aged wine—the best of meats and the finest of wines" (Isa 25:6; see 54:1–8; 62:4–5; Hos 2:7). Jesus adapts the wedding feast as a symbol for the coming of the messianic age.[41] He will not drink again from the fruit of the vine until the eschatological kingdom of God arrives (Mark 14:25; Luke 22:18). The writer of *4 Ezra* pictures a heavenly setting of a complete number of those who sit at the banquet, arrayed in robes of white (*4 Ezra* 2:38–41). All these pictures come to fruition in the wedding

---

38. Claassens, "Wine," 860–61. See Barry Bandstra, "Wine," 1068–72; Beck, *Dictionary of Imagery*, 112–14; Chambers, "Viticulture," 1681–90; Ryken, *Dictionary of Biblical Imagery*, 914–17; Schultz, "Wine and Strong Drink," 1083–87.

39. Osborne, *Revelation*, 538. The phrase can be taken epexegetically, that is, "the wine, which is her immorality" (Aune, *Revelation*, 2:831) or resultantly, "the wine that leads to her immorality" (Osborne, *Revelation*, 539).

40. Claassens, "Wine," 861; Ryken, *Dictionary of Biblical Imagery*, 953–54.

41. See the entry "Wedding Supper of the Lamb" for scriptural references.

supper of the Lamb (19:9). In sum, wine signals final judgment for the wicked but eternal joy for the faithful.

Clothing Images and Accessories

Clothing images serve an important function in Revelation. What the characters wear (or do not wear) speaks volumes. Apparel and decoration underscore John's penchant for contrasts. It highlights faithfulness or unfaithfulness, righteousness or unrighteousness. The condition and color of clothing along with its accoutrements is the subject of this section.[42]

Bow

The bow is a weapon that symbolizes victory through warfare. "Bow" (*toxon*) is found only once in the NT. The rider on a white horse carries a bow, an instrument of war (6:2).[43] Keener explains, "The biblical prophets also used the 'bow' as a metaphor for conquest no less than the 'sword' for war, though the image is associated most frequently with particular peoples known for such skills . . ."[44] The point of the first seal is conquest, militarism, and the lust for war.[45] Several scholars understand the rider in a positive light. This would place the bow as a positive image of the victory of the gospel message.[46] Overall, however, the negativity of the first seal coupled with its close connection with the riders in the subsequent three seals warrants a negative image of the bow as the lust for power and conquest through war.

Clothes

Clothing—whether it be white, soiled, bloodstained, or lacking altogether—is a common metaphor to represent one's faithful or unfaithful lifestyle, righteous or unrighteous activities, purity or pollution, and honor or dishonor. Clothing represents a major symbol in Scripture. "It is no exaggeration to say that one can trace the whole outline of biblical

42. Tōniste (*Ending of the Canon*, 117–18) traces several clothing images to Zech 3. "Holiness," she relates, "is no longer the exclusive privilege of the high priest; through Christ it belongs to all people."

43. See Ryken, *Dictionary of Biblical Imagery*, 41–42, for OT examples. Paul (*Revelation*, 144) associates the bow with Apollo. Thus, he considers pagan religion rather than war as the backdrop.

44. Keener, *Revelation*, 201.

45. So Beale, *Revelation*, 375–78; Beasley-Murray, *Revelation*, 131–32; Boring, *Revelation*, 122; Caird, *Revelation*, 80; Fee, *Revelation*, 93; Harrington, *Revelation*, 91; Alan Johnson, "Revelation," 13:652; Keener, *Revelation*, 201; Morris, *Revelation*, 101; Murphy, *Fallen Is Babylon*, 205; Osborne, *Revelation*, 277; Patterson, *Revelation*, 178; Resseguie, *Revelation*, 127; Roloff, *Revelation*, 86; Smalley, *Revelation*, 147–50; Witherington, *Revelation*, 133.

46. So Hendriksen, *More than Conquerors*, 113–17; Kistemaker, *Revelation*, 223–25; Ladd, *Revelation*, 98; Lupieri, *Apocalypse*, 143; Mulholland, *Revelation*, 168–70; Rowland, "Revelation," 12:611–12; Stefanovic, *Revelation*, 227–28; Sweet, *Revelation*, 137–39.

theology and salvation history through the motif of clothing."[47] Wedding garments symbolize celebration (Ps 45:13; Eccl 9:8; Isa 52:1; Matt 22:11–12) whereas coarse sackcloth symbolizes mourning (Gen 37:34; Ps 69:11; Isa 37:11). Stripping off clothes may symbolize subjection, humility, and humiliation (1 Sam 31:8; Job 12:7; Isa 45:1). Believers must take off their works of darkness and put on Christ (Rom 13:12; Eph 4:32; Col 3:9–10). Heavenly beings and even God wear clothes in order to make significant points, such as majesty (Ps 104:1), righteousness (1 Sam 17:5; Isa 59:17), vengeance (Exod 28:4), and victory (Isa 63:1).[48]

John assuredly has these images in mind for Revelation. Significantly, the noun for "clothes" (*himation*) is found seven times and the verb "to dress" (*periballō*) is found twelve times, indicative of John's numerical symbolism.[49] John utilizes several images to produce a theology of clothes. His areas of emphasis include dazzling clothes (1:13; 12:1; 15:6; 19:14); wedding clothes (21:2, 19); washed clothes (7:14; 22:14); clothes for mourning and repentance (11:3); soiled clothes (3:4); colorful clothes of white (6:11; 7:9; 19:8), purple (17:4), and scarlet (18:16); clothes dipped in blood (19:13); and no clothes at all (3:18; 16:5).

Crown

The crown is a symbol of power, honor, worthiness, royalty, authority, kingship, victory, and reward. Crowns are mentioned over seventy times in the Bible, and used for a variety of purposes. Crown imagery in the NT reveals three distinct senses. First, Paul refers to two churches as "his crown" (Phil 4:1; 1 Thess 2:19). Paul's labors in building these communities were a source of joy and his own royal adornment. Second, crowns are rewards for those who remain faithful to the gospel. Paul awaits his "crown of righteousness" that the Lord will award him "on that day" (2 Tim 4:8). In addition, James mentions the "crown of life" (Jas 1:12) and Peter the "crown of glory" (1 Pet 5:4). Third, Christ, the sinless one, laid aside his crown of honor and put on a crown of thorns. As exalted Lord, however, he will be adorned with a new crown fitting his authority and universal dominion.[50] It is the latter two senses that are used by John in Revelation.

Two Greek words are translated as "crown" in English Bible versions. The first is *stephanos*, found in Revelation eight times. Twice it refers to the victor's crown as a promised reward for faithful believers (2:10; 3:11).[51] The other six times includes the twenty-four elders who wear crowns (4:4, 10); the rider on the white horse in the first seal who is

---

47. Ryken, *Dictionary of Biblical Imagery*, 318.

48. Douglas Edwards, "Dress and Ornamentation," 232–38; Harrison and Yamauchi, "Clothing," 322–36; Mare, "Dress," 183–87; Matthews, "Cloth, Clothes," 691–96; Myers, "Clothe; Clothed," 724–25; Ryken, *Dictionary of Biblical Imagery*, 317–23. See the in-depth studies of Neufeld ("Sumptuous Clothing," 664–89; "Under the Cover of Clothing," 67–75).

49. Other words in John's clothing stockpile include "fine linen" (*byssinos*; five times), "robe" (*stolē*; five times), "dressed" (*endyō*; three times), "adorned" (*kosmeō*; two times), and "long robe" (*podērēs*; once).

50. Raffety, "Crown," 831–32; Ryken, *Dictionary of Biblical Imagery*, 185–86.

51. See the entry "Victor's Crown."

given a crown (6:2); demonic locusts who wear something like crowns (9:7); the woman clothed with the sun who wears a crown (12:1); and one like a son of man who is wearing a crown (14:14). All these picture victory, honor, and power, whether for good or evil.[52]

The second word translated "crown" is *diadēma*. It is usually reserved for a ruler's crown. All three NT uses are in Revelation and reserved for the dragon, the beast, and Christ. The dragon's introduction describes him as having seven crowns on his seven heads (12:3). Then the beast is introduced with ten crowns on his ten horns (13:1). Finally, Christ at his return is pictured with many crowns on his head (19:12). To differentiate *stephanos* from *diadēma* modern versions produce "crown" and "royal crown" (CEB), "crown" and "coronet" (NJB), and "crown" and "diadem crown" (NET). Several select "crown" and "diadem" (ESV, HCSB [except for 19:12], NABR, NASB, NKJV [for 12:1 only], NRSV, REB).[53]

Crowns, therefore, are pictured in two ways. One refers to believers and the crown of life, which represents eternal life. The second refers to royalty and privilege, and is presented as a contrast. For the dragon, beast, the rider in the first seal, and demonic locusts, crowns serve as a parody of Christ's honor and victory. They are nothing but imitations of the true crown-wearer. At the same time, their crowns reflect their own earthly power, and the numbers ten and seven underscore their complete power (see John 12:31; 14:30; 16:11; Eph. 2:2; 2 Cor. 4:4). By contrast, the crowns worn by the elders, the woman, one like the son of man, and the rider on the white horse project authority, dominion, majesty, and everlasting reign.

Fine Linen

Fine linen symbolizes power, status, wealth, and excess when applied to Babylon the Great, but holiness, righteousness, and good works when applied to saints and angels. "Linen" appears about one hundred times in the Bible. In the OT, it is presented as a "power fabric," a sign of status, wealth, and success for people and nations (Gen 41:42; Esth 8:15; Ezek 16:10–13). Linen also comprised part of the priest's garments (Exod 28–29; Lev 16). The Gospel writers connected this to the linen cloths used for Christ's burial (John 20:5–7), and Heb 7–8 identifies Christ as the perfect high priest. Thus, connecting linen to God and his messengers is another biblical motif (Dan 12:7).[54]

John extends these associations in Revelation. First, there is a solitary reference to "shining linen" (*lampron linon*), worn by the seven bowl angels (15:6).[55] Their linen and golden sashes connect them to the priest's adornment and symbolize their royal and

---

52. Koester (*Revelation*, 277–78) prefers the term "wreaths." They were made of laurel, myrtle, ivy, or similar foliage. The most valuable were made of gold. Stevenson ("Golden Crown Imagery," 257–72) makes further distinctions: the gold crowns (4:4, 10; 9:7; 14:14) express victory, royalty, divine glory, and honor.

53. HCSB's updated version, CSB, corrects 19:12.

54. Ryken, *Dictionary of Biblical Imagery*, 513–14.

55. "Shining" (GNT, GW, NCV, NIV, REB) is also translated as "bright" (CEB, CSB, ESV, NASB, NET, NKJV, NRSV) and "white" (CEV, NJB, NLT).

priestly functions.[56] But the primary word John selects for "fine linen" is *byssinos*. All five NT references are found in Rev 18–19. At the fall of Babylon the Great, the merchants of the earth mourn for their lost cargoes, which includes fine linen (18:12). They cry out, "Woe to you, great city, dressed in fine linen" (18:16). These references match OT imagery of fine linen to represent a nation's status and wealth.

The remaining references apply to believers. The wedding of the Lamb has come, and his bride has made herself ready. "Fine linen, bright and clean, was given her to wear. (Fine linen stands for the righteous acts of God's holy people)" (19:8).[57] The wedding clothes of the bride indicate purity (bright and clean), but John's parenthetical statement confirms what fine linen symbolizes—righteous acts performed by the righteous.[58] Thus, a transformed life filled with good works is the proper response to being justified by Christ. The final mention appears on those who follow behind the rider on the white horse. "The armies of heaven were following him, riding on white horses and dressed in fine linen, white and clean" (19:14). Scholars debate over the identity of "the armies of heaven." It seems likely that both angels and believers are in the group. Fine linen, therefore, reflects God's holiness, purchased for humanity by Christ. It is worn by the church when she weds Christ at the eschatological wedding supper, and to dwell for eternity in his glory.[59]

Golden Sash around His Chest

This image is a figure of royalty and authority of the one who wears it in order to deliver end-time judgment. The phrase is found twice in Revelation. In the inaugural vision, John sees Christ, "like a son of man, dressed in a robe reaching down to his feet and with a golden sash around his chest" (1:13). The golden sash may refer to what the high priest wore (Exod 28:4).[60] More likely it is a general reference of royalty that it is taken from Daniel's vision of a man dressed in linen, "with a belt of fine gold from Uphaz around his waist" (Dan 10:5).[61] The latter emphasis also seems closer to the understanding of the second reference. The seven angels who bring the bowls "were dressed in clean, shining linen and wore golden sashes around their chests" (15:6). Osborne states, "a golden sash symbolized royalty or elevated status and with 1:13 may indicate that these angels are

---

56. Smalley, *Revelation*, 390.

57. "The saints' acts of justice" (CEB) is an odd rendering as is "the things that God's holy people do that have his approval" (GW).

58. Osborne (*Revelation*, 674–75) recognizes a general genitive translation, i.e. primarily, righteous acts performed by the righteous. But it also represents righteous acts performed for the saints by God.

59. Ryken, *Dictionary of Biblical Imagery*, 514.

60. So Beale, *Revelation*, 209; Caird, *Revelation*, 25; Easley, *Revelation*, 18; Fee, *Revelation*, 17; Keener, *Revelation*, 94; Kistemaker, *Revelation*, 95; Mounce, *Revelation*, 57; Sweet, *Revelation*, 71; Witherington, *Revelation*, 81.

61. So Aune, *Revelation*, 1:93–94; Beasley-Murray, *Revelation*, 66; Blount, *Revelation*, 44; Brighton, *Revelation*, 50; Morris, *Revelation*, 53; Osborne, *Revelation*, 89; Robert Thomas, *Revelation*, 1:99–100. Some scholars mention both possibilities, including Ladd (*Revelation*, 32–33), Alan Johnson ("Revelation," 13:605), and Smalley (*Revelation*, 54).

emissaries of Christ, pouring out his judicial penalty on the evildoers."[62] Thus, whatever priestly allusions there are appear to be subsumed under the judgment emphasis. The point is royal authority to deliver end-time judgment.

Iron Scepter

This symbolizes the royal scepter and thus sovereign authority of Christ to rule and shepherd over the world, given from the Father and extended to his followers. The noun *rhabdos* ("rod") is mentioned four times in Revelation. Once it is called a "measuring" rod (11:1).[63] The other three times it is rendered in most English versions as an "iron" (*sidērous*) rod (2:27; 12:5; 19:15). However, NIV, CSB, GW, and NJB select "iron scepter" to underscore the aspect of royal rulership. These translations reveal two understandings of the iron rod/scepter. Scholars debate whether this authority (*exousia*) emphasizes rule over the nations (scepter) or to destroy the nations (rod).

The promise to the overcomers at Thyatira is stunning. Christ promises that they will "rule over the nations 'with an iron scepter' and 'dash them to pieces like pottery'— just as I have received authority from my Father" (2:27). This is almost a verbatim quote of Ps 2:8–9. This psalm celebrates the victory of God's anointed one over the kings of the earth, and was interpreted messianically from the first century BC onward (*Pss. Sol.* 17:23–24). John, however, replaces the Psalmist's choice of "inheritance" for "authority" (*exousia*). Thus, the followers of Jesus are in some fashion promised a share in his final rule and final judgment (Matt 19:28; 1 Cor 6:3; 2 Tim 2:12; Rev 1:6; 3:21; 5:10; 20:4, 6).

Scholars disagree not only on whether this authority means to rule over the nations or the power to destroy the nations. John adopts the LXX rendering of *poimainō* ("to shepherd") for the Hebrew verb "to rule." Yet the context of the violence of shattered pottery demands a translation of "rule." This is more in line with the Hebrew.[64] But the LXX rendering of "shepherd" forces interpreters to grapple with John's selection. Unsurprisingly, many exegetes see John stressing the shepherding aspect. Christ rules like the shepherd who wards off attacks with his iron rod.[65] Other scholars, however, maintain the strong language surrounding the verb overrules any idea of shepherding.[66]

A third way is possible. John purposefully gives a double meaning for both shepherd and judge/destroy. Jesus both "shepherds" the faithful and "smashes" the unfaithful.[67]

---

62. Osborne, *Revelation*, 570.

63. See the entry "Measuring Rod."

64. Aune (*Revelation*, 1:210) states that LXX translators simply misunderstood the vowel pointing for the Hebrew verb. See Mark Wilson, *Victor Sayings*, 136.

65. Brighton, *Revelation*, 84; Easley, *Revelation*, 42; Hemer, *Letters to the Seven Churches*, 124–25; Kistemaker, *Revelation*, 142; Morris, *Revelation*, 74; Mounce, *Revelation*, 90; Patterson, *Revelation*, 117; Skaggs and Benham, *Revelation*, 44; Swete, *Apocalypse*, 46; J. C. Thomas, *Apocalypse*, 157; Walvoord, *Revelation*, 77. The HCSB translated "rule" as "shepherd," but the CSB revised it to "rule."

66. Duvall, *Revelation*, 61; Osborne, *Revelation*, 167; Prigent, *Apocalypse*, 188; Robert Thomas, *Revelation*, 1:233. A few (Caird, *Revelation*, 45–46; Charles, *Revelation*, 1:75–76; Smalley, *Revelation*, 78) believe John made the same mistake as the LXX translators.

67. Beale, *Revelation*, 267. So too Keener (*Revelation*, 136), Koester (*Revelation*, 302), and Mark

The final two uses of *rhabdos* confirm this third option. The third interlude (12:1–15:4) begins with a telescopic history of Jesus. The woman clothed with the sun gives birth to a son who will rule all the nations with an iron scepter. Then, "her child was snatched up to God and to his throne" (12:5). This allusion to Christ's ascension implies that the messianic Son of God has fulfilled the prophecy of Ps 2:7–9. Christ's authority is delegated to his followers (Matt 28:18–19). Believers have the authority to rule, discipline, judge, and shepherd (1 Cor 6:2). Then in the rider on the white horse vision (19:11–21), a sword comes from his mouth "with which to strike down the nations. 'He will rule them with an iron scepter.' He treads the winepress of the fury of the wrath of God Almighty" (19:15). With this vision of the second coming, the fulfillment of Ps 2:7–9 is consummated. The faithful overcomers who have persevered now share in the messianic kingdom. They reign and rule, serve and shepherd with Christ.

Naked

Nakedness is a metaphor of humiliation. It reflects a lack of righteousness for the self-sufficient as well as the deserved judgment that comes from unpreparedness for the second coming. Nakedness evokes a wide range of images, including innocence, vulnerability, shame, guilt, judgment, and sexual impropriety (Isa 20:1–6; Ezek 16:37–39; 2 Cor 5:3; Heb 4:13). Even though some of these ideas overlap, each instance must be carefully identified within its biblical context.[68] "Naked" (*gymnos*) is found fifteen times in the NT. John mentions the word three times (3:17; 16:15; 17:16). "Nakedness" (*gymnotēs*) is found three times in the NT, once at Rev 3:18.

In all, three passages speak to nakedness. First, it is one of the five descriptors given to the lazy Laodiceans (3:17). They are charged to come to Christ "so you can cover your shameful nakedness" (3:18). With one article ("the") all five descriptions figuratively undress the arrogant, apathetic, and self-sufficient Laodiceans. Their humiliation will be complete in light of the coming judgment of God at the return of Christ.[69] Second, a parenthetical blessing is made by Christ in the middle of the sixth bowl, reminding persecuted Christians to be ready. "Look, I come like a thief! Blessed is the one who stays awake and remains clothed, so as not to go naked and be shamefully exposed" (16:15). Believers must be ready and alert for the second coming. They do not want to be found "naked" and humiliated at their lack of preparation. Spiritual vigilance is demanded in light of end-time events.[70] Finally, the last usage duplicates the stress on humiliation at judgment. The angel tells John that the beast turns on the great prostitute and will bring

Wilson (*Victor Sayings*, 137), the latter who states that *poimainō* has two meanings, "the first pastoral towards his people and the other authoritarian toward the nations."

68. Ryken, *Dictionary of Biblical Imagery*, 582. See Blaiklock, "Nakedness," 396; Knutson, "Naked," 480; Neufeld, "Sumptuous Clothing," 674–75, 682–83; Silva, "γυμνός," 610–12.

69. Osborne, *Revelation*, 209–10. Resseguie (*Revelation Unsealed*, 41) adds that nakedness symbolizes unrighteousness.

70. Beale, *Revelation*, 837. Smalley (*Revelation*, 411) interprets the idea as being picked up from 3:18, adding that the metaphor was used in the OT to represent God accusing Israel of unfaithful idolatry (Isa 20:1–6; Ezek 16:36; Nah 3:4–5).

her "to ruin and leave her naked" (17:16).[71] The shame of nakedness, then, has nothing to do with social impropriety. It is a metaphor for humanity's sinfulness being uncovered and exposed to the light of truth, and deserving of judgment.

Robe Dipped in Blood

The image of the Divine Warrior Christ dressed in a robe dipped in blood signifies final, complete, end-time judgment on the enemies of God, but may additionally allude to his own blood sacrificially shed to effect salvation for all. Two of John's major symbols are clothing and blood. He combines these two images in a vision of the second coming: "He is dressed in a robe dipped in blood, and his name is the Word of God" (19:13).

Scholars are divided on whose blood is found on the robe of the rider on the white horse. First, a few conclude that the blood-dipped robe is the blood of the martyrs.[72] Second, many surmise the blood is Christ's own, accenting a sacrificial aspect found throughout Revelation (1:5; 5:9; 7:14; 12:11). In addition, "dipped" sounds like his robe is already stained with blood before he arrives to earth.[73] English versions that aid this interpretation include "dyed" (CEB, REB); "stained" (HCSB); "covered" (CEV, GNT); and "soaked" (NJB). The word is *baptō*, found only four times in the NT. Some Greek manuscripts have "sprinkled," but such a reading surely comes from its allusion to Isa 63:3. Older Catholic versions such as Douay-Rheims follow this reading.[74] The majority of scholars, however, select a third possibility. They understand the blood as part of the end-time battle imagery, and thus it represents the blood of Christ's enemies. The imagery is drawn from Isa 63:1–6. Combined with the winepress imagery mentioned a few verses later, it emphasizes the Divine Warrior aspect of Jesus' return.[75]

Intriguingly, a few Bible students attempt to combine the latter two possibilities. Brighton agrees that John alludes primarily to Isa 63:1–6, and that the warrior-judge motif fits. But he adds that John must have had the blood of the Lamb in his mind as well. "For by the shedding of his own blood to defeat the enemy, and thus bring salvation to God's people, Christ earned the right now to judge those enemies by the shedding of their blood . . . Thus, the first blood that covers his garment is his own, but as he comes

---

71. Osborne (*Revelation,* 627) notes the metaphors of these verses "are powerful depictions of judgment."

72. Blount, *Revelation,* 352–53; Caird, *Revelation,* 242–44; Stefanovic, *Revelation,* 552.

73. So Bauckham, *Theology of Revelation,* 106; Boring, *Revelation,* 196–97; Boxall, *Revelation,* 274; Harrington, *Revelation,* 193–94; Krodel, *Revelation,* 323; Morris, *Revelation,* 224; Reddish, *Revelation,* 367; Resseguie, *Revelation,* 238; Rissi, *Future of the World,* 24; Rowland, "Revelation," 12:699; Sweet, *Revelation,* 283; Swete, *Apocalypse,* 252; J. C. Thomas, *Apocalypse,* 578; Wall, *Revelation,* 231.

74. Omanson, *Textual Guide,* 548.

75. So Aune, *Revelation,* 3:1057; Beale, *Revelation,* 957; Beasley-Murray, *Revelation,* 280; Easley, *Revelation,* 353–54; Fee, *Revelation,* 275; Alan Johnson, "Revelation," 13:759; Dennis Johnson, *Triumph of the Lamb,* 270–71; Keener, *Revelation,* 453–54; Kiddle, *Revelation,* 384; Kistemaker, *Revelation,* 521; Ladd, *Revelation,* 254; Mounce, *Revelation,* 353–54; Murphy, *Fallen Is Babylon,* 389; Osborne, *Revelation,* 682–83; Patterson, *Revelation,* 348; Paul, *Revelation,* 317; Roloff, *Revelation,* 218; Skaggs and Benham, *Revelation,* 199; Smalley, *Revelation,* 491; Robert Thomas, *Revelation,* 2:386–87; Walvoord, *Revelation,* 277; Witherington, *Revelation,* 242–43.

in judgment, at his second coming, his garment will be stained with the blood of his enemies (19:15)."[76] Similarly, Smalley holds the warrior-judge motif as primary. "Nevertheless, the sacrificial dimension of Christ's 'blood' would not have entirely escaped the Christian sensitivities of the seer and his audience at this point."[77] Therefore, in this particular end-time context, the warrior-judge idea prevails as John's principal image. Nonetheless, readers should also be mindful of the other metaphors for blood, including the atoning sacrifice of Christ, and even the "blood of the martyrs."

Sackcloth

Sackcloth is worn in times of mourning and repentance, particularly in light of forthcoming end-time judgment. This fabric made from goat hair or camel hair is usually dark in color. Wearing this clothing signified mourning and penitence because of its dark color or because of its being rough and uncomfortable.[78] Sackcloth appears frequently in the OT and often alongside "ashes" in contexts of grief and mourning (Gen 37:34; 2 Kgs 1:8; Isa 20:2; Zech 13:4) or sorrow and repentance over sins (1 Chr 21:16; Dan 9:3; Joel 1:8; Jonah 3:5).

John complements this image with allusions to end-time judgment. "Sackcloth" (*sakkos*) is mentioned twice. First, the cosmic imagery that accompanies the end of the world related in the sixth seal includes, "a great earthquake. The sun turned black like sackcloth made of goat hair, the whole moon turned blood red" (6:12). Thus, the added layer of symbolism that denotes mourning heightens this metaphoric image of the end.[79] The second reference occurs in the ministry of the two witnesses. John is instructed that, "I will appoint my two witnesses, and they will prophesy for 1,260 days, clothed in sackcloth" (11:3). The outward clothing in Revelation consistently reveals inner character. Here sackcloth emphasizes that the two witnesses must "conduct their prophetic ministry in a penitential attitude of humble and sacrificial service."[80] In addition, the plagues directed by the two witnesses and the justice exacted by God for their deaths are acts of judgment.[81] Thus, their message is one of mourning over sins and the necessary call to repentance as long as they are able in view of the nearness of judgment day.

Sickle

The sickle symbolizes the end-time harvesting of believers and unbelievers on judgment day. This entry could be placed under cosmic imagery, nature, or good things and bad things. It is placed here to emphasize its role as an accessory, like a sword or a crown. The sickle was a small, hand-held implement for harvesting standing grain.[82] Since the harvest is

---

76. Brighton, *Revelation*, 505, 521.

77. Smalley, *Revelation*, 491. See also Aune, *Revelation*, 3:1057.

78. Reddish, *Revelation*, 132. See Bratt, "Sackcloth," 229–30.

79. See the entry "Black as Sackcloth."

80. Brighton, *Revelation*, 291.

81. Blount, *Revelation*, 208–9.

82. See Howard, "Sickle," 499.

regularly used by Bible writers as a symbol for final judgment, this cutting tool naturally joins in the metaphor (Hos 6:11; Joel 3:13; Jer 51:33). "Sickle" (*drepanon*) is found eight times in the NT, seven of which are in Revelation. The only other reference to "sickle" is mentioned in Mark 4:29 in a parable that alludes to final judgment. John's mention of "sickle" seven times is intentional, emphasizing numerical symbolism that suggests the completeness and fullness of the judgment of the world is being signaled. The adjective "sharp" is added to four of those seven instances which further hints at full, earthly coverage.[83] All seven occurrences appear in one passage located near the end of the third interlude (14:14–20). The scene depicts the second coming of Christ in deliverance for the faithful and in judgment for the wicked. Thus, the sickle is used both positively and negatively. It reflects the great harvest at the conclusion of history—a grain harvest for the ingathering of the faithful, and a grape harvest for the gathering and judgment of the unfaithful. John utilizes the common instrument of the harvest—the sickle—to envision the action taking place.

Soiled Their Clothes

The image of "soiled clothes" symbolizes sinning in general, especially in idolatrous compromise with pagan culture. Soiled clothing is a symbol for sinfulness and it must be stripped from one's life (Rom 13:12; Eph 4:22; Col 3:9).[84] In Revelation, this expression is related once. The glorified Christ states that there are a few at Sardis who have not "soiled their clothes" (3:4). "Soiled" (*molynō*) is selected by most English translations (ESV, NABR, NASB, NIV, NRSV). Others pick "stained" (CEB, NET), "kept unstained" (NCV, NJB), "polluted" (REB), and "defiled" (CSB, NKJV). A few translations confirm that this image is one of sinfulness by adding a few words—"soiled their clothes with evil" (NLT) and "dirtied your clothes with sin" (CEV). This image builds on a major resource of wealth at Sardis, namely its dye and wool industry. Unlike the clothing they produce, their spiritual garments are "soiled" with sinfulness. Moreover, *molynō* suggests religious connotations. The other two uses in the NT are where one's conscience is "defiled" for eating meat sacrificed to idols (1 Cor 8:7), and where the hundred and forty-four thousand virgins are characterized as not being "defiled" by women (Rev 14:4).[85] Several OT allusions are available for John, but Zech 3:3–5 especially fits. Joshua the high priest stands in filthy clothes before the angel of the Lord. When they are removed and replaced by clean clothes, the angel from God says, "See, I have taken away your sin, and I will put fine garments on you."[86] Soiled clothes, then, are emblematic of polluting oneself with pagan and idolatrous culture. By contrast, overcomers do not stain their clothes with

---

83. Bauckham, *Climax of Prophecy*, 36; Kistemaker, *Revelation*, 5 n. 5. Osborne (*Revelation*, 551) adds that the emphasis on "sharpness" brings out the finality and power behind the judgment

84. For detailed discussions on clothing see Neufeld, "Sumptuous Clothing," 664–89; and Ryken, *Dictionary of Biblical Imagery*, 317–20.

85. Beale, *Revelation*, 276; Mounce, *Revelation*, 95; Osborne, *Revelation*, 178. Resseguie (*Revelation Unsealed*, 41) states that soiled garments signify the inner state of unfaithfulness and unworthiness.

86. J. C. Thomas, *Apocalypse*, 166.

accommodations to pagan culture, but remain faithful to the Lord, dressed in white and walking with Christ (3:5).

Sword

The sword reflects John's dualism. On the one hand, it indicates military, warlike, and state-sponsored execution. On the other hand, it symbolizes the divine, end-time judgment of Christ. The sword was the most important weapon of war in the ancient world. Most of its four hundred references in Scripture are literally understood. Yet symbolism is also noticeable. A sword generally connotes violence (Gen 27:40). The twenty uses in Psalms are outcries to God to deliver his people from the sword (Ps 17:13) or to destroy the wicked by the sword (Ps 7:12). Thus, the sword symbolizes divine judgment (Isa 34:6; Jer 12:12). The power of civil authorities to punish is depicted with a sword (Rom 13:4). The sword can also symbolize good. The Word of God is like a sword that has the power to penetrate and judge every aspect of life (Isa 49:2; Eph 6:17; Heb 4:12).[87]

John uses two words that are translated into English as "sword." First, *machaira* is found four times (6:4; 13:10 [twice], 14). The rider on a red horse is given a "large" (*mega*) sword (6:4), but *machaira* actually refers to a short knife for up close fighting.[88] Sword occurs twice as part of proverb taken from Jer 15:2: "If anyone is to go into captivity, into captivity they will go. If anyone is to be killed with the sword, with the sword they will be killed" (13:10). In other words, do not engage in active resistance against the beast.[89] Finally, the first beast is struck by the sword yet lives (13:14). This is a parody of Christ's death and resurrection. The sword may allude to Nero's suicide by dagger or to the sword of divine judgment.[90] All four references are metonyms for war and emphasize state, military, and political persecution.

Second, John uses *romphaia* six (of seven NT) times (1:16; 2:12, 16; 6:8; 19:15, 21). In 6:8 it refers to fourth horseman who kills with hunger and the sword. The other five references, however, symbolize Christ's role as eschatological judge. The "sharp, two-edged sword" that proceeds from Jesus' mouth (1:16) hearkens back to Isa 11:4 and 49:2 as a symbol of divine judgment. This image is reemphasized for the church at Pergamum (2:12, 16). Thus, Jesus' judgment is not only toward unrepentant enemies, but also against those who fake or compromise their Christian faith. Several scholars choose to emphasize the sword as the powerful and effective words of Christ that include comfort as well

---

87. Mare, "Armor, Arms," 352–59; Plümacher, "μάχαιρα," 397–98; Ryken, *Dictionary of Biblical Imagery*, 835–36; Swartley, "Sword," 409–10.

88. See the entry "Rider on a Red Horse."

89. There are several variants found for 13:10 that nuance the emphasis from perseverance to future vindication. See Mathewson, *Revelation*, 176; and Omanson, *Textual Guide*, 537–38. The reading of UBS5 is preferred and supported by most English versions and commentators. Thorough discussions include those by Aune (*Revelation*, 2:749–51), Beale (*Revelation*, 704–7), Koester (*Revelation*, 575–76, 586–87), Lambrecht ("Rev 13, 9–10," 331–47), Osborne (*Revelation*, 505–6), and Robert Thomas (*Revelation*, 2:166–71). Thus, the more passive resistance reading serves as a corrective to liberation theologians and popular dispensationalists.

90. Bauckham, *Climax of Prophecy*, 433; Osborne, *Revelation*, 515.

as reprimand.[91] This may well rest in the background but the judgment motif appears much stronger and connects better with the final two references (19:15, 21).[92] The sword as an element of end-time judgment is confirmed by the added phrase "in order that he should strike the nations."

Victor's Crown

This image symbolizes eternal salvation, everlasting life, and heavenly rewards yet also challenges believers to live victoriously now even in the midst of persecution. The victor's crown is mentioned twice in Revelation. The majority of versions produce a literal rendering of "crown of life" (*stephanon tēs zōēs*). Exceptions include "life as your victor's crown" (NIV), "crown that is life itself" (NET), "I will reward you with a glorious life" (CEV), and "life as your prize of victory" (GNT). The popular idea of a crown for glorified believers misunderstands the image. The Greek phrase is best understood appositively, that is, "the crown, namely, life."[93] This phrase then is a common metaphor for eternal life along with its heavenly rewards. The first mention is the promise of a victor's crown to the overcomers at Smyrna (2:10). Second, a warning not to fall away is found in the letter to Philadelphia. There Christ states, "I am coming soon. Hold on to what you have, so that no one will take your crown" (3:11). Again, heavenly rewards are in view. Some readers may envision a loss of salvation here, but John's intention is that judgment is for both believers and unbelievers. Similar to 2:5; 21:8; 22:18–19, the believer will also be judged (2 Cor 5:10). Christians must persevere on earth not out of fear of the loss of salvation but out of the loss of reward. It is better, then, to see a challenge to believers to maintain their Christian walk lest they lose the race and forfeit their heavenly rewards. Thus, the metaphor emphasizes future rewards in 2:10 whereas it stresses present status in 3:11. The race is ready to be run in 2:10 and the race is already won in 3:11.[94]

Wash Their Robes

This is a metaphor for the spiritual cleansing which believers receive from Christ through salvation and continual perseverance. Words for washing are generally associated with ceremonial cleansings, but figuratively connected to cleansing from sin and guilt.[95] "Wash" (*plynō*) is found twice in Revelation.[96] On both occasions it refers to the same

91. So Koester, *Revelation*, 253; Ladd, *Revelation*, 33; Patterson, *Revelation*, 69; Rotz, *Revelation*, 56.

92. So Beale, *Revelation*, 211; Duvall, *Revelation*, 53; Mounce, *Revelation*, 60; Osborne, *Revelation*, 92; Skaggs and Benham, *Revelation*, 29; Walvoord, *Revelation*, 45.

93. Beasley-Murray, *Revelation*, 82–83; Smalley, *Revelation*, 67; Robert Thomas, *Revelation*, 1:173. See NET footnote.

94. Osborne, *Revelation*, 195. Even better, as Sandy (*Plowshares and Pruning Hooks*, 28–31) mentions, the crown of life symbolizes a singular reward—the reward of deity and humanity in perfect unity in eternity (Rev 21:3). Zimmerman ("Nuptial Imagery," 153) adds that the crown of life is a bridal wreath, underscoring the rich marital imagery that is found throughout Revelation.

95. See Gay ("Wash," 1022) for biblical examples.

96. In 1:5, NKJV follows TR's reading of *lousanti* ("washed") rather than *lysanti* ("loosed/released/

audience (7:14; 22:14).[97] At the conclusion of the first interlude, one of the elders identifies the great multitude. They "have come out of the great tribulation; they have washed their robes and made them white in the blood of the Lamb'" (7:14). Robes turned white by washing them in blood forms a striking paradox. It hearkens back to Exod 19:10 where the Israelites are entreated to wash their clothes in anticipation of God's descent from the mount. Moreover, Isaiah compares the righteous acts of Israel to "filthy rags" (Isa 64:6) yet elsewhere promises "Though your sins are like scarlet, they shall be as white as snow" (1:18).[98] The most likely background, however, comes from Dan 11:35 where some of the wise will stumble "so that they may be refined, purified, and made white until the time of the end" (ESV). Thus, it is the blood of the Lamb on the cross that provides white robes for the great multitude. The aorist tense suggests a once for all washing, and implies the completeness of the effects of salvation.[99] It is a fitting image as the great multitude stands before the throne on judgment day.

The second "washing" occurs in the final beatitude. "Blessed are those who wash their robes, that they may have the right to the tree of life and may go through the gates into the city" (22:14).[100] The previous mention was addressed to the saints in the eschaton whose robes have been washed once for all (aorist tense). Here Jesus urges the saints on earth (beginning with John's audience onward) to wash their robes again and again (present tense). Thus, the believer's "salvific perseverance" is depicted with an image of continually washing their robes. It connotes the sanctification process of the Christian life. The present tense accentuates the continuing practice of purifying (Heb 9:14; 1 Pet 1:2; 1 John 1:7).[101] Washing robes, then, is a potent picture of the effect of Christ's salvation and the call for believers to grow and persevere in their lives.

---

freed"). Patterson (*Revelation*, 61 n. 12) states that since the two words sound the same the original text cannot be determined with certainty. However, UBS5 gives an {A} rating for *lysanti*. Omanson (*Textual Guide*, 526) confirms the variant reading of "washed" could easily come from an error of sight or hearing.

97. Some interpreters limit the audience of 7:14 to martyrs only or to a select group of end-time saints. For example, Robert Thomas (*Revelation*, 1:496) understands a durative force of the present tense, i.e. "those who are in the process of coming" out of the great tribulation, which for Thomas is still occurring since Christ does not return until chapter 19. Patterson (*Revelation*, 203) agrees with Thomas. The washed saints are the "144,000 Jews and a great company of Gentiles who are actually saved during the great tribulation . . ."

98. Mounce, *Revelation*, 165.

99. Osborne, *Revelation*, 325. Some interpreters (Barr, *Tales*, 88; Prigent, *Apocalypse*, 292–93) understand the washing to refer to baptism. Others (Aune, *Revelation*, 2:474–75; Ford, *Revelation*, 127; Mulholland, *Revelation*, 183) find martyrdom in the image.

100. TR/KJV/NKJV reads "do his commandments" in place of "wash their robes." Few scholars agree with TR's reading. One, however, is Goranson ("Text of Revelation 22:14," 154–57), who cites patristic references, literary analysis, and consistency with the worldview in Revelation. Nevertheless, the best manuscripts confirm "wash their robes," and it is given an {A} rating by UBS4. Interestingly, UBS5 does not show a rating and must be a typographical oversight.

101. Beale, *Revelation*, 1138; Kistemaker, *Revelation*, 590. Mounce (*Revelation*, 407) recalls the story of Jesus washing Peter's feet (John 13:10). A person who has had a bath needs only to wash his feet.

White Clothes/Robes

White clothes and robes emphasize purity, dignity, and victory. Moreover, they signify eternal life and heavenly rewards given to the faithful who persevere through and are purified by suffering. White clothes and robes are a common feature in extratextual literature, usually as a sign of the glory of heavenly reward (*1 En.* 62:16; *2 En.* 22:8; *Ascen. Isa.* 4:16; 8:14; *4 Ezra* 2:39–44). White is also the clothing of God (Dan 7:9) and heavenly beings (Matt 28:3). At Jesus' transfiguration white robes suggested celebration and victory (Matt 17:2; Mark 9:3; Luke 9:29). "White robes, therefore, are an appropriate symbol for eternal life."[102]

John complements these characteristics. The characters in Revelation who wear white clothes and robes are always good people. Most English translations use *himation* ("clothes") and *stolē* ("robes") interchangeably. References to robes (6:11; 7:9, 13, 14), however, stress heavenly rewards more than clothing. A white "long robe" (*podērēs*) is found once (1:13). In Christ's inaugural vision it symbolizes the dress of a priest and perhaps the dignity and honor befitting a person of high rank.[103] Dignity is also evoked in the white robes of the twenty-four elders (4:4). Purity, victory, and heavenly rewards are suggestive in the white clothes of the faithful at Sardis (3:4–5), martyrs under the altar (6:11), the great multitude (7:9, 13), and the armies of heaven (19:14). All these references connote purity and rewards as a result of a persevering faith.

---

102. Reddish, *Revelation*, 72.

103. Winkle ("Clothes Make the [One Like a Son of] Man") presents a full study on the long robe that Jesus wears in chapter 1. He concludes that it is refers to high priestly wear.

8

Institutions and Worship Accoutrements

SEVERAL IMAGES IN REVELATION refer to institutions and their accompanying worship elements. Entries are scattered throughout this study that could serve as candidates for this chapter. For example, "Souls under the Altar," "Hidden Manna," and "God's People" are found elsewhere. This chapter, however, gathers together and summarizes John's developed teaching on the subject.

Institutional Images

This section reflects the great institutions such as synagogue and temple, prophets and priests. These Jewish images are expanded by John to incorporate the church and apostles.

Apostles

John enlarges the role of apostles to designate all believers, underscoring the role that every Christian is an ambassador of Christ. "Apostle" (*apostolos*) is used in the NT in two ways—in a general sense of a representative or messenger, and specifically as a fixed designation of a definite office.[1] John has both usages in mind for the three occurrences of the word (2:2; 18:20; 21:14). It is possible that John reserves the use of "apostles" for leaders chosen by God for the church. Many commentators adopt this view. Yet John consistently expands and universalizes numerous formerly narrow terms. If this is so for his use of apostle, then he is accentuating the role of every believer as one who is sent, a representative, an envoy, an apostle of Christ.

First, the congregation at Ephesus is successful in testing those who claim to be apostles but are not (2:2). Some scholars understand these false apostles as representative messengers who travel from church to church.[2] Thus, they called themselves divinely

---

1. D. Muller, "Apostle," 1:128–35. The verb *apostellō* ("send out") is found three times (1:1; 5:6; 22:6).

2. Morris, *Revelation*, 59; Ladd, *Revelation*, 38. Sweet (*Revelation*, 81) calls them itinerant teachers. Osborne (*Revelation*, 114) suggests that they may claim apostleship and the accompanying authority for themselves, similar to the super-apostles that Paul encountered (2 Cor 11:5; 12:11).

chosen leaders, but the church at Ephesus saw through their deception, tested them, and labeled them heretics.[3] Next, three groups are called on to rejoice because of God's righteous end-time judgment of Babylon. "Rejoice over her, you heavens! Rejoice, you people of God! Rejoice, apostles and prophets! For God has judged her with the judgment she imposed on you" (18:20).[4] Many scholars distinguish between the three groups in this verse. The first group represents all believers and the last two groups are leaders within the early church—apostles and prophets.[5] Other scholars, however, interpret the three groups as believers in general. In other words, all Christians are commanded to rejoice because God's end-time judgment has arrived.[6] The phraseology is balanced. In contrast to the mourning of kings, merchants, and sailors (who represent sinful humanity), the saints, apostles, and prophets rejoice (representing the people of God). Thus, the three groups fall under the "apostleship" (and "prophethood") of all believers. The third reference is found in the vision of the new Jerusalem. John describes its architecture which includes, "The wall of the city had twelve foundations, and on them were the names of the twelve apostles of the Lamb" (21:14). In this instance, the twelve original apostles are clearly intended. Coupled with the twelve tribes, however, they plainly represent the collective people of God. Israel and the church, the old and the new covenants, form a unity in the celestial city.[7] Thus, John may have the official office of apostle in mind for 2:2. But 18:20 and 21:14 imply that John uses the term as another of his numerous designations for the people of God.

Priests

This is a designation for all believers who serve a dual priestly role. On the one hand, they have unlimited access to the presence of God through Christ. On the other hand, it is a reminder that they are the chosen people of God and should reflect Christ's saving light to

3. Many scholars suggest they may be connected to the Nicolaitans (2:6), including Beasley-Murray (*Revelation*, 74), Easley (*Revelation*, 34), Kistemaker (*Revelation*, 113), Osborne (*Revelation*, 113), Patterson (*Revelation*, 84), Smalley (*Revelation*, 61), and Sweet (*Revelation*, 81).

4. The TR/KJV/NKJV reading omits *kai oi* before *apostoloi* at 18:20, resulting in a translation of "holy apostles and prophets." However, modern versions and scholars agree that John refers to three groups, not two.

5. So Aune, *Revelation*, 3:1007; Caird, *Revelation*, 230; Duvall, *Revelation*, 245; Fee, *Revelation*, 259; Koester, *Revelation*, 708; Osborne, *Revelation*, 654; Patterson, *Revelation*, 336–37; Paul, *Revelation*, 300; Prigent, *Apocalypse*, 511; Witherington, *Revelation*, 231. Beasley-Murray (*Revelation*, 268) suggests that "people of God" refer to all the saints, "prophets" to the OT saints, and "apostles" to NT saints. Keener (*Revelation*, 432) finds a distinction to support the ministries of apostles and prophets for every era. Robert Thomas (*Revelation*, 2:342) and Kistemaker (*Revelation*, 500) are even more specific: they represent only the original twelve apostles.

6. So Beale, *Revelation*, 916; Mounce, *Revelation*, 336; Roloff, *Revelation*, 207; Smalley, *Revelation*, 460; J. C. Thomas, *Apocalypse*, 542–43; Waddell, *Spirit in Revelation*, 176–77.

7. A few commentators, however, opt for a more literal understanding of the Holy City with actual gates and foundations with twelve names attached. Robert Thomas (*Revelation*, 2:465) and Walvoord (*Revelation*, 322) suggest that the mention of the two entities teach the election of ethnic Israel and the church and that separate roles for the two peoples will continue in the new Jerusalem. Thus, even in eternity, some interpreters perpetuate ethnic distinctions.

the world. One of the numerous OT terms originally applied to Jews but now applied to Christians is "priests." The majority of references in Scripture involve Jewish priests of the old covenant. Yet being a "priest" referred to one's redeemed status, not their functions and duties. Only a few priests actually ministered in the temple, but all were considered priests in the land. In Exod 19:6, God assigned the nation of Israel to serve as priestly mediators between God and surrounding nations (Isa 43:10–13). Israel's identity then as a nation of priests primarily indicated their redeemed status.[8]

This understanding is sustained in the NT where the image of God's chosen people as a nation of priests is changed into the image of the priesthood of believers in Christ (1 Pet 2:9).[9] "Priest" (*hiereus*) occurs thirty-one times in the NT. In the Gospels and Acts it is found fourteen times and refers to Jewish priests (and once to a priest of Zeus in Acts 14:13). In Hebrews it is found fourteen times, emphasizing how Christ has taken on the high priest's duties by virtue of his exaltation. This leaves three references in Revelation (1:6; 5:10; 20:6).[10] It is here that the priesthood of believers is most evident. Christ's death and resurrection established a twofold office—king and priest. This twofold office was extended to believers who are now kings and priests. Since Jesus mediated God's truth as priest through his sacrifice and faithful witness to the world, believers spiritually fulfill the same two roles by following his example.[11]

John's first mention involves his greeting to the seven churches. It includes a dedication to Jesus who "has made us to be a kingdom and priests to serve his God and Father—to him be glory and power for ever and ever! Amen" (1:6). *Basileian hiereis* has produced a few English translation possibilities. It could be hendiadys, thus "a kingdom and priests" (NIV, NKJV, NRSV). The best rendering, however, is to view "priests" in apposition to "kingdom," thus producing "a kingdom, as priests" (NET), "a kingdom of priests" (GNT, NCV, NJB, NLT), and most popularly, "a kingdom, priests" (CEB, CSB, ESV, GW, NABR, NASB).[12]

Second, heavenly beings conclude their new song to the Lamb with "You have made them to be a kingdom and priests to serve our God, and they will reign on the earth" (5:10). *Basileian kai hiereis* confirms again the effects of Christ's salvific work. The priesthood of all believers in a royal-priestly reign was inaugurated at the cross.[13] The future

---

8. Ryken, *Dictionary of Biblical Imagery*, 663. See Cheung, "Priest as Redeemed Man," 265–75.

9. Feinberg and Fee, "Priests and Levites," 963–85; Moulder, "Priesthood in the NT," 963–65. Boring ("Priests in the NT," 613) states that the use of the term priest to designate a class of ordained Christian ministers distinct from the laity is not found until the second century.

10. Elgvin ("Priests on Earth," 257–78) lists several other possible allusions to priests or the priesthood.

11. Beale, *New Testament Biblical Theology*, 678. See A. J. Bandstra, "Kingship and Priests," 10–25.

12. TR/KJV/NKJV reads "kings and priests" (*basileis kai hiereis*).

13. TR/KJV/NKJV reads you have made "us" to be a kingdom and "we" will reign. However, the pronouns "them" and "they" are given an {A} rating by UBS5. Omanson (*Textual Guide*, 531–32) confirms the "us"/"we" reading is a secondary development that is found only in NJKV among modern editions. Patterson (*Revelation*, 170–73) and Walvoord (*Revelation*, 117–18) prefer the TR reading because it supports their interpretation of a future millennial reign on earth for the saints. It also allows the twenty-four elders to be saints, not angels.

tense "will reign" (*basileusousin*) is a gnomic future, not a predictive future. Thus, it emphasizes how Christians reign now in a spiritual way.[14]

Finally, "Blessed and holy are those who share in the first resurrection. The second death has no power over them, but they will be priests of God and of Christ and will reign with him for a thousand years" (20:6). In the first two references the redeemed are called priests. Here they serve as priests, sharing in Christ's eternal reign. When believers die they continue their function as priests and kings, "because their intimate communion with Christ will last indefinitely (see v. 4)."[15] All three passages parallel and inform each other. The victorious church shares in Christ's royal and priestly status. This priestly kingdom refers to believers who through inaugurated eschatology serve and reign with Christ now and forever.

Prophecy

John's book is a word of prophecy. Although this includes future prediction, it primarily reveals truths which demand from its readers appropriate ethical living in the present. Prophecy was common in the ancient Near East, and a prophet's words were highly esteemed. The themes of prophecy in the Gospels include kingdom warnings (Matt 3:7; 23:33), judgments (Matt 12:30; 25:32–34), requirements (Luke 3:3; 24:47), conditions (Matt 5:43–44), and especially the consummation (Matt 24–25; Mark 13; Luke 17, 21). Prophecies are also found in Paul (1 Thess 4–5; 2 Thess 2; 1 Tim 4; 2 Tim 3), Peter (2 Pet 3), and John (1 John 4).[16] The noun "prophecy" (*prophēteia*) is found seven times in Revelation (1:3; 11:6; 19:10; 22:7, 10, 18–19), signifying numerical symbolism that pictures the Apocalypse as the perfect and consummate fulfillment of all biblical prophecy.

The first reference is in the prologue. Every word of John's book to the churches is a "word of prophecy" (1:3). This confirms that John is not writing only in Jewish apocalyptic terms but is delivering an epistolary-prophetic apocalypse. His numerous OT allusions attest that he continues the prophet's role. Second, the two witnesses (the church) are prophets (11:10) and "it does not rain during the days of their prophecy" (11:6 CSB).[17]

---

14. Koester (*Revelation*, 380–81) notices that several Greek manuscripts have the present tense in place of the future tense. This may be an inadvertent scribal error or more likely intentional to emphasize the believer's current spiritual reign.

15. Kistemaker, *Revelation*, 541. A few commentators (Beckwith, *Apocalypse*, 429; Prigent, *Apocalypse*, 120; Schüssler Fiorenza, *Revelation*, 62) assert this refers only to a future reign. The majority of scholars understand these verses (1:6; 5:10; 20:6) to support a present active reign of believers that consummates in the eschaton. Dispensationalists agree with a present reign but accentuate a future millennial kingdom where the saints share Christ's earthly rule (so Robert Thomas, *Revelation*, 1:71, 402; Walvoord, *Revelation*, 38–39). Beale (*Revelation*, 194–95) lists six reasons why believers presently reign as kings and priests.

16. Grudem, "Prophecy, Prophets," 701–10; Hays, Duvall, and Pate, *Dictionary of Prophecy*, 353–56; MacRae, "Prophets and Prophecy," 992–1028; David Petersen, "Prophet, Prophecy," 622–48; Ryken, *Dictionary of Biblical Imagery*, 667–68; Gary Smith, "Prophet; Prophecy," 986–1004.

17. For stylistic reasons English versions turn the noun "prophecy" into the verb "prophesying" at 11:6. Only CSB and NKJV translate "prophecy" which aids in noticing the numerical symbolism. The verb "prophesy" (*prophēteuō*) is found twice (10:11; 11:3).

Third, the vision of Babylon's fall concludes with the angel's call to "Worship God! For it is the Spirit of prophecy who bears testimony to Jesus" (19:10). Many scholars (followed by English versions) understand "Spirit" (*pneuma*) to mean the "essence" or "heart" of prophecy. Blount, for instance, states that John "is speaking here, then, not about the Spirit of God, but about the role of human witnesses . . ."[18] Nevertheless, a number of commentators accept that John is referring to the Holy Spirit. It is the "Spirit who gave the prophecy" or "the Spirit-inspired prophecy." Robert Thomas comments: "this statement means that the testimony given by Jesus is the substance of what the Spirit inspires Christian prophets to speak."[19] Further support is available through numerical symbolism. If 19:10 is read this way then it confirms exactly fourteen references to the Spirit (7 x 2).[20] The point is that the witness of Jesus is deeply connected to the Holy Spirit of prophecy.[21]

The fourth occurrence is at the close of the new Jerusalem vision: "Look, I am coming soon! Blessed is the one who keeps the words of the prophecy written in this scroll" (22:7).[22] This blessing repeats 1:3. The content of the prophecy is the book itself with all the apocalyptic symbols, imminent events, and hortatory challenges.[23] The last three occurrences are in the epilogue. The angel instructs John, "Do not seal up the words of the prophecy of this scroll, because the time is near" (22:10). The point of the prophecy is to reveal not conceal. The churches must hear and obey its contents. Finally, "I warn everyone who hears the words of the prophecy of this scroll: If anyone adds anything to them, God will add to that person the plagues described in this scroll. And if anyone takes words away from this scroll of prophecy, God will take away from that person any share in the tree of life and in the Holy City, which are described in this scroll" (22:18–19). With a final warning (drawn from Deut 4:2), the risen Christ confirms the importance of this prophecy and warns against those who foster false teaching.[24]

18. Blount, *Revelation*, 348. So too Beale, *Revelation*, 947; Easley, *Revelation*, 352; Harrington, *Revelation*, 187; Hughes, *Revelation*, 202; Ladd, *Revelation*, 251; Michaels, *Revelation*, 214; Mounce, *Revelation*, 351; Murphy, *Babylon Is Fallen*, 385; Patterson, *Revelation*, 346; Reddish, *Revelation*, 365; Witherington, *Revelation*, 234.

19. Robert Thomas, *Revelation*, 2:377. So too Aune, *Revelation*, 3:1039; Beasley-Murray, *Revelation*, 276; Boring, *Revelation*, 194; Brighton, *Revelation*, 502; Caird, *Revelation*, 233; Duvall, *Revelation*, 252; Fee, *Revelation*, 269; Keener, *Revelation*, 452; Kistemaker, *Revelation*, 518; Koester, *Revelation*, 732; Morris, *Revelation*, 222; Osborne, *Revelation*, 678; Paul, *Revelation*, 311; Smalley, *Revelation*, 487; Sweet, *Revelation*, 281; Swete, *Apocalypse*, 249; J. C. Thomas, *Apocalypse*, 572–73; Walvoord, *Revelation*, 273.

20. Bauckham, *Theology of Revelation*, 110. See the entry "(Holy) Spirit."

21. Nevertheless, only the NIV and CEV capitalize "Spirit" (CSB has it as an alternate reading in a footnote). Since a majority of scholars favor "Spirit," then future editions of modern versions should consider capitalizing the word.

22. There is disagreement on who is speaking to John. Many assume it is Christ (Brighton, *Revelation*, 643; Easley, *Revelation*, 417; Fee, *Revelation*, 308; Kistemaker, *Revelation*, 586; Mounce, *Revelation*, 404; Mulholland, *Revelation*, 333). But it is more likely an angel, the same one who speaks at the beginning of the vision (21:9–22:9).

23. Beale, *Revelation*, 1127.

24. Again, who is speaking is debated. John or an angel is possible, but most commentators understand it is Jesus himself, especially since it parallels 22:16, 20. For example, see Blount, *Revelation*, 413; Kistemaker, *Revelation*, 592; Koester, *Revelation*, 844; and Osborne, *Revelation*, 794. Robert Thomas ("Spiritual Gift of Prophecy," 201–16) appeals to 22:18 to support his cessationist perspective on the gift of prophecy. Osborne (*Revelation*, 796 n. 16) offers effective critique to Thomas.

Thus, prophecy nurtures obedience to God. Scott Duvall delivers an effective summary. Prophecy must be understood "primarily as proclamation rather than prediction. The book isn't predicting when Christ will return so much as telling us how to live in light of the imminence of his certain return (cf. Rom. 3:11; 1 Pet. 4:7)."[25]

Prophets

Prophets represent all believers who fulfill the task of delivering God's messages despite persecution and martyrdom. Prophets were important figures in the OT. They were called by God and portrayed a sense of urgency concerning their messages (Isa 6:1–13; Jer 1:5–10). They reproduced God's word (Deut 18:15–18). Many experienced visions and dreams (Dan 7:1–27). Prophets often used symbolic actions to deliver their messages (Hos 1:6–9; Isa 7:1–3; Ezek 4:1–13).[26] When considering the NT, John the Baptist certainly fits the role of a prophet (Matt 3:7–10; Luke 3:7–9). Jesus is identified as a prophet (Luke 4:24; 7:16). Paul mentions prophets, prophetic giftedness, and prophecies in his letters (1 Cor 12:28; 14:1–5; Eph 4:11; 1 Thess 5:19–21). John also fulfills the role of prophet in Revelation (1:3; 10:11; 22:7, 10, 18–19).[27] But John expands the role of prophets to emphasize the "prophethood of all believers."[28]

Prophētai is found eight times (10:7; 11:10, 18; 16:6; 18:20, 24; 22:6, 9), each time in plural form. The final seven references are found near the conclusion of five individual visions, suggesting a stronger role of prophethood near the eschaton.[29] Following other scriptural usages, many Bible students make a distinction of prophets as a specially called group within the Christian community.[30] Several scholars, however, view the term simply as a general description for all believers. Like the "priesthood of the believer" so too the "prophethood of the believer."[31] Thus, God announces his purposes of salvation to his servants the prophets (10:7). The two witnesses—representing all believers—are also prophets (11:10) who "prophesy" (11:3). God rewards the prophets in the eschaton (11:18). Those who persecute and kill the prophets will received due recompense (16:6). But the persecuted prophets rejoice at the judgment of Babylon the Great (18:20, 24), and it is God who inspires the prophets, such as John (22:6, 9). Each usage is easier explained by a general description comprising the Christian community. All believers must prophesy God's message.

---

25. Duvall, *Revelation*, 305.

26. Ryken, *Dictionary of Biblical Imagery*, 670–74. See David Petersen, "Prophet, Prophecy," 4:622–48.

27. Hays, Duvall, and Pate, *Dictionary of Prophecy*, 357–58.

28. Boring, *Revelation*, 142.

29. Jezebel calls herself a "prophetess" (*prophētis*) in 2:20.

30. Bauckham, *Climax of Prophecy*, 160–62; Kistemaker, *Revelation*, 345; Koester, *Revelation*, 840; Mounce, *Revelation*, 295; Osborne, *Revelation*, 446; Robert Thomas, *Revelation*, 2:253, 342, 501.

31. So Beale, *Revelation*, 617, 1128; Blount, *Revelation*, 403; Boring, *Revelation*, 142; Caird, *Revelation*, 129; Prigent, *Apocalypse*, 636–37; Smalley, *Revelation*, 292, 568; J. C. Thomas, *Apocalypse*, 349, 671.

Seven Churches

The seven churches represent the universal church throughout the centuries. The church is charged with being a victorious witness for Christ and exhorted not to compromise. "Church" (*ekklēsia*) occurs over a hundred times in the NT. It can refer to the local assembly of God's people or to the universal community of believers. Acts and Paul's letters hold over half of the references. *Ekklēsia* is found twenty times in Revelation, nineteen times in chapters 1–3 and once at 22:16.[32] The churches that John addressed reside in seven cities of the Roman province of Asia on the west central coast of Asia Minor (1:4, 11, 20). The seven letters form a distinct literary unit (2:1–3:22).[33]

Christ delivers a personal message to each church. The order of the letters is originally geographical, following an ancient postal route.[34] The messages contain praises, calls to repentance, and encouragements to overcome. Christ's intent is to prepare the churches for receiving and applying the messages in the visions found in the remainder of the book.[35] Many interpreters note seven elements to each of the seven letters, which underscores John's numerical symbolism.[36] The primary point is that the symbolism for the number seven stands for completeness.[37] Thus, as synecdoche (one part representing the whole) the seven first-century churches are representatives of all the churches of Asia

---

32. This statistic has prompted dispensationalists such as LaHaye (*Revelation Unveiled*, 100), Lindsey (*New World Coming*, 78), Ryrie (*Revelation*, 42), and Walvoord (*Revelation*, 103) to speculate that since the term "church" is missing after chapter 3, then it is because believers have vacated the earth via a rapture before the judgments commence in the seals, trumpets, and bowls. This is a weak argument for both a possible rapture and for a missing "church" during the judgments. After all, it is the seven churches who receive the subsequent visions of judgment. Using the same formula, it could be argued that since "Jesus" is mentioned five times in chapter 1 but disappears until the last verse of chapter 12, then he must be missing from those middle chapters. Obviously, Jesus is present but is found in one of his many other disguises such as Lamb, Lion, Messiah, and male child. Just as there are numerous images to designate Jesus, so too are there numerous images of the church, as this entry discloses.

33. For background, see Hays, Duvall, and Pate, *Dictionary of Prophecy*, 416–24; Ryken, *Dictionary of Biblical Imagery*, 147–48; and Watson, "Seven Churches," 1143–44. Notable individual treatments on the letters are Culy, *Revelation*; Hemer, *Letters to the Seven Churches*; Mark Wilson, *Victor Sayings*; and Worth, *Seven Cities of the Apocalypse*. Bandy ("Patterns of Prophetic Lawsuits," 178–205) makes a case for the seven letters exhibiting the form and content of the covenant lawsuit. Christ investigates and charges his churches and those assemblies must repent or be judged.

34. Hemer, *Letters to the Seven Churches*, 14–15.

35. Culy (*Revelation*, 22) drives the point home with italics: *"the remainder of Revelation constantly builds on, fleshes out, and drives home each of the messages to the churches in Rev 2–3."*

36. Beale, *Revelation*, 225; Brighton, *Revelation*, 58–59; Duvall, *Revelation*, 36–39; Hailey, *Revelation*, 119; Hendriksen, *More than Conquerors*, 59; Hindson, *Revelation*, 32; Alan Johnson, "Revelation," 13:609; Kistemaker, *Revelation*, 108; Morris, *Revelation*, 58; Osborne, *Revelation*, 105–6; Paul, *Revelation*, 76; Reddish, *Revelation*, 51; Tavo, *Woman, Mother, Bride*, 90; Robert Thomas, *Revelation*, 1:125–26; Wall, *Revelation*, 69.

37. Some find more patterns: Morris (*Revelation*, 58–59), followed by Wall (*Revelation*, 69), note a chiastic pattern of churches in grave danger (1 and 7); excellent shape (2 and 6), and "middling" churches (3–5). Mark Wilson (*Victor Sayings*, 13–16, 18–30), however, corrects this to show Thyatira as the proper peak of the chiasm. Wilson further observes that the seven promises to the churches form a chiasm that matches the new Jerusalem (19:6–22:9). Bauckham (*Climax of Prophecy*, 35) detects several 7 x 4 patterns of numeric symbolism in Revelation, and observes, "there are *four* references to the *seven* churches [1:4, 11, 20 (twice), suggesting that they represent all the churches of the world."

Minor, and by extension, the church universal. Most interpreters, therefore, recognize the churches as a symbol for the universal church, composed of believers throughout the centuries.[38] In Revelation, the church is symbolized in numerous ways. These include lampstands, those in white clothes, pillars in temple, brothers and sisters, fellow servants, prophets, martyrs, saints/holy ones, hundred and forty-four thousand, tribes of Israel, great multitude, Holy City, temple (and altar and outer court), two witnesses, two olive trees, woman clothed with the sun, woman's children, dwelling place (i.e. those who dwell in heaven), virgins, firstfruits, blameless, called, chosen, and faithful, bride of the Lamb, beheaded, camp of God's people, city he loves, new Jerusalem, those who wash their robes, and more. Throughout, John draws from this deep well of metaphors, similes, symbols, and images to describe or emphasize some aspect of the church.

The characteristics found in each church illustrate characteristics that are found in every church and every generation. Ephesus represents an overly zealous church in danger of losing their first love (2:1–7). Smyrna is a suffering and poor church but spiritually rich (2:8–11). Pergamum faces the danger of theological compromise (2:12–17). By contrast, the danger of moral compromise is Thyatira's threat (2:18–29). Sardis is a church that exemplifies the danger of spiritual stagnation (3:1–6). Philadelphia provides a good example for a reputation of loyalty (3:7–13). Finally, the danger of complacency and apostasy are on Laodicea's horizon (3:14–22). The risen Christ's praises and reprimands reverberate through the centuries. The modern church must hear and obey (*tade legei*) his words.

Synagogue of Satan

This refers to Jews in Smyrna and Philadelphia who persecuted believers. John uses the epithet ironically to stress that God's true "synagogue" is the church. The synagogue was a key institution of the Israelite community. Birthed in exile, it became the communal meeting place and outlet for religious instruction. Literally, *synagōgē* comes from two Greek words that mean "gathering together," and stresses the coming together of an assembly to worship God.[39] The institution of the synagogue does not fare well in Revelation. The traditional identification is the local Jewish majority at Smyrna (2:9) and Philadelphia (3:9) whom the risen Christ rejects because of their rejection of him, their hatred of

---

38. Historicists such as Stefanovic (*Revelation*, 117–51) and dispensationalists such as LaHaye (*Revelation Unveiled*, 43–95) and Lindsey (*New World Coming*, 38–73) uncover a prophetic history in chapters 2–3. For them, the seven letters exhibit conditions which characterize subsequent periods of church history from the first advent of Christ to his second advent. Hemer ("Seven Churches," 696–98) traces this methodology through history. A similar but more sustainable theory is practiced by preterists. They purport that John follows other apocalypses by providing *vaticinia ex eventu* prophecies—surveys of history. Thus, Chilton (*Days of Vengeance*, 86–89), Prévost (*How to Read the Apocalypse*, 76–77), and Dulk ("Promises to the Conquerors," 516–22) trace OT salvation history in miniature from the garden of Eden (Ephesus) to the first advent (Laodicea). The majority of scholars on Revelation do not discuss these theories.

39. L&N, 1:128. See also Blickenstaff, "Synagogue in the New Testament," 427; Fine and Brolley, "Synagogue," 416–27; William White, "Synagogue," 648–59.

believers as heretics, and their informing on Christians to Roman authorities.[40] In the OT, Jews were called a synagogue of the Lord (Num 16:3; 20:4). But their persecution of Jesus' followers compels John to refer to them as a synagogue of Satan. Both references in Revelation confirm that the true "synagogue" is now the Christian church. Unbelieving Jews are called the synagogue of Satan because ironically, although they believe they are God's true people, they are not because they reject Christ and oppress his followers. They have forfeited the meaning of their name.[41] This point is made often in the rest of the NT (John 1:12–13; 8:31–47; Rom 2:28–29; 2 Cor 11:14–15).

John's words sound harsh to modern ears, even anti-Semitic. Scholars grapple with his polemical language.[42] But John, who is a Jew himself, is simply making a present judgment of these two cities based on his own relationship to Christ.[43] Application-wise, every church must be careful not to accommodate to the surrounding culture, and fall into the trap of supporting ideals and doctrines which the Bible and Jesus oppose.

Temple

The temple symbolizes God's majestic presence with his people. John moves dually between the heavenly temple and the earthly temple, the latter being represented by his church. The temple holds a central place in Scripture. It became a rich resource for imagery. At its heart, however, the temple symbolized the utter presence of God, his dwelling place on earth. The destruction of Solomon's temple (586 BC), therefore, was especially devastating to Jewish society.[44] Daniel Hays provides an effective summary of temple hopes. After the destruction of the temple, three types of expectation developed in extratextual writings: 1) rebuilt earthly temple; 2) end-time temple (Ezek 40–48); and 3) God's people as the true temple of God. The NT reveals that Jesus fulfills these expectations: 1) his

40. For untraditional offerings see the entry "Those Who Say They Are Jews and Are Not." A few translations regrettably lose the symbolism, translating *synagōgē* with "They are a group that belongs to Satan" (CEV, GNT) and "assembly of Satan" (NABR).

41. Beale (*Revelation*, 94–96) labels this as one of John's inverted uses of the OT. In 3:9, Jewish persecutors ironically bow down before believers instead of vice versa. It has become the opposite of Jewish hopes (Isa 45:14; 49:23; 60:14).

42. Koester (*Revelation*, 280–81), following Yarbro Collins ("Vilification and Self-Identification," 308–20), claims it helped define the congregation's boundaries, giving members a sense of distinctive identity. Duff ("Synagogue of Satan," 149) asserts the phrase was intended to "exacerbate tensions between the churches and synagogues," and foster "enmity against the synagogues and (perhaps more importantly) by promoting fear of hostility from local Jews, John intended to discourage . . . defecting to the synagogues." Friesen ("Sarcasm in Revelation 2–3," 127–44) presents a beneficial approach that views John using irony, satire, and especially sarcasm.

43. See Lambrecht ("Synagogues of Satan," 279–92) for a sensitive approach to the issue of anti-Semitism.

44. Background studies on the temple include those by Beale, *Temple and the Church's Mission*, 365–93; McKelvey, "Temple," 806–11; Roberts, "Temple, Jerusalem," 494–509; Ryken, *Dictionary of Biblical Imagery*, 849–51; Stigers, "Temple, Jerusalem," 716–52; and Westerholm, "Temple," 759–76. Deeper studies include Briggs, *Jewish Temple Imagery*; and Stevenson, *Power and Place*. Briggs stresses how John adapts only OT temple imagery for his work. Stevenson provides a corrective in finding intertestamental texts that John drew from.

resurrection body replaces the physical temple (Mark 14:48; John 2:19); 2) when Christ returns, the eschatological temple will dwell with humanity forever (Rev 21–22); this was the goal of the earthly temple (Exod 25:40; 2 Cor 5:1–10; Gal 4:26; Heb 9:23–24); and 3) the true "temple of the living God" is God's people in Christ through the Spirit (1 Cor 3:11–17; 2 Cor 6:14–7:1; Eph 2:19–22).[45]

Two words are translated as "temple" in the NT. *Hieron* refers to the physical temple complex. It occurs seventy-one times, all in the Gospels and Acts, except once in Paul (1 Cor 9:13). *Naos* refers to the holy of holies within the temple, and symbolizes the very presence of God. *Naos* is used figuratively in the NT; *hieron* never is. *Naos* appears forty-five times, and sixteen times in Revelation (36%). These sixteen references are concentrated in eight passages. John moves dually between the heavenly temple and the earthly temple, the latter being represented by his church, believers in Christ.

First, the overcomer is promised to be made "a pillar in the temple of my God" (3:12). This refers to the new Jerusalem that comes down at the second coming. Believers form part of that very temple, which in actuality refers to the intimate fellowship and presence of God.[46] Second, at the conclusion of the first interlude and in a glimpse of eternity, the faithful will "serve him day and night in his temple; and he who sits on the throne will shelter them with his presence" (7:15). This speaks of the unceasing service which the faithful render to God for eternity, and God's perfect security. Interpreters, however, note the apparent inconsistency with 21:22 which states there is no temple in the eschaton. To offset this, some scholars suppose an interpolation or later editor.[47] A few dispensationalists suggest 7:15 refers to a genuine heavenly temple for the saints upon their deaths whereas 21:2 refers to the time period after ultimate judgment.[48] The point, however, is John's allusion to the role of a high priest who was only able to enter the holy of holies once a year. In the eschaton, believers dwell in God's holy presence not for a few minutes, but forever.[49]

Third, John is instructed to measure the temple and the altar and the worshipers. He is not to measure the outer court which is given over to the gentiles (11:1–2). Preterists and dispensationalists understand a literal, physical temple for this reference. The preterist view finds a description of the destruction of Jerusalem in AD 70 whereas dispensationalists envision a rebuilt future temple.[50] Neither group would deny the symbolic aspects of the temple, but not at the cost of losing their literal understanding. Yet "temple" is used throughout Revelation not as the temple complex (*hieron*) but as the symbolic

---

45. Hays, *Temple and Tabernacle*, 166–84. In addition, Kovacs and Rowland (*Revelation*, 124) and Weinrich (*Revelation*, 154–56) note that patristic writers, beginning with the third century (Hippolytus and Victorinus), understood the temple as the church. For a treatment accentuating all people groups as the one new temple on mission, see Keener, "One New Temple in Christ," 75–92.

46. See the entry "Pillar in the Temple."

47. Charles, *Revelation*, 1:215; Swete, *Apocalypse*, 104.

48. LaHaye, *Revelation Unveiled*, 161; Robert Thomas, *Revelation*, 2:500. Ryrie (*Revelation*, 63), however, pictures 7:15 as a literal future millennial temple.

49. Kistemaker, "Temple in the Apocalypse," 434.

50. Preterist examples include Chilton, *Days of Vengeance*, 275; Clark, *Message from Patmos*, 74; and Roloff, *Revelation*, 129. Futurist examples include LaHaye, *Revelation Unveiled*, 184; Patterson, *Revelation*, 239; and Ryrie, *Revelation*, 83.

presence of God in the holy of holies (*naos*). Since the rest of Revelation's references are used figuratively as the presence of God in heaven, so should 11:1–2 be understood figuratively as Christians being the presence of God on earth. Caird asserts "it is hardly too much to say that in a book in which all things are expressed in symbols, the very last things the 'Temple' and 'holy city' could mean would be the physical Temple and the earthly Jerusalem."[51] The vast majority of commentators on Revelation agree with Caird. The temple symbolizes the people of God, who represent God's presence on earth (1 Cor 3:16–17; 2 Cor 6:16; Eph 2:21; 1 Pet 2:5).[52]

Fourth, at the conclusion of the seventh trumpet, the temple in heaven is opened and the ark of the covenant appears (11:19). This accents the utter presence of God in the holy of holies. In the eschaton the curtain separating his sacred presence is now open. The ark of the covenant is a sign of God's presence and confirms that a merciful God will dwell intimately with his people in the new Jerusalem.[53] Fifth, in the third interlude, the angel who initiates the ingathering of the church at the eschaton does so "from the temple," the very presence of God (14:15). Likewise, another angel who delivers end-time judgment also comes from the temple (14:17). Sixth, the temple is mentioned four times in the launch of the seven bowls. The seven angels come out of the heavenly temple to deliver end-time judgment (15:5–8). This image stresses the vindication of God's judgment on those who have broken his covenant. The mention of the Ten Commandments alludes to the covenant God made with his people on Sinai (Exod 25:16). Thus, from God's presence and from the testimony of his laws divine judgment flows forth.[54] Seventh, the previous temple scene continues with a loud voice coming from the heavenly temple (16:1). Most exegetes believe this is the voice of God (Isa 66:6) sending forth his angels to pour out his judgments.[55] God's voice from the temple resumes at the conclusion of the seventh bowl with "it is done" (16:17).[56] Eighth, and significantly, there is no more temple in the new Jerusalem. The Lord God and the Lamb are the temple. God's presence dwells with his people forever in the new Jerusalem (21:22). The city itself—heavenly Jerusalem—has become a holy of holies. The barrier of sin is gone. God is accessible to everyone in the new Jerusalem.

---

51. Caird, *Revelation*, 131.

52. Cogent discussions appear in Aune, *Revelation*, 2:593–98; Bauckham, *Climax of Prophecy*, 266–73; Beale, *Revelation*, 557–71; idem, *Temple and the Church's Mission*, 313–28; Kistemaker, "Temple in the Apocalypse," 433–41; Schnabel, *40 Questions*, 143–50; Tavo, *Woman, Mother, Bride*, 181–97; and Walker, *Jesus and the Holy City*, 246–48.

53. See the entry "Ark of the Covenant."

54. Kistemaker, "Temple in the Apocalypse," 439–40. See the entry "Tabernacle of the Covenant Law."

55. Bauckham (*Theology of Revelation*, 42) speaks of the common Jewish anthropomorphism that shies away from any reference to God's voice. Thus, it comes "from the throne."

56. Most English versions produce "it is done." There is also "it is finished" (NLT, NCV), "it has happened" (GW), and "it is over" (REB). The rendering that best reflects the eschaton is "the end has come" (NJB).

Worship Accoutrements

The worship of God is accessorized with key elements. These originally Jewish features have been universalized by John and serve as symbols. Major themes include the incorporation of the church and the expectation of suffering for Christ. Strikingly, many of these elements surface at the end of individual visions, suggesting a rising worship motif near the eschaton.

Altar

The altar (like the temple it is part of) symbolizes God's holy presence. John contrastingly moves between the heavenly altar and the earthly altar (where God's presence is symbolized through his people). The people of God's response to his presence combines the two major emphases of worship (altar of incense) and sacrifice (altar of burnt offering). "Altar" occurs over four hundred times in the OT. "It is no exaggeration to say that the most visible sign of one's devotion to the true God in the worship of the old covenant is the building of altars or traveling to them for acts of sacrifice or offering."[57] The main meaning of the altar was its role as a place of sacrifice, located in the temple courtyard. But the temple also contained two more altars—the gold altar for offerings of incense representing the prayers of the people to God, and the table for the perpetual offering of the "bread of presence." The latter altar faded in significance to the ideas of sacrifice and worship. The NT merges all the sacrificial images into the single sacrifice of Christ (Heb 13:10). Jesus' sacrifice made his people "holy through his own blood" (Heb 13:12). Those who have this altar offer up their own sacrifices (Heb 13:15).[58] Thus, the writer of Hebrews proposes the metaphor that Christians are themselves an altar. At the least, they continue to offer their own sacrifices of praise through *the* sacrifice.[59]

If Hebrews is ambiguous, then John makes unambiguous the metaphor of the altar with believers. The "altar" (*thysiastērion*) appears eight times in Revelation, often in connection to the temple (6:9; 8:3 [twice], 5; 9:13; 11:1; 14:18; 16:7). In fact, since it composed the inner part of the temple, the two are practically synonymous. Moreover, like his references to the temple, John refers dually to the heavenly altar (seven times) and the earthly altar (once).[60]

But which altar did John intend to symbolize? Was he alluding to the bronze altar of burnt offering to emphasize sacrifice or to the golden altar of incense with its stress on the worship and prayers of the saints? Some commentators believe that all eight references are consistent with the altar of incense. After all, the time of sacrifices came to an end when Christ died on the cross (Heb 9:26), so John must mean the emphasis is on prayer

---

57. Ryken, *Dictionary of Biblical Imagery*, 20.

58. Minear, *Images of the Church*, 38. See Haak, "Altar," 162–67; van Koppen and van der Toorn, "Altar," 23–24.

59. See George Guthrie, *Hebrews*, 441; and James Thompson, *Hebrews*, 282.

60. Hughes, *Revelation*, 88. Michaels (*Revelation*, 105–6) singularly views the altar of 6:9 as earthly as well.

and worship.[61] Others resolutely view one altar over the other depending on which passage is read.[62]

It is preferable, however, to understand John as intentionally alluding to both altars, but with one altar being stressed at each instance while the other rests in the background. Thus, a combination of sacrifice and worship fits well. Several scholars agree with this blending approach. Both motifs are at work in each of the eight references.[63]

Thus, the broad idea of God's holy presence in the context of both worship and sacrifice works for the seven heavenly references. The one reference to the earthly altar requires more explanation. John was given a measuring rod and told, "Go and measure the temple of God and the altar, with its worshipers" (11:1). If the temple on earth represents the church, then the altar, the inner court of the temple (as well as the worshippers), likewise represents the Christian community. This interpretation is based on regular use found in both the NT (1 Cor 3:16–17; 2 Cor 6:16; Eph 2:19–22; 1 Pet 2:4–10) and early Christian literature (Ign. *Eph.* 9:1; *Barn.* 4:11; 2 Clem. 9:3). Most interpreters believe the burnt offering is stressed more in 11:1. Blending the motifs of both altars, then, leads to understanding the measuring of the altar to symbolize God's people in their sacrificial witness for Christ. They are the suffering Christian community. They are the heavenly community dwelling on earth as a living altar and temple.[64] Yet the worship life of God's people may also be intimated. Their prayer and praise is part of their mission on earth and will be protected and maintained.[65] Finally, John's placement of the altar at the end of four individual visions implies that the actions of worship and sacrifice increase toward the end of history.

Ark of the Covenant

The appearance of the heavenly ark of the covenant is a sign of God's presence and confirms that a merciful God will dwell intimately and eternally with his people in the new Jerusalem. There are nearly two hundred references to the ark of the covenant in the OT. The gold-covered, rectangular-shaped wooden box contained the holy objects, namely the Ten Commandments, a jar of manna, and Aaron's rod. On its top rested the mercy seat, a

61. So Brighton, *Revelation*, 141, 412–13; Easley, *Revelation*, 188; Kistemaker, *Revelation*, 232; Mounce, *Revelation*, 214; Waddell, *Spirit of Revelation*, 167.

62. For example, Aune (*Revelation*, 2:511) states that the altar of incense was intended by John for 8:3; 9:13; but the altar of burnt offerings was intended at 6:9; 11:1; 14:18; 16:7. Stefanovic (*Revelation*, 238, 284, 308, 337, 461, 483) on the other hand, sees the altar of burnt offerings at 6:9; 8:3; 14:18; and 16:7, but the altar of incense at 9:13 and 11:1. Another example is Robert Thomas (*Revelation*, 1:442), who dismisses any idea of blending the two altars "in light of the radically different functions of the two altars," and therefore, for instance, the context of 8:3 "effectively excludes the possibility of this being the altar of burnt offering" (2:9).

63. Beale, *Revelation*, 392; Mounce, *Revelation*, 146; Osborne, *Revelation*, 284. Blount (*Revelation*, 133, 163) understands the imagery of the altar to be one of eschatological judgment. "His main goal, after all, was not to identify a particular altar (i.e., sacrifice or worship) but to clarify what 'altar' in its essence meant: God's judgment." See also Lupieri, *Apocalypse*, 155; Rotz, *Revelation*, 161.

64. Beale, *Revelation*, 563.

65. Brighton, *Revelation*, 285.

covering which included images of cherubim on each side (Exod 25:10–22; Deut 10:1–5). The ark was kept in the temple, in the holy of holies, shielded from human contact, and accessed only once a year by the high priest. It disappeared from history when the Babylonians razed Jerusalem in 586 BC (2 Kgs 25). The ark was a potent image of the presence of God and particularly brought to mind his covenant of mercy.[66]

There are two references to the ark in the NT.[67] First, it is described as being under the first covenant (Heb 9:1–5). The second reference is a vision of the eschatological, heavenly temple that concludes the seventh trumpet (11:19). The cosmic phenomena presented in this verse imply that the final judgment of history has arrived. The seventh trumpet relates the end of evil and the rewards for the faithful. That the ark is mentioned at this moment signals God's gracious presence with his redeemed community and an eternal reminder of his provision of grace by atonement.[68] Closely connected to this heavenly scene is its parallel vision found in 21:1–8, the passage that concludes the thousand years vision (20:1–21:8). There we see John complementing the description of the heavenly temple: "Look! God's dwelling place is now among the people, and he will dwell with them. They will be his people, and God himself will be with them and be their God" (21:3). Therefore, God keeps his covenant with his people. The permanent access to the intimate presence and fellowship of God and the Lamb at the end of time is the picture presented in the ark of the covenant.

Harps

These musical instruments symbolize the joy, praise, and worship that take place in heaven as a result of God's end-time victory and righteous judgment. Music and musical instruments are common expressions of devotion to God. The Psalms, for example, are filled with passages that enjoin the faithful to praise the Lord with the harp, especially for protection or deliverance (Pss 43:4; 57:8; 81:2).[69] Yet harps also accompany the prophetic word of judgment against the nations (Isa 23:16; 24:8; Ezek 26:13). In Daniel the playing of harps accompanies the worship of idols (Dan 3:5–10).[70] References to harps in the NT are usually symbolic.[71]

The dual nature of praise for both deliverance and judgment is expressed well in Revelation. Just as the harp became an instrument used in temple worship (Ps 33:2), so

---

66. Payne, "Ark of the Covenant," 345–50; Ryken, *Dictionary of Biblical Imagery*, 42–43; Hays, *Temple and Tabernacle*, 36–43; Seow, "Ark of the Covenant," 386–93. For interpretations of the ark through history, see Besserman, "Ark of the Covenant," 54–55.

67. "The ark of the covenant" (*hē kibōtos tēs diathēkēs*) is translated as the "Covenant Box" (GNT), "sacred chest" (CEV), "chest containing his covenant" (CEB), "ark of his promise" (GW), and the "Ark that holds the agreement" (NCV).

68. Beale, *Revelation*, 619. Many interpreters, of course, do not view the consummation of the world being pictured at the seventh trumpet.

69. See Braun, "Musical Instruments," 175–83; Matthews and Jones, "Music and Musical Instruments," 930–39.

70. Ryken, *Dictionary of Biblical Imagery*, 364–65.

71. Braun, "Musical Instruments," 183.

too it is an instrument in heavenly temple worship. "Harp" (*kithara*), "harpist," (*kitharodos*), and "to play the harp" (*kitharizō*) are mentioned in four places. First, when the Lamb takes the scroll from the one who sits on the throne, the four living creatures and the twenty-four elders worship him with harps (5:8). This heavenly image is probably drawn from 1 Chr 25. It stresses the worthiness of the Lamb to open the seals and initiate end-time events. Second, in a vision of the second coming, as the Lamb stands triumphantly on Mount Zion, all three cognates of "harp" are mentioned (14:2). Literally, the verse reads "harpers harping with their harps" (KJV). The theme of praise to the Lamb for his end-time victory and deliverance is sounded in these verses. Third, the ultimate victory of the Lamb at his return is explicitly spelled out at the end of the third interlude. Pictured here in this heavenly scene are the redeemed who were victorious over the beast, now celebrating with harps and singing the song of Moses and the Lamb (15:2–4). Finally, the judgment motif appears within the fall of Babylon vision. John utilizes a common expression "will never be again" (*ou mē . . . eti*) five times to emphasize the complete judgment of Babylon the Great. The first use concerns music. This evil empire will never again hear the joyous sounds of the harpist (18:22). John draws from Isa 24:8 and Ezek 26:13 to underscore the bleakness of end-time judgment against those who rejected God and persecuted his people.[72] Each instance of the harp is found near the end of one of John's visions. The image characterizes a high point in the heavenly worship scene through which the saints respond to the victory achieved by the Lamb at his coming.[73]

Incense

Incense is an element of worship that symbolizes acceptable sacrifice and especially the petition of prayers by the faithful to God, who in turn hears and answers in righteous judgment. The fragrant odor of incense is a symbol for acceptable sacrifice, offering, and worship, and is often associated with prayer (Ps 141:2; Luke 1:9–10; Eph 5:2). The fragrance is a metaphor for the knowledge of God or Christ, and for the apostles (2 Cor 2:14–16), and of the Philippians' offering to Paul (Phil 4:18).[74]

Three passages in Revelation refer to incense (*thymiama*). First, in the throne room vision, the Lamb who takes the scroll prompts the four living creatures and the twenty-four elders to fall down. "Each one had a harp and they were holding golden bowls full of incense, which are the prayers of God's people" (5:8). The parenthetical statement "which are the prayers of God's people" interprets the symbol—the incense are the prayers. John uses *phialē* for "bowl," the same word for the seven bowls of God's wrath poured. This implies that the prayers will be answered in righteous end-time judgment.

Second, at the conclusion of the seals, John relates that an angel with a golden censer stood at the altar. "He was given much incense to offer, with the prayers of all God's

---

72. Osborne, *Revelation*, 656.

73. See Beale, *Revelation*, 357, 735–36, 789–91, 919; Beck, *Dictionary of Imagery*, 120–21; Osborne, *Revelation*, 258, 526–27, 561–63, 656; Smalley, *Revelation*, 134; 356, 384–85.

74. See discussions at Beck, *Dictionary of Imagery*, 133–35; Branch, "Incense," 849–64; Nielsen, "Incense," 404–40; J. Alexander Thompson, "Incense," 306–8.

people, on the golden altar in front of the throne. The smoke of the incense, together with the prayers of God's people, went up before God from the angel's hand. Then the angel took the censer, filled it with fire from the altar, and hurled it on the earth; and there came peals of thunder, rumblings, flashes of lightning and an earthquake" (8:3–5). Lev 16:12–13 is echoed here. Once again John connects prayers to incense, although not as a metaphor this time. The passage helps answer the plaintive cries of vindication offered up by the martyrs of the fifth seal (6:9–11). That believers suffered and even gave their lives because they remained faithful is heard and is acceptable to God. He will justifiably avenge. Incense, therefore, "is a symbol showing that their prayers are accepted because of their faithful sacrifice, which was an aroma pleasing to the Lord."[75]

The third reference is found in connection with the fall of Babylon vision. It is among the twenty-eight items listed and lamented over by the merchants of the earth (18:13). Incense, then, is a valuable trade commodity. The purpose of its listing is to show why God's wrath has descended on them—for their ostentatious, self-centered materialism.[76] What then are the petitions that are mentioned in 5:8; 6:9–11; and 8:3–5? Certainly, they are a call for God's vindication from the martyred believers to judge the world. Therefore, incense becomes symbolic not only of worshipful praise but also of appeals for God to dole out justice on those who persecuted his people.

Lampstands

Lampstands signify God's presence with his people, and represent the universal church charged by Christ to be his witnessing light to the world. Lampstands were receptacles for giving off light and serve as positive images in Scripture. Figuratively, they are associated with worship, guidance, illumination, the presence of God, and witness and proclamation. Lampstands formed part of the sacred furniture in the original tabernacle (Exod 25:31–40). Solomon's temple contained ten lampstands (1 Kgs 7:49). Apparently, after Zerubbabel's temple, and certainly before Herod's temple, one lampstand moves to the forefront, adorned with the now customary branches that symbolize the tree of life. This lampstand combined the symbol of the tree of life with the light-giving aspects of the temple (Zech 4:1–14). The lampstands in the tabernacle and temple stood in God's holy presence.[77]

The twin images of eternal life ("tree of life") and eternal presence ("light") carry over to the NT. John imports these ideas for his visions while adapting and adding his own features. The noun "lampstand" (*lychnia*) is found seven times in Revelation. Six times it refers to the seven churches (1:12, 13, 20[twice]; 2:1, 2:5) and once to the two witnesses (11:4), a crucial intratextual link. The total of exactly seven references stresses the full, complete, universal church.

---

75. Beale, *Revelation*, 457. See Smalley, *Revelation*, 135.

76. Osborne, *Revelation*, 647.

77. Hays, Duvall, and Pate, *Dictionary of Prophecy*, 248–50; Carol Meyers, "Lampstand," 141–43; Ryken, *Dictionary of Biblical Imagery*, 485–87.

In the inaugural vision (1:12–20), the one like a son of man walks among the lampstands. In Zech 4, the lampstand represented Israel. John universalizes the term to include all of God's people—both Jew and gentile. Christ provides the interpretive key—the seven lampstands are the seven churches (1:20). There is wide agreement that John refers not only to the churches of Asia Minor but to the church as a whole. The churches, therefore, are depicted as shining lights for God in the world.

The lampstands reappear in the second interlude. The temple is measured and the two witnesses "will prophesy for 1,260 days, clothed in sackcloth" (11:3). The majority of scholarship agrees the two witnesses symbolize the church.[78] They are further identified as "the two olive trees" and "the two lampstands" that "stand before the Lord of the earth" (11:4). Again, the imagery is traced directly to Zech 4. There the lampstand with its seven lamps represented the seven eyes of God which spread over the earth with his presence through his Spirit. The two olive trees referred to Joshua the high priest and Zerubbabel the governor. The two olive trees supply oil to the lampstand. Zechariah's point was that God is in charge of rebuilding the temple. Similarly, this pictures the two witnesses (the church) in their role as priests (Joshua) and kings (Zerubbabel).[79]

At first glance, the numbers prevent some interpreters from connecting and equating the seven churches (lampstands) with the two witnesses (lampstands). But John utilizes multiple images in his visions that include different numbers. For example, believers are symbolized as one woman, two witnesses, seven churches, twelve tribes, hundred and forty-four thousand servants, and an incalculably great multitude. All are various ways to illustrate the full number of saints. Thus, the lampstands are not limited to the seven churches in Asia Minor in the first century or to two individuals at the end of history. The lampstands represent the entire people of God during the interadventual period. Ultimately, lamps and lampstands will no longer be needed in the new Jerusalem. Its lamp is the Lamb (21:23) and he will be their light (22:5).

Outer Court

The outer court of the temple is another metaphor for the church viewed from a different perspective—one that reminds believers that although spiritually preserved, they must nevertheless be prepared for persecution and even martyrdom. John is given a measuring rod and told, "Go and measure the temple of God and the altar, with its worshipers. But exclude the outer court; do not measure it, because it has been given to the Gentiles. They will trample on the holy city for 42 months" (11:1–2).[80] Some scholars suggest the references to the temple, altar, and outer court are literal. Preterists, for example, connect it to the fall of Jerusalem in AD 70, with the measured temple reflecting believers but the

---

78. Many interpreters, however, understand the two witnesses as individuals. See the entry "Two Witnesses."

79. Osborne, *Revelation*, 420–21. Brighton (*Revelation*, 292) suggests the two lampstands represent "the Holy City" and "the temple," i.e. the church.

80. English translations choose either "outer court" or "courtyard outside." NCV selects "yard outside."

unmeasured outer court reflecting unbelieving Jews.[81] For many futurists, this phrase applies to a restored, earthly temple to be rebuilt near the end of history. The gentiles then would refer to wicked unbelievers who trample the Holy City, earthly Jerusalem, and the Jewish remnant of believers would represent the outer court.[82]

The majority of interpreters, however, favor the outer court as another metaphor for the Christian community. It is the church from a different perspective, a contrasting point of view. Since the temple was a customary metaphor for believers by John's day (1 Cor 3:16–17; 2 Cor 6:16; Eph 2:19–22; 1 Pet 2:4–10; Ign. *Eph.* 9:1; Barn. 4:11; 2 Clem. 9:3), it is likely that the outer court serves as a similar symbol.[83] If the outer court symbolizes believers, then two scenarios arise. First, the temple may picture faithful Christians whereas the outer court refers to nominal, compromising, or apostate Christians who God does not protect and who the world tramples.[84] Second, and better, the temple and outer court both refer to faithful Christians. The trampling that the latter receives reminds John's readers once again of the expectation of persecution and even martyrdom. Thus, the church is vulnerable to physical harm while on earth but promised eternal care for eternity. This equals what is true of God's people throughout history as they are rejected, persecuted, and at times killed (Matt 21:39; Mark 12:8; Luke 4:29; John 9:34–35; Heb 13:11–13).[85] This interpretation allows for the sealing of the saints (7:1–8) to be temporally parallel. The sealing ensures faithful Christians their inheritance of eternal life, but it does not guarantee their protection from physical suffering or martyrdom at any time during the interadvental period.[86]

Pillar in the Temple

This symbol is a promise of secure, eternal, and intimate fellowship with God for the victorious believer. Pierre Prigent confirms, "Contemporary Judaism, Christianity, and the

81. So Chilton, *Days of Vengeance*, 273; Clark, *Message from Patmos*, 74; Russell, *Parousia*, 425–27.

82. So Hindson, *Revelation*, 122–25; Patterson, *Revelation*, 241–42; Robert Thomas, *Revelation*, 2:81–84; Walvoord, *Revelation*, 176–77.

83. Beale (*Revelation*, 570–71) makes a solid case for understanding all five images in 11:1–2 (temple, altar, worshippers, outer court, and Holy City) as metaphors for different but complementary aspects of the church, the new people of God.

84. Boxall, *Revelation*, 162; Caird, *Revelation*, 132; Charles, *Revelation*, 1:274–78; Ford, *Revelation*, 176–77; Harrington, *Revelation*, 151–52; Hendriksen, *More than Conquerors*, 127–28; 152–55; Alan Johnson, "Revelation," 13:682; Kiddle, *Revelation*, 189; Kistemaker, *Revelation*, 325; Morris, *Revelation*, 142; Wall, *Revelation*, 143. Michaels (*Revelation*, 137) understands the temple and altar in 11:1–2 to refer to the heavenly temple and altar. Thus, those excluded outside refer to some place on earth—perhaps earth itself.

85. So Aune, *Revelation*, 2:598; Bauckham, *Climax of Prophecy*, 272–73; Beale, *Revelation*, 557–71; Boring, *Revelation*, 143–44; Blount, *Revelation*, 205; Brighton, *Revelation*, 286–87; Caird, *Revelation*, 132; Easley, *Revelation*, 189; Fee, *Revelation*, 149; Hendriksen, *More than Conquerors*, 127–28; 154–55; Hughes, *Revelation*, 120–21; Dennis Johnson, *Triumph of the Lamb*, 166–69; Koester, *Revelation*, 494; Mounce, *Revelation*, 213–14; Mulholland, *Revelation*, 203–4; Osborne, *Revelation*, 412–13; Prigent, *Apocalypse*, 160–63; Resseguie, *Revelation*, 160–61; Smalley, *Revelation*, 270–73; Sweet, *Revelation*, 182–84; Thomas and Macchia, *Revelation*, 200–201.

86. Smalley, *Revelation*, 273.

Hellenistic world at large attested to the prominent metaphorical usage of 'pillar.'"[87] The word "pillar" (*stylos*) is found twice in Revelation (3:12; 10:1). The latter reference is to the mighty angel at the beginning of the second interlude. The angel's power and authority is evident in the symbols attached to his visage, including that "his legs were like fiery pillars." These fiery pillars call attention to the authority the angel has over the entire earth, and may even be allusions to the pillar of cloud by day and the pillar of fire by night.[88] Some modern translations opt for "columns" of fire (CEV, GNT, GW).

The former reference is to the "pillar in the temple," and fills one aspect of a four-part promise given to the Philadelphian faithful. The symbolic nature of "pillar" is mentioned elsewhere in the NT (Gal 2:9; 1 Tim 3:15). It is easy to note that stability and permanence is one image of a pillar. In Revelation, the promise to become a pillar in the temple of God adds a powerful symbol of intimate fellowship for eternity in God's presence. There are several possibilities posited for the background of the imagery on pillars, and which temple John was referencing. Some assert the temple in mind is Solomon's, Ezekiel's, or Herod's. But Aune convincingly states the temple in this context does not refer to any Jewish temple or the Christian church, the new Israel, but rather to the heavenly temple, the dwelling-place of God with his eschatological people.[89] The temple in view is the heavenly temple, the Holy City that comes down in the new heaven and new earth. Ultimately, God himself is the temple (21:22) and the ones who are victorious become "pillars." In addition, the victor is called God's name, the name of the city of my God (the new Jerusalem), and Christ's new name. These are not four distinct promises, but different aspects of the same promise.[90]

Seven Lamps

This represents the Holy Spirit who joins God and the Lamb in delivering end-time judgment. The "seven lamps" is mentioned once by John when describing the throne room vision (4:5).[91] The phrasing of modern versions includes "seven flaming lamps" (NJB), "seven flaming torches" (CEB, GW, NABR, NET, NRSV, REB), "seven torches" (CEV, ESV, NLT), "seven lighted torches" (GNT), and "seven fiery torches" (CSB). Only a few translations choose "seven lamps" (NCV, NIV, NJKV). These lamps allude to the lampstand

87. Prigent, *Apocalypse*, 206.

88. Beale, *Revelation*, 524.

89. Aune, *Revelation*, 1:241–42. See Osborne, *Revelation*, 196–97; Smalley, *Revelation*, 93–94. Wilkinson ("ΣΤΥΛΟΣ of Revelation," 498–501) believes the pillar analogy is rooted in the established coronational rites of ancient Israel and other ancient Near East monarchies. Thus, kingship seems to be the major theme. But see Robert Thomas, *Revelation*, 1:292 n. 71, for refutation. Hemer (*Letters to the Seven Churches*, 166, 175–76) opts for Exod 28:36–38 as the background to "pillar in the temple." Barr (*Tales*, 59) singularly understands the pillar to refer to the earthly temple.

90. Beale, *Revelation*, 293–95. Sandy (*Plowshares and Pruning Hooks*, 30) helpfully lists ten such rewards that all visualize the one reward—deity and humanity in perfect unity (Rev 21:3).

91. The noun "lamp" (*lampas*) is also found at 8:10 but is usually translated as "like a blazing/burning torch." Another noun (*lychnos*) emphasizes light and almost always is rendered as "lamp" (18:23, 21:23, 22:5). The cognate adjective *lampros* is found five times (15:6; 18:14; 19:8; 22:1, 16). It receives a variety of English translations such as "bright," "shining," "splendor," and "elegant."

with its seven branches (Exod 25:31–40) which stood before God's presence in the holy of holies. This echoes Zechariah's prophecy of seven lamps which is interpreted to be the Holy Spirit (Zech 4:2–3). The added information that they are "blazing" probably stems from Ezek 1:13. John confirms the identification of the Holy Spirit by interpreting the lamps himself as "these are the seven spirits of God," which is another allusion to the Spirit.[92] The primary point is that both lightning and the blazing lamps are symbols not only of deity but of judgment. They prepare readers for the coming wrath that a righteous God will soon deliver. The third person of the Trinity, therefore, joins the Father in this activity. The second person of the Trinity, the Lamb, is then promptly introduced in John's throne room vision to complete the image.[93]

Tabernacle of the Covenant Law

This image stresses the righteous vindication of God's end-time judgment on those who have broken his covenant. The "tabernacle of the covenant law" (*skēnēs tou martyriou*) is found once in Revelation at the beginning of the bowl judgments (15:5). The phrase has experienced fluid translations among English Bible versions, and is worthy of listing for comparison.

- "tent of witness" (CEB, ESV, NRSV)
- "sacred tent " (CEV, GNT)
- "tent containing the words of God's promise" (GW)
- "Tent of the Agreement" (NCV)
- "tent of (the) testimony" (NABR, NET, NJB, REB)
- "tabernacle of (the) testimony" (CSB, NASB, NIV 84, NKJV)
- "God's Tabernacle" (NLT)
- "tabernacle of the covenant law" (NIV)

However it is translated, John presents it as an epexegetical genitive, that is, the heavenly temple is the tabernacle of the covenant law (contra GNT's "with the Sacred Tent in it"). This links the heavenly temple with the tabernacle (or "tent") in the wilderness. The extra description of "testimony" is a reference to the Ten Commandments that were placed inside the ark of the covenant. This was a "witness" to the centrality of the Torah (Exod 25:16; Deut 10:1–2; 1 Kgs 8:9). In addition, the holy of holies or the ark of the covenant were often called "the Testimony" (Exod 16:34; Lev 16:13; Num 1:50). The tabernacle and the tent of witness or tent of testimony are all one and the same (Exod 40:34–35; Acts 7:44).[94]

---

92. Not all interpret the seven spirits as the Holy Spirit. See the entry "Seven Spirits."

93. Beale, *Revelation*, 326–27; Osborne, *Revelation*, 231; Smalley, *Revelation*, 119.

94. See Feinberg, "Tabernacle," 664–77; Janzen, "Tabernacle," 447–58. Koester (*Dwelling of God*, 116–51) presents a thorough tracing of the tabernacle/temple, including the tabernacle of the covenant law.

Osborne states, "The purpose for this description is to insert the idea of covenant, with its attendant blessings and cursings. The nations have broken covenant with God and must face the consequences. In 11:19 the ark may have been a sign of mercy, but here it is a sign of judgment."[95] Therefore, in John's vision, arising from the very presence of God and the testimony of these laws, divine judgment flows forth. The seven angels are now empowered to pour out the bowl judgments.[96]

95. Osborne, *Revelation*, 569. See Beale, *Revelation*, 801–2.
96. Hughes, *Revelation*, 171; Kistemaker, *Revelation*, 431–32.

9

Numbers and Colors

APOCALYPTIC WRITINGS MAKE VIGOROUS use of number and color symbolism, and Revelation follows suit. This chapter unfolds these two categories. Numbers were highly symbolic to most Jews and other ancient peoples. When moderns read four, seven, or ten they naturally think of mathematics and literal numbering. But when ancients used numbers, they understood ideas, thoughts, and symbols. Colors also served symbolic roles for the ancients. For example, purple suggested royalty, red was the color of blood, and white signified purity. Readers of Revelation must not take numbers and colors at face value. They must be ready to interpret what the numbers and colors signify.

Numbers

Numbers such as two, four, seven, ten, twelve, along with their multiples, were important for John. Numbers are adjectives. Thus, numbers are scattered throughout the other chapters of this study. Readers will need to see what they modify and refer to the appropriate heading. Numbers and time elements are particularly connected.[1]

First

The adjective "first" signifies primacy, rank, exclusiveness, and excellence. It is found eighteen times in Revelation, more than any other NT book. Often it simply indicates a ranking at the beginning of a series (first angel sounds his trumpet, first angel pours out his bowl) or among groups (first living creature, first beast). In a few instances it refers to something prior (your first love, what you did "at first," the voice I first heard, first heaven

---

1. Farrer (*Rebirth of Images*, 245–60) offers an intriguing study of numbers, positing that John drew his numeric symbolism from 1 Chr 23–27. The majority of scholarship, however, understands John to utilize numerical symbolism from the common stockpile of images that were available throughout the Near East.

and first earth, and first resurrection). Finally, rank and primacy is observable in the antithesis "I am the First and the Last" (1:17; 2:8; 22:13).[2]

Forty

Revelation uses multiples of "forty," a round number that generally symbolizes the sufficient completion of a period of time of testing and trial. The flood was forty days (Gen 7:4–17); Israel's exodus was rounded to forty years (Num 32:13); and Jesus was tested for forty days (Matt 4:2; Luke 4:2). This number became a symbol for the span of a generation.[3] Although "forty" (*tesserakonta*) does not appear by itself in Revelation, it is attached to or connected with multiples in six places—"forty-two months" (11:2; 13:5); "a hundred and forty-four thousand" (7:4; 14:1, 3); and "a hundred and forty-four cubits" (21:17).[4]

Yet there is one more possibility where forty may be serviceable as a numerical symbol for John. In a depiction of judgment day, the wicked are "trampled in the winepress outside the city, and blood flowed out of the press, rising as high as the horses' bridles for a distance of 1,600 stadia" (14:20). This is certainly a numerical symbol that could be viewed as 4 x 4 x 100 or 40 squared. This breakdown becomes a multiple of four, a symbol of completeness and full coverage of the earth (similar to the "four winds of the earth," and "four corners of the earth"). Thus, it should not be limited to a translation of 180 or 200 miles that many modern versions unfortunately update, masking the numerical symbolism, but rather to the total, full coverage of the earth.

Four

This number symbolizes full, total coverage, most often in view of God's creation, the surface of the earth, and universality. The OT is filled with examples of groupings of four to signify completeness (Exod 25–39; Isa 58; Amos 1–2). The *Dictionary of Biblical Imagery* explains that "grouping objects and phrases in fours is a Hebrew literary technique used to picture universality" and that "the number four occurs so often in apocalyptic visions like Daniel, Ezekiel and Revelation that they constitute a category by themselves."[5]

"Four" (*tessares*) is one of John's favorite numbers for symbolism. He mentions "four angels" restraining the "four winds" at the "four corners of the earth" (7:1; 20:8) to signify total earth coverage. The four living creatures who represent the created world appear throughout the book. There are "four horns" on the golden altar (9:13). "Four angels" are

2. Few studies mention the symbolic properties of "first." See Ryken, *Dictionary of Biblical Imagery*, 289–90; Michaelis, "πρῶτος . . .," 865–68; Togtman, "First," 307.

3. Hemer, "Number," 696.

4. Korner ("And I Saw," 178) structured Revelation into forty individual visions based on the forty uses of *kai eidon* and *meta tauta eidon*. He implies the number was purposeful to note the testing and trials of the Apocalypse.

5. Ryken, *Dictionary of Biblical Imagery*, 307–8. See Hailey, *Revelation*, 43–44, for more OT examples and Beale, *Revelation*, 59, for intertestamental examples. Boring ("Numbers, Numbering," 298) relates the number four became so established as a sacred number that Irenaeus argued that the church must accept exactly four Gospels, based on Rev 4:7–8.

bound at the river Euphrates (9:15) in order to symbolize that the restraints of all earthly evil will be unleashed. Bauckham states it is clear that four "is the number of the world."[6] Moreover, four is "the figure of the inhabited earth and thus, in a way, of humanity.[7] But it is John's groupings of four that disclose his literary artistry. The seals, trumpets, and bowls exhibit a 4 + 3 structure. The first four target parts of creation. The numerous groupings of four embedded in Revelation is dramatic, and worthy of listing.

- "Every tribe and language and people and nation" (in different order) symbolizes everyone on earth without exception, and further accentuated by being listed seven times.

- There are four references to the "seven churches" (1:4, 11, 20 [twice]), implying they represent all churches of the world.[8]

- The fourfold division of creation symbolizes total participation of creation with "I heard every creature in heaven and on earth and under the earth and in the sea" (5:13).

- Creation's acclamation to God and the Lamb is also fourfold: "praise and honor and glory and power" (5:13). Note that the other doxologies are sevenfold (5:12; 7:12) or threefold (4:9, 11; 19:1) and match the numerical symbolism of those contexts.

- The sights and sounds from the throne are threefold (4:5), but when judgment comes to earth the formula is extended to fours: "peals of thunder and rumblings and flashes of lightning and an earthquake" (8:5; 16:18).[9]

- The created order consists of earth, sea, rivers/springs, and heaven (8:7–12; 14:7; 16:2–9).

- The fourth seal states the earth will be devastated by sword and famine and disease and wild beasts (6:8).

- At the sixth trumpet's lead up to Armageddon, the four angels are released for "this very hour and day and month and year" (9:15).

- The sixth trumpet also mentions humanity's murders, their witchcraft, their fornication, and their thefts (9:21).

- The blood that flows for one thousand six hundred stadia (14:20) is four squared multiplied by ten squared (4 x 4 x 10 x 10). Since four represents the coverage of earth or creation and ten represents totality, the bloodbath covers the earth completely.[10]

- The title "the one who lives for ever and ever" is found four times (4:9, 10; 10:6; 15:7).

6. Bauckham, *Climax of Prophecy*, 30–31. Beale (*Revelation*, 59) adds that four is "especially connoting something of universal or worldwide scope."

7. Prévost, *How to Read the Apocalypse*, 31.

8. John often attaches four with seven: "great earthquake," sharp sickle," and "shaft" of the "Abyss."

9. Resseguie, *Revelation*, 29.

10. Schüssler Fiorenza, *Revelation*, 91.

- The four references to the seven spirits (1:4; 3:1; 4:5; 5:6) represent the fullness of the Spirit sent throughout the earth.

- John is "in the Spirit" four times (1:10; 4:2; 17:3; 21:10).

- Harps and musicians and flutists and trumpeters will never be heard again (18:22).

- The return of Christ (19:14–16) includes four parts: his mouth issues forth a sharp sword; he shepherds the nations; he treads the winepress; and on his thigh is written a name.[11]

- The new Jerusalem has four sides because it is the new earth (21:16).

- Humanity is divided into four parts: "Let the one who does wrong continue to do wrong; let the vile person continue to be vile; let the one who does right continue to do right; and let the holy person continue to be holy" (22:11).

- The list of cargoes that Babylon imports equals twenty-eight items (7 x 4; 18:11–13). Thus, they "are listed as representative of *all* the products of the whole *world*."[12]

- The "Lamb" as a title of Christ is found twenty-eight times (7 x 4). Seven of these couple God with the Lamb (5:13; 6:16; 7:10; 14:4; 21:22; 22:1, 3). Bauckham states, "Since it is through the Lamb's conquest that God's rule over his creation comes about, the 7 x 4 occurrences of 'Lamb' appropriately indicate the worldwide scope of his complete victory."[13]

- "Time" (*chronos*) is found four times. The other word translated "time" (*kairos*) is found seven times.

- The exclamation "hallelujah" is found four times.

- The verbs "love," "hate," "blaspheme," "know," "bear witness," "shine," "live/dwell," "to shepherd," and "marvel" are found four times.

- The nouns "armies," "brothers," "multitude," "cup," "Hades," "door," "hundred," "John," "key," "faith" (*pistis* is found four times and *pistos* is found eight times), "judgment," "incense," "wine press," "light," "lightning," "hail," "tree," "well/shaft," "mourning," "scarlet," "staff/rod," "sword" (*machaira* is found four times and *romphaia* is found six times), "rich," "wisdom," and "merchants" are found four times each.

Certainly not every single instance in this list was intended as a numerical symbol by John. The sheer volume, however, should give interpreters pause and consider what may be intended by John's intricate structure as an extra theological layer of clarity, emphasis, or intensification.

---

11. See Osborne, *Revelation*, 683–86, who follows this structure. Rissi (*Future of the World*, 19–28) states John's intention is to list four actions in order to symbolize the world, and therefore earthly judgment. Moreover, the preceding context (19:11–13) lists exactly seven traits of the coming Christ, another signal for numerical symbolism. Beale (*Revelation*, 949), however, sees the four and seven as "possible but too tidy to fit the data."

12. Bauckham, *Climax of Prophecy*, 31. See Resseguie, *Revelation Unsealed*, 53.

13. Ibid., 34.

Four Corners of the Earth

The four corners of the earth is a common idiom that indicates the whole earth. Mentioned twice in Revelation (7:1; 20:8) this phrase pictures all of God's creation, the whole earth. The phrase is literally "four quarters of the earth" (NJB, REB), and some scholars contend that John is simply reflecting the ancient cosmology of a flat or square earth.[14] The term, however, seems to have been used as a metaphor long before John's time (Isa 11:12; Jer 49:36; Ezek 7:2; 2 *Bar.* 6:4–7:2; *T. Ash.* 7:1–7) without the need for cosmological decisions. It is common to understand the phrase to encompass the four directions—east, west, south, and north. Moderns continue to use the idiom, along with "four points of a compass" and "four corners of the globe."[15]

The first reference starts the first interlude: "After this I saw four angels standing at the four corners of the earth, holding back the four winds of the earth to prevent any wind from blowing on the land or on the sea or on any tree" (7:1). The abundance of "fours" in this one verse stresses John's point of full earthly coverage. These angels have sovereignty over the entire world. The other mention is in the millennial vision in which the devil musters worldwide forces: "When the thousand years are over, Satan will be released from his prison and will go out to deceive the nations in the four corners of the earth—Gog and Magog—and to gather them for battle" (20:7–8). Kistemaker explains, "His forces are numberless and a vast army reflects his awesome power. The entire non-Christian world from east to west and north to south is at his command."[16] Several modern translations alter or replace the idiom: "far ends of the earth" (CEV); "over the whole world" (GNT); "in all the earth" (NCV); and "every corner of the earth" (NLT). The idiom assists in understanding Armageddon limited not to a few square miles of territory in the Middle East but rather as a global event.

Fourth

Fractions such as "a fourth" reflect something partial, not total. Moreover, as a derivative of "four," it signifies full coverage of the earth. "Fourth" (*tetartos*) is found seven times in Revelation. Six of those times it is used sequentially as the third angel, the fourth angel, and so forth. Once, however, it is used as a fraction. In the fourth seal, the rider was "given power over a fourth of the earth to kill by sword, famine and plague, and by the wild beasts of the earth" (6:8). This fraction generates discussion among Revelation's interpreters.

The two choices are whether the fraction is treated literally or symbolically. Many interpreters chose the literal option. Normally, these are futurist interpreters who estimate the worldwide devastation of one-quarter of the earth's population during a period in the final few years of earth history.[17] The other option is to understand the fraction

---

14. So Ford, *Revelation*, 115; Reddish, *Revelation*, 142; perhaps Aune, *Revelation*, 2:450; Smalley, *Revelation*, 179.

15. Patterson (*Revelation* 190 n. 49) recognizes the figure of speech, but also suggests the ancients were aware of the spherical shape of the earth.

16. Kistemaker, *Revelation*, 542.

17. The numbers keep rising. Walvoord (*Revelation*, 131), writing in 1966, predicts 750 million

as symbolic. If John utilizes numerical symbolism then fractions fit his criteria as well. John did not invent the use of symbolic fractions. In apocalyptic literature a fraction is not intended to be precise. Rather, it represents something large but incomplete. If this fraction is understood symbolically, then John's audience and every successive generation as well must come to grips with its intent.

The fourth seal summarizes the judgment of God on the earth. John draws from the "four dreadful judgments" of Ezek 14:12–23. Whereas Jerusalem's remnant was spared, no such reassurance is found in the first four seals.[18] That "a fourth" is connected to the symbolism of "four" is also conspicuous. In both numerical and rhetorical forms, it is repeated four times in 6:8. Resseguie concludes that, "This heaping-up of fours accentuates the nature and extent of the plagues over the earth."[19]

But if this is not limited to a single, catastrophic event in the distant past or near future, then what does it signify? Throughout the entire time period of the seven seals (the Christian era), "at any given moment a fourth of the earth's population may be dying because of the sword, famine, diseases, and the wild animals of the earth."[20] The countless deaths from self-inflicted wars and famines are traceable throughout the centuries. In other words, Satan is always at work attempting to destroy God's people. But his efforts are permitted to be partial, not total. Nevertheless, toward the end, a release from his chains permits him even more earthly destruction through wars, civil wars, famine, and disease. But attempts to calculate worldwide death totals do not understand how John utilizes numerical symbolism. Like "a third" in 8:7–12, a fourth suggests partial, not total destruction. It becomes a call for unbelievers to repent and believers to persevere.

Full Number

The "full number" of believers to be killed before the eschaton is a common apocalyptic motif that emphasizes the need for patience and perseverance on the part of the faithful as well as the vindication of God. At the fifth seal the answer given to the martyrs' cry of "how long must we wait" is the reward of a white robe (symbolizing purity earned by a persevering faith while on earth; 3:4–5; 4 *Ezra* 2:39–44). Vindication will happen soon, but they must wait "until the full number of their fellow servants, their brothers and sisters, were killed just as they had been" (6:11). The "full number" (NET, NIV, NLT) is also rendered as "complete number" (CEV, GNT), "roll completed" (NJB), and "number. . .complete(d)" (CSB, ESV, NASB, NKJV, NRSV, REB). These words are actually missing from the Greek. The aorist subjunctive *plērōthōsin* ("has been fulfilled") requires added words for sense. Thus, Ladd cautions, "This statement is surely not to be understood in any mathematical way, as though God had decreed that there must be a certain number of martyrs, and

---

dead. Lindsey (*New World Coming*, 106), writing in 1973, raises that to one billion dead. Robert Thomas (*Revelation*, 1:438), writing in 1992, calculates 1.25 billion will perish. LaHaye (*Revelation Unveiled*, 145), writing in 1999, forecasts 1.5 billion, etc. Preterists, on the other hand, point back to first-century fulfillment. Chilton (*Days of Vengeance*, 192) pictures the fall of Jerusalem.

18. Osborne, *Revelation*, 283; Mounce, *Revelation*, 145.

19. Resseguie, *Revelation*, 129.

20. Brighton, *Revelation*, 168.

when this number was slain, the end will come."[21] Nevertheless, the image is intended to stress the sovereignty and vindication of God.

Although a strange concept for modern readers, this was a common motif in apocalyptic literature. God knows each one who is to be martyred and will vindicate them all at the proper time, which must happen soon because the time is near.[22] Bauckham compares apocalyptic texts (*1 En.* 47:1–4; *4 Ezra* 4:35–37; *2 Bar.* 23:4–5) with Rev 6:9–11. The texts all have in common the idea of a set number of people to be killed to be completed at the eschaton.[23] The image of "filling up a measure" goes far back into Greek literature as well (Homer, Apollonius, Rhodius). Likewise, Jews spoke of an appointed period of one's life being filled up: "When your days are fulfilled to walk with your fathers" (1 Chr 17:11, ESV). Paul apparently refers to it as well (1 Thess 2:16). For the faithful this concept underscored the sovereignty of God. For the pagans it referred to fate.[24] Does God answer the martyrs' petition of 6:11? The answer is a resounding yes because the sixth seal (6:12–17) unveils judgment day. Thus, God assures his people that end-time judgment and vindication are certain but only in his sovereign timing. Martyrdom and persecution are not finished. The eschaton is near but not yet. Believers must show patience and perseverance.

Hundred and Forty-Four Cubits

The measurement of the great, high wall of the heavenly city symbolizes eternal protection and complete security for those inside. The cubit was the principal unit for linear measurement in the OT, based on the length of the forearm to the tip of the middle finger (about 17.5 inches).[25] "Cubit" (*pēchys*) is found four times in the NT with an array of renderings. It is translated in Matt 6:27 and Luke 12:25 as "moment," "hour," "a bit longer" (HCSB chooses the more literal "cubit to his height" but CSB revises it to "moment"). The word is usually translated as "yards" in John 21:8. The final usage of *pēchys* is found in Rev 21:17: "The angel measured the wall using human measurement, and it was 144 cubits thick." Many English translations retain the archaic reading of "cubits" for the sake of numerical symbolism. Some versions add "thick" or "high" even though the words are not present in the Greek text. Regrettably, several modern versions update "cubits" into "feet" or "yards." Thus, "216 feet" (CEB, CEV, GNT, NCV, NLT), and "72 yards" (NASB) have been proffered. Such modernizing of measurements found in Revelation undercuts the numerical symbolism that John employs.

---

21. Ladd, *Revelation*, 106.

22. Osborne, *Revelation*, 289.

23. Bauckham, *Climax of Prophecy*, 48–56. See also Murphy, *Apocalypticism*, 107, 150, 158, 340.

24. Keener, *Revelation*, 218 n. 7

25. See Huey, "Weights and Measures," 1061–73.

Scholars and Bible versions divide over whether height[26] or thickness[27] is intended by John. Either way, a literal view is not in mind. Updating cubits into literal measurements is nonsensical when considering the spaciousness of the rest of the heavenly city. Thus, the translation of a hundred and forty-four cubits "high" makes little sense. Likewise, those who choose to add the word "thick" to the heavenly city's wall, picturing a 216-foot thick structure, are similarly hampered. It must be asked, for what purpose are the walls so thick if the twelve gates are left perpetually open? Beale, therefore, reminds us that the wall is measured in the same way as the city was measured in the previous verse—by its height, width, and length. The angel who measures the temple in Ezekiel (40:5) measures the height and width, and they are equal. If one aspect is in mind it is height, not thickness, since in the OT a city's walls emphasize security by their height (Deut 3:5).[28]

Nevertheless, the point is not width or height or length, but the *number*—a hundred and forty-four, the square of twelve, the number of completion for God's people. It multiplies the twelve tribes and the twelve apostles on the foundation of the city.[29] It also brings to mind a hundred and forty-four thousand (12 x 12,000), which is the number of the saints (7:4–8; 14:1–5), the church militant throughout the centuries between Christ's ascension and return. Resseguie states that "the wall, like the city itself, is complete—an eternally secure place for all its inhabitants. The perfect cubic city is the ideal dwelling place for God and his people."[30] This measurement for the heavenly city suggests that the church—the bride of the Lamb—is the Holy City. Therefore, attempts to update cubits into contemporary measurements of feet or yards or height or thickness obscure the figurative nature of the number, reducing the symbol to a bizarre and minimalist meaning. The point is that the wall represents total and complete security and safety for God's people forever.

Hundred and Forty-Four Thousand

The hundred and forty-four thousand servants from every tribe of Israel symbolizes the whole church—Jews and gentiles—the complete number of all believers on the earth throughout the interadvental age, with the emphasis upon their role as militant witnesses. This number is found in the first interlude (7:1–17) and the third interlude (12:1–15:4). The interludes depict the role of God's people, thereby hinting at what the number symbolizes. In the

---

26. Beale, *Revelation*, 1076–77; Beasley-Murray, *Revelation*, 323; Blount, *Revelation,* 390; Morris, *Revelation*, 244; Murphy, *Fallen Is Babylon*, 420; Reddish, *Revelation*, 407; Roloff, *Revelation*, 243; Smalley, *Revelation*, 552; CEV, GNT, NCV, NJB, REB.

27. Aune, *Revelation*, 2:1162; Keener, *Revelation*, 494; Ladd, *Revelation*, 282; Mulholland, *Revelation*, 325; Osborne, *Revelation*, 753; Patterson, *Revelation*, 371; Stefanovic, *Revelation*, 588; Robert Thomas, *Revelation*, 2:468; CEB, NIV, NLT.

28. Beale, *Revelation*, 1076–77.

29. Brighton, *Revelation*, 616; Kistemaker, *Revelation*, 569; Mounce, *Revelation*, 392. Schüssler Fiorenza (*Revelation*, 205) suggests the wall is a symbol for the new Israel itself, the high-priestly people of God, the church.

30. Resseguie, *Revelation*, 254.

first interlude John hears the number of those servants who are sealed: "144,000 from all the tribes of Israel" (7:4). Then in verses 5–8, twelve thousand from each tribe is meticulously listed. This group reappears in the third interlude. John sees the hundred and forty-four thousand standing with the Lamb on Mount Zion. The Lamb's name and the Father's name are written on their foreheads. They are the virgins, the firstfruits, and the blameless (14:1–5).

Numerous possibilities on the identity of these servants have been proposed through the centuries.[31] There are, however, two main views. First, many believe they represent a literal group of Jewish Christians. John's words appear specific. They come from every tribe of the people of Israel, and then he lists the twelve tribes. Dispensationalists advocate this position the most. They understand them as a select group of Jewish Christians who are providentially protected, sealed in order evangelize during the final years of earth history. After they accomplish their task, many are martyred. These Jews are "charged with a special responsibility of witnessing for Christ during the world's darkest hour," states Robert Thomas.[32] Preterists also find the number to refer to a literal remnant of Jewish believers, but relate them to the fall of Jerusalem in AD 70.[33]

The second view is that the number represents the church. The hundred and forty-four thousand servants symbolize the whole church, Jew and gentile, spiritual Israel. The majority of commentators favor this viewpoint.[34] There are several reasons that support the symbolic view over a literal, biological view. First, the NT often uses Jewish terminology to signify the church. For example, "Israel" (Rom 9:6), "Jews" (Rom 2:28–29), "twelve tribes" (Jas 1:1), "the circumcision" (Phil 3:2–3), "chosen people" (1 Pet 2:9–10), and "Abraham's seed" (Rom 4:1–11; 9:6–8; Gal 3:7, 16) are Jewish designations that are applied to the church.[35] For John, Christians are "true Jews" (2:9; 3:9). Keener declares,

31. For a history of views see Aune, *Revelation*, 2:440–47; Kovacs and Rowland, *Revelation*, 102, 161–62; Koester, *Revelation*, 355–56; and Weinrich, *Revelation*, 105–9.

32. Robert Thomas, *Revelation*, 1:478. So too Hindson, *Revelation*, 89; Lindsey, *New World Coming*, 121; Patterson, *Revelation*, 194–99; Ryrie, *Revelation*, 61; Walvoord, *Revelation*, 141–43. Thomas (1:474–78) generates five pages of support for the literal view. Gromacki ("Witnesses, 144,000," 425) follows literalism to its extreme extent. He specifies that these Jews "are further identified as male virgins, obedient followers of Christ redeemed as the possible first converts of the Great Tribulation period, guileless spokesmen, and without fault before God." Another eccentric view is that of LaHaye (*Revelation Unveiled*, 229–31), whose literalism leads him to discover two separate sets of a hundred and forty-four thousand. The first are the Jewish "Billy Grahams" who arrive during humanity's last years (chapter 7). The second set is outstanding gentile saints of history (chapter 14).

33. Adams, *Time Is at Hand*, 63; Buchanan, *Revelation*, 210; Clark, *Message from Patmos*, 60; Charles, *Revelation*, 1:199; Chilton, *Days of Vengeance*, 207–8.

34. In-depth surveys include Aune, *Revelation*, 2:440–47; Bauckham, *Climax of Prophecy*, 210–37; Beale, *Revelation*, 416–23; Mayo, *Those Who Call Themselves Jews*, 77–106; Osborne, *Revelation*, 301–15; Schnabel, *40 Questions*, 85–91; Smalley, *Revelation*, 184–89; and Tavo, *Woman, Mother, Bride*, 135–58. Although most scholars agree the group represents the church, several within this majority view the number more literally or understand that it does not represent the whole church. Thus, the group is in some fashion unique, live only at the time of the eschaton, or most often are seen as a special group of Christian martyrs. These views are found in Beckwith, *Apocalypse*, 353; Caird, *Revelation*, 94; Kiddle, *Revelation*, 135; Murphy, *Fallen Is Babylon*, 313–14; Reddish, *Revelation*, 146–47; Schüssler Fiorenza, *Revelation*, 67; and Skaggs and Benham, *Revelation*, 87.

35. See Minear, *Images of the Church*, 71–84.

"Revelation emphasizes the Jewishness of all believers."[36] Second, the church was widely understood in early Christianity to be the true Israel. Since John applies to the church so many descriptions of the old Israel, "it would be perverse to treat the present case as an exception to the rule."[37] Third, John's peculiar listing of the twelve tribes holds a subtle hint that he is not referring to literal Israel, but to the true, spiritual Israel, the church. The OT lists the twelve tribes twenty-four times and none correspond to John's list. Some scholars suggest this provides an early example of the symbolic use of the tribes to represent the redeemed.[38] Fourth, the context of 9:4 suggests that the church as a whole has been sealed. This implies the sealing of the hundred and forty-four thousand in chapter 7 refers to the church. The mark of the beast symbolizes all unbelievers. The seal of God represents all believers.[39] Fifth, the hundred and forty-four thousand are God's servants without any qualifications. Throughout the rest of Revelation, servants signify all believers (1:1; 2:20; 6:11; 10:7; 11:18; 19:2, 5, 10; 22:3, 6, 9).[40] Therefore, the number combines with many other images in Revelation to highlight the Jewish heritage of all believers.

The key is to understand John's use of numerical symbolism, in this instance the multiples of ten and twelve. Twelve is the number of completeness particularly with God's people in mind. A thousand represents entirety and fullness, and signifies an indefinitely large group. The number then stresses the fullness and comprehensiveness of those sealed and eternally protected. Such numerical symbolism intensifies the complete, inclusive number of the people of God.

Many scholars affirm that John is picturing the whole church as a militant army of the Lord tasked with the assignment of witnessing the gospel.[41] When Israel journeyed in the wilderness they did so organized as a military camp in preparation for the conquest of the promised land. Likewise, believers are a spiritual gospel army. They are spiritually active in the battle for the Lord and face potential martyrdom. They carry the banner of the gospel of Christ to the nations. Therefore, the first mention reflects their militant witness on earth throughout the ages. The second passage reflects their victorious reward at the second coming. God's people will be brought safely through persecution and even martyrdom and into the eternal fellowship of God.

36. Keener, *Revelation*, 232. Patterson (*Revelation*, 196) correctly asks, "How would a first-century Gentile Christian have read this text?" His answer incorrectly states that it must have been taken literally. On the contrary, the evidence supports the gentile church understood what John was doing with this symbol.

37. Caird, *Revelation*, 95.

38. So Boring, *Revelation*, 130; Easley, *Revelation*, 126; Alan Johnson, "Revelation," 13:662; Ladd; *Revelation*, 114–15; Smalley, *Revelation*, 187. But see Tavo, *Woman, Mother, Bride*, 154–55, who cautions against a unique listing by John. For Tavo it is John's numerical symbolism that is most important. See the entry "Tribes of Israel."

39. Beasley-Murray, *Revelation*, 140; Keener, *Revelation*, 232; Osborne, *Revelation*, 311–12; Schnabel, *40 Questions*, 89–91.

40. Keener, *Revelation*, 231–32. Tavo (*Woman, Mother, Bride*, 149–50) supplies a chart. See the entry "Servants."

41. The most compelling arguments for the militant emphasis come from Bauckham, *Climax of Prophecy*, 215–29; Beale, *Revelation*, 422–23; Blount, *Revelation*, 145–46; Boring, *Revelation*, 127–29; Brighton, *Revelation*, 190–91, 370–75; Caird, *Revelation*, 178–81; and Tavo, *Woman, Mother, Bride*, 155–58.

Number

John uses the word "number" as a definite or indefinite term, and for gematria. "Number" (*arithmos*) is found ten times in Revelation.[42] John J. Davis relates that the word follows a threefold usage. It can designate (1) a fixed and definite number; (2) a number whose letters indicate a certain person; and (3) an indefinite number.[43] Revelation's instances fall neatly into all three categories. First, a fixed or definite number is mentioned three times (7:4; 9:16 [twice]). There are a hundred and forty-four thousand sealed and twice ten thousand times ten thousand cavalry. The definite numbers in these two instances stress their symbolism, not their quantity. Second, a number whose letters possibly indicate a certain individual refers to the beast of Rev 13. Calculating the letters of a person's name refers to the ancient practice of gematria. The beast's number is six hundred sixty-six (13:17–18 [four times]; 15:2).[44] Finally, an indefinite number is intended by the thousands of thousands and ten thousands upon ten thousands of angels (5:11), and the incalculable number of Gog and Magog, who are like sand on the seashore (20:8).

Seven

Seven connotes completeness, fullness, totality, and perfection. John's encompassing use of this number emphasizes theological truths and underscores the intricate structuring of his Apocalypse. The number seven along with its multiples is found throughout the ancient Near East as a significant and sacred number. Its symbolism is traceable throughout Scripture, from the seven days of creation (Gen 4:15) to the sevenfold voice of God (Ps 29) to the sevenfold wrath of God (Ps 79:12) to the seven eyes of God (Zech 4:10). The number appears 739 times in the OT, sixty-six times in the Apocrypha, and 108 times in the NT. Boring cautions, "Not all these have a particularly sacred or symbolic meaning, of course, though the majority have at least this tone."[45]

Seven (*hepta*) is the most significant number in John's symbolic arsenal. It is a keystone symbol and John makes extensive use of it in an artistic way to emphasize theological truths.[46] It is found fifty-five times in Revelation, accounting for 63 percent of all NT uses. Seven precedes numerous nouns, including spirits, lampstands, stars, golden lampstands, seals, horns, eyes, angels, trumpets, thunders, crowns, heads, plagues, bowls, hills, and kings. In addition, seven thousand people are killed by an earthquake. Even

---

42. The verb *arithmeō* is found once at 7:9. It is usually translated as "count" but "number" is used by CEB, ESV, NKJV.

43. Davis, *Biblical Numerology*, 40. See also Ryken, *Dictionary of Biblical Imagery*, 599–600; Schmitz, "Number," 683–85.

44. See the entry "Six Hundred Sixty-Six."

45. Boring, "Seven, Seventh, Seventy," 197. See Prévost, *How to Read the Apocalypse*, 31–32; Ryken, *Dictionary of Biblical Imagery*, 774–75; Silva, "ἑπτά," 260–63.

46. Not everyone sees theology behind John's numbers. For example, Davis (*Biblical Numerology*, 104–24) does not find much symbolism beyond the general usage of "seven." Similarly, Moyise ("Word Frequencies in Revelation," 285–99), reacting to Bauckham (*Climax of Prophecy*, 29–37), does not dispute John's meticulous use of numbers, but he does minimize that they are used by John to convey theological truths.

more striking and missing in most scholarly treatments are the quantity of embedded uses in Revelation.

- Two hymns have seven attributes (5:12; 7:12).
- There are seven beatitudes.[47]
- Seven people groups are listed (6:15; 19:18).
- Locusts have seven features (9:7–10).
- The Lamb has "seven horns" and "seven eyes" which are the "seven spirits" (5:6).
- Each of the seven letters contains seven elements.[48]
- The three merisms ("Alpha and Omega," "first and last," "beginning and end") appear a total of seven times.
- The phrase "these are the words" (*tade legei*) is mentioned seven times.[49]
- The fourfold phrase "peoples and languages and tongues and nations" is mentioned seven times.
- "Lord God Almighty" has seven references.
- There are seven occurrences of the "one who sits on the throne."[50]
- The elders and living creatures are mentioned together seven times.
- There are seven promises of the second coming (2:5, 16; 3:11; 16:15; 22:7, 12, 20).[51]
- The hundred and forty-four thousand have seven characteristics (14:4–5).[52]
- The returning Christ is described with seven images (19:11–13).[53]
- The vision of the new Jerusalem falls into seven parts (21:9–27).[54]
- The thrice-mentioned formula (42 months, 1260 days, and time, times, and half a time) add up to seven (11:2, 3, 9, 11; 12:6, 14; 13:5).[55]

47. See the entry "Blessed."

48. See the entry "Seven Churches" for examples.

49. The phrase is found 250 times in the LXX to introduce prophetic oracles from God spoken through the prophets. Thus, the formula now refers to Jesus who is treated on the same level as God. See Mathewson, *Revelation*, 18.

50. Variations of the formula can also be found (4:2, 3; 7:10; 19:4; 20:11), but Bauckham (*Climax of Prophecy*, 34) suggests the variations are deliberately used in order to keep the number of occurrences to seven.

51. Bauckham, *Climax of Prophecy*, 34; Longenecker, "Linked Like a Chain," 107–8. Wendland ("Hermeneutical Significance," 449) observes it from a different angle, finding seven references to the second coming (1:7; 11:17–18; 14:14–20; 16:15; 19:11–16; 21:1–8; 22:12–20).

52. Paul, *Revelation*, 35. Paul follows others who note seven unnumbered visions from 19:11–21:1.

53. See the discussion by Osborne (*Revelation*, 678–83). Rissi (*Future of the World*, 19–28) relates that John purposefully listed seven to accent numerical symbolism (fullness of the Spirit), especially in connection to the four actions of earthly, end-time judgment by the Warrior Messiah found in the subsequent verses (19:14–16). Beale (*Revelation*, 949), however, is not as confident as Rissi.

54. Rissi, *Future of the World*, 60.

55. In addition, many scholars adopt a sevenfold outline for Revelation. Wendland ("Hermeneutical

Thirty words appear exactly seven times in Revelation. Significant nouns and adjectives include Abyss, Christ, cloud, earthquake, lampstand, patient endurance, mark, prophecy, sharp, sickle, sign/signs, time (*kairos*), and worthy. Key verbs include call, prepare, be full, and rule. Moreover, several words appear as multiples of seven. Words found fourteen times (7 x 2) include Jesus (seven of the fourteen occurrences are connected with "witness/testimony" [1:2, 9; 12:17; 17:6; 19:10 (twice); 20:4]), Spirit, God's people (accepting 22:21 as original), servant, star, and woe.[56] Twenty-eight is another key multiple for John (7 x 4). It is used for the Lamb, which among its twenty-eight usages includes seven instances coupled with God (5:13; 6:16; 7:10; 14:4; 21:22; 22:1, 3).[57] The list of cargoes which Babylon imports (18:12–13) equals twenty-eight. Thus, they "are listed as representative of *all* the products of the whole *world*."[58] If the "seven thunders" (10:3–4) are counted as a fourth set of plagues, then a total of twenty-eight plagues are mentioned. It is also intriguing that the three words translated as "scroll" (*biblaridion, biblion, biblos*) and the two words for "thousand" (*chilias, chilioi*) each add up to twenty-eight.

In sum, there are far too many numerical patterns to be coincidental. John is purposeful in utilizing the number seven. He does it for theological reasons. The sevens denote that God controls all the world and practices his sovereignty over it. God guides every event.[59] Yarbro Collins agrees. The frequency of numerical symbolism highlights the notion that there is nothing random or coincidental. John uses numbers to indicate that God's will is behind all the events and guides them so that the ultimate victory of God's people is assured.[60]

Yet the sevens imply even more. The meticulous structuring of John's work with sevens underscores his careful arrangement. The sevens prepare readers to see individual visions coming to a conclusion (churches, seals, trumpets, bowls, and the three interludes). Key words and phrases are found near the conclusion of visions (hymns, beatitudes, words reflecting end-time judgment, and titles of deity). The sevens coupled with the intratextual connections and fuller expansions of vision scenes in later visions confirm John's genius and intentionality.

Significance," 447–76) proposes seven sections with seven subsections beneath each one. Others note seven heavenly throne-room scenes (with different iterations); seven symbolic beings in chapters 12–14 (the woman, the dragon, the child, Michael, the first beast, the second beast, and the Lamb); and seven defeated enemies in chapters 17–20 (Babylon the Great, beast, false prophet, Satan, Gog and Magog, death, and Hades).

56. Bauckham, *Climax of Prophecy*, 34–35. Bauckham assesses only the seven uses of Spirit in the letters and seven other places. Interestingly, there are the twenty-one occurrences (7 x 3) of "authority," "king," and "day."

57. Ibid., 34.

58. Ibid., 31, 350–71.

59. Beale, *Revelation*, 59; Murphy, *Apocalypticism*, 101.

60. See Yarbro Collins, *Cosmology and Eschatology*, 55–138, for several insights on John's symbolism.

Seven Heads/ Seven Hills/ Seven Kings

The "seven" that is attached to each of these words symbolizes all earthly powers and rulers and kingdoms throughout the ages who claim spiritual authority over their subjects, especially in their opposition to Christians. Their demise is certain when Jesus returns. This entry is difficult to categorize. It could be placed under body parts (heads), nature (hills), people (kings), or numbers (seven). The emphasis on numbers wins out. This is one of John's self-interpreting symbols. In the fall of Babylon vision, he is shown the woman sitting on a scarlet beast which had seven heads and ten horns (17:3). The image is interpreted in 17:9–11: "The seven heads are seven hills on which the woman sits. They are also seven kings. Five have fallen, one is, the other has not yet come; but when he does come, he must remain for only a little while. The beast who once was, and now is not, is an eighth king. He belongs to the seven and is going to his destruction."

The seven heads of the beast symbolize the complete power of Satan over his subjects.[61] John next states the seven heads are seven hills. John's readers would think immediately of Rome. The ancient world used the phrase to refer to Rome built on seven hills. John further identifies the heads and hills with seven kings. Many scholars understand Roman emperors for the kings. The difficulty lies in which emperor is counted first. Different calculations have been conjectured through the centuries on the identity of the seven heads, hills, and kings.[62] Three are popular. First, most preterists point to first-century Rome and Nero's reign. He is on the throne and a *Nero Redivivus* legend would make him the eighth king.[63] Second, several commentators, primarily futurists, believe these are not kings, but rather kingdoms. Mountains elsewhere symbolize kingdoms (Isa 2:2; Jer 51:25: Dan 2:35).[64] The five previous empires might be Egypt, Assyria, Babylon, Persia, and Greece. Rome is the sixth. The seventh and eighth empires lie in the future.[65]

A third option, however, fits better and is followed by most scholars. John's use of seven has been consistently symbolic throughout Revelation. The numbers should not be connected to actual emperors or empires. These are apocalyptic symbols. It is better, therefore, to interpret this as complete despotic power and human rule. Ian Paul explains, "There is little point in asking who these seven kings are than in asking for the names of the 144,000 in Revelation 7."[66] The beastly rule of the heads, hills, and kings is not

---

61. See the entry "Heads."

62. Osborne (*Revelation*, 618–21) helpfully lists seven options.

63. So Chilton (*Days of Vengeance*, 435–38) and Gentry (*Beast of Revelation*, 104), who both accent an early date for Revelation's composition. Russell (*Parousia*, 492) attempts to connect the seven hills to Jerusalem. Buchanan (*Revelation*, 496–98) connects the seven heads with the Herodian line. Herod Agrippa I or II would be the eighth.

64. See the entry "Mountain." *Oros* is customarily translated as "mount" or "mountain" throughout Revelation, and it is consistent to translate it "seven mountains" in 17:9. Several versions, however, render it "seven hills," which hinders the intratextual connection (GNT, NABR, NIV, NJB, NLT, REB).

65. Easley, *Revelation*, 310–11; Hendriksen, *More than Conquerors*, 170–71; Hindson, *Revelation*, 178; Kistemaker, *Revelation*, 472; Ladd, *Revelation*, 227; Patterson, *Revelation*, 323; Robert Thomas, *Revelation*, 2:297; Walvoord, *Revelation*, 251.

66. Paul, *Revelation*, 285. Resseguie (*Revelation*, 224) appends, "If a figurative interpretation of the seven kings is adopted, the puzzle is solved."

confined to the first generation or the last generation (the first two options). Brighton declares that "all oppressive rulers that come and go throughout the entire period of time covered by the prophetic message of Revelation (Christ's ascension to his return) are symbolized by these seven kings as well as by the beast itself."[67]

Therefore, it is the fullness and completeness of the beast's power that is the point. The seven heads, mountains, and kings represent Satan's quest for authority. John's riddle of five fallen, one is, one is to come, and then an eighth suggests that all beastly emperors and empires are coming quickly to a close. Their power is demolished a few verses later when Jesus comes (17:14).

Seven Thousand

The number seven thousand is used by John to symbolize the totality of unbelievers who are judged at the return of Christ. "Seven thousand" (*chiliades hepta*) is found only once in Revelation, but the use of two figures, seven and a thousand, alerts readers to the possibility that numerical symbolism is at work. At the conclusion of the second interlude, the two witnesses are whisked to heaven. Then, "At that very hour there was a severe earthquake and a tenth of the city collapsed. Seven thousand people were killed in the earthquake, and the survivors were terrified and gave glory to the God of heaven" (11:13).

Many scholars, especially futurists, accept these numbers literally and often with Jerusalem in mind.[68] However, as with other numbers and places in Revelation, a figurative understanding is meant by seven thousand (as well as the fraction a tenth). The numbers form part of John's symbolic geography—a city that represents the whole world.[69] Thus, seven thousand stresses the idea of completion and signifies "a large number."[70] More specifically, Beale explains, "The two numbers would emphasize the totality of unbelievers judged at the conclusion of history."[71]

The fact that a great earthquake and specific time ("at that hour") accompany the number and that it concludes a vision suggests another picture of the eschaton. If this

67. Brighton, *Revelation*, 449. So also Aune, *Revelation*, 3:948; Beale, *Revelation*, 869; Beasley-Murray, *Revelation*, 256; Boring, *Revelation*, 183; Caird, *Revelation*, 218–19; Duvall, *Revelation*, 227; Farmer, *Revelation*, 116; Fee, *Revelation*, 238; Harrington, *Revelation*, 172; Hughes, *Revelation*, 185; Alan Johnson, "Revelation," 13:742; Dennis Johnson, *Triumph of the Lamb*, 250; Koester, *Revelation*, 691; Morris, *Revelation*, 204; Mounce, *Revelation*, 315; Murphy, *Fallen Is Babylon*, 361; Osborne, *Revelation*, 620; Paul, *Revelation*, 285; Reddish, *Revelation*, 329; Resseguie, *Revelation*, 221; Schnabel, *40 Questions*, 169; Skaggs and Benham, *Revelation*, 175; Smalley, *Revelation*, 436–37; Sweet, *Revelation*, 257; J. C. Thomas, *Apocalypse*, 507; Wall, *Revelation*, 207.

68. Easley, *Revelation*, 195; Hindson, *Revelation*, 126; Ladd, *Revelation*, 159; Mounce, *Revelation*, 223; Ryrie, *Revelation*, 86; Sweet, *Revelation*, 189; Swete, *Apocalypse*, 141; Robert Thomas, *Revelation*, 2:98; Walvoord, *Revelation*, 183. Patterson (*Revelation*, 250) adds that the phrase *onomata anthrōpōn* (literally, "names of men") could refer to particularly significant people who are killed by the quake.

69. Resseguie, *Revelation*, 165.

70. Blount, *Revelation*, 271; Kistemaker, *Revelation*, 338–39; Reddish, *Revelation*, 213.

71. Beale, *Revelation*, 603, who surmises that a "tenth of the city" could be calculated as seven thousand if Jerusalem were in mind. Jerusalem had a population of around 70,000. See the entry "Tenth of the City."

pictures judgment day, then who are "the survivors" (*hoi loipoi*) who in terror give glory to God?[72] Many, if not the majority of scholars, conclude this expresses genuine repentance and true faith near the end of history.[73]

Other scholars, however, understand the survivors as expressing remorse, not repentance. They are forced to recoil in horror and dread.[74] Understood this way, genuine conversion is no longer an option, especially since it describes end-time judgment. It reflects obstinate submission to a greater force (Phil 2:11). It is the end, and a begrudging faithless world is prepared for its judgment. That the seven thousand implies the full number of unbelievers being judged at the end of history is given more support when it is remembered that a previous end-time vision, the sixth seal, included seven social groups (6:15), representing all of humanity, being forced to give end-time homage (6:16–17).[75] Therefore, numerical symbolism, the placement of the numbers at the conclusion of the vision, and the earthquake all signal the end—final judgment.

Six Hundred Sixty-Six

Six hundred sixty-six is the numerical symbol for the beast. It stands for incompleteness and imperfection. The threefold six is a demonic parody of the Trinity. Gematria and triangular numbers suggest Nero was John's original referent. Duvall expresses the exasperation of the modern interpreter: "There may be more proposals for the meaning of 666 than there are verses in Revelation."[76] John states, "This calls for wisdom. Let the person who has insight calculate the number of the beast, for it is the number of a man. That number is 666."[77]

There are three primary approaches to understanding this number.[78] Many commentators overlap, but stress one view over the others. First, it is a triangular number.

---

72. A better translation for "the survivors" is "the rest." See the entry "Rest, The."

73. Aune, *Revelation*, 2:628–29; Bauckham, *Climax of Prophecy*, 278–83; Beasley-Murray, *Revelation*, 187; Brighton, *Revelation*, 302; Caird, *Revelation*, 140; Harrington, *Revelation*, 157; Alan Johnson, "Revelation," 13:688; Keener, *Revelation*, 297; Koester, *Revelation*, 512; Krodel, *Revelation*, 228; Ladd, *Revelation*, 159–60; Murphy, *Fallen Is Babylon*, 268; Osborne, *Revelation*, 433; Patterson, *Revelation*, 251; Prigent, *Apocalypse*, 358–59; Resseguie, *Revelation*, 166; Schüssler Fiorenza, *Justice and Judgment*, 79; Smalley, *Revelation*, 286; Stefanovic, *Revelation*, 361; Tenney, *Interpreting Revelation*, 106; Thomas and Macchia, *Revelation*, 209; Wall, *Revelation*, 148. Duvall (*Revelation*, 151) suggests the passage may teach a large-scale conversion of humanity at the end. Beckwith (*Apocalypse*, 604), Charles (*Revelation*, 1:291), Ladd (*Revelation*, 159), and Robert Thomas (*Revelation*, 2:99) confine the conversion to Jews.

74. Beale, *Revelation*, 604–7; Caird, *Revelation*, 139; Hendriksen, *More than Conquerors*, 158–59; Hughes, *Revelation*, 130; Dennis Johnson, *Triumph of the Lamb*, 175; Kiddle, *Revelation*, 206: Kistemaker, *Revelation*, 339; Mounce, *Revelation*, 229; Roloff, *Revelation*, 134; Rowland, "Revelation," 12:643; Schnabel, *40 Questions*, 218 n. 18; Skaggs and Benham, *Revelation*, 117; Walvoord, *Revelation*, 183.

75. Many interpreters, of course, offer that it is not yet the final end, thus emphasizing the partial nature of a tenth and seven thousand. For example, Mangina (*Revelation*, 141) and Smalley (*Revelation*, 286) see the event not in the realm of ultimate, but only of penultimate things.

76. Duvall, *Revelation*, 186. History has unmasked hundreds of beasts with confidence. See Brady, *Contribution of British Writers*, who cites over a hundred interpretations from 1560 to 1830.

77. This refers to the first beast. Patterson (*Revelation*, 282) uniquely posits the number refers to the second beast.

78. See Aune, *Revelation*, 770–73; Prigent, *Apocalypse*, 423–28; Smalley, *Revelation*, 351–53.

For some interpreters, Revelation reveals triangular numbers (adding up successive numbers), square numbers (sum of sequential odd numbers), and rectangular numbers (sum of successive even numbers). Six hundred sixty-six is a triangular number of thirty-six (adding digits one to thirty-six) which is also a triangular number of eight. This possibly connects the beast to "the eighth" in 17:11. Bauckham champions this view. He concludes that analyzing these numerical values reveals Nero as six hundred sixty-six.[79]

Second, it is gematria. Simply put, gematria is the ancient practice where each letter of the alphabet is assigned a number for counting purposes. If "Neron Caesar" is transliterated from Greek into Hebrew it equates to six hundred sixty-six. Nero was designated as a "beast" (*thērion*) by several Greek writers. The numerical value of *thērion* is six hundred sixty-six. Moreover, an alternate manuscript reading of "616" corrects "Neron Caesar" to "Nero Caesar."[80] Most scholars, therefore, accept the use of gematria at 13:18 and identify Nero.[81]

Third, it is generic numerical symbolism. Like the other numbers in Revelation, this number should be treated symbolically. The figurative significance of six hundred sixty-six begins with the number six which falls short of the perfect number, seven. It falls short of God. Thus, the threefold six is a generic symbol of a humanistic and idolatrous trinity (dragon, beast, and false prophet).[82] This view aids in seeing the beast not only as a contemporary of John, but standing for the Nero-like personalities and Rome-like systems of persecution found in every generation. Numerous interpreters now favor this approach.[83]

There is value in all three approaches and several scholars emphasize more than one approach. The order of priority and worth, however, should place the generic number first. Gematria and triangular numbers are intriguing but must be used with caution.[84]

79. Bauckham, *Climax of Prophecy*, 390–404. Chilton (*Days of Vengeance*, 347–52), Sweet (*Revelation*, 218–19), and J. C. Thomas (*Apocalypse*, 414–17) appeal to this as well.

80. No less than four different numbers are in the Greek manuscript tradition—666, 665, 646, and 616. Although found only in a few manuscripts, Cate ("Text of Revelation," 128) suggests the variant reading of 616 may have been original. Wood ("Simplifying the Number," 131–40) points out that both numbers just as easily refer to the word "beast" (*thērion*) without specifying Nero. Williams "P115 and the Number," 151–53) purports that one manuscript with the reading of 616 mimics the *nomen sacrum* for "Christ." Kirchmayr ("Die Bedeutung von 666," 424–27) conceives a peculiar method of calculation that results in the number being equal to the Tetragrammaton.

81. Bauckham (*Climax of Prophecy*, 389) declares, "The gematria does not merely assert that Nero is the beast: it demonstrates that he is." For discussions supporting gematria see Gentry, *Beast of Revelation*, 29–39; Keener, *Revelation*, 355–56; Koester, *Revelation*, 597–99; Osborne, *Revelation*, 520–21; and Schnabel, *40 Questions*, 190–91.

82. Brighton (*Revelation*, 363) avers, "The number applies to all three members of the unholy trinity, especially to whichever one is most active and most prominent at any given time and in any given situation."

83. Beale, *Revelation*, 721–24; Beasley-Murray, *Revelation*, 220–21; Blount, *Revelation*, 262; Brighton, *Revelation*, 363; Hailey, *Revelation*, 298; Hendriksen, *More than Conquerors*, 148–51; Hughes, *Revelation*, 154–55; Alan Johnson, "Revelation," 13:717; Kistemaker, *Revelation*, 395–96; Michaels, *Revelation*, 166; Morris, *Revelation*, 169; Prigent, *Apocalypse*, 426–28; Resseguie, *Revelation*, 190–91; Smalley, *Revelation*, 352–53; Wallace, *Greek Grammar*, 254; Walvoord, *Revelation*, 210.

84. English versions must also decide their approach. Mathewson (*Revelation*, 184) relates the number of "man" (*anthrōpou*) at 13:18 could be possessive genitive ("belonging to a human"). If so, it affords the possibility of seeing a reference to one man such as Nero or a future antichrist. Most versions adopt

Ten

This number (and multiples) emphasizes indefiniteness and magnitude, often from the point of view of time and humanity, especially with satanic influence and activity in mind. Long ago Isbon Beckwith related that ten (*deka*) is a number signifying fullness and completeness in the Bible and with apocalyptic writers.[85] When connected to its multiples such as a thousand, it is more suggestive of indefiniteness and of magnitude.[86] Resseguie, however, states that, "Commentators fail to distinguish adequately ten from seven and twelve, although John uses ten in strikingly different ways from the other numbers."[87] Thus, ten indicates something more than fullness and completeness. It stresses an indefinite but significant period of time or power or authority. Only when ten is associated with seven and twelve is completion and fullness intended.[88] In the Apocalypse, ten is found within multiples (5:11; 9:16) and fractions (11:13; 21:20). Another occurrence is "ten days" (2:10). But the most uses are found within the ten horns /kings/ crowns (12:3; 13:1; 17:3, 7, 12, 16). This suggests their satanic time of influence and authority is limited to a complete time period.

Tenth of the City

Fractions such as "a tenth" are part of John's numerical symbolism. Fractions denote partialness, yet the context and placement of "a tenth of the city" implies complete and total judgment at the conclusion of history. A "tenth" (*dekatos*) is found twice in Revelation. It occurs once in a series of twelve precious stones which form the foundation of the wall of the new Jerusalem (21:20). The other usage is the fraction "tenth of a city" located at the conclusion of the second interlude: "At that very hour there was a severe earthquake and a tenth of the city collapsed. Seven thousand people were killed in the earthquake, and the survivors were terrified and gave glory to the God of heaven" (11:13). Most scholars understand the fraction as an indication of God's plan that the earthquake not kill all unbelievers at the eschaton.

A "tenth of the city" can also be calculated as seven thousand if Jerusalem is in mind—Jerusalem had around 70,000 people. If so, then Jerusalem could figuratively be representing the whole unbelieving world as pictured in 11:8.[89] The city is an amalgamation

---

this rendering, and NABR includes a footnote naming Nero. GNT has "it is the name of someone." REB has "it represents a man's name." Nevertheless, it could also be an attributive genitive ("human number") and therefore understood more generically. NET translates it as "it is man's number." Soo too NIV 1984, but the 2011 revision inserted "a." NIV and NLT have the attributive genitive reading in their footnotes.

85. Beckwith, *Apocalypse*, 254.

86. Swete, *Apocalypse*, cxxxvii; Boring, "Numbers, Numbering," 4:299. See the entry "Thousand."

87. Resseguie, *Revelation Unsealed*, 60.

88. Ibid., 61.

89. So Beale, *Revelation*, 602–3; Kistemaker, *Revelation*, 338–39; Smalley, *Revelation*, 286. Contra Koester, *Revelation*, 504. Robert Thomas (*Revelation*, 2:98) states it refers to the Jerusalem of the future.

of Rome and Jerusalem that has become representative of all that is unholy, just like Sodom, Egypt, and Babylon the Great.[90]

Several commentators follow Giblin who finds an allusion to the remnant imagery
of the OT prophecies of judgment. In such prophecies a small faithful remnant survives
when God's judgment fell on the unrepentant majority. The remnant is sometimes described as a tenth part (Isa 6:13; Amos 5:3; *Jub.* 10:9). The figure of seven thousand alludes more specifically to Elijah's prophetic commission to bring the judgment on all
except the seven thousand faithful Israelites who had not bowed to Baal. John reverses
the allusion for emphasis.[91]

Thus, the seven thousand (a tenth) of the city matches the seven thousand killed in
the end-time quake. The symbolism of seven and a thousand underscore completeness
and totality. The number seven thousand is used by John to symbolize the totality of
unbelievers who are judged at the return of Christ. If the fraction is pursued, it means
that only a tenth died at the end of history, and nine–tenths are ready to glorify God.
But if this is judgment day, it is too late to repent. Those who give glory to God do so
from forced homage.[92] Therefore, in context with its placement at the conclusion of a
vision which customarily concludes with the eschaton, the end-time earthquake, and the
numerical symbolism, a tenth of the city (equaling 7000) is yet another signal for the end
of history.

Third

Fractions such as "a third" are part of John's numerical symbolism. They mean partial de-
struction and limited judgment of the earth and humanity. The word "third" (*tritos*) is
found twenty-three times in Revelation, often in sequence such as the third angel and the
third seal. But it is also used as a fraction such as a third of humanity is killed (9:15) and a
third of the stars are swept away (12:4). The majority of uses, however, occur is in the first
four trumpets (8:7–12) where it is mentioned twelve times in six verses (plus once more
for the "third angel" in 8:10). Resseguie notes how the repetitive use of a third serves as
a verbal thread throughout chapters 8–9. The cadence of threes and one-third creates the
expectation that time is running out."[93]

The overload of "third"s plus the number twelve may also suggest numerical symbolism. In part, twelve conveys God's ordering of the world and his sovereignty over it.[94]
The divisions of the seals, trumpets, and bowls is generally agreed to follow a four plus

---

90. Osborne, *Revelation*, 433; Resseguie, *Revelation*, 165.

91. Giblin, "Revelation 11:1–13," 445–46.

92. See the entry "Seven Thousand."

93. Resseguie, *Revelation*, 144.

94. Beale, *Revelation*, 59. See the entry "Twelve."

three pattern. The first four demonstrate God's power over all creation.[95] Thus, a third signifies partial destruction and limited judgment of the earth and humanity.[96]

Thousand

The number "thousand" (and its multiples) is a large, round number that represents multiplicity, vastness, entirety, and fullness. The biblical tradition reveals this number was used as hyperbole for quantity, immeasurability, or completeness (Deut 1:10; 1 Sam 18:7; Job 9:3; Ps 50:10; Dan 7:10; 2 Pet 3:8). Since various Bible genres understand "thousand" symbolically, it should also be understood this way in apocalyptic literature, which is grounded in symbolism.[97]

"Thousand" is translated from two words in Revelation—*chilias* (19 of 23 NT uses) and *chilioi* (9 of 11 NT uses), which intriguingly totals twenty-eight occurrences.[98] An additional word, *myrias* is often translated as "thousands." *Myrias* occurs in two passages. First, an innumerable number of angels is mentioned in the throne room vision (5:11). Listed twice, *myriades muriadōn* is often translated as "ten thousand times ten thousand." Some versions update the number to "thousands and millions" (CEB, CEV, GNT, NLT). A few translations transliterate it as "myriads on myriads" (ESV, NASB, NRSV, REB).[99] The phrase comes from Dan 7:10 where the idea of countless is apparent. Second, *dis-myriades myriades* is often updated to two hundred million in modern versions (9:16). Here too the number signifies an incalculable figure.[100]

Chilias is listed twice in 5:11. Its connection with *myrias* affirms these words are synonyms. Most of the listings for *chilias* are in connection with the hundred and forty-four thousand (7:4–8; 14:1, 3). There is also the seven thousand killed by the earthquake (11:13), and the measurements of twelve thousand stadia for the heavenly city (21:16). The occurrences of *chilioi* include the two witnesses prophesying (11:3) and the woman's protection for a thousand two hundred and sixty days (12:6). Blood covers a distance of a

---

95. Osborne (*Revelation*, 357) represents many when he writes, "The purpose of the first four trumpet judgments is primarily to disprove the earthly gods and to show that Yahweh alone is on the throne."

96. Popular dispensationalist readings literalize the fraction. The fourth trumpet's loss of light means day and night are reversed with sixteen hours of darkness and eight hours of daylight, along with a corresponding drop in world temperatures (LaHaye, *Revelation Unveiled*, 167–68; Ryrie, *Revelation*, 69). The sixth trumpet's slaying of a third of humanity (9:15), after a quarter of the world population has already been killed (6:8), means "the remaining population is reduced by another 33 percent!" (Lindsey, *New World Coming*, 139).

97. Boring, "Numbers, Numbering," 299; Ryken, *Dictionary of Biblical Imagery*, 865–66; Silva, "χίλιοι," 671–75.

98. Like the Lamb's twenty-eight occurrences, "thousand" may signify completeness of seven multiplied by the full coverage of four (7 x 4).

99. NCV reduces the incalculable number down to "thousands and thousands." Modern versions that update to "millions" offer readers a sense of the quantity. "Myriads" on the other hand may confuse readers who do not have a dictionary close at hand. The middle of the road attempts at literally producing "tens of thousands times ten thousand" may actually be best for giving a sense of the numeric symbolism. The point is overwhelming innumerability.

100. See the entry "Twice Ten Thousand Times Ten Thousand."

thousand six hundred stadia (14:20). There are six references to a thousand years in 20:2–7. In each instance, the numbers underscore completeness, entirety, and immenseness.[101]

Thousand Six Hundred Stadia

This numerical symbol indicates coverage of the whole earth, and its context confirms the universal judgment of the wicked at the second coming. The phrase "thousand six hundred stadia" occurs once near the conclusion of the third interlude. The angel swings his sickle and gathers the grapes. "They were trampled in the winepress outside the city, and blood flowed out of the press, rising as high as the horses' bridles for a distance of 1,600 stadia" (14:20).

Temporally, this reflects Armageddon, the second coming, and the ushering in of divine judgment. Even extreme futurists recognize the connection to Armageddon at 14:20, using phraseology such as "a reference to Armageddon,"[102] "preview of final events,"[103] "a prophetic fore-glimpse of what is to come,"[104] an "overview" and "proleptic summary"[105] of what follows in greater detail, and "obviously a picture of ultimate judgment of the wickedness of men at the time of the second coming of Christ."[106] For recapitulationists, this verse simply relates one of several retellings in Revelation of the Armageddon event, often signaled at the conclusion of an individual vision.

Unfortunately, only ESV, GW, and NIV translate the number exactly as "1600 stadia" (NKJV and NJB select "furlongs"). Most have updated the distance to "about 180 miles" (CSB, NLT, NCV) or "(almost) 200 miles" (CEB, CEV, GNT, NABR, NASB, NET, NRSV, REB). However, such updates lead to problems when ancient measurements are found in symbolic literature where fondness for numerical symbolism occurs and often plays a significant role in interpretation. This is certainly the case with Revelation. Bible translations which modernize Revelation's measurements not only miss the intended meaning of the number, but also encourage literalistic interpretations for the number. Simply stated, updating numerical measurements in Revelation obscures John's symbolic purposes.

Many interpreters argue that the 180 to 200 miles is a literal measurement, and pictures the length of Palestine. Thus, this last battle is limited to a geographical locale. The bloodbath is 200 miles wide and five feet deep.[107] Yet a few literalists waver on limiting it this way. For example, Walvoord asserts, "There is no reason, however, for limiting the battle to the precise boundary of the holy land, and there is really no serious problem here

---

101. See the entry "Thousand Years."

102. Patterson, *Revelation*, 297.

103. Lindsey, *New World Coming*, 204.

104. LaHaye, *Revelation Unveiled*, 241.

105. Hindson, *Revelation*, 158.

106. Walvoord, *Revelation*, 223.

107. Lindsey, *New World Coming*, 206; Ryrie, *Revelation*, 106.

in taking the distance literally."[108] Thus, Palestine may be emphasized, but even literal proponents suggest an earth-wide catastrophe.

The majority of scholars, however, recognize that John's symbolism is at work again. The number is not a measure of geographical distance. It is a numeric symbol. Theological significance is found in a variety of ways (4 x 4 x 10 x 10; 40 x 40; 4 x 4 x 100). This is hyperbolic imagery at work. The number refers to a slaughter of exceptional proportions, and thus complete, consummative judgment.

A few scholars among the majority deliver even a stronger case for numeric symbolism. Resseguie affirms "Four is the number of the earth or creation and ten represents totality. Thus, the blood covers the earth completely."[109] Paul Rainbow appends that numbers that are squared or cubed intensify their significance. Thus, the square of four multiplied by the square of ten "together represent God's judgment as comprehensive."[110] The beast's kingdom is worldwide and not limited by geography. Therefore, several scholars stress the symbolism not merely as hyperbolic emphasis of Palestine, but in light of numerical symbolism, a figure of complete, worldwide judgment at the end of history.[111]

Three

The number three indicates completeness and unity, especially with reference to deity or counterfeit deity. Three is a noteworthy number in Scripture. After the number seven, it is used most frequently in a symbolic sense. It assumes importance in connection with the Trinity.[112] Surprisingly, three is not as significant for John as is seven, four, ten, and twelve. When inspected closely, the idea of the Trinity is most observable. Three appears eleven times in Revelation. There are "three quarts of barley" (6:6);[113] "three angels" (8:13); "three plagues of fire, smoke, and sulfur" (9:18); "three and a half days" (11:9, 11); "split into three parts" (16:19); three gates east, west, south, and north (21:13); three sets of judgments (seals, trumpets, bowls); and three interludes (7:1–17; 10:1–11:14; 12:1–15:4). None of these examples have divinity necessarily in mind, but do possibly suggest completeness. It is the sequences of threes where deity and counterfeit deity are accentuated.

- "Jesus Christ, God, and his servants" is found in the first verse (1:1).

- John commences with the Trinity—God, the seven spirits, and Christ (1:4–5).

---

108. Walvoord, *Revelation*, 223. See also Hindson, *Revelation*, 159; Patterson, *Revelation*, 297; Robert Thomas, *Revelation*, 2:224. Chilton (*Days of Vengeance*, 376) interprets this as fulfilled in AD 70.

109. Resseguie, *Revelation*, 202.

110. Rainbow, *Pith of the Apocalypse*, 56.

111. So Barr, *Tales*, 130; Boxall, *Revelation*, 215; Brighton, *Revelation*, 394; Duvall, *Revelation*, 204; Hendriksen, *More than Conquerors*, 156; Kistemaker, *Revelation*, 421; Michaels, *Revelation*, 159; Morris, *Revelation*, 181; Murphy, *Fallen Is Babylon*, 328; Roloff, *Revelation*,178; Schüssler Fiorenza, *Revelation*, 91; Thomas and Macchia, *Revelation*, 266.

112. Boring, "Numbers, Numbering," 298; Ryken, *Dictionary of Biblical Imagery*, 866–67; Silva, "τρεῖς," 503.

113. Modern versions have "three quarts" except for NIV ("six pounds"), NABR ("three rations"), and NLT ("three loaves").

- Jesus is the "faithful witness, firstborn from the dead, and ruler of the kings of the earth" (1:5).

- Three times God is described with the past, present, and future threefold title "who is and who was and who is to come" (1:4, 8; 4:8).

- The four living creatures extol God with the triple shout "Holy, holy, holy" and they give "glory and honor and thanks" (4:8–9).

- The twenty-four elders proclaim God is worthy of "glory and honor and power" (4:11).

- God's work as creator is described as "who created heaven and what is in it, the earth and what is in it, and the sea and what is in it" (10:6).

- The voice from heaven announces the arrival of "the salvation and the power and the kingdom of our God" (12:10).

- The heavenly choir sings "salvation and glory and power" to God (19:1).

- Jesus' self-title is "I am the Alpha and the Omega, the first and the last, the beginning and the end" (22:13).

  On the other hand, counterfeit deity is noticeable.

- Three times the beast mimics the divine with its own threefold title "was and is not and is to come" (17:8 [twice], 11).

- The "three impure spirits" (16:13) represent the evil trinity and thus mimic the true Trinity.

- The false trinity is composed of the dragon, the beast, and the false prophet whose end is assured (19:20; 20:10).

Often the series of "threes" accentuate what is said or done. Thus, the "holy, holy, holy" of the four living creatures stresses God's exceeding holiness. The "woe, woe, woe" of the eagle emphasizes the intensification of the last three trumpets (8:13). The three groups—kings, merchants, and sailors—who thrived and exploited on Babylon the Great's power, lament over her fall (18:10–19).[114] Similar to the numbers four and seven, it is the embedded uses of three that draws out John's meticulous structure and inherent symbolism.

Twelve

Twelve symbolizes fullness and completeness, often with humanity in mind, and with special reference to God's people. Twelve is a significant number throughout the Bible. The twelve sons of Israel (Gen 35:22–29) became the twelve tribes of Israel (Gen 49:28), and biblical writers soon employed the number to symbolize the tribes as God's people (Exod 24:4; Num 1:44; Deut 1:23; Josh 4:1–7). Multiples of twelve appear, such as forty-eight Levitical cities (Num 35:6–8), and twenty-four divisions of priests (1 Chr 24:1–19) and musicians

---

114. Resseguie, *Revelation Unsealed*, 49–50.

(1 Chr 25:1–31). Symbolic usage continues in the NT. At the age of twelve Jesus challenges scholars in the temple (Luke 2:41), heals a woman who suffered for twelve years (Matt 9:20; Mark 5:25), raises a twelve-year-old girl (Mark 5:42), and feeds the multitude with twelve baskets left over (Matt 14:20; Luke 9:17). If twelve is understood only in the broadest sense in those passages, then more specificity occurs when Jesus selects twelve disciples as representatives of the new Israel (Matt 10:1–4; Mark 3:13–19: Luke 6:12–16). These will sit on twelve thrones judging the twelve tribes (Matt 19:28; Luke 22:30).[115]

John carries this motif forward. "Twelve" (*dōdeka*) is found twenty-three times in Revelation, comprising one-third of all NT uses. However, if the cognate "twelfth" (*dōkekatos*) is added, then the total comes to twenty-four, underscoring John's numerical symbolism.[116] Unlike seven, which can be used for both divine and demonic symbolism, the number twelve is reserved exclusively for God's people.[117] Jean-Pierre Prévost insists, "So the number twelve has become a consecrated number: it is *the* number of the people of God."[118] Thus, John's readers are treated with the twelve tribes representing the complete number of saints (7:4–8).[119] The woman with twelve stars on her head symbolizes the church (12:1). Twelve is spotlighted in the vision of the new Jerusalem. There are twelve gates, twelve angels, twelve tribes of Israel, twelve foundations, and twelve names of the apostles (21:12–14) to signify completeness.[120] Twelve jewels decorate the twelve foundations (21:21) and the tree of life bears twelve kinds of fruit (22:2). "The heaping up of twelves describes the perfect city, complete in every way, from top to bottom."[121] Multiples are found as well, including the twenty-four elders (who are mentioned exactly twelve times), twelve thousand from each tribe, twelve thousand stadia, a hundred and forty-four cubits, and a hundred forty-four thousand. Altogether, this number is used by John as a key for readers to think of totality and completeness with God's people in mind.

Twelve Thousand Stadia

The measurement of the Holy City pictures perfection, vastness, magnificence, and immeasurability. Twelve thousand stadia combine the symbolism of twelve with a thousand to signify completeness with reference to God's people. The OT relates ten appearances of twelve

115. Ryken, *Dictionary of Biblical Imagery*, 599–600; Scrivner, "Twelve," 689–90; Schmitz, "Number," 694–96.

116. Words that are found exactly twelve times and which John may intend as symbolic include elder (*presbyteros*), repent (*metanoeō*), put on (*periballō*), bowl (*phialē*), speak (*laleō*), know (*oida*), no one (*oudeis*), power (*dynamis*), and smoke (*kapnos*). Words found twenty-four times include "worship" (*proskyneō*), "spirit" (*pneuma*), and "Lord" (*kurios* plus *kuriakos*).

117. Resseguie, *Revelation Unsealed*, 64.

118. Prévost, *How to Read the Apocalypse*, 32. See Bauckham, *Climax of Prophecy*, 36.

119. The number twelve is found twelve times in 7:4–8.

120. See the entry "Twelve Gates."

121. Resseguie, *Revelation*, 32. Giblin (*Revelation*, 203) notes that the words "God" and "Lamb" are found seven times in this section. Moreover, "So obviously important is the number twelve in the account of the New Jerusalem, that it is surely significant that the number can be found to occur twelve times in 21:9–22:5." See also Bauckham, *Climax of Prophecy*, 35–36.

thousand that support symbolic usage (Num 31:5; Josh 8:25; Judg 21:10; 2 Sam 10:6; 17:1; 1 Kgs 4:26; 10:26; 2 Chr 1:14; 9:25; Ps 60).[122] John utilizes twelve thousand at two locations—twelve thousand from each of the twelve tribes (7:4–8) and twelve thousand stadia (21:16). The decision to keep "stadia" by many modern versions is helpful for recognizing John's numerical symbolism.[123] The modern updating of measurements found in several Bible versions, however, obscures John's intentions. For example, "1500 miles" (CEB, CEV, GNT, NABR, NCV, NRSV) and "1400 miles" (NLT, NET) are unfortunate choices.

John states that the angel "measured the city with the rod and found it to be 12,000 stadia in length, and as wide and high as it is long" (21:16). Thus, its length and breadth and height are equal, giving the new Jerusalem a picture of a four-squared, perfectly cubed city. Rainbow explains that "the use of cubic numbers in the Revelation signifies that which is consecrated to God."[124] This image is immediately recognizable as the holy of holies, the most holy place within the temple. "The inner sanctuary was twenty cubits long, twenty wide and twenty high" (1 Kgs 6:20). The city itself is a temple—the utter holy of holies.

Therefore, the Holy City is not limited to fifteen hundred square miles.[125] That may seem like a lot of space, but it stands far from the point John is making. He is not interested in delivering human dimensions. These numbers—like all numbers in Revelation—serve a figurative purpose. The number represents universal totality. Mathematicians have long noted the perfection of the number twelve thousand. It is twelve times ten cubed. Easley explains, "Not coincidentally, a cube has twelve edges. Since each edge measured 12,000 stadia, the total length of the edges is 144,000, exactly the same as the number of the followers of the Lamb (14:1).[126]

Twice Ten Thousand Times Ten Thousand

The number of demonic (perhaps human) mounted troops mentioned in the sixth trumpet is not a literal number, but rather symbolic hyperbole for an incalculable number. An inconceivably large number is found for the angels surrounding the throne. John hears "the voice of many angels, numbering thousands upon thousands, and ten thousand times ten thousand. They encircled the throne and the living creatures and the elders" (5:11). Modern versions normally do well in translating this number and all agree it is an incalculably large number.

The same cannot be said, however, for the number listed at 9:16. John hears "the number of the mounted troops was twice ten thousand times ten thousand." John most likely alludes to previous hyperbolic numbers (Deut 33:2; Ps 68:17; Dan 7:10). Yet many

---

122. Brighton, *Revelation*, 373 n. 1.

123. NJB and REB utilize "furlongs" for their European readership. NKJV's choice to retain "furlongs" from KJV for American audiences is odd.

124. Rainbow, *Pith of the Apocalypse*, 56.

125. LaHaye (*Revelation Unveiled*, 363–64) exemplifies literalism by calculating that each of the estimated twenty billion saints will have a cubic mile for themselves.

126. Easley, *Revelation*, 399.

English versions modernize the number and unwittingly limit and literalize the Greek phrase to "two hundred million." Only a few modern translations make the symbolic number clear with "twice ten thousand times ten thousand" (ESV, NIV, NJB, REB).[127] Any attempt to reduce this expression to an exact arithmetic calculation misses the point. It is an immense, innumerable, and uncountable number. Thus, Smalley explains that "the translation 'two hundred million' is mathematically inaccurate."[128] Nevertheless, many moderns, primarily dispensationalists, lobby for a literal two hundred million troops.[129]

The Greek *dismyriades myriadōn* ("two myriads of myriads") is literally "twice ten thousand of ten thousand" or "twenty thousand of ten thousands." The prefix *dis* is translated as "twice." However, the Hebrew understanding of qualitative aspect reveals this means "times" rather than a doubling of the number.[130] This is carried forward in Greek, and "is an indefinite number of incalculable immensity."[131]

An attendant issue for this passage is the identity of the soldiers. Many understand them as human.[132] More interpreters, however, lean toward demonic armies.[133] Charles Ryrie offers the best solution. "This army might be composed of humans or demons, or demon-possessed human beings."[134] Thus, the number of cavalry mentioned in the sixth trumpet must not be whittled down to "only" two hundred million. It is an apocalyptic number, not an exact number. Its intent is to show the impossibility and futility of resistance. Osborne recognizes that to "get a similar effect, one would have to posit an army of *six billion* demonic cavalry today."[135]

Two

The number two symbolizes completeness, and is often connected to a valid testimony and effectual witness. Two is not as obviously symbolic when compared to three, four, seven, ten, or twelve. Nevertheless, it remains an important symbol in Scripture. The image of two is inherent in the created order, beginning with two genders. Equally, the contrast between good and bad and light and darkness reveal the motif of two sides scattered

127. In addition, KJV reads "two hundred thousand thousand." The awkward English phrasing lends a hand in identifying numerical symbolism.

128. Smalley, *Revelation*, 239.

129. Easley, *Revelation*, 160; Hindson, *Revelation*, 110; Lindsey, *New World Coming*, 140; Ryrie, *Revelation*, 75; LaHaye, *Revelation Unveiled*, 174; Robert Thomas, *Revelation*, 2:46. Walvoord (*Revelation*, 166) wavers but reasons that a literal number is not impossible.

130. Aune, *Revelation*, 2:539; Beale, *Revelation*, 509.

131. BDAG, "δις," 252.

132. Kistemaker, *Revelation*, 297–98; Lindsey, *New World Coming*, 141; Walvoord, *Revelation*, 166–67. Hindson (*Revelation*, 110) supposes an actual army that includes airplanes, modern weaponry, and "tanks, guns, flamethrowers, and laser beams . . ."

133. Aune, *Revelation*, 2:539; Beale, *Revelation*, 509; Beasley-Murray, *Revelation*, 165; Brighton, *Revelation*, 246; Easley, *Revelation*, 160; Fee, *Revelation*, 136; Keener, *Revelation*, 271; LaHaye, *Revelation Unveiled*, 174; Michaels, *Revelation*, 130; Osborne, *Revelation*, 381; Smalley, *Revelation*, 238; Robert Thomas, *Revelation*, 2:46.

134. Ryrie, *Revelation*, 75.

135. Osborne, *Revelation*, 381 n. 9.

throughout the Bible. Although many references to the number lack significance, the majority of them imply some type of completeness—two halves make a whole, two providing a balance, two serving as foils of each other, and so forth. Two is used often in relation to validity for a special assignment. For instance, two angels are sent to Sodom (Gen 19:1). Two spies are sent to Jericho (Josh 2:1). Jesus sent his disciples out "two by two" (Mark 6:7; Luke 10:1). Two is the minimum number for valid witness and testimony (Num 35:30: Deut 17:6; 19:15; Matt 18:16; John 8:17; Heb 10:28; Rev 11:3).[136] The number two is used ten times in Revelation. The fifth trumpet mentions that two more woes are coming (9:12). Twice it is a part of the number forty-two (11:2; 13:5). The woman is given two wings of a great eagle (12:14). The false prophet has two horns (13:11). "Both" (two) the beast and false prophet are thrown into the lake of fire (19:20). But four of its ten occurrences are in regard to the two witnesses (11:3–13), and underscore the symbolic nature of the number. The two witnesses represent the church, particularly its distinguishing characteristic as the complete and effectual witness for Christ. Furthermore, that the number two is mentioned four times hints at a full earthly coverage for the two witnesses.

Colors

Revelation is awash in colors.[137] All of John's visions are colorful. These colors are scattered in several other entries in other chapters. The following entries accent more specifically what each color symbolizes.

Black

The color black symbolizes suffering, mourning, disaster, and distress in the presence of God who comes to deliver end-time judgment. Surprisingly, "black" is found only twice in Revelation. It is also seldom used in the OT. Generally, black describes an object's color, but in one-quarter of its uses it accompanies God's dark and ominous judgment, clearly revealing a symbolic interpretation (Zeph 1:14–16; Joel 2:1–2). The two uses in Revelation are fitting—the rider on the black horse (6:5) and the darkening of the sun which is "black like sackcloth" (6:12). In both cases, they append mourning, famine, and death to the idea of end-time judgment.[138]

Dark Blue

Dark blue is one of the descriptive colors of the demonic cavalry and suggests end-time terror and destruction. Some colors that are normally neutral often take on negative

---

136. Birch, "Number," 558; Resseguie, *Revelation Unsealed*, 48–49; Ryken, *Dictionary of Biblical Imagery*, 901–3.

137. Smalley (*Thunder and Love*, 106–7, 115) and Resseguie (*Revelation*, 36–37) provide helpful discussions on all colors.

138. Beck, *Dictionary of Imagery*, 215–17; Brighton, *Revelation*, 166; Osborne, *Revelation*, 278; Ryken, *Dictionary of Biblical Imagery*, 158–59.

connotations in Revelation. Colors such as blue, purple, and crimson have positive connotations when associated with God. But when such colors are associated with the luxury of the great prostitute, for example, their negativity becomes obvious. "Dark blue" is mentioned only once in the NT and its appearance is found within the sixth trumpet. John's description of the demonic cavalry includes breastplates that were "fiery red, dark blue, and yellow as sulfur" (9:17). English versions offer a wide range of translation for the word. Most select "blue" or "dark blue" (CEB, CEV, NABR, NCV, NET, NIV, NLT), but others suggest "blue as sapphire" (GNT), "sapphire" (ESV, NRSV), "hyacinth blue" (CSB, NKJV, NJB), "hyacinth" (NASB), "pale blue" (GW), and even "turquoise" (REB). The sentence is balanced to reveal that red, blue, and yellow correspond to fire, smoke, and sulfur. Thus, red and fire go together; blue and smoke; and yellow and sulfur. Dark blue then may denote the blue smoke of a sulfurous flame.[139] The whole purpose of this demonic cavalry is death, fire, and destruction. By itself dark blue is a neutral color. But its location at the sixth trumpet that immediately precedes final judgment, along with its company of other colors that display clearer symbolic overtones, grants dark blue the same ominous feel.

Gold/Golden

Gold symbolizes value, indestructibility, purity, riches, and power. In Revelation, it reflects these attributes when speaking of God or is used in parody by the devil. Gold held several meanings. The primary quality of gold was value, but permanence and durability was also symbolized. Gold was also associated with riches and power (Gen 13:2; Isa 60:17). Royal crowns were made of gold (2 Sam 12:30; 1 Chr 20:2).[140] John uses gold more as a precious metal than a color. Several Greek words may be translated as "gold," "golden," "of gold," and even the verb "to glitter like gold." Altogether, Revelation holds twenty-four of the forty-two NT uses, including cognates. There is "gold" (*chrysos*), "gold-covered" (*chrysion*), "golden" (*chrysous*), and "glittering of gold" (*chrysoō*). Gold is often mentioned in connection with the immense power and indestructibility of God (3:18; 5:8; 8:3; 9:13; 21:18, 21) or else in a parody of it by the devil and his minions (9:7), or the value sought by the wicked (18:12, 16).

Gold Refined in the Fire

This image symbolizes the call for persecuted Christians to purify their lives from sin through testing. This phrase is located only at 3:18. The ineffective Laodicean Christians who believe they are "rich" are challenged by the risen Christ "to buy from me gold refined in the fire." This metaphor fits Laodicea well since the church is filled with impurities of pagan culture and lifestyle. "Gold refined by fire" is a common idiom for purifying one's life through the removal of sin (Job 23:10; Prov 27:21; Mal 3:2). Or it could be viewed more positively as a purifying effect of testing God's people, proving them as genuine and

---

139. Kistemaker, *Revelation*, 298; Osborne, *Revelation*, 382.

140. Ryken, *Dictionary of Biblical Imagery*, 340–41. See van der Steen, "Gold," 622–23.

reliable (Prov 17:3; Ps 66:10; Isa 1:25; Zech 13:9; 1 Pet 1:6).[141] Both nuances fit the situation of the self-satisfied Laodiceans. It also fits compromising, unproductive believers of any generation.

Green/Pale

The color green is a metaphor for life and abundance, but in one instance in Revelation it signifies death and judgment. Green (*chlōros*) denotes nature and plant life and is normally considered a positive image of growing plant life (Gen 1:30; Ps 23:2; Jer 17:8; Mark 6:39).[142] The vitality of a green tree can symbolize those who place their trust in the Lord (Ps 92:14; Jer 17:8).[143] This positive image is found twice in Revelation in less than positive circumstances—the first (8:7) and sixth trumpets (9:4). Yet *chlōros* may also be applied to the color of people who are sick or dead, serving as a contrast to their usual skin color when healthy. This is the image found in the final use of the word. John "looked, and there before me was a pale (*chlōros*) horse! Its rider was named Death, and Hades was following close behind him" (6:8). That the horse is pale green is appropriate to its mission of bringing death. John's audience would promptly understand that the use of this color in this context indicates sickness and death.[144]

Purple

The color purple symbolizes status, wealth, power, luxury, and debauchery. It characterizes the great prostitute's corruption and worldliness. Since purple dye was expensive, only people of great rank and royalty were able to wear the color in biblical times (Jer 10:9; Dan 5:7). A purple robe was placed on Jesus to mock him (Mark 15:17; John 19:2).[145] In John's visions, purple becomes strictly a negative symbol. Two words for "purple" (*porphyrous* and *porphyra*) are found three times in the fall of Babylon vision, and all are associated with the corrupt great prostitute. John sees the woman "dressed in purple and scarlet, and was glittering with gold, precious stones and pearls" (17:4). However, the evil merchants of the earth sing a dirge at her end-time judgment. They weep and mourn over her because their precious cargoes which include purple are no longer bought and sold (18:12). These merchants who unfairly gained wealth through the woman now weep and mourn: "'Woe! Woe to you, great city, dressed in fine linen, purple and scarlet, and glittering with gold, precious stones and pearls! In one hour such great wealth has been brought to ruin!'" (18:16–17). The woman, draped with excess and prosperity and so outwardly attractive, is laid bare for what she really is come judgment day. John utilizes

---

141. Beale, *Revelation*, 305; Smalley, *Revelation*, 99.

142. See Ryken, *Dictionary of Biblical Imagery*, 350–51, for more examples.

143. Kenneth Barker, "Green," 893; Boyd, "Green," 698.

144. See the entry "Rider on a Pale Horse."

145. Danker, "Purple," 557–60; Ryken, *Dictionary of Biblical Imagery*, 158; Van Elderen, "Purple," 1103–4; Kevin Wilson, "Purple," 689–90.

the color purple, therefore, as an image of allurement to warn his readers not to be drawn away by the trappings of materialism and consumerism.

Red

The color red emphasizes blood, bloodshed, suffering, persecution, strife, slaughter, and war. John utilizes three words for the color red. One is *kokkinos* which is usually translated "scarlet." The other two are interchangeable cognate words found only in Revelation— *pyrros* is found twice (6:4; 12:3) and *pyrinos* is found once (9:17).[146] That the latter two words are interchangeable is noted by how English versions translate them. The second rider of the seals judgments (6:4) is on a "fiery red" horse (CEB, CEV, CSB, GW, NET, NIV, NKJV), "bright red" (ESV, NJB, NRSV) or simply "red" (GNT, NABR, NASB, NCV, NLT, REB), "symbolizing the terrible bloodshed and slaughter to be wrought upon the world."[147] Similarly, the red color of the enormous dragon introduced in the third interlude (12:3) connotes the oppressive nature of the dragon and his "hatred and murder of the people of God."[148] Finally, the breastplates on the demonic cavalry of the sixth trumpet (9:17) are "fiery red" (CEB, CEV, CSB, GW, NCV, NET, NIV, NLT, REB), "red" (NABR), "red as fire" (GNT), "color of fire" (ESV, NASB, NRSV), and "flame colour" (NJB). Each of these references to the color red indicates persecution, bloodshed, and warfare.

Scarlet

Scarlet emphasizes flagrant sinfulness that arises, for example, from exorbitant luxury as well as from the images of blood, suffering, and persecution. Scarlet is a shade of red and carries much of the same color symbolism. It is the color of blood and also the color of the linen curtains of the tabernacle, perhaps symbolizing that it was covered by (sacrificial) blood. The writer of Hebrews seems to imply this as well (Heb 9:11–28). Scarlet is also an expensive, highly prized dye. It is colorfast and does not fade. This allows scarlet to be used as a metaphor for sin (Isa 1:18). It is still recognized today as a flagrant and offensive symbol.[149] "Scarlet" (*kokkinos*) is found four times in Revelation (17:3, 4; 18:12, 16), all within the fall of Babylon vision. NCV translates the word as "red" and GW has "bright red," but most modern versions properly retain "scarlet" to differentiate the two colors. Concerning the great prostitute (17:3, 4), Beale suggests the scarlet "color of the whore connotes not only her royal associations but especially her persecuting manner, which she exercises in league with the kingly beast and dragon."[150] Moreover, the merchants of

---

146. The verb *pyroō* is mentioned twice by John (1:15; 3:18) and means to burn (red) or to burn with passion, thus renderings such as "glowing" or "refined." Alden ("Red," 58) mentions the well-known verse in Isa 1:18 where three parallel words for red describe sin, and are generally rendered into English as red, crimson, and scarlet.

147. Osborne, *Revelation*, 278.

148. Ibid. CEB, CSB, GW, and REB have "fiery red" dragon.

149. Boyd, "Scarlet," 123–24; Ryken, *Dictionary of Biblical Imagery*, 158.

150. Beale, *Revelation*, 854–55.

the earth mourn over fallen Babylon (18:12, 16), and her fall is pictured in the loss of their exorbitant luxury items. In sum, John utilizes the color symbolism attached to scarlet to characterize the excessive debauchery of Babylon the Great and its excessive persecution of believers.

White

This color attributes the images of victory and purity to God and his people. Once, however, it is used as parody. White is a color that is regularly used in descriptions of transcendence, glory, and redemption. Yet it is also a sign of leprosy. Apocalyptic writers used white often in their visions.[151] In Revelation, the noun *leukos* ("white") is found sixteen times and the verb *leukainō* ("to make white") is found once. Victory and purity overlap but usually one is stressed over the other. The occasions where purity receives emphasis includes the risen Christ's head and hair as white like wool, white as snow (1:14). Like the description of God (Dan 7:9) this adds unity, dignity, and wisdom to the image.[152] Laodiceans are counseled to lay aside their shameful nakedness and buy white clothes from Jesus (3:18). Most occurrences, however, highlight victory over purity.[153] The church at Pergamum is promised a white stone (2:17). The worthy at Sardis will walk with Jesus, dressed in white (3:4–5).[154] The twenty-four elders are dressed in white (4:4). The martyrs under the altar are given white robes (6:11). The great multitude is dressed in white robes (7:9, 13), and they washed their robes and "made them white" in the blood of the Lamb (7:14). One like a son of man is seated on a white cloud (14:14). The rider on a white horse (19:11) has the armies of heaven following him on white horses (victory) and dressed in white linen (purity; 19:14). The riders ride in victory but their garments symbolize acts of righteousness (19:8).[155] The great white throne judgment (20:11) might also stress both ideas equally. Finally, the first rider is on a white horse serves as a contrast and parody of true victory (6:2).

---

151. Boyd, "White," 844–45; Ryken, *Dictionary of Biblical Imagery*, 944.

152. Osborne, *Revelation*, 90.

153. Barr, *Tales*, 85.

154. Beale (*Revelation*, 935–36), however, sees the white clothes of the saints to convey purity that results from a test of persevering faith.

155. See the entry "White Clothes/Robes."

Elements of Time and Miscellaneous Images

READERS OF REVELATION MUST understand how John uses time references. He does not use them the same way moderns do. To interpret elements of time literally is doing a disservice to John the apocalypticist. Similar to numerical symbolism, John insists that readers look for temporal symbolism. This chapter reveals that time elements essentially teach theological truths. Finally, the last section examines a select handful of miscellaneous images that are difficult to fit into other categories.

Elements of Time

All references to time in Revelation are symbolic. Many of the following entries retain their symbolic understanding today. Take note that several time references are coupled with numbers (thousand years, forty-two months, etc.). This results in a good deal of overlap between these two categories of symbols. The flow of time in John's visionary world may be summed up this way—it covers the period between Christ's birth/exaltation and Satan's downfall to the return of Christ and eternity. This interadvental period is short but intense and extends for a symbolic three and a half years (a time of distress). Yet is also reflects the extended period the saints' reign with Christ, effectuated at the cross, and symbolized by a thousand years (a time of completion).[1]

About Half an Hour

"About half an hour" of silence is a symbol for worshipful reverence, answered prayer, and the eschatological judgment that immediately precedes the creation of the new heaven and new earth. Perhaps the strangest time element related by John commences the seventh seal. "When he opened the seventh seal, there was silence in heaven for about half an hour" (8:1). "About half an hour" (*hōs hēmiōrion*) has no equivalent and is found nowhere else in the Bible. Readers certainly resonate with Bauckham's statement that "the

---

1. See Koester, *Revelation*, 120–21, for more insight although he views time more premillennially.

specification of half an hour is puzzling."[2] Bible students generally view it simply as a relatively short period of time. It does slow the narrative down, but for what purpose? Resseguie explains that similar to other "half" numbers (11:9, 11; 12:13), half an hour reflects a fractured period. Its import lies not in being half of an hour but in being a half. Since an hour (*hōra*) represents a momentous or climactic event, a half would represent the sudden interruption of a finalized event. "Half an hour is thus a dramatic pause in the relentless march to the end, heightening the reader's anticipation of what new thing will happen or what more could take place."[3]

Following this understanding, the key to this interruption is the silence that is connected with it. Some Bible students suggest the silence means there is no content to the seventh seal, or that the trumpets and bowls make up the content of the seventh seal, or that there is a temporary stoppage, a dramatic pause, in the forward movement of end-time events. The key for interpretation, however, must begin with how the original audience understood this silence, and how silence is used in the OT and extratextual writings of the time.

Multiple possibilities have been produced to explain the silence of 8:1. Aune and Craig Koester discuss four ways, Robert Thomas lists five, Smalley finds six, and Osborne offers eight options.[4] Most exegetes select one or two among these. Yet most of the options are viable and boast able supporters. It is better to follow those who see most if not all of the possibilities at work.[5] Thus, the purpose of the silence is drawn from several unfolding factors. Awe and reverence is maintained in the worshipful presence of God and forms a necessary prelude to the divine manifestation about to be disclosed (Job 4:16; Hab 2:20; Zeph 1:7; Zech 2:13).[6] The context of silence reveals that the prayers of the suffering saints are now ready to be heard and answered by God (8:3–4).[7] That answer is the end-time judgment that completes the seventh seal (8:5).[8] Lastly, such silence reminds the saints of the primal silence which preceded the first creation (*4 Ezra* 6:39; *2 Bar.* 3:7) and therefore anticipates a new creation that arrives at the eschaton (7:15–17; 21:9–22:9).[9] This scenario fits well if the seventh seal is extended to 8:5. The anticipation of what comes after the interruption of a half is fully answered.

2. Bauckham, *Climax of Prophecy*, 83.

3. Resseguie, *Revelation*, 142. So too Lupieri, *Apocalypse*, 154.

4. Aune, *Revelation*, 2:507–8; Koester, *Revelation*, 431; Osborne, *Revelation*, 336–38; Smalley, *Revelation*, 211–12; Robert Thomas, *Revelation*, 2:2–3. These sources also list representative scholars for each view.

5. Kistemaker, *Revelation*, 266; Osborne, *Revelation*, 337–38; Skaggs and Benham, *Revelation*, 92; J. C. Thomas, *Apocalypse*, 278–79.

6. Aune (*Revelation*, 508) represents this view.

7. Originated from Charles (*Revelation*, 1:233) and championed by Bauckham (*Climax of Prophecy*, 70–71) and Caird (*Revelation*, 107).

8. Beale (*Revelation*, 446–54) presents the best discussion for this option. He notes that "about half an hour" is basically equivalent to an hour which is normally figurative of judgment elsewhere in Revelation (453).

9. The choice of Blount (*Revelation*, 158) and Roloff (*Revelation*, 101).

Day

The designation of "day" stresses a point in time or a short period of time. "Day" appears over three hundred times in the NT and includes several meanings from a temporal time unit to a time of sunlight to a duration of activity ("one's days") to a specific segment in time ("day of atonement") to a measurement of distance ("a day's journey"). Therefore, "day" employs several figurative expressions.[10] These multiple usages are also found in John's twenty-one references. John may refer to theologically insignificant daylight hours (8:12; 21:25). A few times it refers to a short duration of time that stands in the background (2:13; 9:6; 10:7). A period of great tribulation that lasts "ten days" (2:10) also means a short yet completed period of time. Day may also indicate a precise moment in time. For instance, John was in the Spirit "on the Lord's day" (1:10). The sense of its brevity is found when Babylon falls in "one day" (18:8). The precise date fixed by God is this "very hour and day and month and year" (9:15). The "great day" of God's end-time judgment underscores its precise point in time (6:17; 16:14).[11]

A longer period of time, however, is suggested by the Danielic phrase "time, times, and half a time" (12:14) that is usually equated with "1,260 days" (11:3; 12:6). In this case, some interpreters understand the "day" as a literal 24-hour period and then add 1,260 to achieve three and a half years. If "day" is understood as a short period of time, however, it is possible to lengthen the period (e.g. the rhetorical "a day is like a thousand years" of 2 Pet 3:8). The same holds true for the "three and a half days" the two witnesses were refused burial (11:9). Thus, many understand the "1,260 days" and the "three and a half days" as symbolic references to cover the interadvental age between the cross and consummation.

Day and Night

"Day and night" is a common idiom that means unceasing, continuous, and endless. It is an example of hendiadys (two words linked by the conjunction "and" to express the same idea). In this case, continuity between the two words conveys ceaselessness.[12] This common expression is found scores of times in Scripture. The order is insignificant and interchangeable (Luke 2:37; 18:7; Acts 20:31; 26:7). The idiom is found at six places in Revelation. The four living creatures never stop worshiping God (4:8). In a glimpse of eternity, believers will never stop serving God (7:15). Satan never ceases his accusations of believers before the Lord (12:10). The wicked will be tormented "for ever and ever" and receive no rest "day and night" (14:11).[13] Similarly, the unholy trinity will be tormented in the lake of fire day and night for ever and ever, thereby doubling the endlessness of the

---

10. Hasel, "Day," 877-78; Linton, "Time," 1593; Chris Smith, "Day, NT," 47–48.

11. Rissi, *Time and History*, 27–28.

12. Hasel, "Day and Night," 878; Linton, "Time," 1595. Or perhaps it can be considered a merism—day and night and all the time in between. Rissi (*Time and History*, 28) deems it "a designation of the continuity of an event . . ."

13. Beale (*Revelation*, 761–62) suggests that this image of the ceaselessness of torment could indicate that a great judgment will be remembered forever, not one that leads to eternal suffering.

image (20:10). Finally, although not technically in idiomatic form, the Greek words rest next to each other (*hēmeras nux*) in John's vision of the new Jerusalem: "On no day will its gates ever be shut, for there will be no night there" (21:25). This last passage portrays the dwelling place of God's people as perpetual light. Thus, this common phrase continues to hold up well to the present day. It does not refer to the duration of time but to the ceaselessness of it.

Five Months

"Five months" signifies a short intense period of suffering for the wicked in order to give them time to repent. "Five" (*pentē*) does not appear to be a number that John utilizes for numeric symbolism. Biblically, it does seem to be used as a round number to mean "a few."[14] John mentions "five months" twice in the fifth trumpet. Demonic locusts from the Abyss are permitted to torture the inhabitants of the earth (9:5–6, 10). Since "five" is used elsewhere in Scripture to denote "a few" (Lev 26:8; Judg 18:2; Acts 20:6; 1 Cor 14:19), the same idea is intended here. Several commentators note that the normal lifespan of a locust in the ancient Near East is five months. It may mean that this trumpet, though limited, is still intense, and must run its course and be completed. Thus, it is a period of short duration wherein God has placed limitations on the torture probably to give the wicked time to repent (9:20–21).[15] Some commentators, however, consider the period of five months a long period of time rather than a short period. Since locust swarms normally last but a few days, five months is a ferociously long time of torment.[16]

For Ever and Ever

"For ever and ever" is a common idiom that stresses eternity, perpetuity, and the immeasurability of the duration of time, either to everlasting life or to everlasting punishment. The formulaic phrase "for ever and ever" is found over forty times in the Bible. It accentuates timelessness and endlessness. John mentions it twelve times in Revelation.[17] He reserves the phrase for three usages. First, it occurs most often in doxologies with reference to God's and Christ's eternal existence (1:18; 4:9, 10; 10:6; 11:15; 15:7), and the duration of

14. Aune, *Revelation*, 2:530. Resseguie (*Revelation Unsealed*, 54) remarks that when five months is subtracted from twelve months, then the complete period of seven months remains. Thus, five represents a limited period. Davis (*Biblical Numerology*, 122–23) wisely cautions attaching a meaning to the number five by listing several authors who have widely different interpretations. Most preterists (Chilton, *Days of Vengeance*, 244–45; Ford, *Revelation*, 149) and dispensationalists (LaHaye, *Revelation Unveiled*, 172; Ryrie, *Revelation*, 73; Robert Thomas, *Revelation*, 2:32) follow a literal five months.

15. So Charles, *Revelation*, 1:243; Hemer, "Number," 690; Mounce, *Revelation*, 188; Osborne, *Revelation*, 367; Smalley, *Revelation*, 229.

16. So Beasley-Murray, *Revelation*, 161; Rissi, *Time and History*, 25–26. Krodel (*Revelation*, 202), however, concludes that a long or a short period is not to be stressed, but "rather the definiteness and divinely limited nature of the period is the emphasis."

17. This suggests numerical symbolism. However, 14:11 could be added. It is a slight variation with no articles. English translations are consistent in their renderings, but there is also "forever and always" (CEB), and some versions vary with "forevermore." The phrase is missing from GW at 1:18.

praise that is due them (1:6; 5:13; 7:12). Second, the phrase describes the eternal torment of Babylon the Great and the false trinity (14:11; 19:3; 20:10). Finally, it is used to confirm that the reward of the faithful is eternal fellowship with God (22:5). Some Bible students are uneasy with the punishment of the wicked being described as eternal. Instead, they interpret this phrase to refer either to annihilation (the wicked will be destroyed and cease to exist)[18] or to universalism (all will eventually be saved).[19] However, the formula that is applied for the eternality of the saints should also be applied to the wicked for the sake of consistency. The emphatic nature of "for ever and ever," relates Osborne, "makes the point absolutely clear that this terrible punishment will be their continual eternal destiny."[20] It is true that OT prophets often used "forever" without the idea of infinity or temporal perpetuity. Instead, intensity and hyperbole was in mind (Isa 17:1; 32:14; Jer 7:20; 23:40).[21] It is difficult to imagine timelessness when "time shall be no more."[22] But similar to the inconsistency of a "lake of fire," the point is that hyperbolic imagery is at work.

Forty-Two Months

Forty-two months is a numerical symbol for a short yet intense period of persecution for God's people, covering the entire church age. This time designation occurs twice. First, John is not to measure the outer court of the temple "because it has been given to the Gentiles. They will trample on the holy city for 42 months" (11:2). Second, it is the time period for the beast "to exercise its authority for forty-two months" (13:5).[23] Forty-two recalls Israel's wilderness wanderings, which included forty-two encampments (Num 33:5–49).[24] The number is also associated with violence (2 Kgs 2:23–24).[25] For certain,

18. Stefanovic, *Revelation*, 450–51; 570–71. Concerning 14:8, Stefanovic states that the phrase "forever and ever" does not mean endless burning, but "the purpose is destruction, not continuation, consumption, not preservation." So also Mealy, *After the Thousand Years*, 161–89; Paul, *Revelation*, 250, 331; and Steven Thompson, "End of Satan," 257–68. See the critique of this view in Christopher Morgan, "Annihilationism," 195–218.

19. So Boring, *Revelation*, 226–31; Caird, *Revelation*, 186–87; 270–71; Farmer, *Revelation*, 126–33; Harrington, *Revelation*, 229–35; Hughes, *Revelation*, 163–64; Rissi, *Future of the World*, 68, 71–74, 78; Pilgrim, "Universalism in the Apocalypse," 235–43; Smalley, *Revelation*, 367–68, 515. See the critique of this view in Packer, "Universalism," 169–94.

20. Osborne, *Revelation*, 542; see 547–48, 715–16. See also Beale, *Revelation*, 762–63; Fee, *Revelation*, 197; Rissi, *Time and History*, 30–33.

21. Sandy, *Plowshares and Pruning Hooks*, 101–2, 222–23. For comparative discussions on literal, metaphorical, purgatorial, and conditional hell, see Crockett, *Four Views on Hell*; Fudge and Peterson, *Two Views of Hell*; Morgan and Peterson, *Hell under Fire*; and Sprinkle, *Four Views on Hell*.

22. Noble ("Time and Eternity," 912–13) reminds readers that eternity cannot be thought of as a progressive movement from past to future or that God is bound within time.

23. NIV and NLT are inconsistent with renderings of "42 months" and "forty-two months."

24. So Beale, *Revelation*, 565; Morris, *Revelation*, 143; Osborne, *Revelation*, 414.

25. Rotz, *Revelation*, 163. Ford (*Revelation*, 170) and Resseguie (*Revelation Unsealed*, 52) note that forty-two is both a messianic number (3 x 14; Jesus as the new David; Matt 1:1–17) and demonic number (6 x 7; "perfection missing the mark"). Bauckham (*Climax of Prophecy*, 400–402) explains that John uses square numbers to represent the people of God (12; 144), triangular numbers to represent the beast

forty-two months alludes to three and a half years, a common figure signifying a short intense period of suffering of God's people. By John's time, "three and a half" had become a symbol, a metaphor, a standardized expression of persecution of the faithful.[26]

Some interpreters understand the forty-two months literally. Preterists suggest it refers to AD 66–70, the time of tribulation before the fall of Jerusalem.[27] Dispensationalists stress sequence for the structure of Revelation and place this within the final seven years of history.[28] However, this number—and all numbers in Revelation—should be understood figuratively. It is best to view forty-two months (and "thousand two hundred and sixty days" and "time, times, and half a time") as representing the entire Christian era. Koester, for example, relates that "In the visionary world, the three and a half years encompass the entire time between the Messiah's exaltation and final return."[29]

When a thousand two hundred and sixty days with its emphasis on protection and provision is attached, it reveals two perspectives about the saints: "they undergo tribulation (11:2; 12:14; 13:5–6), but are nonetheless protected from ultimate spiritual harm. Their existence as a community is guaranteed until the parousia, so that they can fulfill their corporate call to witness (11:3; 12:4, 14)."[30] The temporal markers are used synonymously and interchangeably. Although forty-two months stresses the persecution aspect, all these ideas—persecution, witness, and protection—are noted in Revelation's uses of the time designations.

Great Day

The great day refers to judgment day—the second coming and the great white throne judgment. The day when Jesus returns in judgment and victory is called by many names. The prophets used the term frequently for any specific time when God decisively intervened in history to save or to judge. Scripture notes "day of trouble" (Ezek 7:7), "day of rebuke" (Hos 1:9), "day of punishment" (Isa 10:3), "day of vengeance" (Isa 63:4), "day of doom"

---

(666), and rectangular numbers to depict the apocalyptic period of the reign of the beast. Thus, forty-two is the sixth rectangular number (6 x 7). A thousand two hundred sixty is the thirty-fifth rectangular number (35 x 36).

26. Easley (*Revelation*, 189) compared it to the typical American expression of a "forty-hour week" for "fully employed" without necessarily meaning an exact length of time. See the entry "Three and a Half Days."

27. Buchanan, *Revelation*, 277; Chilton, *Days of Vengeance*, 275; Russell, *Parousia*, 430. Stefanovic (*Revelation*, 346) offers a historicist understanding. He views these time elements "as referring to the prophetic period of more than twelve centuries, known as the Middle Ages, during which the church, like Israel at the Exodus, suffered the hardship of its 'wilderness' pilgrimage."

28. The time references are added together to equal seven years. Thus, the first mention of forty-two months (11:2) refers to the first half of the great tribulation according to LaHaye (*Revelation Unveiled*, 185), Patterson (*Revelation*, 240), Ryrie (*Revelation*, 84), and Walvoord (*Revelation*, 177), but references the last half according to Hindson (*Revelation*, 122), Lindsey (*New World Coming*, 161), and Robert Thomas (*Revelation*, 2:84–85).

29. Koester, *Revelation*, 562. See the entry "Time, Times, and Half a Time" for more interpreters holding this view.

30. Beale, *Revelation*, 566.

(Jer 51:2), "day of darkness" (Joel 2:2), and "day of the Lord's wrath" (Ezek 7:19). The prophets often abbreviated the reference to "the day when" or "that day" (Isa 2:11–20). Often "that day" refers to events so dreadful that it ends the age (Joel 2–3; Zech 14). It is this latter, more apocalyptic usage that NT writers draw from the most. Thus, in Acts 2, the first coming of Christ ushers in the new era, inaugurating an already-not-yet eschatological understanding. But the majority of NT uses refer to the second coming, the completion of the new era, and accompanying judgment of God.[31] Extratextual writings frequently refer to this day of final judgment (*1 En.* 10:6; 91:7; *2 En.* 65:6; *4 Ezra* 4:30; 7:32; *2 Bar.* 10:2; 59:1–12; *Jub.* 5:10; and Qumran writings).[32] Moreover, these texts add that the Messiah or an equivalent figure would come at the end of time. For instance, *4 Ezra* 12:31–34 states that the Messiah will judge the wicked and deliver the saints at the "end of days."[33]

In the NT, there is "last day" (John 6:39), "day of God" (2 Pet 3:12), "day of the Lord" (Acts 2:20; 1 Thess 5:2), "day of Christ" (Phil 1:6), "day of the Lord Jesus" (1 Cor 1:8), "day of judgment" (Matt 11:15; 1 John 4:17), "judgment on the great day" (Jude 6), "day of slaughter" (Jas 5:5), "day of God's wrath" (Rom 2:5), "day of redemption" (Eph 4:30), "the day" (Luke 17:30; Rom 13:12), "that Day" (Matt 24:36; 2 Tim 1:12), "this day" (1 Thess 5:4), and "his day" (Luke 17:24). This specific day almost always involves the motif of end-time, universal judgment for unbelievers (and a few examples of ultimate redemption and deliverance for the faithful).

John feeds off these synonymous terms for his images of judgment day. Two times he uses the words "great day" (6:17; 16:14). Both references reflect parallel visions of the end that include a gathering of a final battle, cosmic imagery of the dissolution of the world, and arrival of God in judgment.[34] Many interpreters, especially futurists, follow a sequential structure for Revelation. For them, these two references reflect separate events near the end of history. The "great day" of the sixth seal occurs at the beginning of the great tribulation whereas the "great day" of the sixth bowl suggests a fore-glimpse of the second coming.[35]

This study affirms both passages are picturing the same great day—the return of Christ in victory and judgment. First, John narrates the "great day of their wrath" at the sixth seal (6:17).[36] After end-time cosmic imagery (6:12–14), there is an allusion to an Armageddon-like gathering which is described in more detail in later visions (6:15). All unbelievers call out to the mountains and rocks to fall on them and hide them from him

---

31. Allison, "Day of the Lord," 46–47; Hays, Duvall, and Pate, *Dictionary of Prophecy*, 109–10; Hill, "Day of Judgment," 45–46; Ryken, *Dictionary of Biblical Imagery*, 196.

32. Beale, *Revelation*, 121; Smalley, *Revelation*, 172.

33. Beale, *New Testament Biblical Theology*, 125. See also *Apoc. Ab.* 29:9–11; *2 Bar.* 29:3; 30:1.

34. Another possibility is found in the fall of Babylon vision: "Therefore in one day her plagues will overtake her: death, mourning and famine. She will be consumed by fire, for mighty is the Lord God who judges her" (18:8).

35. Fruchtenbaum, "Day of the Lord," 87–88; LaHaye, *Revelation Unveiled*, 147; Walvoord, *Revelation*, 137.

36. Other translations offer "terrible day" (CEV, GNT), "frightening day" (GW), and "Great Day of his Retribution" (NJB). The TR/KJV/NKJV tradition reads "his" in place of "their" wrath. UBS5 gives an "A" rating for "their."

who sits on the throne and from the wrath of the Lamb. "For the great day of their wrath has come, and who can withstand it?" (6:17). This image of a final, righteous judgment receives more description at the great white throne judgment (20:11–15). The use of the article ("the") suggests a specific, eschatological event known to John's original audience. This great day portrays nothing less than the final day of consummation.[37] Second, John speaks of the "Great Day of God Almighty" in the sixth bowl (16:14). The Euphrates River dries up, the false trinity perform miraculous signs, and they drive the kings of the earth to "gather for the battle on the great day of God Almighty" at a "place called Armageddon" (16:14, 16).[38] Therefore, John's usage of the "great day," although confined to two instances, nonetheless includes what his other visions confirm as elements accompanying the arrival of the Messiah at his second coming—gathering for the end-time battle, the destruction of the cosmos, and universal, final judgment.

Great Tribulation

This refers to a time period of hostility, persecution, and suffering that Christians experience from the anti-Christian world. It began with Christ's first coming, continues throughout the centuries, and will intensify near the end. The noun *thlipsis* is translated as trouble, persecution, oppression, distress, anguish, suffering, hardships, and affliction. It is found forty-five times in the NT. John mentions *thlipsis* five times to picture distress as a continual reality for believers. He informs the seven churches that he too is a "brother and companion in the *suffering* and kingdom and patient endurance" (1:9). The risen Christ tells the persecuted Smyrnaeans that "I know your *afflictions* and your poverty . . . Do not be afraid of what you are about to *suffer*" (2:9–10). To false teachers such as Jezebel, Christ "will make those who commit adultery with her *suffer intensely*, unless they repent of her ways" (2:22). The words "suffer intensely" are *thlipsin megalēn* which can be translated as "great tribulation" (NKJV).[39]

The final occurrence of "suffering" emerges near the end of the first interlude. The great multitude stands before the heavenly throne, wearing white robes. The elder conveys to John that these have come out of "the great tribulation" (*tēs thlipseōs tēs megalēs*), and have washed their robes and made them white in the blood of the Lamb" (7:14). The definite articles (lit., "the tribulation, the great one") imply a concept familiar to the original audience.[40] English translations include "terrible suffering" (GW), "great hardship" (CEB), "great distress" (NABR, NCV), "great ordeal" (NRSV, REB), "great trial" (NJB),

---

37. Aune ("Apocalypse of John," 6) lists similarities between 6:15–17 and *1 En.* 62:3–5 under the category of the terror of humanity before judgment day.

38. Alternate readings include "day of God's great victory" (CEV), "frightening day" (GW), "great judgment day" (NLT), and "Great day of God the sovereign Lord" (REB).

39. Thus, several dispensationalists (Hindson, *Revelation*, 41; LaHaye, *Revelation Unveiled*, 70; Lindsey, *New World Coming*, 58; Robert Thomas, *Revelation*, 1:220–21) match 2:22 to the end-of-history "great tribulation" of 7:14. *Thlipsis megalē* is also is mentioned at Matt 24:21 and Acts 7:11.

40. Michaels, "Tribulation, Great," 676–77.

"terrible persecution" (GNT), and "the great suffering" (CEV). Most versions, however, opt for "the great tribulation" (CSB, ESV, NASB, NET, NIV, NKJV, NLT).[41]

The concept of the great tribulation begins with Dan 7–12. The NT affirms that the prophecies concerning it began to be fulfilled in the first coming of Christ and the creation of the church. Specifically, Dan 12:1 refers to the period of persecution for the faithful who triumph through martyrdom. Some "day of the Lord" passages affirm this (Jer 30:7; Zeph 1:14–16; Matt 24:21; Mark 13:19; 1 Macc 9:27).[42]

Interpreters are customarily placed into two camps concerning the great tribulation. It is either a specific time period or a general time period. First, many scholars note Christian persecution throughout history, yet reserve the great tribulation for a final time of intense suffering on earth. Thus, the definite article "the" serves almost like a technical term.[43] Dispensationalists are the most specific, asserting the great tribulation refers to a distinct, short time-period (most often seven years is mentioned) that occurs after a rapture of the saints and before the return of Christ. Those who have come out of this great tribulation are people who come to faith after the rapture. In other words, the great tribulation is judgment geared for the wicked world. Those who come to Christ during this time must experience the world's wrath.[44]

Second, many Bible students define the great tribulation more broadly. It covers the interadvental period between the first and second comings of Christ. It commenced with Jesus' own suffering and applies to all who follow him. All the saints are partakers in the great tribulation. All experience oppression, persecution, and even death throughout history.[45] Thus, for John and his audience, the great tribulation has already begun. The

41. NKJV is consistent in translating *thlipsis* as "tribulation" at all five locations. Other versions use a variety of expressions, but as noted, many choose to reserve the word "tribulation" for an almost technical term for 7:14.

42. For background, see Beale, *New Testament Biblical Theology*, 214–18; Hays, Duvall, and Pate, *Dictionary of Prophecy*, 451–53; Michaels, "Tribulation, Great" 676–77; and Schnabel, *40 Questions*, 77–84.

43. Aune, *Revelation*, 1:473–74; Bauckham, *Climax of Prophecy*, 226; Beasley-Murray, *Revelation*, 147; Brighton, *Revelation*, 197–98; Easley, *Revelation*, 130; Hays, Duvall, and Pate, *Dictionary of Prophecy*, 453; Alan Johnson, "Revelation," 13:664; Keener, *Revelation*, 318–20; Ladd, *Revelation*, 62; Mounce, *Revelation*, 164; Osborne, *Revelation*, 324–25; J. C. Thomas, *Apocalypse*, 273.

44. Hindson, *Revelation*, 91; LaHaye, *Revelation Unveiled*, 154–59; Patterson, *Revelation*, 203; Ryrie, *Revelation*, 63; Robert Thomas, *Revelation*, 1:486–87, 496; Walvoord, *Revelation*, 146. Price ("Tribulation, Old Testament References," 412–15) lists twenty-one OT "day of the Lord" references and links them to the great tribulation. Preterists, on the other hand, advocate the great tribulation occurred as God's punishment on Israel in AD 70. Chilton (*The Great Tribulation*) marshals 200 pages of support for his position. See also idem, *Days of Vengeance*, 219–20; Gentry, *Before Jerusalem Fell*, 233–34; and Russell, *Parousia*, 405–6. Hailey (*Revelation*, 210) confines it to the Roman period from AD 64–313.

45. Beale, *Revelation*, 433–34; Boxall, *Revelation*, 127; Caird, *Revelation*, 102; Fee, *Revelation*, 113–14; Hendriksen, *More than Conquerors*, 113–14; Hughes, *Revelation*, 98; Kistemaker, *Revelation*, 257; Koester, *Revelation*, 421; Morris, *Revelation*, 115; Mulholland, *Revelation*, 183; Paul, *Revelation*, 163; Resseguie, *Revelation*, 139; Schnabel, *40 Questions*, 79–80; Schüssler Fiorenza, *Revelation*, 68; Smalley, *Revelation*, 196; Wall, *Revelation*, 120; Wilcock, *I Saw Heaven Opened*, 82. Pate and Kennard (*Deliverance Now and Not Yet*, 499–516) agree that the great tribulation covers the interadvental era. They suggest Christ inaugurates the "Messianic Woes," but note that Bible writers express differences in how to endure the great tribulation. Paul and John stress realized eschatology. Mark, James, and Peter prefer consistent eschatology. Matthew, Luke, Hebrews, and Revelation tend toward inaugurated eschatology.

time period between the comings of Christ are the great tribulation. Believers do not escape suffering via a rapture. Nevertheless, 20:1–3 suggests that toward the end of history, tribulation will increase, but not necessarily as a specific time-period.

Where John places the great tribulation affirms the second viewpoint as the most viable. The three interludes picture the role of believers. They are an army of the Lord to witness the gospel (7:1–8). They are commissioned to preach to the nations (10:1–11) and be vigilant witnesses (11:3–13; 12:17). While on earth they are trampled and martyred (11:1–2, 7–10). They are harassed by the dragon (12:1–17) and hounded by the two beasts (13:1–18). Although they are afflicted and persecuted, they live victorious lives throughout the great tribulation (7:13–14). The result is eternity sheltered by the presence of their Lord and rewards for their faithfulness (7:9–17; 11:15–19; 14:1–5, 14–16; 15:1–4). Consequently, the great tribulation is a term that describes the role of believers, not unbelievers. They go through the great tribulation, not escape it. John's point, backed up by the rest of the NT, is that Christians are promised spiritual protection. Believers are witnesses even unto death. They follow the example of their Lord and do not seek, hope, or create ways to escape persecution.

Hour

The hour is a figure for a limited, climactic, and appointed period of time. It most often refers to a period of testing and the unexpected quickness of end-time judgment. In later Jewish writings "hour" (*hōra*), like other temporal concepts, acquired a strong eschatological and apocalyptic stress. Like the "day of the Lord," so the "hour of time" (Dan 8:17, 19) or "hour of consummation" (Dan 11:40, 45). It referred to the last days when God comes accompanied by cosmic phenomena to punish the godless and reward the righteous.[46] The "hour" provides several other ideas in the NT. It signifies a brief period of time of no definite length (Matt 26:40), forms part of broad divisions of time (Acts 2:15), reflects a definite period of time (John 4:52), pinpoints when an event occurs (Matt 8:13), and serves as God's appointed time for specific events in the life of Jesus (John 2:4; 12:23; 13:1; 17:1). Primarily, it is understood as an appointed time of God's end-time intervention in history (Matt 24:36; Mark 13:32; Luke 12:12).[47]

John enlarges upon these previous usages.[48] Thus, the hour might refer to a point in time when Jesus returns in judgment. He comes unexpectedly "like a thief, and you will not know at what hour" (3:3 ESV).[49] Four angels are prepared "for this very hour and day and month and year" (9:15). The final, great earthquake occurs "at that hour" (11:13). An

---

46. Hahn, "Time," 847. Beale (*New Testament Theology*, 149–51) traces "the hour" from Dan 7–12. Mihalios (*Danielic Eschatological Hour*, 174–75) does not work through Revelation, but his study of the NT affords parallel fruit on the significance of "hour" in the Johannine corpus. The hour motif has strong connotations of judgment.

47. Barabas, "Hour," 233–34; Ryken, *Dictionary of Biblical Imagery*, 406.

48. That there are exactly ten occurrences of "hour" suggests numerical symbolism, especially since ten often has length of time in mind (e.g. ten days, thousand years).

49. Most versions translate *hōra* as "time" or with a paraphrase of words at least once among the ten occurrences. Only ESV and NASB are consistent with "hour" each time.

angel cries out that "the hour of judgment has come" (14:7, 15). The doom of Babylon happens quickly. In *one* hour its ruin has come (18:10, 17, 19).[50] But hour can also refer to a period of testing before the end. The "hour of trial" that comes upon the whole world lasts for the interadventual age (3:10).[51] For one hour—a limited yet extended period of time—the ten horns receive authority as kings (17:12).[52] The hour, therefore, is a potent symbol for the critical moment of the end or the time period preceding the end.

Hour and Day and Month and Year

This expression specifies an exact moment in time when God will act in end-time judgment along with the assurance that it will happen. The phrase appears only once at the sixth trumpet. The four angels bound at the river Euphrates "who had been kept ready for this very hour and day and month and year were released to kill a third of mankind" (9:15). In apocalyptic thinking, God has fixed in advance the precise, exact time of every earthly event. "The Holy and Great One has designated [specific] days for all things" (*1 En.* 92:2; see also 79:1–3; *4 Ezra* 4:36–43; *Sib. Or.* 2:325–327; *2 En.* 33:1–2). John follows this train of thought. The definite article (*tēn*) precedes all four nouns. This indicates they are one group and further stresses an exact moment in time. Since the sixth trumpet runs parallel to the sixth bowl, this exact moment implies the events leading to the battle of Armageddon. Thus, the precise moment, no later and no sooner, will usher in God's appointed time for end-time events. The timing of the execution of this plague is fixed with complete precision.[53] This cautions humans from calculating or suggesting dates. God determines the exact moment. Osborne offers sound counsel: "Many modern prophecy buffs use these four to justify their attempts to calculate the exact time (or year) of Christ's return. This is hermeneutically impossible and the furthest thing from John's mind here . . . To pretend that this allows one to calculate the exact year for the parousia is nothing but literalistic hubris. The purpose here is clearly *God's* calculation of the exact time, not ours."[54]

Hour of Trial

This refers to the judgments of God upon the wicked in order for them to repent and the testing persecution of believers for them to remain faithful. It covers the interadventual age. In Revelation, an hour can refer to final, climactic moment (3:3; 14:7) or extend to a period of testing (17:12). It is the latter understanding at work for "the hour of trial" (*tēs horas*

---

50. Osborne (*Revelation*, 622) confirms that all three occurrences of "one hour" stress "the sudden and virtually instantaneous destruction of Babylon the Great."

51. See the entry "Hour of Trial."

52. Patterson (*Revelation*, 324) relates, "The fact that they reign for only one hour is to indicate that they have a relatively short reign."

53. Rissi, *Time and History,* 7. However, Keener (*Revelation,* 154) prefers to see 9:15 as a period of time, not an instance in time.

54. Osborne, *Revelation,* 380 n. 7. See Brighton, *Revelation,* 245; Smalley, *Revelation,* 238.

tou peirasmou). Christ promises "Since you have kept my command to endure patiently, I will also keep you from the hour of trial that is going to come on the whole world to test the inhabitants of the earth" (3:10).[55] The main question is whether or not believers go through this hour of trial. Patterson correctly asserts that an honest assessment of the text "leaves us with no ability to resolve the question based on vocabulary, grammar, and syntax alone."[56] Thus, an interpreter's millennial presupposition produces one of two dichotomous solutions—exemption from or protection through.

First, many interpreters find exemption for believers from enduring the hour of trial. The Greek words *se tērēsō ek* are understood as "will keep you from" (i.e. experiencing) or "remove from." The preposition *ek* is understood as "out of." The hour of trial is then connected with the great tribulation (7:14), and the exemption is a rapture that removes believers from the testing that comes upon the earth. Walvoord, for example, affirms that this "implies the rapture of the church before the time of trouble referred to as the great tribulation."[57] The hour of trial is usually limited to the final seven years of earth history.[58]

The second viewpoint contends that believers are spiritually protected yet will go through the hour of trial. The majority of scholars adopt this interpretation. They connect the phrase "keep/protect from" to John 17:15 where Christ prays for his followers: "My prayer is not that you take them out of the world but that you protect them from (*tērēsēs autou ek*) the evil one." Thus, it indicates protection throughout trials, not an escape from them. It means that they are kept safely (spiritually) through the period of distress.[59] A few English translations support this interpretation, including "I will keep you safe through" (CEB); "I will keep you safe during" (GW); and "I'll keep you safe in" (NABR, NJB). Osborne professes that throughout the NT persecution and even martyrdom is not only the believer's lot in life, but a great privilege (Mark 10:29–30; John 15:18—16:4; Phil 3:10; Col 1:24; 1 Pet 3:13–14). Likewise, in Revelation, martyrdom is understood as a victory over Satan, not defeat (6:9–11; 7:14–17; 12:11). "As when he put Christ on the cross, Satan defeats himself whenever he takes the life of one of the saints."[60] The church is

55. The noun *peirasmos* is found only here. The verb *peirazō* is found three times (2:2, 10; 3:10). Other English renderings include "hour of testing" (CSB, NASB, NET), "time of testing" (CEB, CEV, GW, NLT adds 'great'), "time of trouble" (GNT, NCV), "time of trial" (NABR, NJB), and "ordeal" (REB). Almost all English versions have "I will keep/protect you from."

56. Patterson, *Revelation*, 133.

57. Walvoord, *Revelation*, 87. Dispensationalists consider 3:10 a crucial passage for teaching a rapture. For a defense of this position see Essex, "Rapture and Revelation," 215–39.

58. So Patterson (*Revelation*, 130–33), Ryrie (*Revelation*, 34–35), and most pre-tribulationists. Hindson (*Revelation*, 47) conjectures three and a half years. Easley (*Revelation*, 255), following a prewrath approach, opts for some time before the final seven years. Popular dispensationalists follow a historicist approach. Lindsey (*New World Coming*, 65–66) designates the years 1750 to 1925 and LaHaye (*Revelation Unveiled*, 78) posits 1750 to the rapture. The most cogent defense for the exemption view is found in Robert Thomas, *Revelation*, 1:283–90.

59. Detailed discussions supporting this viewpoint include Aune, *Revelation*, 1:239–40; Beale, *Revelation*, 289–92; Schuyler Brown, "Hour of Trial," 308–14; Gundry, *Church and the Tribulation*, 54–61; Keener, *Revelation*, 153–54; Kistemaker, *Revelation*, 161–63; Mounce, *Revelation*, 102–3; Osborne, *Revelation*, 192–94; and Smalley, *Revelation*, 91–92.

60. Osborne, *Revelation*, 194. Osborne specifically addresses Robert Thomas's (*Revelation*, 1:286) question, "What good does it do to be preserved from the physical consequences of divine wrath and

eternally and spiritually protected from the wrath of God that comes against unbelievers, but not necessarily from the physical wrath of Satan. Moreover, the hour of trial covers the entire interadvental age. It "appears to be a generic designation for the entire period before the return of Christ that is characterized by trials."[61] The phrase "is going to come" (*mellousēs erchesthai*) does not relegate this hour of trial to a distant future. It is unfolding now in the life of John's audience, and every generation afterward. Unbelievers, therefore, are challenged to repent and believers are challenged to persevere during the hour of trial, that is, the Christian era.[62]

How Long?

The martyrs of the fifth seal cry out for God to judge the earth. This is a call for justice, not vengeance. Although found only once in the NT, the question "how long?" is a common expression found throughout the OT (Pss 6:3; 13:1; Isa 6:11; Jer 47:6; Dan 12:6; Hab 1:2; Zech 1:12) and other Jewish literature (*1 En.* 9:3–10; *4 Ezra* 4:33–37).[63] Their cry is in "a loud voice" which implies not only volume but repetition and perseverance, like the parable of the widow and the unjust judge (Luke 18:7). The martyrs' cry is addressed to a sovereign Lord who is "holy and true."[64] "The saints are appealing to God to let his holiness and truth shine forth. Inattention to their plea would mean a blot on his being."[65] Thus, their question is not a plea for vengeance but of justice. God will repay at the right time. He will avenge properly and perfectly (Deut 32:35; Rom 12:19; Heb 10:30).

On the Lord's Day

John informs the seven churches that he received his visions on the Lord's day, Sunday, underscoring an emphasis on the resurrection of Christ and worship. The phrase "On the Lord's Day I was in the Spirit" (1:10) relates how John was transported or filled with the Holy Spirit in preparation for his visions. "Lord's Day" (*kyriakē hēmera*) uses the adjective *kyriakē* ("belonging to the Lord") rather than the usually expected noun *kyriou*. The adjective is found only here and in 1 Cor 11:20 ("Lord's supper"). What is the Lord's day? Scholars have produced five possible understandings. First, it refers to Sunday. The phrase does not occur anywhere else although it is possible that Acts 20:7 and 1 Cor 16:2

---

still fall prey to a martyr's death?"

61. Roloff, *Revelation*, 61–62.

62. Morris (*Revelation*, 79) and Smalley (*Revelation*, 92) reason the test motif serves as an opportunity for God's compassion. The wicked are not simply judged and punished, but tested.

63. Keener, *Revelation*, 218. Thus, as N. T. Wright (*New Testament and People of God*, 463) notes, the question could hardly be a Christian innovation. Furthermore, because this is the only plea of supplication found in Revelation, Heil ("Fifth Seal as a Key," 220–43) deems it crucial for the understanding the whole book. Their martyrdom reflects the first four seals which lead to further conflict and eventual vindication in the rest of the book.

64. This phrase is found once more and ascribed to Jesus (3:7). Aune (*Revelation*, 2:406) notes its juridical overtones.

65. Kistemaker, *Revelation*, 233. See Beale, *Revelation*, 392.

allude to it. An understanding of Sunday does appear starting in the early second century (Did. 14:1; Barn. 15:9; Ign. *Magn.* 9:1; Gos. Pet. 35, 50). Thus, John becomes the first in Christian literature to use the Lord's day as a technical term for Sunday, the day Christ rose from the dead. The overwhelming majority of commentators affix this meaning to the phrase.[66]

Second, a few scholars understand the phrase to refer to the annual event of Easter Sunday. Irenaeus apparently referred to the Lord's day in this fashion.[67] Third, a small number see the phrase to refer originally to Emperor's Day and Christians adapted it to Sunday.[68] Fourth, some interpret the expression as John being whisked forward to the eschatological day of the Lord. Thus, John receives prophetic visions of end-time events, and they unfold before him.[69] Finally, a few attempt to make the case for Sabbath as the "Lord's day.[70] In sum, John most likely refers to Sunday. It is not unreasonable to see allusions to the other views, but they reside far into the background. The OT's understanding of Sabbath as the "Lord's day" was altered forever on resurrection Sunday. This day soon became the day when Christians gathered for worship. It is fitting then for John's Revelation, a work so filled with worshipful elements, to have its origin on the day set aside for Christian worship.

Ten Days

This chronological designation symbolizes a limited but complete period of trial and testing that may lead to death yet also implies spiritual protection for God's people. The majority of modern scholars agree that "ten days" stresses an indefinite period of time that is short and limited, yet full and complete.[71] The words are delivered to the suffering church at Smyrna. "I tell you, the devil will put some of you in prison to test you, and you will suffer persecution for ten days. Be faithful, even to the point of death, and I will give you life as your victor's crown" (2:10).

---

66. The most thorough study is Bauckham, "Lord's Day," 221–50, including effective refutations to non-Sunday views. See also Donato, *Perspectives on the Sabbath*; and Jewett, *Lord's Day*.

67. Alan Johnson, "Revelation," 13:603; Prigent, *Apocalypse*, 129–30; Strand, "Another Look at the Lord's Day," 174–80.

68. Beasley-Murray, *Revelation*, 64–65; Charles, *Revelation*, 1:23; Hemer, *Letters to the Seven Churches*, 31; Smalley, *Revelation*, 51; Leonard Thompson, *Revelation*, 56; Witherington, *Revelation*, 80.

69. Bacchiocchi, *From Sabbath to Sunday*, 123–31; LaHaye, *Revelation Unveiled*, 34; Ryrie, *Revelation*, 19; J. C. Thomas, *Apocalypse*, 100–101; Thomas and Macchia, *Revelation*, 34–35; Walvoord, *Revelation*, 42. So too Stefanovic (*Revelation*, 91, 106) who cites older commentators.

70. Many Seventh Day Adventists promote this view, including Specht ("Sunday in the New Testament," 92–113) and Strand ("Another Look at the Lord's Day," 180–81). An attempt to see other allusions to the Sabbath in Revelation is found in Paulien, "Revisiting the Sabbath," 179–86.

71. Some, of course, disagree. Historicists interpret ten historical periods of persecution under ten Roman emperors (Gregg, *Revelation*, 98). Robert Thomas (*Revelation*, 1:169) and Walvoord (*Revelation*, 62) list examples of older commentators who adopted this. LaHaye (*Revelation Unveiled*, 51, 55–56) and Ryrie (*Revelation*, 28) mention the last ten "years" of the historical era that covered AD 100–312, depicting Nero to Diocletian's persecutions.

John alludes to the story of Daniel and his three friends who were tested "for ten days" not to eat food offered to idols (Dan 1:12–15). They did not compromise with the pagan culture that pressured them. The Daniel story became a model for Jews and later for Christians who would rather be persecuted for faithfulness than capitulate to worshipping idols. Although the period of persecution and testing is fixed and limited, it is also complete and thus must be endured. Similarly, other OT references assume complete and thorough time of testing. In Gen 31:7, Jacob uses "ten" as a way of saying "every time" (so too Num 14:22; Job 19:2–3). The ten plagues of Exodus were short, intense, yet all ten were to be fully experienced.[72]

A few interpreters, however, accept a literal period of "ten days." Colin Hemer posits it alludes to the actual time that those sent into gladiatorial combat were imprisoned, to be followed by certain death in the arena.[73] Alan Johnson agrees. "In the first-century Roman world, prison was usually not punitive but the prelude to trial and execution; hence the words 'be faithful, even to the point of death.'"[74] If this indeed rests in Smyrna's background, then it confirms that a short, intense, and complete time period of suffering is in store for believers, and that martyrdom is a future possibility. Following the eclectic method, the first-century church at Smyrna was charged to ready itself for imminent persecution. In like manner, the church in every generation must prepare itself for potential persecution for not compromising or succumbing to pagan incursions. Yet nearer the end of history this type of persecution becomes more intense. Christians will not escape it but they will have the necessary spiritual tools to go through it victoriously. Overcomers at Smyrna, today, and in the future are promised the reward of eternal life ("victor's crown").

Thousand Two Hundred Sixty Days

This time designation emphasizes the church's role in witnessing the gospel. Saints are promised spiritual protection and provision (nourishment) to enable them to witness throughout the church era. The two occurrences of a "thousand two hundred and sixty days" are found in the second (10:1–11:14) and third interludes (12:1–15:4). In the first instance it relates the time period of witnessing for the church (two witnesses). "And I will appoint my two witnesses, and they will prophesy for 1,260 days, clothed in sackcloth'" (11:3). The second mention relates the protective care the people of God (symbolized by the woman) receive during this period. "The woman fled into the wilderness to a place prepared for her by God, where she might be taken care of for 1,260 days" (12:6).[75] "Wilderness"

---

72. Beale, *Revelation*, 242–43; Hughes, *Revelation*, 42; Kistemaker, *Revelation*, 124–25; Osborne, *Revelation*, 134.

73. Hemer, *Letters to the Seven Churches*, 69–70.

74. Alan Johnson, "Revelation," 13:618. So too Patterson, *Revelation*, 98. Robert Thomas (*Revelation*, 1:170–71) understands ten days of tribulation for Smyrna soon after John wrote to them without specifics. Osborne (*Revelation*, 134) states that the gladiatorial arena referent "is interesting but speculative."

75. English translations use a variety of expressions for this number: "1,260 days" (CSB, ESV, GW, GNT, NET, NIV, NLT); "one thousand two hundred and sixty days" (CEB, CEV, NASB [12:6 only], NCV, NKJV, NRSV); and "twelve hundred and sixty days" (NABR, NASB [11:3 only], NJB, REB). The normally consistent NASB is inconsistent at 11:3. KJV has "a thousand two hundred and threescore days."

alludes to the forty years that the Israelites were cared for by God (Exod 16:32; Deut 1:31; Ps 78:52). Thus, a thousand two hundred sixty days "symbolizes not just testing and trial but also divine comfort and protection."[76] Whereas forty-two months stresses the persecution of the saints (11:2; 13:5), a thousand two hundred and sixty days stresses perseverance, protection, and provision for the saints.

Another link to spiritual provision is that the woman is taken care of for "times, time, and half a time" (12:14). This direct allusion to Dan 7:25 confirms that all these time elements correspond to three and a half years, a common expression for persecution of God's people.[77] What John has added is the promise of spiritual protection and nourishment during this time that enables believers to witness. The beast and his forces are allowed to "kill the body" but they "cannot kill the soul" (Matt 10:28).

Although some interpreters limit the time period to the first century or the last days, it should be applied to the entire time period of the church's existence.[78] All of these numbers are synonymous and parallel. They "symbolize the church's character and destiny, which is a paradox of persecution and preservation."[79] During the era between the ascension and return of Christ the church's job is to witness. Persecution is a given, but so is the promise of spiritual protection and nourishment.

Thousand Years

The thousand years describes an indefinite, extended, and complete period of time that spans the Christian era. John employs "a thousand" as part of his repertoire of numerical symbols. The number (and its multiples) represents vastness, entirety, and fullness.[80] Adding the numerical symbol to the time element of "years" accentuates the vastness, extension, and completeness of time.[81] A "thousand years" (*chilia etē*) is mentioned six times in chapter 20 and is centered on verses 1–6. The time period is interpreted in three dramatically distinct ways. First, premillennialists understand Christ to return in order to rule over a thousand-year earthly kingdom. Thus, chapters 19–21 are taken as sequential events.[82] Deriving from a historic premillennial view comes dispensational premillennialism which accents a literal approach to Revelation, a distinction between

---

76. Osborne, *Revelation*, 464.

77. See the entries "Three and a Half Days" and "Forty-Two Months."

78. Some of those who support the entire Christian era are mentioned under the entry "Time, Times, and Half a Time." Beale (*Revelation*, 646–47) offers support for the three and a half years to begin at the death of Christ by the nearby references to the cross event (11:8; 12:5; 13:3). Osborne (*Revelation*, 463), however, questions the connection and states that Phil 3:10 links better. Keener (*Revelation*, 319) takes note that immediately after Jesus' exaltation the tribulation begins (12:5–6).

79. Resseguie, *Revelation Unsealed*, 52.

80. See the entry "Thousand."

81. Rainbow ("Millennium as Metaphor," 210) summarizes, "It is generally recognized that John's millennium is a variation on the apocalyptic theme of a temporary, earthly, messianic kingdom, penultimate to God's final one (cf. *4 Ezra* 7:26–44; 12:31–34; *2 Bar.* 29–30; 40:3; *1 En.* 91:8–17)."

82. For historic premillennial insights see Blomberg and Chung, *Case for Historic Premillennialism*. For exegesis of chapter 20 see Mounce, *Revelation*, 360–71; Osborne, *Revelation*, 696–710; and J. C. Thomas, *Apocalypse*, 592–608.

Israel and the church, and adds a rapture of the saints.[83] Second, postmillennialists view Christ returning after a this-worldly millennium. In other words, Christ established his kingdom by his death, and the progress of the gospel will eventually triumph and bring in a golden millennial age.[84] Third, amillennialism believes there is no distinct thousand-year period. Instead, the millennium symbolizes the era between the first and second comings of Christ.

This study professes what is usually labeled amillennialism concerning the thousand years. Since the "a" means "no" a better designation is "realized millennialism" or "inaugurated millennialism." Several features support that the thousand years vision (20:1–21:8) stands as an independent vision and not a sequential carryover from chapter 19. "And I saw" (20:1) indicates a new vision has started.[85] At Christ's resurrection, Satan was effectively "bound" (20:2–3). His power is limited. He is no longer free to deceive the nations (Matt 12:29; Luke 10:18; John 12:31; Col 2:15; Heb 2:14). Nevertheless, good and evil continue to coexist (Matt 13:24–30). Toward the end of history, Satan will be loosed and permitted to spread havoc. Meanwhile, God's saints reign during the millennium (20:4–6).[86] The "first resurrection" (20:5–6) is the spiritual resurrection that occurs at the believer's physical death (1 Cor 15:22).[87] Christ presently reigns in heaven with the souls of deceased believers. The second resurrection is physical. Glorified bodily resurrection occurs at the second coming (2 Cor 5:1–8; 1 Thess 4:13–18). The resurrection of unbelievers ("rest of the dead") to face judgment is elaborated in 20:12–13. Satan's release and the final battle are envisioned in 20:7–10. But this is not a second "final" battle a thousand years after Armageddon. It is Armageddon—another picture of the same end-time battle described in previous visions. Lastly, Christ's return leads to final judgment for the wicked and eternity for the saints (20:11–15). The thousand years vision concludes with a description of the new heaven and new earth (21:1–8).[88] Therefore, the thousand years

---

83. Dispensationalism is divided further into classic dispensationalists and progressive dispensationalists. For concise dispensational views on millennial options see Couch, "Millennium, New Testament Descriptions," 266–67; LaHaye, *Revelation Unveiled*, 330–38; Stanton, "Millennium, Doctrine of," 259–62; and Walvoord, *Revelation*, 282–90. For dispensational exegesis of chapter 20, see Robert Thomas, *Revelation* 2:407–22; and Walvoord, *Revelation*, 290–300. See also Pate, *Four Views on the Book of Revelation*, for dispensational, historic, and prewrath defenses.

84. For a postmillennial interpretation see Mathison, *Postmillennialism*, 155–59. See Chilton, *Days of Vengeance*, 493–519, for an exegesis of chapter 20.

85. "And I saw" (*kai eidon*) is a discourse marker that functions most often as a literary indicator to introduce a new vision or new scene within a vision. See the Introduction.

86. Resseguie (*Revelation Unsealed*, 61–64) explains that the message of the thousand years is unmistakable: first, the saints are rewarded for their perseverance by reigning for a thousand years with Christ; second, Satan is restrained for the thousand years from deceiving the nations.

87. See the entry "First Resurrection."

88. For amillennial exegesis see Beale, *Revelation*, 984–1021; Brighton, *Revelation*, 533–70; Kistemaker, *Revelation*, 531–42; and Riddlebarger, *Case for Amillennialism*, 195–226. Mathewson ("Re-Examination of the Millennium," 237–51) attempts to bridge premillennialism and amillennialism. He agrees that Armageddon and the second coming in 19:11–21 are recapped in 20:7–10. Thus, there is only one end-time battle, not two separated by a millennial age. Yet he also finds support for the inauguration of the millennium at the second coming, not the first coming. This is an interesting option which should be considered further by modern commentators, but so far has not.

is not a literal, chronological time period. Rather it is a metaphor that symbolizes the completed era between Christ's first and second comings—the Christian era.

Three and a Half Days

"Three and a half" emphasizes the time period of persecution for the church. The three and a half "days" of the humiliation of the two witnesses symbolizes the suffering to the point of martyrdom the church endures during the interadvental age. It matches the other "three and a half" designations ("forty-two months," "thousand two hundred sixty days," "time, times, and half a time"). The phrase is found twice near the conclusion of the second interlude and the ministry of the two witnesses. "For three and a half days some from every people, tribe, language and nation will gaze on their bodies and refuse them burial . . . But after the three and a half days the breath of life from God entered them, and they stood on their feet, and terror struck those who saw them" (11:9, 11).[89]

The number immediately invokes a connection to the three and a half years disguised in forty-two months, a thousand two hundred and sixty days, and time, times, and half a time. Most scholars, however, maintain a distinction between days and years. Thus, three and a half "years" and three and a half "days" signify two distinct short periods of time under God's control. The three and a half days of humiliation is intended to correspond to the three and a half years of ministry, but only analogously.[90]

Interpreters note the three and a half days serves as a reminder to the length of time of Jesus' own death and resurrection "on the third day."[91] It also connotes the length of Jesus' earthly ministry. John's audience would have picked up on the symbolic number from Elijah's drought (1 Kgs 18:1) which Jesus (Luke 4:25) and James (Jas 5:17) utilized. Yet 1 Kgs 18:1 states "in the third year." Thus, "John has converted the 'third day' of Gospel tradition into 'three and a half days,' just as the tradition he followed with regard to Elijah's drought converted the 'third year' of 1 Kings 18:1 into 'three and a half years.'"[92] The point is that John is emphasizing the number three and a half, not the "days" or "years."

89. For "breath of life" the KJV reads "spirit of God." CSB, NIV, and NRSV add a footnote with the option of "spirit." The phrase recalls Ezek 37:1–14. Some commentators, including Fee (*Revelation*, 154), Keener (*Revelation*, 296), Koester (*Revelation*, 502), and J. C. Thomas (*Apocalypse*, 338–39) suggest a connection to the Holy Spirit (Zech 4:6). Blount (*Revelation*, 215) and Mounce (*Revelation*, 222), however, find no connection. Patterson (*Revelation*, 250 n. 130) correctly chastises the NIV for leaving out *megas* ("great") before "terror."

90. So Beale, *Revelation*, 595; Beasley-Murray, *Revelation*, 186; Keener, *Revelation*, 296; Kistemaker, *Revelation*, 334; Koester, *Revelation*, 502; Mounce, *Revelation*, 221; Murphy, *Fallen Is Babylon*, 267; Osborne, *Revelation*, 428; Smalley, *Revelation*, 282. Robert Thomas (*Revelation*, 2:95), on the contrary, finds no connection between three and a half days and three and a half years: "the correspondence to the three and a half years of prophetic ministry being only coincidental."

91. Boxall, *Revelation*, 165; Koester, *Revelation*, 502; Osborne, *Revelation*, 429; J. C. Thomas, *Apocalypse*, 337. Contra Prigent, *Apocalypse*, 356.

92. Bauckham, *Climax of Prophecy*, 280. See Aune, *Revelation*, 2:621; Beale, *Revelation*, 594; Murphy, *Fallen Is Babylon*, 263–64.

Therefore, some interpreters understand that the number "three and a half" is much more significant than the added time elements. Edmondo Lupieri stresses that symbolism is not as significant in the measurement (days, weeks, months, years) as in the numerical value attached to the measurement (one-half, three and a half, seven, ten, twelve).[93] Similarly, Resseguie states that "A broken seven appears once again, but now in terms of days, not years. The numerical portion (three and a half) is more important than the time span (days). The church's life and work is symbolized by the number three and a half, whether three and a half days or three and a half years."[94] John Sweet adds "In other words, John is urging the church to see its whole life and work under the sign of *three and a half*."[95] John is not referring to two separate time periods (days and years), but rather two angles on the same time period—the Christian era.[96]

In sum, "three and a half" emphasizes the time period of the witness of the church. It symbolizes the entire interadvental age from the resurrection to the return of Christ. It matches the other "three and a half" designations.[97] The significance of the number is that the church (two witnesses) testifies and suffers even to the point of martyrdom. When the two witnesses arise after three and a half days, it reflects the second coming and the end of the age.

Time

Two Greek words express time in the NT. Kairos *indicates a decisive and opportune moment of time whereas* chronos *designates linear time or a stretch of time. Both words stress urgency and imminence.* The NT uses *kairos* eighty-five times and *chronos* fifty-four times.[98] John accentuates these two words through his use of numerical symbolism and structural placement within his visions. *Kairos* appears seven times, a sign of completeness and totality (1:3; 11:18; 12:12; 12:14 [3x]; 22:10). This may be divided further into four different phrases. First, "the time is near" (1:3; 22:10) opens and closes John's book. The usage of the word in these two verses "is pregnant with theological meaning."[99] At both places *kairos* signifies the end of history and the in-breaking of the kingdom of God. Second, "the time has come for judging the dead" (11:18), found at the conclusion of the seventh trumpet, pictures the climax of human history. It hints at the more detailed discussion of end-time judgment located at the great white throne judgment (20:11–15). Third, the dragon is angry because he knows his "time is short" (12:12). He has great anger but little

93. Lupieri, *Apocalypse*, 154, 174–75.

94. Resseguie, *Revelation*, 165.

95. Sweet, *Revelation*, 183. So too Aune, *Revelation*, 2:621; Brighton, *Revelation*, 299–300; Tavo, *Woman, Mother, Bride*, 212–13.

96. Chilton (*Days of Vengeance*, 274) provides a chiastic arrangement of "forty-two months," "thousand two hundred sixty days," and "three and a half days," with the last item serving as the peak of the chiasm. This lends support that it should be included with the other designations.

97. See the entries "Forty-Two Months," "Thousand Two Hundred Sixty Days," and "Time, Times, and Half a Time."

98. Linton, "Time," 1594.

99. Rissi, *Time and History*, 22.

time. Finally, the last three occurrences of *kairos* appear in the threefold phrase "time, times, and half a time" (12:14). This temporal designation symbolizes a short yet intense period of persecution and testing for God's people, and a reminder of their call to witness. It is also accompanied with the promise of God's eternal protection, and covers the period between the ascension and return of Christ.

The other word for "time" is *chronos*. It is found four times, a number that highlights full coverage with the earth in mind. That *chronos* designates a linear stretch of time is easily observable. First, Jezebel is "given time" (*edōka chronon*) in order to repent (2:21). The impression is that this is not much time. Second, the martyrs ask how much longer before they are avenged and God is vindicated. Their answer is to wait "a little longer" (*mikron chronon*), literally, "a little time" (6:11). Third, the angel swears "the time is up" (10:6, CEB). God's end-time events are unfolding.[100] Fourth, in 20:3, the dragon is loosed after the thousand years for "a short time" (CSB, NABR, NASB, NCV, NIV).[101] Once again, a period of short duration is understood. Although the different millennial positions have much to say concerning the when of the millennium, all agree that Satan's loosing for a short period of time is chronologically limited. Thus, John utilizes a strong temporal point of view. The end is imminent and humanity must urgently respond. *Kairos* and *chronos* confirm this understanding.

Time Is Near

Alongside "what must soon take place," the phrase "the time is near" emphasizes the swiftness, suddenness, and imminence of the events leading to the second coming as well as the urgency to respond with faith toward God. The phrases "the time is near" and "what must soon take place" both appear twice in the same context and location—the beginning and the end of Revelation (1:1, 3; 22:6, 10). Thus, they serve as an *inclusio* to the entire book.[102] "The time is near" is found at 1:3 and 22:10.[103] The phrase stresses the nearness of the second coming. Futurists, however, interpret this imminence differently. Because two thousand years have passed since John penned these words, the phrase does not refer to the nearness of the event but rather the "certainty" of it. Since the end did not

---

100. Scholars deliberate on the intent of *chronos* in 10:6. Most scholars, followed by English translations, render this as "no more delay," i.e. the present time of waiting will end with the upcoming seventh trumpet. Perhaps better is the nuance of "no more interval of time" (HCSB). Blount (*Revelation*, 195) explains that "While 'There will be no more delay' therefore is an accurate representation of what the angel has to say, the translation 'There will be no more time' is more eloquent and appropriate." See Aune, *Revelation*, 2:568; and Smalley, *Revelation*, 264, for discussion.

101. NET has "a brief period of time." Most other versions produce "a little while."

102. The prologue and epilogue of Revelation repeat numerous key themes, including the sovereignty of God, necessity of conversion for unbelievers, and perseverance on the part of believers in light of the nearness of Christ's return. Hindson (*Revelation*, 225) lists twelve parallels between the locations. Everything between these phrases stresses immediacy and expectation.

103. English renderings include "the time is almost here" and "these things will happen soon" (CEV), "the appointed time is near" (NABR), and "the time of fulfillment is near" (NJB). Two versions produce different renderings for 22:10, and thereby miss the intratextual connection: "the time is at hand" (NKJV) and "the Time is close" (REB).

happen chronologically soon, the expression "indicates nearness from the standpoint of prophetic revelation, not necessarily that the event will immediately occur."[104]

Yet "the time is near" belongs to the whole period of inaugurated eschatology—from the first coming of Christ to his return. It is "already but not yet." Jesus proclaimed "The time has come," and "The kingdom of God has come near. Repent and believe the good news!" (Mark 1:15). His first coming consummated with his death (Matt 26:18; Luke 21:8). The time fully consummates with his return. Thus, believers live between the beginning of the end (cross) and the consummation of the end (second coming).[105] John agrees with the Gospel writers. The death and resurrection of Christ inaugurates the long-awaited kingdom of the end times which the OT predicted and which continues to exist through the church age. The same verbiage appears at the end of a few of John's visions (11:18; 14:15).[106] Eschatological delay, therefore, is as much a feature of Revelation as is eschatological imminence. It is built into the structure.[107]

The nearness of the second coming is frequently used as a summons for believers to live holy lives now (Rom 13:11–14; Phil 4:4–5; Heb 10:25; Jas 5:7; 1 Pet 4:7–11; 2 Pet 3:10–14). Revelation, like the rest of the NT, focuses not only on eschatology but on ethics. Osborne encourages us that "in light of the fact that the 'time is near,' we are called to live decisively and completely for God."[108] Revelation, therefore, begins and closes with the assurance of the immediacy Christ's coming. This constant expectation beckons believers to live holy lives today.

Time, Times, and Half a Time

This temporal designation symbolizes a short yet intense period of persecution of God's people. Nevertheless, spiritual protection and nourishment is promised to the faithful. It covers the period between the ascension and return of Christ. John mentions the enigmatic phrase "time, times, and half a time" once.[109] It depicts the time of protection given to the woman clothed with the sun. She is escorted "to the place prepared for her in the wilderness, where she would be taken care of for a time, times and half a time, out of the serpent's reach" (12:14).[110]

---

104. Walvoord, *Revelation*, 334. See Patterson, *Revelation*, 53–55.

105. Fee and Stuart, *How to Read the Bible*, 152–53.

106. Beale, *Revelation*, 185. Schüssler Fiorenza (*Justice and Judgment*, 64 n. 107) offers that imminent expectation is better termed "constant expectation."

107. Bauckham, *Theology of Revelation*, 157–59.

108. Osborne, *Revelation*, 59. Kistemaker (*Revelation*, 588) appends, "This is not a reference to a calendar or to clock time; rather it means an opportune moment or a time of decision."

109. "Time, times, and half a time" is converted into years in a few Bible translations: "a year, two years, and a half-year" (NABR); "three and a half years" (GNT, REB); and "three and one-half years" (NCV). Most versions, however, retain something like "time and times and half a time." The original form aids in recognizing its derivation from Dan 7:25 and 12:7. Some versions, however, completely muddle the intertextual connections. CEB, for example, has three different renderings for Dan 7:25; 12:7; Rev 12:14.

110. The words "taken care of" come from *trephetai*. Other versions have "nourished" (CSB, ESV, NASB, NKJV, NRSV), "looked after" (NJB, REB), "fed" (HCSB), and "cared for and protected" (NLT).

This coincides temporally, synonymously, and equivalently with forty-two months (11:2; 13:5), a thousand two hundred sixty days (11:3; 12:6), and three and a half years (a designation not in Revelation, but three and a half days is: 11:9, 11). The events include the trampling of the Holy City (church), prophesying of the two witnesses (church), protection of the woman (church) during which the dragon makes war with her offspring, and the beast's war with saints. As Frederick Murphy concludes, "All of these are the same thing seen from different angles."[111]

Dispensationalists interpret these time designations literally and locate them in the final years of earth history, after a rapture has whisked faithful believers away. Robert Thomas correctly notes that times, times, and half a time is used as an expression "to depict the same period as is designated in months (11:2; 13:5) and days (11:3; 12:6) elsewhere (cf. Dan. 7:25; 12:7)."[112] But Thomas assigns the time to the final three and a half years of history.[113]

Yet John uses these figures to tell us about kind of time, not length of time.[114] Most scholars understand the numbers as figurative. Indeed, many interpret these temporal designations to cover the entire interadventual age. The Christian era is the time when the church must witness, the time that Satan and the beast persecute the church, and the time that the church is nourished, tested, trained, and spiritually protected.[115]

The phrase comes directly from Dan 7:25 and 12:7. The context of Dan 7–12 includes a future tribulation centered on the temple, one who comes and speaks words against God, the "abomination of desolation," and the coming of God's kingdom of saints, including "one like a son of man." Daniel asks how much longer until the end (Dan 12:6). The answer is "time, times, and half a time." The historical backdrop is the persecution of Antiochus Epiphanes IV (167–164 BC).[116] Thus, John is confirming this Danielic period has arrived and the conflict between the dragon and the woman (church) takes place in this time period. Although the saints are persecuted physically, they will be protected and nourished spiritually (3:10; 6:9–11; 7:3–4, 14–17; 10:9–10; 11:1–2; 12:6).[117]

Daniel referred to the persecution of the saints. By contrast, John calls it a time of nourishment for the saints. Thus, a subtle inversion confirms the time of persecution is

---

Mounce (*Revelation*, 241) adds the idea of "training" as well. The verb was used in the rearing of children (Luke 4:16).

111. Murphy, *Fallen Is Babylon*, 262.

112. Robert Thomas, *Revelation*, 2:139.

113. Preterists such as Buchanan (*Revelation*, 322), Chilton (*Days of Vengeance*, 321), and Mazzaferri (*Genre of Revelation*, 83) follow a literal time period of AD 66–70. Historicists such as Stefanovic (*Revelation*, 402) mark off AD 538–1798.

114. Keener, *Revelation*, 319.

115. Commentators who agree with the interadventual time period include Beale (*Revelation*, 646–47, 669), Brighton (*Revelation*, 287–91, 339), Duvall (*Revelation*, 173), Harrington (*Revelation*, 121), Hendriksen (*More than Conquerors*, 129), Hughes (*Revelation*, 141), Keener (*Revelation*, 319), Kistemaker (*Revelation*, 368), Koester (*Revelation*, 562), Prigent (*Apocalypse*, 345–46), and Schnabel (*40 Questions*, 82–83).

116. Beale (*Revelation*, 566) relates this is specified as "three years and six months" in 1 Macc 1–4; 2 Macc 5; and Josephus, *J.W.* 1.19; 5.394.

117. Osborne, *Revelation*, 482–83.

also a time of protection.[118] All of these numerical/time symbols, therefore, stress persecution, the need to be faithful witnesses, and the promise of spiritual protection and nourishment from God. When contrasted with the security of eternity in God's presence, the time of testing and persecution on earth is microscopic by comparison.

Wait a Little Longer

This answer to the cry of "how long?" from the martyrs under the altar accents the imminence of Christ's coming, the sovereignty of God, and the need for patience endurance on the part of the faithful. In the fifth seal, the answer from heaven to the martyrs' cry of "how long?" is to "wait a little longer." The phrase literally means "rest still a little time." The verb *anapauō* is found only twelve times in the NT, usually with "rest" or "refresh" in mind. John uses the word twice (6:11; 14:13). The majority of English versions translate the verb as "rest." In fact, only NIV and NCV have "wait." Both meanings, however, do fit.[119] Nevertheless, rest is a stronger term. This is because the idea of "rest" parallels "perseverance," which is a key theme in Revelation. The martyrs are called upon to have patience, the same patience that characterized their lives of patient endurance while living.[120] The full significance of the term is found in its parallel use in 14:13. For the wicked there is no rest (14:11) but the righteous will rest from their labors.[121]

Thus, saints (living and dead) are to be patient and at rest with God's perfect, consummate timing on their behalf. The fifth seal's "wait a little longer," like "the time is near" and "what must soon take place," stresses the imminence of the end. If a progressive recapitulation methodology is followed, then "a little longer" is answered immediately by the sixth seal (6:12–17) which pictures judgment day. The theme of delay that is frequently found in John continues to resonate today since we are one day closer than yesterday. The answer remains the same—wait, rest, and even more so, "be patient" (NABR) for a little while longer.[122]

What Must Soon Take Place

Alongside "the time is near," this phrase emphasizes the swiftness, suddenness, and immediacy of the events leading to the second coming as well as the urgency to respond to them with faith toward God. The twin phrases "what must soon take place" and "the time is near" appear twice in the same context and location—the prologue and epilogue of John's

118. J. C. Thomas, *Apocalypse*, 377.

119. Osborne (*Revelation*, 289) understands that both meanings fit the word. Patterson (*Revelation*, 185) adopts the singular idea of "stop" instead of "rest" or "wait." The noun *anapausis* can contain the idea of "ceasing" (Rev 4:8). No other resource, however, carries this noun idea over to the verb as Patterson does. In fact, the notion of calling on the martyrs to "stop" their cry to God implies the idea for them to limit or control their impatience. Robert Thomas (*Revelation*, 1:447) calls this "an unworthy trait to attribute to glorified beings in heaven."

120. See the entry "Patient Endurance."

121. Beale, *Revelation*, 768; Murphy, *Fallen Is Babylon*, 211; Resseguie, *Revelation*, 131.

122. See Beale, *Revelation*, 394; Pattemore, *People of God*, 88; J. C. Thomas, *Apocalypse*, 253.

Apocalypse (1:1, 3; 22:6, 10). They serve as an *inclusio* for the entire book. Everything between these phrases stresses immediacy and expectation. "What must soon take place" occurs at 1:1 and 22:6.[123]

The imminence of Christ's coming raises questions for many Bible readers because almost two thousand years have passed since "soon" was recorded by John. Preterists and historicists answer that "soon" was indeed fulfilled in the fall of Jerusalem and/or the fall of Rome. Chilton, for example, states that "Christians needed the Revelation as a stable guide during the period of dramatic change which was to come. The end of the world was approaching—not the destruction of the physical universe, but the passing away of the old world-order, the governing of the world around the central sanctuary in Jerusalem."[124]

Many futurists, on the other hand, are not inclined to stress immediacy. This allows for the urgency of John's audience, and other biblical passages on imminence, while at the same time allowing for the passage of time. Walvoord relates that *tachei* means "quickly or suddenly coming to pass," thus indicating rapidity of execution after the beginning takes place. The idea is not that the event may occur soon, but that when it does, it will be sudden."[125]

The word "soon" indeed contains an element of "suddenly." Its placement, however, in the context of "the time is near" on both occasions confirms "soonness" over "suddenness." Mounce advises, "The most satisfying solution is to take the expression 'must soon take place' in a straightforward sense, remembering that in the prophetic outlook the end is always imminent."[126]

John's approach differs from apocalyptic writings that were written for future generations (Dan 8:26; 12:4; *T. Mos.* 1:17–18; *1 En.* 1:2). Thus, Revelation was meant to be relevant for John's original audience. The "coming soon" includes the discipline that the seven churches faced from the risen Christ.[127] But it also holds consummative force of the second coming. Therefore, it is better to see this as apocalyptic language similar to what is found elsewhere in the NT (Luke 18:8; Rom 16:20; 1 Pet 4:7). Such language does not mean that there are no events left to occur but that there is a period of time before fulfillment (6:11). Thus, expectation is coupled with responsibility.[128]

Sandy relates what the prophets understood about "suddenly" and "soon." Like the word "forever," words that emphasize brevity and swiftness are used to intensify the situation. Impending judgment is much worse when it is understood as imminent. "Words of swiftness raise the bar. It will be severe, and it will be sudden and unexpected."[129] Sandy

123. Other renderings include "that/what must happen (very) soon" (CEV, GNT, GW, NABR, NCV, NET, NLT [22:6]); "which must shortly take place" (NKJV); and "what must quickly take place" (HCSB). Two versions (NLT, NJB) miss the intratextual connection by translating the two passages differently.

124. Chilton, *Days of Vengeance,* 55. See also Caird, *Revelation,* 12, 32, 49; Clark, *Message from Patmos,* 22–23; Russell, *Parousia,* 367–70.

125. Walvoord, *Revelation,* 35. See also Hitchcock, "Critique of the Preterist View," 467–78; Patterson, *Revelation,* 53–55; Robert Thomas, *Revelation,* 1:54–56; 2:496–98.

126. Mounce, *Revelation,* 41.

127. Bauckham, *Theology of Revelation,* 157–59; Koester, *Revelation,* 222–23.

128. Osborne, *Revelation,* 55.

129. Sandy, *Plowshares and Pruning Hooks,* 101.

continues that "If this insight is applied to 1:1; 22:6, for example, a problem is resolved swiftly. Expressions of brevity and imminency in the prophets must be interpreted beyond the range of dictionaries. They generally intensify the severity of judgment."[130] Thus, the church today—like the churches of John's generation and all subsequent generations—eagerly awaits the return of Christ. The weight placed on its immediacy here and elsewhere in the NT is a clarion call for believers to live holy lives.

Miscellaneous Images

This final section serves as a catch all of entries that are not easily placed in the other categories. Strictly speaking, some are not symbols. Nonetheless, they are significant additions to the overall understanding and structure of Revelation.

Blessed

John expertly distributes seven beatitudes throughout Revelation to stress ethical living for persecuted believers in light of the nearness of the second coming. The fact that there are seven beatitudes or macarisms (*makarioi*) scattered throughout John's Apocalypse accents the fullness and completeness of the blessings (1:3; 14:13; 16:15; 19:9; 20:6; 22:7; 22:14).[131] Most English versions translate *makarios* as "blessed" at all seven locations.[132] Exceptions include "favored" (CEB) and "happy" (GNT). It is difficult to find a one-to-one correspondence between Greek and English for *makarios*. A translation of "happy," however, seems particularly weak.[133]

Several studies have analyzed the seven beatitudes in Revelation.[134] Briefly, beatitudes are expressions of praise or congratulation and as such belong to the subgenre known as ascription.[135] Typically, beatitudes have four components: the ascription, object of ascription, reason for the ascription, and commentary.[136] At first sight, it appears there

---

130. Ibid., 102.

131. Resseguie (*Revelation*, 64) states, "The selection of seven—the perfect number—underscores the fullness of blessing that is given to those who hear and keep what is written in the book."

132. HCSB unfortunately has "fortunate" at 19:9, breaking up its intratextual connections. The CSB revision corrects it. REB is consistent with "happy" except for its switch to "blessed" at 20:6.

133. Nonetheless, Prévost (*How to Read the Apocalypse*, 60–61) stresses the idea of happiness. Yet this may also reflect the decision of Prévost's English translators, John Bowden and Margaret Lydamore. Pennington (*Sermon on the Mount*, 41–68), although concentrating on the Matthean beatitudes, suggests a translation of "human flourishing."

134. This includes Cruz, "Beatitudes of the Apocalypse," 269–83; Giesen, "Heilszusage angesichts der Bedragnis," 191–223; Hatfield, "Function of the Seven Beatitudes"; and Nwachukwu, *Beyond Vengeance and Protest*.

135. Warren Carter, "Beatitudes," 415–16; Raymond Collins, "Beatitudes," 629.

136. Nwachukwu, *Beyond Vengeance and Protest*, 183. Alternatively, Mark Wilson (*Victory through the Lamb*, 33) produces seven themes: (1) God/Obedience; (2) Heavenly Voice and the Spirit/Persecution; (3) Jesus/Preparation/watchfulness; (4) Angel/Fellowship; (5) John/ Eternal Life; (6) Jesus/Obedience; and (7) Jesus/Restoration.

is no structural significance to where the seven are located.[137] A closer inspection, however, reveals the blessings are placed at key locations. The first and seventh beatitudes are found in the prologue (1:3) and epilogue (22:14), and serve as an effective *inclusio*. The remaining five are situated at or near the end of five different visions (14:13; 16:15; 19:9; 20:6; 22:7). Their placement prepares readers to know the end of an individual vision is forthcoming. Most importantly, John is giving ethical statements in light of the near end.[138]

Thus, the theological teaching from the beatitudes encourages the faithful to read, hear, and obey God's words (1:3; 22:7). They are to persevere and be ever ready for the return of Christ (16:15). They are to remain faithful unto death (14:13; 22:14). As a result, they will rest from their labor (14:13). They are invitees to the Lamb's wedding supper (19:9) and participants in the first resurrection (20:6). The tree of life and entry into the new Jerusalem is theirs (22:14).[139] The seven beatitudes therefore accentuate the challenge of holy living in light of the nearness of the second coming.

First Resurrection

This refers to the spiritual resurrection of all believers upon physical death into the presence of God. In the thousand years vision (20:1–21:8), John describes those who were beheaded coming back to life to rule with Christ during the millennium, twice mentioning the first resurrection (20:4–6). Resurrection is a central theme in the NT. "The first resurrection," however, is related only here. Bible students disagree over whether this first resurrection and that "they came to life" (*ezēsan*) is spiritual or physical as well as over when this resurrection takes place. Indeed, the position Christians take on this places them into the different millennial camps.

Many interpreters, particularly futurists, believe this refers to a *physical* resurrection that occurs at the second coming for all believers or perhaps a select group (e.g. restricted only to martyrs) who will then reign with Christ for a thousand years on earth.[140] Others, arising from the ranks of preterists, idealists, and eclectics, understand the first resurrection as a *spiritual* resurrection, and the "coming to life" occurs either at the time of an individual believer's conversion to Christ or more likely at the time of physical death.

---

137. Several scholars note a lack of structural placement, including Bauckham (*Theology of Revelation*, 26–27), Lupieri (*Apocalypse*, 99), and Prévost (*How to Read the Apocalypse*, 60).

138. Kuykendall, "Twelve Visions of John," 549–50. In addition, Giblin (*Revelation*, 217 n. 164) and Mark Wilson (*Victor Sayings*, 8–9) note chiastic structure in the seven blessings. If so, this also underscores the literary genius of John.

139. Bauckham, *Climax of Prophecy*, 30, who appends that "these are only *representative* of the complete blessing indicated by the number seven. The seven beatitudes comprise a kind of summary of Revelation's message."

140. So Beasley-Murray, *Revelation*, 295; Duvall, *Revelation*, 269; Easley, *Revelation*, 372; Hindson, *Revelation*, 203; Alan Johnson, "Revelation," 13:768–69; Keener, *Revelation*, 464; Koester, *Revelation*, 775; LaHaye, *Revelation Unveiled*, 326; Ladd, *Revelation*, 265–67; Mealy, *After the Thousand Years*, 208; Mounce, *Revelation*, 366; Murphy, *Fallen Is Babylon*, 399; Osborne, *Revelation*, 707; Patterson, *Revelation*, 354; Paul, *Revelation*, 329; Reddish, *Revelation*, 383; Stefanovic, *Revelation*, 565; J. C. Thomas, *Apocalypse*, 603; Robert Thomas, *Revelation*, 2:412–22; Walvoord, *Revelation*, 296–98.

Such an understanding may have also been intended by other NT writers. Paul states, "For as in Adam all die, so in Christ all will be made alive" (1Cor 15:22). Certainly the Holy Spirit as a pledge or down payment of the kingdom of God (2 Cor 1:22; Eph 1:14) implies a distinction between those who are resurrected with Christ and those who do not unite with him. This also fits with an understanding of the intermediate state of the believer found (2 Cor 5:1–8; Phil 1:21–23; 1 Thess 4:13–18). In other words, absent from the physical body, but spiritually present with the Lord. This is followed by the glorified bodily resurrection that occurs at the second coming. Thus, throughout the thousand years (the time period between the first and second comings) believers reign with Christ. Kistemaker relates that when the saints depart earth they enter eternal life. "They remain without their resurrected bodies until the return of Christ. The saints live and rule with Christ a thousand years, but where is Christ? He is in heaven, where he sits on the throne and rules; all authority has been given to him (Matt. 28:18). And the saints redeemed from sin and death are seated on heavenly thrones and are privileged to rule as royalty with Christ in heaven."[141] This group who receives the first resurrection is described as martyrs, and some Bible students will thus limit them. It is more likely this is yet another portrayal of the church whose mission and possible martyrdom comes "with the job" of witnessing for Christ. Thus, all the saints who have lived and died is best understood.[142]

The "rest of the dead" (20:5) then refer to unbelievers.[143] Translating the verse as a parenthetical comment (GNT, NCV, NET, NIV, NLT, NRSV) assists in understanding the first resurrection to apply only to believers whereas "the rest" applies to the general resurrection discussed in 20:12–13. Said another way, believers have a first (physical) death followed by a first (spiritual) resurrection. When Christ comes again they will experience a second (physical) resurrection. By contrast, unbelievers also face a first (physical) death. But they are raised after the thousand years is completed, on judgment day, in order to face a second (spiritual) death, followed by a second (physical) "resurrection" into the lake of fire. Thus, those who belong to Christ die once but rise twice (spiritually and physically) whereas those who reject Christ rise once but die twice (physically and spiritually).[144] To conclude, these verses are among the most hotly contested among scholars, dividing the millennial viewpoints into their respective camps. The position of this study is that believers reign now. Whereas another yet future reign is conceivable, it is unnecessary. "They came to life" reflects a spiritual resurrection, a new spiritual life.

---

141. Kistemaker, *Revelation*, 539. So too Beale, *Revelation*, 1000–1016; Brighton, *Revelation*, 556–58; Farmer, *Revelation*, 125; Hailey, *Revelation*, 394; Hendriksen, *More than Conquerors*, 232; Hughes, *Revelation*, 213; Dennis Johnson, *Triumph of the Lamb*, 291–92; Morris, *Revelation*, 231; Mulholland, *Revelation*, 310; Rainbow, "Millennium as Metaphor," 209–21; Storms, *Kingdom Come*, 451. Alternatively, Hughes ("First Resurrection," 315–18) opted that the first resurrection referred to Christ's resurrection and the second resurrection refers to the believer's resurrection. Smalley (*Revelation*, 509–10) chooses the resurrection to occur at conversion.

142. See the entry "Beheaded."

143. See the entry "Rest, The."

144. Kistemaker, *Revelation*, 540–41. See Beale, *Revelation*, 1005; Smalley, *Revelation*, 507–8; Storms, *Kingdom Come*, 451–74.

I Am Coming

The second coming is a major theme of John's message. Jesus' return is imminent. There-fore, believers are challenged to be ready, to witness, and to lead holy lives. Unbelievers are warned to repent now. The favored NT word to refer to the second coming is *parousia* ("appearance"). Seventeen of its twenty-four occurrences refer to Christ's return. But *parousia* is not found in Revelation. Instead, John prefers *erchomai* ("I am coming"). This verb occurs thirty-six times, and twenty-one of those refer to the second coming. In ad-dition, the compound words *eiserchomai* (3:20; 11:11; 15:8; 21:27; 22:14), *exerchomai* (3:12; 6:2, 4; 9:3; 14:15, 17, 18, 20; 15:6; 16:17; 18:4; 19:5, 21; 20:8), and the similar word *ekporeuomai* (1:16; 4:5; 9:17, 18; 11:5; 16:14; 19:15; 22:1) are found. Noticeably, these words often appear at the end of individual visions.

Six of the seven messages to the churches contain references to his coming. In three instances Jesus promises to come and deliver his faithful from persecution, and in three he threatens to come and judge the unfaithful. Smyrna does not receive a message of coming. All six references reflect an imminent return either for deliverance or for judg-ment.[145] Thus, when Christ returns it will be to vindicate and reward the righteous and to judge the unrighteous.

For the remainder of Revelation, several observations can be made. Four instances of "coming" are connected to the significant title "the one who is and who was and is to/ has come" (1:4, 8; 4:8; 11:17–18). Several occurrences to "coming" emphasize the divine judgment for unbelievers (1:7; 6:17; 14:7; 18:10) and for warning believers (2:5, 16; 3:11; 16:15). Other references include the harvest of the earth (14:14–20) and the wedding supper of the Lamb (19:7). There are seven references found in chapter 22, a final chal-lenge for believers to persevere.

Several occurrences emphasize the imminence of his coming. The simile "I come like a thief" is common (Matt 24:43; Luke 12:39; 1 Thess 5:2–4; 2 Pet 3:10), and ap-pears twice in Revelation to sustain the idea of surprise and suddenness of his return (3:3; 16:15).[146] Several times imminence is heightened by the phrase "I am coming soon." "Soon" is translated from two Greek words. First, *tachos* is found twice and used in the phrase "what must soon take place" (1:1; 22:6). Second, *tachys* is found six times, five of which are used in the phrase "I am coming soon" (2:16; 3:11; 22:7, 12, 20).[147] The

---

145. For Robert Thomas ("The 'Comings' of Christ in Revelation 2–3," 153–81), the only way this can happen is for the deliverance—the rapture of the church—and the final (seven) years of judgment—to occur simultaneously. For non–dispensationalists, it simply reflects the contrast of the second com-ing—either reward or condemnation. Several interpreters do not view the second coming in Rev 2–3. Instead, a more historical visitation of Christ to those specific churches is in mind (so Beale, *Revelation*, 275; Beasley-Murray, *Revelation* 97; Caird, *Revelation*, 48–49; Alan Johnson, "Revelation," 13:628; Mor-ris, *Revelation*, 76; Mounce, *Revelation*, 95; Murphy, *Fallen Is Babylon*, 344; Smalley, *Revelation*, 83, 411). Osborne (*Revelation*, 146) states it best. These "comings" refer "both to a present judgment upon the church and at the final judgment at the 'parousia.'"

146. Several versions note the interruption at 16:15 by inserting parentheses around the verse (CEB, ESV, NABR, NASB, NET, NRSV).

147. The sixth use also corresponds to the idea of imminence: "the third woe is coming soon" (11:14). The third woe is the seventh trumpet, which ushers in the end. Almost all English versions translate both words "soon." There are exceptions. NASB translates *tachos* as "soon" and *tachys* as "quickly." NKJV

repetition of the phrase at the end of Revelation increases the urgency associated with the imminent return of Christ.[148]

Finally, several of John's visions portray this futuristic event ("is coming,"; "will come") as already happened—"has come" (6:17; 11:18; 14:7, 15; 18:10; 19:7). This helps in identifying John's structuring for his visions since these past tense usages are found near the end of individual visions, namely the sixth seal, the seventh trumpet, the third interlude, and the fall of Babylon.[149]

Jesus is coming soon. This produces a challenge and a warning. Believers must be ever ready, living holy lives and witnessing the gospel. Faltering Christians and non–Christians must repent now. For the faithful, however, it also becomes a promise of hope and encouragement. Jesus concludes his prophecy with "Yes, I am coming soon," which John and all believers should answer with, "Amen. Come, Lord Jesus" (22:20).

No More

*John uses negative language (*via negativa*) to describe what the new heaven and new earth will be like.* Apophatic (or negative) theology is the attempt to describe God by what cannot be said of him. God is unknowable and human language is inadequate to describe him. Thus, listing what he is not is one way to understand God. John enters into this type of thinking with his many references to "no more."[150] What is eternity for believers like? The end of the first interlude attempts to explain it: "Never again will they hunger; never again will they thirst. The sun will not beat down on them, nor any scorching heat" (7:16). This introduction of negative language gives way to fuller expressions at the conclusion of Revelation.

Negative language permeates the description of the two cities. Resseguie explains that Babylon is deprived of all good and greatness. Terms such as "no one," "never," "lost,"

---

translates the words as "shortly" and "quickly." HCSB translates both words as "quickly."

148. Again, not everyone understands the imminent second coming here. For example, Beale (*Revelation*, 1127) understands this as inaugurating a series of comings in blessing and judgment, but most commentators disagree. For preterists, Jesus' promise of "I am coming soon" is rooted in the first-century fall of Jerusalem (Chilton, *Days of Vengeance*, 129–30; 575, 577; Clark, *Message from Patmos*, 143–46; Gentry, *Before Jerusalem Fell*, 142–45). Futurists answer the problem of imminence by understanding the word "soon" to mean "suddenly" or "quickly." Furthermore, dispensationalists generally interpret most if not all of the examples of "I am coming" to refer to the rapture (Hindson, *Revelation*, 47; LaHaye, *Revelation Unveiled*, 371; Patterson, *Revelation*, 133, 381; Robert Thomas, *Revelation*, 1:290–91; Walvoord, *Revelation*, 87, 333–37). See the entry "What Must Soon Take Place."

149. Caution should be exercised on what weight to give to this mixing of verb tenses in Revelation. Beale (*Revelation*, 102) writes that John mixes "his verb tenses and moods for no explicit reason (e.g., 21:24–27) . . ." Nevertheless, Bauckham (*Climax of Prophecy*, 286) relates that the switch from future tense ("will come") to past tense ("has come") connected to the significant phrase "the one who is, who was, and who will/has come" occurs at "points in the vision which anticipate the end, when God will have 'come' in his eschatological kingdom."

150. *Via negativa* is an apocalyptic characteristic. Aune (*Revelation*, 2:1183) notes that *4 Ezra* 7:38–42 lists twenty-seven things that will disappear at the final judgment: sun, moon, stars, cloud, thunder, lightning, wind, water, air, darkness, evening, morning, summer, spring, heat, winter, frost, cold, hail, rain, dew, noon, night, dawn, shining, brightness, and light.

"laid waste," and "no more" (six times) describe the great city's downfall (18:11–23). New Jerusalem, on the other hand, is "deprived" of all evil. Terms such as "no more" (*ou mē eti*), "never" (*ou mē*), "not" (*ouk*), and "nothing" (*ou mē pan*) accentuate this. John's use of "no more" intentionally echoes the sixfold refrain of the dirge over Babylon.[151] In chapters 21–22, John lists several items that will be "no more" when the new heaven and new earth arrives at the eschaton. There will be no more sea (21:1), death, mourning, crying, pain, (21:4), temple (21:22), sun, moon (21:23), closed gates (21:25), impure, shameful or deceitful person (21: 27), curse (22:3), and night (22:5).[152]

John produces two vice lists of those who are excluded from entering the new Jerusalem. "No more" applies to them (21:8; 22:15). Keener traces these uninvited throughout Revelation. He notes the "cowardly" (11:18; 14:7; 15:4; 19:5); "unbelieving" (2:13, 19; 13:10; 14:12); "vile" (17:4; 21:27); "murderers" (9:21; 22:15); "sexually and spiritually immoral" (2:14, 20; 9:21; 17:1–5, 15–16; 18:3, 9; 19:2); "idolaters" (2:14, 20; 13:15); and "liars" (2:14, 20; 3:9; 14:5).[153] The number of those excluded equals seven to stress totality and completeness.

Patient Endurance

Enduring resistance, active perseverance, and constant persistence is highlighted in Revelation as the expected character of the faithful Christian toward the powers of evil, especially in light of the near end. The perseverance of the saints is a chief characteristic of apocalyptic literature. God's people are exhorted to remain faithful no matter what befalls them. Osborne affirms, "Every passage dealing with the return of Christ ends with a call to conduct one's life with both vigilance and diligence."[154] Thus, perseverance is a key ethical term in Revelation.

"Patient endurance" translates the word *hupomonē*, found seven times, underlining numerical symbolism on John's part (1:9; 2:2, 3, 19; 3:10; 13:10; 14:12). Most Bible translations use a variety of words and expressions including "patience," "endurance," "patient endurance," "steadfast endurance," "perseverance," "patience to continue," "strength to endure," "endure patiently," and "never give up." Only a few versions, however, retain consistency with all seven uses, thereby aiding the intratextual connection. These include CEB and GW ("endurance") and NASB and NJB ("perseverance.")

The first occurrence is in the prologue. John essentially summarizes the Christian experience. He is a brother and companion in the suffering and kingdom and patient

---

151. Resseguie, *Revelation Unsealed*, 74–76.

152. "No more curse" is the promise of the eternal removal of sin and permanent peace and security. Aune (*Revelation*, 3:1179) suggests it alludes to the curses (*cherem*) hurled upon evil nations or apostate Israel (Isa 34:1–2). The context, however, alludes farther back to the garden of Eden and the curses of sin, disease, and death (Gen 3:14–19). Minear ("Far as the Curse Is Found," 71–77) also connects 12:15–16 to the curses of Eden. Another key passage is "People will live there, and never again will there be a curse of complete destruction. So Jerusalem will dwell in security" (Zech 14:11 CSB). Zechariah's promise is fulfilled in the new Jerusalem.

153. Keener, *Revelation*, 489–91.

154. Osborne, *Revelation*, 42.

endurance with the churches (1:9). The next four references are in the letters to the churches where patient endurance is so critical. The risen Christ knows the perseverance of the Ephesians, who have endured hardships in the name of Christ (2:2–3). Likewise, the faithful of Thyatira are praised by Christ for their deeds, love and faith, and service and perseverance (2:19). The victorious at Philadelphia kept Christ's command to endure patiently (3:10).

The final two mentions are in the third interlude. The pressure to conform to the beast means the faithful must persevere. "'If anyone is to go into captivity, into captivity they will go. If anyone is to be killed with the sword, with the sword they will be killed.' This calls for patient endurance and faithfulness on the part of God's people" (13:10). The end is eternal judgment for those who follow the beast. Thus, "this calls for patient endurance on the part of the people of God who keep his commands and remain faithful to Jesus" (14:12). These last two references allude to Jer 15:2. The point is not to pick up arms and fight against the beast with weaponry. Rather it is a powerful perseverance and endurance in the face of physical abuse and threats.[155] Christopher Rowland concludes, "In 13:10 and 14:12 we see that this characteristic is defined by resisting capitulation to the beast and thereby continuing the witness of Jesus."[156]

Patient endurance flies in the face of many modern westerners who strive to fight for their rights and privileges. But *hupomonē* is not passive capitulation according to Scripture. Some exegetes recognize that *hupomonē* should be understood as "consistent resistance" to the powers of evil that seek to undermine God's rule.[157] Jeffrey Meyers suggests a translation of "enduring resistance." He states, "This does not mean a heroic violent resistance, but a steadfast and enduring nonviolent resistance through noncooperation and witness to the supremacy of the power of the Lamb over the power of the Empire."[158] Walter Wink addresses the word this way. "It is usually somewhat limply rendered 'patient endurance,' but it is in fact closer to 'absolute intransigence,' 'unbending determination,' 'an iron will,' 'the capacity to endure persecution, torture, and death without yielding one's faith.' It is one of the fundamental attributes of nonviolent resistance."[159] This more active sense, therefore, is better than any passive type of understanding.

Prepare

This word emphasizes divine sovereignty and guidance in the unfolding events of history. The fact that John mentions "prepared" or "make ready" (*hetoimazō*) seven times should

---

155. Streett (*Here Comes the Judge*, 146) asserts that endurance is the believer's response to whatever threat there is in a violent world. It "is not an active or violent response." Streett then challenges the novels of popular dispensationalists whose protagonists take up arms and fight the beast with modern weapons of warfare.

156. Rowland, "Revelation," 12:585.

157. Barr, *Tales*, 38–39; Schüssler Fiorenza, *Revelation*, 51; Zerbe, "Revelation's Expose of Two Cities," 55–56.

158. Jeffrey Meyers, "*Hupomonē* as Enduring Resistance," 43.

159. Wink, *Naming the Powers*, 127–28. This is also quoted by Reddish, *Revelation*, 256. Duvall (*Heart of Revelation*, 183–85) offers sound applications on perseverance.

alert readers to numerical symbolism. In all seven instances, the word indicates that God's will is perfectly planned out. If John intended to use the word exactly seven times, then extra stress is added to this concept of divine action at work. "Prepare" is found in key verses in the NT (Matt 25:34; John 14:2–3), leading Osborne to call the word "a major term for God's predestined will."[160] In Revelation, only CSB consistently renders the word the same way all seven times ("prepared").[161] The seven passages include the seven angels preparing to blow their trumpets (8:6); demonic locusts who look like horses prepared for battle (9:7); the four angels prepared for this exact moment in history (9:15); the woman who is nourished and protected by divine preparation (12:6); the Euphrates River drying up to prepare the way for end-time battle (16:12); the preparation of the bride of the Lamb by means of faithfulness and perseverance (19:7); and finally, the new Jerusalem, prepared like a bride adorned for her husband (21:2). In particular, the last two offer striking examples of divine sovereignty at work. Beale summarizes this word well. Throughout Revelation *hetoimazō* "is used of events that occur *ultimately* as a result of God's decrees and not human actions . . ."[162]

Second Death

This refers to the final, total, and eternal judgment of unbelievers who are cast into the lake of fire. "The second death" (*ho deuteros thanatos*) could also be situated under the entry of bad places. It is mentioned only four times in the NT, all in Revelation (2:11; 20:6, 14; 21:8). The phrase is not found in the OT either but its origin may come from there (Gen 19:24; Ezek 38:22). Certainly, later Judaism teaches the idea in Targums on Deut 33:6; Jer 51:39; and Isa 52:14. In fact, Tg. Isa. 65:5–6 explicitly identifies the second death with the constant fire of Gehenna.[163]

All four occurrences are closely linked. The first mention is found in the promise to the victorious of Smyrna. They are promised the crown of life (eternal life) and "will not be hurt at all by the second death" (2:11). Although they are presently being threatened with physical death, their eternal victory through Christ is assured. Next, John mentions the second death twice in chapter 20. Concerning the millennium, John states, "(The rest of the dead did not come to life until the thousand years were ended.) This is the first resurrection. Blessed and holy are those who share in the first resurrection. The second death has no power over them, but they will be priests of God and of Christ and will reign with him for a thousand years" (20:5–6). Thus, it is the rest of the dead (unbelievers) who face the second death. The third mention occurs at the great white throne judgment. John says, "Then death and Hades were thrown into the lake of fire. The lake of fire is the second death. Anyone whose name was not found written in the book of life was thrown into the lake of fire" (20:14–15). This verse specifically identifies the second death as the lake

160. Osborne, *Revelation*, 380.

161. ESV, HCSB, and NKJV come close with six out of seven.

162. Beale, *Revelation*, 940.

163. See Hays, Duvall, and Pate, *Dictionary of Prophecy*, 369–72; 412–13; Watson, "Death, Second," 111–12.

of fire, and helps to clarify 20:6. The second death is defined as the lake of fire. Finally, the second death is referred to in the new Jerusalem vision (21:9–22:9). "But the cowardly, the unbelieving, the vile, the murderers, the sexually immoral, those who practice magic arts, the idolaters and all liars—they will be consigned to the fiery lake of burning sulfur. This is the second death" (21:8). The second death is again affirmed to be the fiery lake of burning sulfur.

Some Bible students understand these terms to refer to annihilation, not eternal torment. John, however, consistently uses words such as "everlasting" and "forever" to describe what is in store for believers in the heavenly city. Consistency dictates that the terms mean the same for unbelievers.[164] Therefore, the second death is synonymous with eternal, spiritual death and the lake of fire. Those who suffer the second death will not enter into the eternal new Jerusalem. It is God's final condemnation upon sin carried out at the great white throne judgment.

164. See the entry "For Ever and Ever."

Conclusion

THIS STUDY ATTEMPTED SEVERAL things that previous studies on Revelation have not done or have underemphasized. First, the symbols of Revelation were systematically categorized. By necessity there was overlapping of categories and some repetition between entries. In addition, many of John's images were used contrastingly, making it difficult to categorize them. Overall, however, the creation of categories assists readers to visualize more clearly the stockpile of imagery from which John drew. John's choice of symbols was not original, but he adapted and enlarged the common imagery available to challenge his audience afresh. As a NT prophet, he sustained the OT prophetic role of being a forth-teller more than a foreteller.

Second, in order to interpret John's images a seven-step approach was adopted. The steps took into account historical, cultural, intertextual, extratextual, and particularly intratextual allusions and connections. These connections help modern readers to see what John's original audience had at their disposal for interpreting the images and structuring the visions. Numerous intratextual connections were uncovered for the first time. The first beatitude promises blessings to the "one who reads aloud the words of this prophecy, and blessed are those who hear it and take to heart what is written in it, because the time is near" (1:3). Those original readers and hearers were well-equipped to discover John's intratextual connections. Modern readers are two thousand years removed from the circumstances. They are often dependent on translations of the original Greek. Following the seven-step approach aids modern readers to interpret the images with more precision. It also tempers extreme views that disregard the steps.

Third, the study followed an original twelve-vision outline. Scholarly support was found for the parameters of each individual vision, but the result of twelve visions was unique. The outline was anchored on the intratextual cross-references supplied by John coupled with a progressive recapitulation methodology. The individual visions, especially their conclusions, give readers different points of view on the same topics. Subsequent visions enlarge and elaborate previous visions. A result of this approach affirmed that John intended to portray one end-time battle, one second coming, and one final judgment.

Fourth, more representative resources were accessed and categorized than many previous studies. On most of the nearly three hundred entries readers can find where their favorite interpreters land. This resulted in more detailed footnotes, but this may save time and money for many who research, teach, and preach on Revelation. Moreover, multiple English Bible translations were used. Bible versions are often the first and final decision maker that modern readers have at their disposal. The twenty versions consulted revealed numerous interpretive choices on several entries. There were also intratextual inconsistencies noted. One outcome of this study is for future Bible editions to consider revising these inconsistencies.

This study was not an exhaustive accounting of all of John's images. The amount, however, should guide readers, teachers, and preachers of Revelation. Hopefully, it will serve as a practical resource for many. The church deserves to hear God's word from Revelation.

Bibliography

Aasgaard, Reidar. "Brother, Brotherhood." In *NIDB* 1:505–7.

Adams, Jay Edward. *The Time Is at Hand*. Phillipsburg, NJ: P&R, 1966.

Alden, Robert L. "Cloud." In *ZEB* 1:936.

———. "Red." In *ZEB* 5:58.

———. "Sodom." In *ZEB* 5:550–52.

Allison, Dale C. Jr. "Day of the Lord." In *NIDB* 2:46–47.

Appler, Deborah A. "Hand." In *NIDB* 2:731.

———. "Jezebel." In *NIDB* 3:313–14.

Archer, Melissa L. *"I Was in the Spirit on the Lord's Day": A Pentecostal Engagement with Worship in the Apocalypse*. Cleveland, TN: CPT, 2015.

Aune, David E. "The Apocalypse of John and Palestinian Jewish Apocalyptic." *Neot* 40 (2006) 1–33.

———. *Apocalypticism, Prophecy, and Magic in Early Christianity: Collected Essays*. Tübingen: Mohr Siebeck, 2006.

———. "Demonology." In *ISBE* 1:919–23.

———. "The Form and Function of the Proclamations to the Seven Churches (Revelation 2–3)." *NTS* 36 (1990) 182–204.

———. *Prophecy in Early Christianity and the Ancient Mediterranean World*. Grand Rapids: Eerdmans, 1983.

———. *Revelation*. 3 vols. WBC. Dallas: Word, 1997–1998.

———. "Son of Man." In *ISBE* 4:574–81.

Bacchiocchi, Samuele. *From Sabbath to Sunday: A Historical Investigation of the Rise of Sunday Observance in Early Christianity*. Berrien Springs, MI: Biblical Perspectives, 2000.

Bailleul-Lesuer, Rozenn. "Birds." In *DDL* 176–89.

Baines, Matthew Charles. "The Identity and Fate of the Kings of the Earth in the Book of Revelation." *RTR* 75 (2016) 73–88.

Balz, Horst. "οἰκουμένη." In *EDNT* 2:504.

Bandstra, A. J. "'A Kingship and Priests': Inaugurated Eschatology in the Apocalypse." *CTJ* 27 (1992) 10–25.

Bandstra, Barry L. "Wine." In *ISBE* 4:1068–72.

Bandy, Alan S. "The Hermeneutics of Symbolism: How to Interpret the Symbols of John's Apocalypse." *SBJT* 14 (2010) 46–58.

———. "The Layers of the Apocalypse: An Integrative Approach to Revelation's Macrostructure." *JSNT* 31 (2009) 469–99.

———. "Patterns of Prophetic Lawsuits in the Oracles to the Seven Churches in the Book of Revelation." *Neot* 45 (2011) 178–205.

———. *The Prophetic Lawsuit in the Book of Revelation*. Sheffield: Sheffield Academic, 2010.

Bandy, Alan S., and Benjamin L. Merkle. *Understanding Prophecy: A Biblical-Theological Approach*. Grand Rapids: Kregel, 2015.

Banks, Robert. "'Walking' as a Metaphor of the Christian Life: The Origins of a Significant Pauline Usage." In *Perspectives on Language and Text: Essays in Honor of Francis I. Andersen's Sixtieth Birthday*, edited by Edgar W. Conrad and Edward G. Newing, 303–13. Winona Lake, IN: Eisenbrauns, 1987.

Barabas, Steven. "Almighty." In *ZEB* 1:125.

———. "Gog." In *ZEB* 2:806.

———. "Hour." In *ZEB* 3:233–34.

Barker, Kenneth L. "Abaddon." In *ZEB* 1:7.

———. "Green." In *ZEB* 2:893.

Barker, Margaret. *The Revelation of Jesus Christ*. London: T. & T. Clark, 2000.

———. "The Servant in the Book of Revelation." *HeyJ* 36 (1995) 493–511.

Barr, David L. *Tales of the End: A Narrative Commentary on the Book of Revelation*. Santa Rosa, CA: Polebridge, 1998.

Bartchy, S. S. "Servant." In *ISBE* 4:420–21.

Batey, Richard A. *New Testament Nuptial Imagery*. Leiden: Brill, 1971.

Bauckham, Richard J. *The Climax of Prophecy: Studies on the Book of Revelation*. Edinburgh: T. & T. Clark, 1993.

———. "Creation's Praise of God in the Book of Revelation." *BTB* 38 (2008) 55–63.

———. "The List of Tribes in Revelation 7 Again." *JSNT* 42 (1991) 99–115.

———. "The Lord's Day." In *From Sabbath to Lord's Day: A Biblical, Historical, and Theological Investigation*, edited by D. A. Carson, 221–50. Eugene, OR: Wipf & Stock, 1999.

———. "The Role of the Spirit in the Apocalypse." *EvQ* 52 (1980) 66–83.

———. *The Theology of the Book of Revelation*. Cambridge: Cambridge University Press, 1993.

Bauckham, Richard J., James R. Davila, and Alexander Panayotov, edtiors. *Old Testament Pseudepigrapha: More Noncanonical Scriptures*. Grand Rapids: Eerdmans, 2013.

Beagley, Alan James. *The 'Sitz im Leben' of the Apocalypse with Particular Reference to the Role of the Church's Enemies*. New York: de Gruyter, 1987.

Beale, Gregory K. *The Book of Revelation: A Commentary on the Greek Text*. NIGTC. Grand Rapids: Eerdmans, 1999.

———. *Handbook on the New Testament Use of the Old Testament: Exegesis and Interpretation*. Grand Rapids: Baker, 2012.

———. "The Hearing Formula and the Visions of John in Revelation." In *A Vision of the Church: Studies in Early Christian Ecclesiology in Honour of J. P. M. Sweet*, edited by Markus Bockmuehl and Michael B. Thompson, 167–80. Edinburgh: T. & T. Clark, 1997.

———. *A New Testament Biblical Theology: The Unfolding of the Old Testament in the New*. Grand Rapids: Baker, 2011.

———. "The Origin of the Title 'King of Kings and Lord of Lords' in Rev. 17:14." *NTS* 31(1985) 618–20.

———. *The Temple and the Church's Mission: A Biblical Theology of the Dwelling Place of God*. Downers Grove, iL: InterVarsity, 2004.

———. *We Become What We Worship: A Biblical Theology of Idolatry*. Downers Grove, IL: InterVarsity, 2008.

Beale, Gregory K., and Sean M. McDonough. "Revelation." In *A Commentary on the New Testament Use of the Old Testament*, edited by G. K. Beale and D. A. Carson, 1081–161. Grand Rapids: Baker, 2007.

Bean, Adam L., and R. K. Harrison. "Seals." In *DDL* 1505–14.

Beasley-Murray, George R. *The Book of Revelation*. NCB. Greenwood, SC: Attic, 1974.

Beck, James A., editor. *Zondervan Dictionary of Biblical Imagery*. Grand Rapids: Zondervan, 2011.

Beckwith, Isbon T. *The Apocalypse of John*. New York: Macmillan, 1919.

Besserman, Lawrence. "Ark of the Covenant." In *DBTEL* 54–55.

Biguzzi, Giancarlo. "Is the Babylon of Revelation Rome or Jerusalem?" *Bib* 87 (2006) 371–86.

Birch, Bruce C. "Number." In *ISBE* 3:558.

———. "Scorpion." In *ISBE* 4:357–58.

Blaiklock, David A. "Nakedness." In *ZEB* 4:396.

Blaising, Craig A., and Darrell L. Bock. *Progressive Dispensationalism*. Colorado Springs, CO: Victor, 1993.

Blickenstaff, Marianne. "Synagogue in the New Testament." In *NIDB* 5:427.

Blomberg, Craig L. *Matthew*. NAC. Nashville: Broadman & Holman, 1992.

Blomberg, Craig L., and Sung Wook Chung, editors. *A Case for Historic Premillennialism: An Alternative to "Left Behind" Eschatology*. Grand Rapids: Baker, 2009.

Blount, Brian K. "Reading Revelation Today: Witness as Active Resistance." *Int* 54 (2000) 398–412.

———. *Revelation: A Commentary*. NTL. Louisville: Westminster John Knox, 2009.

Blount, Brian, and Marianne Blickenstaff. "Whore of Babylon." In *NIDB* 5:845–46.

Bock, Darrell L. *Luke*. BECNT. 2 vols. Grand Rapids: Baker, 1994, 1996.

Bøe, Sverre. *Gog and Magog: Ezekiel 38–39 as Pre-Text to Revelation 19,17–21 and 20,7–10*. Tübingen: Mohr Siebeck, 2001.

Bond, Ronald B. "Scales." In *DBTEL* 683–84.

———. "Whore of Babylon." In *DBTEL* 826–28.

Boone, N. S. "The Five Armageddons of Revelation." *ResQ* 55 (2013) 107–15.

Boring, M. Eugene. "Numbers, Numbering." In *NIDB* 4:294–99.

———. "Priests in the NT." In *NIDB* 4:613–14.

———. *Revelation*. IBC. Louisville: Westminster John Knox, 1989.

———. "Seven, Seventh, Seventy." In *NIDB* 5:197–99.

Borowski, Oded. "Lion." In *NIDB* 3:669–70.

Bowes, Donald R. "Brimstone." In *ZEB* 1:678.

———. "Bronze." In *ZEB* 1:679–80.

Bowker, John. "The Son of Man." *JTS* 28 (1977) 19–48.

Boxall, Ian. *The Revelation of St. John*. BNTC. Peabody, MA: Hendrickson, 2006.

———. "'Who Rides the White Horse?' Truth and Deception in the Book of Revelation." *ScrB* 41 (2011) 76–88.

Boyd, Mary Petrina. "Green." In *NIDB* 2:698.

———. "Scarlet." In *NIDB* 5:123–24.

———. "White." In *NIDB* 5:844–45.

Brady, David. *The Contribution of British Writers between 1560 and 1830 to the Interpretation of Revelation 13:16–18*. Tübingen: Mohr Siebeck, 1983.

Branch, Robin G. "Incense." In *DDL* 849–64.

Bratt, John H. "Sackcloth." In *ZEB* 5:229–30.

Braun, Joachim. "Musical Instruments." In *NIDB* 4:175–83.

Bredin, Mark R. "God the Carer: Revelation and the Environment." *BTB* 38 (2008) 76–86.

———. "Hate Never Dispelled Hate: No Place for the *Pharmakos*." *BTB* 34 (2004) 105–13.

———. "The Synagogue of Satan Accusation in Revelation 2:9." *BTB* 28 (1999) 160–64.

Briggs, Robert. *Jewish Temple Imagery in the Book of Revelation*. StBibLit 10. New York: P. Lang, 1999.

Brighton, Louis A. *Revelation*. ConcC. St. Louis: Concordia, 1999.

Brown, Ian R. "The Two Witnesses of Revelation 11:1–13: Arguments, Issues of Interpretation, and a Way Forward." PhD diss., Andrews University, 2016.

Brown, Schuyler. "The Hour of Trial (Rev. 3, 10)." *JBL* 85 (1966) 308–14.

Bruce, F. F. "The Spirit in the Apocalypse." In *Christ and Spirit in the New Testament: In Honour of C. F. D. Moule*, edited by Barnabas Lindars and Stephen Smalley, 333–44. Cambridge: Cambridge University Press, 1973.

Brueggemann, Walter. *The Land: Place as Gift, Promise, and Challenge in Biblical* Faith. 2nd ed. Minneapolis: Fortress, 2002.

Buchanan, George Wesley. *The Book of Revelation: Its Introduction and Prophecy*. Eugene, OR: Wipf & Stock, 2005.

Bullard, Reuben G. "Stones, Precious." In *ISBE* 4:623–30.

Burge, Gary M. *Jesus and the Land: The New Testament Challenge to "Holy" Land Theology*. Grand Rapids: Baker, 2010.

———. "Land." In *NIDB* 3:570–75.

Caird, G. B. *The Revelation of St. John the Divine*. HNTC. 2nd ed. New York: Harper & Row, 1984.

Campbell, Gordon. "Antithetical Feminine-Urban Imagery and a Tale of Two Women-Cities in the Book of Revelation." *TynB* 55 (2004) 81–108.

Cansdale, George S. "Scorpion." In *ZEB* 5:350–51.

———. "Serpent." In *ZEB* 5:427–29.

Carey, Greg. "Dragon." In *NIDB* 2:161–62.

———. *Ultimate Things: An Introduction to Jewish and Christian Apocalyptic Literature*. St. Louis: Chalice, 2005.

Cargal, Timothy B. "Nicolaitans." In *NIDB* 4:270–71.

Carr, G. Lloyd. "Manna." In *ISBE* 3:239–40.

Carrell, Peter R. *Jesus and the Angels: Angelology and the Christology of the Apocalypse of John*. Cambridge: Cambridge University Press, 1997.

Carter, Charles W. "Son of Man." In *ZEB* 5:579–81.

Carter, Warren. "Beatitudes." In *NIDB* 1:415–16.

Cartledge, Tony W. "Hair, Hairs." In *NIDB* 2:719.

Cate, Jeffrey J. "How Green Was John's World? Ecology and Revelation." In *Essays on Revelation: Appropriating Yesterday's Apocalypse in Today's World*, edited by Gerald L. Stevens, 145–55. Eugene, OR: Pickwick, 2010.

———. "The Text of Revelation: Why neither Armageddon nor 666 May Be Exactly What You Think." In *Essays on Revelation: Appropriating Yesterday's Apocalypse in Today's World*, edited by Gerald L. Stevens, 116–29. Eugene, OR: Pickwick, 2010.

Chamberlain, Gary. "Smoke; Smoking." In *ISBE* 4:554.

Chambers, Adam C. "Viticulture." In *DDL* 1681–90.

Charles, R. H. *The Revelation of St. John*. 2 vols. ICC. Edinburgh: T. & T. Clark, 1920.

Charlesworth, James H., editor. *Old Testament Pseudepigrapha: Apocalyptic Literature and Testaments*. 2 vols. Peabody, MA: Hendrickson, 1983, 1985.

———. "Paradise." In *ABD* 5:154–55.

Cheung, Alex T. M. "The Priest as Redeemed Man: A Biblical-Theological Study of the Priesthood." *JETS* 29 (1986) 265–75.

Chilton, David. *The Days of Vengeance: An Exposition of Revelation*. Fort Worth: Dominion, 1987.

———. *The Great Tribulation*. Fort Worth: Dominion, 1987.

Claassens, L. Juliana. "Wine." In *NIDB* 5:860–61.

Clark, David S. *The Message from Patmos: A Postmillennial Commentary on the Book of Revelation*. Grand Rapids: Baker, 1989.

Collins, John J. *The Apocalyptic Imagination: An Introduction to Jewish Apocalyptic Literature*. 3rd ed. Grand Rapids: Eerdmans, 2016.

Collins, Raymond F. "Beatitudes." In *ABD* 1:629.

Comfort, Philip W. *New Testament Text and Translation Commentary*. Carol Stream, IL: Tyndale, 2008.

Conrad, Edgar W. "Satan." In *NIDB* 5:112–16.

Coogan, Michael D. "Sea." In *NIDB* 5:139–40.

Couch, Mal. "Millennium, New Testament Descriptions of." In *DPT* 266–67.

Couch, Mal, and Joseph Chambers. "Babylon." In *DPT* 61–62.

Cousland, J. R. C. "Michael." In *NIDB* 4:77–78.

Crockett, William, editor. *Four Views on Hell*. Grand Rapids: Zondervan, 1996.

Cruz, Victor P. "The Beatitudes of the Apocalypse: Eschatology and Ethics." in *Perspectives on Christology: Essays in Honor of Paul K. Jewett*, edited by Marguerite Shuster and Richard A. Muller, 269–83. Grand Rapids: Zondervan, 1991.

Culver, R. D. "Jezebel." In *ZEB* 3:670–71.

Culy, Martin M. *The Book of Revelation: The Rest of the Story*. Eugene, OR: Pickwick, 2017.

Curtis, Edward C. "Idol, Idolatry." In *ABD* 3:380–81.

Dalrymple, Rob. *Revelation and the Two Witnesses: The Implications for Understanding John's Depiction of the People of God and Its Hortatory Intent*. Eugene, OR: Wipf & Stock, 2011.

Danker, Frederick W. "Purple." In *ABD* 5:557–60.

Davidson, Maxwell J. "Angel." In *NIDB* 1:148–55.

Davies, G. I. "Wilderness Wanderings." In *ABD* 6:912–14.

Davis, John J. *Biblical Numerology: A Basic Study of the Use of Numbers in the Bible*. Grand Rapids: Baker, 1968.

Day, Alfred E., and R. K. Harrison. "Dog." In *ISBE* 1:980–81.

Day, Alfred E., and Gregory D. Jordan. "Serpent." In *ISBE* 4:417–18.

Day, John. "Dragon and the Sea, God's Conflict with." In *ABD* 2:228–31.

———. "The Origin of Armageddon: Revelation 16:16 as an Interpretation of Zechariah 12:11." In *Crossing the Boundaries: Essays in Biblical Interpretation in Honour of Michael D. Goulder*, edited by Stanley E. Porter, Paul Joyce, and David E. Orton, 315–26. Leiden: Brill, 1994.

Decker, Rodney. "People of God." In *DPT* 297-300.

Declaisse-Walford, Nancy. "Tree of Knowledge, Tree of Life." In *NIDB* 5:659–61.

DeFelice, John F. "Slavery." In *DDL* 1515–39.

———. "The Use of the Expression *ho Christos* in the Apocalypse of John." In *L'Apocalypse Johannique et l'Apocalyptique dans le Nouveau Testament*, edited by Jan Lambrecht, 267–81. Leuven: Leuven University Press, 1980.

DeSilva, David. "'The Image of the Beast' and the Christians in Asia Minor: Escalation of Sectarian Tension in Revelation 13." *TJ* 12 (1991) 185–208.

———. *Seeing Things John's Way: The Rhetoric of the Book of Revelation*. Louisville: Westminster John Knox, 2009.

Donato, Christopher John, editor. *Perspectives on the Sabbath: 4 Views*. Nashville: Broadman & Holman, 2011.

Downing, Jonathan. "The Women Clothed with the Sun: The Reception of Revelation 12 among Female British Prophets 1780-1814." In *The Book of Revelation: Currents in British Research on the Apocalypse*, edited by Garrick V. Allen, Ian Paul, and Simon P. Woodman, 65–80. Tübingen: Mohr Siebeck, 2015.

Draper, J. A. "The Heavenly Feast of Tabernacles: Revelation 7.1–17." *JSNT* 19 (1983) 133–47.

———. "The Twelve Apostles as Foundation Stones of the Heavenly Jerusalem and the Foundation of the Qumran Community." *Neot* 22 (1988) 41–63.

Drinkard, Joel F. Jr. "Seal, to." In *NIDB* 5:141.

———. "Throne." In *NIDB* 5:589–90.

Duff, Paul B. "'I Will Give to Each of You as Your Works Deserve': Witchcraft Accusations and the Fiery-Eyed Son of God in Rev. 2:18–23." *NTS* 43 (1997) 116–33.

———. "The Synagogue of Satan: Crisis Mongering and the Apocalypse of John." In *The Reality of the Apocalypse: Rhetoric and Politics in the Book of Revelation*, edited by David L. Barr, 147–68. Atlanta: Society of Biblical Literature, 2006.

———. *Who Rides the Beast? Prophetic Rivalry and the Rhetoric of Crisis in the Churches of the Apocalypse*. New York: Oxford University Press, 2001.

Duling, Dennis C. "Kingdom of God, Kingdom of Heaven." In *ABD* 4:49–69.

Dulk, Matthijs den. "The Promises to the Conquerors in the Book of Revelation." *Bib* 87 (2006) 516–22.

Dumbrell, William J. *The End of the Beginning: Revelation 21–22 and the Old Testament*. Eugene, OR: Wipf & Stock, 2001.

Dutcher-Walls, Patricia. *Jezebel: Portraits of a Queen*. Collegeville, MN: Glazier, 2004.

Duvall, J. Scott. *The Heart of Revelation*. Grand Rapids: Baker, 2016.

———. *Revelation*. TTCS. Grand Rapids: Baker, 2014.

Duvall, J. Scott, and J. Daniel Hays. *Grasping God's Word*. 3rd ed. Grand Rapids: Zondervan, 2012.

Dyer, Charles H. *The Rise of Babylon: Sign of the End Times*. Wheaton, IL: Tyndale, 1991.

Easley, Kendell. *Revelation*. HolNTC. Nashville: Broadman & Holman, 1998.

Edwards, David M., and Carl E. Armerding. "Drunkenness." In *ISBE* 1:994–95.

Edwards, Douglas R. "Dress and Ornamentation." In *ABD* 2:232–38.

Elgvin, Torleif. "Priests on Earth as in Heaven: Jewish Light on the Book of Revelation." In *Echoes from the Caves: Qumran and the New Testament*, edited by Florentino García Martínez, 257–78. STDJ 85. Leiden: Brill, 2009.

Emmerson, Richard K. "Gog and Magog." In *DBTEL* 311–12.

———. "Mark of the Beast." In *DBTEL* 481–82.

———. "Woman Clothed with the Sun." In *DBTEL* 846–47.

Essex, Keith H. "The Rapture and the Book of Revelation." *TMSJ* 13 (2002) 215–39.

Farmer, Ronald L. *Revelation*. CCT. St. Louis: Chalice, 2005.

Farrell, Robert, and Catherine Karkov. "Serpent." In *DBTEL* 693–95.

Farrer, Austin. *A Rebirth of Images: The Making of St. John's Apocalypse*. London: Dacre, 1949.

———. *The Revelation of St. John the Divine*. London: Oxford University Press, 1964.

Fee, Gordon D. *Revelation*. NCCS. Eugene, OR: Wipf & Stock, 2011.

Fee, Gordon D., and Douglas Stuart. *How to Read the Bible for All Its Worth*. 4th ed. Grand Rapids: Zondervan, 2014.

Feinberg, Charles L. "Bitter, Bitterness." In *ZEB* 1:644.

———. "Tabernacle." In *ZEB* 5:664–677.

Feinberg, Charles L., and Gordon D. Fee. "Priests and Levites." In *ZEB* 4:963–85.

Fekkes, Jan. "His Bride Has Prepared Herself: Revelation 19–21 and Isaian Nuptial Imagery." *JBL* 109 (1990) 269–87.

———. *Isaiah and Prophetic Traditions in the Book of Revelation*. LNTS 93. Sheffield: Sheffield Academic, 1994.

Feldmeier, Reinhard. "Almighty." In *DDD* 20–23.

Ferguson, Everett. "Angels of the Churches in Revelation 1–3: *Status Quaestionis* and Another Proposal." *BBR* 21 (2011) 371–86.

Filho, José Adriano. "The Apocalypse of John as an Account of a Visionary Experience: Notes on the Book's Structure." *JSNT* 25 (2002) 213–34.

Fine, Steven, and John David Brolley. "Synagogue." In *NIDB* 5:416–27.

Fitzpatrick, Paul E. "People of God." In *NIDB* 4:440–41.

Follis, Elaine R. "Sea." In *ABD* 5:1058–59.

Foos, Harold D. "Jerusalem in Biblical Prophecy." In *DPT* 207–10.

Ford, J. Massyngberde. *Revelation: A New Translation with Introduction and Commentary*. AB. Garden City, NY: Doubleday, 1975.

Foreman, Benjamin A. *Animal Metaphors and the People of Israel in the Book of Jeremiah*. Göttingen: Vandenhoeck & Ruprecht, 2011.

Fortune, A. W. "Babylon, NT." In *ISBE* 1:391.

Frankfurter, David. "Jews or Not? Reconstructing the 'Other' in Rev 2:9 and 3:9." *HTR* 94(2001) 403–25.

Friesen, Steven J. "Babylon, NT." In *NIDB* 1:379.

———. "The Beast from the Land: Revelation 13:11–18 and Social Setting." In *Reading the Book of Revelation: A Resource for Students*, edited by David L. Barr, 49–64. Atlanta: Society of Biblical Literature, 2003.

———. *Imperial Cults and the Apocalypse of John: Reading Revelation in the Ruins*. New York: Oxford University Press, 2001.

———. "Sarcasm in Revelation 2–3." In *The Reality of the Apocalypse: Rhetoric and Politics in the Book of Revelation*, edited by David L. Barr, 127–44. Atlanta: Society of Biblical Literature, 2003.

———. "Satan's Throne, Imperial Cults, and the Social Settings of Revelation." *JSNT* 27 (2005) 351–73.

Fruchtenbaum, Arnold G. "Day of the Lord." in *DPT* 87–88.

Fudge, Edward William, and Robert A. Peterson. *Two Views of Hell: A Biblical and Theological Dialogue*. Downers Grove, IL: InterVarsity, 2000.

Fuller, Daniel P. "Satan." In *ISBE* 4:340–44.

Fuller, Robert C. *Naming the Antichrist: The History of an American Obsession*. New York: Oxford University Press, 1996.

Funderburk, Gus D. "Amen." In *ZEB* 1:147–48.

———. "Angel." In *ZEB* 1:183–91.

Gallusz, Laszlo. "The Exodus Motif in Revelation 15–16: Its Background and Nature." *AUSS* 46 (2008) 21–43.

———. *The Throne Motif in the Book of Revelation.* LNTS 487. New York: T. & T. Clark, 2014.

Gasque, W. Ward. "Jew." In *ISBE* 2:1056.

Gay, George A. "Wash." In *ISBE* 4:1022.

Gentry, Kenneth L. Jr. *The Beast of Revelation.* Tyler, TX: Institute for Christian Economics, 1989.

———. *Before Jerusalem Fell: Dating the Book of Revelation.* Rev. ed. Powder Springs, GA: American Vision, 1998.

Giacumakis, George Jr. "Forehead." In *ZEB* 2:630–31.

Giblin, Charles H. *The Book of Revelation: The Open Book of Prophecy.* Collegeville, MN: Glazier, 1991.

———. "Recapitulation and the Literary Coherence of John's Apocalypse." *CBQ* 56 (1994) 81–95.

———. "Revelation 11:1–13—Its Form, Function, and Contextual Integration." *NTS* 30 (1984) 433–59.

———. "Structural and Thematic Correlations in the Theology of Revelation 16–22," *Bib* 55 (1974) 487–504.

Gieschen, Charles A. "The Identity of Michael in Revelation 12: Created Angel or the Son of God?" *CTQ* 74 (2010) 139–43.

Giesen, Heinz. "Heilszusage angesichts der Bedragnis: Zu den Makarismen in der Offenbarung des Johannes." *SNTSU* 6–7 (1981–1982) 191–223.

Gilchrest, Eric J. "The Topography of Utopia: Revelation 21–22 in Light of Ancient Jewish and Greco-Roman Utopianism." PhD diss., Baylor University, 2012.

Gill, David W. "City, Biblical Theology of." In *ISBE* 1:713–15.

Goranson, Stephen. "The Text of Revelation 22:14." *NTS* 43 (1997) 154–57.

Gordon, Victor R. "Paradise." In *ISBE* 3:660–61.

———. "Saints." In *ISBE* 4:282–83.

Gorman, Michael J. "Saint." In *NIDB* 5:41–43.

Goulder, M. D. "The Apocalypse as an Annual Cycle of Prophecies." *NTS* 27 (1981) 342–67.

Grant, Deena. "Wrath of God." In *NIDB* 5:932–37.

Green, Mark D. "Mount, Mountain." In *NIDB* 4:159–60.

Gregg, Steve, editor. *Revelation: Four Views, A Parallel Commentary.* Rev. ed. Nashville: T. Nelson, 2012.

Grenz, Stanley J. *The Millennial Maze: Sorting Out Evangelical Options.* Downers Grove, IL: InterVarsity, 1992.

Grether, Herbert G. "Abyss, the." In *ABD* 1:49.

Gromacki, Robert G. "Revelation, Twenty-Four Elders of." In *DPT* 377–78.

———. "Witnesses, 144,000." In *DPT* 425.

Grudem, Wayne A. "Prophecy, Prophets." In *NDBT* 701–10.

Gundry, Robert H. *The Church and the Tribulation.* Grand Rapids: Zondervan, 1973.

———. "The New Jerusalem: People as Place, Not Place for People." *NovT* 29 (1987) 254–64.

Guthrie, Donald. "Jesus Christ." In *ZEB* 3:567–661.

———. "The Lamb in the Structure of the Book of Revelation." *VE* 12 (1981) 64–71.

Guthrie, George H. *Hebrews.* NIVAC. Grand Rapids: Zondervan, 1998.

Haak, R. D. "Altar." In *ABD* 1:162–67.

Habel, Norman C. *The Land Is Mine: Six Biblical Land Ideologies*. Minneapolis: Fortress, 1995.

Hackett, Jo Ann. "Balaam." In *ABD* 1:569–72.

Hahn, Hans-Christoph. "Time." In *NIDNTT* 3:847.

Hailey, Homer. *Revelation: An Introduction and Commentary*. Grand Rapids: Baker, 1979.

Hall, Mark Seaborn. "The Hook Interlocking Structure of Revelation: The Most Important Verses in the Book and How They May Unify Its Structure." *NovT* 44 (2002) 278–96.

Hall, Robert G. "Living Creatures in the Midst of the Throne: Another Look at Revelation 4.6." *NTS* 36 (1990) 609–13.

Hamilton, F. E., and R. Laird Harris. "Saint." In *ZEB* 5:260–61.

Hamilton, Victor P. "Satan." In *ABD* 5:985–89.

Handy, Lowell K. "Serpent (Religious Symbol)." In *ABD* 5:1113–16.

Hannah, Darrell D. *Michael and Christ: Michael Traditions and Angel Christology in Early Christianity*. Tübingen: Mohr Siebeck, 1999.

Hanson, K. C. "Blood and Purity in Leviticus and Revelation." *List* 28 (1993) 215–30.

Harrington, Wilfred J. *Revelation*. SP. Collegeville, MN: Liturgical, 1994.

Harris, Murray J. *Slave of Christ: A New Testament Metaphor for Total Devotion to Christ*. Downers Grove, IL: InterVarsity, 1999.

Harrison, R. K. "Horn." In *ISBE* 2:757.

———. "Leopard." In *ISBE* 3:102–3.

———. "Water. In *ISBE* 4:1024–26.

Harrison, R. K., and Edwin M. Yamauchi. "Banquets." In *DDL* 127–35.

———. "Clothing." In *DDL* 322–36.

Hartley, John E. "Star." In *ISBE* 4:611–12.

Hartopo, Yohanes Adrie. "The Marriage of the Lamb: The Background and Function of the Marriage Imagery in the Book of Revelation." PhD diss., Westminster Theological Seminary, 2005.

Hasel, Gerhard F. "Day." In *ISBE* 1:877–78.

———. "Day and Night." In *ISBE* 1:878.

Hatfield, Daniel Earl. "The Function of the Seven Beatitudes in Revelation." PhD diss., Southern Baptist Theological Seminary, 1987.

Hawkins, Ralph K. "Hail, Hailstones." In *NIDB* 2:718–19.

Hays, J. Daniel. *The Temple and the Tabernacle: A Study of God's Dwelling Places from Genesis to Revelation*. Grand Rapids: Baker, 2016.

Hays, J. Daniel, J. Scott Duvall, and C. Marvin Pate. *Dictionary of Biblical Prophecy and End Times*. Grand Rapids: Zondervan, 2007.

Heater, Homer Jr. "Do the Prophets Teach that Babylonia Will Be Rebuilt in the Eschaton?" *JETS* 41 (1998) 23–43.

Heide, Gale Z. "What Is New about the New Heaven and the New Earth? A Theology of Creation from Revelation 21 and 2 Peter 3." *JETS* 40 (1997) 37–56.

Heil, J. P. *The Book of Revelation: Worship for Life in the Spirit of Prophecy*. Eugene, OR: Cascade, 2014.

———. "The Fifth Seal (Rev 6, 9–11) as a Key to the Book of Revelation." *Bib* 74 (1993) 220–43.

Hemer, Colin J. *The Letters to the Seven Churches in Their Local Setting*. LNTS 11. Sheffield: Sheffield Academic, 1986.

———. "Number." In *NIDNTT* 2:690–96.

———. "Seven Churches." In *DBTEL* 696–98.

Hendriksen, William. *More than Conquerors*. Grand Rapids: Baker, 1962.

Henten, Jan Willem van. "Archangel." In *DDD* 80–82.

Herms, Ronald. *An Apocalypse for the Church and for the World: The Narrative Function of Universal Language in the Book of Revelation*. BZNW 143. Berlin: de Gruyter, 2006.

Hill, Craig C. "Day of Judgment." In *NIDB* 2:45–46.

Hillyer, Norman. "'The Lamb' in the Apocalypse." *EvQ* 39 (1967) 228–36.

Hindson, Edward. *The Book of Revelation*. TFCBC. Chattanooga, TN: AMG, 2002.

Hitchcock, Mark. "A Critique of the Preterist View of 'Soon' and 'Near' in Revelation." *BibSac* 163 (2006) 467–78.

———. *Russia Rising: Tracking the Bear in Bible Prophecy*. Carol Stream, IL: Tyndale, 2017.

———. *The Second Coming of Babylon*. Eugene, OR: Multnomah, 2003.

Hock, Andreas. "From Babel to the New Jerusalem (Gen 11,1–9 and Rev 21,1–22, 5)." *Bib* 89 (2008) 109–18.

Homcy, Stephen L. "'To Him Who Overcomes': A Fresh Look at What 'Victory' Means for the Believer according to the Book of Revelation." *JETS* 38 (1995) 193–201.

Howard, David M. Jr. "Sickle." In *ISBE* 4:499.

———. "Sodom." In *ISBE* 4:560–61.

———. "Sodom and Gomorrah Revisited." *JETS* 27 (1984) 385–400.

Huber, Lynn R. *Like a Bride Adorned: Reading Metaphor in John's Apocalypse*. New York: T. & T. Clark, 2007.

Huey, F. B. Jr. "Idolatry." In *ZEB* 3:270–75.

———. "Weights and Measures." In *ZEB* 5:1061–73.

Hughes, Philip E. *The Book of Revelation*. Grand Rapids: Eerdmans, 1990.

———. "The First Resurrection: Another Interpretation." *WTJ* 39 (1977) 315–18.

Hultberg, Alan "A Case for the Prewrath Rapture." In *Three Views on the Rapture: Pretribulation, Prewrath, or Postribulation*, edited by Stanley N. Gundry, 109–54. 2nd ed. Grand Rapids: Zondervan, 2010.

Humphrey, Edith M. *And I Turned to See the Voice: The Rhetoric of Vision in the New Testament*. Grand Rapids: Baker, 2007.

Hurtado, Larry W., and Paul L. Owens, editors. *"Who Is This Son of Man?": The Latest Scholarship on a Puzzling Expression of the Historical Jesus*. LNTS 390. New York: T. & T. Clark, 2011.

Hutter, Manfred. "Abaddon." In *DDD* 1.

Hylen, Susan E. "Lamb." In *NIDB* 3:563.

———. "New Heaven, New Earth." In *NIDB* 4:263–64.

———. "Sea of Glass, Glassy Sea." In *NIDB* 5:140.

Ice, Thomas D. "The Meaning of 'Earth-Dwellers' in Revelation." *BibSac* 166 (2009) 350–65.

Janzen, Waldemar. "Tabernacle." In *NIDB* 5:447–58.

Jauhiainen, Marko. "The OT Background to *Armageddon* (Rev. 16:16) Revisited." *NovT* 47 (2005) 381–93.

———. "Recapitulation and Chronological Progression in John's Apocalypse: Towards a New Perspective." *NTS* 49 (2003) 543–49.

Jenks, Alan W. "Eating and Drinking in the Old Testament." In *ABD* 2:250–54.

Jeske, Richard L. "Spirit and Community in the Johannine Apocalypse." *NTS* 31 (1985) 452–66.

Jewett, Paul K. *The Lord's Day*. Grand Rapids: Eerdmans, 1971.

Jocz, Jakob. "Jew." In *ZEB* 3:666–67.

Johns, Loren L. *The Lamb Christology of the Apocalypse of John.* Tübingen: Mohr Siebeck, 2003.

Johnson, Alan F. "Revelation." In *EBC*, edited by Tremper Longman III and David E. Garland, 13:572–789. Rev. ed. Grand Rapids: Zondervan, 2006.

Johnson, David R. "The Mark of the Beast, Reception History, and Early Pentecostal Literature." *JPT* 25 (2016) 184–202.

Johnson, Dennis E. *Triumph of the Lamb: A Commentary on Revelation.* Phillipsburg, NJ: P&R, 2001.

Johnston, Eleanor B. "Jezebel." In *ISBE* 2:1057–59.

Johnston, Philip, and Peter Walker, editors. *The Land of Promise: Biblical, Theological and Contemporary Perspectives.* Downers Grove, IL: InterVarsity, 2000.

Jones, Brian C. "Wilderness." In *NIDB* 5:848–52.

Jonge, Marinus de. "Christ." In *ABD* 1:914–21.

Joy, Alfred H. "Cloud." In *ISBE* 1:725–26.

———. "Dark; Darkness." In *ISBE* 1:868–69.

Keener, Craig. S. "One New Temple in Christ (Ephesians 2:11–22; Acts 21:7–9; Mark 11:17; John 4:20–24)." *AJPS* 12 (2009) 75–92.

———. *Revelation.* NIVAC. Grand Rapids: Zondervan, 2000.

Keener, Craig S., Jeremy S. Crenshaw, and Jordan Daniel May, editors. *"But These Are Written . . . ": Essays on Johannine Literature in Honor of Benny C. Aker.* Eugene, OR: Wipf & Stock, 2014.

Keown, Gerald L. "Locust." In *ISBE* 3:149–50.

Kerkeslager, Allen. "Apollo, Greco-Roman Prophecy, and the Rider on the White Horse in Rev. 6:2." *JBL* 112 (1993) 116–21.

Keylock, L. R. "Key." In *ZEB* 3:898–900.

Kiddle, Martin. *The Revelation of St. John.* MNTC. 2nd ed. London: Hodder & Stoughton, 1941.

Kirchmayr, Karl. "Die Bedeutung von 666 und 616 (Offb 13, 18)." *Bib* 95 (2014) 424–27.

Kissling, Paul J. "Rainbow." In *NIDB* 4:729.

Kistemaker, Simon J. *Exposition of the Book of Revelation.* NTC. Grand Rapids: Baker, 2001.

———. "The Temple in the Apocalypse." *JETS* 43 (2000) 433–41.

Klauck, Hans-Josef. "Do They Never Come Back? Nero Redivivus and the Apocalypse of John." *CBQ* 63 (2001) 683–98.

Kline, Meredith C. "Har Magedon: The End of the Millennium." *JETS* 39 (1996) 207–22.

Klingbeil, Gerald A. "'Eating' and 'Drinking' in the Book of Revelation: A Study of New Testament Thought and Theology." *JATS* 16 (2005) 75–92.

———. "Water." In *NIDB* 5:818–21.

Knapp, Gary L. "Walk." In *ISBE* 4:1003–5.

Knutson, F. Brent. "Dwell; Dweller; Dwelling." In *ISBE* 1:999–1000.

———. "Naked." In *ISBE* 3:480.

Koester, Craig R. "Antichrist." In *NIDB* 1:177–78.

———. *The Dwelling of God: The Tabernacle in the Old Testament, Intertestamental Jewish Literature, and the New Testament.* Washington, DC: Catholic Biblical Association of America, 1989.

———. *Revelation.* AYBC. New Haven, CT: Yale University Press, 2014.

Koosed, Jennifer L. "Dwelling Place." In *NIDB* 2:168.

Koppen, Frans van, and Karel van der Toorn. "Altar." In *DDD* 23–24.

Korner, Ralph J. "'And I Saw . . .': An Apocalyptic Literary Convention for Structural Identification in the Apocalypse." *NovT* 42 (2000) 160–83.

Köstenberger, Andreas J. *John*. BECNT. Grand Rapids: Baker, 2004.

Köstenberger, Andreas J., and Richard D. Patterson. *For the Love of God's Word: An Introduction to Biblical Interpretation*. Grand Rapids: Kregel, 2015.

Kovacs, Judith, and Christopher Rowland. *Revelation*. BBC. Malden, MA: Blackwell, 2003.

Kraybill, J. Nelson. *Imperial Cult and Commerce in John's Apocalypse*. LNTS 132. Sheffield: Sheffield Academic, 1996.

Krodel, Gerhard A. *Revelation*. ACNT. Minneapolis: Augsburg, 1989.

Kurschner, Alan. *Antichrist before the Day of the Lord*. Pompton Lakes, NJ: Eschatos, 2013.

Kuykendall, Michael. "Marriage of the Lamb." In *LDB*.

———. "Sea of Glass." In *LDB*.

———. "The Twelve Visions of John: Another Attempt at Structuring the Book of Revelation." *JETS* 60 (2017) 533–55.

Labahn, Michael, and Outi Lehtipuu, editors. *Imagery in the Book of Revelation*. Walpole, MA: Peeters, 2011.

Ladd, George Eldon. *A Commentary on the Revelation of John*. Grand Rapids: Eerdmans, 1972.

LaHaye, Tim. *Revelation Unveiled*. Grand Rapids: Zondervan, 1999.

Lambrecht, Jan. "Rev 13,9–10 and Exhortation in the Apocalypse." In *New Testament Textual Criticism and Exegesis: Festschrift Joel Delobel*, edited by Adelbert Denaux, 331–47. Leuven: Peeters, 2002.

———. "'Synagogues of Satan' (Rev 2.9 and 3.9): Anti-Judaism in the Book of Revelation." In *Anti-Judaism and the Fourth Gospel*, edited by R. Bieringer, Didier Pollefeyt, and F. Vandecasteele-Vanneuville, 279–92 Louisville: Westminster John Knox, 2001.

Laughlin, John C. H. "Idol," "Idolatry." In *NIDB* 3:8–14.

Lawlor, John I. "Sit, Dwell." In *NIDB* 5:295–96.

———. "Thunder and Lightning." In *NIDB* 5:590–91.

Lay, Herbert W., and Ralph W. Vunderink. "Foot." In *ISBE* 2:332–33.

Lee, G. A. "Hill, etc." In *ISBE* 3:713–16.

Lee, Hee Youl. *A Dynamic Reading of the Holy Spirit in Revelation*. Eugene, OR: Wipf & Stock, 2014.

Lee, Pilchan. *The New Jerusalem in the Book of Revelation: A Study of Revelation 21–22 in the Light of Its Background in Jewish Tradition*. Tübingen: Mohr Siebeck, 2001.

Lemcio, Eugene E. *Navigating Revelation: Charts for the Voyage*. Eugene, OR: Wipf & Stock, 2011.

Lemon, Joel M. "Smoke." In *NIDB* 5:308–9.

Lewis, Gordon R. "Paradise." In *ZEB* 4:665–67.

Lewis, Jack P. "Firstfruits." In *ZEB* 2:578.

Lewis, Scott M. "Light and Darkness." In *NIDB* 3:662–63.

Lindsey, Hal. *Late Great Planet Earth*. Grand Rapids: Zondervan, 1970.

———. *There's a New World Coming*. Santa Ana, CA: Vision House, 1973.

Linton, Gregory L. "Time." In *DDL* 1593–95.

Lioy, Dan. *The Book of Revelation in Christological Focus*. StBibLit 58. New York: P. Lang, 2003.

Litwak, Kenneth D. "Face." In *NIDB* 2:407.

Liu, Rebekah Yi. "The Backgrounds and Meaning of the Image of the Beast in Rev. 13:14, 15." PhD diss., Andrews University, 2016.

Longenecker, Bruce W. "'Linked Like a Chain': Rev 22.6–9 in Light of an Ancient Transition Technique." *NTS* 47 (2001) 105–17.

Lupieri, Edmondo F. *A Commentary on the Apocalypse of John*. Translated by Maria Poggi Johnson. Grand Rapids: Eerdmans, 2006.

MacLeod, David J. "The Sixth 'Last Thing': The Last Judgment and the End of the World (Rev. 20:11–15)." *BibSac* 157 (2000) 315–30.

MacPherson, Anthony. "The Mark of the Beast as a 'Sign Commandment' and 'Anti-Sabbath' in the Worship Crisis of Revelation 12–14." *AUSS* 43 (2005) 267–83.

MacRae, Allan A. "Prophets and Prophecy." In *ZEB* 4:992–1028.

Maier, Harry O. *Apocalypse Recalled: The Book of Revelation after Christendom*. Minneapolis: Fortress, 2002.

Mangina, Joseph L. *Revelation*. BTC. Grand Rapids: Baker, 2010.

Mare, W. Harold. "Armor, Arms." In *ZEB* 1:352–59.

———. "Dress." In *ZEB* 1:183–87.

———. "Moon." In *ZEB* 4:308–10.

Marshall, I. H. "Kingdom of God (of Heaven)." In *ZEB* 3:911–22.

Marshall, John W. *Parables of War: Reading John's Jewish Apocalypse*. Waterloo, ON: Wilfrid Laurier University Press, 2001.

Martin, Ralph P. "Jesus Christ." In *ISBE* 2:1034–49.

Mathewson, David L. "The Destiny of the Nations in Revelation 21:1–22:5." *TynB* 53 (2002) 121–42.

———. "New Exodus as a Background for 'The Sea Was No More' in Revelation 21:1C." *TJ* 24 (2003) 243–58.

———. A New Heaven and a New Earth: The Meaning and Function of the Old Testament in Revelation 21:1—22:5. LNTS 238. London: Sheffield, 2003.

———. "A Note on the Foundation Stones in Revelation 21.14, 19–20." *JSNT* 25 (2003) 487–98.

———. "A Re-Examination of the Millennium in Rev 20:1–6: Consummation and Recapitulation." *JETS* 44 (2001) 237–51.

———. *Revelation: A Handbook on the Greek Text*. Waco, TX: Baylor University Press, 2016.

Mathison, Keith A. *Postmillennialism: An Eschatology of Hope*. Phillipsburg, NJ: P&R, 1999.

Matthews, Victor H. "Cloth, Clothes." In *ZEB* 1:691–96.

Matthews, Victor H., and Ivor H. Jones. "Music and Musical Instruments." In *ABD* 4:930–39.

Mayhew, Eugene. "Revelation 11, the Two Witnesses." In *DPT* 364–66.

Mayo, Philip L. *"Those Who Call Themselves Jews": The Church and Judaism in the Apocalypse of John*. Eugene, OR: Pickwick, 2006.

Mazzaferri, Frederick David. *The Genre of the Book of Revelation from a Source-Critical Perspective*. New York: de Gruyter, 1989.

McDonough, Sean M. *YHWH at Patmos*. Tübingen: Mohr Siebeck, 1999.

McFall, Leslie "Serpent." In *NDBT* 773–75.

McGinn, Bernard. *Antichrist: Two Thousand Years of Human Fascination with Evil*. San Francisco: HarperCollins, 1994.

McKelvey, Robert J. "Temple." In *NDBT* 806–11.

McKim, Donald K. "Door." In *ISBE* 1:983–84.

McNichol, Allan J. *The Conversion of the Nations in Revelation*. LNTS 438. London: T. & T. Clark, 2011.

Mealy, J. Webb. *After the Thousand Years: Resurrection and Judgment in Revelation 20*. LNTS 70. Sheffield: Sheffield Academic, 1992.

Metzger, Bruce M. *A Textual Commentary on the Greek New Testament*. 2nd ed. New York: United Bible Societies, 1994.

Meyer, Ben F. "Jesus Christ." In *ABD* 3:773–96.

Meyers, Carol. "Lampstand." In *ABD* 4:141–43.

Meyers, Jeffrey D. "*Hupomonē* as 'Enduring Resistance': Finding Nonviolence in the Book of Revelation." *BT* 69 (2018) 40–55.

Michaelis, Wilhelm. "πρῶτος . . ." In *TDNT* 6:865–68.

Michaels, J. Ramsey. *Interpreting the Book of Revelation*. Grand Rapids: Baker, 1992.

———. *Revelation*. IVPNTC. Downers Grove, IL: InterVarsity, 1997.

———. "Servant." In *ZEB* 5:429–31.

———. "Tribulation, Great." In *NIDB* 5:676–77.

Middleton, J. Richard. "A New Heaven and a New Earth: The Case for a Holistic Reading of the Biblical Story of Redemption." *JCTR* 11 (2006) 73–97.

———. *A New Heaven and a New Earth: Reclaiming Biblical Eschatology*. Grand Rapids: Baker, 2014.

Mihalios, Stefanos. *The Danielic Eschatological Hour in the Johannine Literature*. LNTS 436. New York: T. & T. Clark, 2011.

Miles, John R. "Lamb." In *ABD* 4:132–34.

Millar, J. Gary "Land." In *NDBT* 623–27.

———. "People of God." In *NDBT* 684–87.

Minear, Paul S. "Far as the Curse Is Found: The Point of Revelation 12:5–6." *NovT* 33 (1991) 71–77.

———. *Images of the Church in the New Testament*. Philadelphia: Westminster, 1960.

———. *I Saw a New Earth: An Introduction to the Visions of the Apocalypse*. Eugene, OR: Wipf & Stock, 2003.

Mixter, Russell L. "Face." In *ZEB* 2:513–14.

———. "Hand." In *ZEB* 3:34–35.

———. "Head." In *ZEB* 3:63–64.

Moo, Jonathan. "The Sea that Is No More: Rev. 21:1 and the Function of Sea Imagery in the Apocalypse of John." *NovT* 51 (2009) 148–67.

Morgan, Christopher W. "Annihilationism: Will the Unsaved Be Punished Forever?" In *Hell under Fire*, edited by Christopher W. Morgan and Robert A. Peterson, 195–218. Grand Rapids: Zondervan, 2004.

Morgan, Donn F. "Horse." In *ISBE* 2:759–60.

Morris, Leon. *The Book of Revelation*. TNTC. 2nd ed. Grand Rapids: Eerdmans, 1987.

———. *The Epistle to the Romans*. Grand Rapids: Eerdmans, 1988.

Morton, Russell S. *One upon the Throne and the Lamb: A Tradition Historical/Theological Analysis of Revelation 4–5*. StBibLit 104. New York: P. Lang, 2007.

Moulder, William J. "Priesthood in the NT." In *ISBE* 3:963–65.

Mounce, Robert H. *Revelation*. NICNT. 2nd ed. Grand Rapids: Eerdmans, 1998.

Moyise, Steve. "Word Frequencies in the Book of Revelation." *AUSS* 43 (2005) 285–99.

Mulder, Martin J. "Sodom and Gomorrah." In *ABD* 6:99–103.

Mulholland, M. Robert, Jr. *Revelation: Holy Living in an Unholy World.* Grand Rapids: Zondervan, 1990.

Muller, D. "Apostle." In *NIDNTT* 1:128–35.

Müller, Ekkehardt. "The Two Witnesses of Revelation 11." *JATS* 13 (2002) 30–45.

Murphy, Frederick J. *Apocalypticism in the Bible and in Its World: A Comprehensive Introduction.* Grand Rapids: Baker, 2012.

———. *Fallen Is Babylon: The Revelation to John.* London: T. & T. Clark, 1998.

Murphy-O'Connor, Jerome. "Jerusalem." In *NIDB* 3:246–59.

Myers, Allen C. "Clothe; Clothed." In *ISBE* 1:724–25.

Neufeld, Dietmar. "Sumptuous Clothing and Ornamentation in the Apocalypse." *HTS* 58 (2002) 664–89.

———. "Under the Cover of Clothing: Scripted Clothing Performances in the Apocalypse of John." *BTB* 35 (2005) 67–75.

Newsom, Carol A., and Duane F. Watson. "Angels." In *ABD* 1:248–55.

Nicholas, David R. "Judgments, Various." In *DPT* 225–27.

Nickelsburg, George W. E. *Jewish Literature between the Bible and the Mishnah.* 2nd ed. Nashville: Fortress, 2005.

———. "Son of Man." In *ABD* 6:137–50.

Nielsen, Kjeld. "Incense." In *ABD* 3:404–40.

Noble, T. A. "Time and Eternity." In *NDT* 912–13.

Noll, Stephen F. *Angels of Light, Powers of Darkness: Thinking Biblically about Angels, Satan, and Principalities.* Eugene, OR: Wipf & Stock, 2003.

Nwachukwu, Oliver O. *Beyond Vengeance and Protest: A Reflection on the Macarisms in Revelation.* StBibLit 71. New York: P. Lang, 2005.

Olson, Daniel C. "'Those Who Have Not Defiled Themselves with Women': Revelation 14:4 and the Book of Enoch." *CBQ* 59 (1997) 492–510.

Omanson, Roger L. *A Textual Guide to the Greek New Testament.* Stuttgart: Deutsche Bibelgesellschaft, 2006.

Osborne, Grant. R. *The Hermeneutical Spiral: A Comprehensive Introduction to Biblical Interpretation.* Rev. ed. Downers Grove, IL: InterVarsity, 2006.

———. *Revelation.* BECNT. Grand Rapids: Baker, 2002.

Packer, J. I. "Universalism: Will Everyone Ultimately Be Saved? In *Hell Under Fire*, edited by Christopher W. Morgan and Robert A. Peterson, 169–94. Grand Rapids: Zondervan, 2004.

Parsons, Marnie. "Jezebel." In *DBTEL* 401–2.

Pate, C. Marvin. *Interpreting Revelation and Other Apocalyptic Literature: An Exegetical Handbook.* HNTE. Grand Rapids: Kregel, 2016.

Pate, C. Marvin, editor. *Four Views on the Book of Revelation.* Grand Rapids: Zondervan, 1998.

Pate, C. Marvin, and Douglas W. Kennard. *Deliverance Now and Not Yet: The New Testament and the Great Tribulation.* StBibLit 54. New York: P. Lang, 2003.

Pattemore, Stephen. *The People of God in the Apocalypse: Discourse, Structure, and Exegesis.* Cambridge: Cambridge University Press, 2004.

Paterson, John H. "Sea." In *ZEB* 5:370–72.

Patterson, Paige. *Revelation.* NAC. Nashville: Broadman & Holman, 2012.

Paul, Ian. *Revelation.* TNTC. Downers Grove, IL: InterVarsity, 2018.

———. "Source, Structure, and Composition in the Book of Revelation." In *The Book of Revelation: Currents in British Research on the Apocalypse*, edited by Garrick V. Allen, Ian Paul, and Simon P. Woodman, 41–54. Tübingen: Mohr Siebeck, 2015.

Paulien, Jon. "Armageddon." In *ABD* 1:394–95.

———. "Revisiting the Sabbath in the Book of Revelation." *JATS* 9 (1998) 179–86.

Payne, J. Barton. "Ark of the Covenant." In *ZEB* 1:345–50.

———. "Jerusalem." In *ZEB* 3:528–64.

Peach, Michael E. *Paul and the Apocalyptic Triumph: An Investigation of the Usage of Jewish and Greco-Roman Imagery in 1 Thess. 4:13–18.* New York: P. Lang, 2016.

Pennington, Jonathan T. *The Sermon on the Mount and Human Flourishing: A Theological Commentary.* Grand Rapids: Baker, 2017.

Petersen, David L. "Prophet, Prophecy." In *NIDB* 4:622–48.

Petersen, Rodney L. *Preaching in the Last Days: The Theme of "Two Witnesses" in the 16th and 17th Centuries.* New York: Oxford University Press, 1993.

Pilgrim, Walter E. "Universalism in the Apocalypse." *WW* 9 (1989) 235–43.

Pitre, Brant. "Jesus, the Messianic Banquet, and the Kingdom of God." *L&S* 5 (2009) 145–66.

Platt, Elizabeth E. "Jewelry, Ancient Israelite." In *ABD* 3:823–34.

Price, J. Randall. "Tribulation, Old Testament References to the." In *DPT* 412–15.

Plümacher, E. "μάχαιρα." In *EDNT* 2:397–98.

Pollard, Leslie N. "The Function of *Loipos* in Contexts of Judgment and Salvation in the Book of Revelation." PhD diss., Andrews University Dissertation, 2007.

Porter, Stanley E. "Why the Laodiceans Received Lukewarm Water (Revelation 3:15–18)." *TynB* 38 (1987) 143–49.

Poythress, Vern S. *The Returning King: A Guide to the Book of Revelation.* Phillipsburg, NJ: P&R, 2000.

Prévost, Jean-Pierre. *How to Read the Apocalypse.* New York: Crossroad, 1993.

Priest, J. "A Note on the Messianic Banquet." In *The Messiah: Developments in Earliest Judaism and Christianity*, edited by James H. Charlesworth, 222–38. Minneapolis: Fortress, 1992.

Prigent, Pierre. *Commentary on the Apocalypse of St. John.* Translated by Wendy Pradels. Tübingen: Mohr Siebeck, 2004.

Provan, Charles D. *The Church Is Israel Now: The Transfer of Conditional Privilege.* Vallecito, CA: Ross House, 2003.

Raffety, W. E. "Crown." In *ISBE* 1:831–32.

Rainbow, Paul A. "Millennium as Metaphor in John's Apocalypse." *WTJ* 58 (1996) 209–21.

———. *The Pith of the Apocalypse: Essential Message and Principles for Interpretation.* Eugene, OR: Wipf & Stock, 2008.

Railton, Nicholas M. "Gog and Magog: The History of the Symbol." *EvQ* 75 (2003) 23–43.

Räpple, Eva Maria. *The Metaphor of the City in the Apocalypse of John.* StBibLit 67. New York: P. Lang, 2004.

Rasmussen, Carl G. "City, theology of." In *ZEB* 1:917.

Rea, John. "Cup." In *ZEB* 1:1111.

Reader, William W. "The Twelve Jewels of Revelation 21:19–20: Tradition, History, and Modern Interpretations." *JBL* 100 (1981) 433–57.

Reddish, Mitchell G. "Alpha and Omega." In *ABD* 1:161–62.

———. "Gog and Magog." In *ABD* 2:1056.

———. *Revelation.* SHBC. Macon, GA: Smyth & Helwys, 2001.

Redditt, Paul L. "Locust." In *NIDB* 3:684–85.

Reese, David George. "Demons." In *ABD* 2:140–42.

Reeves, Marjorie. "Dragon of the Apocalypse." In *DBTEL* 210–13.

———. "Seven Seals." In *DBTEL* 703–6.

Resseguie, James L. *The Revelation of John: A Narrative Commentary*. Grand Rapids: Baker, 2009.

———. *Revelation Unsealed: A Narrative Critical Approach to John's Apocalypse*. Leiden: Brill, 1998.

Reynolds, Edwin. "The Feast of Tabernacles and the Book of Revelation." *AUSS* 38 (2000) 245–68.

———. "The Sodom/Egypt/Babylon Motif in the Book of Revelation." PhD diss., Andrews University, 1994.

———. "The Trinity in the Book of Revelation." *JATS* 17 (2006) 55–72.

Riddlebarger, Kim. *A Case for Amillennialism: Understanding the End Times*. Grand Rapids: Baker, 2003.

Rigsby, Richard O. "First Fruits." In *ABD* 2:796–97.

Rissi, Mathias. *The Future of the World: An Exegetical Study of Revelation 19:11—22:15*. London: SCM, 1972.

———. *Time and History: A Study on the Revelation*. Translated by Gordon C. Winsor. Richmond, VA: John Knox, 1966.

Roberts, J. J. M. "Temple, Jerusalem." In *NIDB* 5:494–509.

Robertson, O. Palmer. *God's People in the Wilderness: The Church in Hebrews*. Geanies House, Fearn, Scotland: Christian Focus, 2009.

Roloff, Jürgen. *The Revelation of John*. CC. Translated by John E. Alsup. Minneapolis: Fortress, 1993.

Rosenthal, Marvin. *The Pre-Wrath Rapture of the Church*. Nashville: T. Nelson, 1990.

Ross, J. M. "The Ending of the Apocalypse." In *Studies in New Testament Language and Text: Essays in Honour of George D. Kilpatrick*, edited by J. K. Elliott, 338–44. Leiden: Brill, 1976.

Rosscup, James E. "Firstborn." In *ZEB* 2:577–78.

———. "New Jerusalem." In *ZEB* 4:461–62.

———. "The Overcomer in the Apocalypse." *GTJ* 3 (1982) 261–86.

Rossing, Barbara. *The Choice between the Two Cities: Whore, Bride, and Empire in the Apocalypse*. Harrisburg, PA: Trinity, 1999.

———. "River of Life in God's New Jerusalem: An Ecological Vision for Earth's Future." *CurTM* 25 (1998) 487–99.

Rotz, Carol. *Revelation: A Commentary in the Wesleyan Tradition*. NBBC. Kansas City: Beacon Hill, 2012.

Rowland, Christopher C. "Revelation." In *NIB*, edited by Leander Keck, 12:501–743. Nashville: Abingdon, 1998.

Russell, James Stuart. *The Parousia: A Critical Inquiry into the New Testament Doctrine of Our Lord's Second Coming*. Grand Rapids: Baker, 1983.

Ryken, Leland, et al., editors. *Dictionary of Biblical Imagery*. Downers Grove, IL: InterVarsity, 1998.

Ryrie, Charles C. *Revelation*. Chicago: Moody, 1996.

Sandy, D. Brent. *Plowshares and Pruning Hooks: Rethinking the Language of Biblical Prophecy and Apocalyptic*. Downers Grove, IL: InterVarsity, 2002.

Schley, Donald G. "Sun." In *ISBE* 4:662–64.

Schmidt, Brian. "Moon." In *DDD* 585–93.

Schmidt, Thomas E. "'And the Sea Was No More': Water as People, Not Place." In *To Tell the Mystery: Essays on New Testament Eschatology in Honor of Robert H. Gundry*, edited by T. E. Schmidt and Moisés Silva, 233–49. LNTS 100. Sheffield: Sheffield Academic, 1994.

Schmitz, E. D. "Number." In *NIDNTT* 2:683–85, 694–96.

Schnabel, Eckhard J. *40 Questions about the End Times*. Grand Rapids: Kregel, 2011.

———. "John and the Future of the Nations." *BBR* 12 (2002) 243–71.

Schöpflin, Karin. "Fire." In *NIDB* 2:454–55.

Schreiner, Thomas R. *Romans*. BECNT. Grand Rapids: Baker, 1998.

Schultz, Arnold C. "Wine and Strong Drink." In *ZEB* 5:1083–87.

Schüssler Fiorenza, Elisabeth. *The Book of Revelation: Justice and Judgment*. 2nd ed. Nashville: Fortress, 1998.

———. *Revelation: Vision of a Just World*. PC. Minneapolis: Fortress, 1991.

Scrivner, Joseph F. "Twelve." In *NIDB* 5:689–90.

Scurlock, Joann. "Euphrates River." In *NIDB* 2:356.

Seal, David. "Shouting in the Apocalypse: The Influence of First-Century Acclamations on the Praise Utterances in Revelation 4:8 and 11." *JETS* 51 (2008) 339–52.

Seebass, H. "Babylon." In *NIDNTT* 1:140–42.

Seow, C. L. "Ark of the Covenant." In *ABD* 1:386–93.

Shargel, Steve. "A Hearer-Centric Approach to Identifying, Confirming, and Interpreting the Allusions to the Old Testament in Revelation." PhD diss., Gateway Seminary, 2017.

Shin, E. C. "The Conqueror Motif in Chapters 12–13: A Heavenly and an Earthly Perspective in the Book of Revelation." *VeE* 28 (2007) 207–23.

Showers, Renald. "Gog and Magog." In *DPT* 124–26.

———. *The Pre-Wrath Rapture View*. Grand Rapids: Kregel, 2001.

Siew, Antoninus King Wai. *The War between the Two Beasts and the Two Witnesses: A Chiastic Reading of Revelation 11.1—14.5*. LNTS 283. London: T. & T. Clark, 2005.

Silva, Moisés, editor. "ἅγιος." In *NIDNTTE* 1:124–33.

———. "ἀδελφός." In *NIDNTTE* 1:150–51.

———. "βιβλίος." In *NIDNTTE* 1:510–15.

———. "γυμνός." In *NIDNTTE* 1:610–12.

———. "δοῦλος." In *NIDNTTE* 1:767–73.

———. "ἑπτά." In *NIDNTTE* 2:260–63.

———. "κεφαλή." In *NIDNTTE* 2:669–74.

———. "ὀρός." In *NIDNTTE* 3:548–53.

———. "σείω." In *NIDNTTE* 4:279.

———. "τρεῖς." In *NIDNTTE* 4:503.

———. "χίλιοι." In *NIDNTTE* 4:671–75.

Skaggs, Rebecca, and Priscilla Benham. *Revelation*. PCS. Dorset, UK: Deo, 2009.

Skaggs, Rebecca, and Thomas Doyle. "Lion/Lamb in Revelation." *CBR* 7 (2009) 362–75.

———. "Revelation 7: Three Critical Questions." In *Imagery in the Book of Revelation*, edited by Michael Laban and Outi Lehtipuu, 161–81. Walpole, MA: Peeters, 2011.

Slater, Thomas B. "'King of Kings and Lord of Lords' Revisited." *NTS* 39 (1993)159–60.

———. "One Like a Son of Man in First-Century CE Judaism." *NTS* 41 (1995) 183–98.

Smalley, Stephen S. *The Revelation to John: A Commentary on the Greek Text of the Apocalypse*. Downers Grove, IL: InterVarsity, 2005.

———. *Thunder and Love: John's Revelation and John's Community*. Milton Keynes, UK: Word, 1994.

Smick, Elmer B. "Tree of Knowledge; Tree of Life." In *ISBE* 4:901–3.

Smidt, J. C. de. "The Holy Spirit in the Book of Revelation—Nomenclature." *Neot* 28 (1994) 229–44.

Smidt, Kobus de. "Hermeneutical Perspectives on the Spirit in the Book of Revelation." *JPT* 7 (1999) 27–47.

Smith, Chris M. "Day, NT." In *NIDB* 2:47–48.

Smith, Christopher R. "The Portrayal of the Church as the New Israel in the Names and Order of the Tribes in Revelation 7.5–8." *JSNT* 39 (1990) 111–18.

———. "The Structure of the Book of Revelation in Light of Apocalyptic Literary Conventions." *NovT* 36 (1994) 373–93.

———. "The Tribes of Revelation 7 and the Literary Competence of John the Seer." *JETS* 38 (1995) 213–18.

Smith, Gary V. "Prophet; Prophecy." In *ISBE* 3:986–1004.

Song, Seung-In. "Water as an Image of the Spirit in the Johannine Literature." PhD diss., Golden Gate Baptist Theological Seminary, 2015.

Sorke, Ingo Willy. "The Identity and Function of the Seven Spirits in the Book of Revelation." PhD Diss., Southwestern Baptist Theological Seminary, 2009.

Specht, Walter F. "Sunday in the New Testament." In *The Sabbath in Scripture and History*, edited by Kenneth A. Strand, 92–113. Washington, DC: Review and Herald, 1982.

Sprinkle, Preston, editor. *Four Views on Hell*. 2nd ed. Grand Rapids: Zondervan, 2016.

Stanton, Gerald B. "Millennium, Doctrine of." In *DPT* 259–62.

Steen, Eveline J. van der. "Gold." In *NIDB* 2:622–23.

Stefanovic, Ranko. *Revelation of Jesus Christ: Commentary on the Book of Revelation*. 2nd ed. Berrien Springs, MI: Andrews University Press, 2009.

Stephens, Mark B. *Annihilation or Renewal? The Meaning and Function of New Creation in the Book of Revelation*. Tübingen: Mohr Siebeck, 2011.

Stevenson, Gregory. "Conceptual Background to Golden Crown Imagery in the Apocalypse of John." *JBL* 114 (1995) 257–72.

———. *Power and Place: Temple and Identity in the Book of Revelation*. Berlin: de Gruyter, 2001.

Stibbs, Alan M. *His Blood Works: The Meaning of the Word "Blood" in Scripture*. 3rd ed. Carol Stream, IL: Tyndale, 1962.

Stigers, Harold G. "Temple, Jerusalem." In *ZEB* 5:716–52.

Stolz, Fritz. "Sea." In *DDD* 737–42.

Storms, Sam. *Kingdom Come: The Amillennial Alternative*. Geanies House, Fearn, Scotland: Mentor, 2013.

Stramara, Daniel F. Jr. *God's Timetable: The Book of Revelation and the Feast of Seven Weeks*. Eugene, OR: Pickwick, 2011.

Strand, Kenneth A. "Another Look at 'Lord's Day' in the Early Church and Revelation 1:10." *NTS* 13 (1967) 174–80.

———. "'Overcomer': A Study in the Macrodynamic of Theme Development in the Book of Revelation." *AUSS* 28 (1990) 237–54.

———. "The Two Olive Trees of Zechariah 4 and Revelation 11." *AUSS* 20 (1982) 257–61.

———. "The Two Witnesses of Rev 11:3–12." *AUSS* 19 (1981) 127–35.

Strawn, Brent A. *What Is Stronger than a Lion?: Leonine Image and Metaphor in the Hebrew Bible and the Ancient Near East.* Göttingen: Vandenhoeck & Ruprecht, 2005.

Streett, Matthew J. *Here Comes the Judge: Violent Pacifism in the Book of Revelation.* LNTS 462. London: T. & T. Clark, 2012.

Strelan, Rick. "'Outside Are the Dogs and the Sorcerers . . .': Revelation 22:15." *BTB* 33 (2003) 148–57.

Suring, Margit L. "The Horn-Motifs of the Bible and the Ancient Near East." *AUSS* 22 (1984) 327–40.

Swanson, Kristin A. "Serpent." In *NIDB* 5:190–91.

Swartley, Willard M. "Sword." In *NIDB* 5:409–10.

Sweet, John P. M. *Revelation.* TPINTC. Philadelphia: Trinity, 1979.

Swete, Henry Barclay. *The Apocalypse of St. John.* 3rd ed. New York: Macmillan, 1922.

Tan, Christine Joy. "A Critique of Idealist and Historicist Views of the Two Witnesses in Revelation 11." *BibSac* 171 (2014) 328–51.

———. "A Critique of Preterist Views of the Two Witnesses in Revelation 11." *BibSac* 171 (2014) 210–25.

———. "A Futurist View of the Two Witnesses in Revelation 11." *BibSac* 171 (2014) 452–71.

———. "Preterist Views on the Two Witnesses in Revelation 11." *BibSac* 171 (2014) 72–95.

Tanner, J. Paul. "Rethinking Ezekiel's Invasion of Gog." *JETS* 39 (1996) 29–46.

Tavo, Felise. *Woman, Mother and Bride: An Exegetical Investigation into the "Ecclesial" Notions of the Apocalypse.* Leuven: Peeters, 2007.

Tenney, Merrill C. *Interpreting Revelation.* Grand Rapids: Eerdmans, 1957.

Thomas, John Christopher. *The Apocalypse: A Literary and Theological Commentary.* Cleveland, TN: CPT, 2012.

Thomas, John Christopher, and Frank Macchia. *Revelation.* THNTC. Grand Rapids: Eerdmans, 2016.

Thomas, Robert L. "An Analysis of the Seventh Bowl of the Apocalypse." *TMSJ* 5 (1994) 73–95.

———. "The 'Comings' of Christ in Revelation 2–3." *TMSJ* 7 (1996) 153–81.

———. "Marriage Supper of the Lamb." In *DPT* 248.

———. *Revelation.* 2 vols. WEC. Chicago: Moody, 1992, 1995.

———. "The Spiritual Gift of Prophecy in Rev 22:18." *JETS* 32 (1989) 201–16.

———. "The Structure of the Apocalypse: Recapitulation or Progression?" *TMSJ* 4 (1993) 45–66.

Thompson, J. Alexander. "Incense." In *ZEB* 3:306–8.

Thompson, James W. *Hebrews.* PCNT. Grand Rapids: Baker, 2008.

Thompson, Leonard L. *The Book of Revelation: Apocalypse and Empire.* New York: Oxford University Press, 1990.

———. *Revelation.* ANTC. Nashville: Abingdon, 1998.

Thompson, Steven. "The End of Satan." *AUSS* 37 (1999) 257–68.

Thuesen, Peter J. *In Disconcordance with the Scriptures.* New York: Oxford University Press, 1999.

Togtman, R. C. "First." In *ISBE* 2:307.

Tõniste, Külli. *The Ending of the Canon: A Canonical and Intertextual Reading of Revelation 21–22.* LNTS 526. London: Bloomsbury, 2016.

Tooman, William. *Gog of Magog.* Tübingen: Mohr Siebeck, 2011.

Trail, Ronald. *An Exegetical Summary of Revelation*. 2 vols. 2nd ed. Dallas: SIL International, 2008.

Tucker, Gordon C. "Trees." In *DDL* 1632–58.

Twelftree, Graham H. "Demon." In *NIDB* 2:91–100.

———. "Devil, Devils." In *NIDB* 2:117–18.

Ulfgard, Hakan. *Feast and Future: Revelation 7:9–17 and the Feast of Tabernacles*. Lund: Almqvist & Wiksel, 1989.

Umstattd, Rustin. *The Spirit and the Lake of Fire*. Eugene, OR: Wipf & Stock, 2017.

Valentine, Kendra Haloviak. "Cleopatra: New Insights for the Interpretation of Revelation 17." *EvQ* 87 (2015) 310–30.

Van Broekhoven, Harold Jr. "Fire." In *ISBE* 2:305–6.

Van Elderen, Bastiaan. "Purple." In *ZEB* 4:1103–4.

Van Kampen, Robert. *The Sign*. 3rd ed. Wheaton, IL: Crossway, 2000.

Vanzant, Michael G. "Eye." In *NIDB* 2:386.

Villeneuve, André. *Nuptial Symbolism in Second Temple Writings, the New Testament and Rabbinic Literature: Divine Marriage at Key Moments of Salvation History*. Leiden: Brill, 2016.

Villiers, Pieter G. R. de. "The Lord Was Crucified in Sodom and Egypt: Symbols in the Apocalypse of John." *Neot* 22 (1988) 125–38.

———. "The Role of Composition in the Interpretation of the Rider on the White Horse and the Seven Seals in Revelation." *HvTSt* 60 (2004) 125–53.

Volohonsky, Henri. "Is the Color of that Horse Really Pale?" *IJTP* 18 (1999) 167–68.

Vos, Johannes G. "Alpha and Omega." In *ZEB* 1:128–29.

Waddell, Robby. *The Spirit of the Book of Revelation*. Blandford Forum, UK: Deo, 2006.

Waechter, Steven Lloyd. "An Analysis of the Literary Structure of the Book of Revelation according to Textlinguistic Methods." ThD diss., Mid-America Baptist Theological Seminary, 1994.

Wainwright, Arthur W. *Mysterious Apocalypse: Interpreting the Book of Revelation*. Nashville: Abingdon, 1993.

Waite, J. C. J. "Balaam." In *ISBE* 1:404–5.

Walker, Peter W. L. *Jesus and the Holy City: New Testament Perspectives on Jerusalem*. Grand Rapids: Eerdmans, 1996.

Wall, Robert W. *Revelation*. NIBCNT. Peabody, MA: Hendrickson, 1991.

Wallace, Daniel B. *Greek Grammar beyond the Basics*. Grand Rapids: Zondervan, 1996.

Waltke, Bruce K. "Birds." In *ISBE* 1:511–13.

Walvoord, John F. *The Revelation of Jesus Christ*. Chicago: Moody, 1989.

Watson, Duane F. "Death, Second." In *ABD* 2:111–12.

———. "Devil." In *ABD* 2:183–84.

———. "Michael." In *ABD* 4:811.

———. "New Earth, New Heaven." In *ABD* 4:1094–95.

———. "New Jerusalem." In *ABD* 4:1095–96.

———. "Nicolaitans." In *ABD* 4:1106–7.

———. "Seven Churches." In *ABD* 5:1143–44.

Watts, Rikki E. "Wilderness." In *NDBT* 841–43.

Weber, Timothy P. "Millennialism." In *OHE*, edited by Jerry L. Walls, 365–83. Oxford: Oxford University Press, 2008.

Weima, Jeffrey A. D. *1–2 Thessalonians*. BECNT. Grand Rapids: Baker, 2014.

Weinrich, William C., editor. *Revelation.* ACCS. Downers Grove, IL: InterVarsity, 2005.

Wendland, Ernst R. "The Hermeneutical Significance of Literary Structure in Revelation." *Neot* 48 (2014) 447–76.

Westerholm, Stephen. "Temple." In *ISBE* 4:759–76.

Whitaker, Muriel. "River of Life." In *DBTEL* 667.

White, R. Fowler. "Reexamining the Evidence for Recapitulation in Rev. 20:1–10." *WTS* 51 (1989) 319–44.

White, William Jr. "Synagogue." In *ZEB* 5:648–59.

———. "Sun." In *ZEB* 5:632–34.

———. "Thunder." In *ZEB* 5:852.

———. "Wrath." In *ZEB* 5:1153–58.

Wiarda, Tim. "Revelation 3:20: Imagery and Literary Context." *JETS* 38 (1995) 203–12.

Wilcock, Michael. *I Saw Heaven Opened: The Message of Revelation.* BST. Downers Grove, IL: InterVarsity, 1991.

Wilkinson, Richard H. "The ΣΤΥΛΟΣ of Revelation 3:12 and Ancient Coronation Rites." *JBL* 107 (1988) 498–501.

Williams, Peter J. "P115 and the Number of the Beast." *TynB* 58 (2007) 151–53.

Williamson, Ricky Lee. "Thrones in the Book of Revelation." PhD diss., Southern Baptist Theological Seminary, 1993.

Wilson, Jim L., et al. *Impact Preaching: A Case for the One-Point Expository Sermon.* Wooster, OH: Weaver, 2018.

Wilson, Kevin A. "Foot." In *NIDB* 2:476.

———. "Purple." In *NIDB* 4:689–90.

Wilson, J. Macartney. "Angels." In *ISBE* 1:124–27.

Wilson, Mark. "Revelation." In *ZIBBC*, edited by Clinton E. Arnold, 4:244–383. Grand Rapids: Zondervan, 2002.

———. *The Victor Sayings in the Book of Revelation.* Eugene, OR: Wipf & Stock, 2007.

———. *Victory through the Lamb: A Guide to Revelation in Plain Language.* Wooster, OH: Weaver, 2014.

Wilson, Marvin R. "Alcoholic Beverages." In *DDL* 43–52.

———. "Doors and Keys." In *DDL* 536–46.

Wilson, Marvin R., and Seth Rodriquez. "Hair." In *DDL* 765–78.

Wilson, Walter L. *Dictionary of Bible Types.* Peabody, MA: Hendrickson, 1999.

Wink, Walter. *Naming the Powers: The Language of Power in the New Testament.* Philadelphia: Fortress, 1984.

Winkle, Ross. "Another Look at the List of Tribes in Revelation 7." *AUSS* 27 (1989) 53–67.

———. "'Clothes Make the (One Like a Son of) Man': Dress Imagery in Revelation 1 as an Indicator of High Priestly Status." PhD Diss., Andrews University, 2012.

Wiseman, Donald J. "Babylon [NT]." In *ZEB* 1:479.

Witetschek, Stephan. "The Dragon Spitting Frogs: On the Imagery of Revelation 16.13–14." *NTS* 54 (2008) 557–72.

Witherington, Ben III. *Revelation.* NCBC. New York: Cambridge University Press, 2003.

Wolf, Herbert M. "Harvest." In *ZEB* 3:45–46.

Wong, Daniel K. K. "The Beast from the Sea in Revelation 13." *BibSac* 160 (2003) 337–48.

———. "The Hidden Manna and the White Stone in Revelation 2:17." *BibSac* 155 (1998) 346–54.

———. "The First Horseman of Revelation 6." *BibSac* 153 (1996) 212–26.

———. "The Tree of Life in Revelation 2:7." *BibSac* 155 (1998) 211–26.

———. "The Two Witnesses in Revelation 11." *BibSac* 154 (1997) 344–54.

Wood, Shane J. "Simplifying the Number of the Beast (Rev 3:18): An Interpretation of 666 and 616." In *Dragons, John, and Every Grain of Sand: Essays on the Book of Revelation*, edited by Shane J. Wood, 131–40 Joplin, MO: College Press, 2011.

Woodbridge, Paul D. "Lamb." In *NDBT* 620–22.

Woods, Richard. "Seven Bowls of Wrath: The Ecological Relevance of Revelation." *BTB* 38 (2008) 64–75.

Worth, Roland H. Jr. *The Seven Cities of the Apocalypse and Greco-Asian Culture.* Mahweh, NJ: Paulist, 1999.

Woudstra, Sierd. "Eat." In *ISBE* 2:6–8.

Wray, T. J. and Gregory Mobley. *The Birth of Satan: Tracing the Devil's Biblical Roots.* New York: Palgrave Macmillan, 2005.

Wright, Archie T. "Firstborn." In *NIDB* 2:457–58.

Wright, N. T. *The New Testament and the People of God.* Minneapolis: Fortress, 1992.

Yamauchi, Edwin M. "Demons." In *DDL* 410–27.

———. "Dogs." In *DDL* 519–27.

———. "Horses." In *DDL* 817–24.

———. "Insects." In *DDL* 886–904.

Yarbro Collins, Adela. *The Apocalypse.* Wilmington, DE: Glazier, 1979.

———. *The Combat Myth in the Book of Revelation.* Eugene, OR: Wipf & Stock, 2001.

———. *Cosmology and Eschatology in Jewish and Christian Apocalypticism.* Leiden: Brill, 1996.

———. *Crisis and Catharsis: The Power of the Apocalypse.* Philadelphia: Westminster, 1984.

———. "The 'Son of Man' Tradition and the Book of Revelation." In *The Messiah: Developments in Earliest Judaism and Christianity*, edited by James H. Charlesworth, 536–68. Minneapolis: Fortress, 1992.

———. "Vilification and Self-Identification in the Book of Revelation." *HTR* 79 (1986) 308–20.

———. "'What the Spirit Says to the Churches': Preaching the Apocalypse." *QR* 4 (1984) 69–84.

Zerbe, Gordon. "Ecology according to the New Testament." *Dir* 22 (1992) 15–26.

———. "Revelation's Expose of Two Cities: Babylon and New Jerusalem." *Dir* 32 (2003) 46–60.

Zimmerman, Ruben. "Nuptial Imagery in the Revelation of John." *Bib* 84 (2003) 153–83.

Author Index

Aasgaard, Reidar, 159
Adams, Jay Edward, 39, 178, 281
Alden, Robert L., 84, 129, 302
Allison, Dale C. Jr., 310
Appler, Deborah A., 185, 204
Archer, Melissa L., 34, 35
Armerding, Carl E., 232
Aune, David E. , 1, 10–11, 17, 30–32, 34,
    37–38, 40–41, 43, 45, 47, 49–52, 56, 60,
    65–67, 72, 79–80, 82, 87, 94, 99, 101–2,
    111–12, 117, 123, 128, 130–32, 135–37,
    142, 145, 148, 154–55, 160, 162–64,
    166–68, 170, 172, 174–75, 178–79, 184,
    186–87, 189, 199, 201–2, 204, 207–9,
    215, 219, 225, 227, 238, 242–43, 245–46,
    248, 250, 253, 256, 262, 264, 269–70, 277,
    280–81, 287–88, 298, 305, 307, 311–12,
    315–16, 321–23, 332–33

Bacchiocchi, Samuele, 317
Bailleul–Lesuer, Rozenn, 214
Baines, Matthew Charles , 187, 189
Bandstra, A. J., 254
Bandstra, Barry L., 238
Bandy, Alan S., 7, 10, 258
Banks, Robert, 210
Barabas, Steven, 48, 180, 313
Barker, Kenneth L., 56, 301
Barker, Margaret, 38, 167
Barr, David L., 34, 49, 69, 76, 94, 163, 176, 204,
    250, 270, 294, 303, 334
Bartchy, S. S., 167
Batey, Richard A., 158
Bauckham, Richard J. 2, 4, 8, 10, 12, 17, 34¬¬–
    38, 40–41, 43, 47–48, 52–55, 65, 72, 89,
    92–95, 99, 108, 112–14, 116, 118–19,
    124, 136–37, 140, 143, 151, 153–54, 160,
    163–64, 167, 169, 171, 173, 178, 181, 184,
    187–90, 196–97, 213, 220–21, 223, 245,
    247–48, 256–58, 262, 269, 275–76, 279,
    281–85, 288–89, 296, 304–5, 308, 312,
    317, 321, 324, 327, 329, 332

Beagley, Alan James, 119, 163, 184
Beale, Gregory K., 1–2, 5, 8, 10–13, 17, 30–34,
    37–38, 40–49, 51–56, 58–61, 64–69,
    71–73, 76, 78–83, 85–86, 88–92, 94–95,
    97, 99, 101–5, 107, 109, 111–12, 114,
    116–22, 124–25, 127–35, 137, 139–40,
    142–43, 145–46, 148–52, 154–55, 157–58,
    160–66, 168–78, 180–81, 183–84, 186–87,
    189–90, 192, 194–95, 197, 201, 206–9,
    213, 216–20, 223, 225–27, 229, 231–32,
    234–36, 239, 242–45, 247–50, 253–58,
    260, 262, 264–67, 269–72, 274–76,
    280–82, 284–85, 287–91, 298, 301–3,
    305–6, 308–10, 312–13, 315–16, 318–21,
    324–26, 330–32
Bean, Adam L. , 138
Beasley-Murray, George R., 11, 13, 17, 32–33,
    37–38, 40, 42, 47, 49, 55, 59–60, 76,
    80, 82, 90, 92, 95, 99, 103, 106, 111–12,
    117–19, 124, 128, 132–33, 136–37, 143,
    146, 151, 156, 160, 162–64, 171, 173, 175,
    178, 181, 184–85, 189, 208, 214, 219,
    227–28, 231, 234, 239, 242, 245, 249, 253,
    256, 280, 282, 287–89, 298, 307, 312, 317,
    321, 329, 331
Beck, James, 93, 119, 140–41, 211, 215, 235,
    238, 266, 299
Beckwith, Isbon T. , 39, 80, 98, 133, 164, 193,
    208, 255, 281, 288, 290
Benham, Priscilla , 11, 37, 40, 42, 65, 71, 99,
    113–14, 157, 163, 173, 186, 243, 245, 249,
    281, 287–88, 305
Besserman, Lawrence, 265
Biguzzi, Giancarlo, 119
Birch, Bruce C., 225, 299
Blaiklock, David A., 244
Blaising, Craig A., 7
Blickenstaff, Marianne 183, 259
Blomberg, Craig L. , 91, 170, 319
Blount, Brian K. , 17, 32–33, 37, 40, 49–50, 56,
    60, 64, 66, 70, 80, 83, 86, 89, 92, 95, 97,
    99, 102, 104–5, 107, 111–12, 119, 124,

Scripture Index

Ancient Document Index

Jubilees

1:27–29	39
1:29	112
2:1–2	39
2:2	30–31, 88
4:26	98
5:3–11	116
5:10	310
5:14	85
8:25	180
10:9	291
15:27	39
31:14	39

Psalms of Solomon

14:9	85
15:9	146
17:23–24	243

Sirach

18:1	48
39:30	225
47:2	55

Testament of Abraham

5:9	202
12:14	31
13:11–14	31

Testament of Asher

7:1–7	277

Testament of Dan

5:12–13	114
5:12	75

Testament of Joseph

19:6–8	218

Testament of Levi

4:1	84–85, 94
5	37
5:1	142
18:10–14	75

Testament of Moses

1:17–18	327
10	71
10:1–7	91
10:3–6	97

Testament of Naphtali

5:4	66

Testament of Solomon

2:2–4	229
13:1	201
20:14–17	103

Tobit

3:8–18	114

Dead Sea Scrolls

1QM

1:2–3	81
11:15–16	180
11:16–18	87

1QS

4:11–13	85
4:19–20	80
4:21	69
8:1–16	74
8:13–15	80
9:3–7	74
11:7–9	74

CPSIA information can be obtained
at www.ICGtesting.com
Printed in the USA
LVHW101506271021
701711LV00006B/321

9 781532 6408